Becoming a MASTER STUDENT

16e
Dave Ellis

Contributing Editor:
Doug Toft

Australia • Brazil • Mexico • Singapore • United Kingdom • United States

Becoming A Master Student, Sixteenth Edition

Dave Ellis

Product Director: Lauren Murphy

Product Manager: Sarah Seymour

Content Developer: Courtney Triola

Product Assistant: Chip Moreland

Senior Content Project Manager: Aimee Bear

Art Director: Diana Graham

Manufacturing Planner: Bev Breslin

IP Analyst: Ann Hoffman

IP Project Manager: Kathryn Kucharek

Design and Production Service: MPS Limited

Compositor: MPS Limited

Cover and Interior Designer: Diana Graham

Cover Image: Rawpixel.com/Shutterstock.com

For product information and technology assistance, contact us at
Cengage Learning Customer & Sales Support, 1-800-354-9706

For permission to use material from this text or product, submit all requests online at **cengage.com/permissions**
Further permissions questions can be emailed to
permissionrequest@cengage.com

Library of Congress Control Number: 2016942156

Student Edition:

ISBN: 978-1-337-09710-9

Loose-leaf Edition:

ISBN: 978-1-337-27916-1

Cengage Learning
20 Channel Center Street
Boston, MA 02210
USA

Cengage Learning is a leading provider of customized learning solutions with employees residing in nearly 40 different countries and sales in more than 125 countries around the world. Find your local representative at **www.cengage.com**

Cengage Learning products are represented in Canada by Nelson Education, Ltd.

To learn more about Cengage Learning Solutions, visit **www.cengage.com**

Purchase any of our products at your local college store or at our preferred online store **www.cengagebrain.com**

Printed in the United States of America
Print Number: 01   Print Year: 2016

Brief Contents

1 Introduction
The Master Student

23 Chapter 1
Discovering Yourself

59 Chapter 2
Time

111 Chapter 3
Memory

137 Chapter 4
Reading

169 Chapter 5
Notes

201 Chapter 6
Tests

231 Chapter 7
Thinking

271 Chapter 8
Communicating

321 Chapter 9
Money

355 Chapter 10
Next Steps

Contents

xi   **Preface**

Introduction:

The Master Student

2   Power Process: Discover what you want

3   Rewrite this book

3   **Practicing Critical Thinking 1:** Textbook reconnaissance

4   Master student qualities

7   **Practicing Critical Thinking 2:** The master student in you

8   The master student process: Discovery

9   The master student process: Intention

10   *Be on the lookout*

11   The master student process: Action

12   Keep the process alive

12   *The secret of student success*

13   Get the most from this book

14   *Here's the sales pitch*

15   Motivation: I'm just not in the mood

17   Ways to change a habit

19   **Journal Entry 1:** Declare what you want

20   *Do you have a minute?*

21   **Practicing Critical Thinking 3:** Plan to change a habit

22   **Journal Entry 2:** Commitment

chapter 1

Discovering Yourself

24   Power Process: Ideas are tools

25   First Step: Truth is a key to mastery

27   **Practicing Critical Thinking 4:** Taking the First Step

28   The Discovery Wheel

32   **Skills Snapshot:** Discovery wheel

33   Learning styles: Discovering how you learn

34   **Journal Entry 3:** Prepare for the Learning Style Inventory (LSI)

35   *Directions for completing the learning style inventory*

36   Learning Style Inventory

37   *Scoring Your Inventory*

38   *Learning Style Graph*

39   *Interpreting Your Learning Style Graph*

40   *Developing All Four Modes of Learning*

41   *Balancing Your Preferences*

42   Using your learning style profile to succeed

47   **Journal Entry 4:** Choosing your purpose

48   Claim your multiple intelligences

49   **Practicing Critical Thinking 5:** Develop your multiple intelligences

52 Learning through your senses: The VARK system

55 **Journal Entry 5:** Get back to the big picture about learning styles

55 *Master Student Profiles*

56 Master Student Profile: Joshua Williams

57 **Quiz Chapter 1**

58 **Skills Snapshot Chapter 1**

chapter **2**

Time

60 Power Process: Be here now

61 You've got the time

62 Make choices about multitasking

63 **Practicing Critical Thinking 6:** The Time Monitor/Time Plan

68 **Journal Entry 6:** Discover the impact of technology on your time and attention

69 Define your values

70 Setting and achieving goals

71 **Practicing Critical Thinking 7:** Create a lifeline

73 **Practicing Critical Thinking 8:** Get real with your goals

74 The ABC daily to-do list

76 **Practicing Critical Thinking 9:** Create your to-do list

78 Planning sets you free

80 Making the transition to higher education

82 *Avoid high-tech time wasters*

83 Making time for school as an adult learner

85 **Practicing Critical Thinking 10:** Master monthly calendar

88 Break it down, get it done—using a long-term planner

91 Create a work flow that works

92 There's an app for that—using technology for time management

93 Stop procrastination now

95 *The 7-step antiprocrastination plan*

96 25 ways to get the most out of now

99 *Setting limits on screen time*

101 Making time for health

104 **Practicing Critical Thinking 11:** Taking a First Step about health

106 Beyond time management: Stay focused on what matters

107 **Journal Entry 7:** Create a not-to-do list

108 Master Student Profile: Ramit Sethi

109 **Quiz Chapter 2**

110 **Skills Snapshot Chapter 2**

chapter **3**

Memory

112 Power Process: Love your problems

113 Your memory and your brain—6 key principles

115 **Journal Entry 8:** Reflect on the care and feeding of your brain

116 The memory jungle

118 25 memory techniques

125 **Practicing Critical Thinking 12:** Use Q-cards to reinforce memory

126 Set a trap for your memory

126 **Practicing Critical Thinking 13:** Remembering your car keys—or anything else

127 Mnemonic devices

129 *Making connections in memory-friendly ways*

130 Retool your memory

131 **Practicing Critical Thinking 14:** Get creative

131 **Journal Entry 9:** Revisit your memory skills

132 Remembering names

133 **Practicing Critical Thinking 15:** Move from problems to solutions

134 Master Student Profile: Maria Popova

135 **Quiz Chapter 3**

136 **Skills Snapshot Chapter 3**

chapter **4**

Reading

138 Power Process: Notice your pictures and let them go

139 Muscle Reading

140 How Muscle Reading works

141 Phase 1: Before you read

142 Phase 2: While you read

143 *Five smart ways to highlight a text*

144 Phase 3: After you read

145 *Muscle Reading: A leaner approach*

146 Extending Muscle Reading to web pages and ebooks

146 **Journal Entry 10:** Experiment with Muscle Reading

147 Muscle Reading at work

148 **Journal Entry 11:** Reflect on your online reading habits

149 When reading is tough

151 Getting past roadblocks to reading

153 *Get SPUNKI with your reading*

154 **Practicing Critical Thinking 16:** Plan to complete your reading assignments

155 Beyond speed reading: Becoming a flexible reader

156 Word power—expanding your vocabulary

158 *Checklist: Review these common word parts*

159 Mastering the English language

161 Developing information literacy

166 Master Student Profile: Matias Manzano

167 **Quiz Chapter 4**

168 **Skills Snapshot Chapter 4**

chapter **5**

Notes

170 Power Process: I create it all

171 The note-taking process flows

172 Observe: The note-taking process flows

173 *What to do when you miss a class*

175 **Journal Entry 12:** Create more value from lectures

176 Record: The note-taking process flows

181 Review: The note-taking process flows

182 **Practicing Critical Thinking 17:** Reflect on your review habits

184 Turn PowerPoints into powerful notes

185 When your instructor talks quickly

186 **Practicing Critical Thinking 18:** Taking notes under pressure

187 Taking notes while reading

188 *Note this information about your sources*

190 Visualize ideas with concept maps

192 Taking effective notes for online coursework

195 *Taking notes during meetings*

196 Note taking 2.0

198 Master Student Profile: Teresa Amabile

199 **Quiz Chapter 5**

200 **Skills Snapshot Chapter 5**

chapter **6**

Tests

202 Power Process: Detach

203 Think beyond the grade

204 What to do before the test

205 *How to cram (even though you "shouldn't")*

206 **Journal Entry 13:** Explore your feelings about tests

207 Ways to predict test questions

208 **Journal Entry 14:** Notice your excuses and let them go

209 Cooperative learning: Studying in groups

211 What to do during the test

212 *Words to watch for in essay questions*

215 The high costs of cheating

215 *Perils of high-tech cheating*

216 Let go of test anxiety

217 *Have some FUN!*

218 Getting ready for math tests

222 **Practicing Critical Thinking 19:** Use learning styles for math success

222 Studying across the curriculum

224 The test isn't over until . . .

225 *F is for Feedback*

226 Celebrate mistakes

227 Notable failures

227 **Practicing Critical Thinking 20:** 20 things I like to do

228 Master Student Profile: Lalita Booth

229 **Quiz Chapter 6**

230 **Skills Snapshot Chapter 6**

chapter **7**

Thinking

232 Power Process: Embrace the new

233 Critical thinking: A survival skill

235 Six kinds of thinking

238 A process for critical thinking

241 **Practicing Critical Thinking 21:** Critical thinking scenarios

243 Finding "aha!": Creativity fuels critical thinking

243 *Tangram*

244 **Journal Entry 15:** Use divergent thinking to brainstorm goals

245 Ways to create ideas

246 **Journal Entry 16:** Use convergent thinking to plan habits

247 *Create on your feet*

249 **Practicing Critical Thinking 22:** Explore emotional reactions

250 Attitudes, affirmations, and visualizations

251 **Practicing Critical Thinking 23:** Reprogram your attitude

251 *Simple attitude replacements*

252 Don't fool yourself: 15 common mistakes in logic

254 *Cognitive biases: More ways we fool ourselves*

256 Think critically about information on the Internet

257 Gaining skill at decision making

258 Four ways to solve problems

260 Asking questions: Learning through inquiry

261 *15 questions to try on for size*

263 Thinking about your major

265 Service-learning: Turn thinking into contribution

268 Master Student Profile: Irshad Manji

269 **Quiz Chapter 7**

270 **Skills Snapshot Chapter 7**

chapter 8

Communicating

272 Power Process: Employ your word

273 Communication: Keeping the channels open

273 **Practicing Critical Thinking 24:** Practice sending or receiving

274 Choosing to listen

277 *Five ways to say "I"*

278 Choosing to speak

280 **Practicing Critical Thinking 25:** Write an "I" message

281 **Journal Entry 17:** Discover communication styles

282 Developing emotional intelligence

283 Communicating in teams: Getting things done as a group

285 *Using technology to collaborate*

287 Managing conflict

289 **Journal Entry 18:** Recreate a relationship

290 Five ways to say no . . . respectfully

291 **Practicing Critical Thinking 26:** VIPs (very important persons)

292 Five steps to effective complaints

292 *Criticism is constructive*

293 Communicating with instructors

294 *Communicating respect for your instructors*

295 Diversity is real—and valuable

297 Communicating across cultures

299 *Students with disabilities: Ask for what you want*

300   *You deserve compliments*

301   **Practicing Critical Thinking 27:**
Becoming a culture learner

302   Communicating as a first-generation
student

303   Staying safe on social networks

306   Three phases of effective writing

307   *Writing for online readers*

308   *Befriend your word processor*

311   Academic integrity: Avoid plagiarism

313   Mastering public speaking

317   *Making the grade in group presentations*

318   Master Student Profile: Chimamanda
Adichie

319   **Quiz Chapter 8**

320   **Skills Snapshot Chapter 8**

chapter **9**

Money

322   Power Process: Risk being a fool

323   The end of money worries

324   **Practicing Critical Thinking 28:** The
Money Monitor/Money Plan

325   **Journal Entry 19:** Reflect on your
experience of money

329   Make more money

330   **Journal Entry 20:** Reflect on your
Money Monitor/Money Plan

332   *No budgeting required*

333   Spend less money

334   *Free fun*

335   **Practicing Critical Thinking 29:** Show
me the money

336   Managing money during tough times

338   Take charge of your credit

340   *Common credit terms*

342   **Journal Entry 21:** Create a new
experience of money

342   *If you get into trouble . . .*

343   Education pays off—and you can pay
for it

344   **Practicing Critical Thinking 30:**
Education by the hour

345   Money for the future

346   **Practicing Critical Thinking 31:** Plan
to pay for your degree

349   Use tools to tame your money

351   Your money and your values

352   Master Student Profile: Leo Babauta

353   **Quiz Chapter 9**

354   **Skills Snapshot Chapter 9**

chapter **10**

Next Steps

356   Power Process: Persist

357   Jump-start your education with
transferable skills

359   **Practicing Critical Thinking 32:**
Recognize your skills

360   *65 transferrable skills*

363   **Practicing Critical Thinking 33:** Plan
to develop a new skill

364   Taking the road to graduation

365 **Practicing Critical Thinking 34:** Make a trial choice of a major

367 Transferring to a new school

369 Start creating your career

370 **Journal Entry 22:** Plan a career by naming names

371 *Another option: Don't plan your career*

372 Start creating your résumé

373 Discover the hidden job market

376 Develop interviewing skills

377 **Practicing Critical Thinking 35:** Plan to explore your career

378 Join a diverse workplace

380 Put your health to work

381 Persist on the path of mastery

384 **Practicing Critical Thinking 36:** Plan to persist with an academic plan

386 Tools for lifelong learning

387 **Practicing Critical Thinking 37:** This book shouts, "Use me!"

388 The Discovery Wheel: Coming full circle

392 **Skills Snapshot:** Revisiting your Discovery Wheels

393 **Journal Entry 23:** Celebrate your gains, clarify your intentions

394 **Practicing Critical Thinking 38:** Are you getting there?

396 Master Student Profile: Ben Barry

397 **Quiz Chapter 10**

398 **Skills Snapshot Chapter 10**

399 The Master Guide to *Becoming a Master Student*

402 Endnotes

405 Additional Reading

407 Index

Preface

Children are great students. They quickly master complex skills like language, and they have fun doing it. For young children, learning is a high-energy process that involves experimentation, discovery, and sometimes broken dishes.

Then comes school. Drill and drudgery can replace discovery and dish breaking. Learning may become a drag.

Use this book to reverse that process. Rediscover what you knew as a child—that joy and learning go hand in hand. Becoming a master student is about gaining knowledge and skills by unleashing the natural learner within you.

This book is full of suggestions for doing that. Every chapter is packed with tips, techniques, methods, tools, and processes for you to play with.

Sometimes people feel overwhelmed by this fact. "There are more ideas in here than I could ever use this term—or even during the rest of my education," they say.

Exactly. That's the whole point. And there are several reasons for this.

One is that *Becoming a Master Student* is designed for long-term use. You'll find enough ideas to play with for years beyond graduation—for the rest of your life, in fact.

There are also many suggestions here because some of them may work well for you and others might not. Consider note-taking methods, for example. Some students rave about mind mapping—a visual way of recording ideas. Other students find mind mapping too messy and swear by traditional outlines instead. This book offers detailed instructions for both methods—and many more. Feel free to play with all of them, combine them, modify them, and invent new methods of your own.

That's the biggest reason for the density of ideas in this book. Underlying every paragraph and every page is an invitation to *actively experiment* with the content. Find out what truly works for you.

People who excel in any field are experimenters. They're willing to consider many options—even the ones that sound crazy at first. When faced with a new idea, their first reaction is not to say: *That will never work.* Instead, they ask: *How might that work?* Then they take action to find out.

It took hundreds of people to produce *Becoming a Master Student.* Besides the author, there were editors, designers, proofreaders, and advisors. Beyond them were hundreds of educators and students who contributed everything from a single comment to the inspiration for entire chapters.

The true author of this book, however, is you. Your responses to any suggestion can lead you to think new thoughts, say new things, and do what you never believed you could do. If you're willing to experiment with new ways of learning, the possibilities are endless. This process is more fundamental and more powerful than any individual tool or technique you'll ever read about.

Consider the possibility that you can create the life of your dreams. There are people who scoff at this idea, and they have a perspective that is widely shared. Please set it aside. The process of experimenting with your life is sheer joy, and it never ends.

Begin now. ✖

Acknowledgments

Jose Adames, *Central Texas College*
Deb Butler, *Victoria College*
Dale Haralson, *Hinds Community College*
Judy Isonhood, *Hinds Community College*
Wendy Jansen, *Killian Community College*
Kami Kurtenbach, *South Dakota State University*

Krista LeBrun, *East Central Community College*
Stacey Macchi, *Western Illinois University*
Jenny Middleton, *Seminole State College of Florida*
LeAnne Olson, *Mountwest Community and Technical College*
Jennifer Perkins, *Central Piedmont Community College*
Jason Walker, *Salem International University*

WHAT'S NEW
to this Edition

The foundations and themes for student success in *Becoming a Master Student* have been used by millions of students. Since the first edition, students and instructors have helped shape this book by providing strategies, insights, and suggestions. As a result of its continuous evaluation and refinement, students are inspired and motivated by this book to adopt, develop, and commit to using the skills needed for success in college and throughout life. These ideas are now a part of the 16th edition. Every word in every article has been evaluated for its helpfulness to students. Statistics have been updated; recent research has been included; and articles have been shortened or lengthened as necessary to maximize clarity of concepts and strategies. Here are some of the major changes you will see in this edition.

KEY UPDATES

- *Becoming a Master Student* has a new chapter structure based on extensive feedback from instructors about how they actually use the text. Core content from the Diversity and Health chapters in the Fifteenth Edition are now integrated throughout the text. The remaining chapters— those that instructors and students use most often—are expanded.
- Master Student Profiles now emphasize specific strategies that people use to overcome obstacles and achieve their goals.
- Exercises throughout the text focus on critical thinking and have new titles to reflect this change. Many of the new Practicing Critical Thinking exercises are worksheets with step-by-step instructions. These guide students to move to higher levels of thinking in Bloom's taxonomy of educational objectives.
- Chapter quizzes also focus on higher levels of thinking and direct students to more of the core concepts in the text.

- The Master Student Map at the beginning of each chapter now includes "Do you have a minute?"—actions that students can take in 60 seconds or less to move toward mastery.

CHAPTER-BY-CHAPTER UPDATES
Introduction: The Master Student

- **New focus on mastery** Mastery and qualities of a master student are the centerpiece of this revised chapter. Articles and interactives about motivation and habit change support the master student process—the continuous cycle of discovery, intention, and action.
- **Revised article** "Ways to change a habit" offers more strategies for behavior change.
- **New exercise** "Practicing Critical Thinking: Plan to change a habit" guides students to specify a cue, new behavior, and reward for a habit that they want to adopt.
- **New sidebar** "Do you have a minute?" gives more examples of "baby steps" that students can take to make meaningful progress toward their goals.
- **Revised journal entry** "Commitment" is expanded.

Chapter 1: Discovering Yourself

- **Revised Learning Styles Inventory (LSI)** Students can now complete this assessment without having to remove pages from the book.
- **Revised article** "Learning through your senses: The VARK system" describes the Read–Write style in more detail and offers related strategies.
- **New master student profile** Joshua Williams demonstrated the courage to take a First Step and tell the truth about being homeless as student. He persisted to graduation, founded a scholarship that helps students pay for textbooks, worked as a case manager for delinquent teenagers, and entered graduate school.

Chapter 2: Time

- **New articles** "Making the transition to higher education" and "Making time for school as an adult learner" focus on time management as a key to balancing education with work and family commitments. "Making time for health" suggests ways for students to exercise, rest, eat well, and manage stress in the midst of their busy lives.
- **New exercises** Students can use "Practicing Critical Thinking: Take a first step about health" to assess their health-related habits and plan changes in these behaviors. "Practicing Critical Thinking: Create your to-do list" is a worksheet that guides students to apply strategies from "The ABC daily to-do list."
- **New master student profile** Ramit Sethi wrote the book *I Will Teach You To Be Rich* and created an online community "focused on personal finance and entrepreneurship for college students, recent college grads, and everyone else."

Chapter 3: Memory

- **Revised article** "Mnemonic devices" offers additional suggestions for using these popular memory techniques.
- **New sidebar** "Making connections in memory-friendly ways" reveals the mnemonic devices that are baked into *Becoming a Master Student* and suggests ways for students to use similar strategies.
- **New master student profile** Maria Popova grew Brain Pickings from a weekly email newsletter to one of the world's most visited websites, demonstrating how a side project can bloom into a career.

Chapter 4: Reading

- **New articles** "Muscle reading at work" suggests ways to use the three phases of Muscle Reading to extract meaning from documents of all types, including reports, emails, training materials, and websites. "Checklist: Review these common word parts" defines word prefixes, roots, and suffixes that are useful for students to know. "Beyond speed reading: Becoming a flexible reader" guides students to think critically about claims for speed reading techniques and offers research-based strategies as alternatives.

- **New exercise** "Practicing Critical Thinking: Plan to complete your reading assignments" is a worksheet based on "Getting past roadblocks to reading," with detailed guidance for estimating and scheduling reading time.

Chapter 5: Notes

- **Revised article** "Visualize ideas with concept maps" is expanded with an additional example.

Chapter 7: Thinking

- **New articles** "Six kinds of thinking" presents Bloom's taxonomy of educational objectives—the theoretical basis of this chapter—with examples of each level of thinking. "Attitudes, affirmations and visualizations" suggests creative ways for students to change attitudes and behaviors.
- **New exercise** "Practicing Critical Thinking: Reprogram your attitude" guides students to create their own affirmations.
- **New sidebars** "Simple attitude replacements" offers examples of effective affirmations. "Cognitive biases: More ways we fool ourselves" expands on "Don't fool yourself: 15 common mistakes in logic" with additional examples of errors in reasoning.

Chapter 8: Communicating

- **New articles** "Communicating with instructors" suggests ways for students to develop positive, long-term relationships with teachers. "Communicating respect in the classroom" emphasizes the benefits civility for both students and instructors. "Communicating respect at work" offers strategies for develop a work ethic that employers value. "Communicating across cultures" explains the concept of cultural competence and includes strategies for thriving with diversity. "Communicating as a first-generation student" guides students who are new to higher education to build alliances with instructors and maintain positive relationships with family members. In addition, "Diversity is real and valuable" encourages students to use higher education as a laboratory for learning to bridge culture gaps.
- **Revised article** "Choosing to listen" is expanded with additional techniques.
- **New exercise** "Practicing Critical Thinking: Becoming a culture learner" guides students to question their assumptions about members of other cultures, interpret their observations in alternative ways, and choose new behaviors to thrive with diversity.

Chapter 9: Money

- **New article** "Money for the future" suggests ways for students to make decisions about saving, investing, insurance, home ownership, car shopping, and signing contracts.
- **New exercises** "Practicing Critical Thinking: Plan to pay for your degree" guides students to predict their income and expenses for each school term and prevent financial issues that might disrupt their education.

- **New journal entry** "Reflect on your experience of money" asks students to state their current financial concerns and preview the chapter for potential solutions.

Chapter 10: Next Steps
- **New articles** "Join a diverse workplace" suggests how students can become master employees who enter the global marketplace with ease. "Put your health to work" underlines the connection between wellness and success in the workplace.
- **New exercises** Look for four new worksheets in this chapter. "Practicing Critical Thinking: Plan to develop a new skill" guides students to apply strategies from "Jump-start your education with transferable skills." "Practicing Critical

Thinking: Plan to explore your career" prompts students to test their career choices through internships, employment, and other experiences. "Practicing Critical Thinking: Plan to persist with an academic plan" allows students to track their academic progress each term and ensure that they're on track to graduate. And "Practicing Critical Thinking: Are you getting there?" suggests that students revisit their long-term goals to assess how their daily activities align with those goals.
- **New master student profile** Ben Barry worked for Facebook as one of the company's first communication designers and now heads his own design studio in San Francisco. He demonstrates strategies for staying focused in the midst of everyday distractions. ✶

Embracing
TECHNOLOGY

MindTap® College Success for *Becoming a Master Student* combines tools like readings, videos, flashcards, quizzes, and digital activities to help guide students through their course and transform into master students.

The College Success Factors Index (CSFI) is a personal success indicator that helps students identify their strengths and areas for growth in 10 key factors identified by researchers to affect college success. The CSFI now kicks off MindTap® College Success for *Becoming a Master Student*!

For Instructors
Visit the Instructor Companion Site for additional resources and course support to support your teaching with *Becoming a Master Student*. This site includes an Instructor's Manual, test banks, sample syllabi, and more. To access the Instructor Companion Site, visit **login.cengage.com**. ✶

Alberto Masnovo/Fotolia; Robert Churchill/E+/Getty Images

DISCOVERY
& INTENTION STATEMENT

GUIDELINES

DISCOVERY STATEMENTS

- [ ] Record the specifics about your thoughts, feelings, and behavior.

- [ ] Notice your thoughts, observe your actions, and record them accurately.

- [ ] Use discomfort as a signal.

- [ ] Feeling uncomfortable, bored, or tired might be a signal that you're about to do valuable work.

- [ ] Suspend judgment.

- [ ] When you are discovering yourself, be gentle.

- [ ] Tell the truth.

- [ ] The closer you get to the truth, the more powerful your Discovery Statements.

INTENTION STATEMENTS

- [ ] Make intentions positive.

- [ ] Focus on what you want rather than what you don't want.

- [ ] Make intentions observable.

- [ ] Be specific about your intentions.

- [ ] Make intentions small and achievable.

- [ ] Break large goals into small, specific tasks that can be accomplished quickly.

- [ ] Set timelines.

- [ ] Set a precise due date for tasks you intend to do.

- [ ] Move from intention to action.

If you want new results in your life, then take action. ✖

© wavebreakmedia/Shutterstock.com

The Master Student

why

You can ease your transition to higher education and set up a lifelong pattern of success by starting with some key strategies.

how

Take a few minutes to skim this chapter. Find three suggestions that look especially useful. Make a note to yourself, or mark the pages where the strategies that you intend to use are located in the chapter.

what if...

I could use the ideas in this book to more consistently get what I want in my life?

what is included . . .

2   Power Process: Discover what you want

3   Rewrite this book

4   Master student qualities

8   The master student process—Discovery

9   The master student process—Intention

11   The master student process—Action

12   Keep the process alive

13   Get the most from this book

15   Motivation—I'm just not in the mood

17   Ways to change a habit

do you have a minute?

Take a minute to make a list of anything about your life that's nagging at you as incomplete or unresolved. Possibilities for this list include:

- Longstanding problems that are still not solved
- Projects that you'd like to finish and haven't yet started
- Tasks that you've been putting off
- Habits that you'd like to stop—or start

Save this list and refer to it as you read and work through this chapter. *Everything you wrote down is a clue about something that's important to you.* This chapter is filled with strategies for getting clear about what you want and taking immediate steps to get it.

Discover what you want

Imagine a man who tries to buy a plane ticket for his next vacation, with no destination in mind. He pulls out his iPad and logs in to his favorite website for trip planning. He gets a screen that prompts him for details about his destination. And he leaves all the fields blank.

"I'm not fussy," says the would-be vacationer. "I just want to get away. I'll just accept whatever the computer coughs up."

Compare this person to another traveler who books a flight to Ixtapa, Mexico, departing on Saturday, March 23, and returning Sunday, April 7—window seat, first class, and vegetarian meals.

Now, ask yourself which traveler is more likely to end up with a vacation that he'll enjoy.

The same principle applies in any area of life. Knowing where we want to go increases the probability that we will arrive at our destination. Discovering what we want makes it more likely that we'll attain it.

Okay, so the example about the traveler with no destination is far-fetched. Before you dismiss it, though, do an informal experiment: Ask three other students what they want to get out of their education. Be prepared for hemming, hawing, and vague generalities.

This is amazing, considering the stakes involved. Students routinely invest years of their lives and thousands of dollars, with only a hazy idea of their destination in life.

Now suppose that you asked someone what she wanted from her education, and you got this answer: "I plan to get a degree in journalism, with double minors in earth science and Portuguese, so I can work as a reporter covering the environment in Brazil." The details of a person's vision offer clues to his or her skills and sense of purpose.

Another clue is the presence of "stretch goals"—those that are big *and* achievable. A 40-year-old might spend years talking about his desire to be a professional athlete someday. Chances are, that's no longer achievable. However, setting a goal to lose 10 pounds by playing basketball at the gym three days a week is another matter. That's a stretch—a challenge. It's also doable.

Discovering what you want helps you succeed in higher education. Many students quit school simply because they are unsure about what they want from it. With well-defined goals in mind, you can look for connections between what you want and what you study. The more connections, the more likely you'll stay in school—and get what you want in every area of life. ◼

Gil C/Shutterstock.com

REWRITE
this book

Some books should be preserved in pristine condition. This book isn't one of them.

Something happens when you get involved with a book by writing in it. *Becoming a Master Student* is about learning, and learning results when you are active. When you make notes in the margin, you can hear yourself talking with the author. When you doodle and underline, you see the author's ideas taking shape. You can even argue with the author and come up with your own theories and explanations. In all of these ways, you can become a coauthor of this book. Rewrite it to make it yours.

While you're at it, you can create symbols or codes that will help you when reviewing the text later on. You might insert a "Q" where you

have questions, or put exclamation points or stars next to important ideas. You could also circle words to look up in a dictionary.

Remember, if any idea in this book doesn't work for you, you can rewrite it. Change the exercises to fit your needs. Create a new technique by combining several others. Create a technique out of thin air!

Find something you agree or disagree with and write a short note in the margin about it. Or draw a diagram. Better yet, do both. Let creativity be your guide. Have fun.

Begin rewriting now. ✂

practicing
CRITICAL THINKING

1

Textbook reconnaissance

Start becoming a master student this moment by doing a 15-minute "textbook reconnaissance." First, read the table of contents. Do it in three minutes or less. Next, look at every page in the text. Move quickly. Scan headlines. Look at pictures. Notice forms, charts, and diagrams.

Look especially for ideas you can use. When you find one, note the location and a short description of the idea. You also can use sticky notes to flag pages that look useful. (If you're reading *Becoming a Master Student* as an ebook, you can flag pages electronically.)

Master student
QUALITIES

Oliver Cleve/Photographer's Choice/Getty Images

This book is about something that cannot be taught. It's about becoming a master student.

Mastery means attaining a level of skill that goes beyond technique. For a master, work is effortless. Struggle evaporates. The master carpenter is so familiar with her tools that they are part of her. To a master chef, utensils are old friends. Because these masters don't have to think about the details of the process, they bring more of themselves to their work.

Mastery can lead to flashy results: an incredible painting, for example, or a gem of a short story. In basketball, mastery might result in an unbelievable shot at the buzzer. For a musician, it might be the performance of a lifetime, the moment when everything comes together. You could describe the experience as "flow" or "being in the zone."

Often, the result of mastery is a sense of profound satisfaction, wellbeing, and timelessness. Distractions fade. Time stops. Work becomes play. After hours of patient practice, after setting clear goals and getting precise feedback, the master has learned to be fully in control.

At the same time, he lets go of control. Results happen without effort, struggle, or worry. Work seems self-propelled. The master is in control by being out of control. He lets go and allows the creative process to take over. That's why after a spectacular performance by an athlete or performer, observers often say, "He played full out—and made it look like he wasn't even trying."

Likewise, the master student is one who makes learning look easy. She works hard without seeming to make any effort. She's relaxed *and* alert, disciplined *and* spontaneous, focused *and* fun-loving.

You might say that those statements don't make sense. Actually, mastery does *not* make sense. It cannot be captured with words. It defies analysis. Mastery cannot be taught. It can only be learned and experienced.

By design, you are a learning machine. As an infant, you learned to walk. As a toddler, you learned to talk. By the time you reached age 5, you'd mastered many skills needed to thrive in the world. And you learned all these things without formal instruction, without lectures, without books, without conscious effort, and without fear. You can rediscover that natural learner within you. Each chapter of this book is about a step you can take on this path.

Master students share certain qualities. These are attitudes and core values. Although they imply various strategies for learning, they ultimately go beyond what you do. Master student qualities are ways of *being* exceptional.

Following is a list of master student qualities. Remember that the list is not complete. It merely points in a direction. As you read, look to yourself. Put a check mark next to each quality that you've already demonstrated. Put another mark—say, an exclamation point— next to each quality you want to actively work on possessing. This is not a test. It is simply a chance to celebrate what you've accomplished so far—and start thinking about what's possible for your future.

☐ **Inquisitive.** The master student is curious about everything. By posing questions, she can generate interest in the most mundane, humdrum situations. When she is bored during a biology lecture, she thinks to herself, "I always get bored when I listen to this instructor. Why is that? Maybe it's because he reminds me of my boring Uncle Ralph, who always tells those endless fishing stories. He even looks like Uncle Ralph. Amazing! Boredom is certainly interesting." Then she asks herself, "What can I do to get value out of this lecture, even though it seems boring?" And she finds an answer.

☐ **Able to focus attention.** Watch a 2-year-old at play. Pay attention to his eyes. The wide-eyed look reveals an energy and a capacity for amazement that keep his attention absolutely focused in the here and now. The master student's focused attention has a childlike quality. The world, to a child, is always new. Because the master student can focus attention, to him the world is always new too.

☐ **Willing to change.** The unknown does not frighten the master student. In fact, she welcomes it—even the unknown in herself. We all have pictures of who we think we are, and these pictures can be useful. But they also can prevent learning and growth. The master student embraces new ideas and new strategies for success.

☐ **Able to organize and sort.** The master student can take a large body of information and sift through it to discover relationships. He can play with information, organizing data by size, color, function, timeliness, and hundreds of other categories. He has the guts to set big goals—and the precision to plan carefully so that those goals can be achieved.

☐ **Competent.** Mastery of skills is important to the master student. When she learns mathematical formulas, she studies them until they become second nature. She

practices until she knows them cold—then puts in a few extra minutes. She also is able to apply what she learns to new and different situations.

☐ **Joyful.** More often than not, the master student is seen with a smile on his face—sometimes a smile at nothing in particular other than amazement at the world and his experience of it.

☐ **Able to suspend judgment.** The master student has opinions and positions, and she is able to let go of them when appropriate. She realizes she is more than her thoughts. She can quiet her internal dialogue and listen to an opposing viewpoint. She doesn't let judgment get in the way of learning. Rather than approaching discussions with a "prove it to me and then I'll believe it" attitude, she asks herself, "What if this is true?" and explores possibilities.

☐ **Energetic.** Notice the master student with a spring in his step, the one who is enthusiastic and involved in class. When he reads, he often sits on the very edge of his chair, and he plays with the same intensity. He is determined and persistent.

☐ **Well.** Health is important to the master student, though not necessarily in the sense of being free of illness. Rather, she values her body and treats it with respect. She tends to her emotional and spiritual health as well as her physical health.

☐ **Self-aware.** The master student is willing to evaluate himself and his behavior. He regularly tells the truth about his strengths and those aspects that could be improved.

☐ **Responsible.** There is a difference between responsibility and blame, and the master student knows it well. She is willing to take responsibility for everything in her life—even for events that most people would blame on others. For example, if a master student takes a required class that most students consider boring, she chooses to take responsibility for her interest level. She looks for ways to link the class to one of her goals and experiments with new study techniques that will enhance her performance in any course.

☐ **Willing to take risks.** The master student often takes on projects, with no guarantee of success. He participates in class dialogues at the risk of looking foolish. He tackles difficult subjects in term papers. He welcomes the risk of a challenging course.

☐ **Willing to participate.** Don't look for the master student on the sidelines. She's a collaborator—a team player who can be counted on. She is engaged at school, at work, and with friends and family. She is willing to make a commitment and to follow through on it.

☐ **A generalist.** The master student is interested in everything around him. In the classroom, he is fully present. Outside the classroom, he actively seeks out ways to deepen his learning—through study groups, campus events, student organizations, and team-based projects. Through such experiences, he develops a broad base of knowledge in many fields that can apply to his specialties.

☐ **Willing to accept paradox.** The word *paradox* comes from two Greek words, *para* ("beyond") and *doxen* ("opinion"). A paradox is something that is beyond opinion or, more accurately, something that might seem contradictory or absurd yet might actually have meaning. For example, the master student can be committed to managing money and reaching her financial goals. At the same time, she can be totally detached from money, knowing that her real worth is independent of how much money she has.

☐ **Courageous.** The master student admits his fear and fully experiences it. For example, he will approach a tough exam as an opportunity to explore feelings of anxiety and tension related to the pressure to perform. He does not deny fear; he embraces it. If he doesn't understand something or if he makes a mistake, he admits it. When he faces a challenge and bumps into his limits, he asks for help.

And he's just as willing to give help as to receive it.

☐ **Self-directed.** Rewards or punishments provided by others do not motivate the master student. Her desire to learn comes from within, and her goals come from herself. She competes like a star athlete—not to defeat other people, but to push herself to the next level of excellence.

☐ **Spontaneous.** The master student is truly in the here and now. He is able to respond to the moment in fresh, surprising, and unplanned ways.

☐ **Relaxed about grades.** Grades make the master student neither depressed nor euphoric. She recognizes that sometimes grades are important. At the same time, grades are not the only reason she studies. She does not measure her worth as a human being by the grades she receives.

☐ **"Tech" savvy.** A master student defines *technology* as any tool that's used to achieve a human purpose. From this point of view, computers become tools for deeper learning, higher productivity, and greater success. When faced with a task to accomplish, the master student chooses effectively from the latest options in hardware and software. He doesn't get overwhelmed with unfamiliar technology. Instead, he embraces learning about the new technology and finding ways to use it to help him succeed at the given task. He also knows when to go "offline" and fully engage with his personal community of friends, family members, classmates, instructors, and coworkers.

☐ **Intuitive.** The master student has an inner sense that cannot be explained by logic alone. She trusts her "gut instincts" as well as her mind.

☐ **Creative.** Where others see dull details and trivia, the master student sees opportunities to create. He can gather pieces of knowledge from a wide range of subjects and put them together in new ways. The master student is creative in every aspect of his life.

☐ **Willing to be uncomfortable.** The master student does not place comfort first. When discomfort is necessary to reach a goal, she is willing to experience it. She can endure personal hardships and can look at unpleasant things with detachment.

☐ **Optimistic.** The master student sees setbacks as temporary and isolated, knowing that he can choose his response to any circumstance.

☐ **Willing to laugh.** The master student might laugh at any moment, and her sense of humor includes the ability to laugh at herself. Although going to school is a big investment, with high stakes, you don't have to enroll in the deferred-fun program. A master student celebrates learning, and one of the best ways of doing that is to laugh now and then.

☐ **Hungry.** Human beings begin life with a natural appetite for knowledge. In some people, it soon gets dulled. The master student has tapped that hunger, and it gives him a desire to learn for the sake of learning.

☐ **Willing to work.** Once inspired, the master student is willing to follow through with sweat. She knows that genius and creativity are the result of persistence and work. When in high gear, the master student works with the intensity of a child at play.

☐ **Caring.** A master student cares about knowledge and has a passion for ideas. He also cares about people and appreciates learning from others. He collaborates on projects and thrives on teams. He flourishes in a community that values win–win outcomes, cooperation, and love. ✄

practicing CRITICAL THINKING

2

The master student in you

The purpose of this exercise is to demonstrate to yourself that you truly are a master student. Start by remembering a time in your life when you learned something well or demonstrated mastery. This experience does not have to relate to school. It might be a time when you aced a test, played a flawless soccer game, created a work of art that won recognition, or burst forth with a blazing guitar solo. It might be a time when you spoke from your heart in a way that moved someone else. Or it might be a time when you listened deeply to another person who was in pain, comforted him, and connected with him at a level beyond words.

Step 1

Describe the details of such an experience in your life. Include the place, time, and people involved. Describe what happened and how you felt about it.

Step 2

Now, review the article "Master student qualities," and take a look at the master student qualities that you checked off. These are the qualities that apply to you. Give a brief example of how you demonstrated at least one of those qualities.

Step 3

Now think of other qualities of a master student—characteristics that were not mentioned in the article. List those qualities along with a one-sentence description of each.

The master student process:
DISCOVERY

One way to become a better student is to grit your teeth and try harder. There is a better way—the master student process. The purpose of using this process is to develop the qualities of a master student.

You can use the master student process to learn about any subject, change your habits, and acquire new skills.

That is a large claim. If you're skeptical, that means you're already developing one quality of a master student—being inquisitive. Balance it with another quality—the ability to suspend judgment while considering a new idea.

First, get an overview of the master student process. There are three phases:

Brian A Jackson/Shutterstock.com

- Discovery—observing your thoughts, feelings, behaviors, and current circumstances
- Intention—choosing the new outcomes you'd like to create
- Action—following through on your intentions with new behaviors

As you experiment with the master student process, remember that there's nothing you need to take on faith. Experience it firsthand. Test the process in daily life. Then watch the results unfold.

Throughout this book, you'll see Journal Entries. These are suggestions for writing that guide you through the master student process.

Some of these Journal Entries are called Discovery Statements. Their purpose is to help you gain awareness of "where you are"—your current thoughts, feelings, and behaviors. Use Discovery Statements to describe your strengths and the aspects of your life that you'd like to change. The result is a running record of how you are learning and growing.

Sometimes Discovery Statements capture an "aha!" moment—a sudden flash of insight. Perhaps a new solution to an old problem suddenly occurs to you. Maybe a life-changing insight

wells up from the deepest part of your mind. Don't let such moments disappear. Capture them in Discovery Statements.

To get the most value from Discovery Statements, keep the following guidelines in mind.

Record the specifics. Thoughts include inner voices. We talk to ourselves constantly in our head. When internal chatter gets in the way, write down what you tell yourself. If this seems difficult at first, just start writing. The act of writing can trigger a flood of thoughts.

Thoughts also include mental pictures. These are especially powerful. Picturing yourself flunking a test is like a rehearsal to do just that. One way to take away the power of negative images is to describe them in detail.

Also notice how you feel when you function well. Use Discovery Statements to pinpoint exactly where and when you learn most effectively.

In addition, observe your emotions and actions, and record the facts. If you spent 90 minutes chatting online with a favorite cousin instead of reading your anatomy text, write about it. Include the details—when you did it, where you did it, and how it felt.

Use discomfort as a signal. When you approach a hard task, such as a difficult math problem, notice your physical sensations. These might include a churning stomach, shallow breathing, and yawning. Feeling uncomfortable, bored, or tired can be a signal that you're about to do valuable work. Stick with it. Write about it. Tell yourself you can handle the discomfort just a little bit longer. You will be rewarded with a new insight.

Suspend judgment. As you learn about yourself, be gentle. Suspend self-judgment. If you continually judge your behaviors as "bad" or "stupid," your mind will quit making discoveries rather than put up with abuse. For your own benefit, be kind to yourself.

Tell the truth. Suspending judgment helps you tell the truth about yourself. "The truth will set you free" is a saying that endures for a reason. The closer you get to the truth, the more powerful your Discovery Statements. And if you notice that you are avoiding the truth, don't blame yourself. Just tell the truth about it. ✖

The master student process:
INTENTION

Some Journal Entries in this book are called Intention Statements. These are about your commitment to take action. Use Intention Statements to describe how you will change your thinking and behavior.

leedsn/Shutterstock.com

In terms of the master student process, Intention Statements and Discovery Statements are linked.

Whereas Discovery Statements promote insights, Intention Statements are blueprints for action based on those insights.

To remind you of this connection, many Journal Entries in this book are labeled as Discovery/Intention Statements.

The act of writing will focus your energy on specific tasks and help you aim at particular goals. Here are ways to create Intention

Statements that make a positive difference in your life.

Make intentions observable. Rather than writing "I will work harder on my history assignments," write, "I intend to review my class notes, and I intend to make summary sheets of my reading." Then when you review your progress, you can actually tell whether you did what you intended to do.

Make intentions small and achievable. Give yourself the chance to succeed. Set goals that you can meet. Break large goals into small, specific tasks that can be accomplished quickly. If you want to get an A in biology, ask yourself, *What can I do today?* You might choose to talk to three classmates about forming a study group. Make that your intention.

Anticipate self-sabotage. Be aware of what you might do, consciously or unconsciously, to undermine your best intentions. If you intend to study differential equations at 9:00 p.m., notice when you sit down to watch a two-hour movie that starts at 8:00 p.m.

Be careful with intentions that depend on other people. If you intend for your study group to complete an assignment by Monday, then your success depends on the students in the group. However, you can support your group's success by writing an Intention Statement about completing your part of the assignment.

Set timelines. Timelines can focus your attention. For example, if you are assigned a paper to write, break the assignment into small tasks and set a precise due date for each one. For example, you might write, *I will select a topic for my paper by 9:00 a.m. Wednesday.*

Timelines are especially useful when your intention is to experiment with a technique suggested in this book. The sooner you act on a new idea, the better. Plan to practice a new behavior within 24 hours after you first learn about it.

Remember that you create timelines for your own benefit—not to feel guilty. And you can always adjust the timeline to allow for unplanned events.

Create reminders. Even the most carefully crafted intentions can fizzle when they're forgotten. If you intend to do something at a specific time or on a specific day, then make a note in your calendar. Other intentions can go on your to-do list. (For more about using these tools, see the Time chapter in this text.)

Reward yourself. When you carry out your intention on time, celebrate that fact. Remember that some rewards follow directly from your accomplishment. For example, one possible reward for earning your degree is a career that you enjoy.

Other rewards are more immediate and related to smaller tasks. When you turn in a paper on time, you could reward yourself with a movie or a long bike ride in the park.

In either case, rewards work best when you are willing to withhold them. If you plan to take a nap on Sunday afternoon whether or not you complete a reading assignment, then the nap is not an effective reward.

Another way to reward yourself is to sit quietly after finishing a task and savor the feeling. One reason that success breeds success is that it feels good. ✸

Be on the lookout

Be on the lookout for the Journal Entries throughout this text to begin writing Discovery and Intention Statements, and put the Master Student Process to work.

Sergey Nivens/Shutterstock.com

The master student process:
ACTION

Here's the deal: Life responds to what you *do*. The action phase of the master student process is where you jump "off the page" and into your life. This is where the magic happens.

A well-written Discovery Statement can move you to tears. A carefully crafted Intention Statement can fill you with inspiration. And if they fail to change your behavior, both kinds of Journal Entries are useless.

There's an old saying: If you do what you've always done, you'll get what you've always gotten. That seems so obvious. To get new results, be willing to experiment with new behaviors.

Successful people consistently produce the results that they want. And results follow from specific, consistent behaviors. There are some useful guidelines to keep in your back pocket as you move into action.

As you move into action, welcome discomfort, your old friend. Changing your behavior might lead to feelings of discomfort. Instead of going back to your old behaviors, befriend the yucky feelings. Taking action has a way of dissolving discomfort.

Discover the joy of "baby steps." Even simple changes in behavior can produce results. If you feel like procrastinating, then tackle just one small, specific task related to your intention. Find something you can complete in five minutes or less, and do it *now*. For example, access just one website related to the topic of your next assigned paper. Spend just three minutes previewing a reading assignment. Taking tiny steps like these can move you into action with grace and ease.

If you're unsure about what to do, then tweak your intentions. Make sure that your Intention Statements include specific behaviors. Describe what you'll actually *do*—the kind of physical actions that would show up on a video recording. Get your legs, arms, and mouth moving.

When you get stuck, tell the truth about it. As you become a student of human behavior, you'll see people expecting new results from old behaviors—and then wondering why they feel stuck. Don't be surprised if you discover this tendency in yourself. Just tell the truth about it, review your intentions, and take your next action.

Look for prompts to action throughout this book. In addition to Journal Entries, you'll see exercises scattered throughout *Becoming a Master Student*. These are suggestions for taking specific actions based on the ideas in the text. To get the most out of this book, do the exercises.

Remember that it's not about self-improvement. If you walk into a bookstore or browse an online bookseller, you might notice titles listed under a category called "self-improvement." *Becoming a Master Student* is not a "self-improvement" book. It's based on the idea that you already *are* a master student. All that's needed is a process to unlock what's already present within you.

Actually, this is a *self-experimenting* book. It's about defining what matters to you and choosing what to do as a result. There's nothing mysterious or "New Age" about it. Just discover what works for you. Then do it. ✴

Keep the process
ALIVE

Julianka/Shutterstock.com

The first edition of this book began with a memorable sentence: *This book is worthless.* Many students thought that this was a trick to get their attention. It wasn't.

Others thought it was "reverse psychology." It wasn't that either.

What was true of that first edition is true of this one as well: This book is worthless *if reading it is all you do.*

When you consistently move through the master student process—from discovery to intention and all the way to action—prepare for a different outcome. Practicing the process is what keeps it alive.

Think about the process as flying a plane. Airplanes are seldom exactly on course. Human and automatic pilots are always checking an airplane's positions and making corrections. The resulting path looks like a zigzag. The plane is almost always flying in the wrong direction. Yet through constant observation and course correction, it flies to the planned destination.

That's how the master student process works. Discovery Statements call for constant observation. Intention Statements call for course

correction. And moving into action keeps you on course, headed in your desired direction.

By the way, straying off course is normal. Don't panic when you forget a Discovery Statement or fail to complete an intended task. Simply make the necessary corrections.

Work smarter, not harder. Sometimes—and especially in college—learning *does* take effort. As you become a master student, you can learn many ways to get the most out of that effort.

Though the following statement might strike you as improbable, you may well discover that it's true: It can take the same amount of energy to get what you *don't* want in school as it takes to get what you *do* want. Sometimes getting what you don't want takes even more effort. An airplane burns the same amount of fuel flying away

The secret of student success

Okay, we're done kidding around. It's time to reveal the secret of student success.

(Provide your own drum roll here.)

The secret is . . .

. . . *there are no secrets.*

The strategies that successful students use are well known. You have hundreds of them at your fingertips right now, in this book.

Use those strategies. Modify them. Invent new ones. With the master student process, you become the authority on what works for you.

What makes any strategy work is discovery, intention, and action. Without them, the pages of *Becoming a Master Student* are just 2.1 pounds of expensive mulch.

Add your participation and these pages become priceless.

from its destination as it does flying toward it. It pays to stay on course.

Take a path to self-actualization. Abraham Maslow is an important figure in the history of psychology. One of his most memorable discoveries is that we are meant to do more than just satisfy our basic needs for physical safety and survival. We also need to

- love and be loved;
- experience accomplishment and self-esteem;
- fully develop our unique talents; and
- go beyond self-centeredness and find fulfillment in contributing to other people.

When we are meeting this full range of needs, we are self-actualizing.[1]

Maslow's ideas are a major inspiration for this book. One goal of the master student process is to put you on a path to self-actualization. As you gain experience with writing Discovery and Intention Statements, you'll learn to think more critically and creatively. And as you move into action, you'll learn to overcome procrastination and manage your behaviors in the midst of constantly changing moods. Each time that you increase your skill in the master student process, you move higher up the hierarchy of needs.

See the process as a lifelong adventure. Remember that this book is big for a reason. There are far more ideas in this book than you can possibly put into action during a single term.

This is not a mistake. In fact, it is quite intentional. There are many ideas in this book because no one expects all of them to work for you. If one technique fizzles out, you have dozens more to choose from.

Consider the first word in the title of this book—*becoming*. This word implies that mastery is not an end state or final goal. Rather, mastery is a continuous process. ✶

Get the most from
THIS BOOK

GET USED TO A NEW LOOK AND TONE
This book looks different from traditional textbooks. *Becoming a Master Student* presents major ideas in magazine-style articles. There are lots of lists, blurbs, one-liners, pictures, charts, graphs, illustrations, and even a joke or two.

SKIP AROUND
Feel free to use this book in several different ways. Read it straight through. Or pick it up, turn to any page, and find an idea you can use right now. You might find that this book presents similar ideas in several places. This repetition is intentional. Repetition reinforces key points. A technique that works in one area of your life might work in others as well.

USE WHAT WORKS
If there are sections of this book that don't apply to you at all, skip them—unless, of course, they are assigned. In that case, see whether you can

HERE'S THE SALES PITCH

The purpose of this book is to help you make a successful transition to higher education by setting up a pattern of success that will last the rest of your life. You probably won't take action and use the ideas in this book until you are convinced that you have something to gain.

Before you stiffen up and resist this sales pitch, remember that you have already bought the book. Now you can get value for your money by committing yourself to becoming a master student. Here's what's in it for you.

Get full value for your money. Your college education is one of the most expensive things you will ever buy. When you add up all the direct and indirect expenses, you might be paying $100 an hour or more to sit in class.

At the same time, you control the value you get out of your education. And that value can be considerable. The joy of learning aside, higher levels of education relate to higher lifetime income and more consistent employment.[2] It pays to be a master student.

Get suggestions from thousands of students. The ideas and techniques in this book are here not just because learning theorists, educators, and psychologists say they work. They're here because tens of thousands of students from all kinds of backgrounds use them.

Get a tested product. The previous editions of this book have proved successful for millions of students. In particular, students with successful histories have praised the techniques in this book.

gain value from those sections anyway. When you commit to get value from this book, even an idea that seems irrelevant or ineffective at first can turn out to be a powerful tool in the future. If it works, use it. If it doesn't, lose it.

RIP 'EM OUT

The pages of *Becoming a Master Student* are loose or perforated because some of the information here is too important to leave in the book. You can rip out pages, then reinsert them later by sticking them into a binder or the spine of the book with a piece of tape.

PRACTICE CRITICAL THINKING

Practicing Critical Thinking activities appear throughout this book. Other elements of this text, including Journal Entries and Skills Snapshots, also promote critical thinking.

LEARN ABOUT LEARNING STYLES

Check out the Learning Style Inventory and related articles in the Discovering Yourself chapter. This material can help you discover your preferred learning styles and allow you to explore new styles. Then, throughout the rest of this book, you'll find suggestions for applying your knowledge of learning styles. The modes of learning can be

accessed by asking four basic questions: *Why? What? How?* and *What if?* You can use this four-part structure to effectively learn anything.

EXPERIENCE THE POWER OF THE POWER PROCESSES

A Power Process is a suggestion to shift your perspective or try a new behavior. Look for this feature near the beginning of each chapter. Users of *Becoming a Master Student* often refer to these articles as their favorite part of the book. Approach them with a sense of play and possibility. Start with an open mind, experiment with the ideas, and see what works.

READ THE SIDEBARS

Look for sidebars—short bursts of words placed between longer articles—throughout the book. These short pieces might offer insights that transform your experience of higher education.

wavebreakmedia/Shutterstock.com

MOTIVATION:
I'm just not in the mood

In large part, this chapter is about your motivation to succeed in school.

There are at least two ways to think about motivation. One is that the terms *self-discipline, willpower,* and *motivation* describe something missing in ourselves. We use these words to explain another person's success or our own shortcomings: "If I were more motivated, I'd get more involved in school." "Of course she got an A. She has self-discipline." "Losing weight takes a lot of willpower. I must not have enough." It seems that certain people are born with lots of motivation, whereas others miss out on it.

A second approach to thinking about motivation is to stop assuming that motivation is mysterious, determined at birth, or hard to come by. Perhaps there's nothing missing in you. What we call motivation could be something that you already possess—the ability to do a task even when you don't feel like it. This is a habit that you can develop with practice. The following suggestions offer ways to do that.

Promise it. Motivation can come simply from being clear about your goals and acting on them. Say that you want to start a study group. You can commit yourself to inviting people and setting a time and place to meet. Promise your

classmates that you'll do this, and ask them to hold you accountable. Self-discipline, willpower, motivation—none of these mysterious characteristics has to get in your way. Just make a promise and keep your word.

Befriend your discomfort. Sometimes keeping your word means doing a task you'd rather put off. The mere thought of doing laundry, reading a chapter in a statistics book, or proofreading a term paper can lead to discomfort. In the face of such discomfort, you can procrastinate. Or you can use this barrier as a means to getting the job done.

Begin by investigating the discomfort. Notice the thoughts running through your head, and speak them out loud: "I'd rather walk on a bed of coals than do this." "This is the last thing I want to do right now."

Also observe what's happening with your body. For example, are you breathing faster or slower than usual? Are your shoulders tight? Do you feel any tension in your stomach?

Once you're in contact with your mind and body, stay with the discomfort a few minutes longer. Don't judge it as good or bad. Accepting the

thoughts and body sensations robs them of power. They might still be there, but in time they can stop being a barrier for you.

Change your mind—and your body. You can also get past discomfort by planting new thoughts in your mind or changing your physical stance. For example, instead of slumping in a chair, sit up straight or stand up. You can also get physically active by taking a short walk. Notice what happens to your discomfort.

Work with your thoughts also. Replace "I can't stand this" with "I'll feel great when this is done" or "Doing this will help me get something I want."

Sweeten the task. Sometimes it's just one aspect of a task that holds you back. You can stop procrastinating merely by changing that aspect. If distaste for your physical environment keeps you from studying, you can change that environment. Reading about social psychology might seem like a yawner when you're alone in a dark corner of the house. Moving to a cheery, well-lit library can sweeten the task.

When you're done with an important task, reward

wavebreakmedia/Shutterstock.com

yourself for a job well done. The simplest rewards—such as a walk, a hot bath, or a favorite snack—can be the most effective.

Talk about how bad it is. One way to get past negative attitudes is to take them to an extreme. When faced with an unpleasant task, launch into a no-holds-barred gripe session. Pull out all the stops: "There's no way I can start my income taxes now. This is terrible beyond words—an absolute disaster. This is a catastrophe of global proportions!" Griping taken this far can restore perspective. It shows how self-talk can turn inconveniences into crises.

Turn up the pressure. Sometimes motivation is a luxury. Pretend that the due date for your project has been moved up one month, one week, or one day. Raising the stress level slightly can spur you into action. Then the issue of motivation seems beside the point, and meeting the due date moves to the forefront.

Turn down the pressure. The mere thought of starting a huge task can induce anxiety. To get past this feeling, turn down the pressure by taking "baby steps." Divide a large project into small tasks. In 30 minutes or less, you could preview a book, create a rough outline for a paper, or solve two or three math problems.

Careful planning can help you discover many such steps to make a big job doable.

Ask for support. Other people can become your allies in overcoming procrastination. For example, form a support group and declare what you intend to accomplish before each meeting. Then ask members to hold you accountable. If you want to begin exercising regularly, ask another person to walk with you three times weekly. People in support groups ranging from Alcoholics Anonymous to Weight Watchers know the power of this strategy.

Adopt a model. One strategy for succeeding at any task is to hang around the masters. Find someone you consider successful, and spend time with her. Observe this person and use her as a model for your own behavior. You can "try on" this person's actions and attitudes. Look for tools that feel right for you. This person can become a mentor for you.

Compare the payoffs to the costs. All behaviors have payoffs and costs. Even unwanted behaviors such as cramming for exams or neglecting exercise have payoffs. Cramming might give you more time that's free of commitments. Neglecting exercise can give you more time to sleep.

One way to let go of such unwanted behaviors is first to celebrate them—even embrace them. We can openly acknowledge the payoffs.

Celebration can be especially powerful when you follow it up with the next step—determining the costs. For example, skipping a reading assignment can give you time

to go to the movies. However, you might be unprepared for class and have twice as much to read the following week.

Maybe there is another way to get the payoff (going to the movies) without paying the cost (skipping the reading assignment). With some thoughtful weekly planning, you might choose to give up a few hours of television and end up with enough time to read the assignment *and* go to the movies.

Comparing the costs and benefits of any behavior can fuel our motivation. We can choose new behaviors because they align with what we want most.

Do it later. At times, it's effective to save a task for later. For example, writing a résumé can wait until you've taken the time to analyze your job skills and map out your career goals. Putting it off does not show a lack of motivation—it shows planning.

When you do choose to do a task later, turn this decision into a promise. Estimate how long the task will take, and schedule a specific date and time for it on your calendar.

Heed the message. Sometimes lack of motivation carries a message that's worth heeding. An example is the student who majors in accounting but seizes every chance to be with children. His chronic reluctance to read accounting textbooks might not be a problem. Instead, it might reveal his desire to major in elementary education. His original career choice might have come from the belief that "real men don't teach kindergarten." In such cases, an apparent lack of motivation signals a deeper wisdom trying to get through. ✄

Jason Stitt/Shutterstock.com

Ways to change a
HABIT

Consider a new way to think about the word *habit*. Imagine for a moment that many of our most troublesome problems and even our most basic traits are just habits.

The expanding waistline that your friend blames on her spouse's cooking—maybe that's just a habit called overeating.

The fit of rage that a student blames on a teacher—maybe that's just the student's habit of closing the door to new ideas.

Procrastination, stress, and money shortages might just be names that we give to collections of habits—scores of simple, small, repeated behaviors that combine to create a huge result. The same goes for health, wealth, love, and many of the other things that we want from life.

One way of thinking about success or failure is to focus on habits. Behaviors such as failing to complete reading assignments or skipping class might be habits leading to outcomes that "could not" be avoided, including dropping out of school. In the same way, behaviors such as completing assignments and attending class might lead to the outcome of getting an A.

When you discover a behavior that undermines your goals or creates a circumstance that you don't

want, consider a new attitude: *That behavior is just a habit. And it can be changed.*

Thinking about yourself as a creature of habit gives you power. Then you are not faced with the monumental task of changing your very nature. Rather, you can take on the doable job of changing your habits. Even a change in behavior that seems small can have positive effects that ripple throughout your life. Following are ways to move successfully through the stages of habit change.

TELL THE TRUTH

Telling the truth about our current habits—from chewing our fingernails to cheating on tests—frees us. Without taking this step, our efforts to change can be as ineffective as rearranging the deck chairs on the *Titanic*. Telling the truth allows us to see what's actually sinking the ship.

When we admit what's really going on in our lives, our defenses are down. We're open to change and accepting help from others. The support we need to change a habit has an opportunity to make an impact.

START SMALL

Many people sabotage their success by planning habit changes that are too big or too hard. Avoid this mistake by starting with a small, easy change. Take what you think you "should" do and reduce it. Then reduce it again. Whittle down the task until it's easy to start.

Draw on the "power of one." Change one habit at a time—a behavior that you will do once each day. Instead of planning to floss all your teeth, for example, plan to floss just one. Instead of planning to walk one mile, plan to walk one block. Set yourself up for success by making the new habit easy to start. Instead of planning a big change in your diet, plan to eat just one extra piece of fruit each day.

Do not be deceived by the simplicity of this approach. It works for a simple reason: The hardest part of developing a new habit is simply getting started. Once you succeed with a tiny habit change, it's easier to extend the behavior. Over time, flossing one tooth can gradually and naturally extend to flossing all your teeth. Spending 1 minute on the mat can extend to 10 or 15. Walking a block can extend to a mile.

Learn more about the power of changing behaviors in small steps. For example, check out the 3 Tiny Habits course (**tinyhabits.com**) created by B. J. Fogg, professor of psychology at Stanford University. One of his main suggestions for habit change is to make sure that your new behavior is truly tiny—one that you can easily do in less than 30 seconds.

REHEARSE THE NEW HABIT

Before committing to the new behavior on a daily basis, make sure that it's something you can and *will* do. You can pave the way for a new behavior by clearing a mental path for it. Before you apply the new behavior, rehearse it in your mind. Mentally picture what actions you will take and in what order.

Say that you plan to improve your handwriting when taking notes. Imagine yourself in class with a blank notebook poised before you. See yourself taking up a finely crafted pen. Notice how comfortable it feels in your hand. See yourself writing clearly and legibly. You can even picture how you will make individual letters: the *e*'s, *i*'s, and *r*'s. Then, when class is over, see yourself reviewing your notes and taking pleasure in how easy they are to read.

Whenever possible, rehearse the new habit *physically* as well. If you plan to do one push up every time you start the microwave, for instance, then try out this new behavior right away. See how it feels and notice how the new movement registers in your body.

TRIGGER THE HABIT

To increase your success at behavior change, link a new habit to an existing habit—one that's stable and predictable. If you want to develop the habit of flossing, for example, then do it right after brushing your teeth. If you want to do yoga early in the day, then step on that mat right after using the bathroom in the morning.

B. J. Fogg suggests that you plan new habits using this format: *After I . . . , I will . . .* For instance:

- After I sit down at my desk, I will drink a sip of water.
- After I clean up from breakfast, I will do one pushup.
- After I answer the phone, I will stand up.

PRACTICE THE NEW HABIT

Learning is a stable change in behavior that comes as a result of practice. This is key to changing habits. Act on your intention over and over again. If you fail or forget, then let go of any self-judgment. Just review your intention and go back to practicing the new habit.

Also accept any feelings of discomfort that come with a new behavior. Keep practicing the new habit, even if it feels unnatural at first.

GIVE IT TIME

Perhaps you've heard people say that it takes a certain number of days to change a habit. This can lead to needless worries about whether your habit change is taking too much time.

Instead, consider a more practical approach: It takes what it takes. You might find that some habits take longer to develop than others. That's fine. Trust the process. Do what works. Give yourself enough time to make the change—whatever it takes. When your new behavior develops into a stable habit, you'll know that you've succeeded.

BE WILLING TO REVISE YOUR PLANS

If your planned habit change doesn't work, then simply note what happened. Notice any feelings of guilt or blame and let them go. Write a Discovery Statement about what you learned from the experience. Then select a new habit and begin again.

Making mistakes as you practice doesn't mean that you've failed. Even when you don't get the results you want from a new behavior, you learn something valuable in the process. Once you understand ways to change one habit, you understand ways to change *any* habit.

GET FEEDBACK AND SUPPORT

Getting feedback and support is a crucial step in adopting a new behavior. It is also a point at which many plans for change break down. It's easy to practice your new behavior with enthusiasm for a few days. After the initial rush of excitement, though, things can get a little tougher. You begin to find excuses for slipping back into old habits: "One more cigarette won't hurt." "I can get back to my paper tomorrow." "It's been a tough day. I deserve to skip class."

One way to get feedback is to bring other people into the

picture. Ask others to remind you that you are changing your habit if they see you backsliding. Starting new habits might call for the more focused, long-lasting support that close friends or family members can give. Support from others can be as simple as a quick phone call: "Hi. Have you started that outline for your research paper yet?" Or it can be as formal as a support group that meets once a week to review everyone's goals and action plans.

MONITOR YOUR BEHAVIOR

Jerry Seinfeld told one aspiring comedian that "the way to be a better comic was to create better jokes, and the way to create better jokes was to write every day."[3] Seinfeld also revealed his own system for creating a writing habit: He bought a big wall calendar that displayed the whole year on one page. On each day that he wrote jokes, Seinfeld marked a big red X on the appropriate day on the wall calendar. He knew that he'd established a new habit when he looked at the calendar and saw an unbroken chain of X's. You can use the same strategy to take a series of small steps that add up to a big change.

Search for habit change apps. Examples are Habit List (**habitlist.com**) and Way of Life (**wayoflifeapp.com**). Some apps allow you to create a Seinfeld-style calendar for tracking your daily behavior.

CELEBRATE SUCCESS

Every time that you practice your new habit, celebrate. This can be as simple as using a word or phrase—*Yes!* or *Victory!* or *Way to go!* or *I rock!* Say it to yourself or even out loud. Draw on the power of positive emotions to reinforce new behaviors.

Choose a celebration that supports your goals and values. Eating a high-calorie snack is not an effective way to celebrate the fact that you exercised, especially if your goal is to lose weight.

CHANGE YOUR ENVIRONMENT

Consider the student who always snacks when he studies. Each time he sits down to read, he positions a bag of potato chips within easy reach. For him, opening a book is a cue to start chewing. Snacking is especially easy, given the place he chooses to study—the kitchen.

This student decides to change this habit by studying at a desk in his bedroom instead of at the kitchen table. And every time he feels the urge to bite into a potato chip, he drinks from a glass of water that he's placed nearby.

You can use this strategy to change many habits in short order. Just set up your environment so that the undesired behaviors become harder—and desired behaviors become easier.

If you want to stop snacking on junk foods, for example, then throw them in the garbage. If you want to drink less alcohol at home, then store the

bottles in an out-of-the way closet. And if you want to develop a daily habit of doing yoga, then lay out a mat in your bedroom and leave it there.

The beauty of this strategy is that habit change doesn't depend on motivation or willpower. That's a big step toward success at habit change. ✄

---

journal entry 1

DISCOVERY STATEMENT

Declare what you want

Review the articles that you've read so far in this chapter. Then use this Journal Entry to start experiencing the master student process—the ongoing cycle of discovery, intention, and action.

Brainstorm many possible ways to complete this sentence: *I discovered that what I want most from my education is . . .* When you're done, choose the ending that feels best to you and write it down.

I discovered that what I want most from my education is . . .

do you have a
MINUTE?

Sometimes the hardest part of meeting a goal or changing a habit is simply getting started. To get past this obstacle, take a "baby step" right away. In 60 seconds or less, you can often do something right away that takes you in your desired direction.

Review the following chart for examples. Then plan a few baby steps of your own.

If you want to . . .	Then take a minute to . . .
Exercise every day right after getting up in the morning.	Lay out your exercise clothes and shoes the night before.
Spend less time on email.	Unsubscribe from email lists that no longer interest you.
Capture important ideas as soon as they occur to you.	Grab a few 3 × 5 cards and pen to stick in a pocket or purse. Or download a note-taking app for your smartphone.
Clean out that pile of unopened mail on top of your desk.	Throw away the junk mail and stuff that you'll never respond to.
Empty your email inbox.	Look for one email that you can respond to in 60 seconds, and handle it now. Set up a separate folder for emails that require follow-up action. Set up a separate folder for "read later" emails that don't require follow-up action.
Organize your desk.	Find a small metal tray, basket, or other container to temporarily store new pieces of mail, class handouts, notes to yourself, and other papers.
Organize your list of contacts.	Take one business card and enter the name, address, and phone number into the Contacts app on your computer, tablet, or smartphone.
Write more useful notes.	Take your notes from one of today's classes and fix a sentence that's unclear.
Communicate more effectively with instructors.	Write down three questions you'd like to ask one of your instructors during an office meeting.
Start reviewing for tests earlier.	Use a 3 × 5 card or smartphone app to create one flash card for one of your courses. Enter upcoming test dates in your calendar.
Get started on an assigned paper to write.	Make a list of three possible topics. Write one sentence that you might be able to include in the paper. Brainstorm three questions about your topic.
Express gratitude to the key people in your life.	Send one person a short text with a specific thank-you.
Get financial aid.	Search your school's website for the location, phone number, and email address of the financial aid office.
Reduce the amount of time that you spend sitting every day.	Stand up right now for one minute. Stand up whenever you answer a phone call.
Manage stress more effectively.	Take 60 seconds to scan your body for any points of tension and relax those muscles.
Develop a career plan.	Go online to make an appointment with your school's career center to find out more about the resources that are available to you.
Protect your privacy when you go online.	Create a new password that's stronger than one of your current passwords. Bookmark a search engine with built-in privacy features, such as Epic Search (**epicsearch.in**) and DuckDuckGo (**duckduckgo.com**).

practicing
CRITICAL THINKING

Plan to change a habit

In his book *The Power of Habit*, Charles Duhigg explains that any habit has three elements:[3]

- **Routine.** This is a behavior that we repeat, usually without thinking. Examples are taking a second helping at dinner, biting fingernails, or automatically hitting the snooze button when the alarm goes off in the morning.
- **Cue.** Also known as a *trigger*, this is an event that occurs right before we perform the routine. It might be an internal event, such as a change in mood. Or it could be an external event, such as seeing an advertisement that triggers food cravings.
- **Reward.** This is the payoff for the routine—usually a feeling of pleasure or a reduction in stress.

Taken together, these elements form a habit loop: You perceive a *cue* and then perform a *routine* in order to get a *reward*. Use this Practicing Critical Thinking exercise to test Duhigg's ideas for yourself.

Step 1: Identify your current routine.

Describe the habit that you want to change. Refer to a specific behavior that anyone could observe—preferably a physical, visible action that you perform every day.

I discovered that the habit I want to change is . . .

Step 2: Identify the cue.

Next, think about what takes place immediately before you perform the routine. For instance, drinking a cup of coffee (cue) might trigger the urge to eat a cookie (routine).

I discovered that the cue for the behavior I described is . . .

Step 3: Identify the reward.

Now for the "goodie." Reflect on the reward you get from your routine. Do you gain a distraction from discomfort? A pleasant sensation in your body? A chance to socialize with friends or coworkers? Describe the details.

I discovered that my reward for my current routine is . . .

Step 4: Choose a new routine.

Now choose a different routine that you can perform in response to the cue. The challenge is to choose a behavior that offers a reward with as few disadvantages as possible. Instead of eating a whole cookie, for example, you could break off just one small section and eat it slowly, with full attention. This would allow you to experience a familiar pleasure with a fraction of the calories. Describe your new routine.

The new routine that I intend to do is . . .

Step 5: Create a visual summary of your experience with habit change.

After practicing your new routine for at least seven days, fill in the following chart to summarize what you did. Use the "Notes" column to describe what you learned, including anything that surprised you, consequences of the new routine, and things that will be useful to remember when you plan habit changes in the future.

Current Routine	Cue	Reward	New Routine	Notes

journal
entry 2

Commitment

This book is worthless *unless* you actively participate in its activities and exercises.

One powerful way to begin taking action is to make a commitment. Conversely, if you don't make a commitment, then sustained action is unlikely. The result is a worthless book.

Therefore, in the interest of saving your valuable time and energy, this exercise gives you a chance to declare your level of involvement upfront.

From the options that follow, choose the sentence that best reflects your commitment to using this book.

1. Well, I'm reading this book right now, aren't I?
2. I will skim the book and read the interesting parts.
3. I will read the book, think about it, and do the exercises that look interesting.
4. I will read the book, do some exercises, and complete some of the Journal Entries.
5. I will read the book, do some exercises and Journal Entries, and use some of the techniques.
6. I will read the book, do most of the exercises and Journal Entries, and use some of the techniques.
7. I will study this book, do most of the exercises and Journal Entries, and use some of the techniques.
8. I will study this book, do most of the exercises and Journal Entries, and experiment with many of the techniques in order to discover what works best for me.
9. I promise myself that I will create value from this course by studying this book, doing all the exercises and Journal Entries, and experimenting with most of the techniques.
10. I will use this book as if the quality of my education depended on it—doing all the exercises and Journal Entries, experimenting with most of the techniques, inventing techniques of my own, and planning to reread this book in the future.

Enter today's date and the number of the sentence that reflects your commitment level:

Date: _____   Commitment level: _____

If you selected commitment level 1 or 2, you probably won't create a lot of value in this class. Consider passing this book on to a friend.

If your commitment level is 9 or 10, you are on your way to terrific success in school.

If your level is somewhere in between, then experiment with three suggestions from this chapter. Also set a date to return to this exercise and consider raising your level of commitment based on the results of your experiment.

I intend to . . .

Date: _____   Commitment level: _____

Monkey Business/Fotolia

Discovering Yourself

what is included . . .

24   Power Process: Ideas are tools

25   First Step: Truth is a key to mastery

28   The Discovery Wheel

33   Learning styles: Discovering how you learn

36   Learning Style Inventory

42   Using your learning style profile to succeed

48   Claim your multiple intelligences

52   Learning through your senses: the VARK system

56   Master Student Profile: Joshua Williams

why

Success starts with telling the truth about what *is* working—and what *isn't*—in your life right now.

how

Skim this chapter for three techniques that you'd like to use in school or in your personal life during the upcoming week. Make a note to yourself or mark the pages where the strategies that you intend to use are located in the chapter.

what if...

I could start to create new outcomes in my life by accepting the way I am right now?

do you have a minute?

Take a minute to write down a "baby step"—a task that takes 60 seconds or less—that can help you move toward completing a current project or assignment. For example, brainstorm a list of topics for a paper that you plan to write.

If you can spare another minute, then do that task immediately.

Ideas are tools

There are many ideas in this book. When you first encounter them, don't believe any of them. Instead, think of the ideas as tools.

For example, you use a hammer for a purpose—to drive a nail. You don't try to figure out whether the hammer is "right." You just use it. If it works, you use it again. If it doesn't work, you get a different hammer.

People have plenty of room in their lives for different kinds of hammers, but they tend to limit their openness to different kinds of ideas. A new idea, at some level, is a threat to their very being—unlike a new hammer, which is simply a new hammer.

Most of us have a built-in desire to be right. Our ideas, we often think, represent ourselves.

Some ideas are worth dying for. But please note: This book does not contain any of those ideas. The ideas on these pages are strictly "hammers."

Imagine someone defending a hammer. Picture this person holding up a hammer and declaring, "I hold this hammer to be self-evident. Give me this hammer or give me death. Those other hammers are flawed. There are only two kinds of people in this world: people who believe in this hammer and people who don't."

That ridiculous picture makes a point. This book is not a manifesto. It's a toolbox, and tools are meant to be used.

If you read about a tool in this book that doesn't sound "right" or one that sounds a little goofy, remember that the ideas here are for using, not necessarily for believing. Suspend your judgment. Test the idea for yourself. If it works, use it. If it doesn't, don't use it.

Any tool—a hammer, a computer program, a study technique—is designed to do a specific job. A master mechanic carries a variety of tools because no single tool works for all jobs. If you throw a tool away because it doesn't work in one situation, you won't be able to pull it out later when it's just what you need. So if an idea doesn't work for you and you are satisfied that you gave it a fair chance, don't throw it away. File it away instead. The idea might come in handy soon.

And remember, this book is not about figuring out the "right" way. Even the "ideas are tools" approach is not "right."

It's just a tool.

Anteromite/Shutterstock.com

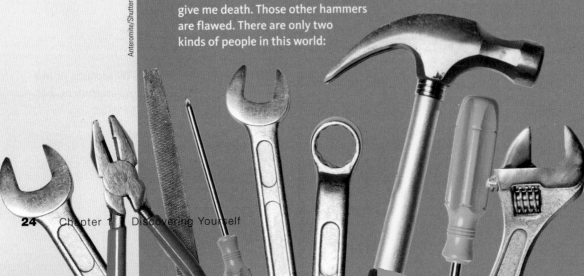

Akva/Shutterstock.com

FIRST STEP:

Truth is a key to mastery

The First Step is one of the most valuable tools in this book. It magnifies the power of all the other techniques. It is a key to becoming a master student.

The First Step technique is simple: Tell the truth about who you are and what you want. End of discussion. Now proceed to the next chapter. Well . . . it's not *quite* that simple.

To succeed in school, tell the truth about what kind of student you are and what kind of student you want to become. Success starts with telling the truth about what *is* working—and what is *not* working—in your life right now.

An article about telling the truth might sound like pie-in-the-sky moralizing. However, there is nothing pie-in-the-sky or moralizing about a First Step. It is a practical, down-to-earth principle to use whenever you want to change your behavior.

When we acknowledge our strengths, we gain an accurate picture of what we can accomplish. When we admit that we have a problem, we are free to find a solution. Ignoring the truth, on the other hand, can lead to problems that stick around for decades.

FIRST STEPS ARE UNIVERSAL

When you see a doctor, the First Step is to tell the truth about your current symptoms. That way you can get an accurate diagnosis and effective treatment plan. This principle is universal. It works for just about any problem in any area of life.

First Steps are used by millions of people who want to turn their lives around. No technique in this book has been field-tested more often or more successfully—or under tougher circumstances.

For example, members of Alcoholics Anonymous start by telling the truth about their drinking. Their First Step is to admit that they are powerless over alcohol. That's when their lives start to change.

When people join Weight Watchers, their First Step is telling the truth about how much they currently weigh.

When people go for credit counseling, their First Step is telling the truth about how much money they earn, how much they spend, and how much they owe.

People dealing with a variety of other challenges—including troubled relationships with food, drugs, sex, and work—also start by telling the truth. They use First Steps to change their behavior, and they do it for a reason: First Steps work.

FIRST STEPS ARE JUDGMENT-FREE

Let's be honest: It's not easy to tell the truth about ourselves.

It's not fun to admit our weaknesses. Many of us approach a frank evaluation of ourselves about as enthusiastically as we'd greet a phone call from the bank about an overdrawn account. We might end up admitting that we're afraid of algebra, that we don't complete term papers on time, or that coming up with the money to pay for tuition is a constant challenge.

There is another way to think about self-evaluations. If we could see them as opportunities to solve problems and take charge of our lives, we might welcome them. Believe it or not, we can begin working with our list of weaknesses by celebrating them.

Consider the most accomplished, "together" people you know. If they were totally candid with you, they would talk about their mistakes and regrets as well as their rewards and recognition. The most successful people tend to be the most willing to look at their flaws.

It may seem natural to judge our own shortcomings and feel bad about them. Some people believe that such feelings are necessary to correct their errors. Others think that a healthy dose of shame can prevent the moral decay of our society.

Think again. In fact, consider the opposite idea: We can gain skill without feeling rotten about the past. We can change the way things *are* without having to criticize the way things *have been*. We can learn to see shame or blame as excess baggage and just set them aside.

If the whole idea of telling the truth about yourself puts a knot in your stomach, that's good. Notice the knot. It is your friend. It is a reminder that First Steps call for courage and compassion. These are qualities of a master student.

FIRST STEPS POINT US TOWARD GOALS

Master students get the most value from a First Step by turning their perceived shortcomings into goals. "I don't exercise enough" turns into "I will walk briskly for 30 minutes at least three times per week."

"I don't take clear notes" becomes "I will review my notes within 24 hours after class and rewrite them for clarity."

"I am in conflict with my parents" transforms into "When my parents call, I will take time to understand their point of view before disagreeing with them."

"I get so nervous during the night before a big test that I find it hard to sleep" turns into "I will find ways to reduce stress during the 24 hours before a test so that I sleep better."

Another quality of master students is that they refuse to let their First Steps turn into excuses. These students avoid using the phrase "I can't" and its endless variations.

The key is to state First Steps in a way that allows for new possibilities in the future. Use language in a way that reinforces your freedom to change.

For example, "I can't succeed in math" is better stated like this: "During math courses, I tend to get confused early in the term and find it hard to ask questions. I could be more assertive in asking for help right away."

"I can't say no to my underage friends who like to drink until they get drunk" is better stated as "I have friends who drink illegally and drink too much. I want to be alcohol-free and still be friends with them."

Telling the truth about what we don't want gives us more clarity about what we *do* want. By taking a First Step, we can free up all the energy that it takes to deny our problems and avoid change. We can redirect that energy and use it to take actions that align with our values.

FIRST STEPS INCLUDE STRENGTHS

For some of us, it's even harder to recognize our strengths than to recognize our weaknesses. Maybe we don't want to brag. Maybe we're attached to a poor self-image.

The reasons don't matter. The point is that using the First Step technique in *Becoming a Master Student* means telling the truth about our positive qualities too.

Remember that weaknesses are often strengths taken to an extreme. The student who carefully revises her writing can make significant improvements in a term paper. If she revises too much and hands in the paper late, though, her grade might suffer. Any success strategy carried too far can backfire.

FIRST STEPS ARE SPECIFIC

Whether written or verbal, the ways that we express our First Steps are more powerful when they are specific. For example, if you want to improve your note-taking skills, you might write, "I am an awful note taker," but it would be more effective to write, "I can't read 80 percent of the notes I took in Introduction to Psychology last week, and I have no idea what was important in that class."

Be just as specific about what you plan to achieve. You might declare, "I want to take legible notes that help me predict what questions will be on the final exam."

The exercises and Journal Entries in this chapter are all about getting specific. They can help you tap resources you never knew you had. For example, do the Discovery Wheel to get a big-picture view of your personal effectiveness. And use the Learning Style Inventory, along with the articles about multiple intelligences and the VARK system, to tell the truth about how you perceive and process information.

As you use these elements of *Becoming a Master Student*, you might feel surprised at what you discover. You might even disagree with the results of an exercise. That's fine. Just tell the truth about it. Use your disagreement as a tool for further discussion and self-discovery.

This book is full of First Steps. It's just that simple. The truth has power. ✠

practicing
CRITICAL THINKING

4

Taking the First Step

The purpose of this exercise is to give you a chance to discover and acknowledge your own strengths, as well as areas for improvement. For many students, this exercise is the most difficult one in the book. To make the exercise worthwhile, do it with courage. Some people suggest that looking at areas for improvement means focusing on personal weaknesses. They view it as a negative approach that runs counter to positive thinking. Well, perhaps. Positive thinking is a great technique. So is telling the truth, especially when we see the whole picture—the negative aspects as well as the positive ones.

If you admit that you can't add or subtract, and that's indeed the truth, then you have taken a strong, positive First Step toward learning basic math. On the other hand, if you say that you are a terrible math student, but that's not the truth, then you are programming yourself to accept unnecessary failure.

The point is to tell the truth. This exercise is similar to the Discovery Statements that appear in every chapter. The difference is that, in this case, for reasons of confidentiality, you won't write down your discoveries in the book.

You are likely to disclose some things about yourself that you wouldn't want others to read. You might even write down some truths that could get you into trouble. Do this exercise on separate sheets of paper; then hide or destroy them. Protect your privacy. To make this exercise work, follow these suggestions.

- **Be specific.** It is not effective to write, "I can improve my communication skills." Of course you can. Instead, write down precisely what you can *do* to improve your communication skills—for example, "I can spend more time really listening while the other person is talking, instead of thinking about what I'm going to say next."
- **Be self-aware.** Look beyond the classroom. What goes on outside school often has the greatest impact on your ability to be an effective student. Consider your strengths and weaknesses that you may think have nothing to do with school.
- **Be courageous.** This exercise calls for an important master student quality—courage. It is a waste of time if this exercise is done halfheartedly. Be willing to take risks. You might open a door that reveals a part of yourself that you didn't want to admit was there. The power of this technique is that once you know what is there, you can do something about it.

Part 1	Part 2	Part 3	Part 4
Time yourself, and for 10 minutes write as fast as you can, completing each of the following sentences at least 10 times with anything that comes to mind. If you get stuck, don't stop. Just write something—even if it seems crazy.	When you have completed the first part of the exercise, review what you have written, crossing off things that don't make any sense. The sentences that remain suggest possible goals for becoming a master student.	Here's the tough part. Time yourself, and for 10 minutes write as fast as you can, completing the following sentences with anything that comes to mind. As in Part 1, complete each sentence at least 10 times. Just keep writing, even if it sounds silly.	Review what you have written, and circle the things that you can fully celebrate. This list is a good thing to keep for those times when you question your own value and worth.

I never succeed when I . . .

I'm not very good at . . .

Something I'd like to change about myself is . . .

I always succeed when I . . .

I am very good at . . .

Something I like about myself is . . .

The Discovery Wheel

The Discovery Wheel gives you an in-depth opportunity to practice the master student process—the ongoing cycle of discovery, intention, and action. Like many other students, you might find the Discovery Wheel to be the most valuable exercise in this book.

This is not a test. There are no trick questions, and the answers will have meaning only for you.

Here are two suggestions to make this exercise more effective. First, think of it as the beginning of an opportunity to change. Second, lighten up. A little laughter can make self-evaluations a lot more effective.

Here's how the Discovery Wheel works. By the end of this exercise, you will have filled in a circle similar to the example. The Discovery Wheel circle is a picture of how you see yourself as a student. The closer the shading comes to the outer edge of the circle, the higher the evaluation of a specific skill. In Figure 1.1, the student has rated her reading skills low and her note-taking skills high.

The terms *high* and *low are* not meant to reflect judgment. The Discovery Wheel is not a permanent picture of who you are. It is a picture of how you view your strengths and weaknesses as a student today. To begin this exercise, read

5 points	This statement is always or almost always true of me.
4 points	This statement is often true of me.
3 points	This statement is true of me about half the time.
2 points	This statement is seldom true of me.
1 point	This statement is never or almost never true of me.

the following statements and award yourself points for each one, using the point system described here. Then add up your point total for each section, and shade the Discovery Wheel in Figure 1.2 to the appropriate level.

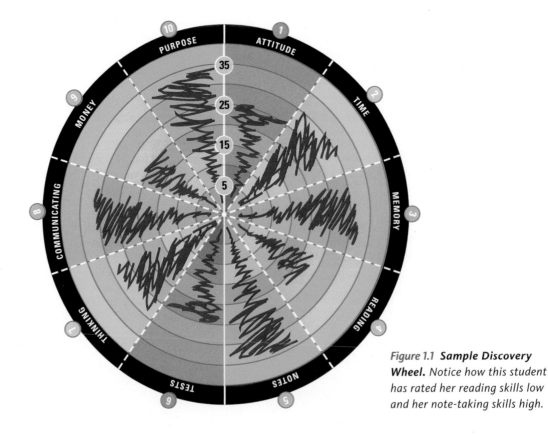

Figure 1.1 **Sample Discovery Wheel.** *Notice how this student has rated her reading skills low and her note-taking skills high.*

1 Attitude

_____ I enjoy learning.

_____ I understand and apply the concept of multiple intelligences.

_____ I connect my courses to my purpose for being in school.

_____ I make a habit of assessing my personal strengths and areas for improvement.

_____ I am satisfied with how I am progressing toward achieving my goals.

_____ I use my knowledge of learning styles to support my success in school.

_____ I am willing to consider any idea that can help me succeed in school.

_____ I regularly remind myself of the benefits I intend to get from my education.

_____ **Total Score: Attitude**

2 Time

_____ I set long-term goals and periodically review them.

_____ I set short-term goals to support my long-term goals.

_____ I write a plan for each day and each week.

_____ I assign priorities to what I choose to do each day.

_____ I plan review time so I don't have to cram before tests.

_____ I plan regular recreation time.

_____ I adjust my study time to meet the demands of individual courses.

_____ I have adequate time each day to accomplish what I plan.

_____ **Total Score: Time**

3 Memory

_____ I am confident of my ability to remember.

_____ I can remember people's names.

_____ At the end of a lecture, I can summarize what was presented.

_____ I apply techniques that enhance my memory skills.

_____ I can recall information when I'm under pressure.

_____ I remember important information clearly and easily.

_____ I can jog my memory when I have difficulty recalling.

_____ I can relate new information to what I've already learned.

_____ **Total Score: Memory**

4 Reading

_____ I preview and review reading assignments.

_____ When reading, I ask myself questions about the material.

_____ I underline or highlight important passages when reading.

_____ When I read textbooks, I am alert and awake.

_____ I relate what I read to my life.

_____ I select a reading strategy to fit the type of material I'm reading.

_____ I take effective notes when I read.

_____ When I don't understand what I'm reading, I note my questions and find answers.

_____ **Total Score: Reading**

5 Notes

_____ When I am in class, I focus my attention.

_____ I take notes in class.

_____ I know about many methods for taking notes and choose those that work best for me.

_____ I distinguish important material and note key phrases in a lecture.

_____ I copy down material that the instructor writes on the board or overhead display.

_____ I can put important concepts into my own words.

_____ My notes are valuable for review.

_____ I review class notes within 24 hours.

_____ **Total Score: Notes**

6 Tests

_____ I use techniques to manage stress related to exams.

_____ I manage my time during exams and am able to complete them.

_____ I am able to predict test questions.

_____ I adapt my test-taking strategy to the kind of test I'm taking.

_____ I understand what essay questions ask and can answer them completely and accurately.

_____ I start reviewing for tests at the beginning of the term.

_____ I continue reviewing for tests throughout the term.

_____ My sense of personal worth is independent of my test scores.

_____ **Total Score: Tests**

7 Thinking

_____ I have flashes of insight and think of solutions to problems at unusual times.

_____ I use brainstorming to generate solutions to a variety of problems.

_____ When I get stuck on a creative project, I use specific methods to get unstuck.

_____ I learn by thinking about ways to contribute to the lives of other people.

_____ I am willing to consider different points of view and alternative solutions.

_____ I can detect common errors in logic.

_____ I construct viewpoints by drawing on information and ideas from many sources.

_____ As I share my viewpoints with others, I am open to their feedback.

_____ **Total Score: Thinking**

8 Communicating

_____ I am honest with others about who I am, what I feel, and what I want.

_____ Other people tell me that I am a good listener.

_____ I can communicate my upset and anger without blaming others.

_____ I can make friends and create valuable relationships in a new setting.

_____ I am open to being with people I don't especially like in order to learn from them.

_____ I can effectively plan and research a large writing assignment.

_____ I create first drafts without criticizing my writing, then edit later for clarity, accuracy, and coherence.

_____ I know ways to prepare and deliver effective speeches.

_____ **Total Score: Communicating**

9 Money

_____ I am in control of my personal finances.

_____ I can access a variety of resources to finance my education.

_____ I am confident that I will have enough money to complete my education.

_____ I take on debts carefully and repay them on time.

_____ I have long-range financial goals and a plan to meet them.

_____ I make regular deposits to a savings account.

_____ I pay off the balance on credit card accounts each month.

_____ I can have fun without spending money.

_____ **Total Score: Money**

10 Purpose

_____ I see learning as a lifelong process.

_____ I relate school to what I plan to do for the rest of my life.

_____ I see problems and tough choices as opportunities for learning and personal growth.

_____ I use technology in a way that enriches my life and supports my success.

_____ I am developing skills that will be useful in the work-place.

_____ I take responsibility for the quality of my education—and my life.

_____ I live by a set of values that translates into daily actions.

_____ I am willing to accept challenges even when I'm not sure how to meet them.

_____ **Total Score: Purpose**

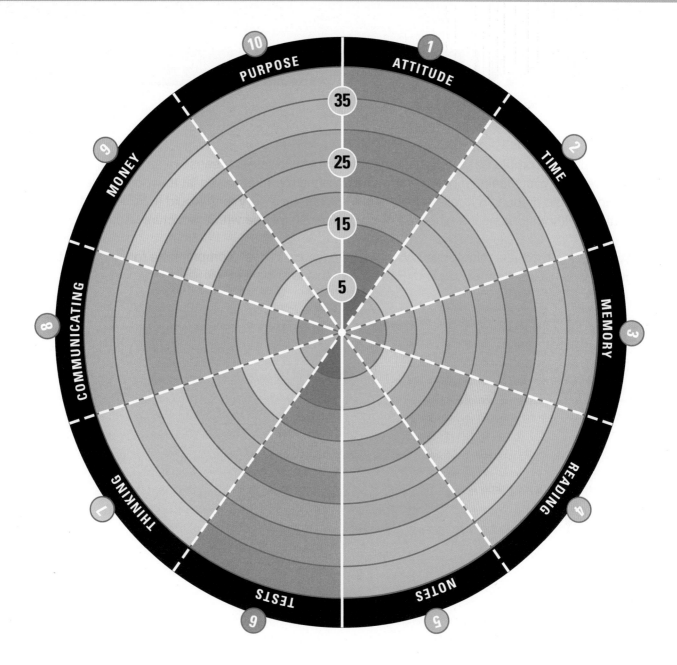

Figure 1.2 **Your Discovery Wheel.**

Filling in your Discovery Wheel

Using the total score from each category, shade in each corresponding wedge of the
Discovery Wheel in Figure 1.2. Use different colors, if you want. For example, you could use green
to denote areas you want to work on. When you have finished, complete the Skills Snapshot that follows.

SKILLS
snapshot

Now that you have completed your Discovery Wheel, it's time to get a sense of its weight, shape, and balance. Can you imagine running your hands around it? If you could lift it, would it feel light or heavy? How would it sound if it rolled down a hill? Would it roll very far? Would it wobble? Make your observations without judging the wheel as good or bad. Simply be with the picture you have created.

After you have spent a few minutes studying your Discovery Wheel, complete the following sentences. Just put down whatever comes to mind. Remember, this is not a test.

Overview

This wheel is an accurate picture of my ability as a student because . . .

My self-evaluation surprises me because . . .

Strengths

One area where I show strong skills is . . .

Another area of strength is . . .

Goals

The area in which I most want to improve is . . .

It is also important for me to get better at . . .

I want to concentrate on improving these areas because . . .

To meet my goals for improvement, I intend to . . .

© Huntstock/yes

LEARNING STYLES:
Discovering how you learn

Right now, you are investing substantial amounts of time, money, and energy in your education. What you get in return for this investment depends on how well you understand the process of learning and use it to your advantage.

If you don't understand learning, you might feel bored or confused in class. Over time, frustration can mount to the point where you question the value of being in school.

Some students answer that question by dropping out of school. These students lose a chance to create the life they want. You can prevent that outcome for yourself.

Start by understanding the different ways that people create meaning from their experience and change their behavior. In other words, learn about *how* we learn.

WE LEARN BY PERCEIVING AND PROCESSING

When we learn well, says psychologist David Kolb, two things happen.[1] First, we *perceive.* That is, we notice events and "take in" new experiences.

Second, we *process.* We "deal with" experiences in a way that helps us make sense of them.

Some people especially prefer to perceive through *feeling* (also called *concrete experience*). They like to absorb information through their five senses. They learn by getting directly involved in new experiences. When solving problems, they rely on intuition as much as intellect. These people typically function well in unstructured classes that allow them to take initiative.

Other people like to perceive by *thinking* (also called *abstract conceptualization*). They take in information best when they can think about it as a subject separate from themselves. They analyze, intellectualize, and create theories. Often these people take a scientific approach to problem solving and excel in traditional classrooms.

Some people prefer to process by *watching* (also called *reflective observation*). They prefer to stand back, watch what is going on, and think about it. They consider several points of view as they attempt to make sense of things and generate many ideas about how something happens. They value patience, good judgment, and a thorough approach to learning.

Other people like to process by *doing* (also called *active experimentation*). They prefer to jump in and start doing things immediately. These people do not mind taking risks as they attempt to make sense of things; this helps them learn. They are results oriented and look for practical ways to apply what they have learned.

PERCEIVING AND PROCESSING—AN EXAMPLE

Suppose that you get a new cell phone. It has more features than any phone you've used before. You have many options for learning how to use it. For example:

- Just get your hands on the phone right away, press some buttons, and see whether you can dial a number or send a text message.

- Read the instruction manual and view help screens on the phone before you try to make a call.
- Recall experiences you've had with phones in the past and what you've learned by watching other people use their cell phones.
- Ask a friend who owns the same type of phone to coach you as you experiment with making calls and sending messages.

These actions illustrate the different approaches to learning:

- Getting your hands on the phone right away and seeing whether you can make it work is an example of learning through *feeling* (or *concrete experience*).
- Reading the manual and help screens before you use the phone is an example of learning through *thinking* (or *abstract conceptualization*).
- Recalling what you've experienced in the past is an example of learning

through *watching* (or *reflective observation*).

- Asking a friend to coach you through a "hands-on" activity is an example of learning through *doing* (or *active experimentation*).

In summary, your learning style is the unique way that you blend thinking, feeling, watching, and doing. You tend to use this approach in learning anything. Reading the next few articles and doing the recommended activities will help you explore your learning style in more detail. ✕

DISCOVERY STATEMENT

journal entry 3

Prepare for the Learning Style Inventory (LSI)

As a "warm-up" for the LSI, spend a minute or two thinking about times in the past when you felt successful at learning. Underline or highlight any of the following statements that describe those situations:

- I was in a highly structured setting with a lot of directions about what to do and feedback on how well I did at each step.
- I was free to learn at my own pace and in my own way.
- I learned as part of a small group.
- I learned mainly by working alone in a quiet place.
- I learned in a place where there was a lot of activity going on.
- I learned by forming pictures in my mind.
- I learned by *doing* something—moving around, touching

something, or trying out a process for myself.

- I learned by talking to myself or explaining ideas to other people.
- I got the "big picture" before I tried to understand the details.
- I listened to a lecture and then thought about it after class.
- I read a book or article and then thought about it afterward.
- I used a variety of media—such as videos, films, audio recordings, or computers—to assist my learning.
- I went beyond taking notes and wrote in a personal journal.

- I was considering where to attend school and knew I had to actually set foot on each campus before choosing.
- I was shopping for a car and paid more attention to how I felt about test-driving each one than to the sticker prices or mileage estimates.
- I was thinking about going to a movie and carefully read the reviews before choosing one.

Reviewing the list, do you see any patterns in the way you prefer to learn? Briefly describe them.

To help you become more aware of learning styles, a psychologist named David Kolb developed the Learning Style Inventory (LSI). Responding to the items in the LSI can help you discover a lot about ways you learn. Following the LSI are suggestions for using the LSI results to promote your success.

The LSI is not a test. There are no right or wrong answers. Your goal is simply to develop a profile of your current learning style. So, take the LSI quickly. You might find it useful to recall a recent time when you learned something new at school, home, or work. However, do not agonize over your responses.

Note that the LSI consists of 12 sentences, each with four different endings. Read each sentence, and then rank each ending using the following scale:

4 = Most like you
3 = Second most like you
2 = Third most like you
1 = Least like you

Only use each number one time per sentence. This is a forced-choice inventory, so you must rank each ending. *Do not leave any endings blank.* Use each number only once for each question.

Read the instructions at the top of the LSI. When you understand example A, you are ready to begin.

Learning Style Inventory

Read the first sentence and its four possible endings. Put a 4 next to the ending that best describes the way you currently learn. Then continue ranking the other endings with a 3, 2, and 1, which represents the ending that is least like you. Do this for each sentence. Use the following example as a guide:

A. When I learn: _2_ I am happy.   _3_ I am fast.   _4_ I am logical.   _1_ I am careful.

Remember: *4 = Most like you   3 = Second most like you   2 = Third most like you   1 = Least like you*

Do not leave any endings blank. Use each number only once for each question.

1. When I learn:	_____ I like to deal with my feelings.	_____ I like to think about ideas.	_____ I like to be doing things.	_____ I like to watch and listen.
2. I learn best when:	_____ I listen and watch carefully.	_____ I rely on logical thinking.	_____ I trust my hunches and feelings.	_____ I work hard to get things done.
3. When I am learning:	_____ I tend to reason things out.	_____ I am responsible about things.	_____ I am quiet and re-served.	_____ I have strong feelings and reactions.
4. I learn by:	_____ feeling.	_____ doing.	_____ watching.	_____ thinking.
5. When I learn:	_____ I am open to new experiences.	_____ I look at all sides of issues.	_____ I like to analyze things, break them down into their parts.	_____ I like to try things out.
6. When I am learning:	_____ I am an observing person.	_____ I am an active person.	_____ I am an intuitive person.	_____ I am a logical person.
7. I learn best from:	_____ observation.	_____ personal relationships.	_____ rational theories.	_____ a chance to try out and practice.
8. When I learn:	_____ I like to see results from my work.	_____ I like ideas and theories.	_____ I take my time before acting.	_____ I feel personally involved in things.
9. I learn best when:	_____ I rely on my observations.	_____ I rely on my feelings.	_____ I can try things out for myself.	_____ I rely on my ideas.
10. When I am learning:	_____ I am a reserved person.	_____ I am an accepting person.	_____ I am a responsible person.	_____ I am a rational person.
11. When I learn:	_____ I get involved.	_____ I like to observe.	_____ I evaluate things.	_____ I like to be active
12. I learn best when:	_____ I analyze ideas.	_____ I am receptive and open-minded.	_____ I am careful.	_____ I am practical.

Scorecard

....

Brown F   Total _____

Teal W   Total _____

Purple T   Total _____

Orange D   Total _____

....

Grand Total _____

Scoring Your Inventory

Now that you've finished taking the LSI, you probably have some questions about what it means. You're about to discover some answers!

STEP 1 First, copy your numbers from the Learning Style Inventory to the corresponding lines on this page. When you've finished, add up all of the numbers you gave to the items marked with brown F letters. Then write down that total on your Scorecard next to "**Brown F**." Next, add up all of the numbers for "**Teal W**," "**Purple T**," and "**Orange D**." Write down those totals in the Scorecard box as well.

STEP 2 Add the four totals to arrive at a **Grand Total** and write down that figure in the Scorecard box. (*Note:* The grand total should equal 120. If you have a different amount, go back and re-add the colored letters. It was probably just an addition error.)

	First Column Ranking	Second Column Ranking	Third Column Ranking	Fourth Column Ranking
1. When I learn:	___ **F**	___ **T**	___ **D**	___ **W**
2. I learn best when:	___ **W**	___ **T**	___ **F**	___ **D**
3. When I am learning:	___ **T**	___ **D**	___ **W**	___ **F**
4. I learn by:	___ **F**	___ **D**	___ **W**	___ **T**
5. When I learn:	___ **F**	___ **W**	___ **T**	___ **D**
6. When I am learning:	___ **W**	___ **D**	___ **F**	___ **T**
7. I learn best from:	___ **W**	___ **F**	___ **T**	___ **D**
8. When I learn:	___ **D**	___ **T**	___ **W**	___ **F**
9. I learn best when:	___ **W**	___ **F**	___ **D**	___ **T**
10. When I am learning:	___ **W**	___ **F**	___ **D**	___ **T**
11. When I learn:	___ **F**	___ **W**	___ **T**	___ **D**
12. I learn best when:	___ **T**	___ **F**	___ **W**	___ **D**

Learning Style Graph

STEP 3 Transfer your totals from Step 2 to the lines on the Learning Style Graph below. On the brown (F) line, find the number that corresponds to your "**Brown F**" total from your Scorecard. Then write an X on this number. Do the same for your "**Teal W**," "**Purple T**," and "**Orange D**" totals. The graph on this page is for you to keep. The graph on the page about "Developing all four modes of learning" is for you to turn in to your instructor if required to do so.

STEP 4 Now draw four straight lines to connect the four X's. Then shade in the area to form a "kite." *This is your learn-*

ing style profile. (For an example, see the illustration below.) Each X that you placed on these lines indicates your preference for a different aspect of learning as described here.

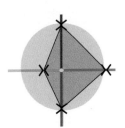

F: Feeling
Concrete Experience
The number where you put your X on this line indicates your preference for learning things that have personal meaning. The higher your score on this line, the more you like to learn things that you feel are important and relevant to yourself.

W: Watching
Reflective Observation
Your number on this line indicates how important it is for you to reflect on the things you are learning. If your score is high on this line, you probably find it important to watch others as they learn about an assignment and then report on it to the class. You probably like to plan things out and take the time to make sure that you fully understand a topic.

T: Thinking
Abstract Conceptualization
Your number on this line indicates your preference for learning ideas, facts, and figures. If your score is high on this line, you probably like to absorb many concepts and gather lots of information on a new topic.

D: Doing
Active Experimentation
Your number on this line indicates your preference for applying ideas, using trial and error, and practicing what you learn. If your score is high on this line, you probably enjoy hands-on activities that allow you to test out ideas to see what works.

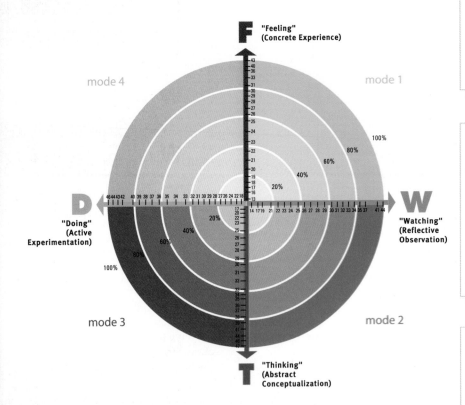

Interpreting Your Learning Style Graph

When you examine your completed Learning Style Graph, you will notice that your learning style profile (the "kite" that you drew) might be located primarily in one part of the graph. This will give you an idea of your preferred mode of learning—the kind of behaviors that feel most comfortable and familiar to you when you are learning something.

Using the descriptions below and the sample graphs, identify your preferred learning mode.

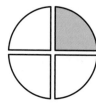

Mode 1 blends feeling and watching.
If the majority of your learning style profile is in the upper right-hand corner of the Learning Style Graph, you probably prefer Mode 1 learning. You seek a purpose for new information and a personal connection with the content. You want to know why a course matters and how it challenges or fits in with what you already know. You embrace new ideas that relate directly to your current interests and goals.

Mode 2 blends watching and thinking.
If your learning style profile is mostly in the lower right-hand corner of the Learning Style Graph, you probably prefer Mode 2 learning. You are interested in knowing what ideas or techniques are important. You seek a theory to explain events and are interested in what experts have to say. You enjoy learning lots of facts and then arranging these facts in a logical and concise manner. You break a subject down into its key elements or steps and master each one in a systematic way.

Mode 3 blends thinking and doing. If most of your learning style profile is in the lower left-hand corner of the Learning Style Graph, you probably prefer Mode 3 learning. You hunger for an opportunity to try out what you're studying. You get involved with new knowledge by testing it out. You investigate how ideas and techniques work, and you put into practice what you learn. You thrive when you have well-defined tasks, guided practice, and frequent feedback.

Mode 4 blends doing and feeling. If most of your learning style profile is in the upper left-hand corner of the Learning Style Graph, you probably prefer Mode 4 learning. You get excited about going beyond classroom assignments. You like to take what you have practiced and find other uses for it. You seek ways to apply this newly gained skill or information at your workplace or in your personal relationships.

It might be easier for you to remember the modes if you summarize each one as a single question:

> **Mode 1** means asking, *Why* learn this?

> **Mode 2** means asking, *What* is this about?

> **Mode 3** means asking, *How* does this work?

> **Mode 4** means asking, *What if* I tried this in a different setting?

Combinations
Some learning style profiles combine all four modes. The profile to the left reflects a learner who is focused primarily on gathering information—*lots* of information! People with this profile tend to ask for additional facts from an instructor, or they want to know where they can go to discover more about a subject.

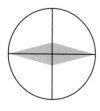

The profile to the left applies to learners who focus more on understanding what they learn and less on gathering lots of information. People with this profile prefer smaller chunks of data with plenty of time to process it. Long lectures can be difficult for these learners.

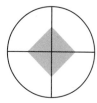

The profile to the left indicates a learner whose preferences are fairly well balanced. People with this profile can be highly adaptable and tend to excel no matter what the instructor does in the classroom.

Developing All Four Modes of Learning

Each mode of learning represents a unique blend of feeling, watching, thinking, and doing. No matter which of these you've tended to prefer, you can develop the ability to use all four modes:

- **To develop Mode 1,** ask questions that help you understand *why* it is important for you to learn about a specific topic. You might also want to form a study group.

- **To develop Mode 2,** ask questions that help you understand *what* the main points and key facts are. Also, learn a new subject in stages. For example, divide a large reading assignment into sections and then read each section carefully before moving on to the next one.

- **To develop Mode 3,** ask questions about *how* a theory relates to daily life. Also allow time to practice what you learn. You can do experiments, conduct interviews, create presentations, find a relevant work or internship experience, or even write a song that summarizes key concepts. Learn through hands-on practice.

- **To develop Mode 4,** ask *what-if* questions about ways to use what you have just learned in several different situations. Also, seek opportunities to demonstrate your understanding. You could coach a classmate about what you have learned, present findings from your research, explain how your project works, or perform your song.

Developing all four modes offers many potential benefits. For example, you can excel in many types of courses and find more opportunities to learn outside the classroom. You can expand your options for declaring a major and choosing a career. You can also work more effectively with people who learn differently from you.

In addition, you'll be able to learn from instructors no matter how they teach. Let go of statements such as "My teachers don't get me" and "The instructor doesn't teach to my learning style." Replace those excuses with attitudes such as "I am responsible for what I learn" and "I will master this subject by using several modes of learning."

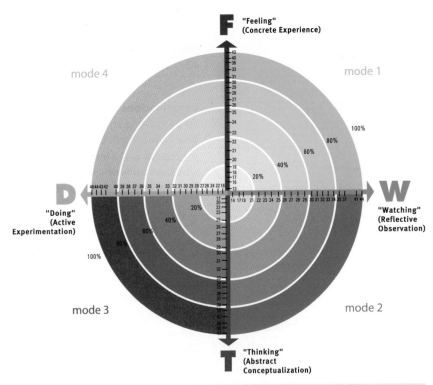

The graph on this page is here for you to turn in to your instructor if required to do so.

Balancing Your Preferences

The chart below identifies some of the natural talents people have, as well as challenges for people who have a strong preference for any one mode of learning. For example, if most of your "kite" is in Mode 2 of the Learning Style Graph, then look at the lower right-hand corner of the following chart to see whether it gives an accurate description of you.

After reviewing the description of your preferred learning mode, read all of the sections that start with the words "People with other preferred modes." These sections explain what actions you can take to become a more balanced learner.

Feeling

mode 4

Strengths:
• Getting things done
• Leadership
• Risk taking

Too much of this mode can lead to:
• Trivial improvements
• Meaningless activity

Too little of this mode can lead to:
• Work not completed on time
• Impractical plans
• Lack of motivation to achieve goals

People with other preferred modes can develop Mode 4 by:
• Making a commitment to objectives
• Seeking new opportunities
• Influencing and leading others
• Being personally involved
• Dealing with people

mode 1

Strengths:
• Imaginative ability
• Understanding people
• Recognizing problems
• Brainstorming

Too much of this mode can lead to:
• Feeling paralyzed by alternatives
• Inability to make decisions

Too little of this mode can lead to:
• Lack of ideas
• Not recognizing problems and opportunities

People with other preferred modes can develop Mode 1 by:
• Being aware of other people's feelings
• Being sensitive to values
• Listening with an open mind
• Gathering information
• Imagining the implications of ambiguous situations

Doing ←→ **Watching**

Strengths:
• Problem solving
• Decision making
• Deductive reasoning
• Defining problems

Too much of this mode can lead to:
• Solving the wrong problem
• Hasty decision making

Too little of this mode can lead to:
• Lack of focus
• Reluctance to consider alternatives
• Scattered thoughts

People with other preferred modes can develop Mode 3 by:
• Creating new ways of thinking and doing
• Experimenting with fresh ideas
• Choosing the best solution
• Setting goals
• Making decisions

mode 3

Strengths:
• Planning
• Creating models
• Defining problems
• Developing theories

Too much of this mode can lead to:
• Vague ideals ("castles in the air")
• Lack of practical application

Too little of this mode can lead to:
• Inability to learn from mistakes
• No sound basis for work
• No systematic approach

People with other preferred modes can develop Mode 2 by:
• Organizing information
• Building conceptual models
• Testing theories and ideas
• Designing experiments
• Analyzing quantitative data

mode 2

Thinking

Take your time to absorb all this material. Be willing to read through it several times and ask questions.

Your efforts will be rewarded. In addition to discovering more details about *how* you learn, you'll gain a set of strategies for applying this knowledge to your courses. With these strategies, you can use your knowledge of learning styles to succeed in school.

Above all, aim to recover your natural gift for learning as a master student. Rediscover a world where the boundaries between learning and fun, between work and play, all disappear. While immersing yourself in new experiences, blend the sophistication of an adult with the wonder of a child. This is a path that you can travel for the rest of your life.

Using your learning style profile to SUCCEED

James Baigrie/Digital Vision/Getty Images

DEVELOP ALL FOUR MODES OF LEARNING

Each mode of learning highlighted in the Learning Style Inventory represents a unique blend of concrete experience, reflective observation, abstract conceptualization, and active experimentation. You can explore new learning styles simply by adopting new habits related to each of these activities. Consider the following suggestions as places to start. Also remember that any idea about learning styles will make a difference in your life only when it leads to changes in your behavior.

To gain concrete experiences:

- See a live demonstration or performance related to your course content.
- Engage your emotions by reading a novel or seeing a video related to your course.
- Interview an expert in the subject you're learning or a master practitioner of a skill you want to gain.
- Conduct role-plays, exercises, or games based on your courses.
- Conduct an informational interview with someone in your chosen career, or "shadow" that person for a day on the job.
- Look for a part-time job, internship, or volunteer experience that complements what you do in class.
- Deepen your understanding of another culture and extend your foreign language skills by studying abroad.

To become more reflective:

- Keep a personal journal, and write about connections among your courses.
- Form a study group to discuss and debate topics related to your courses.
- Set up a website, blog, email listserv, or online chat room related to your major.

- Create analogies to make sense of concepts; for instance, see whether you can find similarities between career planning and putting together a puzzle.
- Visit your course instructor during office hours to ask questions.
- During social events with friends and relatives, briefly explain what your courses are about.

To develop abstract thinking:

- Take notes on your reading in outline form; consider using word-processing software with an outlining feature.
- Supplement assigned texts with other books, magazine and newspaper articles, and related websites.
- Attend lectures given by your current instructors and others who teach the same subjects.
- Take ideas presented in text or lectures and translate them into visual form—tables, charts, diagrams, and maps.
- Create visuals and use computer software to recreate them with more complex graphics and animation.

To become more active:

- Conduct laboratory experiments or field observations.
- Go to settings where theories are being applied or tested.
- Make predictions based on theories you learn, and then see whether events in your daily life confirm your predictions.
- Try out a new behavior described in a lecture or reading, and observe its consequences in your life.

LOOK FOR EXAMPLES OF THE MODES IN ACTION

To understand the modes of learning, notice when they occur in your daily life. You are a natural learner and this means that the modes are often at work. You use them when you solve problems, make choices, and experiment with new ideas.

Suppose that your family members ask about your career plans. You've just enrolled for your first semester of classes, and you think it's too early to think about careers. Yet you choose to brainstorm some career options anyway. If nothing else, it might be fun, and you'll have some answers for when people ask you what you're going to do after college. This is an example of Mode 1: You asked, "Why learn about career planning?" and came up with an answer.

During the next meeting of your psychology class, your instructor mentions the career planning center on campus. You visit the center's website and discover its list of services. While you're online, you also register for one of the center's workshops because you want more information about writing a career plan. This illustrates Mode 2: You asked, "What career planning options are available?" and discovered several answers.

In this workshop, you learn about the role that internships and extracurricular activities play in career planning. All of these are ways to test an early career choice and discover whether it appeals to you. You enjoy being with children, so you choose to volunteer at a campus-based childcare center. You want to discover how this service-learning experience might help you choose a career. This is Mode 3: You asked, "How can I use what I learned in the workshop?" This led you to working with children.

Your experience at the center leads to a work-study assignment there. On the basis of this new experience, you choose to declare a major in early childhood education. This is an example of Mode 4: You asked, "What if this assignment points to a new direction for my future?" The answer led to a new commitment.

USE THE MODES WHILE CHOOSING COURSES

Remember your learning style profile when you're thinking about which classes to take and how to study for each class. Look for a fit between your preferred mode of learning and your course work.

If you prefer Mode 1, for example, then look for courses that sound interesting and seem worthwhile to you. If you prefer Mode 2, then consider classes that center on lectures, reading, and discussion. If you prefer Mode 3, then choose courses that include demonstrations, lab sessions, role-playing, and others ways to take action. And if you enjoy Mode 4, then look for courses that could apply to many situations in your life—at work, at home, and in your relationships.

You won't always be able to match your courses to your learning styles. View those situations as opportunities to practice becoming a flexible learner. By developing your skills in all four modes, you can excel in many types of courses.

USE THE MODES TO EXPLORE YOUR MAJOR

If you enjoy learning in Mode 1, you probably value creativity and human relationships. When choosing a major, consider the arts, English, psychology, or political science.

If Mode 2 is your preference, then you enjoy gathering information and building theories. A major related to math or science might be ideal for you.

If Mode 3 is your favorite, then you like to diagnose problems, arrive at solutions, and use technology. A major related to health care, engineering, or economics is a logical choice for you.

And if your preference is Mode 4, you probably enjoy taking initiative, implementing decisions, teaching, managing projects, and moving quickly from planning into action. Consider a major in business or education.

As you prepare to declare a major, remain flexible. Use your knowledge of learning styles to open up possibilities rather than restrict them. Remember that regardless of your mode, you can excel at any job or major; it just may mean developing new skills in other modes.

USE THE MODES OF LEARNING TO EXPLORE YOUR CAREER

Knowing about learning styles becomes especially useful when planning your career.

People who excel at Mode 1 are often skilled at tuning in to the feelings of clients and coworkers. These people can listen with an open mind, tolerate confusion, be sensitive to people's feelings, open up to problems that are difficult to define, and brainstorm a variety of solutions. If you like Mode 1, you may be drawn to a career in counseling, social services, the ministry, or another field that centers on human relationships. You might also enjoy a career in the performing arts.

People who prefer Mode 2 like to do research and work with ideas. They are skilled at gathering data, interpreting information, and summarizing—arriving at the big picture. They may excel at careers that center on science, math, technical communications, or planning. Mode 2 learners may also work as college teachers, lawyers, technical writers, or journalists.

People who like Mode 3 are drawn to solving problems, making decisions, and checking on progress toward goals. Careers in medicine, engineering, information technology, or another applied science are often ideal for them.

People who enjoy Mode 4 like to influence and lead others. These people are often described as "doers" and "risk takers." They like to take action and complete projects. Mode 4 learners often excel at managing, negotiating, selling, training, and teaching. They might also work for a government agency.

Keep in mind that there is no strict match between certain learning styles and certain careers. Learning is essential to success in all careers. Also, any career can attract people with a variety of learning styles. For instance, the health care field is large enough to include people who prefer Mode 3 and become family physicians—*and* people who prefer Mode 2 and become medical researchers.

EXPECT TO ENCOUNTER DIFFERENT STYLES

As higher education and the workplace become more diverse and technology creates a global marketplace, you'll meet people who differ from you in profound ways. Your fellow students and coworkers will behave in ways that express a variety of preferences for perceiving information, processing ideas, and acting on what they learn. Consider these examples:

- A roommate who's continually moving while studying—reciting facts out loud, pacing, and gesturing—probably prefers concrete experience and learning by taking action.
- A coworker who talks continually on the phone about a project may prefer to learn by listening, talking, and forging key relationships.
- A supervisor who excels at abstract conceptualization may want to see detailed project plans and budgets submitted in writing well before a project swings into high gear.
- A study group member who always takes the initiative, manages the discussion, delegates any work involved, and follows up with everyone probably prefers active experimentation.

Differences in learning style can be a stumbling block—or an opportunity. When differences intersect, there is the potential for conflict as well as for creativity. Succeeding with peers often means seeing the classroom and workplace as a laboratory for learning from experience. Resolving conflict and learning from mistakes are all part of the learning cycle.

LOOK FOR SPECIFIC CLUES TO ANOTHER PERSON'S STYLE

You can learn a lot about other people's styles of learning simply by observing them during the workday. Look for clues such these:

Approaches to a task that requires learning. Some people process new information and ideas by sitting quietly and reading or writing. When learning to use a piece of equipment, such as a new computer, they'll read the instruction manual first. Others will skip the manual, unpack all the boxes, and start setting up equipment. And others might ask a more experienced colleague to guide them in person, step by step.

Word choice. Some people like to process information visually. You might hear them say, "I'll look into that" or "Give me the big picture first." Others like to solve problems verbally: "Let's talk though this problem" or "I hear you!" In contrast, some people focus on body sensations ("This product feels great") or action ("Let's run with this idea and see what happens").

Body language. Notice how often coworkers or classmates make eye contact with you and how close they sit or stand next to you. Observe their gestures as well as the volume and tone of their voice.

Content preferences. Notice what subjects coworkers or classmates openly discuss and which topics they avoid. Some people talk freely about their feelings, their families, and even their personal finances. Others choose to remain silent on such topics and stick to work-related matters.

Process preferences. Look for patterns in the way that your coworkers and classmates meet goals. When attending meetings, for example, some of them might stick closely to the agenda and keep an eye on the clock. Other people might prefer to go with the flow, even if it means working an extra hour or scrapping the agenda.

ACCOMMODATE DIFFERING STYLES

Once you've discovered differences in styles, look for ways to accommodate them. As you collaborate on projects with other students or coworkers, keep the following suggestions in mind:

Remember that some people want to reflect on the big picture first. When introducing a project plan, you might say, "This process has four major steps." Before explaining the plan in detail, talk about the purpose of the project and the benefits of completing each step.

Allow time for active experimentation and concrete experience. Offer people a chance to try out a new product or process for themselves—to literally get the feel of it.

Allow for abstract conceptualization. When leading a study group or conducting a training session, provide handouts that include plenty of visuals and step-by-step instructions. Visual learners and people who like to think abstractly will appreciate these. Also schedule periods for questions and answers.

When planning a project, encourage people to answer key questions. Remember the four essential questions that guide learning. Answering *Why?* means defining the purpose and desired outcomes of the project. Answering *What?* means assigning major tasks, setting due dates for each task, and generating commitment to action. Answering *How?* means carrying out assigned tasks and meeting regularly to discuss things that are working well and ways to improve the project. And answering *What if?* means discussing what the team has learned from the project and ways to apply that learning to the whole class or larger organization.

When working on teams, look for ways that members can complement one another's strengths. If you're skilled at planning, find someone who excels at doing. Also seek people who can reflect on and interpret the team's experience. Pooling different styles allows you to draw on everyone's strengths.

RESOLVE CONFLICT WITH RESPECT FOR STYLES

When people's styles clash in educational or work settings, you have several options. One is to throw up your hands and resign yourself to personality conflicts. Another option is to recognize differences, accept them, and respect them as complementary ways to meet common goals. Taking that perspective allows you to act constructively. You might do one of the following:

Resolve conflict within yourself. You might have mental pictures of classrooms and workplaces as places where people are all supposed to have the same style. Notice whether you have

Succeeding with peers often means seeing the classroom and workplace as a laboratory for learning from experience. Resolving conflict and learning from mistakes are all part of the learning cycle.

those pictures, and gently let them go. If you *expect* to find differences in styles, you can more easily respect those differences.

Introduce a conversation about learning styles. Attend a workshop on learning styles. Then bring such training directly to your classroom or office.

Let people take on tasks that fit their learning styles. People gravitate toward the kinds of tasks they've succeeded at in the past, and that's fine. Remember, though, that learning styles are both stable and dynamic. People gravitate toward the kinds of tasks they've succeeded at in the past. People can also broaden their styles by tackling new tasks to reinforce different modes of learning.

Rephrase complaints as requests. "This class is a waste of my time" can be recast as "Please tell me what I'll gain if I participate actively in class." "The instructor talks too fast" can become "What strategies can I use for taking notes when the instructor covers the material rapidly?"

ACCEPT CHANGE—AND OCCASIONAL DISCOMFORT

Seek out chances to develop new modes of learning. If your instructor asks you to form a group to complete an assignment, avoid joining a group where everyone shares your learning style. Work on project teams with people who learn differently than you. Get together with people who both complement and challenge you.

Also look for situations where you can safely practice new skills. If you enjoy reading, for example, look for ways to express what you learn by speaking, such as leading a study group on a textbook chapter.

Discomfort is a natural part of the learning process. Allow yourself to notice any struggle with a task or lack of interest in completing it. Remember that such feelings are temporary and that you are balancing your learning preferences. By choosing to move through discomfort, you consciously expand your ability to learn in new ways. ✠

Choosing your purpose

Success is a choice—your choice. To *get* what you want, it helps to *know* what you want. That is the purpose of this two-part Journal Entry.

You can begin choosing success by completing this Journal Entry right now. If you choose to do it later, then plan a date, time, and place and then block out the time on your calendar.

Date: _____ Time: _____ Place: _____

Part 1

Select a time and place when you know you will not be disturbed for at least 20 minutes. (The library is a good place to do this exercise.) Relax for two or three minutes, clearing your mind. Next, complete the following sentences—and then keep writing.

When you run out of things to write, stick with it just a bit longer. Be willing to experience a little discomfort. Keep writing. What you discover might be well worth the extra effort.

What I want from my education is . . .

When I complete my education, I want to be able to . . .

I also want . . .

Part 2

After completing Part 1, take a short break. Reward yourself by doing something that you enjoy. Then come back to this Journal Entry.

Now review the list you just created of things that you want from your education. See whether you can summarize them in one sentence. Start this sentence with "My purpose for being in school is . . ."

Allow yourself to write many drafts of this mission statement, and review it periodically as you continue your education. With each draft, see whether you can capture the essence of what you want from higher education and from your life. State it in a vivid way—in a short sentence that you can easily memorize, one that sparks your enthusiasm and makes you want to get up in the morning.

You might find it difficult to express your purpose statement in one sentence. If so, write a paragraph or more. Then look for the sentence that seems most charged with energy for you.

Following are some sample purpose statements:

- My purpose for being in school is to gain skills that I can use to contribute to others.
- My purpose for being in school is to live an abundant life that is filled with happiness, health, love, and wealth.
- My purpose for being in school is to enjoy myself by making lasting friendships and following the lead of my interests.

Now write at least one draft of your purpose statement.

Claim your
MULTIPLE INTELLIGENCES

People often think that being smart means the same thing as having a high IQ and that having a high IQ automatically leads to success. However, psychologists are finding that IQ scores do not always predict which students will do well in academic settings—or after they graduate.[2]

Vladgrin/Shutterstock.com

Howard Gardner of Harvard University believes that no single measure of intelligence can tell us how smart we are. Instead, Gardner defines intelligence in a flexible way as "the ability to solve problems, or to create products, that are valued within one or more cultural settings." He also identifies several types of intelligence, as described here and in Table 1.1.[3]

People using **verbal/linguistic intelligence** are adept at language skills and learn best by speaking, writing, reading, and listening. They are likely to enjoy activities such as telling stories and doing crossword puzzles.

People who use **mathematical/logical intelligence** are good with numbers, logic, problem solving, patterns, relationships, and categories. They are generally precise and methodical, and are likely to enjoy science.

When people learn visually and by organizing things spatially, they display **visual/spatial intelligence.** They think in images and pictures, and understand best by seeing the subject. They enjoy charts, graphs, maps, mazes, tables, illustrations, art, models, puzzles, and costumes.

People using **bodily/kinesthetic intelligence** prefer physical activity. They enjoy activities such as building things, woodworking, dancing, skiing, sewing, and crafts. They generally are coordinated and athletic, and they would rather participate in games than just watch.

Individuals using **musical/rhythmic intelligence** enjoy musical expression through songs, rhythms, and musical instruments. They are responsive to various kinds of sounds, remember melodies easily, and might enjoy drumming, humming, and whistling.

People using **intrapersonal intelligence** are exceptionally aware of their own feelings and values. They are generally reserved, self-motivated, and intuitive.

Outgoing people show evidence of **interpersonal intelligence**. They do well with cooperative learning and are sensitive to the feelings, intentions, and motivations of others. They often make good leaders.

People using **naturalist intelligence** love the outdoors and recognize details in plants, animals, rocks, clouds, and other natural formations. These people excel in observing fine distinctions among similar items.

Each of us has all of these intelligences to some degree. And each of us can learn to enhance them. Experiment with learning in ways that draw on a variety of intelligences—including those that might be less familiar. When we acknowledge all of our intelligences, we can constantly explore new ways of being smart. ✖

practicing
CRITICAL THINKING

5

Develop your multiple intelligences

Gardner's theory of multiple intelligences complements the discussion of different learning styles in this chapter. The main point is that there are many ways to gain knowledge and acquire new behaviors. You can use Gardner's concepts to explore a range of options for achieving success in school, work, and relationships.

Table 1.1 summarizes the content of "Claim your multiple intelligences" and suggests ways to apply the main ideas. Instead of merely glancing through this chart, get active. Place a check mark next to any of the "Possible characteristics" that describe you. Also check off the "Possible learning strategies" that you intend to use.

Finally, underline or highlight any of the "Possible Careers" that spark your interest. Follow up with Discovery Statements about how these possibilities align with your interests, connect to your career plans, and align with your choice of a major.

Remember that the chart is *not* an exhaustive list or a formal inventory. Take what you find merely as points of departure. You can invent strategies of your own to cultivate different intelligences.

Table 1.1 Multiple Intelligences

Type of Intelligence	Possible Characteristics	Possible Learning Strategies	Possible Careers
Verbal/linguistic	☐ You enjoy writing letters, stories, and papers. ☐ You prefer to write directions rather than draw maps. ☐ You take excellent notes from textbooks and lectures. ☐ You enjoy reading, telling stories, and listening to them.	☐ Highlight, underline, and write notes in your textbooks. ☐ Recite new ideas in your own words. ☐ Rewrite and edit your class notes. ☐ Talk to other people often about what you're studying.	Librarian, lawyer, editor, journalist, English teacher, radio or television announcer
Mathematical/logical	☐ You enjoy solving puzzles. ☐ You prefer math or science class to English class. ☐ You want to know how and why things work. ☐ You make careful, step-by-step plans.	☐ Analyze tasks so you can order them in a sequence of steps. ☐ Group concepts into categories, and look for underlying patterns. ☐ Convert text into tables, charts, and graphs. ☐ Look for ways to quantify ideas—to express them in numerical terms.	Accountant, auditor, tax preparer, mathematician, computer programmer, actuary, economist, math or science teacher

Type of Intelligence	Possible Characteristics	Possible Learning Strategies	Possible Careers
Visual/spatial	☐ You draw pictures to give an example or clarify an explanation. ☐ You understand maps and illustrations more readily than text. ☐ You assemble things from illustrated instructions. ☐ You especially enjoy books that have a lot of illustrations.	☐ When taking notes, create concept maps, mind maps, and other visuals. ☐ Code your notes by using different colors to highlight main topics, major points, and key details. ☐ When your attention wanders, focus it by sketching or drawing. ☐ Before you try a new task, visualize yourself doing it well.	Architect, commercial artist, fine artist, graphic designer, photographer, interior decorator, engineer, cartographer
Bodily/kinesthetic	☐ You enjoy physical exercise. ☐ You tend not to sit still for long periods of time. ☐ You enjoy working with your hands. ☐ You use a lot of gestures when talking.	☐ Be active in ways that support concentration; for example, pace as you recite, read while standing up, and create flash cards. ☐ Carry materials with you, and practice studying in several different locations. ☐ Create hands-on activities related to key concepts; for example, create a game based on course content. ☐ Notice the sensations involved with learning something well.	Physical education teacher, athlete, athletic coach, physical therapist, chiropractor, massage therapist, yoga teacher, dancer, choreographer, actor
Musical/rhythmic	☐ You often sing in the car or shower. ☐ You easily tap your foot to the beat of a song. ☐ You play a musical instrument. ☐ You feel most engaged and productive when music is playing.	☐ During a study break, play music or dance to restore energy. ☐ Put on background music that enhances your concentration while studying. ☐ Relate key concepts to songs you know. ☐ Write your own songs based on course content.	Professional musician, music teacher, music therapist, choral director, musical instrument sales representative, musical instrument maker, piano tuner
Intrapersonal	☐ You enjoy writing in a journal and being alone with your thoughts. ☐ You think a lot about what you want in the future. ☐ You prefer to work on individual projects rather than group projects. ☐ You take time to think things through before talking or taking action.	☐ Connect course content to your personal values and goals. ☐ Study a topic alone before attending a study group. ☐ Connect readings and lectures to a strong feeling or significant past experience. ☐ Keep a journal that relates your course work to events in your daily life.	Minister, priest, rabbi, professor of philosophy or religion, counseling psychologist, creator of a home-based or small business

Type of Intelligence	Possible Characteristics	Possible Learning Strategies	Possible Careers
Interpersonal	☐ You enjoy group work over working alone. ☐ You have plenty of friends and regularly spend time with them. ☐ You prefer talking and listening to reading or writing. ☐ You thrive in positions of leadership.	☐ Form and conduct study groups early in the term. ☐ Create flash cards, and use them to quiz study partners. ☐ Volunteer to give a speech or lead group presentations on course topics. ☐ Teach the topic you're studying to someone else.	Manager, school administrator, salesperson, teacher, counseling psychologist, arbitrator, police officer, nurse, travel agent, public relations specialist, creator of a midsize to large business
Naturalist	☐ As a child, you enjoyed collecting insects, leaves, or other natural objects. ☐ You enjoy being outdoors. ☐ You find that important insights occur during times you spend in nature. ☐ You read books and magazines on nature-related topics.	☐ During study breaks, take walks outside. ☐ Post pictures of outdoor scenes where you study, and play recordings of outdoor sounds while you read. ☐ Invite classmates to discuss course work while taking a hike or going on a camping trip. ☐ Focus on careers that hold the potential for working outdoors.	Environmental activist, park ranger, recreation supervisor, historian, museum curator, biologist, criminologist, mechanic, woodworker, construction worker, construction contractor or estimator

Learning through your senses:
THE VARK SYSTEM

Another way to approach the topic of learning styles is with a simple and powerful system that focuses on your senses and your ability to use language. According to this system, you learn by:

Tara Moore/Riser/Getty Images

- Seeing, or **visual** learning
- Hearing, or **auditory** learning
- Using words, or **read/write** learning
- Moving, or **kinesthetic** learning

To recall this system, remember the letters **VARK**, which stand for *Visual, Auditory, Read/Write,* and *Kinesthetic.*

The theory is that each of us prefers to learn in some of these ways more than in others. And we can enrich our learning with activities that draw on all four preferences.

SIGNS OF THE FOUR PREFERENCES

People with a preference for **visual** learning are interested in how things look. They are sensitive to shape, color, and design. To understand and explain concepts, they like to see and create drawings, maps, and diagrams. Getting an overview of a topic—the "big picture"—is important to these learners.

Learners with an **auditory** preference enjoy conversation, discussion, and debate. For them, the spoken word matters more than the written word. If they're excited about something they learned in class or at work, they'll tell you about it in person before sending you an email or a photo.

In contrast, **read/write** learners prefer the written word. Their notes will include more paragraphs and lists than drawings and diagrams. While a lecture or discussion might be fine with these learners, they also like to see text-based handouts or web pages that capture the main points and key details.

People with a **kinesthetic** preference like to move. They learn by doing and experimenting. When faced with a new idea, they ask: *How does that work? How can I use this?* They're interested in examples, case studies, and exercises that allow them to test concepts in action.

DISCOVERING YOUR VARK PREFERENCES

To reflect on your own VARK preferences, answer the following questions. Each question has four possible answers. Circle the answer that best describes how you would respond in the stated situation. This is not a formal inventory—just a way to prompt some self-discovery.

You enjoy courses the most when you get to do which of the following?

1. View slides, overhead displays, videos, and readings with plenty of charts, tables, and illustrations.

2. Ask questions, engage in small-group discussions, and listen to guest speakers.
3. Read texts that interest you, write papers, and take detailed notes.
4. Take field trips, participate in lab sessions, or apply the course content while working as a volunteer or intern.

When giving someone directions on how to drive to a destination, which of these do you prefer to do?
1. Pull out a piece of paper and sketch a map.
2. Give verbal directions.
3. Write down your directions.
4. Say, "I'm driving to a place near there, so just follow me."

When planning an extended vacation to a new destination, which of the following do you prefer to do?
1. Read colorful, illustrated brochures or look at photo essays about that place.
2. Talk directly to someone who's been there.
3. Read books and articles about the destination.
4. Spend a day or two at the destination on a work-related trip before taking a vacation there.

You've made a commitment to learn to play the guitar. What is the first thing you do?
1. Go to a library or music store and find an instruction book with plenty of diagrams and chord charts.
2. Pull out your favorite recordings, listen closely to the guitar solos, and see whether you can play along with them.
3. Search out books and articles with specific strategies for learning the guitar.
4. Buy or borrow a guitar, pluck the strings, and ask someone to show you how to play a few chords.

You've saved up enough money to lease a car. Which of the following is the most important factor in your decision when choosing from among several new models?
1. Your visual impressions of the car's interior, exterior, and engine.
2. The information you get by talking to people who own the cars you're considering.
3. Reading information about the car from sources like *Consumer Reports*.
4. The overall impression you get by taking each car on a test drive.

You're browsing the Internet with the intention to learn a new skill. What features are most important to you in choosing the websites you'll explore in detail?
1. Design, color, and videos that demonstrate the skill.
2. Podcasts that feature interviews with experts.
3. Text-heavy pages with clearly written explanations.
4. Links that you can click on to produce an effect, such as rearranging the elements on a page.

You've just bought a new computer system. When setting up the system, what is the first thing you do?
1. Take all the components out of the box, lay them out, and see how they connect.
2. Call someone with a similar system and ask her for directions.
3. Skim through the printed instructions that come with the equipment.
4. Assemble the components as best as you can, see whether everything works, and consult the instructions only as a last resort.

You get a scholarship to study abroad next semester, which starts in just three months. You will travel to a country where French is the most widely spoken language. To learn as much French as you can before you depart, which of these do you do?
1. Buy a video-based language course that's recorded on a DVD.
2. Set up tutoring sessions with a friend who's fluent in French.
3. Find workbooks with exercises that guide you through the basics of reading and speaking French.
4. Sign up for a short immersion course in an environment in which you speak only French, starting with the first class.

Now take a few minutes to reflect on the meaning of your responses. All of the answers numbered 1 are examples of visual learning. The 2s refer to auditory learning. The 3s refer to read/write learning and the 4s illustrate kinesthetic learning. Finding a consistent pattern in your answers indicates that you prefer learning through one of these channels more than the others. Or you might find that your preferences are fairly balanced.

When you approach your classes with the VARK system in mind, you can turn even the driest subjects into rich, multisensory experiences. Experiment with the following techniques and then create more of your own. Use them to build on your current preferences and develop another set of options for learning.

TO ENHANCE VISUAL LEARNING:

- Preview reading assignments by looking for elements that are highlighted visually—bold headlines, charts, graphs, illustrations, and photographs.
- When taking notes in class, leave plenty of room to add your own charts, diagrams, tables, and other visuals later.
- Whenever an instructor writes information on a blackboard or overhead display, copy it exactly in your notes.
- Transfer your handwritten notes to your computer. Use word-processing software that allows you to format your notes in lists, add headings in different fonts, and create visuals in color.
- Before you begin an exam, quickly sketch a diagram on scratch paper. Use this diagram to summarize the key formulas or facts you want to remember.
- During tests, see whether you can visualize pages from your handwritten notes or images from your computer-based notes.

TO ENHANCE AUDITORY LEARNING:

- Reinforce memory of your notes and readings by talking about them. When studying, stop often to recite key points and examples in your own words.
- After reciting several summaries of key points and examples, record your favorite version.
- Read difficult passages in your textbooks slowly and out loud.
- Join study groups, and create short presentations about course topics.
- Visit your instructors during office hours to ask questions.

TO ENHANCE READ/WRITE LEARNING:

- Find a reliable way to capture ideas that occur to you at random moments, such as a notes app on your smartphone.
- Take detailed notes during classes and meetings.
- Later, reduce your notes to lists of major topics, main points, and key details.
- Study for exams by predicting test questions and writing out your answers.
- Write to restate ideas from a textbook or lecture in your own words.
- Supplement your textbooks with related books and articles.

TO ENHANCE KINESTHETIC LEARNING:

- Look for ways to translate course content into three-dimensional models that you can build. While studying biology, for example, create a model of a human cell, using different colors of clay.
- Supplement lectures with trips to museums, field observations, lab sessions, tutorials, and other hands-on activities.
- Recite key concepts from your courses while you walk or exercise.
- Intentionally set up situations in which you can learn by trial and error.
- Create a practice test, and write out the answers in the room where you will actually take the exam.

MIXING THE PREFERENCES

The official **VARK** questionnaire allows for learners who rely on more than preference.[4] Some of these people use different strategies in different situations. Others regularly use two or more sets of strategies. While mixing the preferences can take extra time, it can lead to a broader, deeper level of understanding and skill.

You can get the most value from VARK by using the master student process. Discover the details about the preferences and strategies. Create an intention to experiment with them. Then move into action and write about the results. This is a process that works for any approach to learning styles—and all the other ideas in this book. ✄

Get back to the big picture about learning styles

This chapter introduces many ideas about how people learn—four modes, multiple intelligences, and the VARK system. That's a lot of information! And these are just a few of the available theories.

Remember that there is one "big idea" to take away from all of this material—*metacognition* (pronounced "metta-cog-ni-shun"). *Meta* means "beyond" or "above." *Cognition* refers to everything that goes on inside your brain: perceiving, thinking, and feeling. So, metacognition refers to your ability to stand "above" your current mental activities and observe them. From this larger point of view, you can choose to think and act in new ways.

Metacognition is the heart of the master student process. It's also a major benefit of higher education.

Take a few minutes right now to practice metacognition. Complete the following sentences.

The most important thing that I discovered about myself by doing the learning styles activities in this chapter is . . .

I also discovered that . . .

I discovered that what I would most like to change about the way I learn is . . .

In order to make that change, I intend to . . .

I also intend to . . .

Remember that teachers in your life will come and go. Some are more skilled than others. None of them are perfect. With skill in metacognition, you can see any experience as a chance to learn in ways that work for you. In your personal path toward mastery, you become your own best teacher.

Master Student Profiles

An example of a person who embodies one or more of the master student qualities mentioned in the Introduction to this book is in each chapter of this text, like the one that follows. As you read about these people and others like them, ask yourself: "How can I apply this?" Look for the timeless qualities in the people you read about. Many of the strategies used by master students from another time or place are tools that you can use today.

The master students in this book demonstrate unusual and effective ways to learn. Remember that these are just 10 examples of master students (one for each chapter).

As you read the Master Student Profiles, also ask questions based on each mode of learning: Why is this person considered a master student? What attitudes or behaviors helped to create her mastery? How can I develop those qualities? What if I could use his example to create positive new results in my own life?

Also reflect on other master students you've read about or know personally. Focus on people who excel at learning. The master student is not a vague or remote ideal. Rather, master students move freely among us.

In fact, there's one living inside your skin.

Joshua Williams }

After spending much of his first three college years homeless and hungry, graduated from Bethune-Cookman University in Daytona Beach, Florida.

As an undergraduate at Bethune-Cookman University, Joshua Williams established a scholarship to help students pay for textbooks and found donors willing to fund the program.

Williams knew from personal experience what a difference the program would make. For much of his time as an undergraduate, Williams couldn't afford textbooks. He was dealing with a bigger problem—being homeless.

Bethune-Cookman is a private school, one of America's historically black colleges and universities. When Williams arrived there in the fall of 2008, he had $3,000 that he'd saved while working at a gas station in his native Miami. That wasn't nearly enough to cover the cost of tuition, room, and board for his freshman year.

Williams had no idea where to get the rest of the money. Financial support from his parents was not an option. He'd never met his father and seldom saw his mother. As a child, Williams lived with a great-grandmother in Atlanta and then an aunt in Miami.

What Williams *did* know is that he wanted a new start in life. He remembered drive-by shootings and drug dealers working the corners in his aunt's neighborhood. He vowed never to end up on the streets. He decided he'd rather be homeless in Daytona Beach than back in Miami.

Bethune-Cookman offered support in the form of a temporary dorm room. Williams lived there for his first semester while applying for financial aid. When the room was no longer available, Williams merely said that he planned to move off campus. The truth was that he had no money for rent.

Williams stayed with friends whenever he could. Sometimes he snuck into a dormitory to shower and get a few hours of sleep on a couch in the lobby. And sometimes he just walked the beach all night.

During his junior year, Williams spoke at a school assembly and revealed that he was homeless. An advisor at Bethune-Cookman was in the audience and later arranged to place Williams in a dormitory.

In addition, Williams was named Mr. Bethune-Cookman University. The honorary title made him an ambassador for the school—and guaranteed him room and board for his senior year.

Williams graduated from Bethune-Cookman in 2013 with a degree in criminal justice and safety studies. After graduation he joined the Florida Department of Juvenile Justice as a case manager, working with teenagers who'd committed crimes. In addition, he became a public speaker, making presentations at the National Urban League, the United Negro College Fund, Delta Sigma Theta, and other organizations.

In 2014, Williams moved to Washington, D.C., to spend the summer as a congressional intern for the second district of Louisiana. That fall he returned to the South, enrolling in graduate school at Alabama A&M University to earn a master's degree in counseling psychology—a career, he says that "will allow me to change lives."

"Education is the movement from darkness to light," says Williams in a video about the Keeper of Light Book Scholarship. "We are all the light of the world."

Joshua Williams *demonstrated the courage to take a First Step and tell the truth about being homeless.*

QUIZ

Name _____

Date _____

Chapter 1

1. The Power Process: "Ideas are tools" states that if you want to use an idea, then you must first believe that it's true.
   a. True
   b. False

2. Effective First Steps are:
   a. Broad
   b. Full of self-judgments such as "I'm really bad at doing . . ."
   c. Used to create goals
   d. Include weaknesses but not strengths

3. Which of the following statements is an example of telling the truth about your current abilities in a way that creates the most possibilities for change?
   a. "I find it hard to read the notes I took in Introduction to Psychology last week."
   b. "I am an awful note taker."
   c. "When reviewing my notes, I find it hard to see the difference between main points and details."
   d. Both a and c

4. Getting your hands on a new cell phone right away to see if you can make it work is an example of:
   a. Learning through thinking
   b. Learning through feeling
   c. Learning through doing
   d. Learning through watching

5. Reading the manual for a new cell phone before you try to make a call is an example of:
   a. Learning through thinking
   b. Learning through feeling
   c. Learning through doing
   d. Learning through watching

6. An example of learning through concrete experience is:
   a. Seeing a live demonstration
   b. Taking notes in outline form
   c. Attending lectures by several instructors
   d. Translating idea from a textbook into a chart or map

7. The word *kinesthetic* refers to:
   a. Moving
   b. Hearing
   c. Seeing
   d. Listening

8. The recommended strategies for using learning styles to succeed include:
   a. Developing all four modes of learning
   b. Looking for examples of the modes in action
   c. Using the modes to explore your major
   d. Using the modes to explore your career
   e. All of the answer choices

9. The Discovery Wheel is:
   a. A test that will be graded
   b. Not a test, though it contains trick questions
   c. Intended to be a permanent picture of your skills
   d. An opportunity to tell the truth about your current skills without judgment

10. Clues to another person's learning style include:
    a. Approaches to a task that requires learning
    b. Word choice
    c. Body language
    d. All of the answer choices

SKILLS *snapshot*

You'll find a Skills Snapshot at the end of each chapter in this book. Use these exercises to stay aware of your changing attitudes and behaviors—including your progress in developing the qualities of a master student.

Before moving on to a new chapter in this book, take a snapshot of attitudes that can affect your success in school. Clarify your intentions to develop insights into yourself that lead to clear intentions and new behaviors.

Discovery
My score on the Attitude section of the Discovery Wheel was . . .

One of my attitudes that supports my success in school is . . .

One of my attitudes that does not support my success is . . .

Intention
The idea from this chapter that can make the biggest difference in my life right now is . . .

A habit that I can adopt to put this idea into practice is . . .

This habit will be useful in my career if I . . .

Action
The specific new behavior that I will practice is . . .

My cue for doing this behavior is . . .

My reward for following through on this intention will be . . .

Alex Staroseltsev/Shutterstock.com

why

Procrastination and lack of planning can quickly undermine your success in school.

how

Take a few minutes to skim this chapter. Find at least three techniques that you intend to use. Make a note or mark the pages where these strategies are located.

what if...

I could meet my goals with time to spare?

Time

what is included . . .

60	Power Process: Be here now
61	You've got the time
62	Make choices about multitasking
69	Define your values
70	Setting and achieving goals
74	The ABC daily to-do list
78	Planning sets you free
80	Making the transition to higher education
83	Making time for school as an adult learner
88	Break it down, get it done—using a long-term planner
91	Create a work flow that works
92	There's an app for that—using technology for time management
93	Stop procrastination now
96	25 ways to get the most out of now
101	Making time for health
106	Beyond time management: Stay focused on what matters
108	Master Student Profile: Ramit Sethi

do you have a minute?

Write down an important outcome for today. This is not a to-do list. It is a *result* that you intend to produce by getting one or more items on your to-do list done. Complete this sentence: *Before I go to bed tonight, I want to make sure that I've . . .*

POWERPROCESS

Be here now

Being right here, right now is such a simple idea. It seems obvious. Where else can you be but where you are? When else can you be there but when you are there?

The answer is that you can be somewhere else at any time—in your head. It's common for our thoughts to distract us from where we've chosen to be. Sometimes technology becomes the source of distraction: The arrival of every new text message, Facebook update, or email comes with an attention-grabbing alert. When we let this happen without conscious choice, we lose the benefits of focusing our attention on what's important to us in the present moment.

To "be here now" means to do what you're doing when you're doing it. It means to be where you are when you're there. Students consistently report that focusing attention on the here and now is one of the most powerful tools in this book.

We all have a voice in our head that hardly ever shuts up. If you don't believe it, conduct this experiment: Close your eyes for 10 seconds, and pay attention to what is going on in your head. Please do this right now.

Notice something? Perhaps a voice in your head was saying, "Forget it. I'm in a hurry." Another might have said, "I wonder when 10 seconds is up?" Another could have been saying, "What little voice? I don't hear any little voice."

That's the voice.

This voice can take you anywhere at any time—especially when you are studying. When the voice takes you away, you might appear to be studying, but your brain is somewhere else.

All of us have experienced this voice, as well as the absence of it. When our inner voices are silent, we can experience something that's called "flow": Time no longer seems to exist. We forget worries, aches, pains, reasons, excuses, and justifications. We fully experience the here and now. Life is magic.

Do not expect to be rid of the voice entirely. That is neither possible nor desirable. Inner voices serve a purpose. They enable us to analyze, predict, classify, and understand events out there in the "real" world. The trick is to consciously choose when to be with your inner voice and when to let it go.

Instead of trying to force a stray thought out of your head, simply notice it. Accept it. Tell yourself, "There's that thought again." Then gently return your attention to the task at hand. That thought, or another, will come back. Your mind will drift. Simply notice again where your thoughts take you, and gently bring yourself back to the here and now.

Also remember that planning supports this Power Process. Goals are tools that we create to guide our action in the present. Time-management techniques—calendars, lists, and all the rest—have only one purpose. They reveal what's most important for you to focus on right *now*. Ironically, one way to create flow experiences is to plan for them.

The idea behind this Power Process is simple. When you listen to a lecture, listen to a lecture. When you read this book, read this book. And when you choose to daydream, daydream. Do what you're doing when you're doing it. Be where you are when you're there.

Be here now . . . and now . . . and now. ✄

© iko/Shutterstock.com

A Stock-Studio/Shutterstock.com

You've got the TIME

When you say you don't have enough time, you might really be saying that you are not spending the time you do have in the way that you want. This chapter is about ways to solve that problem.

The words time management may call forth images of restriction and control. You might visualize a prune-faced Scrooge hunched over your shoulder, stopwatch in hand, telling you what to do every minute. Bad news.

Good news: You do have enough time for the things you want to do. All it takes is thinking about the possibilities and making conscious choices.

Time is an equal opportunity resource. All of us, regardless of gender, race, creed, national origin, and so on, have exactly the same number of hours in a week. No matter how famous we are, no matter how rich or poor, we get 168 hours to spend each week—no more, no less.

Time is an unusual commodity. It cannot be saved. You can't stockpile time like wood for the stove or food for the winter. It can't be seen, heard, touched, tasted, or smelled. You can't sense time directly. Even scientists and philosophers find it hard to describe. Because time is

so elusive, it is easy to ignore. That doesn't bother time at all. Time is perfectly content to remain hidden until you are nearly out of it. And when you are out of it, you are out of it.

Time is a nonrenewable resource. If you're out of wood, you can chop some more. If you're out of money, you can earn a little extra. If you're out of love, there is still hope. If you're out of health, it can often be restored. But when you're out of time, that's it. When this minute is gone, it's gone.

Time seems to pass at varying speeds. Sometimes it crawls, and sometimes it's faster than a speeding bullet. On Friday afternoons, classroom clocks can creep. After you've worked a 10-hour day, reading the last few pages of an economics assignment can turn minutes into hours. A year in school can stretch out to an eternity.

At the other end of the spectrum, time flies. There are moments when you are so absorbed in what you're doing that hours disappear like magic.

Everything written about time management can be reduced to three main ideas:

1. Discover exactly *what* you want. State your wants as clear, specific goals. And put them in writing.
2. Know *how* to get what you want. Determine what you'll do *today* to get what you want in the future. Put those intentions in writing as well.
3. Follow up by doing what you intend to do.

When we forget these principles, we can easily spend most of our time responding to interruptions, last-minute projects, and emergencies. Life feels like a scramble to just survive. We're so busy achieving someone else's goals that we forget about getting what *we* want.

Sometimes it seems that your friends control your time; your boss controls your time; your teachers or your parents or your kids or somebody else controls your time. Maybe that is not true, though. Approach time as if you are in control.

According to Stephen R. Covey, the purpose of planning is to carve out space in your life for things that are not urgent, but are truly important.[1] Examples are exercising regularly, reading, praying or meditating, spending quality time alone or with family members and friends, traveling, and cooking nutritious meals. Each of these contributes directly to our personal goals for the future and to the overall quality of our lives in the present.

Yet when schedules get tight, we often drop important activities. We postpone them for that elusive day when we'll finally "have more time."

Don't wait for that time to come. *Make* the time. Use the exercises in this chapter to let go of being "crazy busy" and align your daily activities with your values. Think of time management as time *investment.* Then spend your most valuable resource in the way you choose. ✳

Make choices about
MULTITASKING

When we get busy, we get tempted to do several things at the same time. It seems like such a natural solution: Watch TV *and* read a textbook. Talk on the phone *and* outline a paper. Write an email *and* listen to a lecture. These are examples of multitasking.

There's a problem with this strategy: Multitasking is much harder than it looks. Despite the awe-inspiring complexity of the human brain, research reveals that we are basically wired to do one thing at a time.[2]

The solution is an old-fashioned one: Whenever possible, take life one task at a time. Develop a key quality of master students—focused attention—with the following strategies.

UNPLUG FROM TECHNOLOGY
To reduce the temptation of multitasking, turn off distracting devices. Shut off your TV and cell phone. Disconnect from the Internet unless it's required for your planned task. Later, you can take a break to make calls, send texts, check email, and browse the Web. When you go online, do so with a clear intention and a time to quit.

Mike Kemp/Blend Images/Getty Images

CAPTURE FAST-BREAKING IDEAS WITH MINIMAL INTERRUPTION
Your brain is an expert nagger. After you choose to focus on one task, it might issue urgent reminders about 10 more things you need to

do. Keep 3 × 5 cards or paper and a pen handy to write down those reminders. You can take a break later and add them to your to-do list. Your mind can quiet down once it knows that a task has been captured in writing.

HANDLE INTERRUPTIONS WITH CARE

Some breaking events are so urgent that they call for your immediate attention. When this happens, note what you were doing when you were interrupted. For example, write down the number of the page you were reading or the name of the computer file you were creating. When you return to the task, your notes can help you get up to speed again.

COMMIT TO "SINGLE TASKING"

Today's technology—email, text messages, social media—seems to require multitasking. The key word in the previous sentence is *seems*. Multitasking is actually an option, not a requirement. You can still choose to do one thing at a time with full attention. You might find yourself in a minority. And, you'll enjoy the benefits, including greater effectiveness at whatever you choose to do and lower levels of stress.

Planning helps. Set a goal to keep your daily to-do list short—three items, maximum. Focus on getting these done, one at a time, before tackling other tasks. Even if you fail to achieve this goal, you'll benefit from the increased focus and practice at single tasking.

MULTITASK WITH SKILL

If multitasking seems inevitable in certain situations, then do it as effectively as possible. Pair one activity that requires concentration with another activity that you can do almost automatically. For example, studying for your psychology exam while downloading music is a way to reduce the disadvantages of multitasking. Pretending to listen to your children while watching TV is not.

ALIGN YOUR ACTIVITIES WITH YOUR PASSIONS

Handling routine tasks is a necessary part of daily life. But if you find that your attention frequently wanders throughout the day, ask yourself: "Am I really doing what I want to do? Do my work and my classes connect to my interests?" If the answer is no, then the path beyond multitasking might call for a change in your academic and career plans. Whenever an activity aligns with your passion, the temptation to multitask loses power. ✕

practicing
CRITICAL THINKING

6

The Time Monitor/Time Plan

The purpose of this exercise is to transform time into a knowable and predictable resource. To do this, monitor your time in 15-minute intervals, 24 hours a day, for seven days. Record how much time you spend sleeping, eating, studying, attending lectures, traveling to and from class, working, watching television, listening to music, taking care of the kids, running errands—everything.

If this sounds crazy, hang on for a minute. This exercise is not about keeping track of the rest of your life in 15-minute intervals. It is an opportunity to become conscious of how you spend your time—your life. Use the Time Monitor only for as long as it helps you do that. When you know exactly how you spend your time, you can make choices with open eyes.

You can plan to spend more time on the things that are most important to you and less time on the unimportant. Monitoring your time puts you in control of your life. To do this exercise, complete the following steps.

Step 1

Look at Figure 2.1, a sample Time Monitor. On Monday, the student got up at 6:45 a.m., showered, and got dressed. He ate breakfast from 7:15 to 7:45. It took him 15 minutes to walk to class (7:45 to 8:00), and he attended classes from 8:00 to 11:00.

List your activities in the same way. When you begin an activity, write it down next to the time you begin. Round off to the nearest 15 minutes. If, for example, you begin eating at 8:06, enter your starting time as 8:00.

Step 2

Fill out your Time Monitor. Now it's *your* turn. Using the blank Time Monitor, Figure 2.2, choose a day to begin monitoring your time. On that day, start filling out your Time Monitor. Keep it with you all day and use it for one full week. Take a few moments every couple of hours to record what you've done. Or enter a note each time that you change activities.

Step 3

After you've monitored your time for one week, group your activities together into categories. List them in the "Category" column in Figure 2.3, which includes the categories "Sleep," "Class," "Study," and "Meals." Think of other categories to add. "Grooming" might include showering, putting on makeup, and getting dressed. "Travel" could include walking, taking the bus, and riding your bike. Other categories might be "Exercise," "Entertainment," "Work," "Television," and "Children." Write in the categories that work for you.

Step 4

List your estimated hours for each category of activity. Guess how many hours you *think* you spent on each category of activity. List these hours in the "Estimated" column in Figure 2.3.

Then, list your *actual* hours for each category of activity. Add up the figures from your daily time monitoring. List these hours in the "Actual" column in Figure 2.3. Make sure that the grand total of all categories is 168 hours.

Step 5

Reflect on the results of this exercise. Compare the "Estimated" and "Actual" columns. You might feel disappointed or even angry about where your time goes. Use those feelings as motivation to make different choices. Think about how you would complete these sentences:

- I was surprised at the amount of time I spent on . . .
- I want to spend more time on . . .
- I want to spend less time on . . .

Step 6

Repeat this exercise. Do this exercise as many times as you want. The benefit is developing a constant awareness of your activities. With that awareness, you can make informed choices about how to spend the time of your life.

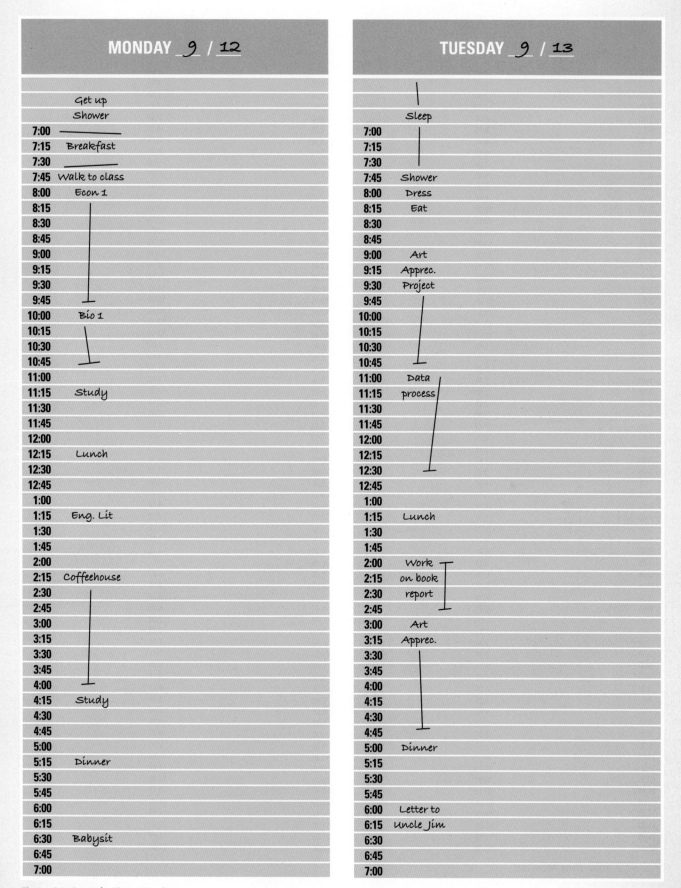

MONDAY _9_ / _12_		TUESDAY _9_ / _13_
Get up		Sleep
Shower		
7:00 ————		7:00
7:15 Breakfast		7:15
7:30 ————		7:30
7:45 Walk to class		7:45 Shower
8:00 Econ 1		8:00 Dress
8:15		8:15 Eat
8:30		8:30
8:45		8:45
9:00		9:00 Art
9:15		9:15 Apprec.
9:30		9:30 Project
9:45		9:45
10:00 Bio 1		10:00
10:15		10:15
10:30		10:30
10:45		10:45
11:00		11:00 Data
11:15 Study		11:15 process
11:30		11:30
11:45		11:45
12:00		12:00
12:15 Lunch		12:15
12:30		12:30
12:45		12:45
1:00		1:00
1:15 Eng. Lit		1:15 Lunch
1:30		1:30
1:45		1:45
2:00		2:00 Work
2:15 Coffeehouse		2:15 on book
2:30		2:30 report
2:45		2:45
3:00		3:00 Art
3:15		3:15 Apprec.
3:30		3:30
3:45		3:45
4:00		4:00
4:15 Study		4:15
4:30		4:30
4:45		4:45
5:00		5:00 Dinner
5:15 Dinner		5:15
5:30		5:30
5:45		5:45
6:00		6:00 Letter to
6:15		6:15 Uncle Jim
6:30 Babysit		6:30
6:45		6:45
7:00		7:00

Figure 2.1 **Sample Time Monitor**

MONDAY ___ / ___ / ___ /	TUESDAY ___ / ___ / ___ /	WEDNESDAY ___ / ___ / ___ /	THURSDAY ___ / ___ / ___ /
7:00	7:00	7:00	7:00
7:15	7:15	7:15	7:15
7:30	7:30	7:30	7:30
7:45	7:45	7:45	7:45
8:00	8:00	8:00	8:00
8:15	8:15	8:15	8:15
8:30	8:30	8:30	8:30
8:45	8:45	8:45	8:45
9:00	9:00	9:00	9:00
9:15	9:15	9:15	9:15
9:30	9:30	9:30	9:30
9:45	9:45	9:45	9:45
10:00	10:00	10:00	10:00
10:15	10:15	10:15	10:15
10:30	10:30	10:30	10:30
10:45	10:45	10:45	10:45
11:00	11:00	11:00	11:00
11:15	11:15	11:15	11:15
11:30	11:30	11:30	11:30
11:45	11:45	11:45	11:45
12:00	12:00	12:00	12:00
12:15	12:15	12:15	12:15
12:30	12:30	12:30	12:30
12:45	12:45	12:45	12:45
1:00	1:00	1:00	1:00
1:15	1:15	1:15	1:15
1:30	1:30	1:30	1:30
1:45	1:45	1:45	1:45
2:00	2:00	2:00	2:00
2:15	2:15	2:15	2:15
2:30	2:30	2:30	2:30
2:45	2:45	2:45	2:45
3:00	3:00	3:00	3:00
3:15	3:15	3:15	3:15
3:30	3:30	3:30	3:30
3:45	3:45	3:45	3:45
4:00	4:00	4:00	4:00
4:15	4:15	4:15	4:15
4:30	4:30	4:30	4:30
4:45	4:45	4:45	4:45
5:00	5:00	5:00	5:00
5:15	5:15	5:15	5:15
5:30	5:30	5:30	5:30
5:45	5:45	5:45	5:45
6:00	6:00	6:00	6:00
6:15	6:15	6:15	6:15
6:30	6:30	6:30	6:30
6:45	6:45	6:45	6:45
7:00	7:00	7:00	7:00
7:15	7:15	7:15	7:15
7:30	7:30	7:30	7:30
7:45	7:45	7:45	7:45
8:00	8:00	8:00	8:00
8:15	8:15	8:15	8:15
8:30	8:30	8:30	8:30
8:45	8:45	8:45	8:45
9:00	9:00	9:00	9:00
9:15	9:15	9:15	9:15
9:30	9:30	9:30	9:30
9:45	9:45	9:45	9:45
10:00	10:00	10:00	10:00
10:15	10:15	10:15	10:15
10:30	10:30	10:30	10:30
10:45	10:45	10:45	10:45
11:00	11:00	11:00	11:00
11:15	11:15	11:15	11:15
11:30	11:30	11:30	11:30
11:45	11:45	11:45	11:45
12:00	12:00	12:00	12:00

Figure 2.2 *Your Time Monitor*

FRIDAY ___ / ___ / ___ /	SATURDAY ___ / ___ / ___ /	SUNDAY ___ / ___ / ___ /
7:00	7:00	7:00
7:15	7:15	7:15
7:30	7:30	7:30
7:45	7:45	7:45
8:00	8:00	8:00
8:15	8:15	8:15
8:30	8:30	8:30
8:45	8:45	8:45
9:00	9:00	9:00
9:15	9:15	9:15
9:30	9:30	9:30
9:45	9:45	9:45
10:00	10:00	10:00
10:15	10:15	10:15
10:30	10:30	10:30
10:45	10:45	10:45
11:00	11:00	11:00
11:15	11:15	11:15
11:30	11:30	11:30
11:45	11:45	11:45
12:00	12:00	12:00
12:15	12:15	12:15
12:30	12:30	12:30
12:45	12:45	12:45
1:00	1:00	1:00
1:15	1:15	1:15
1:30	1:30	1:30
1:45	1:45	1:45
2:00	2:00	2:00
2:15	2:15	2:15
2:30	2:30	2:30
2:45	2:45	2:45
3:00	3:00	3:00
3:15	3:15	3:15
3:30	3:30	3:30
3:45	3:45	3:45
4:00	4:00	4:00
4:15	4:15	4:15
4:30	4:30	4:30
4:45	4:45	4:45
5:00	5:00	5:00
5:15	5:15	5:15
5:30	5:30	5:30
5:45	5:45	5:45
6:00	6:00	6:00
6:15	6:15	6:15
6:30	6:30	6:30
6:45	6:45	6:45
7:00	7:00	7:00
7:15	7:15	7:15
7:30	7:30	7:30
7:45	7:45	7:45
8:00	8:00	8:00
8:15	8:15	8:15
8:30	8:30	8:30
8:45	8:45	8:45
9:00	9:00	9:00
9:15	9:15	9:15
9:30	9:30	9:30
9:45	9:45	9:45
10:00	10:00	10:00
10:15	10:15	10:15
10:30	10:30	10:30
10:45	10:45	10:45
11:00	11:00	11:00
11:15	11:15	11:15
11:30	11:30	11:30
11:45	11:45	11:45
12:00	12:00	12:00

Figure 2.2 *(Continued)*

WEEK OF ___ / ___ / ___ /		
Category	Estimated Hours	Actual Hours
Sleep		
Class		
Study		
Meals		

Figure 2.3 *Your Estimated and Actual Hours*

DISCOVERY/INTENTION STATEMENT

journal entry 6

Discover the impact of technology on your time and attention

Many students find that the Internet becomes a major time drainer. Discover whether this is true for you. For one day, keep track of how much time you spend online. Use a simple system for gathering data. For instance, keep a 3 × 5 card and pen handy. On this card, write down the times when you start using the Internet and when you stop. Another option is to use a Web-based time tracker such as SlimTimer (**slimtimer.com**) or RescueTime (**rescuetime.com**).

If possible, include short descriptions of how you spent your online time. For example: *visit Facebook, check email, read the news, do course work,* or *watch videos.* After monitoring your online time, complete the following sentences:

I discovered that the number of minutes I spent online today was . . .

The things that I did online were . . .

Next, think about any changes that you want to make in the amount of time you spend online. For example, you could close your web browser for defined periods each day. Complete the following sentence:

I intend to . . .

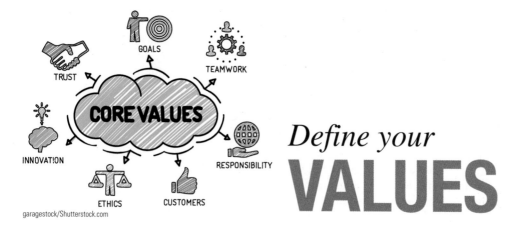

Define your VALUES

Values are the things in life that you want for their own sake. They define who you want to be. They also guide your moment-by-moment choices about what to do and what to have.

Values have little meaning unless they change our daily behavior. Our values are truly affirmed in a public way—through behaviors that anyone can observe.

People often say that they live a values-based life—and then act in ways that contradict what they say. They might say that they value contribution and yet avoid doing volunteer work. Students might say that they value education even though they skip classes to party.

One way to take charge of your time and attention is to define your values and then carefully choose your actions. If you discover a mismatch between what you say and what you do, then set a clear intention to use your time differently.

Don't be content with a vague set of ideals. Make your values so clear that they guide you on when to say yes to an activity—and when to say no.

CONSIDER ONE SET OF VALUES

Becoming a Master Student is based on a specific set of values:

- *Focusing attention* means "being here now"—fully awake, aware, and present to any task that occupies you in the present moment. People with focused attention can be centered even in the midst of chaos.
- *Showing self-responsibility* means being the victor rather than the victim. This value is based on the idea that in any circumstance—no matter how difficult—you can still choose how to respond.
- *Having integrity* means being someone that people can count on. When you practice integrity, your words and your actions are aligned. People can trust you to keep your agreements.
- *Taking risks* means being willing to change. People who live by this value are open-minded and courageous. They know that learning calls on us to consider new ideas and experiment with new behaviors—even when we feel fear.
- *Contributing* means being a person who discovers the meaning of life in serving others. People who practice this value gain knowledge and skills so that they can give something back to the world.

If you look carefully, you'll find one or more of these values reflected on every page of this text. For example, the qualities of a master student are a detailed statement of the core values listed here.

TRANSLATE YOUR VALUES INTO VISIBLE BEHAVIORS

One way to define your values is to reflect on the qualities of people you appreciate. Describe their behaviors. Then ask yourself what values might serve as the source of those behaviors.

You can also define your values by creating your eulogy. This is a detailed statement of how you want to be remembered after you die. After you've put this statement in writing, set goals about what you will *do* to create that legacy. This is not about focusing on death. It's about choosing how to spend your time while you're alive.

Yet another option is to define your values as high-priority activities. In your journal, brainstorm ways to complete this sentence: *It's extremely important that I make time for* . . . Then use your answers to set goals, schedule events, and write daily to-do lists. This strategy translates your values into plans that directly affect the way you manage time.

For example, perhaps it's important for you to make time for staying healthy. Then you can set goals to exercise regularly and manage your weight. In turn, those goals can show up as items on your to-do list and calendar—commitments to go to the gym, take an aerobics class, and include low-fat foods on your grocery list.

You might also place a high value on creating loving relationships. If so, then block out regular times on your calendar for spending time with family members and close friends.

If you value financial security, then set specific goals for increasing your income and reducing your expenses.

In any case, the ultimate time-management skill is defining your values and aligning your actions. ✄

Setting and achieving
GOALS

Marekuliasz/Shutterstock.com

Many people have no goals or have only vague, idealized notions of what they want. They are wonderful, fuzzy, safe thoughts such as "I want to be a good person," "I want to be financially secure," or "I want to be happy."

General outcomes such as these have potential as achievable goals. When we *keep* these goals in a general form, however, we may become confused about ways to actually achieve them.

Make your goal as real as a finely tuned engine. There is nothing vague or fuzzy about engines. You can see them, feel them, and hear them. You can take them apart and inspect the moving parts.

Goals can be every bit as real and useful. If you really want to meet a goal, then take it apart. Inspect the moving parts—the physical actions that you will take to make the goal happen and fine-tune your life.

There are many useful methods for setting goals. You're about to learn one of them. This method is based on writing goals that relate to several time frames and areas of your life. Experiment, and modify as you see fit.

Write down your goals. Writing down your goals greatly increases your chances of meeting them. Writing exposes undefined terms, unrealistic time frames, and other symptoms of fuzzy thinking. If you've been completing Intention Statements as explained in the Introduction to this book, then you've already had experience writing goals. Both goals and Intention Statements address changes you want to make in your behavior, your values, your circumstances—or all of these.

Write specific goals. State your goals in writing as observable outcomes or measurable results. Think in detail about how things will be different once your goals are attained. List the changes in what you'll see, feel, touch, taste, hear, be, do, or have.

Suppose that one of your goals is to become a better student by studying harder. You're headed in a powerful direction; now translate that goal into a concrete action, such as "I will study two hours for every hour I'm in class."

Specific goals make clear what actions are needed or what results are expected. Consider these examples:

Vague Goal	Specific Goal
Get a good education.	Graduate with BS degree in engineering, with honors, by 2021.
Get good grades.	Earn a 3.5 grade point average next semester.
Enhance my spiritual life.	Join a church in my neighborhood with a strong tradition of community service.
Improve my appearance.	Lose 6 pounds during the next six months.
Get control of my money.	Have $5,000 in my savings account by July 1 of next year.

Write goals in several time frames. To get a comprehensive vision of your future, write down the following:

- **Long-term goals.** Long-term goals represent major targets in your life. These goals can take 5 to 20 years to achieve. In some cases, they will take a lifetime. They can include goals in education, careers, personal relationships, travel, financial security—whatever is important to you. Consider the answers to the following questions as you create your long-term goals: What do you

want to accomplish in your life? Do you want your life to make a statement? If so, what is that statement?

- **Midterm goals.** Midterm goals are objectives you can accomplish in one to five years. They include goals such as completing a course of education, paying off a car loan, or achieving a specific career level. These goals usually support your long-term goals.

- **Short-term goals.** Short-term goals are the ones you can accomplish in a year or less. These goals are specific achievements, such as completing a particular course or group of courses, hiking down the Appalachian Trail, or organizing a family reunion. A short-term financial goal would probably include an exact dollar amount. Whatever your short-term goals are, they will require action now or in the near future.

Create a lifeline

On a large sheet of paper, draw a horizontal line. This line will represent your lifetime. Now add key events in your life to this line, in chronological order. Examples are birth, first day at school, graduation from high school, and enrollment in higher education.

Now extend the lifeline into the future. Write down key events you would like to see occur 1 year, 5 years, and 10 or more years from now. Choose events that align with your core values. Work quickly in the spirit of a brainstorm, bearing in mind that this plan is not a final one.

Afterward, take a few minutes to review your lifeline. Select one key event for the future, and list any actions you could take in the next month to bring yourself closer to that goal. Do the same with the other key events on your lifeline. You now have the rudiments of a comprehensive plan for your life.

Finally, extend your lifeline another 50 years beyond the year when you would reach age 100. Describe in detail what changes in the world you'd like to see as a result of the goals you attained in your lifetime.

Write goals in several areas of life. People who set goals in only one area of life—such as their career—may find that their personal growth becomes one-sided. They might experience success at work while neglecting their health or relationships with family members and friends.

To avoid this outcome, set goals in a variety of categories. Consider what you want to experience in these areas:

- Education
- Career
- Financial life
- Family life or relationships
- Social life
- Contribution (volunteer activities, community services)
- Spiritual life
- Level of health

Add goals in other areas as they occur to you.

Reflect on your goals. Each week, take a few minutes to think about your goals. You can perform the following spot checks:

- **Check in with your feelings.** Think about how the process of setting your goals felt. Consider the satisfaction you'll gain in attaining your objectives. If you don't feel a significant emotional connection with a written goal, consider letting it go or filing it away to review later.
- **Check for alignment.** Look for connections among your goals. Do your short-term goals align with your midterm goals? Will your midterm goals help you achieve your long-term goals? Look for a fit between all of your goals and your purpose for taking part in higher education as well as your overall purpose in life.
- **Check for obstacles.** All kinds of things can come between you and your goals, such as constraints on time and money. Anticipate obstacles and start looking now for workable solutions.
- **Check for next steps.** Here's a way to link goal setting to time management. Decide on a list of small, achievable steps you can take right away to accomplish each of your short-term goals. Write these small steps down on a daily to-do list. If you want to accomplish some of these steps by a certain date, enter them in a calendar that you consult daily. Then, over the coming weeks, review your to-do list and calendar. Take note of your progress and celebrate your successes.

Move into action immediately. The idea of making New Year's resolutions is the butt of countless jokes. On January 1, we swear to start exercising regularly. By February 1, we're reaching for the TV remote instead of the jogging shoes.

Don't let your goals suffer such a fate. To increase your odds of success, take immediate action. Decrease the gap between stating a goal and starting to achieve it. If you slip and forget about the goal, you can get back on track at any time by *doing* something about it. Make those jokes about resolutions a part of your past, not a predictor of your future. ✶

practicing
CRITICAL THINKING

Get real with your goals

One way to make goals effective is to examine them up close. That's what this exercise is about. Using a process of brainstorming and evaluation, you can break a long-term goal into smaller segments until you have taken it completely apart. When you analyze a goal to this level of detail, you're well on the way to meeting it.

Make sure you have a watch with a second hand while you work on this exercise. (A digital watch with a built-in stopwatch feature is even better.) Timing is an important part of the brainstorming process, so follow the stated time limits. This entire exercise takes about an hour.

Part 1: Long-term goals

Brainstorm. Begin with an eight-minute brainstorm. For eight minutes, write down everything you think you want in your life. Write as fast as you can, and write whatever comes into your head. Leave no thought out. Don't worry about accuracy. The object of a brainstorm is to generate as many ideas as possible.

Evaluate. After you have finished brainstorming, spend the next six minutes looking over your list. Analyze what you wrote. Read the list out loud. If something is missing, add it. Look for common themes or relationships among your goals. Then select three long-term goals that are important to you—goals that will take many years to achieve. Write these goals down.

Before you continue, take a minute to reflect on the process you've used so far. What criteria did you use to select your top three goals?

Part 2: Midterm goals

Brainstorm. Read out loud the three long-term goals you selected in Part 1. Choose one of them. Then brainstorm

a list of goals you might achieve in the next one to five years that would lead to the accomplishment of that one long-term goal. These are midterm goals. Spend eight minutes on this brainstorm. Go for quantity.

Evaluate. Analyze your brainstorm of midterm goals. Then select three that you determine to be important in meeting the long-term goal you picked. Allow yourself six minutes for this part of the exercise. Write your selections down.

Again, pause for reflection before going on to the next part of this exercise. Why do you see these three goals as more important than the other midterm goals you generated? Write about your reasons for selecting these three goals.

Part 3: Short-term goals

Brainstorm. Review your list of midterm goals and select one. In another eight-minute brainstorm, generate a list of short-term goals—those you can accomplish in a year or less that will lead to the attainment of that midterm goal. Write down everything that comes to mind. Do not evaluate or judge these ideas yet. For now, the more ideas you write down, the better.

Evaluate. Analyze your list of short-term goals. The most effective brainstorms are conducted by suspending judgment, so you might find some bizarre ideas on your list. That's fine. Now is the time to cross them out. Next, evaluate your remaining short-term goals, and select three that you are willing and able to accomplish. Allow yourself six minutes for this part of the exercise. Then write your selections down.

The more you practice, the more effective you can be at choosing goals that have meaning for you. You can repeat this exercise, employing the other long-term goals you generated or creating new ones.

The ABC daily
TO-DO LIST

One of the most effective ways to stay on track and actually get things done is to use a daily to-do list. While the Time Monitor/Time Plan gives you a general picture of the week, your daily to-do list itemizes specific tasks you want to complete within the next 24 hours.

chrupka/Shutterstock.com

One advantage of keeping a daily to-do list is that you don't have to remember what to do next. It's on the list. A typical day in the life of a student is full of separate, often unrelated tasks—reading, attending lectures, reviewing notes, working at a job, writing papers, researching special projects, running errands. It's easy to forget an important task on a busy day. When that task is written down, you don't have to rely on your memory.

The following steps present one method for creating and using to-do lists. This method involves ranking each item on your list according to three levels of importance—A, B, or C. Experiment with these steps, modify them as you see fit, and invent new techniques that work for you.

BRAINSTORM TASKS

To get started, list all of the tasks you want to get done tomorrow. Each task will become an item on a to-do list. Don't worry about putting the entries in order or scheduling them yet. Just list everything you want to accomplish on a sheet of paper or planning calendar or in a special notebook. You can also use 3 × 5 cards, writing one task on each card. Cards work well because you can slip them into your pocket or rearrange them, and you never have to copy to-do items from one list to another.

ESTIMATE TIME

For each task you wrote down in Step 1, estimate how long it will take you to complete it. This can be tricky. If you allow too little time, you end up feeling rushed. If you allow too much time, you become less productive. For now, give it your best guess. If you are unsure, overestimate rather than underestimate how long it will take for each task.

Overestimating has two benefits: (1) It avoids a schedule that is too tight, missed deadlines, and the resulting feelings of frustration and failure; and (2) it allows time for the unexpected things that come up every day—the spontaneous to-dos. Now pull out your calendar or Time Monitor/Time Plan. You've probably scheduled some hours for activities such as classes or work. This leaves the unscheduled hours for tackling your to-do lists.

Add up the time needed to complete all your to-do items. Also add up the number of unscheduled hours in your day. Then compare the two totals. The power of this step is that you can spot overload in advance. If you have eight hours' worth of to-do items but only four unscheduled hours, that's a potential problem. To solve it, proceed to Step 3.

RATE EACH TASK BY PRIORITY

To prevent overscheduling, decide which to-do items are the most important, given the time you have available. One suggestion for making this decision comes from the book *How to Get Control of Your Time and Your Life,* by Alan Lakein: Simply label each task A, B, or C.[3]

The As on your list are those things that are the most critical. They include assignments that are coming due or jobs that need to be done immediately. Also included are activities that lead directly to your short-term goals.

The Bs on your list are important, but less so than the As. Bs might someday become As. For the present, these tasks are not as urgent as As. They can be postponed, if necessary, for another day.

The Cs do not require immediate attention. C priorities include activities such as "shop for a new blender" and "research genealogy on the Internet." Cs are often small, easy jobs with no set time line. They too can be postponed.

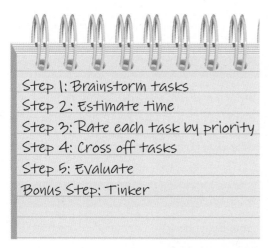

Step 1: Brainstorm tasks
Step 2: Estimate time
Step 3: Rate each task by priority
Step 4: Cross off tasks
Step 5: Evaluate
Bonus Step: Tinker

Alexey Grigorev/Shutterstock.com

Once you've labeled the items on your to-do list, schedule time for all of the As. The Bs and Cs can be done randomly during the day when you are in between tasks and are not yet ready to start the next A. Even if you get one or two of your As done, you'll still be moving toward your goals.

CROSS OFF TASKS

Keep your to-do list with you at all times. Cross off activities when you finish them, and add new ones when you think of them. If you're using 3 × 5 cards, you can toss away or recycle the cards with completed items. Crossing off tasks and releasing cards can be fun—a visible

reward for your diligence. This step fosters a sense of accomplishment.

When using the ABC priority method, you might experience an ailment common to students: C fever. Symptoms include the uncontrollable urge to drop that A task and begin crossing Cs off your to-do list. If your history paper is due tomorrow, you might feel compelled to vacuum the rug, call your third cousin in Tulsa, and make a trip to the store for shoelaces. The reason C fever is so common is that A tasks are usually more difficult or time-consuming to achieve, with a higher risk of failure.

If you notice symptoms of C fever, ask yourself, "Does this job really need to be done now? Do I really need to alphabetize my CD collection, or might I better use this time to study for tomorrow's data-processing exam?" Use your to-do list to keep yourself on task, working on your As. But don't panic or berate yourself when you realize that in the last six hours, you have completed nine Cs and not a single A. Just calmly return to the As.

EVALUATE

At the end of the day, evaluate your performance. Look for A priorities you didn't complete. Look for items that repeatedly turn up as Bs or Cs on your list and never seem to get done. Consider changing them to As or dropping them altogether. Similarly, you might consider changing an A that didn't get done to a B or C priority.

Be willing to admit mistakes. You might at first rank some items as As only to realize later that they are actually Cs. And some of the Cs that lurk at the bottom of your list day after day might really be As. When you keep a daily to-do list, you can adjust these priorities *before* they become problems.

When you're done evaluating, start on tomorrow's to-do list. That way you can wake up and start getting things done right away.

TINKER

When it comes to to-do lists, one size does not fit all. Feel free to experiment. Tweak the format of your list so that it works for you.

For example, the ABC system is not the only way to rank items on your to-do list. Some people prefer the 80-20 system. This method is based on the idea that 80 percent of the value of any to-do list comes from only 20 percent of the tasks on that list. So on a to-do list of 10 items, find the 2 that will contribute most to your life today. Complete those tasks without fail.

Another option is to rank items as "yes," "no," or "maybe." Do all of the tasks marked "yes." Delete those marked "no." And put all of the "maybes" on the shelf for later. You can come back to the "maybes" at a future point and rank them as "yes" or "no."

You might find that grouping items by categories such as "Errands" and "Calls" works best. Be creative.

In any case, use your to-do list in close connection with your calendar. On your calendar, note appointments, classes, and other events that take place on a specific date, a specific time, or both. Use your to-do list for items that

practicing
CRITICAL THINKING

9

Create your to-do list

The purpose of this exercise is to break down the suggestions from "The ABC daily to-do list" into a series of steps. When you're done, you'll have a to-do list that you can use today.

Step 1: Brainstorm things to do

Take at least 15 minutes to write a list of things that you want or need to do. Write down *everything* that's on your mind as urgent, important, or unfinished. Your list can include anything from *change my career* to *pick up dog food*. Include things that you want to get done today, this week, this month, or any time in the future.

If your list gets long, then celebrate that fact. It means that your mind is getting clear. Take a short break to notice how good that feels.

Step 2: Separate goals from tasks

Now review your list. Some of the items are probably outcomes that will take more than one action to complete (such as changing your career). Label those items clearly as *goals*. The remaining items are tasks.

Step 3: Fill out the following chart to create your to-do list for today

a. *From your tasks, find a maximum of seven tasks that you want to get done today.* List these in the *Tasks* column. This is the first draft of your to-do list.
b. *Predict how much time each of the tasks on your to-do list will take.* Estimate these times in 15-minute increments, just as you did with the Time Monitor/Time Plan exercise. If you're not sure how long a task will take, then allow at least 15 extra minutes. For complex tasks, consider adding an extra 30 to 90 minutes. Finish this step by adding up your estimates. This is your total estimate of the time needed to finish your to-do list for today.
c. *Compare estimated time to available time.* Now, check your calendar. Figure out how many unscheduled hours you have today. Then compare this number to your total estimate. If you have more tasks than time, realize that you have a common problem. Consider taking some tasks away from the table and moving them back to your master list of tasks.
d. *Set priorities.* Now assign a priority to each task that remains in the table. Use the ABC system or one of the alternatives explained in "The ABC daily to do-list." Remember that the purpose of making a to-do list is not necessarily to finish *all* the tasks on your list. Rather, your goal is to complete the most *important* and *urgent* tasks for today.

you can complete between scheduled events. Keeping a separate to-do list means that you don't have to clutter up your calendar with all those reminders.

In addition, consider planning a whole week or even two weeks in advance. Planning in this way can make it easier to put activities in context and see how your daily goals relate to your long-term goals. Weekly planning can also free you from feeling that you have to polish off your whole to-do list in one day. Instead, you can spread tasks out over the whole week.

In any case, make starting your own to-do list an A priority. ✖

e. ***Cross off tasks.*** Here's a fun step: When you finish a task during the day, note that fact. Cross off each completed task rather than erasing or deleting it. That way you'll have a record of what you get done today.

Task	Time	Priority

Step 4: Evaluate

Before you go to sleep tonight, reflect on your experience with creating today's to-do list. Write a Discovery Statement about how well it worked and how you felt about doing this exercise. Follow up with an Intention Statement to describe anything you'll do differently when creating tomorrow's to-do list.

Step 5: Celebrate and continue

This exercise involves creative and critical thinking. Though the process might seem simple at first glance, it's not always easy. Give yourself credit for completing the earlier steps. Then make it a daily habit to create a to-do list. You are taking control of your time—and your life.

Planning sets you
FREE

Graphixmania/Shutterstock.com

Planning sets you free. When you set goals and manage time, your life does not just happen by chance. You are on equal terms with the greatest sculptor, painter, or playwright. You are doing more than creating a work of art: You are designing a life.

Without planning, we simply "dig in." We forget the difference between busy and being productive. Planning helps us to prevent this problem. We define our core values, set clear goals, and choose the next steps to achieve them. As we focus on our most important activities, we are free to let go of everything else. We can actually end up doing less and being more effective at the same time.

An effective plan creates options. It is not carved in stone. You can change your plans frequently and still preserve the advantages of planning—choosing your overall direction and taking charge of your life. Even when other people set the goals, you can choose how to achieve them.

Planning is a self-creative venture that lasts for a lifetime. Following are suggestions that flow directly from this point of view.

Schedule for flexibility and fun. Be realistic. Don't set yourself up for failure by telling yourself you can do a four-hour job in two hours. There are only 168 hours in a week. If you schedule 169 hours, you're sunk.

Expect the unexpected. Allow for emergencies by leaving some holes in your schedule—blocks of unplanned time. Consider setting aside time each week marked "flex time" or "open time." Use these hours for spontaneous activities, catching up, or seizing new opportunities.

Include time for errands. The time we spend buying groceries, paying bills, and doing laundry is easy to overlook. These small tasks can destroy a tight schedule and make us feel rushed and stressed all week. Plan for them. Also remember to allow for travel time between locations.

One immediate way to lower your stress level is set *personal* due dates for two or three

days before *actual* due dates. If you have a paper to submit on March 15, for example, enter the due date on your calendar as March 13. You now have a two-day buffer to get that writing done.

Also make room for fun. This is important. Brains that are constantly stimulated by new ideas and new challenges need time off to digest them.

Back up to a bigger picture. When choosing activities for the day or week, take some time to lift your eyes to the horizon. Step back for a few minutes and consider your longer-range goals—what you want to accomplish in the next six months, the next year, the next five years, and beyond.

Ask whether the activities you're about to schedule actually contribute to those goals. If they do, great. If not, ask whether you can delete some items from your calendar or to-do list to make room for goal-related activities. See if you can free up at least one hour each day for doing something you love instead of putting it off to a more "reasonable" or "convenient" time.

Look boldly for things to change. When creating your future, be bold. You can write goals related to money, marriage, career, or anything else. Don't accept the idea that you have to put up with substandard results in a certain area of your life. Staying open-minded about what is possible to achieve can lead to a future you never dreamed was possible.

Look for what's missing—and what to maintain. Goals often arise from a sense of what's missing in our lives. Goal setting is fueled by problems that are not resolved, projects that are incomplete, relationships we want to develop, and careers we still want to pursue.

However, not all planning has to spring from a sense of need. You can set goals to maintain things that you already have, or to keep doing the effective things that you already do. If you exercise vigorously three times each week, you can set a goal to keep exercising. If you already have a loving relationship with your spouse, you can set a goal to nurture that relationship for the rest of your life.

Think even further into the future. To have fun and unleash your creativity, set goals as far in the future as you can. The specific length of time doesn't matter. For some people, long-range planning might mean 10, 20, or even 50 years from now. For others, imagining three years feels right. Do whatever works for you.

Return to the present. Once you've stated your longest-range goals, work backward until you can define a next step to take. Suppose your 30-year goal is to retire and maintain your present standard of living. Ask yourself, "To do that, what financial goals do I need to achieve in 20 years? In 10 years? In a year? In a month? In a week?" Put the answers to these questions in writing. Some people refer to this as "backward planning." It's a way to drill down to details after thinking forward into the future.

To make backward planning more effective, remember the suggestion to schedule for flexibility. Leave some space in your schedule for unplanned events. Give yourself some time to deal with obstacles before they derail from your dreams.

Schedule fixed blocks of time first. When planning your week, start with class time and work time. These time periods are usually determined in advance, so other activities must be scheduled around them. Then schedule essential daily activities such as sleeping and eating. In addition, schedule some time each week for actions that lead directly to one of your written goals.

Set clear starting and stopping times. Tasks often expand to fill the time we allot to them. "It always takes me an hour just to settle into a reading assignment" might become a self-fulfilling prophecy.

As an alternative, schedule a certain amount of time for a reading assignment. Set a timer, and stick to it. Students often find that they can decrease study time by forcing themselves to read faster. They can usually do so without sacrificing comprehension.

A variation of this technique is called *time boxing*. Set aside a specific number of minutes or hours to spend on a certain task. Instead of working on that task until it's done, commit to work on it just for that specific amount of time. Then set a timer, and get to work. In effect, you're placing the task inside a definite "box"— a specific space on your daily calendar.

Feeling rushed or sacrificing quality is not the goal here. The point is to push yourself a little and discover what your time requirements really are.

Plan for changes in your workload. You might find yourself with a lighter load of assignments to complete during the first few days or weeks of any course. Faced with this situation, some students are tempted to let early homework slide. They figure that they'll have plenty of time to catch up later. These students often get a rude surprise when the course shifts into warp speed.

To stay on top of your workload over the entire term, plan for such a change of pace. Stay on top of your assignments right from the start. Whenever possible, work ahead. This tactic gives you an edge when the load for a course gets heavier or when big assignments for several courses are due during the same week.

Involve others when appropriate. Statements such as these often follow a communications breakdown: "I just assumed you were going to pick up the kids from school on Tuesday." "I'm working overtime this week and hoped that you'd take over the cooking for a while." When you schedule a task that depends on another person's involvement, let that person know— the sooner, the better.

Start the day with your Most Important Task. Review your to-do list and calendar first thing each morning. Then visualize the rest of your day as a succession of tasks. For an extra level of clarity, pretend that you have to condense your to-do list to only one top-priority item. This is the thing that you want to complete today *without fail*. Behold your Most Important Task (MIT). Do it as early in the day as possible. Also do your MIT impeccably, with total attention.

Plan in a way that works for you. Even in this high-tech culture, there are many people who prefer to use low-tech tools for planning. This chapter includes paper-and-pencil exercises for students with a more kinesthetic learning style.

Planning that sets you free can be done with any set of tools. What matters above all is clear thinking and specific intentions. You can take any path that gets you there.

Stay on top of your assignments right from the start. Whenever possible, work ahead. This tactic gives you an edge when the load for a course gets heavier or when big assignments for several courses are due during the same week. ✄

Making the transition to
HIGHER EDUCATION

You share one thing in common with other students at your school: Entering higher education represents a major change in your life. You've joined a new culture with its own set of rules—both spoken and unspoken.

Perhaps you've just graduated from high school. Or maybe you've been out of the classroom for decades. Either way, you'll discover big differences between secondary and post-secondary education. Many of those differences call for new skills in managing time.

Begin by taking a minute to relax and remember something: You don't have to do it all at once. To enter the culture of higher education, start by dealing with some common challenges. Then learn to manage time in ways that help you make a successful transition.

DEAL WITH COMMON CHALLENGES

The moment that you enter higher education, you're immediately faced with:

- **New academic standards.** Once you enter higher education, you'll probably find yourself working harder in school than ever before. Instructors will often present more material at a faster pace. There probably will be fewer tests in higher education than in high school, and the grading might be tougher. Compared to high school, you'll have more to read, more to write, more problems to solve, and more to remember.

- **A new level of independence.** College instructors typically give less guidance about how or when to study. You may not get reminders about when assignments are due or when quizzes and tests will take place. Overall, you might receive less consistent feedback about how well you are doing in each of your courses.

- **Differences in teaching styles.** Instructors at colleges, universities, and vocational schools are often steeped in their subject matter. Many did not take courses on how to teach and might not be as interesting as some of your high school teachers.

- **A larger playing field.** The sheer size of your campus, the variety of courses offered, the large number of departments can add up to a confusing array of options.
- **More students and more diversity.** The school you're attending right now might enroll hundreds or thousands more students than your high school. And the range of diversity among these students might surprise you.

Decrease the unknowns. To reduce surprise, anticipate changes. Before classes begin, get a map of the school property and walk through your first day's schedule, perhaps with a classmate or friend. Visit your instructors in their offices and introduce yourself. Anything you can do to get familiar with the new routine will help. In addition, consider buying your textbooks before class begins. Scan them to get a preview of your courses.

Admit your feelings— whatever they are. Simply admitting the truth about how you feel—to yourself and to someone else—can help you cope. And you can almost always do something constructive in the present moment, no matter how you feel.

If your feelings about this transition make it hard for you to carry out the activities of daily life—going to class, working, studying, and relating to people—then get professional help. Start with a counselor at the student health service on your campus. The mere act of seeking help can make a difference.

Allow time for transition. You don't have to master the transition to higher education right away. Give it some time. Also, plan your academic schedule with your needs for transition in mind. Balance time-intensive courses with others that don't make as many demands.

Find and use resources. For example, visit the career planning center and financial aid office. Check out tutoring services and computer labs. Check the schedule for on-campus concerts, films, and plays. Extracurricular activities include athletics, fraternities, sororities, student newspapers, debate teams, service-learning projects, internships, student government, and political action groups, to name just a few. Check your school's website for more.

Accessing resources is especially important if you are the first person in your family to enter higher education. As a first-generation student, you are having experiences that people in your family may not understand. Talk to your relatives about your activities at school. If they ask how they can help you, give specific answers. Also, ask your instructors about programs for first-generation students on your campus.

Take the initiative in meeting new people. Of all resources, people are the most important. You can isolate yourself, study hard, and get a good education. When you build relationships with teachers, staff members, fellow students, and employers, you can get a *great* education. Create a network of people who will personally support your success in school.

Introduce yourself to class-mates and instructors. Just before or after class is a good time. Realize that most of the people in this new world of higher education are waiting to be welcomed. You can help them and help yourself at the same time. Connecting to school socially as well as academically promotes your success and your enjoyment.

Meet with your academic advisor. One person in particular—your academic advisor—can help you access resources and make the transition to higher education. Meet with this person regularly. Advisors generally know about course requirements, options for declaring majors, and the resources available at your school. Peer advisors might also be available.

When you work with an advisor, remember that you're a paying customer and have a right to be satisfied with the service you get. Don't be afraid to change advisors when that seems appropriate.

Learn the language of higher education. Terms such as *grade point average (GPA), prerequisite, accreditation, matriculation, tenure,* and *syllabus* might be new to you. Ease your transition to higher education by checking your school catalog or school website for definitions of these words and others that you don't understand. Also ask your academic advisor for clarification.

MANAGE TIME WITH TRANSITION IN MIND

Devote study time to deep processing. Stephen Chew, a professor of psychology at

AVOID HIGH-TECH TIME WASTERS

Time management is about to take on a new meaning in your life. What you do *outside* class will matter as much as—or even more than—what you do during class. To make a successful transition to higher education, start taking charge of your time and attention. The following suggestions are ways to begin.

Limit your time on social networks. Track how much time you spend each day on websites such as Facebook, Twitter, LinkedIn, Google+, and Pinterest. Focus on just one or two of them. Check them just once or twice daily, and for just a few minutes at a time. If you don't post updates every day, your friends will forgive you. Remind them that you're going to school.

Save online activity for down times. During the times of the day when your energy peaks, tackle more demanding tasks such as homework and exercising.

Start your day as a student, not a consumer. The first things that you do in the morning set the tone for the entire day. Instead of surfing the Web or checking social networks, start off with a task that supports your success in school.

Simplify email. Most email programs provide an option to save messages into folders for future reference. You can manage all your email with three folders. One is for messages that require follow-up action. A second is for interesting messages to read later. And the third is an archive of messages you might want to refer to in the future. Trash everything else.

Turn off notifications. You don't need to hear an alert from your digital devices whenever someone posts a Facebook update or sends you an email. Savor the silence and extra space for concentration.

Samford University, reminds students that they can struggle in school even if they spend a lot of time studying. The goal, he says, is to make the most of study time. Study *smarter* rather than harder.

To do this, start with your mindset—the beliefs that shape your behaviors. Chew says that certain beliefs can undermine your success in school. Examples are:

- Smart people don't have to study much.
- It's okay to multitask.
- Mastery of a subject is based on talent rather than effort.[4]

In reality, students tend to *underestimate* how much time it takes to master a subject, even for "smart" people. Many students also *overestimate* how effective they are at multitasking, which leads to wasted study time. And they overlook the power of effort, which matters much more than talent or native intelligence.

The crucial factor for effective study time is something that Chew calls *deep processing*. This involves relating new information to what you already know, putting concepts into your own words, and creating mental images that make ideas easier to recall. In contrast, *shallow processing* is seeing a subject as a collection of isolated facts that you memorize without understanding or connection to your current knowledge.

One purpose of *Becoming a Master Student* is to help you move from shallow processing to deep processing. Each chapter of this book is loaded with suggestions for making this transition.

Ease into it. If you're new to higher education, consider easing into it. You can choose to attend school part-time before making a full-time commitment. If you've taken college-level classes in the past, find out if any of those credits will transfer into your current program.

Make time for class. In higher education, teachers generally don't take attendance. Yet you'll find that attending class is essential to your success. The amount that you pay in tuition and fees makes a powerful argument for going to classes regularly and getting your money's worth. In large part, the material that you're tested on comes from events that take place in class.

Manage out-of-class time. Instructors give you the raw materials for understanding a subject while a class meets. You then take those materials, combine them, and *teach yourself* outside of class.

To allow for this process, schedule two hours of study time for each hour that you spend in class. Also, get a calendar that covers the entire academic year. With the syllabus for each of your courses in hand, note key events for the entire term—dates for tests, papers, and other projects. Getting a big picture of your course load makes it easier to get assignments done on time and prevent all-night study sessions.

Plan ahead. By planning a week or month at a time, you get a bigger picture of your multiple roles as a student, an employee, and a family member. With that awareness, you can make conscious adjustments in the number of hours you devote to each domain of activity in your life. For example:

- If your responsibilities at work or home will be heavy in the near future, then register for fewer classes next term.
- Choose recreational activities carefully, focusing on those that relax you and recharge you the most.
- Don't load your schedule with classes that require unusually heavy amounts of reading or writing.

"Publish" your schedule. After you plan your study and class sessions for the week, write up your schedule and post it in a place where others who live with you will see it. If you use an online calendar, print out copies to put in your school binder or on your refrigerator door, bathroom mirror, or kitchen cupboard.

Enlist your employer's support. If you're working while going to school, then let your employer in on your educational plans. Point out how the skills you gain in the classroom will help you meet work objectives. Offer informal seminars at work to share what you're learning in school. You might find that your company reimburses its employees for some tuition costs or even grants time off to attend classes.

Also find ways to get extra mileage out of your current tasks at work. Look for ways to relate your schoolwork to your job. For example, when you're assigned a research paper, choose a topic that relates to your current job tasks. Some schools even offer academic credit for work and life experience. ✖

Making time for school as an
ADULT LEARNER

Stockbyte/Getty Images

Perhaps you're entering higher education as a "nontraditional student" or "adult learner" (age 25 or older). If so, you might find some of these thoughts crossing your mind:

- I'll be the oldest person in all my classes.
- I've been out of the classroom too long.
- I'm concerned about my math, reading, and writing skills.
- I'm worried about making tuition payments.
- How will I ever make the time to study, on top of everything else I'm doing?
- I won't be able to keep up with all the new technology.

Those concerns are understandable. Many of them have to do with making time for all the people and projects that are important to you.

Now consider a couple of facts.

First, in terms of age, classrooms are more diverse than ever before. You can verify this for yourself by noticing how many nontraditional students you see on campus.

Second, you are now enrolled in a course that can help boost your skills at math, reading, writing, note taking, time management, and other key skills for succeeding in school. Every strategy that you discover in this course can help you balance school with work, family, and other major commitments in your life. Get started right away with the following suggestions.

Get to know other adult learners. Introduce yourself to other nontraditional students. Being in the same classroom gives you an immediate bond. You can exchange work, home, or cell phone numbers and build a network of mutual support. Some students adopt a buddy system, pairing up with another student in each class to complete assignments and prepare for tests.

In addition, learn about student services and organizations. Many schools have a learning assistance center with workshops geared to adult learners. Sign up and attend. Meet people on campus. Personal connections are key to your success.

Find common ground with traditional students. Traditional (younger) and nontraditional students have many things in common. They seek to gain knowledge and skills for their chosen careers. They desire financial stability and personal fulfillment. And, like their older peers, many younger students are concerned about whether they have the skills to succeed in higher education.

Consider pooling resources with younger students. Share notes, edit one another's papers, and form study groups. Look for ways to build on one another's strengths. If you want help with using a computer for assignments, you might ask a younger student for help. In group projects and case studies, you can expand the discussion by sharing insights from your experiences.

Remember that being an adult learner puts you on a strong footing. With a rich store of life experiences, you can ask meaningful questions and make connections between course work and daily life. Any abilities that you've developed to work on teams, manage projects, meet deadlines, and solve problems are assets. Many instructors will especially enjoy working with you.

Review your subjects before you start classes. Say that you've registered for trigonometry and you haven't taken a math class since high school. Consider brushing up on the subject before classes begin. Also, talk with future instructors about ways to prepare for their classes.

Delegate tasks. If you have children, delegate some of the household chores to them. Or start a meal co-op in your neighborhood. Cook dinner for yourself and someone else one night each week. In return, ask that person to furnish you with a meal on another night. A similar strategy can apply to childcare and other household tasks.

Enroll family and friends in your success. School can cut into your social life. Prepare friends and family members by discussing this issue ahead of time.

You can also involve your spouse, partner, children, or close friends in your schooling. Offer to give them a tour of the campus, introduce them to your instructors and classmates, and encourage them to attend social events at school with you. Share ideas from this book, and from your other courses.

Take this process a step further, and ask the key people in your life for help. Share your reason for getting a degree, and talk about what your whole family has to gain from this change in your life. Ask them to think of ways that they can support your success in school and to commit to those actions. Make your own education a joint mission that benefits everyone. ✴

practicing
CRITICAL THINKING 10

Master monthly calendar

This exercise will give you an opportunity to step back from the details of your daily schedule and get a bigger picture of your life. The more difficult it is for you to plan beyond the current day or week, the greater the benefit of this exercise.

Your basic tool is a one-month calendar. Use it to block out specific times for upcoming events such as study group meetings, due dates for assignments, review periods before tests, and other time-sensitive tasks. To get started, you might want to copy the blank monthly calendars in Figure 2.5 onto both sides of a sheet of paper. Or make copies of these pages and tape them together so that you can see several months at a glance.

Be creative. Experiment with a variety of uses for your monthly calendar. For instance, you can note day-to-day changes in your health or moods, list the places you visit while you are on vacation, or circle each day that you practice a new habit. Figure 2.4 shows a sample monthly calendar.

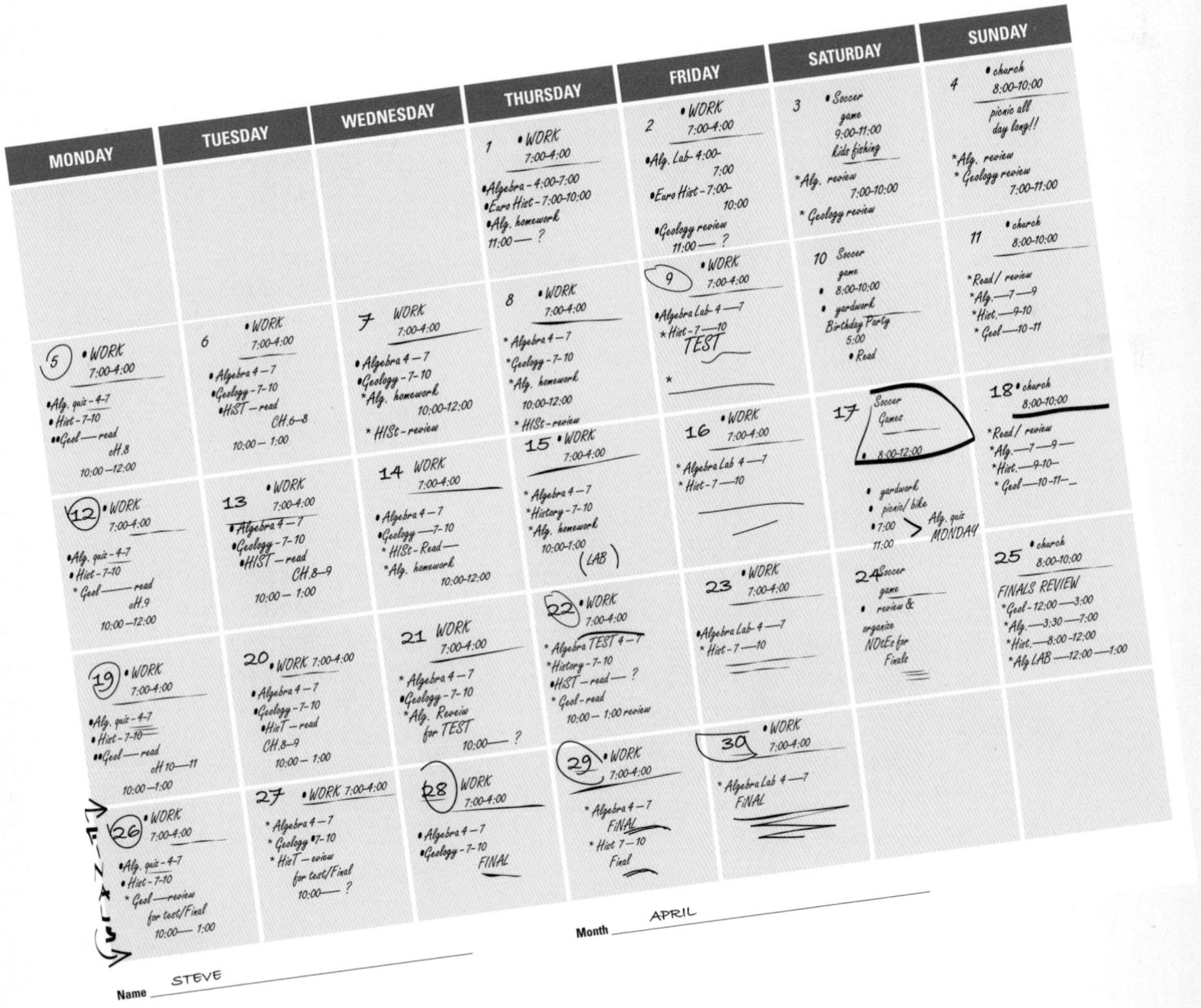

Figure 2.4 ***Sample Monthly Calendars***

MONDAY	TUESDAY	WEDNESDAY	THURSDAY	FRIDAY	SATURDAY	SUNDAY

Month _____

Name _____

Figure 2.5 Your Monthly Calendar

MONDAY	TUESDAY	WEDNESDAY	THURSDAY	FRIDAY	SATURDAY	SUNDAY

Name _____

Month _____

Figure 2.5 (Continued)

Break it down, get it done—using a long-term
PLANNER

Planning a day, a week, or a month ahead is a powerful practice. Using a long-term planner—one that displays an entire quarter, semester, or year at a glance—can yield even more benefits.

With a long-term planner, you can eliminate a lot of unpleasant surprises. Long-term planning allows you to avoid scheduling conflicts—the kind that obligate you to be in two places at the same time three weeks from now. You can also anticipate busy periods, such as finals week, and start preparing for them now. Good-bye, all-night cram sessions. Hello, serenity.

Find a long-term planner or make your own.
Many office supply stores carry academic planners in paper form that cover an entire school year. Computer software for time management offers the same features. You can also be creative and make your own long-term planner. A big roll of newsprint pinned to a bulletin board or taped to a wall will do nicely. You can also search the Internet for a computer application or smartphone app that's designed for planning.

Enter scheduled dates that extend into the future. Use your long-term planner to list commitments that extend beyond the current month. Enter test dates, lab sessions, days that classes will be canceled, and other events that will take place over this term and next term. See Figure 2.6 for an example.

Create a master assignment list. Find the syllabus for each course you're currently taking. Then, in your long-term planner, enter the due dates for all of the assignments in all of your courses. This step can be a powerful reality check.

The purpose of this technique is not to make you feel overwhelmed with all the things you have to do. Rather, its aim is to help you take a First Step toward recognizing the demands on your time. Armed with the truth about how you use your time, you can make more accurate plans.

Include nonacademic events. In addition to tracking academic commitments, you can use your long-term planner to mark significant events in your life outside school. Include birthdays, doctor appointments, concert dates, credit card payment due dates, and car maintenance schedules.

Use your long-term planner to divide and conquer. For some people, academic life is a series of last-minute crises punctuated by periods of exhaustion. You can avoid that fate. The trick is to break down big assignments and projects into smaller assignments and subprojects, each with their own due date.

When planning to write a paper, for instance, enter the final due date in your long-term planner. Then set individual due dates for each milestone in the writing process—creating an outline, completing your research, finishing a first draft, editing the draft, and preparing the final copy. By meeting these interim due dates, you make steady progress on the assignment throughout the term. That sure beats trying to crank out all those pages at the last minute. Try using the blank long-term planner in Figure 2.7. ✂

Week of	Monday	Tuesday	Wednesday	Thursday	Friday	Saturday	Sunday
9 / 5							
9 / 12		English quiz					
9 / 19			English paper due		Speech #1		
9 / 26	Chemistry test					Skiing at the lake	
10 / 3		English quiz			Speech #2		
10 / 10				Geography project due			
10 / 17				--- No classes ---			

Figure 2.6 **Sample Long-Term Planner**

LONG-TERM PLANNER ___ / ___ / ___ to ___ / ___ / ___

Week of	Monday	Tuesday	Wednesday	Thursday	Friday	Saturday	Sunday
__ / __							
__ / __							
__ / __							
__ / __							
__ / __							
__ / __							
__ / __							
__ / __							
__ / __							
__ / __							
__ / __							
__ / __							

Figure 2.7 *Your Long-Term Planner*

Name _____

LONG-TERM PLANNER ___ / ___ / ___ to ___ / ___ / ___

Week of	Monday	Tuesday	Wednesday	Thursday	Friday	Saturday	Sunday
___ / ___							
___ / ___							
___ / ___							
___ / ___							
___ / ___							
___ / ___							
___ / ___							
___ / ___							
___ / ___							
___ / ___							
___ / ___							
___ / ___							

Figure 2.7 **(Continued)**

Freer/Shutterstock.com

Create a
WORK
FLOW
that works

This chapter offers dozens of strategies for time management. To get the most value from them, weave these strategies into a *work flow*—an organized way of taking projects from start to finish.

The beauty of a work flow is that you can use it for projects at work, school, and home. And once you establish a reliable work flow, you can use it for the rest of your life.

Everyone's work flow is a little different. However, they usually include the following four habits. To aid your memory, each habit starts with the letter C.

1. COLLECT

Use inboxes to collect:

- Pieces of mail, brochures, handouts from classes, and other printed items
- Notes to yourself—Journal Entries, shopping lists, any ideas that occur to you while you're on the run
- Messages from other people

You will probably use several inboxes. Start with a physical one—a tray for loose papers. Also create a folder on your computer desktop for email attachments and other digital documents. In addition,

think of your email software and the voice mail on your phone as inboxes.

As you develop the collection habit, welcome feelings of relief. True, all that you're doing is dumping stuff into physical and digital "buckets." The benefit is that you're no longer wondering: *Did I forget something?* The stuff you need to deal with is out of your head and safely collected. This frees up space in your mind to apply the Power Process: "Be here now" and focus on what you're doing in the present moment.

2. CHOOSE

Next, choose what to do about each collected item. Pick any item from any of your inboxes (you can do them in any order). Then make a decision about how to respond to it. You have three basic options:

- *Delete* it. Throw it in the trash or recycling bin.
- *Do* it now. This works well for tasks that you can finish in a minute or two, such as making a quick phone call.
- *Defer* the item—that is, write yourself a reminder to take action at a later time. This reminder can go on your calendar (for scheduled events) or on a to-do list.

Set a goal to empty your inboxes at least once per week. On your calendar, block off an hour for this purpose at a regular time each week. Friday afternoon and Sunday night are popular choices.

David Allen, author of *Getting Things Done: The Art of Stress-Free Productivity*, describes this activity as a weekly review.[5] This is a time to ask yourself: "What are all my current goals? And what is the *very next action* that I can take to achieve each goal?"

Remember that next actions are specific behaviors. They involve physical movement. For instance, you send an email, run an errand, or walk down the hall to ask someone a question.

With practice, your weekly review can become an enjoyable activity. This is when you will do some of your most important thinking for the next seven days.

3. CLASSIFY

Some of the things that you collect will not require any follow-up action. Even so, you might want to keep them on hand so that you can refer to them later. Examples are insurance policies, owner manuals, and contact information for your friends and family members.

Set up simple filing systems for these reference materials. Use file folders for pieces of paper. Give each folder a name, and store the folders in alphabetical order. On your computer, create separate folders for each of your current classes and projects. Once a year, go through all of these folders—paper-based and digital—and purge the items that no longer matter to you.

4. COMPLETE

There's one more C, by the way—completing. When you form the habits of collecting, clarifying, and classifying, you get a calendar and to-do list that you can trust. With them in hand, you can make informed, moment-to-moment choices about how to spend the time of your life. And you can actually get things done. Congratulations. ✖

There's an app for that— using technology for TIME MANAGEMENT

Time-management activities generally fall into two major categories: making lists and using calendars. Today you can choose from dozens of applications for doing both. Many are Web-based and synchronize with apps for smartphones and tablets.

A few options are described here. To find more, search the Web, using the key words *calendar apps, goal setting apps, time-management apps,* and *to-do list managers.*

CALENDAR APPLICATIONS

These tools allow you to keep track of scheduled events and share them with other people if you choose. Some examples are listed here:

- Google Calendar (**www.google.com/calendar**)
- 30 Boxes (**www.30boxes.com**)
- Zoho Calendar (**www.zoho.com/calendar**)

Also check the built-in calendar software that comes with your computer, tablet, or smartphone. It may do everything you want.

LIST MANAGERS

You might wonder why you need sophisticated software just to keep lists of stuff to do. That's a fair question, and it has three answers. First, when a to-do list gets longer than an average grocery list, it gets tough to manage on paper. Second, you'll probably have more than one list to manage—lists of values, goals, to-do items, work-related projects, household projects, and more. And finally, it's convenient to access your lists from any device with an Internet connection.

Some list managers let you add items, delete or cross off items, assign due dates, and send yourself reminders. Here are some options:

- Gubb (**www.gubb.net**)
- Remember the Milk (**www.rememberthemilk.com**)
- Todoist (**www.todoist.com**)

Other list managers offer you access to a community of people who make some of their goals public. You can cheer one another on when progress occurs and suggest strategies. Some of these websites offer a library of action plans based on expert-recommended content. Examples are:

- HabitForge (**www.habitforge.com**)
- IRUNURUN (**www.irunurun.com**)

Another option is to just create lists with plain text editors that come without all the bells and whistles of word-processing software. Examples are Notepad for Windows and TextEdit for Mac OSX.

MORE POSSIBILITIES
You have many options for taking notes and accessing them from any digital device. One-Note from Microsoft is free and popular with students. Others swear by Evernote. Both of these allow you to organize notes (text, audio, video, and images) into notebooks, sections, and pages. Another option is Notes, which is built in to Apple's products.

Trello (**trello.com**) is a full-featured and free way to manage group projects. Each project gets its own "board" that's shared among group members. You can assign "cards" to each board with any kind of list. For example, list project-related tasks, who's responsible for doing each one, and when each task is due.

WHAT TO CONSIDER BEFORE YOU CHOOSE
You'll be spending a lot of time with your calendar, list manager, and other apps. Choose carefully and be willing to read reviews and test-drive several before making a final choice. Be sure to consider these aspects:

- Speed
- Stability
- Appearance
- Search functions
- Ease of use and syncing
- Ease of customizing
- Voice commands
- Alarms and reminders
- Options for backing up your data
- The developer's track record

Price is not always a major factor. You can spend $50 or more for a time-management app or find a freebie that meets your needs perfectly.

Also remember that all of these tools are optional. People lived organized lives long before computers were invented. Even today, there are plenty of people who plan effectively with pencil and paper.

The goal is to actually get stuff done. Keep it simple, make it easy, and do what works. ✖

Diego Cervo/Shutterstock.com

Stop procrastination
NOW

Consider a bold idea: The way to stop procrastinating is to stop procrastinating. Giving up procrastination is actually a simple choice. People just make it complicated.

Sound crazy? Well, test this idea for yourself.

Think of something that you've been putting off. Choose a small, specific task—one that you can complete in five minutes or less. Then do that task today.

Tomorrow, choose another task and do it. Repeat this strategy each day for one week. Notice what happens to your habit of procrastination.

Discover the costs. Find out whether procrastination keeps you from getting what you want. Clearly seeing the side effects of procrastination can help you kick the habit.

Discover your procrastination style. Psychologist Linda Sapadin identifies different styles of procrastination.[6] For example, *dreamers* have big goals that they seldom translate into specific plans. *Worriers* focus on the worst-case scenario and are likely to talk more about problems than about solutions. *Defiers* resist new tasks or promise to do them and then don't follow through. *Overdoers* create extra work for themselves by refusing to delegate tasks and neglecting to set priorities. And *perfectionists* put off tasks for fear of making a mistake.

Awareness of your procrastination style is a key to changing your behavior. If you exhibit the characteristics of an overdoer, for example, then say no to new projects. Also ask for help in completing your current projects.

To discover your procrastination style, observe your behavior. Avoid judgments. Just be a scientist: Record the facts. Write Discovery Statements about specific ways you procrastinate. Follow up with Intention Statements about what to do differently.

Trick yourself into getting started. If you have a 50-page chapter to read, then grab the book and say to yourself, "I'm not really going to read this chapter right now. I'm just going to flip through the pages and scan the headings for 10 minutes." Tricks like these can get you started on a task you've been dreading.

Let feelings follow action. If you put off exercising until you feel energetic, you might wait for months. Instead, get moving now. Then watch your feelings change. After 5 minutes of brisk walking, you might be in the mood for a 20-minute run. This principle—action generates motivation—can apply to any task that you've put on the back burner.

Choose to work under pressure. Sometimes people thrive under pressure. As one writer puts it, "I don't do my *best* work under deadline. I do my *only* work under deadline." Used selectively, this strategy might also work for you.

Put yourself in control. If you choose to work with a due date staring you right in the face, then schedule a big block of time during the preceding week. Until then, enjoy!

Think ahead. Use a monthly calendar or long-term planner to list due dates for assignments in all your courses. Using these tools, you can anticipate heavy demands on your time and take action to prevent last-minute crunches. Make *Becoming a Master Student* your home base—the first place to turn in taking control of your schedule.

Play with antiprocrastination apps. There are apps for everything these days, including procrastination. Many of these are based on the Pomodoro Technique (**pomodorotechnique.com**). This method is simple—a key benefit for procrastinators: Set a timer for 25 minutes. During that period, get started on just one task that you've been putting off. Then take a five-minute break.

The beauty of this technique is twofold. First, you can do just about anything for 25 minutes—especially when you know a break is coming up. Second, 25 minutes is enough to actually accomplish something. It might even make you interested in going for another 25 minutes.

Find apps for the Pomodoro Technique by searching the Web. Even simpler: Use a kitchen timer or the alarm on your smartphone.

Create goals that draw you forward. A goal that grabs you by the heartstrings is an inspiration to act now. If you're procrastinating, then set some goals that excite you. Then you might wake up one day and discover that procrastination is part of your past. ✂

The 7-step antiprocrastination plan

STEP 1 Make it meaningful. What is important about the task you've been putting off? List all the benefits of completing that task. Look at it in relation to your short-, mid-, or long-term goals. Be specific about the rewards for getting it done, including how you will feel when the task is completed.

STEP 2 Take it apart. Break big jobs into a series of small ones you can do in 15 minutes or less. If a long reading assignment intimidates you, divide it into two- or three-page sections. Make a list of the sections, and cross them off as you complete them so you can see your progress. Even the biggest projects can be broken down into a series of small tasks.

STEP 3 Write an Intention Statement. If you can't get started on a term paper, you might write, "I intend to write a list of at least 10 possible topics by 9:00 p.m. I will reward myself with an hour of guilt-free recreational reading." Write your intention on a 3 × 5 card. Carry it with you or post it in your study area, where you can see it often.

STEP 4 Tell everyone. Publicly announce your intention to get a task done. Tell a friend that you intend to learn 10 irregular French verbs by Saturday. Tell your spouse, roommate, parents, and children. Include anyone who will ask whether you've completed the assignment or who will suggest ways to get it done. Make the world your support group.

STEP 5 Find a reward. Construct rewards to yourself carefully. Be willing to withhold them if you do not complete the task. Don't pick a movie as a reward for studying biology if you plan to go to the movie anyway. And when you legitimately reap your reward, notice how it feels.

STEP 6 Settle it now. Do it now. The minute you notice yourself procrastinating, plunge into the task. Imagine yourself at a cold mountain lake, poised to dive. Gradual immersion would be slow torture. It's often less painful to leap. Then be sure to savor the feeling of having the task behind you.

STEP 7 Say no. When you keep pushing a task into a low-priority category, re-examine your purpose for doing that task at all. If you realize that you really don't intend to do something, quit telling yourself that you will. That's procrastinating. Just say no. Then you're not procrastinating. You don't have to carry around the baggage of an undone task.

Note: You can use a handy trick to remember these strategies. Tie a key word for each one to a specific day of the week:

- Link Make it meaningful with the word *Monday*.
- Link Take it apart with *Tuesday*.
- Link Write an intention statement with *Wednesday*.
- Link Tell everyone with *Thursday*.
- Link Find a reward with *Friday*.
- Link Settle it now with *Saturday*.
- Link Say no with *Sunday*.

This memory trick offers a reminder: Each day of your life is an opportunity to stop the cycle of procrastination.

25 ways to get the most out of NOW

The following techniques are about getting the most from your coursework. They're listed in four categories:

- **Choosing your time**
- **Choosing your place**
- **Getting focused**
- **Questions that keep you focused**

Ammentorp Photography/Shutterstock.com

Don't feel pressured to use all of the techniques or to tackle them in order. As you read, note the suggestions you think will be helpful. Pick one technique to use now. When it becomes a habit, come back to this article and select another one. Repeat this cycle, and enjoy the results as they unfold in your life.

CHOOSING YOUR TIME

Study difficult (or boring) subjects first. If your chemistry problems put you to sleep, get to them first, while you are alert. We tend to give top priority to what we enjoy studying, yet the courses that we find most difficult often require the most creative energy. Save your favorite subjects for later. If you find yourself avoiding a particular subject, get up an hour earlier to study it before breakfast. With that chore out of the way, the rest of the day can be a breeze.

Continually being late with course assignments indicates a trouble area. Further action is required. Clarify your intentions about the course by writing down your feelings in a journal, talking with an instructor, or asking for help from a friend or counselor. Consistently avoiding study tasks can also be a signal to re-examine your major or course program.

Be aware of your best time of day. Many people learn best in daylight hours. If this is true for you, schedule study time for your most difficult subjects or most difficult people before nightfall.

Unless you grew up on a farm, the idea of being conscious at 5:00 a.m. might seem ridiculous. Yet many successful businesspeople begin the day at 5:00 a.m. or earlier. Athletes and yoga practitioners use the early morning too. Some writers complete their best work before 9:00 a.m.

Others experience the same benefits by staying up late. They flourish after midnight. If you aren't convinced, then experiment. When you're in a time crunch, get up early or stay up late. You might even see a sunrise.

Use waiting time. Five minutes waiting for a subway, 20 minutes waiting for the dentist, 10 minutes in between classes—waiting time adds up fast. Have short study tasks ready to do during these periods, and keep your study materials handy. For example, carry 3 × 5 cards with facts, formulas, or definitions and pull them out anywhere. A mobile phone with an audio recording app can help you use commuting time to your advantage. Make a recording of yourself reading your notes. Play back the recording as you drive, or listen through headphones as you ride on the bus or subway.

Study two hours for every hour you're in class. Students in higher education are regularly advised to allow two hours of study time for every hour spent in class. If you are taking 15 credit hours, then plan to spend 30 hours a week studying. That adds up to 45 hours each week for school—more than a full-time job. The benefits of thinking in these terms will be apparent at exam time.

This guideline is just that—a guideline, not an absolute rule. Consider what's best for you. If you do the Time Monitor/Time Plan exercise in this chapter, note how many hours you actually spend studying for each hour of class. Then ask how your schedule is working. You might want to allow more study time for some subjects.

Keep in mind that the "two hours for one" rule doesn't distinguish between focused time and unfocused time. In one four-hour block of study time, it's possible to use up two of those hours with phone calls, breaks, daydreaming, and doodling. With study time, quality counts as much as quantity.

Avoid marathon study sessions. With so many hours ahead of you, the temptation is to tell yourself, "Well, it's going to be a long day. No sense rushing into it. Better sharpen about a dozen of these pencils and change the light bulbs." Three 3-hour sessions are usually more productive than one 9-hour session.

If you must study in a large block of time, work on several subjects. Avoid studying similar topics one after the other.

Whenever you study, stop and rest for a few minutes every hour. Give your brain a chance to take a break. Simply moving to a new location might be enough to maintain your focus. When taking breaks fails to restore your energy, it's time to close the books and do something else for a while.

Monitor how much time you spend online.
To get an accurate picture of your involvement in social networking and other online activities, use the Time Monitor/Time Plan process in this chapter. Then make conscious choices about how much time you want to spend on these activities. Staying connected is fine. Staying on constant alert for a new text, Tweet, or Facebook update distracts you from achieving your goals.

CHOOSING YOUR PLACE
Use a regular study area. Your body and your mind know where you are. Using the same place to study, day after day, helps train your responses. When you arrive at that particular place, you can focus your attention more quickly.

Study where you'll be alert. In bed, your body gets a signal. For most students, that signal is more likely to be "Time to sleep!" than "Time to study!" Just as you train your body to be alert at your desk, you also train it to slow down near your bed. For that reason, don't study where you sleep.

Easy chairs and sofas are also dangerous places to study. Learning requires energy. Give your body a message that energy is needed. Put yourself in a situation that supports this message. For example, some schools offer empty classrooms as places to study. If you want to avoid distractions, look for a room where friends are not likely to find you.

Use a library. Libraries are designed for learning. The lighting is perfect. The noise level is low. A wealth of material is available. Entering a library is a signal to focus the mind and get to work. Many students can get more done in a shorter time frame at the library than anywhere else. Experiment for yourself.

GETTING FOCUSED
Pay attention to your attention. Breaks in concentration are often caused by internal interruptions. Your own thoughts jump in to divert you from your studies. When this happens, notice these thoughts and let them go. Perhaps the thought of getting something else done is distracting you. One option is to handle that other task now and study later. Or you can write yourself a note about it or schedule a specific time to do it.

Agree with living mates about study time. This agreement includes roommates, family, spouses, and children. Make the rules about study time clear, and be sure to follow them yourself. Explicit agreements—even written contracts—work well. One student always wears a colorful hat when he wants to study. When his wife and children see the hat, they respect his wish to be left alone.

Get off the phone. The phone is the ultimate interrupter. People who wouldn't think of distracting you in person might call or text you at the worst times because they can't see that you are studying. You don't have to be a victim of your cell phone. If a simple "I can't talk; I'm studying" doesn't work, use dead silence. It's a conversation killer. Or short-circuit the whole problem: Turn off your phone or silence it.

Learn to say no. Saying no is a time-saver and a valuable life skill for everyone. Some people feel it is rude to refuse a request. But you can say no effectively and courteously. Others want you to succeed as a student. When you tell them that you can't do what they ask because you are busy educating yourself, most people will understand.

Hang a "Do not disturb" sign on your door. Many hotels will give you a free sign, for the advertising. Or you can create a sign yourself. They work. Using signs can relieve you of making a decision about cutting off each interruption—a time-saver in itself.

Get ready the night before. Completing a few simple tasks just before you go to bed can help you get in gear the next day. If you need to make some phone calls first thing in the morning, look up those numbers, write them on 3 × 5 cards, and set them near the phone. If you need to drive to a new location, make a note of the address and put it next to your car keys. If you plan to spend the next afternoon writing a paper, get your materials together: dictionary, notes, outline, paper, pencil, flash drive, laptop—whatever you need. Pack your lunch or put gas in the car. Organize the baby's diaper bag and your briefcase or backpack.

Call ahead. We often think of talking on the telephone as a prime time-waster. Used wisely, though, the telephone can actually help manage time. Before you go shopping, call the store to see whether it carries the items you're looking for. A few seconds on the phone or computer can save hours in wasted trips and wrong turns.

Avoid noise distractions. To promote concentration, avoid studying in front of the television, and turn off the radio. Many students insist that they study better with background noise, and it might be true. Some students report good results with carefully selected and controlled music. For many others, silence is the best form of music to study by.

At times noise levels might be out of your control. A neighbor or roommate might decide to find out how far she can turn up her music before the walls crumble. Meanwhile, your ability to concentrate on the principles of sociology goes down the drain. To avoid this scenario, schedule study sessions during periods when your living environment is usually quiet. If you live in a residence hall, ask whether study rooms are available. Or go somewhere else where it's quiet, such as the library. Some students have even found refuge in quiet coffee shops, self-service laundries, and places of worship.

Manage interruptions. Notice how others misuse your time. Be aware of repeat offenders. Ask yourself whether there are certain friends or relatives who consistently interrupt your study time.

If avoiding the interrupter is impractical, send a clear message. Sometimes others don't realize that they are breaking your concentration. You can give them a gentle, yet firm, reminder: "What you're saying is important. Can we schedule a time to talk about it when I can give you my full attention?" If this strategy doesn't work, there are other ways to make your message more effective.

See whether you can "firewall" yourself for selected study periods each week. Find a place where you can count on being alone and working without interruption.

Sometimes interruptions still happen, though. Create a system for dealing with them. One option is to take an index card and write a quick note about what you're doing the moment an interruption occurs. As soon as possible, return to the card and pick up the task where you left off.

QUESTIONS THAT KEEP YOU FOCUSED

Ask: "What is one task I can accomplish toward achieving my goal?" This technique is helpful when you face a big, imposing job. Pick out one small accomplishment, preferably one you can complete in about five minutes; then do it. The satisfaction of getting one thing done can spur you on to get one more thing done. Meanwhile, the job gets smaller.

Ask: "Am I being too hard on myself?" If you are feeling frustrated with a reading assignment; your attention wanders repeatedly; or you've fallen behind on math problems that are due tomorrow, take a minute to listen to the messages you are giving yourself. Are you scolding yourself too harshly? Lighten up. Allow yourself to feel a little foolish, and then get on with the task at hand. Don't add to the problem by berating yourself.

Worrying about the future is another way people beat themselves up: "How will I ever get all this done?" "What if every paper I'm assigned turns out to be this hard?" "If I can't do the simple calculations now, how will I ever pass the final?" Instead of promoting learning, such questions fuel anxiety and waste valuable time.

Labeling and generalizing weaknesses are other ways people are hard on themselves. Being objective and specific in the messages you send yourself will help eliminate this form of self-punishment and will likely generate new possibilities. An alternative to saying "I'm terrible in algebra" is to say, "I don't understand factoring equations." This rewording suggests a plan to improve.

You might be able to lighten the load by discovering how your learning styles affect your behavior. For example, you may have a bias toward concrete experience rather than abstract thinking. If so, after setting a goal, you might want to move directly into action.

In large part, the ability to learn through concrete experience is a valuable trait. After all, action is necessary to achieve goals. At the same time, you might find it helpful to allow extra time to plan. Careful planning can help you avoid unnecessary activity. Instead of using a planner that shows a day at a time, experiment with a calendar that displays a week or month at a glance. The expanded format can help you look further into the future and stay on track as you set out to meet long-term goals.

Ask: "Is this a piano?" Carpenters who construct rough frames for buildings have a saying they use when they bend a nail or accidentally hack a chunk out of a two-by-four: "Well, this ain't no piano." It means that perfection is not necessary. Ask yourself whether what you are doing needs to be perfect. Perhaps you don't have to apply the same standards of grammar to lecture notes that you would apply to a term paper. If you can complete a job 95 percent perfectly in two hours and 100 percent perfectly in four hours, ask yourself whether the additional 5 percent improvement is worth doubling the amount of time you spend.

Sometimes, though, it *is* a piano. A tiny miscalculation can ruin an entire lab experiment. A misstep in solving a complex math problem can negate hours of work. Computers are notorious for turning little errors into nightmares. Accept lower standards only when appropriate.

A related suggestion is to weed out low-priority tasks. The to-do list for a large project can include dozens of items, not all of which

Setting limits on screen time

Access to the Internet and wireless communication offers easy ways to procrastinate. We call it "surfing," "texting," "IMing,"—and sometimes "researching" or "working." In his book *Crazy Busy: Overstretched, Overbooked, and About to Snap*, Edward Hallowell coined a word to describe these activities when they're done too often—*screensucking*.

Discover how much time you spend online. People who update their Twitter feed or Facebook page every hour may be sending an unintended message—that they have no life offline.

To get an accurate picture of your involvement in social networking and other online activity, monitor how much time you spend on them for one week. Then make conscious choices about how much time you want to spend online and on the phone. Don't let social networking distract you from meeting personal and academic goals.

Use technology to tame technology. See if you can set your smartphone for "airplane mode." This disables calls and text messages. While using your laptop or desktop computer, consider applications such as Freedom (**freedom.to**), SelfControl (**selfcontrolapp.com**), and Cold Turkey (**getcoldturkey.com**). These limit or block Internet access for an amount of time that you determine in advance.

Go offline to send the message that other people matter. It's hard to pay attention to the person who is right in front of you when you're hammering out text messages or updating your Twitter feed. You can also tell when someone else is doing these things and only half listening to you.

An alternative is to close up all your devices and "be here now." When you're eating, stop answering the phone. Notice how the food tastes. When you're with a friend, close up your laptop. Hear every word he says. Rediscover where life actually takes place—in the present moment.

Developing emotional intelligence requires being with people and away from a computer or smartphone. People who break up with a partner through text messaging are not developing that intelligence. True friends know when to go offline and head across campus to resolve a conflict. They know when to go back home and support a family member in crisis. When it counts, your presence is your greatest present.

are equally important. Some can be done later, while others can be skipped altogether, if time is short.

Apply this idea when you study. In a long reading assignment, look for pages you can skim or skip. When it's appropriate, read chapter summaries or article abstracts. As you review your notes, look for material that might not be covered on a test, and decide whether you want to study it.

Ask: "Can I do just one more thing?" Ask yourself this question at the end of a long day. Almost always you will have enough energy to do just one more short task. The overall increase in your productivity might surprise you.

Ask: "Can I delegate this?" Instead of slogging through complicated tasks alone, you can draw on the talents and energy of other people. Busy executives know the value of delegating tasks to coworkers. Without delegation, many projects would flounder or die.

You can apply the same principle in your life. Instead of doing all the housework or cooking by yourself, for example, you can assign some of the tasks to family members or roommates. Rather than making a trip to the library to look up a simple fact, you can call and ask a library assistant to research it for you. Instead of driving across town to deliver a package, you can hire a delivery service to do so. All of these tactics can free up extra hours for studying.

It's not practical to delegate certain study tasks, such as writing term papers or completing reading assignments. However, you can still draw on the ideas of others in completing such tasks. For instance, form a writing group to edit and critique papers, brainstorm topics or titles, and develop lists of sources.

If you're absent from a class, find a classmate to summarize the lecture, discussion, and any upcoming assignments. Presidents depend on briefings. You can use the same technique.

Ask: "How did I just waste time?" Notice when time passes and you haven't accomplished what you had planned to do. Take a minute to review your actions and note the specific ways you wasted time. We tend to operate by habit, wasting time in the same ways over and over again. When you are aware of things you do that drain your time, you are more likely to catch yourself in the act next time. Observing one

small quirk might save you hours. But keep this in mind: Asking you to notice how you waste time is not intended to make you feel guilty. The point is to increase your skill by getting specific information about how you use time.

Ask: "Would I pay myself for what I'm doing right now?" If you were employed as a student, would you be earning your wages? Ask yourself this question when you notice that you've taken your third snack break in 30 minutes. Then remember that you are, in fact, employed as a student. You are investing in your own productivity and are paying a big price for the privilege of being a student. Doing a mediocre job now might result in fewer opportunities in the future.

Ask: "Could I find the time if I really wanted to?" The way people speak often rules out the option of finding more time. An alternative is to speak about time with more possibility.

The next time you're tempted to say, "I just don't have time," pause for a minute. Question the truth of this statement. Could you find four more hours this week for studying? Suppose that someone offered to pay you $10,000 to find those four hours. Suppose too that you will get paid only if you don't lose sleep, call in sick for work, or sacrifice anything important to you. Could you find the time if vast sums of money were involved?

Remember that when it comes to school, vast sums of money *are* involved.

Ask: "Am I willing to promise it?" This time-management idea might be the most powerful of all: If you want to find time for a task, promise yourself—and others—that you'll get it done. Unleash one of the key qualities of master students and take responsibility for producing an outcome.

To make this technique work, do more than say that you'll try to keep a promise or that you'll give it your best shot. Take an oath, as you would in court. Give it your word.

One way to accomplish big things in life is to make big promises. There's little reward in promising what's safe or predictable. No athlete promises to place seventh in the Olympic Games. Chances are that if you're not making big promises, you're not stretching yourself.

The point of making a promise is not to chain yourself to a rigid schedule or impossible expectations. You can promise to reach goals without unbearable stress. You can keep schedules flexible and carry out your plans with ease, joy, and satisfaction.

At times, though, you might go too far. Some promises may be truly beyond you, and you might break them. However, failing to keep a promise is just that—failing to keep a promise. A broken promise is not the end of the world.

Promises can work magic. When your word is on the line, it's possible to discover reserves of time and energy you didn't know existed. Promises can push you to exceed your expectations. ✸

GaudiLab/Shutterstock.com

Making time for HEALTH

Even when you're pressed for time, you have choices. You can become aware of current habits (discovery), choose new habits (intention), and take appropriate action. Begin with any of the following suggestions.

CHOOSE YOUR FUEL

The demands of higher education and a heavy work schedule are bound to affect the amount of time that you spend on planning and preparing meals.

If you're confused about nutrition, join the crowd. The official recommendations for eating well change from time to time. Nutrition is an evolving science, and new studies appear every year.

Michael Pollan, a writer for the *New York Times*, spent several years sorting out the scientific literature on nutrition.[7] He boiled the key guidelines down to seven words in three statements:

- ***Eat food.*** In other words, choose whole, fresh foods over processed products with a lot of ingredients.
- ***Mostly plants.*** Fruits, vegetables, and grains are loaded with natural chemicals that help to prevent disease. Plant-based foods also make fewer demands on the environment than animal-based foods.
- ***Not too much.*** Notice portion sizes. Pass on snacks, seconds, and desserts—or indulge just occasionally.

Discover what works for you by doing personal experiments. For example, reduce the amount of carbohydrates (sugar and refined grains) that you eat. Then see how this change affects your weight and energy level.

Also remember that *how* you eat is important. If you want to eat less, then eat slowly. Savor each bite. Stop when you're satisfied instead of when you feel full. Use meal times as a chance to relax, reduce stress, and connect with people.

CHOOSE TO EXERCISE

Exercise refreshes your body and your mind. Find simple ways to include more physical activity in your life.

Stay active throughout the day. Park a little farther from work or school. Walk some extra blocks. Take the stairs instead of the elevator. For an extra workout, climb two stairs at a time. An hour of daily activity is ideal, but do whatever you can.

Adapt to your campus environment. Look for exercise facilities on campus. Search for classes in aerobics, swimming, volleyball, basketball, golf, tennis, and other sports. Intramural sports are another option.

Get active early. Work out first thing in the morning. Then it's done for the day.

Before beginning any vigorous exercise program, consult a health care professional. This is critical if you are overweight, over age 60, in poor condition, a heavy smoker, or if you have a history of health problems.

CHOOSE TO REST

A lack of rest can decrease your immunity to illness and impair your performance in school. If you have trouble sleeping, then experiment with the following suggestions:

- Exercise daily. For many people, regular exercise promotes sounder sleep. However, finish exercising several hours before you want to go to sleep.
- Avoid naps during the daytime.
- Monitor your caffeine intake, especially in the afternoon and evening.
- Avoid using alcohol to feel sleepy. Drinking alcohol late in the evening can disrupt your sleep during the night.
- Develop a sleep ritual—a regular sequence of calming activities that end your day. You might take a warm bath and do some light reading. Turn off the TV and computer at least one hour before you go to bed.
- Use your bed for sleeping. Avoid studying in bed.
- Keep your sleeping room cool.
- Keep a regular schedule for going to sleep and waking up.
- Sleep in the same place each night. When

you're there, your body gets the message: "It's time to go to sleep."
- Practice relaxation techniques while lying in bed. A simple one is to count your breaths and release distracting thoughts as they arise.
- Make tomorrow's to-do list before you go to sleep so you won't lie there worrying that tomorrow you'll forget about something you need to do.
- Get up and study or do something else until you're tired.
- See a doctor if sleeplessness persists.

While studying for finals or completing a big project at work, you might be tempted to cut back drastically on your sleep. You can avoid this fate by managing your time.

CHOOSE FREEDOM FROM SEXUALLY TRANSMITTED INFECTION

The most effective ways to prevent sexually transmitted infection (STI) are to abstain from sex. Or, have sex exclusively with one person who is free of infection and has no other sex partners. See your family doctor or someone at the student health center to ask about getting screened for STIs.

Before you have sex with someone, talk about the risk of STIs. If you are infected, tell your partner. Also have sex only when you and your partner are sober, and don't share needles or other paraphernalia with drug users.

CHOOSE EMOTIONAL HEALTH

A little tension before a test, a presentation, or a date is normal. The problem comes when tension is persistent and extreme. That's when stress turns into *distress*. You can take immediate steps toward freedom from distress.

Protect your overall health. Your thoughts and emotions can get scrambled if you go too long feeling hungry or tired. Eating well, exercising daily, and getting plenty of sleep are powerful ways to reduce stress.

Make contact with the present moment. If you feel anxious, see whether you can focus your attention on a specific sight, sound, or other sensation that's happening in the present moment. In a classroom, for example, take a few seconds to listen to the sounds of squeaking chairs, the scratching of pencils, the muted coughs. Focus all of your attention on one point—anything other than the flow of thoughts through your head.

Don't believe everything you think. Some beliefs set us up for misery. One example is: People should always behave in exactly the way I expect. Some more sane ways to think are: I can control my own behavior but not the behavior of others. And: Some events are beyond my control. Changing unrealistic beliefs can reduce stress significantly.

Solve problems. Although you can't "fix" an unpleasant feeling in the same way that you can fix a machine, you can choose to change a situation *associated* with that feeling. There might be a problem that needs a solution. Use distress as your motivation to take action.

Stay active. It is appropriate to feel upset sometimes. It is also possible to go to class, study, work, eat, and feel miserable at the same time. Unless you have a diagnosable problem, continue normal activities until the distress passes.

Share what you're thinking and feeling. Tell a family member or friend about your feelings. This is a powerful way to gain perspective. The simple act of describing a problem can sometimes reveal a solution or give you a fresh perspective.

Ask for help. Student health centers are not just for treating colds and flu symptoms. Seek help whenever problems with your thinking, moods, or behaviors consistently interfere with your ability to sleep, eat, go to class, work, or sustain relationships.

CHOOSE A RESPONSIBLE RELATIONSHIP WITH DRUGS

Some people will choose to stop using a drug when the consequences get serious enough. Other people don't stop. Their top priority in life becomes finding and using drugs. At that point, the problem might be addiction (technically called *substance use disorder.*)

Use responsibly. Show people that you can have a good time without drugs. If you do choose to drink, consume alcohol with food and water. Pace yourself. Take time between drinks. Stay out of games that encourage

people to guzzle. Also avoid people who make fun of you for choosing not to drink.

On a day when you might be sexually active, avoid alcohol so that you can think clearly and stay safe. For women who become pregnant, this also reduces the risk of having a baby with fetal alcohol syndrome.

Pay attention. Whenever you use alcohol or another drug, do so with awareness. Then pay attention to the consequences. Before going out to a restaurant or bar, set a limit for the number of drinks you will consume. If you consistently break this promise to yourself and experience negative consequences afterward, then you have a problem.

Get help. Nobody plans to become addicted. If you have pneumonia, you seek treatment without shame. Approach drug problems in the same way. Your options for help include counseling, self-help groups, and treatment programs.

USE THE POWER OF SMALL DAILY CHOICES

Choosing health on a daily basis doesn't have to take a lot of time. Consider the followings suggestions from Tom C. Rath, senior scientist at Gallup and author of *Eat Move Sleep: How Small Choices Lead to Big Changes*.[8]:

- Ask yourself whether the next food you put in your mouth is a net gain or a net loss. Repeat throughout the day.
- Gradually add sleep to your nightly schedule in 15-minute increments. Continue until you feel fully rested each morning.
- Put the healthiest foods in your home on a shelf at eye level or in a bowl on the counter.
- Pick one food or drink you sweeten regularly—artificially or with sugar—and consume it without the added sweetener for a week.
- Always leave serving dishes in the kitchen; don't bring them to the table.
- Engineer activity into your work. Have a standing or walking meeting. Get up and move every time you are on the phone.
- Use smaller cups, plates, and serving sizes to eat less.
- Go through the food in your house today. Get rid of a few unhealthy items that have been sitting on a shelf for months.
- Start every meal with the most healthy item on your plate, and end with the least. ✄

practicing
CRITICAL THINKING

11 ●

Taking a First Step about health

Your success in school and at work is directly tied to your health. Any health habit that undermines your physical energy and mental clarity can prevent you from doing your best.

Taking charge of your health starts with telling the truth. With the facts in hand, you can create an intention to choose new habits with a big impact on your health.

Discover your current level of health in more detail by completing the following sentences. If a statement does not apply to you, then skip it.

Note: You may want to keep your responses to this exercise confidential.

Eating

What I know about the way I eat is . . .

What I would most like to change about my diet is . . .

My eating habits lead me to be . . .

Exercise

The way I usually exercise is . . .

The last time I did 20 minutes or more of aerobic exercise was . . .

As a result of my physical conditioning, I feel . . .

And I look . . .

It would be easier for me to work out regularly if I . . .

The most important benefit I can get from exercising more is . . .

Substances

My history of cigarette smoking is . . .

An objective observer would say that my use of alcohol is . . .

In the last seven days, the number of alcoholic drinks I have had is . . .

I would describe my use of coffee, colas, and other caffeinated drinks as . . .

I have used the following illegal drugs in the past week:

When it comes to drugs, what I am sometimes concerned about is . . .

I take the following prescription drugs:

Emotional Health and Relationships

Someone who knows me fairly well would describe my emotional health as . . .

If I am upset or worried about something, I can talk about it with . . .

The last time that I felt too upset to work, study, or go to classes was . . .

I would describe the overall quality of my relationships as . . .

Sleep

The number of hours I sleep each night is . . .

On weekends I normally sleep . . .

I have trouble sleeping when . . .

The quality of my sleep is usually . . .

Choosing your next steps

Next, take a few minutes to reflect on your responses and create powerful intentions.

Based on what I just wrote, the aspects of my health that I am most concerned about are . . .

The new health habits that I intend to practice over the next week are . . .

BEYOND TIME MANAGEMENT:

Stay focused on what matters

Ask some people about managing time, and a dreaded image appears in their minds. They see a person with a 100-item to-do list clutching a calendar chock full of appointments. They imagine a robot who values cold efficiency, compulsively accounts for every minute, and has no time for people.

These stereotypes about time management hold a kernel of truth. Sometimes people fixate so much on time management that they fail to appreciate what they are doing. Time management becomes a burden, a chore, a process that prevents them from actually enjoying the task at hand.

At other times, people who pride themselves on efficiency are merely keeping busy. In their rush to check items off a to-do list, they might be fussing over activities that create little value in the first place.

It might help you to think beyond time management to the larger concept of *planning*. The point of planning is not to load your schedule with obligations. Instead, planning is about getting the important things done and still having time to be human. An effective planner is productive and relaxed at the same time.

FOCUS ON VALUES

View your activities from the perspective of an entire lifetime. Given the finite space between birth and death, determine what matters most to you.

As a way to define your values, write your own obituary. Describe the ways you want to be remembered. List the contributions you intend to make during your lifetime and the kind of person you wish to become. Or simply write your life purpose—a sentence or short paragraph that describes what's most important to you. Keep this handy when scheduling your day and planning your week.

FOCUS ON OUTCOMES

You might feel guilty when you occasionally stray from your schedule and spend two hours napping or watching soap operas. But if you're regularly meeting your goals, there's probably no harm done.

Managing time and getting organized are not ends in themselves. It's possible to be efficient, organized, and miserable. Larger outcomes such as personal satisfaction and effectiveness count more than the means used to achieve them.

igor.stevanovic/Shutterstock.com

Visualizing a desired outcome can be as important as having a detailed action plan. Here's an experiment: Write a list of goals you plan to accomplish over the next six months. Next, create a vivid mental picture of yourself attaining those goals and enjoying the resulting benefits. Visualize this image several times in the next few weeks. Then file the list away, making a note on your calendar to review it in six months. When six months have passed, look over the list and note how many of your goals you have actually accomplished.

DO LESS

Planning is as much about dropping worthless activities as about adding new ones. See whether you can reduce or eliminate activities that contribute little to your values. When you add a new item to your calendar or to-do list, consider dropping a current one.

BUY LESS

Before you purchase an item, estimate how much time it will take to locate, assemble, use, repair, and maintain it. You might be able to free up hours by doing without. If the product comes with a 400-page manual or 20 hours of training, beware. Before rushing to the store to add another possession to your life, see whether you can reuse or adapt something you already own.

SLOW DOWN

Sometimes it's useful to hurry, such as when you're late for a meeting or about to miss a plane. At other times, haste is a choice that serves no real purpose. If you're speeding through the day like a launched missile, consider what would happen if you got to your next destination a few minutes later than planned. Rushing might not be worth the added strain.

HANDLE IT NOW

A long to-do list can result from postponing decisions and procrastinating. An alternative is to handle a task or decision immediately. Answer that letter now. Make that phone call as soon as it occurs to you. Then you don't have to add the task to your calendar or to-do list.

The same idea applies when someone asks you to volunteer for a project and you realize immediately that you don't want to do it. Save time by graciously telling the truth up front. Saying "I'll think about it and get back to you" just postpones the conversation until later, when it might take more time.

REMEMBER PEOPLE

Few people on their deathbeds ever say, "I wish I'd spent more time at the office." They're more likely to say, "I wish I'd spent more time with my family and friends." The pace of daily life can lead us to neglect the people we cherish.

Efficiency is a concept that applies to things—not people. When it comes to maintaining and nurturing relationships, we can often benefit from loosening up our schedules. We can allow extra time for conflict management, spontaneous visits, and free-ranging conversations.

FORGET ABOUT TIME

Take time away from time. Schedule downtime—a space in your day where you ignore to-do lists, appointments, and accomplishments. This period is when you're accountable to no one else and have nothing to accomplish. Even a few minutes spent in this way can yield a sense of renewal. One way to manage time is periodically to forget about it.

Experiment with decreasing your overall awareness of time. Leave your watch off for a few hours each day. Spend time in an area that's free of clocks. Notice how often you glance at your watch, and

Create a not-to-do list

One of the key skills in time management is choosing what not to do. You can discover this for yourself. Make a list of all your activities during the past 24 hours. (If you did the Time Monitor/Time Plan exercise, then review a day's worth of activity.) Next, review your list and circle any activities that have no relationship to any of your goals. Behold your *not-to-do* list.

Creating a not-to-do list is a simple, useful, and often neglected strategy for building more breathing space into your life. Some items you might want to put on this list are listed here:

- Attending meetings with no clear agenda or end time
- Checking email more than twice per day
- Answering calls from numbers that you don't recognize
- Watching television on weeknights (or any night)
- Carrying a smartphone with you everywhere

Declare your own commitment to simplify your life:

I intend to stop . . .

make a conscious effort to do so less often.

Strictly speaking, time cannot be managed. The minutes, hours, days, and years simply march ahead. What we can do is manage ourselves with respect to time. A few basic principles can help us do that as well as a truckload of cold-blooded techniques. ⚑

Ben Baker/Redux

Ramit Sethi }

Wrote the book I Will Teach You To Be Rich *and created an online community "focused on personal finance and entrepreneurship for college students, recent college grads, and everyone else."*

Ramit Sethi has a problem with "tips"— especially when they come from people who don't actually test them.

It all started with his goal to attend Stanford University. His parents couldn't afford the tuition, so Sethi created his own system for applying for financial aid. It worked: He won 60 scholarships.

Flush with success, he followed some tips and invested his first scholarship check in the stock market. Immediately, half of the money was lost.

Sethi responded to this setback with a decision to master personal finance and avoid costly mistakes in the future.

Sethi read widely on the topic and found the same tips in book after book: Keep a budget. Be ruthless in reducing expenses. Don't go out to eat. Stop buying lattés.

He had little use for this.

"Be honest," says Sethi on his website, I Will Teach You To Be Rich (**iwillteachyoutoberich.com**). "Almost nobody keeps a budget. Almost nobody wants to cut back on lattés. Who wants to be told what they CAN'T do with money— no new shoes, no vacations, no going out with friends?"

After testing conventional advice about money, Sethi rejected most of it. He now coaches people to focus on the "big wins" in their money life: landing a job that pays well. Negotiating a higher salary. Getting a higher credit score. Starting a business on the side.

Over the course of a career, he says, strategies such as these can put hundreds of thousands of extra dollars in your pocket. You won't ever do that by denying yourself lattés and other small pleasures.

On the topic of time management, Sethi proceeds with the same irreverence. Sethi scolds people for depending on random tips and "life hacks" in their quest to get more done in less time. The problem with this approach, he says, is the same as the problem with conventional money management—it ignores the fundamental strategies that actually work.

Sethi talks about five big mistakes in time management and ways to avoid them.[9]

First, **stop trying to do everything yourself.** The top performers in every field are clear about what deserves their time—and what does not. Sethi urges you to ask: What activities are the best use of my time? Can I delegate other activities to someone else?

He concedes that paying someone to run errands or cook meals for you can cost money. But online services such as TaskRabbit and On The Run are reducing the cost of this strategy. And over time, as you increase your income, you can afford to delegate more.

Second, **remember that you have limited energy and willpower.** If you create a to-do list of 25 items and expect to get them all done in the next 24 hours, then you set yourself up for failure.

Instead, says Sethi, reduce the pressure. Start by taking one low-priority item off of your list or your calendar for this week. Do this next week, and the week after. Repeat the process until you're focused on activities that yield the biggest benefits.

Third, **allow space in your schedule for rest, recreation, and regular vacations.** You'll be rewarded with more energy, which can help you get more done.

Fourth, **let go of "productivity porn"**—the latest apps and devices for time management. You can go through lots of these while ignoring bigger challenges, such as getting distracted and forgetting to plan.

Sethi suggests an experiment: For the next week, stop using any productivity tools beyond a basic calendar and notepad for writing lists. Then gradually add other time-management tools only if they truly add value.

Finally, **assess your performance—honestly and often.** On Friday afternoon ask, "What did I say that I was going to get done this week? And, what did I *actually* get done?"

Then list your top three tasks for next week. If you get them done, then consider choosing slightly harder tasks for the following week. And if you don't get them done, then diagnose the problem and look for solutions.

Ramit Sethi *suggests the cycle of discovery, intention, and action as a way to fuel success in every area of life.*

QUIZ

Chapter 2

1. The Power Process: "Be here now" rules out planning.
   a. True
   b. False

2. Suggested strategies for reflecting on your goals include:
   a. Check in with your feelings
   b. Check for alignment
   c. Check for obstacles
   d. Check for next steps
   e. All of the answer choices

3. Examples of an effectively stated goal include:
   a. Make peace with money
   b. Lose 1 pound this month
   c. Graduate with an AA degree by 2019
   d. Both a and c
   e. Both b and c

4. "C fever" refers to:
   a. Skipping a high-priority task to do something that does not require immediate attention
   b. Scheduling too many items on your calendar each day
   c. Checking your cell phone for messages every few minutes
   d. None of the answer choices

5. Alternatives to the ABC system for creating priorities in to-do lists include:
   a. The 80–20 system
   b. Ranking tasks as "yes," "no," or "maybe"
   c. Grouping tasks by category
   d. All of the answer choices

6. According to the text, overcoming procrastination is a complex process that must take months or even years.
   a. True
   b. False

7. The suggested strategies for "creating a work flow that works" do *not* include:
   a. Use one inbox to collect mail, messages, class hand-outs, and notes to yourself
   b. Delete, do, or defer items that you collect
   c. Empty your inboxes once per week
   d. Set up a simple filing system for reference materials

8. According to the text, everything written about time management can be reduced to:
   a. Discover exactly *what* you want
   b. Know *how* to get what you want
   c. Follow up by doing what you intend to do
   d. All of the answer choices

9. The text suggests that you approach "25 ways to get the most out of now" by:
   a. Using all of the techniques
   b. Tackling the techniques in numerical order
   c. Picking 10 techniques to start using now
   d. Choosing 1 technique at a time and use it until it becomes a habit
   e. None of the answer choices

10. The text suggests that the most powerful time-management technique might be:
    a. Promising yourself and other people that you'll get a task done
    b. Focusing on A-priority tasks
    c. Using a long-term planner
    d. Performing tasks as perfectly as possible

SKILLS
snapshot

Before moving on to a new chapter in this book, take a snapshot of your current skills in time management. Clarify your intentions to develop more mastery in this area of your life. Then clear a path to taking action.

Discovery

My score on the Time section of the Discovery Wheel was . . .

When it comes to time management, I am skilled at . . .

To get better at time management, I could . . .

A suggestion from this chapter that can help me achieve one of my personal goals is . . .

Intention

A suggestion from this chapter that I will use as long as I'm in school is . . .

A suggestion from this chapter that I will use in my career is . . .

Action

To put the suggestions I just listed into practice, the next actions I will take are . . .

Some possible obstacles to taking those actions are . . .

To overcome these obstacles, I will . . .

Soul wind/Shutterstock.com

Memory

why

Learning memory techniques can boost your skills at test taking, reading, note taking, and many other tasks.

how

Think of a time when you struggled to remember something that was important. Perhaps you were trying to remember someone's name or recall some key information for a test. Then scan this chapter and find at least three strategies that you will use to prevent this problem in the future.

what if...

I could use my memory to its full potential?

what is included . . .

112   Power Process: Love your problems

113   Your memory and your brain—6 key principles

116   The memory jungle

118   25 memory techniques

126   Set a trap for your memory

127   Mnemonic devices

130   Retool your memory

132   Remembering names

134   Master Student Profile: Maria Popova

do you have a minute?

Take action to make sure that you remember the important commitments in your academic life right now. Take a minute to pull out your calendar and enter due dates for your current assignments.

Love your problems

We all have problems and barriers that block our progress or prevent us from moving into new areas. Often the way we respond to our problems places limitations on what we can be, do, and have.

Problems often work like barriers. When we bump up against one of our problems, we usually turn away and start walking along a different path. And all of a sudden—bump!—we've struck another barrier. And we turn away again.

As we continue to bump into problems and turn away from them, our lives stay inside the same old boundaries. Inside these boundaries, we are unlikely to have new adventures. We are unlikely to keep learning.

If we respond to problems by loving them instead of resisting them, we can expand the boundaries in which we live our lives.

The word *love* might sound like an overstatement. In this Power Process, the word means to unconditionally accept the fact that your problems exist. The more we deny or resist a problem, the stronger it seems to become. When we accept the fact that we have a problem, we can find effective ways to deal with it.

Suppose one of your barriers is taking a final exam in one of your courses. You fear that you'll forget everything you tried to memorize.

One option for dealing with this barrier is denial. You could walk into the exam room and pretend that you're not afraid. You could tell yourself, "I'm not going to be scared," and then try to force a smile on your face.

A more effective approach is to love your fear. Go into the room, notice how you actually feel, and say to yourself, "I am afraid. I notice that my knees are shaking and my mouth feels dry, and I'm having a rush of thoughts about what might happen if I screw up this exam. Yup, I'm scared, and I'm not going to fight it. I'm going to take this exam anyway."

You can apply the same approach to just about any fear—fear of math courses, fear of sounding silly when learning a new language, fear of making mistakes when learning a musical instrument, fear of looking silly when dancing, and much more.

The beauty of this Power Process is that you continue to stay in action—by taking the exam, for example—no matter what you feel. You walk right up to the barrier and then *through* it. You might even find that if you totally accept and experience a barrier, such as fear, it shrinks or disappears. When you relax, you reclaim your natural abilities. You can more easily recall the main points from your notes and readings and maybe even crack a real smile. Even if this does not happen right away, you can still open up to a new experience, apply a strategy for reducing test anxiety, and learn something.

It is impossible to live a life that's free of problems. In fact, problems serve a purpose. They provide opportunities to participate in life. Problems stimulate us and pull us forward.

Seen from this perspective, our goal becomes not to eliminate problems, but to find problems that are worthy of us. The problems worth loving are those that can be solved with the greatest benefits for ourselves and others. Engaging with big problems changes us for the better. Bigger problems give more meaning to our lives.

Loving a problem does not mean *liking* it, by the way. Instead, loving a problem means admitting the truth about it. This helps us take effective action—which can free us of the problem once and for all.

iStockphoto.com/sturti

Your memory and your brain—
6 KEY PRINCIPLES

Sharpening your memory starts with understanding how memory depends on a squishy organ that's inside your head—your brain.

Following are six key things to remember about how you remember and learn. They will introduce you to ideas and suggestions that are presented in more detail in the rest of this chapter.

PRINCIPLE 1: SEE MEMORY AS SOMETHING YOU *DO*—NOT SOMETHING YOU HAVE

Once upon a time, people talked about human memory as if it were a closet. You stored individual memories there as you would old shirts and stray socks. Remembering something was a matter of rummaging through all that stuff. If you were lucky, you found what you wanted.

This view of memory creates some problems. For one thing, closets can get crowded. Things too easily disappear. Even with the biggest closet, you eventually run out of space. If you want to pack some new memories in there—well, too bad. There's no room.

Brain researchers shattered this image to bits. Memory is

not a closet. It's not a place or a thing. Instead, memory is a *process* that's based in the brain.

On a conscious level, memories appear as distinct and unconnected mental events: words, sensations, images. They can include details from the distant past—the smell of cookies baking in your grandmother's kitchen, or the feel of sunlight warming your face through the window of your first-grade classroom.

On a biological level, each of those memories involves millions of brain cells, or neurons, firing chemical messages to one another. If you could observe these exchanges in real time, you'd see regions of cells all over the brain glowing with electrical charges at speeds that would put a computer to shame.

When a series of brain cells connects several times in a similar pattern, the result is a memory. Psychologist Donald Hebb explains it this way: "Neurons which fire together, wire together."[1]

It means that memories are not really stored. Instead, remembering is a process in

which you *encode* information as links between active neurons that fire together. You also *decode*, or reactivate, neurons that wired together in the past.

Memory is the probability that certain patterns of brain activity will occur again in the future. In effect, you recreate a memory each time you recall it.

Scientists tell us that the human brain is "plastic." Whenever you efficiently encode and decode, your brain changes physically. You grow more connections between neurons. The more you learn, the greater the number of connections.

For all practical purposes, there's no limit to how many memories your brain can process. Knowing this allows you to step out of your crowded mental closet into a world of infinite possibilities.

PRINCIPLE 2: REMEMBER THAT THE MEMORY PROCESS WORKS IN STAGES

The memory process consists of a series of events. To make the most of your memory, apply an appropriate memory strategy when one of these events takes place:

- **Pay attention to sense experiences.** Memories start as events that we see, hear, feel, touch, or taste. Memory strategies at this stage are about choosing where to focus your attention.

- **"Move" sense experiences to short-term memory.** Sensory memories last for only a few seconds. If you don't want them to disappear, then immediately apply a strategy for moving them into short-term memory, such as reciting the information to yourself several times. Short-term memory is a place where you can "hold" those fleeting sensory memories for up to several minutes.

- **Encode for long-term memory.** If you want to recall information for more than a few minutes, then wire the new neural connections in a more stable way. This calls for a more sophisticated memory strategy—one that allows you to refire the connections for days, weeks, months, or even years into the future.

- **Decode important information on a regular basis.** The more often you recall information, the more stable the memory becomes. To remember it, retrieve it.

PRINCIPLE 3: SINK DEEPLY INTO SENSE EXPERIENCE

Your brain's contact with the world comes through your five senses. So, anchor your learning in as many senses as possible. For example:

- **Create images.** Draw mind map summaries of your readings and lecture notes. Include visual images. Put main ideas in larger letters and brighter colors.

- **Translate ideas in physical objects.** If one of your career goals is to work from a home office, for example, then create a model of your ideal workspace. Visit an art supplies store to find appropriate materials.

- **Immerse yourself in concrete experiences.** Say that you're in a music appreciation class and learning about jazz. Go to a local jazz club or concert to see and hear a live performance.

PRINCIPLE 4: CHOOSE STRATEGIES FOR ENCODING

Signs of encoding mastery are making choices about *what* to remember and *how* to remember it. This in turn makes it easier for you to decode, or recall, the material at a crucial point in the future—such as during a test.

Say that you're enjoying a lecture in introduction to psychology. It really makes sense. In fact, it's so interesting that you choose to just sit and listen—without taking notes. Two days later, you're studying for a test and wish you'd made a different choice. You remember that the lecture was interesting, but you don't recall much else. In technical terms, your decision to skip note taking was an *encoding error.*

So, you decide to change your behavior and take extensive notes during the next psychology lecture. Your goal is to capture everything the instructor says. This too has mixed results—a case of writer's cramp and 10 pages of dense, confusing scribbles. Oops!—another encoding error.

Effective encoding is finding a middle ground between these two extremes. Make moment-to-moment choices about what you want to remember. As you read or listen to a lecture, distinguish between key points, transitions, and minor details. Predict what material is likely to appear on a test. You also stay alert for ideas you can actively apply. These are things you capture in your notes.

Another strategy for effective encoding is to find and create patterns. Your brain is a pattern-making machine. It excels at taking random bits of information and translating them into meaningful wholes. For instance:

- **Use your journal.** Write Discovery and Intention Statements like the ones in this book. Journal Entries prompt you to elaborate on what you hear in class and read in your textbooks. You can create your own writing prompts. For example: "In class today, I discovered that . . ." "In order to overcome my confusion about this topic, I intend to . . ."

- **Send yourself a message.** Imagine that an absent classmate has asked you to send her an email about what happened in class today. Write up a reply and send this email to yourself. You'll actively process your recent learning—and create a summary that you can use to review for tests.

- **Play with ideas.** Copy your notes onto 3 × 5 cards, one fact or idea per card. Then see whether you can arrange them into new patterns—chronological order, order of importance, or main ideas and supporting details.

PRINCIPLE 5: CHOOSE STRATEGIES FOR DECODING

You've probably experienced the "tip of the tongue" phenomenon. You know that the fact or idea that you want to remember is just within reach—so close that you can almost feel it. Even so, the neural connections stop just short of total recall. This is an example of a decoding glitch.

No need to panic. You have many options at this point. These are known as decoding strategies. For example:

- **Relax.** Your mood affects your memory. The information that you want to recall is less likely to appear if you're feeling overly stressed. Taking a long, deep breath and relaxing muscles can work wonders for your body and your brain.
- **Let it go for the moment.** When information is at the tip of your tongue, one natural response is to try hard to remember it. However, this can just create more stress that in turn interferes with decoding. Another option is to stop trying to decode and to do something else for the moment. Don't be surprised if the memory you were seeking

suddenly pops into your awareness while you're in the midst of an unrelated activity.

- **Recall something else.** Many encoding strategies are based on association—finding relationships between something you already know and something new that you want to remember. This means that you can often recall information by taking advantage of those associations. Say that you're taking a multiple-choice test and can't remember the answer to a question. Instead of worrying about this, just move on. You might come across a later question on the same topic that triggers the answer to the earlier question. This happens when a key association is activated.
- **Recreate the original context.** Encoding occurs at specific times and places. If a fact or idea eludes you at the moment, then see whether you can recall where you were when you first learned it. Think about what time of day that learning took place and what kind of mood you were in. Sometimes you can decode the information merely by remembering where you wrote the information in your class notes or where on the page you saw it in a book.

PRINCIPLE 6: TAKE CARE OF YOUR BRAIN

Because memory is a brain-based process, it's important to take care of your brain. Starting now, adopt habits to keep your brain lean and fit for life.

journal entry 8

DISCOVERY/INTENTION STATEMENT

Reflect on the care and feeding of your brain

Review the list of suggestions for taking care of your brain in "Your memory and your brain—6 key principles." Then complete the following sentences:

I discovered that brain health habits I already practice include . . .

To take even better care of my brain, I intend to adopt a new habit of . . .

Consider these research-based suggestions from the Alzheimer's Association.[2]

- **Stay mentally active.** Play challenging games and work crossword puzzles. Seek out museums, theaters, concerts, and other cultural events. Consider learning another language, taking up a musical instrument, traveling to another country, or starting a part-time business. Lifelong learning gives your brain a workout, much like sit-ups condition your abs.
- **Stay socially active.** Having a network of supportive friends can reduce stress levels. In turn, stress management helps to maintain connections between brain cells. Stay socially active by working, volunteering, and joining clubs.

- **Stay physically active.** Physical activity promotes blood flow to the brain. It also reduces the risk of diabetes, cardiovascular disease, and other diseases that can impair brain function. Exercise that includes mental activity—such as learning to dance or doing yoga—offers added benefits.
- **Adopt a brain-healthy diet.** A diet rich in dark-skinned fruits and vegetables boosts your supply of antioxidants—natural chemicals that nourish your brain. Examples of these foods are raisins, blueberries, blackberries, strawberries, raspberries, kale, spinach, brussels sprouts, alfalfa sprouts, and broccoli. Avoid foods that are high in saturated fat and cholesterol, which may increase the risk of Alzheimer's disease.
- **Protect your heart.** In general, what's good for your heart is good for your brain. Protect both organs by eating well, exercising regularly, managing your weight, staying tobacco-free, and getting plenty of sleep. These habits reduce your risk of heart attack, stroke, and other cardiovascular conditions that interfere with blood flow to the brain. ✖

The memory JUNGLE

Think of your memory as a vast, overgrown jungle. This memory jungle is thick with wild plants, exotic shrubs, twisted trees, and creeping vines. It spreads over thousands of square miles—dense, tangled, forbidding.

In the jungle there are animals—millions of them. The animals represent all of the information in your memory. Imagine that every thought, mental picture, or perception you ever had is represented by an animal in this jungle.

Also imagine that the jungle is encompassed on all sides by towering mountains. There is only one entrance to the jungle, a small meadow that is reached by a narrow pass through the mountains.

The memory jungle has two rules: Each thought animal must pass through the meadow at the entrance to the jungle. And once an animal enters the jungle, it never leaves.

Every single event ever perceived by any of your five senses—sight, touch, hearing, smell, or taste—is a thought animal that passed through the meadow and entered the jungle. Some of the thought animals, such as the color of your seventh-grade teacher's favorite sweater, are well hidden. Other thoughts, such as your cell phone number or the position of the reverse gear in your car, are easier to find.

The meadow represents short-term memory. You use this kind of memory when you look up a telephone number and hold it in your memory long enough to make a call. Short-term memory appears to have a limited capacity (the meadow is small) and disappears fast (animals pass through the meadow quickly).

The jungle itself represents long-term memory. This kind of memory allows you to recall information from day to day, week to week, and year to year. Remember that thought animals never leave the long-term memory jungle. The following visualizations can help you recall useful concepts about memory.

VISUALIZATION 1:
A WELL-WORN PATH

Imagine what happens as a thought—in this case, we'll call it an elephant—bounds across short-term memory and into the jungle. The elephant leaves a trail of broken twigs and hoof prints that you can follow.

Brain research suggests that thoughts can wear "paths" in the brain.[3] These paths consist of

dendrites—string-like fibers that connect brain cells. The more these connections are activated, the easier it is to retrieve (recall) the

thought. In other words, the more often the elephant retraces the path, the clearer the path becomes. The more often you recall information and the more often you put the same information into your memory, the easier it is to find.

When you buy a new car, for example, the first few times you try to find reverse, you have to think for a moment. After you have found the reverse gear every day for a week, the path is worn into your memory. After a year, the path is so well worn that when you dream about driving your car backward, you even dream the correct motion for putting the gear in reverse.

VISUALIZATION 2:
A HERD OF THOUGHTS

The second picture you can use to your advantage in recalling concepts about memory is the picture of many animals gathering at a clearing—like thoughts gathering at a central location in memory. It is easier to retrieve

thoughts that are grouped together, just as it is easier to find a herd of animals than it is to find a single elephant.

Pieces of information are easier to recall if you can associate them with similar information. For example, you can more readily remember a particular player's batting average if you can associate it with other baseball statistics.

VISUALIZATION 3:
TURNING YOUR BACK

Imagine releasing the elephant into the jungle, turning your back, and counting to 10. When you turn around, the elephant is gone. This is exactly what happens to most of the information you receive.

Psychological research consistently shows that we start forgetting new material almost

as soon as we learn it. The memory loss is steep, with most of it occurring within the first 24 hours.[4] This means that much of the

material is not being encoded. It is wandering around, lost in the memory jungle.

The remedy is simple: Review quickly. Do not take your eyes off the thought animal as it crosses the short-term memory meadow. Look at it again (review it) within 24 hours after it enters the long-term memory jungle. Wear a path in your memory immediately.

VISUALIZATION 4:
DIRECTING THE ANIMAL TRAFFIC

The fourth picture is one you are in. You are standing at the entrance to the short-term memory meadow, directing herds of thought animals as they file through the pass, across the meadow, and into your long-term memory. You are taking an active role in the learning process. You are paying attention. You are doing more than sitting on a rock and watching the animals file past into your brain. You have

become part of the process, and in doing so, you have taken control of your memory. ✕

25 *memory techniques*

Experiment with these techniques to develop a flexible, custom-made memory system that fits your style of learning. These techniques are divided into five groups, each of which represents a general principle for improving memory.

Violetkaipa/Shutterstock.com

Your first task is to escape the short-term memory trap. Capture new information before it disappears from your attention.

Don't stop there. Then you can encode it by *thinking*—playing with information to make it more vivid in your mind. Also encode by *feeling*—by making an emotional connection with ideas and information. And, encode by *moving*—using your body as well as your brain.

In addition, decode by recalling key information on a regular basis. And instead of saying, "I don't remember," say, "It will come to me." The latter statement implies that the information you want is encoded in your brain and that you can retrieve it—just not right now.

Adopt the attitude that you never forget. You might not believe this right now. That's okay. Just be willing to test the idea and see where it leads.

ESCAPE THE SHORT-TERM MEMORY TRAP

1 Start by understanding the nature of short-term memory. It's different from the kind of memory you'll need during exam week. For example, most of us can look at an unfamiliar seven-digit phone number once and remember it long enough to dial it. See whether you can recall that number the next day. Short-term memory can fade after a few minutes, and it rarely lasts more than several hours. Come to the rescue with any of the following techniques.

2 Chunk it. You already use this technique to dial phone numbers with an area code. For instance, 8006128030 gets chunked into several groups of numbers: 800-612-8030. Chunking works with many other types of information as well. To help you remember the techniques in this article, for instance, they are already chunked into five groups.

3 Recite and repeat. When you repeat something out loud, you anchor the concept in two different senses. First, you get the physical sensation in your throat, tongue, and lips when voicing the concept. Second, you hear it. The combined result is synergistic, just as it is when you create pictures. That is, the effect of using two different senses is greater than the sum of their individual effects.

The "out loud" part is important. Reciting silently in your head can be useful—in the library, for example. Yet it is not as effective as making noise. Your mind can trick itself into thinking it knows something when it doesn't. Your ears are harder to fool.

Don't forget to move your mouth. During a lecture, ask questions. Read key passages from textbooks out loud. Use a louder voice for the main points.

The repetition part is important too. Repetition is a common memory device because it works. Repetition blazes a trail through the pathways of your brain, making the information easier to find. Repeat a concept out loud until you know it; then say it five more times.

Recitation works best when you recite concepts in your own words. For example, if you want to remember that the acceleration of a falling body due to gravity at sea level equals 32 feet per second per second, you might say, "Gravity makes an object accelerate 32 feet per second faster for each second that it's in the air at sea level." Putting a concept into your own words forces you to think about it.

Have some fun with this technique. Recite by writing a song about what you're learning.

Sing it in the shower. Or imitate someone. Imagine your textbook being read by Will Ferrell, Madonna, or Johnny Depp.

4 Review as soon as possible. A short review within minutes of a class or study session can move material from short-term memory into long-term memory. That quick mini-review—paired with a weekly review of all your class notes—can save you hours of study time when exams roll around.

ENCODE BY THINKING

5 Be selective. There's a difference between gaining understanding and drowning in information. During your stay in higher education, you will be exposed to thousands of facts and ideas. No one expects you to memorize all of them. To a large degree, the art of memory is the art of selecting what to remember in the first place.

As you dig into your textbooks and notes, make choices about what is most important to learn. Imagine that you are going to create a test on the material, and consider the questions you would ask.

When reading, look for chapter previews, summaries, and review questions. Pay attention to anything printed in bold type. Also notice visual elements—tables, charts, graphs, and illustrations. They are all clues pointing to what's important. During lectures, notice what the instructor emphasizes. Anything that's presented visually—on the board, in overheads, or with slides—is probably key.

6 Elaborate with questions. *Elaboration* means consciously encoding new information. Repetition is one basic way to elaborate. However, current brain research indicates that other types of elaboration are more effective for long-term memory.

One way to elaborate is to ask yourself questions about incoming information: "Does this remind me of something or someone I already know?" "Is this similar to a technique that I already use?" and "Where and when can I use this information?"

When you learned to recognize Italy on a world map, your teacher probably pointed out that the country is shaped like a boot. This is a simple form of elaboration.

The same idea applies to more complex material. When you meet someone new, for example, ask yourself, "Does she remind me of someone else?" Or when reading this book, preview the material using the first page of each chapter.

7 Organize it. You remember things better if they have meaning for you. One way to create meaning is to learn from the general to the specific. Before you begin your next reading assignment, skim the passage to locate the main ideas. If you're ever lost, step back and look at the big picture. The details then might make more sense.

You can organize any list of items—even random items—in a meaningful way to make them easier to remember. Although there are probably an infinite number of facts, there are only a finite number of ways to organize them.

One option is to organize any group of items by *category*. You can apply this suggestion to long to-do lists. For example, write each item on a separate index card. Then create a pile of cards for calls to make, errands to run, and household chores to complete. These will become your working categories.

The same concept applies to the content of your courses. In chemistry, a common example of organizing by category is the periodic table of chemical elements. When reading a novel for a literature course, you can organize your notes in categories such as theme, setting, and plot. Then take any of these categories and divide them into subcategories such as major events and minor events in the story.

Another option is to organize by *chronological order*. Any time that you create a numbered list of ideas, events, or steps, you are organizing by chronological order. To remember the events that led up to the stock market crash of 1929, for instance, create a timeline. List the key events on index cards. Then arrange the cards by the date of each event.

A third option is to organize by *spatial order*. In plain English, this means making a map. When studying for a history exam, for example, you can create a rough map of the major locations where events take place.

Fourth, there's an old standby for organizing lists—putting a list of items in *alphabetical order*. It's simple and it works.

8 Create associations. The data already encoded in your neural networks are arranged according to a scheme that makes sense to you. When you introduce new data, you can remember them more effectively if you associate them with similar or related data.

Think about your favorite courses. They probably relate to subjects that you already know something about. If you have been interested in politics over the last few years, you'll find it easier to remember the facts in a modern history course. Even when you're tackling a new subject, you can build a mental store of basic background information—the raw material for creating associations. Preview reading assignments, and complete those readings before you attend lectures. Before taking upper-level courses, master the prerequisites.

Ironically, you can also create associations by using contrasts. Ask yourself: "How does this new information *differ* from what I already know?" Concepts that directly contradict your current knowledge will seem unusual. This makes them distinct and memorable.

9 Create pictures. Draw diagrams. Make cartoons. Use these images to connect facts and illustrate relationships. You can "see" and recall associations within and between abstract concepts more easily when you visualize both the concepts and the associations. The key is to use your imagination. Creating pictures reinforces visual and kinesthetic learning styles.

For example, Boyle's law states that at a constant temperature the volume of a confined ideal gas varies inversely with its pressure. Simply put, cutting the volume in half doubles the pressure. To remember this concept, you might picture someone "doubled over," using a bicycle pump. As she increases the pressure in the pump by decreasing the volume in the pump cylinder, she seems to be getting angrier. By the time she has doubled the pressure (and halved the volume), she is boiling ("Boyle-ing") mad.

Another reason to create pictures is that visual information is associated with a part of the brain that is different from the part that processes verbal information. When you create a picture of a concept, you are anchoring the information in a second part of your brain. Doing so increases your chances of recalling that information.

To visualize abstract relationships effectively, create an action-oriented image, such as the person using the pump. Make the picture vivid too. The person's face could be bright red. And involve all of your senses. Imagine how the cold metal of the pump would feel and how the person would grunt as she struggled with it.

You can also create pictures as you study by using *graphic organizers*. These preformatted charts prompt you to visualize relationships between facts and ideas.

One example is a *topic–point–details* chart. At the top of this chart, write the main topic of a lecture or reading assignment. In the left column, list the main points you want to remember. And in the right column, list key details related to each point. Figure 3.1 is the beginning of a chart based on this article.

Topic: 25 Memory Techniques	
Point	**Details**
1. Understand the nature of short-term memory.	Know that information can only be kept in memory for short period unless other techniques are used.
2. Chunk it.	Chunk things into smaller groups to remember them more easily, like phone numbers.
3. Recite and repeat.	Say things out loud, many times.
4. Review as soon as possible.	Reviewing right after learning something new helps move it from short-term to long-term memory.

Figure 3.1 **Topic–Point–Details Chart**

You could use a similar chart to prompt critical thinking about an issue. Express that issue as a question, and write it at the top. In the left column, note the opinion about the issue. In the right column, list notable facts, expert opinions, reasons, and examples that support each opinion. Figure 3.2 is about tax cuts as a strategy for stimulating the economy.

Sometimes you'll want to remember the main actions in a story or historical event. Create a time line by drawing a straight line. Place points in order on that line to represent key events. Place earlier events toward the left end of the line and later events toward the right. Figure 3.3 shows the start of a time line of events relating the US war with Iraq.

Stimulate the Economy with Tax Cuts?	
Opinion	Support
Yes	Savings from tax cuts allow businesses to invest money in new equipment.
	Tax cuts encourage businesses to expand and hire new employees.
No	Years of tax cuts under the Bush administration failed to prevent the mortgage credit crisis.
	Tax cuts create budget deficits.
Maybe	Tax cuts might work in some economic conditions.
	Budget deficits might be only temporary.

Figure 3.2 **Question–Opinion–Support Chart**

When you want to compare or contrast two things, play with a Venn diagram. Represent each thing as a circle. Draw the circles so that they overlap. In the overlapping area, list characteristics that the two things share. In the outer parts of each circle, list the unique characteristics of each thing. Figure 3.4 compares the two types of Journal Entries included in this book—Discovery Statements and Intention Statements.

The graphic organizers described here are just a few of the many kinds available. To find more examples, do an Internet search. Have fun and invent graphic organizers of your own.

10 Restate it. One way to test your understanding and aid your memory at the same time is to put ideas into your own words. For example, you could define decoding simply as the act of recalling information that you learned earlier. Using this technique helps you avoid the trap of memorizing information that you do not understand.

11 Write it down. The technique of writing things down is obvious, yet easy to forget. Writing a note to yourself helps you remember an idea, even if you never look at the note again. Writing notes in the margins of your textbooks can help you remember what you read.

You can extend this technique by writing down an idea not just once but many times. Let go of the old image of being forced to write "I will not throw paper wads" a hundred times on the chalkboard after school. When you choose to remember something, repetitive writing is a powerful tool.

Writing engages a different kind of memory than speaking. Writing prompts us to be more logical, coherent, and complete. Written reviews reveal gaps in knowledge that oral reviews miss, just as oral reviews reveal gaps that written reviews miss.

Another advantage of written reviews is that they more closely match the way you're asked to remember materials in school. During your academic career, you'll probably take far more written exams than oral exams. Writing can be an effective way to prepare for such tests.

Finally, writing is physical. Your arm, your hand, and your fingers join in. Remember, learning is an active process—you remember what you *do*.

12 Make flash cards. Write a sample test question on one side of a 3 × 5 card, and write the answer to that question on the other side of the card. Use these cards to quiz yourself. Or ask someone else to read the questions, listen to your answers, and compare them to the answers on the card.

You can also use PowerPoint or other presentation software to create flash cards. Add illustrations, color, and other visual effects— a simple and fun way to activate your visual intelligence.

A related option is to go online. Do an Internet search with the keywords *flash card*. One of the most popular flash card apps is

3/19/03	3/30/03	4/9/03	5/1/03	5/29/03
U.S. invades Iraq	Rumsfeld announces location of WMD	Soldiers topple statue of Saddam	Bush declares mission accomplished	Bush: We found WMD

Figure 3.3 **Time Line**

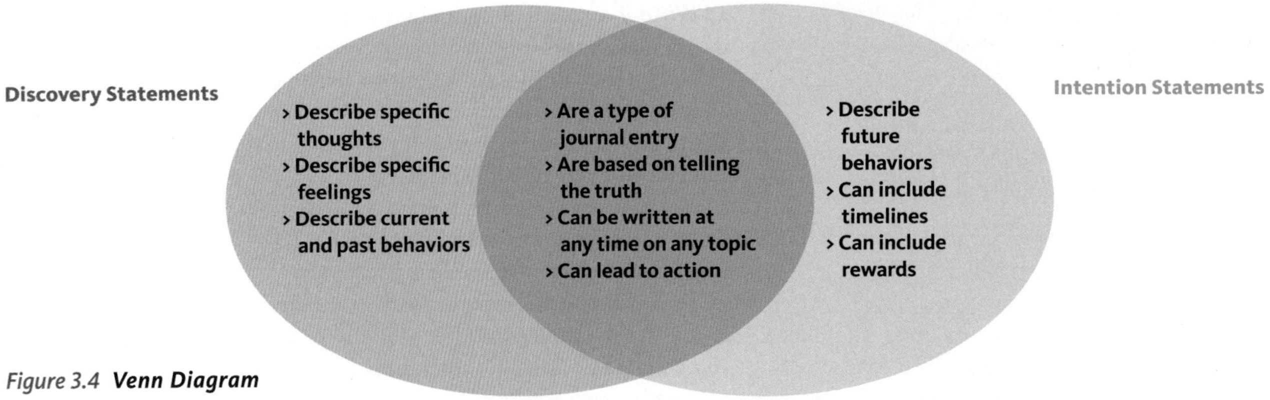

> Describe specific
  thoughts
> Describe specific
  feelings
> Describe current
  and past behaviors

> Are a type of
  journal entry
> Are based on telling
  the truth
> Can be written at
  any time on any topic
> Can lead to action

> Describe
  future
  behaviors
> Can include
  timelines
> Can include
  rewards

Figure 3.4 **Venn Diagram**

Anki (**ankisrs.net**), which is based on the principle of spaced repetition (gradually increasing the amount of time between review sessions). Anki allows you to create your own flash card decks with audio, video, and images as well as text. You can also download decks created by other people.

13 Overlearn. One way to fight mental fuzziness is to learn more than you need to know about a subject simply to pass a test. You can pick a subject apart, examine it, add to it, and go over it until it becomes second nature.

This technique is especially effective for problem solving. Do the assigned problems and then do more problems. Find another textbook and work similar problems. Then make up your own problems and solve them. When you pretest yourself in this way, the potential rewards are speed, accuracy, and greater confidence at exam time. Being well prepared can help you prevent test anxiety.

14 Intend to remember. To instantly enhance your memory, form the simple intention to *learn it now* rather than later. The intention to remember can be more powerful than any single memory technique.

You can build on your intention with simple tricks. During a lecture, for example, pretend that you'll be quizzed on the key points at the end of the period. Imagine that you'll get a $5 reward for every correct answer.

Also pay attention to your attention. Each time your mind wanders during class, make a tick mark in the margins of your notes. The act of writing re-engages your attention.

If your mind keeps returning to an urgent or incomplete task, then write an Intention

Statement about how you will handle it. With your intention safely recorded, return to what's important in the present moment.

ENCODE BY FEELING

15 Make friends with your amygdala. This area of your brain lights up with extra neural activity each time you feel a strong emotion. When a topic excites love, laughter, or fear, the amygdala sends a flurry of chemical messages that say, in effect, *"This information is important and useful. Don't forget it."*

16 Relax. When you're relaxed, you absorb new information quickly and recall it with greater ease and accuracy. Students who can't recall information under the stress of a final exam can often recite the same facts later when they are relaxed.

Relaxing might seem to contradict the idea of active learning, but it doesn't. Being relaxed is not the same as being drowsy, zoned out, or asleep. Relaxation is a state of alertness, free of tension, during which your mind can play with new information, roll it around, create associations with it, and apply many of the other memory techniques. You can be active *and* relaxed.

17 Use your times of peak energy. Study your most difficult subjects during the times when your energy peaks. Some people can concentrate more effectively during daylight hours. The early morning hours can be especially productive, even for those who hate to get up with the sun. Observe the peaks and valleys in your energy flow during the day, and adjust study times accordingly. Perhaps you experience surges in memory power during the late afternoon or evening.

18 Be aware of attitudes. People who think history is boring tend to have trouble remembering dates and historical events. People who believe math is difficult often have a hard time recalling mathematical equations and formulas. All of us can forget information that contradicts our opinions.

If you think a subject is boring, remind yourself that everything is related to everything else. Look for connections that relate to your own interests.

For example, consider a person who is fanatical about cars. He can rebuild a motor in a weekend and has a good time doing so. From this apparently specialized interest, he can explore a wide realm of knowledge. He can relate the workings of an engine to principles of physics, math, and chemistry. Computerized parts in newer cars can lead him to the study of data processing. He can research how the automobile industry has changed our cities and helped create suburbs, a topic that relates to urban planning, sociology, business, economics, psychology, and history.

Being aware of your attitudes is not the same as fighting them or struggling to give them up. Just notice your attitudes and be willing to put them on hold.

19 Relate the material to a personal goal. You're more likely to remember course material when you relate it to a goal—whether academic, personal, or career—that you feel strongly about. This is one reason why it pays to be specific about what you want. The more goals you have and the more clearly they are defined, the more channels you create for incoming information.

You can use this strategy even when a subject seems boring at first. If you're not naturally interested in a topic, then create interest. Find a study partner in the class—if possible, someone you know and like—or form a study group. Also consider getting to know the instructor personally. When a course creates a bridge to human relationships, you engage the content in a more emotional way.

ENCODE BY MOVING

20 Sit at full attention, stand up, and move. Action is a great memory enhancer. Test this theory by studying your assignments with the same energy that you bring to the dance floor or the basketball court.

You can use simple, direct methods to infuse your learning with action. When you sit at your desk, sit up straight. Sit on the edge of your chair as if you were about to spring out of it and sprint across the room.

Also experiment with standing up when you read, write, or recite. It's harder to fall asleep in this position. Some people insist that their brains work better when they stand.

In addition, you can pace back and forth and gesture as you recite material out loud. Use your hands. Go jogging while listening to a recordings of lectures. Get your body moving.

21 Use it. Many courses in higher education lean heavily toward abstract thinking. These courses might not offer opportunities to actively experiment with ideas or test them in daily life.

Create those opportunities yourself. For example, your introductory psychology book probably offers some theories about how people remember information. Choose one of those theories, and test it on yourself. See whether it helps you learn.

Your sociology class might include a discussion about how groups of people resolve conflict. See whether you can apply any of those ideas to resolving conflict in your own life right now.

The point behind these examples is the same: To remember an idea, go beyond thinking about it. Make it personal. *Do* something with it.

At the very least, do something to embed new information in two or more of your senses. For example, outlining a chapter allows you to *see* the main points and *write* them, drawing on your sense of touch. You could add another sense by reciting each point out loud as you outline it and recording your speaking with an app on your smartphone. Also, translate the material from an outline to a picture, which allows you to see the ideas in a new way.

RECALL IT

22 Distribute learning. As an alternative to marathon study sessions, experiment with several shorter sessions spaced out over time. You might find that you can get far more done in three 2-hour sessions than in one 6-hour session.

For example, when you are preparing for your American history exam, study for an hour or two and then wash the dishes. While you are washing the dishes, part of your mind will be reviewing what you studied. Return to American history for a while, then call a friend. Even when you are deep in conversation, part of your mind will be reviewing history.

You can get more done if you take regular breaks. You can even use the breaks as mini-rewards. After a productive study session, give yourself permission to surf the Web, listen to a song, or play 10 minutes of hide-and-seek with your kids.

Distributing your learning is a brain-friendly activity. You cannot absorb new information and ideas during all of your waking hours. If you overload your brain, it will find a way to shut down for a rest—whether you plan for it or not. By taking periodic breaks while studying, you allow information to sink in. During these breaks, your brain is taking the time to rewire itself by growing new connections between cells. Psychologists call this process *consolidation*.[5]

The idea of allowing time for consolidation does have an exception. When you are so engrossed in a textbook that you cannot put it down, when you are consumed by an idea for a term paper and cannot think of anything else—keep going. The master student within you has taken over. Enjoy the ride.

23 Remember something else. When you are stuck and can't remember something that you're sure you know, remember something else that is related to it. If you can't remember your great-aunt's name, remember your great-uncle's name. During an economics exam, if you can't remember anything about the aggregate demand curve, recall what you do know about the aggregate supply curve. If you cannot recall specific facts, remember the example that the instructor used during her lecture. Any piece of

To remember something, access it a lot. Test yourself on it. Read it, write it, speak it, listen to it, apply it. Find some way to make contact with the material regularly. Each time you do so, you widen the neural pathway to the material and make it easier to recall the next time.

information is encoded in the same area of the brain as a similar piece of information. You can unblock your recall by stimulating that area of your memory. A brainstorm is a good memory jog. If you are stumped when taking a test, start writing down lots of answers to related questions, and—pop!—see whether the answer you need suddenly appears.

24 Recall it often. Even information encoded in long-term memory becomes difficult to recall when we don't use it regularly. The pathways to the information become faint with disuse. For example, you can probably remember the names of the courses that you're currently taking. What courses did you take as a freshman in high school?

This example points to a powerful memory technique. To remember something, access it a lot. Test yourself on it. Read it, write it, speak it, listen to it, apply it. Find some way to make contact with the material regularly. Each time you do so, you widen the neural pathway to the material and make it easier to recall the next time.

This is where memory techniques overlap with test preparation. Ask yourself: "How will the instructor ask me to *apply* this concept?" On a test, you might be asked to solve a problem with it, recognize it in a multiple choice question, or explain it in an essay question. Create a practice test with the appropriate types of questions.

25 Teach it. Another way to make contact with the material is to teach it. Teaching demands mastery. When you explain the function of the pancreas to a fellow student, you discover quickly whether you really understand it yourself. Study groups are especially effective because they put you on stage. The friendly pressure of knowing that you'll teach the group helps focus your attention. ✶

Use Q-cards to reinforce memory

One memory strategy you might find useful involves a special kind of flash card. It's called a *Question Card*, or *Q-Card* for short.

To create a standard flash card, you write a question on one side of a 3 × 5 card, and its answer on the other side. Q-Cards have a question on *both* sides. Here's the trick: The question on one side of the card contains the answer to the question on the other side.

The questions you write on Q-Cards can draw on both lower- and higher-order thinking skills. Writing these questions forces you to encode material in different ways. You activate more areas of your brain and burn the concepts even deeper into your memory.

For example, say that you want to remember the subject of the Eighteenth Amendment to the US Constitution—the one that prohibited the sale of alcohol. On one side of a 3 × 5 card, write, *Which amendment prohibited the sale of alcohol?* Turn the card over, and write, *What did the Eighteenth Amendment do?*

To get the most from Q-Cards:

* Add a picture to each side of the card. Doing so helps you learn concepts faster and develop a more visual learning style.
* Read the questions and recite the answers out loud. Two keys to memory are repetition and novelty, so use a different voice whenever you read and recite. Whisper the first time you go through your cards, then shout or sing the next time. Doing this develops an auditory learning style.
* Carry Q-Cards with you, and pull them out during waiting times. To develop a kinesthetic learning style, handle your cards often.
* Create a Q-Card for each new and important concept within 24 hours after attending a class or completing an assignment. This is your *active stack* of cards. Keep answering the questions on these cards until you learn each new concept.
* Review all of the cards for a certain subject on one day each week. For example, on Monday, review all cards from biology; on Tuesday, review all cards from history. These cards make up your *review stacks*.

Get started with Q-Cards right now. One blank represents the front of the card; the other blank represents the back. Start by creating a Q-Card about remembering how to use Q-Cards!

How do living organisms obtain ENERGY?

Why do living things need METABOLISM?

What is the formula for factoring the difference of squares?

$a^2 - b^2 = (a+b)(a-b)$

Robert Harding/Photodisc/Getty Images

NOAA's Sanctuaries Collection/National Oceanic and Atmospheric Administration (NOAA)

Set a trap for your MEMORY

When you want to remind yourself to do something, link this activity to another event you know will take place. The key is to "trap" your memory by picking events that are certain to occur.

Say that you're walking to class and suddenly remember that your accounting assignment is due tomorrow. If you wear a ring, then switch it to a finger on the opposite hand. Now you're "trapped." Every time you glance at your hand and notice that you switched the ring, you get a reminder that you were supposed to remember something else. If you empty your pockets every night, put an unusual item in your pocket in the morning to remind yourself to do something before you go to bed. For example, to remember to call your younger sister on her birthday, pick an object that

reminds you of her—a photograph, perhaps—and put it in your pocket. When you empty your pocket that evening and find the photo, you're more likely to make the call.

Everyday rituals that you seldom neglect, such as feeding a pet or unlacing your shoes, provide opportunities for setting traps. For example, tie a triple knot in your shoelace as a reminder to set the alarm for your early morning study group meeting.

You can even use imaginary traps. To remember to pay your phone bill, visualize a big, burly bill collector knocking on your front door to talk to

you about how much you owe. The next time your arrive at your front door, you'll be glad that you got there before he did. You still have time to make your payment!

Mobile devices work well for setting memory traps. To remind yourself to bring your textbook to class, for example, set an alarm on your cell phone to go off 10 minutes before you leave the house. Visualize yourself picking up the book when the alarm goes off.

Link two activities together, and make the association unusual. ✄

practicing CRITICAL THINKING

13

Remembering your car keys—or anything else

Pick something you frequently forget. Some people chronically lose their car keys or forget to write down checks in their check register. Others let anniversaries and birthdays slip by.

Pick an item or a task you're prone to forget. Then design a strategy for remembering it. Use any of the techniques

from this chapter, research others, or make up your own from scratch. Describe your technique and the results.

In this exercise, as in most of the exercises in this book, a failure is also a success. Don't be concerned with whether your technique will work. Design it, and then find out whether it works. If it doesn't work for you this time, use another method.

MNEMONIC *devices*

Kristin Chiasson/Shutterstock.com

It's pronounced "ne-MON-ik." Mnemonic devices are memory techniques based on *unusual* mental associations rather than *logical* associations.

Some entertainers use mnemonic devices to perform "impossible" feats of memory, such as recalling the names of everyone in a large audience after hearing them just once. Using mnemonic devices, speakers can go for hours without looking at their notes.

There is a catch, though. Mnemonic devices have serious limitations. They don't always help you understand material. Mnemonics rely only on rote memorization. They can be complex and hard to recall. And if you fail to get them exactly right, they quickly lead to errors.

In spite of their limitations, mnemonic devices can be useful. The trick is to have fun and create devices that are simple enough to learn quickly.

There are five main types of mnemonic devices:

- New words
- Creative sentences
- Rhymes and songs
- The loci system
- The peg system

Make up new words. *Acronyms* are words created from the initial letters of a series of words. Examples include NASA (National Aeronautics and Space Administration) and laser (light amplification by stimulated emission of radiation).

You can make up your own acronyms to recall a series of facts. A common mnemonic acronym is Roy G. Biv, which has helped millions of students remember the colors of the visible spectrum (red, orange, yellow, green, blue, indigo, and violet).

IPMAT helps biology students remember the stages of cell division (interphase, prophase, metaphase, anaphase, and telophase).

SKILL can help you recall the organs of the human body that excrete waste: skin, kidneys, intestines, liver, lungs.

OCEAN helps psychology students recall the five major personality factors: open-mindedness, conscientiousness, extraversion, agreeableness, and neuroticism. (You can also use CANOE for this list.)

Speaking of water, the acronym HOMES helps people remember the names of the Great Lakes: Huron, Ontario, Michigan, Erie, Superior.

There's also FOIL, which helps algebra students remember the order for multiplying elements in a binomial equation: first, outer, inner, last.

Use creative sentences. Acrostics are sentences that help you remember a series of letters that stand for something. For example, the first letters of the words in the sentence *Every good boy does fine* (E, G, B, D, and F) are the music notes of the lines of the treble clef staff.

In biology, you might be required to memorize the major categories of living things in the animal world:

- Kingdom
- Phylum
- Class
- Order
- Family
- Genus
- Species
- Variety

Believe it or not, there's a creative sentence for that: *Kings play cards on fairly good soft velvet.*

And if you want to remember the names of the Great Lakes in order from west to east, there's *Super machine heaved earth out.* That stands for *Superior, Michigan, Huron, Erie, Ontario.*

Create rhymes and songs. Madison Avenue advertising executives spend billions of dollars a year on advertisements designed to burn their messages into your memory. The song "It's the Real Thing" was used to market Coca-Cola, despite the soda's artificial ingredients.

Rhymes have been used for centuries to teach basic facts. Here's one that has helped many a student on spelling tests:

> I *before* E *except after* C
> *Or when sounding like* A
> *As in* neighbor *and* weigh.

To remember how many days are in each month of the year, you can say:

> *Thirty days hath September,*
> *April, June, and November.*
> *All the rest have 31*
> *Except February alone.*

Use the loci system. The word *loci* is the plural of *locus*, a synonym for *place* or *location*. Use the loci system to create visual associations with familiar locations. Unusual associations are the easiest to remember.

The loci system is an old one. Ancient Greek orators used it to remember long speeches, and politicians use it today. For example, if a politician's position were that road taxes must be raised to pay for school equipment, his loci visualizations before a speech might look like the following.

First, as he walks in the door of his house, he imagines a large porpoise jumping through a hoop. This reminds him to begin by telling the audience the purpose of his speech.

Next, he visualizes his living room floor covered with paving stones, forming a road leading into the kitchen. In the kitchen, he pictures dozens of schoolchildren sitting on the floor because they have no desks.

Now it's the day of the big speech. The politician is nervous. He's perspiring so much that his clothes stick to his body. He stands up to give his speech and his mind goes blank. Then he starts thinking to himself:

I can remember the rooms in my house. Let's see, I'm walking in the front door and— wow!—I see a porpoise. That reminds me to talk about the purpose of my speech. And then there's that road leading to the kitchen. Say, what are all those kids doing there on the floor? Oh, yeah, now I remember—they have no desks! We need to raise taxes on roads to pay for their desks and the other stuff they need in classrooms.

Use the peg system. The peg system is a technique that employs key words that are paired with numbers. Each word forms a "peg" on which you can "hang" mental associations. To use this system effectively, learn the following peg words and their associated numbers well:

> *Bun* goes with 1.
> *Shoe* goes with 2.
> *Tree* goes with 3.
> *Door* goes with 4.
> *Hive* goes with 5.
> *Sticks* goes with 6.
> *Heaven* goes with 7.
> *Gate* goes with 8.
> *Wine* goes with 9.
> *Ben* goes with 10.

You can use the peg system to remember the Bill of Rights (the first 10 amendments to the US Constitution). For example, amendment number *four* is about protection from unlawful search and seizure. Imagine people knocking at your *door* who are demanding to search your home. This amendment means that you do not have to open your door unless those people have a proper search warrant. ✄

PhotoSpin   National Archives and Records Administration

Making connections in memory-friendly ways

You can think of *Becoming a Master Student* as a huge mnemonic device. It's written and designed to help you make unusual associations. This was done to aid your memory—and to help the book's creators have fun.

To see this for yourself, scan the chapters and look for lists. Yes, there are *lots* of them in this book. Many of the articles and interactive elements are basically lists of suggestions to use and steps to take.

One common use of mnemonics is to remember lists of items. The challenge is to organize lists so that they are more than random collections of ideas. That's why many of the lists in this book are based on certain patterns. By noticing them, you can see how articles are constructed and connect ideas across chapters. Following are a couple of examples.

Numbered Lists

Often the pattern is based on a number:

- **Twos.** Take the number 2, for example. There are two main phases in both the Time Monitor/Time Plan exercise and the Money Monitor/Money Plan exercise—monitoring and planning.
- **Threes.** You'll find many 3s as well. For example, the master student process includes three phases—*discovery, intention*, and *action*. You'll see the same phases in the Skills Snapshots at the end of each chapter. There are also three phases in Muscle Reading—things to do *before, during*, and *after* you dive into a text. Notice that the suggestions for writing papers and making presentations in the Communicating chapter are based on the same *before, during*, and *after* format.
- **Fours.** This number is important, too. The Discovering Yourself chapter presents four types of intelligence in the VARK system (visual, auditory, read-write, kinesthetic) and four modes in the cycle of learning (why, what, how, what if?). In the chapter about Time, there are four "Cs" for getting organized and creating a workflow—collect, choose, classify, and complete. And in the Thinking chapter, look for four steps in solving problems and four ways to choose your major.
- **And more.** When there's too much content for a relatively small list, give yourself permission to make it longer. For instance, give yourself

permission to go all the way up to 25. That's how "25 memory techniques" in this chapter and "25 ways to get the most out of now" in the Time chapter came to be.

Behind all of these examples is a memory-technique: Look for a numbered list, or make one up. Sometimes, just knowing that there's a certain number of items to remember can prompt you to think until you finish recalling them: *Let's see . . . there were four suggestions for things to include when taking notes on meetings—attendance, agenda, agreements, and . . . and . . . actions. That's it—actions!*

Contrasting Pairs

Sometimes you can encode two ideas in your memory by contrasting them as opposites, contradictions, or *paradoxes* (things that are true even though they seem like contradictions).

Contrasting items are often linked by the word *but*. However, the editors of this book prefer to think creatively by using the word *and*. Here are some examples:

- This book is about mastery—*and* it is something that cannot be taught.
- Set specific goals in all areas of your life—*and* use the Power Process: "Detach" to be fulfilled even if you do not meet them.
- To manage time more effectively, create a to-do list—*and* a not-to-do list with activities that you intend to stop.
- Manage time by remembering to do the Time Monitor/Time Plan exercise—*and* by taking your eyes off the clock and forgetting about time once in a while.
- Problems can be difficult—*and* you can use a Power Process in this book to practice "loving" them.
- You can manage your career by setting long-term goals—*and* by taking one immediate step in a desired direction while forgetting about long-term goals.
- Practice divergent and convergent thinking by creating many ideas—*and* being willing to let most of them go.

This is something that you can do as well. Be willing to hold ideas in creative tension by inventing contrasting pairs of your own—the more outrageous, the better.

RETOOL
your memory

Back in the eighteenth century, writer Samuel Johnson noted that the "art of true memory is the art of attention."

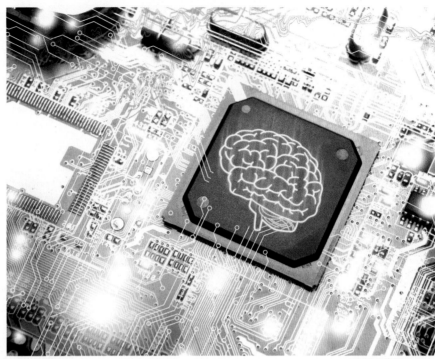

max sattana/Shutterstock.com

Johnson focused enough attention on his own work to produce essays, novels, poems, literary criticism, and a two-volume dictionary of the English language.

The demands on our attention have accelerated steadily since Johnson's day. Current technology provides us with ample means to multitask and scatter our concentration.

Yet technology can also be used to increase our mental focus and enhance our memory.

STORE IMPORTANT INFORMATION WHERE IT'S JUST ONE CLICK AWAY

Imagine how useful—and fun—it would be to download everything you've ever read or thought and then instantly locate what you want to remember about a particular topic. Websites and computer applications give you a variety of ways to store text and images, organize, search them, and even share them. These applications fall into two major categories.

First are websites for social bookmarking. These allow you to store, tag, share, and search links to specific pages. Examples are:

- Delicious (**del.icio.us**)
- Diigo (**www.diigo.com**)
- Pinboard (**https://pinboard.in**)

Also check out online notebooks and note-taking apps, such as:

- Evernote (**www.evernote.com**)
- Zoho Notebook (**notebook.zoho.com**)
- OneNote (**www.onenote.com**)
- Google Keep (**keep.google.com**)
- Notes (an app that comes with Apple computers and iOS devices)

With these, you can "clip" images and text from various web pages, categorize all that content, search it, and add your own notes.

Evernote also allows you to add "offline" content such as digital photos of business cards and receipts. You can search it by using tags and key words.

NAME DIGITAL DOCUMENTS FOR EASY RECALL

No matter where you store documents—on your digital device or online (in the "cloud"), do yourself a favor. Name them so that they're easy to remember.

Avoid generic names such as *agenda.doc* and *notes.doc*. Instead consider adding specific key words that will help you recall what the document contains. For example, include the name of the course and date that the document was created: *biology 2000 12.1.17.doc*. Documents created for work can include the name of a project or coworker.

USE OUTLINING SOFTWARE TO ENCODE INFORMATION

The outlining feature of a word-processing program offers a way to combine several memory techniques in this chapter. Outlining allows you to organize information in a meaningful way. Stating key points in your own words also helps you learn actively.

To create outlined summaries of your textbooks and lecture notes:

- Divide a book chapter or set of handwritten notes into sections.
- Open up a new document in your word-processing program, and list the main points from each section.
- Shift to the outline view of your document, and turn each point into a level-one heading.
- Enter key facts and other details as normal text under the appropriate heading.
- When reviewing for a test, shift your document into outline view so that only the headings are

displayed. Scan them as you would scan the headlines in a newspaper.

In the outline view, see whether you can recall the details you included. Then open up the normal text underneath each headline to check the accuracy of your memory.

Also go online for outlining options. An example is Workflowy (**workflowy.com**). It allows you to create bulleted lists, turn each list item into *another* list, and view as many lists as you want at one time. Checkvist (**checkvist.com**) and Fargo (**fargo.io**) offer similar features.

MAKE CONSCIOUS CHOICES ABOUT WHAT TO REMEMBER

It's true that you can look up just about any fact in seconds with a smartphone and a search engine. Even so, consider the advantages of continuing to memorize the information that matters to your performance at school and at work. For example, coworkers will be impressed if you can deliver a short presentation without notes, recall the main points of a proposal, and instantly match names with faces.

The ultimate memory app is one that's fast, free, and always available—your brain. ✕

practicing CRITICAL THINKING

14

Get creative

Construct your own mnemonic device for remembering some of the memory techniques in this chapter. Make up a poem, jingle, acronym, or acrostic. Or use another mnemonic system. Describe your mnemonic device.

DISCOVERY STATEMENT

journal entry 9

Revisit your memory skills

Take a minute to reflect on the memory techniques in this chapter. You probably use some of them already without being aware of it. List at least three memory techniques you have used in the past, and describe how you have used them.

Remembering
NAMES

New friendships, job contacts, and business relationships all start with remembering names. Here are some suggestions for remembering them.

Rawpixel.com/Shutterstock.com

Recite and repeat in conversation. When you hear a person's name, repeat it. Immediately say it to yourself several times without moving your lips. You can also repeat the name out loud in a way that does not sound forced or artificial: "I'm pleased to meet you, Maria."

Ask the other person to recite and repeat. You can let other people help you remember their names. After you've been introduced to someone, ask that person to spell her name and pronounce it correctly for you. Most people will be flattered by the effort you're making to learn their names.

While you're at it, verify what name people want to be called. "Bob" may actually prefer "Robert."

Visualize. After the conversation, construct a brief visual image of the person. For a memorable image, make it unusual. Imagine the name painted in hot pink fluorescent letters on the person's forehead.

Admit you don't know. Admitting that you can't remember someone's name can actually put people at ease. Most of them will sympathize if you say, "I'm working to remember names better. Yours is right on the tip of my tongue. What is it again?"

Introduce yourself again. Most of the time we assume introductions are one-shot affairs. If we miss a name the first time around, our hopes for remembering it are dashed. Instead of giving up, reintroduce yourself: "We met earlier. I'm Jesse. Please tell me your name again."

Use associations. Link each person you meet with one characteristic that you find interesting or unusual. For example, you could make a mental note: "Vicki Cheng-long, black hair" or "James Washington—horn-rimmed glasses." To reinforce your associations, write them on 3 × 5 cards as soon as you can.

Limit the number of new names you learn at one time. Occasionally, we find ourselves in situations where we're introduced to several people at the same time: "Dad, these are all the people in my Boy Scout troop." "Let's take a tour so you can meet all 32 people in this department."

When meeting a large group of people, concentrate on remembering just two or three names. Free yourself from feeling obligated to remember everyone. Few of the people in mass introductions expect you to remember their names. Another way to avoid memory overload is to limit yourself to learning just first names. Last names can come later.

Ask for photos. In some cases, you might be able to get photos of all the people you meet. For example, a small business where you work might have a brochure with pictures of all the employees. If you're having trouble remembering names the first week of work, ask for individual or group photos, and write in the names if they're not included. You can use these photos as flash cards to drill yourself on names.

Go early. Consider going early to conventions, parties, and classes. Sometimes just a few people show up on time for these occasions. That's fewer names for you to remember. And as more people arrive, you can overhear them being introduced to others—an automatic review for you.

Make it a game. In situations where many people are new to one another, consider pairing up with another person and staging a contest. Challenge one another to remember as many new names as possible. Then choose an award— such as a movie ticket or free meal—for the person who wins.

Use technology. After you meet new people, enter their names as contacts in your email, add them to a database, or enter them into your cell phone. If you get business cards, enter phone numbers, email addresses, and other contact information as well.

Intend to remember. The simple act of focusing your attention at key moments can do wonders for your memory. Test this idea for yourself. The next time you're introduced to someone, direct 100 percent of your attention to hearing that person's name. Do this consistently, and see what happens to your ability to remember names. ✂

practicing CRITICAL THINKING

15

Move from problems to solutions

Many students find it easy to complain about school and to dwell on problems. This exercise gives you an opportunity to change that habit and respond creatively to any problem you're currently experiencing—whether it be with memorizing or some other aspect of school or life.

The key is to dwell more on solutions than on problems. Do that by inventing as many solutions as possible for any given problem. See whether you can turn a problem into a *project* (a plan of action) or a *promise* to change some aspect of your life. Shifting the emphasis of your conversation from problems to solutions can raise your sense of possibility and unleash the master learner within you.

Describe at least three problems that could interfere with your success as a student. The problems can be related to courses, teachers, personal relationships, finances, or anything else that might get in the way of your success.

My problem is that . . .

My problem is that . . .

My problem is that . . .

Next, brainstorm at least three possible solutions to each of those problems. Ten solutions would be even better. You might find it hard to come up with that many ideas. That's okay. Stick with it. Stay in the inquiry, give yourself time, and ask other people for ideas.

I can solve my problem by . . .

I can solve my problem by . . .

I can solve my problem by . . .

Maria Popova }

Grew Brain Pickings from a weekly email newsletter to one of the world's most visited websites, demonstrating how a side project can bloom into a career.

Maria Popova presides over an online empire. Her website Brain Pickings (**brainpickings.org**) attracts over two million visitors each month. Brain Pickings is reader-supported, and Popova makes a living doing it.

The whole project started as a labor of love. In 2006 Popova was working part-time at an advertising agency while attending the University of Pennsylvania. One of her coworkers sent emails with clippings from the work of the agency's competitors.

Popova liked the idea of sharing ideas via email, but she wanted to go in a different direction. Her idea was to share clippings from the most interesting things she was reading at the moment. The range was wide—anything from poetry and novels to biographies and other nonfiction books on just about any topic. Reviews of children's books were in the mix as well. If Popova liked it, she featured it.

Popova's first email went out to seven friends. They started forwarding those emails to *their* friends. Readership continued to grow, eventually convincing Popova to collect her newsletters and post them online. Brain Pickings was born.

Popova describes her website as a "LEGO treasure chest" of the mind. Like many writers on creativity, she believes that new ideas arise when we combine existing insights from many sources in surprising ways. The more people we can draw from, the richer and more powerful the results.

On Brain Pickings, Popova puts it this way: "In order for us to truly create and contribute to the world, we have to be able to connect countless dots, to cross-pollinate ideas from a wealth of disciplines, to combine and recombine these pieces and build new ideas."

Popova often describes herself simply as a reader and writer. Few people do these with as much intensity, however. Researching, curating, and maintaining Brain Pickings takes hundreds of hours of her time each month.

Popova believes that the health of the mind and the health of the body work together. She begins her day by working out at a gym. While she's on the elliptical trainer, she's often highlighting passages from a printed book or reading on her iPad.

Afterward she returns to her office at home to publish at least one new piece per weekday on Brain Pickings. She's active on Twitter, Facebook, Instagram, and Tumblr as well.

Besides doing Brain Pickings, Popova is Futures of Entertainment Fellow at the Massachusetts Institute of Technology. Her background also includes writing for *Wired* UK, *The Atlantic*, *The New York Times*, and Harvard's Nieman Journalism Lab.

During an interview posted on **99u.com**[6], Popova shared the purpose behind all this activity:

> *I feel very fortunate in that to a large extent what I do is exactly what I want to be doing for myself, and I still write for an audience of one. I read things that stimulate me and inspire me and help me figure out how to live and then I write about them. The fact that there are other people who enjoy it is nice, but it's just a byproduct.*

Popova said that she gets emails from people who want to get rich by reaching an audience of millions online. She suggests that they go deeper and focus on doing something that resonates personally with them and with other people at the same time. She urged people not to confuse getting noticed with being happy.

In sum, Popova's business model is simple: Share useful ideas. Respect her audience by keeping Brain Pickings uncluttered and ad-free. And, ask readers to support her work by making a donation.

All these strategies run counter to conventional wisdom about how to make money on the Internet. And, they work.

Maria Popova *preserves our cultural memory by curating and sharing her favorite ideas from books.*

QUIZ

Chapter 3

1. The word *love* as it is used in the Power Process: "Love your problems" means:
   a. Trying hard to enjoy problems
   b. Practicing positive thinking
   c. Focusing only on problems that involve your family members
   d. Accepting the fact that your problems exist

2. According to research, memory is:
   a. The probability that certain patterns of brain activity will occur again in the future
   b. A process of encoding and decoding
   c. A process that takes place in stages
   d. Something you *do*—not something you *have*
   e. All of the answer choices

3. The psychologist Donald Hebb said that "Neurons which fire together, _____ together."

4. In general, the activities that are good for your heart are also good for your brain.
   a. True
   b. False

5. To remember the content of a lecture more effectively:
   a. Wait at least two hours to review your notes on that lecture
   b. Wait at least 24 hours to review your notes on that lecture
   c. Review your lecture notes within the first 24 hours after class
   d. Wait to review your lecture notes until you study for a major test

6. The area of your brain that lights up with extra neural activity each time you feel a strong emotion is called the _____.

7. A _____ is a preformatted chart that prompts you to visualize relationships among facts and ideas.

8. In spite of their limitations, mnemonic devices can be useful.
   a. True
   b. False

9. Connecting a fact or idea to something that you feel strongly about is not recommended, since emotions are not supposed to play a role in critical thinking.
   a. True
   b. False

10. In order to test the idea that "you never forget," you have to believe it first.
    a. True
    b. False

SKILLS
snapshot

Before moving on to a new chapter in this book, reflect on what you learned and how you will gain value from this chapter. Clarify your intention to adopt a new behavior to promote your success in school and at work.

Discovery
My score on the Memory section of the Discovery Wheel was . . .

Some ideas about memory that I read and already knew about in this chapter include . . .

The most surprising thing about memory that I learned from reading this chapter is . . .

Intention
The idea from this chapter that could make the biggest difference in my life right now is . . .

A habit that I could adopt to put this idea into practice is . . .

A suggestion from this chapter that I will likely use in my career is . . .

Action
The specific new behavior that I will practice is . . .

My cue for doing this behavior is . . .

My reward for following through on this intention will be . . .

Digital Vision/Getty Images

Reading

why

Higher education requires extensive reading of complex material.

how

Recall a time when you encountered problems with reading, such as finding words you didn't understand or pausing to reread paragraphs more than once. Then identify at least three specific reading skills you want to gain from this chapter.

what if...

I could finish my reading with time to spare and easily recall the key points?

what is included . . .

138   Power Process: Notice your pictures and let them go

139   Muscle Reading

140   How Muscle Reading works

141   Phase 1: Before you read

142   Phase 2: While you read

144   Phase 3: After you read

146   Extending Muscle Reading to web pages and ebooks

147   Muscle Reading at work

149   When reading is tough

151   Getting past roadblocks to reading

155   Beyond speed reading: Becoming a flexible reader

156   Word power—expanding your vocabulary

159   Mastering the English language

161   Developing information literacy

166   Master Student Profile: Matias Manzano

do you have a minute?

Find a tool for building your vocabulary. For example, test your web browser to see if it will display definitions when you control-click on a word. You could also search for a dictionary app and download it to your mobile phone or tablet.

Notice your pictures and let them go

One of the brain's primary jobs is to manufacture images. We use mental pictures to make predictions about the world, and we base much of our behavior on those predictions.

Pictures can sometimes get in our way. Take the student who plans to attend a school he hasn't visited. He chose this school for its strong curriculum and good academic standing, but his brain didn't stop there. In his mind, the campus has historic buildings with ivy-covered walls and tree-lined avenues. The professors, he imagines, will be as articulate as Barack Obama and as entertaining as Jimmy Fallon. The cafeteria will be a cozy nook serving everything from delicate quiche to strong coffee. He will gather there with fellow students for hours of stimulating, intellectual conversation. The library will have every book, and the computer lab will boast the newest technology.

The school turns out to be four gray buildings downtown, next to the bus station. The first class he attends is taught by an overweight, balding professor wearing a plaid suit that went out of style sometime during the previous century. The cafeteria is a nondescript hall with machine-dispensed food, and the student's apartment is barely large enough to accommodate his roommate's tuba. This hypothetical student gets depressed. He begins to think about dropping out of school.

It's no wonder that pictures have this kind of power. Your brain is incredibly efficient at processing images. In a matter of seconds, for example, you can recognize a familiar face and "read" it for signs of that person's emotional state. If the emotion is not what you expected, then you could find yourself bracing for conflict. The reason:

Reality has failed to match up with one of your precious mental pictures.

The problem with pictures is that they can prevent us from seeing what is really there. That is what happened to the student in this story. His pictures prevented him from noticing that his school is in the heart of a culturally vital city—close to theaters, museums, government offices, clubs, and all kinds of stores. The professor with the weird suit is not only an expert in his field but also a superior teacher. The school cafeteria is skimpy because it can't compete with the variety of inexpensive restaurants in the area.

Our pictures often lead to our being angry or disappointed. We set up expectations of events before they occur. Sometimes we don't even realize that we have these expectations. The next time you discover you are angry, disappointed, or frustrated, look to see which of your pictures aren't being fulfilled.

When you notice that pictures are getting in your way, in the gentlest manner possible let your pictures go. Let them drift away like wisps of smoke picked up by a gentle wind.

This Power Process can be a lifesaver when it comes to reading. Some students enter higher education with pictures about all the reading they'll be required to do before they graduate. They see themselves feeling bored, confused, and worried about keeping up with assignments. If you have such pictures, be willing to let them go. This chapter can help you recreate your whole experience of reading, which is crucial to your success.

Sometimes when we let go of old pictures, it's helpful to replace them with new, positive pictures. These new images can help you take a fresh perspective. Your new pictures might not feel as comfortable and genuine as your old ones. That's okay. Give it time. It's your head, and you're ultimately in charge of the pictures that live there.

Muscle
READING

Effective textbook reading is an active, energy-consuming, sit-on-the-edge-of-your-seat business. That's why this strategy is called Muscle Reading.

Picture yourself sitting at a desk, a book in your hands. Your eyes are open, and it looks as if you're reading. Suddenly your head jerks up. You blink. You realize your eyes have been scanning the page for 10 minutes, and you can't remember a single thing you have read.

Finally, you get to your books at 8:00 p.m. You begin a reading assignment on something called the *equity method of accounting for common stock investments.* "I am preparing for the future," you tell yourself as you plod through two paragraphs and begin the third.

Suddenly, the clock reads 11:00 p.m. Say good-bye to three hours. Sometimes the only difference between a sleeping pill and a textbook is that the textbook doesn't have a warning on the label about operating heavy machinery.

Contrast this scenario with the image of an active reader, who exhibits the following behaviors:

- Stays alert, poses questions about what she reads, and searches for the answers
- Recognizes levels of information within the text, separating the main points and general principles from supporting details

- Quizzes herself about the material, makes written notes, and lists unanswered questions
- Instantly spots key terms and takes the time to find the definitions of unfamiliar words
- Thinks critically about the ideas in the text and looks for ways to apply them

That sounds like a lot to do. Yet skilled readers routinely accomplish all these things and more—while enjoying the process. Master students engage actively with reading material. They're willing to grapple with even the most challenging texts. They wrestle meaning from each page. They fill the margins with handwritten questions. They underline, highlight, annotate, and nearly rewrite some books to make them their own.

Master students also practice the deepest level of information literacy: They commit to change their lives based on what they read. Of every chapter, they ask, "What's the point? And what's the payoff? How can I use this to live my purpose and achieve my goals?" These students are just as likely to create to-do lists as to take notes on their reading. And when they're done with a useful book, master students share it with others for continuing conversation. Reading becomes a creative act and a tool for building community.

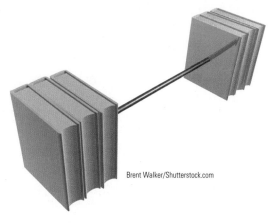
Brent Walker/Shutterstock.com

One way to experience this kind of success is to approach reading with a system in mind. An example is Muscle Reading. You can use Muscle Reading to avoid mental mini-vacations and reduce the number of unscheduled naps during study time, even after a hard day. Muscle Reading is a way to decrease difficulty and struggle by increasing energy and skill. Once you learn this system, you might actually spend less time on your reading and get more out of it.

Boosting your reading skills will promote your success in school. It can also boost your income. According to a report from the National Endowment for the Arts, proficient readers earn more than people with only basic reading skills. In addition, better readers are more likely to work as managers or other professionals.[1]

This is not to say that Muscle Reading will make your job or education a breeze. Muscle Reading might even look like more work at first. That's a normal reaction to have when learning any new skill. Persist with the process. Allow time to develop your new muscles for reading. With time and patience, you'll reap the rewards—understanding more of what you read and remembering more of what you understand. ✄

How Muscle Reading
WORKS

Muscle Reading is a three-phase technique you can use to extract the ideas and information you want:

- Phase 1 includes steps to take *before* you read.
- Phase 2 includes steps to take *while* you read.
- Phase 3 includes steps to take *after* you read.

Each phase has several steps.

PHASE 1:
Before you read
Step 1: Preview
Step 2: Outline
Step 3: Question

PHASE 2:
While you read
Step 4: Focus
Step 5: Flag Answers

PHASE 3:
After you read
Step 6: Recite
Step 7: Review
Step 8: Review again

To assist your recall of Muscle Reading strategies, memorize three short sentences:

Pry out questions.
Focus and flag answers.
Recite, review, and review again.

These three sentences correspond to the three phases of the Muscle Reading technique. Each sentence is an acrostic. The first letter of each word stands for one of the steps in Muscle Reading.

g-stockstudio/Shutterstock.com

Take a moment to invent images for each of those sentences.

For Phase 1, visualize or feel yourself prying out questions from a text. These questions are ones you want answered based on a brief survey of the assignment. Make a mental picture of yourself scanning the material, spotting a question, and reaching into the text to pry it out. Hear yourself saying, "I've got it. Here's my question."

Then for Phase 2, focus on finding answers to your questions. Feel free to underline, highlight, or mark up your text in other ways. Make the answers so obvious that they lift up from the page.

Finally, you enter Phase 3. Hear your voice reciting what you have learned. Listen to yourself making a speech or singing a song about the material as you review it.

To jog your memory, write the first letters of the Muscle Reading acrostic in a margin or at the top of your notes. Then check off the steps you intend to follow. Or write the Muscle Reading steps on 3 × 5 cards and then use them for bookmarks.

Muscle Reading might take a little time to learn. At first you might feel it's slowing you down. That's natural when you're gaining a new skill. Mastery comes with time and practice. ✖

PHASE 1:

Before you read

STEP 1: PREVIEW

Before you start reading, preview the entire assignment. You don't have to memorize what you preview to get value from this step. Previewing sets the stage for incoming information by warming up a space in your mental storage area.

If you are starting a new book, look over the table of contents and flip through the text page by page. If you're going to read one chapter, flip through the pages of that chapter. Even if your assignment is merely a few pages in a book, you can benefit from a brief preview of the table of contents.

Read all chapter headings and subheadings. Like the headlines in a newspaper, these are usually printed in large, bold type. Often headings are brief summaries in themselves. For a more thorough preview, read the first few paragraphs and last few paragraphs of a chapter, or the first sentence of each paragraph.

Keep an eye out for summary statements. If the assignment is long or complex, read the summary first. Many textbooks have summaries in the introduction or at the end of each chapter.

When previewing, seek out familiar concepts, facts, or ideas. These items can help increase comprehension by linking new information to previously learned material. Take a few moments to reflect on what you already know about the subject—even if you think you know nothing. This technique prepares your brain to accept new information.

Look for ideas that spark your imagination or curiosity. Inspect drawings, diagrams, charts, tables, graphs, and photographs.

Imagine what kinds of questions will show up on a test. Previewing helps to clarify your purpose for reading. Ask yourself what you will do with this material and how it can relate to your long-term goals. Will you be reading just to get the main points? Key supporting details? Additional details? All of the above? Your answers will guide what you do with each step that follows.

Keep your preview short. If the entire reading assignment will take less than an hour, your preview might take five minutes. Previewing is also a way to get started when an assignment looks too big to handle. It is an easy way to step into the material.

STEP 2: OUTLINE

With complex material, take time to understand the structure of what you are about to read. Outlining actively organizes your thoughts about the assignment and can help make complex information easier to understand.

If your textbook provides chapter outlines, spend some time studying them. When an outline is not provided, sketch a brief one in the margin of your book or at the beginning of your notes, on a separate sheet of paper. Later, as you read and take notes, you can add to your outline.

Have fun with this technique. Make the questions playful or creative. You don't need to answer every question that you ask. The purpose of making up questions is to get your brain involved in the assignment. Take your unanswered questions to class, where they can be springboards for class discussion.

Headings in the text can serve as major and minor entries in your outline. For example, the heading for this article is "Phase 1: Before you read," and the subheadings list the three steps in this phase. When you outline, feel free to rewrite headings so that they are more meaningful to you.

The amount of time you spend on this outlining step will vary. For some assignments, a 10-second mental outline is all you might need. For other assignments (fiction and poetry, for example), you can skip this step altogether.

STEP 3: QUESTION

Before you begin a careful reading, determine what you want from the assignment. Then write down a list of questions, including any questions that resulted from your preview of the materials.

Another useful technique is to turn chapter headings and subheadings into questions. For example, if a heading is "Transference and Suggestion," you can ask yourself, "What are *transference* and *suggestion*? How does *transference* relate to *suggestion*?" Make up a quiz as if you were teaching this subject to your classmates.

If there are no headings, look for key sentences and turn them into questions. These sentences usually show up at the beginnings or ends of paragraphs and sections.

To read at a deeper level, ask deeper questions. Unless you're reading solely to gain facts, go beyond simple yes–no and true–false questions. Create questions that prompt you to define key terms, separate the main points from minor details, and make connections between ideas. Often these questions will have more than one correct answer.

Have fun with this technique. Make the questions playful and creative. You don't need to answer every question that you ask. The purpose of making up questions is to get your brain involved in the assignment. Take your unanswered questions to class, where they can be springboards for class discussion. Demand your money's worth from your textbook. If you do not understand a concept, write specific questions about it. The more detailed your questions, the more powerful this technique becomes. ✴

PHASE 2:

While you read

STEP 4: FOCUS

You have previewed the reading assignment, organized it in your mind or on paper, and formulated questions. Now you are ready to begin reading.

It's easy to fool yourself about reading. Just having an open book in your hand and moving your eyes across a page doesn't mean that you are reading effectively. Reading takes mental focus.

As you read, be conscious of where you are and what you are doing. When you notice your attention wandering, gently bring it back to the present moment. There are many ways to do this.

To begin, get in a position to stay focused. If you observe chief executive officers, you'll find that some of them wear out the front of their chair first. They're literally on the edge of their seat. Approach your reading assignment in the same way. Sit up. Keep your spine straight. Avoid reading in bed, except for fun.

Avoid marathon reading sessions. Schedule breaks and set a reasonable goal for the entire session. Then reward yourself with an enjoyable activity for 10 or 15 minutes every hour or two.

For difficult reading, set more limited goals. Read for a half hour and then take a break. Most students find that shorter periods of reading distributed throughout the day and week can be more effective than long sessions.

Visualize the material. Form mental pictures of the concepts as they are presented. If you read that a voucher system can help control cash disbursements, picture a voucher handing out dollar bills. Using visual imagery in this way can help deepen your understanding of the text while allowing information to be transferred into your long-term memory.

Read material out loud, especially if it is complicated. Some of us remember better and understand more quickly when we hear an idea.

Get a "feel" for the subject. For example, let's say you are reading about a microorganism—a paramecium—in your biology text. Imagine what it would feel like to run your finger around the long, cigar-shaped body of the organism. Imagine feeling the large fold of its gullet on one side and the tickle of the hairy little cilia as they wiggle in your hand.

In addition, predict how the author will answer your key questions. Then read to find out if your predictions were accurate.

STEP 5: FLAG ANSWERS

As you read, seek out the answers to your questions. You are a detective, watching for every clue. When you do find an answer, flag it so that it stands out on the page.

Deface your books. Have fun. Flag answers by highlighting, underlining, writing comments, filling in your outline, or marking up pages in any other way that helps you. Indulge yourself as you never could with your grade school books.

Marking up your books offers other benefits. When you read with a highlighter, pen, or pencil in your hand, you involve your kinesthetic senses of touch and motion. Being physical with your books can help build strong neural pathways in your memory.

You can mark up a text in many ways. For example:

- Place an asterisk (*) or an exclamation point

Five smart ways to highlight a text

Step 5 in Muscle Reading mentions a popular tool: highlighting. It also presents a danger—the ever-present temptation to highlight too much text. Excessive highlighting leads to wasted time during reviews. Get the most out of all that money you pay for books and the time you spend reading. Highlight in an efficient way that leaves texts readable for years to come and provides you with an easy reviewing method.

Pindyurin Vasily/Shutterstock.com

Read carefully first. Read an entire chapter or section at least once before you begin highlighting. Don't be in a hurry to mark up your book. Get to know the text first. Make two or three passes through difficult sections before you highlight.

Make choices up front about what to highlight. Perhaps you can accomplish your purposes by highlighting only certain chapters or sections of a text. When you highlight, remember to look for passages that directly answer the questions you posed during Step 3 of Muscle Reading. Within these passages, highlight individual words, phrases, or sentences rather than whole paragraphs. The important thing is to choose an overall strategy before you put highlighter to paper.

Recite first. You might want to apply Step 6 of Muscle Reading before you highlight. Talking about what you read—to yourself or with other people—can help you grasp the essence of a text. Recite first; then, go back and highlight. You'll probably highlight more selectively.

Underline, then highlight. Underline key passages lightly in pencil. Then close your text and come back to it later. Assess your underlining. Perhaps you can highlight less than you underlined and still capture the key points.

Use highlighting to monitor your comprehension. Critical thinking plays a role in underlining and highlighting. When highlighting, you're making moment-by-moment decisions about what you want to remember from a text. You're also making inferences about what material might be included on a test.

Take your critical thinking a step further by using highlighting to check your comprehension. Stop reading periodically and look back over the sentences you've highlighted. See whether you are making accurate distinctions between main points and supporting material. Highlighting too much (more than 10 percent of the text) can be a sign that you're not making this distinction and that you don't fully understand what you're reading. Review the rest of this chapter for suggestions that can help.

- (!) in the margin next to an especially important sentence or term.
- Circle key terms and words to look up later in a dictionary.
- Write short definitions of key terms in the margin.
- Write a *Q* in the margin to highlight possible test questions, passages you don't understand, and questions to ask in class.
- Write personal comments in the margin—points of agreement or disagreement with the author.
- Write mini-indexes in the margin—that is, the numbers of other pages in the book where the same topic is discussed.
- Write summaries in your own words.
- Rewrite chapter titles, headings, and subheadings so that they're more meaningful to you.
- Draw diagrams, pictures, tables, or maps that translate text into visual terms.
- Number each step in a list or series of related points.
- In the margins, write notes about the relationships between elements in your reading. For instance, note connections between an idea and examples of that idea.
- If you infer an answer to a question or come up with another idea of your own, write that down as well.

Avoid marking up a text too soon. Wait until you complete a chapter or section to make sure you know the key points. Then mark up the text. Sometimes, flagging answers after you read each paragraph works best.

Also remember that the purpose of making marks in a text is to call out important concepts or information that you will review later. Flagging key information can save lots of time when you are studying for tests. With this in mind, highlight or underline sparingly—usually less than 10 percent of the text. If you mark up too much on a page, you defeat the purpose: to flag the most important material for review.

Finally, jot down new questions, and note when you don't find the answers you are looking for. Ask these questions in class, or see your instructor personally. Demand that your textbooks give you what you want—answers. ✖

PHASE 3:
After you read

STEP 6: RECITE

Talk to yourself about what you've read. Or talk to someone else. When you finish a reading assignment, make a speech about it. When you recite, you practice an important aspect of metacognition—synthesis, or combining individual ideas and facts into a meaningful whole.

One way to get yourself to recite is to look at each underlined point. Note what you marked; then, put the book down and start talking out loud. Explain as much as you can about that particular point.

To make this technique more effective, do it in front of a mirror. It might seem silly, but the benefits can be enormous. Reap them at exam time.

A related technique is to stop reading periodically and write a short, free-form summary of what you just read. In one study, this informal "retrieval practice" helped students recall information better than other study techniques.[2]

Classmates are even better than mirrors. Form a group and practice teaching one another what you have read. One of the best ways to learn anything is to teach it to someone else.

In addition, talk about your reading whenever you can. Tell friends and family members what you're learning from your textbooks.

Talking about your reading reinforces a valuable skill—the ability to summarize. To practice this skill, pick one chapter (or one section of one chapter) from any of your textbooks. State the main topic covered in this chapter. Then state the main points that the author makes about this topic.

For example, the main topic up to this point in this chapter is Muscle Reading. The main point about this topic is that Muscle Reading includes three phases—steps to take before you read, while you read, and after you read. For a more detailed summary, you could name each of the steps.

Note: This topic-point method does not work so well when you want to summarize short stories, novels, plays, and other works of fiction. Instead, focus on action. In most stories, the main character confronts a major problem and takes a series of actions to solve it. Describe that problem and talk about the character's key actions—the turning points in the story.

STEP 7: REVIEW

Plan to do your first complete review within 24 hours of reading the material. Sound the trumpets! This point is critical: A review within 24 hours moves information from your short-term memory to your long-term memory.

Review within one day. If you read it on Wednesday, review it on Thursday. During this review, look over your notes and clear up anything you don't understand. Recite some of the main points again.

STEP 8: REVIEW AGAIN

The final step in Muscle Reading is the weekly or monthly review. This step can be very short—perhaps only four or five minutes per assignment. Simply go over your notes. Read the highlighted parts of your text. Recite one or two of the more complicated points.

The purpose of these reviews is to keep the neural pathways to the information open and to make them more distinct. That way, the information can be easier to recall. You can accomplish these short reviews anytime, anywhere, if you are prepared.

Conduct a five-minute review while you are waiting for a bus, for your socks to dry, or for the water to boil. Three-by-five cards are a handy review tool. Write ideas, formulas, concepts, and facts on cards, and carry them with you. These short review periods can be effortless and fun.

Sometimes longer review periods are appropriate. For example, if you found an assignment difficult, consider rereading it. Start over, as if you had never seen the material before. Sometimes a second reading will provide you with surprising insights.

Decades ago, psychologists identified the primacy-recency effect, which suggests that we most easily remember the first and last items in any presentation.[3] Previewing and reviewing your reading can put this theory to work for you. ✄

MUSCLE READING: A LEANER APPROACH

Keep in mind that Muscle Reading is an overall approach, not a rigid, step-by-step procedure. Here's a shorter variation that students have found helpful. Practice it with any chapter in this book:

- **Preview and question.** Flip through the pages, looking at anything that catches your eye—headings, subheadings, illustrations, photographs. Turn the title of each article into a question. For example, "How Muscle Reading works" can become "How does Muscle Reading work?" List your questions on a separate sheet of paper, or write each question on a 3 × 5 card.

- **Read to answer your questions.** Read each article. Then go back over the text and underline or highlight answers to the appropriate questions on your list.

- **Recite and review.** When you're done with the chapter, close the book. Recite by reading each question—and answering it—out loud. Review the chapter by looking up the answers to your questions. (It's easy—they're already highlighted.) Review again by quizzing yourself one more time with your list of questions.

This review can be short. You might spend as little as 15 minutes reviewing a difficult two-hour reading assignment. Investing that time now can save you hours later when studying for exams.

EXTENDING

Muscle Reading to web pages and ebooks

The techniques suggested in this chapter work for more than printed textbooks.

Alex Segre/Alamy Stock Photo

You can still use the three phases of Muscle Reading when accessing a web page or ebook on a computer, mobile phone, or tablet.

PHASE 1: BEFORE YOU READ

For this phase, the core Muscle Reading techniques are previewing, outlining, and posing questions. These are all about *preparing* to dig into a text. Digital texts offer another level of preparation that allows you to create more readable pages.

To begin, change the appearance of the text. Adjust the size and choose from different fonts. Many ebook readers also allow you to change the color of the text and the amount of contrast between text and background. These settings can be useful when you're reading in a place with dim lighting.

In addition, cut the clutter. Web pages abound with ads, pop-up windows, and animations. Getting rid of all that stuff makes it easier to focus your attention on the core content of the page and avoid time-wasting distractions.

Readability (**readability.com**) offers extensions and bookmarklets for your web browser that allow you to do just that. (Bookmarklets are tiny programs that add a specific function to a browser.) Safari and other web browsers also come with a built-in "reader" mode that does much the same thing as Readability.

DISCOVERY/INTENTION STATEMENT

journal entry **10**

Experiment with Muscle Reading

After reading the steps included in Muscle Reading, reflect on your reading skills. Are you a more effective reader than you thought you were? Less effective? Record your observations.

I discovered that I . . .

Many students find that they only do the "read" step with their textbooks. You've just read about the advantages of seven additional steps you should perform. Depending on the text, reading assignment, your available time, and your commitment level to the material, you may discover through practice which additional steps work best for you. Right now,

make a commitment to yourself to experiment with all or several of the additional Muscle Reading steps by completing the following Intention Statement.

I intend to use the following Muscle Reading steps for the next two weeks in my _____ class:

- ☐ Preview
- ☐ Outline
- ☐ Question
- ☐ Focus
- ☐ Flag answers
- ☐ Recite
- ☐ Review
- ☐ Review again

PHASE 2: WHILE YOU READ

During this phase, skilled readers focus on finding answers to their questions and flagging them in the text. Ebooks offer features that help with these steps:

- **Access the table of contents.** For a bigger picture of the text, look for a table of contents that lists chapter headings and subheadings. Click on any of these headings to expand the text for that part of the book. Note that charts, illustrations, photos, tables, diagrams, and other visuals might be listed separately in the table of contents.
- **Use navigation tools.** To flip electronic pages, look for *previous* and *next* buttons or arrows on the right and left borders of each page. Many ebooks also offer a "go to page" feature that allows you to key in a specific page number.
- **Search the text.** Look for a search box that allows you to enter key words and find all the places in the text where those words are mentioned.
- **Follow links to definitions and related information.** Many ebook readers will supply a definition of any word in the text. All you need to do is highlight a word and click on it. Also find out if your ebook reader will connect you to websites related to the topic of your ebook.

- **Highlight and annotate.** Ebook readers allow you to select words, sentences, or entire paragraphs and highlight them in a bright color. You can also annotate a book by keying in your own notes tied to specific pages.

Even with features such as these, you might find that you sometimes prefer the printed version of a book. This is likely to happen when a text includes large illustrations and charts that don't translate well to a small screen. Go to the library or bookstore to see whether you can find those pages in a printed copy of your ebook. Use the print and ebook versions of a text to supplement each other.

PHASE 3: AFTER YOU READ

The final phase of Muscle Reading is about moving information into your long-term memory by reciting and reviewing. These steps call on you to locate the main points in a text and summarize them.

Ebooks can help you create instant summaries. For example, the Amazon Kindle allows you to view all your highlighted passages at once. Another option is to copy these passages and then paste them into a word-processing file. To avoid plagiarism, put these passages within quotation marks and note the source. ✖

Dragon Images/Shutterstock.com

Muscle Reading at
WORK

Knowledge workers read a lot. They consume technical manuals, sales manuals, policies and procedures, memos, emails, websites, newsletters, invoices, application forms, meeting minutes, brochures, annual reports, job descriptions—and more.

DISCOVERY/INTENTION STATEMENT

Reflect on your online reading habits

Take a few minutes to reflect on your experience of reading web pages and ebooks. Suppose that you were able to read a book in three versions—online, print, and ebook. Based on your current experience, do you think that one of these versions would better support your understanding of the content and efficient use of reading time? Would you use different reading strategies for the different versions? Complete the following sentences:

With web pages and ebooks, I discovered that I read most effectively when I . . .

I read less effectively when I . . .

To get the most from online reading and ebooks in the future, I intend to . . .

The techniques of Muscle Reading can help you plow through all that material and extract what you want.

Start with a purpose. At work, your purpose for reading is probably to produce a specific outcome—to gain a skill or gather information needed to complete a task. Fix that purpose in mind before you read in depth about a topic.

This is where step 3 of Muscle Reading—asking questions—comes in handy. See if you can express your purpose as a question.

Suppose that your purpose for reading is to learn more about marketing. Turn that purpose into a question: *What are the elements of extraordinary marketing?* Then read books and articles for specific answers.

Extract value with nonlinear reading. Consider how you first learned to read as a child. You opened up a book, fixed your eyes on the first word, and worked straight through until the end of the sentence or page.

As you got older, you approached longer and longer documents with essentially the same strategy: Start at the beginning and plow through word by word until you reach the last period of the last paragraph.

Instead, read with the alertness of someone who's in a large group of people and searching for someone she knows. Her eyes scan the crowd at high speed until—presto!—they land on the familiar face. When reading, your brain can operate with that kind of efficiency. Rather than looking for people, however, you're scanning to land on the paragraphs that contain answers to your questions.

The key is to make several passes through the material. Make your first pass a preview—step 1 of Muscle Reading.

Then go for a second pass. Read the first sentence of each paragraph or the first and last paragraphs of each section.

If you want more detail, then make additional passes. Slow down and pick up a little more detail each time.

During each pass through a document, you can skip entire sections or take them out of order. This is the nonlinear technique. You might even want to start at the end of a chapter or article to see if there's a summary or review section placed there. This section might be all that you need.

Create a "To Read" folder. Much of the paper that crosses your field of attention at work will probably consist of basic background material—items that are important, but not urgent. Place these documents in a paper or digital folder, label it "To Read," and pull it out the next time you have a few minutes to spare.

Beware of blog overload. Reading blogs can be useful. It can also become an activity that devours too many hours. To get the most value from blogs:

- *Create a schedule.* Rather than checking blogs for updates at random points throughout the workday, set specific times for visiting these sites.
- *Set limits.* If you're an avid blog reader, monitor how much time you spend on them each week. The results might surprise you.
- *Use an RSS reader to monitor blogs.* RSS readers are online tools that create summaries of frequently updated websites. (RSS stands for "Rich Site Summary" or "Really Simple Syndication.") Examples include NetNewsWire, My Yahoo!, and Google Reader. For each article posted on a

website, an RSS reader displays a headline. You can add several sets of headlines, or "feeds," to your RSS reader. This allows you to scan the contents of many websites in one window—much like you'd skim the headlines in a newspaper.

- *Limit the number of blogs you read.* If you add a new feed to your RSS reader, see if you can delete an old one.

Read with a bias toward action.
Your reading might include passages that call for action on your part. Mark these passages with an appropriate symbol in the margin. For example, write a big letter "A" for *action* next to the relevant paragraph. Or draw a small box there and check off the box after taking the appropriate action. Another option is to enter actionable items directly in your calendar or add them to your to-do list.

The bottom line is that reading at work ultimately means one thing—getting something done. ✖

wavebreakmedia/Shutterstock.com

When reading is
TOUGH

Sometimes ordinary reading methods are not enough. It's easy to get bogged down in a murky reading assignment The solution starts with a First Step: When you are confused, tell the truth about it.

Successful readers monitor their understanding of reading material. They do not see confusion as a mistake or a personal shortcoming. Instead, they take it as a cue to change reading strategies and process ideas at a deeper level.

Somehow, students get the idea that reading means opening a book and slogging through the text in a straight line from the first word until the last. Actually, this method can be an ineffective way to read.

Feel free to shake up your routine. Make several passes through tough reading material. During a preview, for example, just scan the text to look for key words and highlighted material.

Then, skim the entire chapter or article again, spending a little more time and taking in more than you did during your preview. Finally, read in more depth, proceeding word by word through some or all of the text. Also consider the following suggestions.

Look for essential words.
If you are stuck on a paragraph, mentally cross out all of the adjectives and adverbs, and then read the sentences without them. Find the important words—usually verbs and nouns.

Hold a mini-review. Pause briefly to summarize—either verbally or in writing—what you've read so far. Stop at the end of a paragraph and recite, in your own words, what you have just read. Jot down some notes, or create a short outline or summary.

Read it out loud. Make noise. Read a passage out loud several times, each time using a different inflection and emphasizing a different part of the sentence. Be creative. Imagine that you are the author talking.

Stand up. Changing positions periodically can combat fatigue. Experiment with standing as you read, especially if you get stuck on a tough passage and decide to read it out loud.

Skip around. Jump to the next section or to the end of a tough article or chapter. You might have lost the big picture. Simply seeing the next step, the next main point, or a summary might be all you need to put the details in context. Retrace the steps in a chain of ideas, and look for examples. Absorb facts and ideas in whatever order works for you, which may be different from the author's presentation.

Use another text. Find a similar text in the library. Sometimes a concept is easier to understand if it is expressed another way. Children's books—especially children's encyclopedias—can provide useful overviews of baffling subjects.

Note where you get stuck. When you feel stuck, stop reading for a moment and diagnose what's happening. At these stop points, mark your place in the margin of the page with a penciled S for *Stuck*. A pattern to your marks over several pages might indicate a question you want to answer before going further.

This is the essence of the *Corson technique*, named after Dale Corson, the eighth president of Cornell University. Before asking for help, Corson said, ask yourself: *What exactly do I not understand?* When reading, locate the first sentence, paragraph, or page that confused you. Then set a timer and spend 15 minutes trying to overcome your confusion. Keep a record of everything you do during that time period. If you're still confused when the timer goes off, then proceed to the next suggestion.

Talk to someone who can help. Admit when you are stuck. Then bring questions about reading assignments to classmates, members of your study group, or a tutor. Many schools provide free tutoring services. If your school does not, ask your instructor whether other students who have completed the course can assist you.

Also make an appointment with your instructor. Most of them welcome the opportunity to work individually with students. If you used the Corson technique, you'll be able to pinpoint the source of your confusion and explain what you've already done to overcome it. This can save time—and impress your instructor.

Stop reading. When none of the above suggestions work, do not despair. Admit your confusion and then take a break. Catch a movie, go for a walk, study another subject, or sleep on it. The concepts you've already absorbed might come together at a subconscious level as you move on to other activities. Allow some time for that process. When you return to the reading material, see it with fresh eyes. ✳

Somehow, students get the idea that reading means opening a book and slogging through the text in a straight line from the first word until the last. Actually, this method can be an ineffective way to read.

Getting past
ROADBLOCKS
to reading

Even your favorite strategies for reading can fail when you're dealing with bigger issues. Those roadblocks to getting your reading done can come from four major sources:

- Finding enough time to keep up with your reading
- Making choices about what to read once you find the time
- Getting interrupted by other people while you're reading
- Remembering the main ideas from what you read

For solutions to each of these problems, read on.

MAKING CHOICES ABOUT WHAT TO READ

Books about time management often mention the "80–20" principle. According to this principle, 80 percent of the value created by any group derives from only 20 percent of its members. If you have a to-do list of 10 items, for example, you'll get 80 percent of your desired results by doing only two items on the list.

The point is not to take these figures literally but to remember the underlying principle: *Focus on what creates the most value.* Look at your

reading in light of the 80–20 principle. For instance:

- In a 10-paragraph article, you might find 80 percent of the crucial facts in the headline and first paragraph. (In fact, journalists are *taught to* write this way.)
- If you have a 50-page assignment, you may find the most important facts and ideas in 10 pages of that total.
- If you're asked to read five books for a course, you may find that most exam questions come from just one of them.

A caution is in order here. The 80–20 principle is not a suggestion to complete only 20 percent of your reading assignments. That choice can undermine your education. To find the most important parts of anything you read, first get familiar with the whole. Only then can you make sound choices about where to focus.

Skilled readers constantly make choices about what to read and what *not* to read. They realize that some texts are more valuable for their purposes than others and that some passages within a single text are more crucial than the rest. When reading, they instantly ask, "What's most important here?"

The answer to this question varies from assignment to assignment, and even from page to page within a single assignment. Pose this question each time that you read, and look for clues to the answers. Pay special attention to the following:

- Any readings that your instructor refers to in class
- Readings that are emphasized in a class syllabus
- Readings that generate the most questions on quizzes and tests
- Parts of a text that directly answer the questions you generated while previewing
- Chapter previews and summaries (usually found at the beginning and end of a chapter or section)

Henk Badenhorst/Taxi/Getty Images

DEALING WITH INTERRUPTIONS

Sometimes the people you live with and care about the most—a friend, roommate, spouse, or child—can become a temporary roadblock to reading. The following strategies can help you stay focused on your reading:

Attend to people first. When you first come home from school, keep your books out of sight. Spend some time with your roommates or family members before you settle in to study. Make small talk and ask them about their day. Give the important people in your life a short period of full, focused attention rather than a longer period of partial attention. Then explain that you have some work to do. Set some ground rules for the amount of time you need to focus on studying. You could be rewarded with extra minutes or hours of quiet time.

Plan for interruptions. It's possible that you'll be interrupted even if you set up guidelines for your study time in advance. If so, schedule the kind of studying that can be interrupted. For instance, you could write out or review flash cards with key terms and definitions. Save the tasks that require sustained attention for more quiet times.

Use "pockets" of time. See whether you can arrange a study time in a quiet place at school before you come home. If you arrive at school 15 minutes earlier and stay 15 minutes later, you can squeeze in an extra half hour of reading that day. Also look for opportunities to study on campus between classes.

When you can't read everything, read something. Even if you can't absorb an entire chapter while your roommates are blasting music, you can skim a chapter. Or you can just read the introduction and summary. When you can't get it *all* done, get *something* done.

    Caution: If you always read this way, your education will be compromised. Supplement this strategy with others from this chapter so that you can get your most important reading done.

Read with children underfoot. It is possible to have both effective study time and quality time with your children. The following suggestions come mostly from students who are also parents. The specific strategies you use will depend on your schedule and the ages of your children.

- **Find a regular playmate for your child.** Some children can pair off with close friends and safely retreat to their rooms for hours of private play. You can check on them occasionally and still get lots of reading done.
- **Create a special space for your child.** Set aside one room or area of your home as a play space. Childproof this space. The goal is to create a place where children can roam freely and play with minimal supervision. Consider allowing your child in this area *only* when you study. Your homework time then becomes your child's reward. If you're cramped for space, just set aside some special toys for your child to play with during your study time.
- **Use television responsibly.** Whenever possible, select educational programs that keep your child's mind active and engaged. Also see whether your child can use headphones while watching television. That way, the house stays quiet while you study.
- **Schedule time to be with your children when you've finished studying.** Let your children in on the plan: "I'll be done reading at 7:30. That gives us a whole hour to play before you go to bed."
- **Ask other adults for help.** Getting help can be as simple as asking your spouse, partner, neighbor, or fellow student to take care of the children while you study. Offer to trade childcare with a neighbor: You will take his kids and yours for two hours on Thursday night if he'll take them for two hours on Saturday morning.
- **Find community activities and services.** Ask whether your school provides a day care service. In some cases, these services are available to students at a reduced cost.

REMEMBERING WHAT YOU READ

Think about the last book you read. How many pages did it have? How many hours did you spend reading it? And how much of it do you remember?

    These simple questions remind us that it's easy to forget most of what we read—unless we take steps to prevent that outcome. Following are four suggestions.

Write informal Discovery Statements. After you finish an article or book chapter, set aside your reading material. Grab a pen and paper, or open up a document on your computer, tablet, or smartphone. Then spend two minutes writing a free-form Discovery Statement about what you just read.

Don't worry about the format of this Journal Entry. Don't worry about making it complete or detailed or clear enough for someone else to read. Just capture what you want to remember from the chapter or article you just read. It doesn't matter whether you write a sentence, a paragraph, a page, or even more. Just summarize what is important, memorable, and useful to you.

File these Journal Entries in a place where you can easily find them in the future. Spending even a few minutes rereading these Discovery Statements can make books you read years ago come back to life in the present.

Write short Intention Statements. For many business, self-help, and other "how-to" books you can go directly to application. Ask yourself: "What is my intention after reading this? How will I use this? What will I say or do differently based on what I just read?" Don't worry about following up on all the author's suggestions. Simply write Intention Statements to plan a few new behaviors that will make a huge positive difference in your life.

Use the Feynman technique. This strategy is named after Richard Feynman, a physicist who won the Nobel Prize in 1965 and author of many popular science books. While reading, Feynman often took out a blank sheet of paper and wrote a key topic from a book at the top of the page. Then he wrote out what he would say about this topic if he were teaching it to someone who knew nothing about it.

When he got stuck, Feynman went back to the book to find what he missed. Then he went back to writing. He kept revising until he eliminated the gaps in his understanding of the topic.

To get the most from this technique, use your own words as much as possible. Simplify the language and create analogies that relate new ideas to something your imaginary student would already understand.

Copy the passages you want to remember. During the Middle Ages, books were hard to find and expensive. When people did manage to put their hands on a book, they copied out their favorite passages from the author into a personal journal called a *commonplace book.*

Quotations were collected from many books and organized by date or topic. In addition, some people added a table of contents, an index, or both to their commonplace books.

The commonplace book is still a powerful tool. Experiment with creating one of your own. If you use a digital app for this purpose, you'll have a searchable database of the "greatest hits" from all your favorite authors. At your fingertips will be nuggets of wisdom from a lifetime of reading. ✂

Get SPUNKI with your reading

SPUNKI is an acronym that stands for six words:

- *Surprising*
- *Puzzling*
- *Useful*
- *New*
- *Knew*
- *Interesting*

These are the key words in six questions you can ask about anything you want to read and remember.

After finishing a book chapter or article, take a few minutes to complete any or all of the following sentences in writing:

- What I found *surprising* in this reading is . . .
- What I found *puzzling* in this reading is . . .
- What I found *useful* in this reading is . . .
- What I found *new* in this reading is . . .
- What I already *knew* in this reading is . . .
- What I found *interesting* in this reading is . . .

Use these questions to create discussions, organize your notes, and—above all—to have more fun with reading.

Plan to complete your reading assignments

Planning dispels panic *(I've got 300 pages to read before tomorrow morning!)* and helps you finish off your entire reading load for a term. Creating a reading plan is relatively simple if you use the following steps. Have your calendar handy.

Step 1. Estimate the total number of pages that you'll read.

To arrive at this figure, check the course syllabus for each class that you're taking. Look for lists of reading assignments. Based on what you find, estimate the total number of pages that you'll read for all your classes.

Step 2. Estimate how many pages you can read during one hour.

Remember that your reading speed will be different for various materials. It depends on everything from the layout of the pages to the difficulty of the text. To give your estimate some credibility, base it on actual experience. During your first reading assignment in each course, keep track of how many pages you read per hour.

Step 3. Estimate your total number of reading hours.

Divide the total number of pages from Step 1 by your pages-per-hour from Step 2. For example, look at this calculation:

600 (total number of pages for all courses this term) ÷ 10 (pages read per hour)
= 60
The result is the total number of hours you'll need to complete
your reading assignments this term—60 hours in this case.

Remember to give yourself some "wiggle room." Allow extra hours for rereading and unplanned events. Consider taking your initial number of projected hours and doubling it. You can always back off from there to an estimate that seems more reasonable.

Step 4. Schedule reading time.

Take the total number of hours from Step 3 and divide it by the number of weeks in your current term. That will give you the number of hours to schedule for reading each week. For example:

60 (total reading hours needed for the term) ÷ 16 (weeks in the term)
= 3.75 (hours per week to schedule for reading)

Now, go to your calendar or long-term planner and reflect on it for a few minutes. Look for ways to block out your reading hours for next week.

Step 5. Refine your reading plan.

Scheduling your reading takes time. The potential benefits are beyond calculation. With a plan, you can be more confident that you'll actually get your reading done. Even if your estimates are off, you'll still go beyond blind guessing or leaving the whole thing to chance. Your reading matters too much for that.

Chris Pancewicz/Alamy Stock Photo

Beyond speed reading: Becoming a
FLEXIBLE READER

There are plenty of apps, books, and courses that promise to turn you into a speed reader. Want to read a novel in one night? No problem! Want to power through 500 emails on your lunch break with time to spare? Easy! Want to "mentally photograph" whole pages instead of plodding through paragraphs? That's just the beginning!

All of this sounds too good to be true. That's because it is.

A 2016 report from the Association for Psychological Science reviewed decades of studies on speed reading programs and found little evidence to support any of them.[4] The researchers concluded that big increases in speed came with dramatic drops in comprehension.

The good news is that speed isn't everything. What counts is *flexibility*. Skillful readers vary their reading rate according to their purpose and the nature of the material. An advanced text in analytic geometry calls for a different reading rate than the Sunday comics.

Flexible readers also use different reading rates on the same material. For example, you can take one pass through an assigned chapter to spot the key words and sentences. Then make a second pass to get an overview of the main points. Follow up with a third pass to slow down and reread the difficult parts.

Other ways to become a flexible reader include psuedo-skimming, reading widely, and reading wisely.

PRACTICE PSUEDO-SKIMMING

While research debunked the benefits of speed reading, there is skimming. This is what you do for the first 3 steps of Muscle Reading: preview an assignment, create an outline, and pose questions to answer. For many of the documents that you encounter in daily life— magazine articles, blog posts, emails, memos—this might be all you need to fulfill your purpose for reading.

Author Cal Newport talks about a related approach that falls between previewing and reading for detail. He calls it *pseudo-skimming*.[5] This calls for

distinguishing between two kinds of paragraphs. *Important* paragraphs contain the main points, key details, and major events in a story. *Filler* paragraphs include minor details, stories about how the author arrived at her conclusions, digressions, answers to critics, rare exceptions to rules, and other optional material.

To practice pseudo-skimming, read the first sentence of each paragraph. If it seems like the beginning of an important idea, then read the whole paragraph. If not, mentally label it as filler and proceed to the next paragraph.

READ WIDELY

Speed-reading teachers often tell you to:

- Reduce eye movements.
- Avoid regressions (going back to reread passages that you didn't understand).

- Stop sub-vocalizing (hearing words in your mind as you read them).

Yet the faster you try to read with these techniques, the less you'll understand. When it comes to reading speed, the size of your vocabulary and the prior knowledge that you bring to a topic are more important factors. These develop gradually over time as you continue your education and gain new experiences.

While there are no "hacks," tips, tricks, secrets, or shortcuts to personal development, there is one thing you *can* do: read more. Choose books that challenge you and introduce you to new subjects. Also read more actively by joining book groups and distilling what you learn into Discovery and Intention Statements.

READ WISELY

Some people like to boast about how many books they read each week, month, or year. That's like taking a trip across the country and boasting about how many miles you covered. For most of us, the purpose of a trip is not to drive as far or fast as possible. Rather, it's to relax, see the sights, connect with people, and gain a new perspective on life.

In a similar way, reading is not about winning a race. It's about becoming a better human being. When you read to pass a test or certification exam, you aim for comprehension and recall. When you read for a lifetime, you aim for wisdom. You think critically. You look for logic, evidence, and quality. And you evaluate an author's message in the light of your lifetime of personal experiences.

In addition, you open up to change. Reading widely and well allows you to think new thoughts, make new decisions, and master new skills. That takes time—and it's worth it. ✴

Word power— expanding your
VOCABULARY

Having a large vocabulary makes reading more enjoyable and increases the range of materials you can explore.

In addition, building your vocabulary gives you more options for self-expression when speaking or writing. With a larger vocabulary, you can think more precisely by making finer distinctions between ideas. And you won't have to stop to search for words at crucial times—such as a job interview.

Stockbyte

Strengthen your vocabulary by taking delight in words. Look up unfamiliar terms. Pay special attention to words that arouse your curiosity.

Before the age of the Internet, students used two kinds of printed dictionaries: the desk dictionary and the unabridged dictionary. A desk dictionary is an easy-to-handle abridged dictionary that you can use many times in the course of a day. You can keep this book within easy reach (maybe in your lap) so you can look up unfamiliar words while reading.

In contrast, an unabridged dictionary is large and not made for you to carry around. It provides more complete information about words and definitions not included in your desk dictionary, as well as synonyms, usage notes, and word histories. Look for unabridged dictionaries in libraries and bookstores.

You might prefer using one of several online dictionaries, such as **dictionary.com**. Another common option is to search for definitions by using a search engine such as **google.com**. If you do this, inspect the results carefully. They can vary in quality and be less useful than the definitions you'd find in a good dictionary or thesaurus.

Construct a word stack. When you come across an unfamiliar word, write it down on a 3 × 5 card. Below the word, copy the sentence in which it was used, along with the page number. You can look up each word immediately, or you can accumulate a stack of these cards and look up the words later. Write the definition of each word on the back of the 3 × 5 card, adding the *diacritics*—marks that tell you how to pronounce it.

To expand your vocabulary and learn the history behind the words, take your stack of cards to an unabridged dictionary. As you find related words in the dictionary, add them to your stack. These cards become a portable study aid that you can review in your spare moments.

Learn—even when your dictionary is across town. When you are listening to a lecture and hear an unusual word or when you are reading on the bus and encounter a word you don't know, you can still build your word stack. Pull out a 3 × 5 card and write down the word and its sentence. Later, you can look up the definition and write it on the back of the card.

Divide words into parts. Another suggestion for building your vocabulary is to divide an unfamiliar word into syllables and look for familiar parts. This strategy works well if you make it a point to learn common prefixes (beginning syllables) and suffixes (ending syllables). For example, the suffix *-tude* usually refers to a condition or state of being. Knowing this makes it easier to conclude that *habitude* refers to a usual way of doing something and that *similitude* means being similar or having a quality of resemblance.

Infer the meaning of words from their context. You can often deduce the meaning of an unfamiliar word simply by paying attention to its context—the surrounding words, phrases, sentences, paragraphs, or images. Later, you can confirm your deduction by consulting a dictionary.

Practice looking for context clues such as these:

- **Definitions.** A key word might be defined right in the text. Look for phrases such as *defined as* or *in other words*.
- **Examples.** Authors often provide examples to clarify a word meaning. If the word is not explicitly defined, then study the examples. They're often preceded by the phrases *for example, for instance,* or *such as*.
- **Lists.** When a word is listed in a series, pay attention to the other items in the series. They might define the unfamiliar word through association.
- **Comparisons.** You might find a new word surrounded by synonyms—words with a similar meaning. Look for synonyms after words such as *like* and *as*.
- **Contrasts.** A writer might juxtapose a word with its antonym. Look for phrases such as *on the contrary* and *on the other hand*. ✳

Make an investment in your word power by learning the following word parts. Use each of the example words in a sentence and check off each prefix, root, or suffix as you do.

Prefixes

- *a* [not, without] *Example*: amoral ("without a sense of moral responsibility")
- *acro* [high] *Example*: acrophobia ("fear of height")
- *anti* [against] *Example*: anticommunist ("someone who is against communism")
- *bi* [both, double, twice] *Example*: biweekly ("occurring twice per week")
- *cerebro* [brain] *Example*: cerebral ("relating to the workings of the brain")
- *circum* [around] *Example*: circumnavigate ("to walk around an object")
- *deca* [ten] *Example*: decagon ("a ten-sided figure")
- *extra* [beyond, outside] *Example*: extraneous ("outside the topic")
- *fore* [before in time] *Example*: foreshadow ("to predict an event before it happens")
- *hyper* [over, above] *Example*: hypersensitive ("to react over and above what is considered normal in a situation")
- *infra* [beneath] *Example*: infrastructure ("the underlying organization")
- *macro* [large] *Example*: macrocosm ("a larger viewpoint or system")
- *neo* [new] *Example*: neologism ("a new word")
- *oct* [eight] *Example*: octagon ("an eight-sided figure")
- *poly* [many] *Example*: polygamy ("having many wives")
- *quad* [four] *Example*: quadruple ("to increase by a factor of four")
- *retro* [backward] *Example*: retrospective ("to look back over a body of work")
- *sub* [below] *Example*: subhuman ("beneath ordinary standards of human conduct")
- *ultra* [exceedingly] *Example*: ultraconservative ("extremely opposed to change")

Roots

- *acu* [sharp] *Example*: acupuncture ("treatment with needles")
- *amor* [love] *Example*: amorous ("feeling affectionate")
- *brev* [short] *Example*: abbreviate ("to make shorter")
- *bio* [life] *Example*: biopsy ("to take a sample of living tissue")
- *cide* [kill] *Example*: fratricide ("to kill a sibling")
- *dorm* [sleep] *Example*: dormant ("remaining in a state of sleep or otherwise inactive")
- *dox* [opinion] *Example*: heterodox ("embracing many opinions")
- *erg* [work] *Example*: ergonomics ("relating to working conditions")
- *gastro* [stomach] *Example*: gastrointestinal ("relating to the stomach and intestines")
- *greg* [herd, group, crowd] *Example*: gregarious ("enjoying the presence of crowds")
- *hetero* [different] *Example*: heterogeneous ("having many different elements")
- *uni* [one] *Example*: unicorn ("an imaginary horse with one horn")
- *vor* [eat greedily] *Example*: voracious ("eating many foods or absorbing many stimuli")

Suffixes

- *algia* [pain] *Example*: neuralgic ("a medication to relieve pain")
- *ate* [cause, make] *Example*: liquidate ("to dissolve or make obsolete")
- *escent* [in the process of] *Example*: obsolescent ("in the process of passing or becoming extinct")
- *ize* [make] *Example*: idolize ("to make an object of worship")
- *oid* [resembling] *Example*: spheroid ("resembling a sphere")
- *ology* [study, science, theory] *Example*: neurology ("the study of the nervous system")
- *tude* [state of] *Example*: multitude ("a state of having many elements")
- *ward* [in the direction of] *Example*: eastward ("turning in the opposite direction of west")

exopixel/Shutterstock.com

MASTERING
the English language

The complexity of English makes it a challenge for people who grew up with another language—and for native speakers of English as well. To get the most benefit from your education, analyze the ways that you speak and write English. Look for patterns that might block your success. Then take steps to increase your mastery.

LEARN TO USE STANDARD ENGLISH WHEN IT COUNTS

Standard English (also called *standard written English*) is the form of the language used by educated speakers and writers. It is the form most likely to be understood by speakers and writers of English, no matter where they live.

Using non-standard English in the classroom or workplace might lead people to doubt your skills, your intentions, or your level of education. Non-standard English comes in many forms, including these:

- **Slang.** These informal expressions often create vivid images. When students talk about "acing" a test or "hanging loose" over spring break, for example, they're using slang.
- **Idioms.** These are colorful expressions with meanings that are not always obvious. For instance, a "fork in the road" does not refer to an eating utensil discarded on a street but rather to a place where a part of the road branches off. Even native speakers of English can find idioms hard to understand.

- **Dialects.** A sentence such as "I bought me a new phone" is common in certain areas of the United States. If you use such an expression in a paper or presentation, however, your audience might form a negative impression of you.
- **Jargon.** Some terms are used mainly by people who work in certain professions. If you talk about "hacking a site" or finding a "workaround," for example, then only students majoring in software engineering might understand you.

Any community of English speakers and writers can reshape the language for its own purposes. People who send text messages are doing that now. So are people who post on Twitter, a website that limits updates to 140 characters. Even your family, friends, and coworkers might develop expressions that no one else comprehends.

Learning when and how to use non-standard English is part of mastering the language. However, save nonstandard expressions for informal conversations with friends. In

that context, you can safely try out new words and ask for feedback about how you're using them. If you're not sure whether a particular expression is standard English, then talk to an instructor. And if someone points out that you're using non-standard English, be willing to learn from that experience. You can do this even when the feedback is not given with skill or sensitivity.

BUILD CONFIDENCE

Students who grew up with a language other than English might fall under the category of English as a Second Language (ESL) student, or English Language Learner (ELL). Many ESL/ELL students feel insecure about using English in social settings, including the classroom. Choosing not to speak, however, can delay your mastery of English and isolate you from other students.

As an alternative, make it your intention to speak up in class. List several questions beforehand and plan to ask them. Also schedule a time to meet with your instructors during office hours to discuss any material that you find confusing. These strategies can help you build relationships while developing English skills.

In addition, start a conversation with at least one native speaker of English in each of your classes. For openers, ask about their favorite instructors or ideas for future courses to take.

English is a complex language. Whenever you extend your vocabulary and range of expression, the likelihood of making mistakes increases. The person who wants to master English yet seldom makes mistakes is probably being too careful. Do not look upon mistakes as a sign of weakness. Mistakes can be your best teachers—if you are willing to learn from them.

Remember that the terms *English as a Second Language* and *English Language Learner* describe a difference—not a deficiency. The fact that you've entered a new culture and are mastering another language gives you a broader perspective than people who speak only one language.

And if you currently speak two or more languages, you've already demonstrated your ability to learn.

ANALYZE ERRORS IN USING ENGLISH

To learn from your errors, make a list of those that are most common for you. Next to the error, write a corrected version. For examples, see the chart. Remember that native speakers of English also use this technique—for instance, by making lists of words they frequently misspell.

LEARN BY SPEAKING AND LISTENING

You probably started your English studies by using textbooks. Writing and read-

Errors	Corrections
Sun is bright.	The sun is bright.
He cheerful.	He is cheerful.
I enjoy to play chess.	I enjoy playing chess.
Good gifts received everyone.	Everyone received good gifts.
I knew what would present the teachers.	I knew what the teachers would present.
I like very much burritos.	I like burritos very much.
I want that you stay.	I want you to stay.
Is raining.	It is raining.
My mother, she lives in Iowa.	My mother lives in Iowa.
I gave the paper to she.	I gave the paper to her.
They felt safety in the car.	They felt safe in the car.
He has three car.	He has three cars.
I have helpfuls family members.	I have helpful family members.
She don't know nothing.	She knows nothing.

ing in English are important. Both can help you add to your English vocabulary and master grammar. To gain greater fluency and improve your pronunciation, also make it your goal to *hear* and *speak* standard English.

For example, listen to radio talk shows hosted by educated speakers with a wide audience. Imitate the speaker's pronunciation by repeating phrases and sentences that you hear. During TV shows and personal conversations, notice the facial expressions and gestures that accompany certain English words and phrases.

If you speak English with an accent, do not be concerned. Many people speak clear, accented English. Work on your accent only if you can't be easily understood.

Take advantage of opportunities to read and hear English

at the same time. For instance, turn on English subtitles when watching a film on DVD. Also, check your library for audiobooks. Check out the printed book, and follow along as you listen.

USE ONLINE RESOURCES

Some online dictionaries allow you to hear words pronounced. They include Answers.com (**www.answers.com**) and Merriam-Webster Online (**www.m-w.com**).

Other resources include online book sites with a read-aloud feature. An example is Project Gutenberg (**www.gutenberg.org**; search on "Audio Books").

Also, check general websites for ESL students. A popular one is Dave's ESL Café (**www.eslcafe.com**), which will lead you to others.

GAIN SKILLS IN NOTE TAKING AND TESTING

When taking notes, remember that you don't have to capture everything that an instructor says. To a large extent, the art of note taking consists of choosing what *not* to record. Listen for key words, main points, and important examples. Remember that instructors will often repeat these things. You'll have more than one chance to pick up on the important material. When you're in doubt, ask for repetition or clarification.

Taking tests is a related challenge. You may find that certain kinds of test questions—such as multiple-choice items—are more common in the United States than in your native country.

The suggestions for reading, note taking, and memorizing in this book can help you master these and many other types of tests.

CREATE A COMMUNITY OF ENGLISH LEARNERS

Learning as part of a community can increase your mastery. For example, when completing a writing assignment in English, get together with other people who are learning the language. Read one another's papers and suggest revisions. Plan on revising your paper a number of times based on feedback from your peers.

You might feel awkward about sharing your writing with other people. Accept that feeling—and then remind

yourself of everything you have to gain by learning from a group. In addition to learning English more quickly, you can raise your grades and make new friends.

Native speakers of English might be willing to assist your group. Ask your instructors to suggest someone. This person can benefit from the exchange of ideas and the chance to learn about other cultures.

CELEBRATE YOUR GAINS

Every time you analyze and correct an error in English, you make a small gain. Celebrate those gains. Taken together over time, they add up to major progress in mastering English. ✺

Jasminko Ibrakovic/Shutterstock.com

Developing
INFORMATION LITERACY

Master students find information from appropriate sources, evaluate the information, organize it, and use it to achieve a purpose. The ability to do this in a world where data is literally at your fingertips is called information literacy.

Information literacy is a set of skills that you can use for many purposes. For example, you might want to learn more about a product, a

service, a vacation spot, or a potential job. You might want to follow up on something you heard on the radio or saw on TV. Or you might want to develop a topic for a paper or presentation. In each case, success depends on information literacy.

Information literacy happens in a continuous cycle. You ask questions and gather answers. Those answers lead to more questions, which lead to more research. At each stage, you dig deeper. You understand your topic in a more refined way. You ask better questions and find better answers.

To begin, choose your topic with care. A topic that's too broad is hard to cover in a single presentation or paper. A topic that's too narrow won't lead you to many sources of information. The trick is to find a topic that falls in between these two extremes.

GET IDEAS FOR A TOPIC

You can use the Web to get some initial ideas for a topic. Go to a search engine such as Google (**google.com**), Bing (**bing.com**), or DuckDuckGo (**duckduckgo.com**). In the search box, enter a key word followed by *research paper topics*—for example, *astronomy research paper topics.*

Another source of topic ideas is Alltop (**alltop.com**). It lists hundreds of websites organized by major topics. You'll find links to the five most recent articles on each site.

If you are writing a paper or preparing a presentation for class, ask your instructor for guidance in choosing your topic. She may have requirements about how many sources and what kind of sources to use. Choose a topic to meet those requirements.

DISCOVER QUESTIONS ABOUT YOUR TOPIC

One of the early steps in Muscle Reading involves asking questions. Start with your *main question* about the topic you chose. This is the thing that sparked your curiosity in the first place. Answering it is your purpose for doing research.

Your main question will raise a number of smaller, related questions. These are *supporting questions.* They also call for answers.

DISCOVERING QUESTIONS— AN EXAMPLE

Suppose that you're interested in the economic recession that began during 2008 in the United States. You know that one factor in this recession was the mortgage credit crisis. This occurred when banks loaned large amounts of money to people to buy a house, even if those people had little income and a low credit rating.

Your main question might be: "Leading up to the mortgage credit crisis of 2008, what led banks to lend money to people with a poor credit history?" Your list of supporting questions might include the following:

- What banks were involved in the mortgage credit crisis?
- What is the criteria for a mortgage worthy borrower?
- How do banks discover a person's credit history?
- What are the signs of a poor credit history?

FIND SOURCES

Next, find sources of answers to your questions. Sources include books, articles, websites, and people you can interview.

Start with sources that give an overview of your topic. One is an encyclopedia. Through your campus or community library, you might have full access to Encyclopedia Britannica (**www.britannica.com**) and other encyclopedia databases that are not available to the general public. To find out more, make both an online and in-person visit to the library.

Another option is Wikipedia (**wikipedia.org**). Because the quality of Wikipedia articles varies so much, they are *not* acceptable sources to use for a final paper or presentation. However, many Wikipedia articles mention *other* respected sources.

Google Books (**books.google.com**) and Google Scholar (**scholar.google.com**) offer more ways to find sources. For each site, enter your topic and key words from your questions in the search box. Google Scholar is especially useful for finding peer-reviewed articles in professional journals.

Following are more encyclopedias and search engines to check:

- Dogpile (**www.dogpile.com**)
- Pandia Metasearch (**www.pandia.com/articles/metasearch**)
- Mamma (**www.mamma.com**)
- **www.bartleby.com**
- **www.encyclopedia.com**
- **www.Answers.com**
- **www.About.com**

You might find that certain sources appear over and over again in the results that you get from your searches. These are important sources for you to find and read for yourself.

REFINE YOUR TOPIC

A common problem at this point is to discover that your topic is too broad. Fortunately, there are several ways to narrow it down.

One option is DMOZ (**www.dmoz.org**). What you'll see first is a page with a list of major categories. Click on any of these to find narrower topics (subcategories). Enter some key words in the search box to narrow the topic even more. Clusty (**www.clusty.com**) works in a similar way.

REFINE YOUR QUESTIONS

As you skim these sites and the other sources, review the main question and supporting questions that you asked at the beginning of your research. You might choose to drop some of those questions, reword them, or ask new questions based on what you've discovered so far.

REFINE YOUR KEY WORDS

One crucial skill for information literacy is using key words. Your choice of key words determines the quality of results that you get from search engines. For better search results:

Use specific key words. Entering *firefox* or *safari* will give you more focused results than entering *web browser*. *Reading strategies* or *note-taking strategies* will get more specific results than *study strategies*. Do not type in your whole research question as a sentence. The search engine will look for each word and give you a lot of useless results.

Use unique key words. Whenever possible, use proper names. Enter *Beatles* or *Radiohead* rather than *British rock bands*. If you're looking for nearby restaurants, enter *restaurant* and your zip code rather than the name of your city.

Use quotation marks if you're looking for certain words in a certain order. *"Audacity of hope"* will return a list of pages with that exact phrase.

Discover the pleasures of emerging insights and sudden inspiration. You just might get hooked on the adventure of information literacy.

Search within a site. If you're looking only for articles about college tuition from the *New York Times*, then add *new york times* or *nytimes.com* to the search box.

Remember to think of synonyms. For example, "hypertension" is often called "high blood pressure."

When you're not sure of a key word, add a wild card character. In most search engines, the wild card character is the asterisk (*). If you're looking for the title of a film directed by Clint Eastwood and just can't remember the name, enter *clint eastwood directed *.

Look for more search options. Many search engines also offer advanced search features and explain how to use them. Look for the word *advanced* or *more* on the site's home page, and click on the link. If in doubt about how to use your library's search engines, ask a librarian for help.

DIG DEEPER INTO THE WEB

When people talk about the Internet, they usually mean the *free Web*—sites that anyone can access through popular search engines. However, this adds up to less than half of all websites. Other sites are created by organizations for their employees, partners, or subscribers rather than the general public. Together these make up the *deep Web*.

The deep Web offers several benefits. Here you will find articles written by recognized experts for an audience of scholars. Plus, deep websites often have their own search engines, such as:

- H. W. Wilson (**www.hwwilson.com**)
- Highbeam Research (**https://www.highbeam.com**)
- NewsBank (**www.newsbank.com**)
- Wolters Kluwer UpToDate (**www.uptodate.com**)

To access such sources, go to your school or community library. It will probably have access to a number of deep websites.

GET TO KNOW YOUR LIBRARY

Remember that many published materials are available in print as well as online. This is another reason to visit a library. Start by talking to a reference librarian. Tell this person about the questions you want to answer, and ask for good sources of information. Also visit your library's website.

Remember that libraries—from the smallest one in your hometown to the Smithsonian in Washington, D.C.—consist of just three basic elements:

- **Catalogs**—databases that list all of the library's accessible sources.
- **Collections**—materials, such as periodicals (magazines, journals, and newspapers), books, pamphlets, ebooks, audiobooks, and materials available from other libraries via interlibrary loan.
- **Computer resources**—online databases that allow you to look at full-text articles from magazines, journals, and newspapers.

TALK TO PEOPLE

Making direct contact with people can offer a welcome relief from hours of solitary research time and give you valuable hands-on involvement. Your initial research will uncover the names of experts on your chosen topic. Consider doing an interview with one of these people—in person, over the phone, or via email.

To get the most from interviews:

- Schedule a specific time for the interview— and a specific place, if you're meeting the expert in person. Agree on the length of the interview in advance and work within that time frame.
- Enter the interview with a short list of questions to ask. Allow time for additional questions that occur to you during the interview.
- If you want to record the interview, ask for permission in advance. When talking to people who don't want to be recorded, be prepared to take handwritten notes.
- Ask experts for permission to quote their comments.
- Be courteous before, during, and after the interview; thank the person for taking time to talk with you.
- End the interview at your agreed-on time.
- Follow up on interviews with a thank-you note.
- Be sure to cite your interview as a source for your research.

EVALUATE INFORMATION

Some students assume that anything that's published in print or on the Internet is true. Unfortunately, that's not the case. Some sources of information are more reliable than others, and some published information is misleading or mistaken.

Before evaluating any source of information, make sure that you understand what it says. Use the techniques of Muscle Reading to comprehend an author's message. Then think critically about the information. Be sure to look for the following:

- **Publication date**. If your topic is time-sensitive, then set some guidelines about how current you want your sources to be—for example, that they were published during the last five years.
- **Credibility.** Scan the source for biographical information about the author. Look for educational degrees, training, and work experience that qualify this person to publish on the topic of your research.
- **Bias.** Determine what the website or other source is "selling"—the product, service, or point of view it promotes. Political affiliations or funding sources might color the author's point of view. For instance, you can predict that a pamphlet on gun control policies that's printed with funding from the National Rifle Association will promote certain points of view. Round out your research with other sources on the topic.

EVALUATE INTERNET SOURCES WITH EXTRA CARE

Ask the following questions:

Who pays for the site? Carefully check information from an organization that sells advertising. Look for an "About This Site" link—a clue to sources of funding. You want to avoid sources that may pose a conflict of interest.

Who runs the site? Look for a clear description of the person or organization responsible for the content. If the sponsoring person or organization did not create the site's content, then find out who did.

How is the site's content selected? Look for a link that lists members of an editorial board or other qualified reviewers.

Does the site support claims with evidence?
Credible sites base their editorial stands on expert opinion and facts from scientific studies. If you find grandiose claims supported only by testimonials, beware. When something sounds too good to be true, it probably is.

Does the site link to other sites? Think critically about these sites as well.

How can readers connect with the site?
Look for a way to contact the site's publisher with questions and comments. See whether you can find a physical address, email address, and phone number. Sites that conceal this information might conceal other facts. Also inspect reader comments on the site to see whether a variety of opinions are expressed.

Many websites from government agencies and nonprofit organizations have strict and clearly stated editorial policies. These are often good places to start your research.

DISTINGUISH BETWEEN PRIMARY AND SECONDARY SOURCES

In addition, distinguish between primary and secondary sources. *Primary sources* can lead to information treasures. Primary sources are firsthand materials—personal journals, letters, speeches, government documents, scientific experiments, field observations, interviews with recognized experts, archeological digs, artifacts, and original works of art. Primary sources can also include scholarly publications such as the *New England Journal of Medicine*.

Secondary sources summarize, explain, and comment on primary sources. Examples are popular magazines such as *Time* and *Newsweek* and general reference works such as *Encyclopedia Britannica*. Secondary sources are useful places to start your research. Use them to get an overview of your topic. Depending on the assignment, these may be all you need for informal research.

TAKE NOTES AND REFLECT ON THEM

Take careful notes on your sources. Remember to keep a list of all your sources of information and avoid plagiarism. Be prepared to cite your sources in footnotes or endnotes, and a bibliography.

Also make time to digest all the information you gather. Ask yourself:

- Do I have answers to my main question?
- Do I have answers to my supporting questions?
- What are the main ideas from my sources?
- Do I have personal experiences that can help me answer these questions?
- If a television talk show host asked me these questions, how would I answer?
- On what points do my sources agree?
- On what points do my sources disagree?
- Do I have statistics and other facts that I can use to support my ideas?
- What new questions do I have?

The beauty of these questions is that they stimulate your thinking. Discover the pleasures of emerging insights and sudden inspiration. You just might get hooked on the adventure of information literacy. ✂

Courtesy of Matias Manzano

Matias Manzano }

Taught at Jose de Diego Middle School and International Studies Charter High School, now candidate for a J.D. degree, Benjamin N. Cardozo School of Law.

I struggled early on with reading. In fourth grade, I scored a 23 percent on a reading proficiency assessment. Many people would have written me off at that young age—a poor, Latino, illegal immigrant who ended up in New York and was destined to fail. I remember thinking in elementary school that it wasn't fair that the other kids spoke English at home and for that reason, they were better readers than I was. There were times when I would try to read something, and the words would float around the page as if they didn't want to be understood.

I had a teacher in fifth grade, Ms. Leventhaul, who really made me want to improve my reading. She was inspirational. There was something about her demeanor, the way that she carried herself, which was both intimidating and motivational at the same time. She treated me as if she knew that I could achieve greatness.

My brother also challenged me to just read more books. I read at least 20 R. L. Stine *Goosebumps* books in a competition that I had one year with him. We used to have conversations after reading the books. I didn't realize it at the time, but having those conversations allowed me to develop reading skills like making comparisons, identifying main ideas, describing settings, and identifying foreshadowing. By sixth grade, I had scored a 99 percent on the reading assessment.

After high school, I decided to follow in my brother's footsteps and attend Stony Brook University in New York. Money was tight. We would roam around the college, staying with different friends who allowed us to sleep on their floor for the night. I guess I was, in a way, homeless.

Toward the end of my sophomore year, the letter came that our application for legal residence was accepted. I was able to receive financial aid. I no longer had to work 40 hours a week to pay for tuition. I could focus my energy on academics.

The reading skills that I started developing in elementary school became the foundation for my success in college. As a history major and Latin American Caribbean studies minor, I found that my assignments were based on reading scholarly journals and books. My vocabulary improved exponentially. I learned to read entire books in just a few hours.

I can tell you first-hand what the research says is true: The greatest factor impacting the education of our nation's poorest children is the quality of the teacher that they get. All of my students have talents. All of my students have a spark. I joined Teach for America and the staff at Jose De Diego Middle School in Miami because I know that the children living in poverty can achieve at the highest rates.

If I had taken certain tests in Florida when I was in fourth grade, the state would have projected me as a future prison inmate. My apologies to the statisticians who use elementary student achievement scores to predict future prison needs. Soon I will finish my master's degree in educational leadership. I am driven by a desire to be the best and to achieve greatness in all aspects of my life, because I believe that no task is insurmountable.

Matias Manzano *demonstrates the master student quality of being self-directed. You can be self-directed by focusing your energy on what matters most to you.*

QUIZ

Chapter 4

1. The Power Process: "Notice your pictures and let them go" states that mental pictures are useless.
   a. True
   b. False

2. Muscle Reading is designed to:
   a. Ensure that you spend more time on your reading assignments
   b. Help you relax so that reading will eventually feel easy and effortless
   c. Increase your energy and skill as a reader
   d. All of the answer choices

3. You must complete all the steps of Muscle Reading to get the most out of any reading assignment.
   a. True
   b. False

4. The steps in Phase 1 of Muscle Reading take place:
   a. Before you read
   b. While you read
   c. After you read

5. The Corson technique includes:
   a. Asking yourself: What exactly do I *not* understand?
   b. Locating the first sentence, paragraph, or page in a reading assignment that confuses you
   c. Spending 15 minutes to overcome your confusion
   d. Keeping a record of what you do to overcome your confusion
   e. All of the answer choices

6. According to the text, effective alternatives to "speed reading" include:
   a. Becoming a flexible reader
   b. Psuedo-skimming
   c. Reading widely
   d. Reading wisely
   e. All of the answer choices

7. To get the most benefit from marking a book, underline at least 33 percent of the text.
   a. True
   b. False

8. The primacy-recency effect suggests that we most easily remember:
   a. The first items in any presentation
   b. The middle items in any presentation
   c. The last items in any presentation
   d. Both the first and last items in any presentation

9. The part of a word with its core meaning is the:
   a. Root
   b. Prefix
   c. Suffix

10. Information literacy is a skill that includes:
    a. Finding information from appropriate sources
    b. Evaluating information
    c. Organizing information
    d. Using information to achieve a purpose
    e. All of the above

SKILLS
snapshot

After studying this chapter, you might want to make some changes in the way you read. First, take a snapshot of your current reading skills. Then set a goal to adopt a habit that will take your reading skills to a new level. Complete the following sentences.

Discovery

My score on the Reading section of the Discovery Wheel was . . .

If someone asked me how well I keep up with my assigned reading, I would say that . . .

To get the most out of a long reading assignment, I start by . . .

When I don't understand something that I've read, I overcome confusion by . . .

Intention

I'll know that I've reached a new level of mastery with reading when . . .

The idea from this chapter that could make the biggest difference in my experience of reading is . . .

Action

The new reading habit that I plan to adopt is . . .

This new habit can help me succeed in the workplace by . . .

At the end of this course, I would like my *Reading* score on the Discovery Wheel to be . . .

A. and I. Kruk/Shutterstock.com

Notes

what is included . . .

170   Power Process: I create it all

171   The note-taking process flows

172   Observe: The note-taking process flows

176   Record: The note-taking process flows

181   Review: The note-taking process flows

184   Turn PowerPoints into powerful notes

185   When your instructor talks quickly

187   Taking notes while reading

190   Visualize ideas with concept maps

192   Taking effective notes for online coursework

196   Note taking 2.0

198   Master Student Profile: Teresa Amabile

why

Note taking helps you remember information and influences how well you do on tests.

how

Recall a recent incident in which you had difficulty taking notes. Perhaps you were listening to an instructor who talked fast, or you got confused and stopped taking notes altogether. Then preview this chapter to find at least three strategies that you can use right away to help you take better notes.

what if...

I could take notes that remain informative and useful for weeks, months, or even years to come?

do you have a minute?

Look at today's notes from a course that you're taking this term. Take a minute to do a quick edit. For instance, fix passages that are illegible. Label the notes with the date and the name of the class. If you have a few seconds to spare, then number the pages.

I create it all

This article describes a powerful tool for times of trouble. In a crisis, "I create it all" can lead the way to solutions. The main point of this Power Process is to treat experiences, events, and circumstances in your life *as if* you created them.

"I create it all" is one of the most unusual and bizarre suggestions in this book. It certainly is not a belief. Use it when it works. Don't when it doesn't. Keeping that in mind, consider how powerful this Power Process can be. It is really about the difference between two distinct positions in life: being a victim or being responsible.

A victim of circumstances is controlled by outside forces. We've all felt like victims at one time or another. Sometimes we felt helpless.

In contrast, we can take responsibility. Responsibility is "response-ability"—the ability to choose a *response* to any event. You can choose your *response* to any event, even when the event itself is beyond your control.

Many students approach grades from the position of being victims. When the student who sees the world this way gets an F, she reacts probably like this:

"Another F! That teacher couldn't teach her way out of a wet paper bag. She can't teach English for anything. There's no way to take notes in that class. And that textbook—what a bore!"

The problem with this viewpoint is that in looking for excuses, the student is robbing herself of the power to get any grade other than an F. She's giving all of her power to a bad teacher and a boring textbook.

There is another way, called *taking responsibility*. You can recognize that you choose your grades by choosing your actions. Then you are the source, rather than the result, of the grades you get. The student who got an F could react like this:

"Another F! Oh, shoot! Well, hmmm . . . What did I do to create it?"

Now, that's power. By asking, "How did I contribute to this outcome?" you are no longer the victim. This student might continue by saying, "Well, let's see. I didn't review my notes after class. That might have done it." Or, "I went out with my friends the night before the test. Well, that probably helped me fulfill some of the requirements for getting an F."

The point is this: When the F is the result of your friends, the book, or the teacher, you probably can't do anything about it. However, if you *chose* the F, you can choose a different grade next time. You are in charge. ◢

Mark Chen/E+/Getty Images

iStockphoto.com/Chad McDermott/cmcderm1

The note-taking
PROCESS FLOWS

One way to understand note taking is to realize that taking notes is just one part of the process. Effective note taking consists of three parts: observing, recording, and reviewing.

First, you observe an "event." This can be a statement by an instructor, a lab experiment, a slide show of an artist's works, or a chapter of required reading.

Then you record your observations of that event. That is, you "take notes." These can be recorded in a variety of formats—paragraphs, outlines, diagrams, and more.

Finally, you review what you have recorded. You memorize, reflect, apply, and rehearse what you're learning. This step lifts ideas off the page and turns them into a working part of your mind.

Each part of the note-taking process is essential, and each depends on the others. Your observations determine what you record. What you record determines what you review. And the quality of your review can determine how effective your next observations will be. If you review your notes on the Sino-Japanese War of 1894, for example, the next day's lecture on the Boxer Rebellion of 1900 will make more sense.

Legible and speedy handwriting is also useful in taking notes. Knowledge of outlining is handy too. A nifty pen, a new notebook, and a laptop computer are all great note-taking devices.

And they're all worthless—unless you participate as an energetic observer *in* class and regularly review your notes *after* class. If you take those two steps, you can turn even the most disorganized chicken scratches into a powerful tool.

This is a well-researched aspect of student success in higher education. Study after study

points to the benefits of taking notes. The value is added in two ways. First, you create a set of materials that refreshes your memory and helps you prepare for tests. Second, taking notes prompts you to listen effectively during class. You translate new ideas into your own words and images. You impose a personal and meaningful structure on what you see, read, and hear. You move from passive observer to active participant.[1] It's not that you take notes so that you can learn from them later. Instead, you learn *while* taking notes.

Computer technology takes traditional note taking to a whole new level. You can capture key notes with word-processing, outlining, database, and publishing software. Your notes become living documents that you can search, bookmark, tag, and archive like other digital files.

In short, note taking is a "brain-friendly" activity. Taking notes leads you to actively encode the material in your own words and images—an effective strategy for moving new information into long-term memory.

Sometimes note taking looks like a passive affair, especially in large lecture classes. One person at the front of the room does most of the talking. Everyone else is seated and silent, taking notes. The lecturer seems to be doing all of the work.

Don't be deceived.

Look more closely. You'll see some students taking notes in a way that radiates energy. They're awake and alert, poised on the edge of their seats. They're writing—a physical activity that expresses mental engagement. These students listen for levels of ideas and information, make choices about what to record, and compile materials to review.

In higher education, you might spend hundreds of hours taking notes. Making them more effective is a direct investment in your success.

Think of your notes as a textbook that *you* create—one that's more current and more in tune with your learning preferences than any textbook you could buy. ✖

OBSERVE

The note-taking process flows

Sherlock Holmes, a fictional master detective and student of the obvious, could track down a villain by observing the fold of his scarf and the mud on his shoes. In real life, a doctor can save a life by observing a mole—one a patient has always had—that undergoes a rapid change.

Lucky Business/Shutterstock.com

An accountant can save a client thousands of dollars by observing the details of a spreadsheet. A student can save hours of study time by observing that she gets twice as much done at a particular time of day.

Keen observers see facts and relationships. They know ways to focus their attention on the details and then tap their creative energy to discover patterns.

Observation starts with preparation. Arrive early, and then put your brain in gear by reviewing your notes from the previous class. Scan your reading assignment. Look at the sections you have underlined or highlighted. Review assigned problems and exercises. Note questions you intend to ask.

To further sharpen your classroom observation skills, experiment with the following techniques, and continue to use those that you find most valuable. Many of these strategies can be adapted to the notes you take while reading.

SET THE STAGE

Complete outside assignments. Nothing is more discouraging (or boring) than sitting through a lecture about the relationship of Le Chatelier's principle to the principle of kinetics if you've never heard of Henri Louis Le Chatelier or kinetics. The more familiar you are with a subject, the more easily you can absorb important information during class lectures. Instructors usually assume that students complete assignments, and they construct their lectures accordingly.

Bring the right materials. A good pen does not make you a good observer, but the lack of a pen or notebook can be distracting enough to take the fine edge off your concentration. Make sure you have a pen, pencil, notebook, or any other materials you need. Bring your textbook to class, especially if the lectures relate closely to the text.

If you are consistently unprepared for a class, that might be a message about your intentions concerning the course. Find out if it is. The next time you're in a frantic scramble to borrow pen and paper 37 seconds before the class begins, notice the cost. Use the borrowed pen and paper to write a Discovery Statement about your lack of preparation. Consider whether you intend to be successful in the course.

Sit front and center. Students who get as close as possible to the front and center of the classroom often do better on tests for several reasons. The closer you sit to the lecturer, the harder it is to fall asleep. The closer you sit to the front, the fewer interesting or distracting classmates are situated between you and the instructor. Material on the board is easier to read from up front. Also, the instructor can see you more easily when you have a question.

Instructors are usually not trained to perform. Some can project their energy to a large audience, but some cannot. A professor who sounds boring from the back of the room might sound more interesting up close.

Sitting up front enables you to become a constructive force in the classroom. By returning the positive energy that an engaged teacher gives out, you can reinforce the teacher's enthusiasm and enhance your experience of the class.

In addition, sound waves from the human voice begin to degrade at a distance of 8 to 12 feet. If you sit more than 15 feet from the speaker, your ability to hear and take effective notes might be compromised. Get close to the source of the sound. Get close to the energy.

Sitting close to the front is a way to commit yourself to getting what you want out of school. One reason students gravitate to the back of the classroom is that they think the instructor is less likely to call on them. Sitting in back can signal a lack of commitment. When you sit up front, you are declaring your willingness to take a risk and participate.

Clarify your intentions. Take a 3 × 5 card to class with you. On that card, write a short Intention Statement about what you plan to get from the class. Describe your intended level of participation or the quality of attention you will bring to the subject. Be specific. If you found your previous class notes to be inadequate, write down what you intend to do to make your notes from this class session more useful.

WHAT TO DO WHEN YOU MISS A CLASS

For most courses, you'll benefit by attending every class session. This allows you to observe and actively participate. If you miss a class, then catch up as quickly as possible. Find additional ways to observe class content.

Clarify policies on missed classes. On the first day of classes, find out about your instructors' policies on absences. See whether you will be allowed to make up assignments, quizzes, and tests. Also inquire about doing extra-credit assignments. If you know in advance that you'll miss some classes, let your instructor know as soon as possible. Create a plan for staying on top of your coursework.

Contact a classmate. Early in the semester, identify a student in each class who seems responsible and dependable. Exchange email addresses and phone numbers. If you know you won't be in class, contact this student ahead of time. When you notice that your classmate is absent, pick up extra copies of handouts, make assignment lists, and offer copies of your notes.

Contact your instructor. If you miss a class, email or call your instructor, or put a note in his mailbox. Ask whether he has another section of the same course that you can attend so you won't miss the lecture information. Also ask about getting handouts you might need before the next class meeting.

Consider technology. If there is a website for your class, check it for assignments and handouts you missed. Also, course management software, such as BlackBoard, might allow you to stay in contact with your instructor and fellow students during your absence.

"BE HERE NOW" IN CLASS

Accept your wandering mind. Focusing your attention is useful when your head soars into the clouds. Don't fight daydreaming, however. When you notice your mind wandering during class, look at this as an opportunity to refocus your attention. If thermodynamics is losing out to beach parties, let go of the beach.

Notice your writing. When you discover yourself slipping into a fantasyland, feel the weight of your pen in your hand. Notice how your notes look. Paying attention to the act of writing can bring you back to the here and now.

You also can use writing in a more direct way to clear your mind of distracting thoughts. Pause for a few seconds to write those thoughts down. If you're distracted by thoughts of errands you need to run after class, list them on a 3 × 5 card and stick it in your pocket. Or simply put a symbol, such as an arrow or asterisk, in your notes to mark the places where your mind started to wander. Once your distractions are out of your mind and safely stored on paper, you can gently return your attention to taking notes.

Be with the instructor. In your mind, put yourself right up front with the instructor. Imagine that you and the instructor are the only ones in the room and that the lecture is a personal conversation between the two of you. Pay attention to the instructor's body language and facial expressions. Look the instructor in the eye.

Remember that the power of this suggestion is immediately reduced by digital distractions—web surfing, email checking, or text messaging. Taking notes is a way to stay focused. The physical act of taking notes signals your mind to stay in the same room as the instructor.

Notice your environment. When you become aware of yourself daydreaming, bring yourself back to class by paying attention to the temperature in the room, the feel of your chair, or the quality of light coming through the window. Run your hand along the surface of your desk. Listen to the chalk on the blackboard or the sound of the teacher's voice. Be in that environment. Once your attention is back in the room, you can focus on what's happening in class.

Postpone debate. When you hear something you disagree with, note your disagreement and let it go. Don't allow your internal dialogue to drown out subsequent material. If your disagreement is persistent and strong, make note of it and then move on. Internal debate can prevent you from absorbing new information. It's okay to absorb information you don't agree with. Just absorb it with the mental tag "My instructor says . . . , but I don't agree with it."

Let go of judgments about lecture styles. Human beings are judgment machines. We evaluate everything, especially other people. If another person's eyebrows are too close together (or too far apart), if she walks a certain way or speaks with an unusual accent, we in-

stantly make up a story about her. We do this so quickly that the process is usually not a conscious one.

Don't let your attitude about an instructor's lecture style, habits, or appearance get in the way of your education. You can decrease the power of your judgments if you pay attention to them and let them go.

You can even let go of judgments about rambling, unorganized lectures. Turn them to your advantage. Take the initiative and organize the material yourself. While taking notes, separate the key points from the examples and supporting evidence. Note the places where you got confused, and make a list of questions to ask.

Participate in class activities. Ask questions. Volunteer for demonstrations. Join in class discussions. Be willing to take a risk or look foolish if that's what it takes for you to learn. Chances are, the question you think is dumb is also on the minds of several of your classmates.

Relate the class to your goals. If you have trouble staying awake in a particular class, write at the top of your notes how that class relates to a specific goal. Identify the reward or payoff for reaching that goal.

Think critically about what you hear. This suggestion might seem contrary to the previously mentioned technique "postpone debate." It's not. You might choose not to think critically about the instructor's ideas during the lecture. That's fine. Do it later, as you review and edit your notes. This is the time to list questions or write down your agreements and disagreements.

WATCH FOR CLUES ABOUT IMPORTANT MATERIAL

Be alert to repetition. When an instructor repeats a phrase or an idea, make a note of it. Repetition is a signal that the instuctor thinks the information is important.

Listen for introductory, concluding, and transition words and phrases. Introductory, concluding, and transition words and phrases include phrases such as *the following three factors, in conclusion, the most important consideration, in addition to,* and *on the other hand.* These phrases and others signal relationships, definitions, new subjects, conclusions, cause and effect, and examples. They reveal the structure of the lecture. You can use these phrases to organize your notes.

Watch the board or PowerPoint presentation. If an instructor takes the time to write something down on the board or show a PowerPoint presentation, consider the material to be important. Copy all equations, names, places, dates, statistics, and definitions. If your instructor presents pictures, graphics, or tables, pay special attention. Ask for copies of these, recreate them, or summarize their key points in your notes.

Watch the instructor's eyes. If an instructor glances at her notes and then makes a point, it is probably a signal that the information is especially important. Anything she reads from her notes is a potential test question.

Highlight the obvious clues. Instructors often hint strongly or tell students point-blank that certain information is likely to appear on an exam. Make stars or other special marks in your notes next to this information. Instructors are not trying to hide what's important.

Notice the instructor's interest level. If the instructor is excited about a topic, it is more likely to appear on an exam. Pay attention when she seems more animated than usual. ✂

DISCOVERY/INTENTION STATEMENT — journal entry **12**

Create more value from lectures

Think back on the last few lectures you have attended. How do you currently observe (listen to) lectures? What specific behaviors do you have as you sit and listen? Do you listen more closely in some classes than others? Briefly describe your responses.

I discovered that I . . .

Now create an Intention Statement about any changes you want to make in the way you respond to lectures.

I intend to . . .

RECORD

The note-taking process flows

The format and structure of your notes are more important than how fast you write or how elegant your handwriting is. The following techniques can improve the effectiveness of your notes.

GENERAL TECHNIQUES FOR NOTE TAKING

Use key words. An easy way to sort the extraneous material from the important points is to take notes using key words. Key words or phrases contain the essence of communication. They include these:

- Concepts, technical terms, names, and numbers
- Linking words, including words that describe action, relationship, and degree (e.g., *most, least,* and *faster*)

Key words evoke images and associations with other words and ideas. They trigger your memory. That characteristic makes them powerful review tools. One key word can initiate the recall of a whole cluster of ideas. A few key words can form a chain from which you can reconstruct an entire lecture.

To see how key words work, take yourself to an imaginary classroom. You are now in the middle of an anatomy lecture. Picture what the room looks like, what it feels like, how it smells. You hear the instructor say:

Okay, what happens when we look directly over our heads and see a piano falling out of the sky? How do we take that signal and translate it into the action of getting out of the way? The first thing that happens is that a stimulus is generated in the neurons—receptor neurons—of the eye. Light reflected from the piano reaches our eyes. In other words, we see the piano.

The receptor neurons in the eye transmit that sensory signal—the sight of the piano—

Dragon Images/Shutterstock.com

to the body's nervous system. That's all they can do—pass on information. So we've got a sensory signal coming into the nervous system. But the neurons that initiate movement in our legs are effector neurons. The information from the sensory neurons must be transmitted to effector neurons, or we will get squashed by the piano. There must be some kind of interconnection between receptor and effector neurons. What happens between the two? What is the connection?

Key words you might note in this example include *stimulus, generated, receptor neurons, transmit, sensory signals, nervous system, effector neurons,* and *connection.* You can reduce the instructor's 163 words to these 12 key words. With a few transitional words, your notes might look like this:

Stimulus (piano) generated in receptor neurons (eye)
↓
Sensory signals transmitted by nervous system to effector neurons (legs)

What connects receptor to effector?

Note the last key word of the lecture: *connection.* This word is part of the instructor's question and leads to the next point in the lecture. Be on the lookout for questions like this. They can help you organize your notes and are often clues for test questions.

Use pictures and diagrams. Make relationships visual. Copy all diagrams from the board, and invent your own. A drawing of a piano falling on someone who is looking up, for example, might be used to demonstrate the relationship of receptor neurons to effector neurons. Label the eyes "receptor" and the feet "effector." This picture implies that the sight of the piano must be translated into a motor response. By connecting the explanation of the process with the unusual picture of the piano falling, you can link the elements of the process together.

Write notes in paragraphs. When it is difficult to follow the organization of a lecture or put information into outline form, create a series of informal paragraphs. These paragraphs should contain few complete sentences. Reserve complete sentences for precise definitions, direct quotations, and important points that the instructor emphasizes by repetition or other signals—such as the phrase "This is an important point."

Copy material from the board and a Power-Point presentation. Record key formulas, diagrams, and problems that the teacher presents on the board or in a PowerPoint presentation. Copy dates, numbers, names, places, and other facts. You can even use your own signal or code to flag important material.

Use a three-ring binder. Three-ring binders have several advantages over other kinds of notebooks. First, pages can be removed and spread out when you review. This way, you can get the whole picture of a lecture. Second, the three-ring-binder format allows you to insert handouts right into your notes. Third, you can insert your own out-of-class notes in the correct order.

Use only one side of a piece of paper. When you use one side of a page, you can review and organize all your notes by spreading them out side by side. Most students find the benefit well worth the cost of the paper. Perhaps you're concerned about the environmental impact of consuming more paper. If so, you can use the blank side of old notes and use recycled paper.

Use 3 × 5 cards. As an alternative to using notebook paper, use 3 × 5 cards to take lecture notes. Copy each new concept onto a separate 3 × 5 card.

Keep your own thoughts separate. For the most part, avoid making editorial comments in your lecture notes. The danger is that when you return to your notes, you might mistake your own ideas for those of the instructor. If you want to make a comment, clearly label it as your own.

Use an "I'm lost" signal. No matter how attentive and alert you are, you might get lost and confused in a lecture. If it is inappropriate to ask a question, record in your notes that you were lost. Invent your own signal—for example, a circled question mark. When you write down your code for "I'm lost," leave space for the explanation or clarification that you will get later. The space will also be a signal that you missed something. Later, you can speak to your instructor or ask to see a fellow student's notes.

Label, number, and date all notes. Develop the habit of labeling and dating your notes at the beginning of each class. Number the page too. Sometimes the sequence of material in a lecture is important. Write your name, phone number, and email in each notebook in case you lose it.

Leave blank space. Notes tightly crammed into every corner of the page are hard to read and difficult to use for review. Give your eyes a break by leaving plenty of space. Later, when you review, you can use the blank spaces in your notes to clarify points, write questions, or add other material.

Take notes in different colors. You can use colors as highly visible organizers. For example, you can signal important points with red. Or use one color of ink for notes about the text and another color for lecture notes.

Use graphic signals. The following ideas can be used with any note-taking format:

- Use brackets, parentheses, circles, and squares to group information that belongs together.
- Use stars, arrows, and underlining to indicate important points. Flag the most important points with double stars, double arrows, or double underlines.
- Use arrows and connecting lines to link related groups.
- Use equal signs and greater-than and less-than signs to indicate compared quantities.

To avoid creating confusion with graphic symbols, use them carefully and consistently. Write a master key, or legend, of your symbols in the front of your notebooks; an example is shown here.

[ ], ( ), ○, ☐	=	info that belongs together
*, ↘, —	=	important
**, ↘↘, ▭, !!!	=	extra important
>	=	greater than
<	=	less than
=	=	equal to
→	=	leads to, becomes
ex: school → job → money		
?	=	huh?, lost, question
??	=	big trouble, clear up immediately

Use recorders effectively. Some students record lectures with audio or digital recorders, but there are persuasive arguments against doing so. When you record a lecture, there is a strong temptation to daydream. After all, you can always listen to the lecture again later on. Unfortunately, if you let the recorder do all of the work, you are skipping a valuable part of the learning process.

There are other potential problems as well. Listening to recorded lectures can take a lot of time—more time than reviewing written notes. Recorders can't answer the questions you didn't ask in class. Also, recording devices malfunc-

tion. In fact, the unscientific Hypothesis of Recording Glitches states that the tendency of recorders to malfunction is directly proportional to the importance of the material.

With those warnings in mind, you can use a recorder effectively if you choose. For example, you can use recordings as backups to written notes. Turn the recorder on; then take notes as if it weren't there. Recordings can be especially useful if an instructor speaks fast.

Note: Before you hit the "record" button, check with your instructor. Some prefer not to be recorded.

THE CORNELL METHOD

A note-taking system that has worked for students around the world is the *Cornell method*.[2] Originally developed by Walter Pauk at Cornell University during the 1950s, this approach continues to be taught across the United States and in other countries as well.

The cornerstone of this method is what Pauk calls the *cue column*—a wide margin on the left-hand side of the paper. The cue column is the key to the Cornell method's many benefits. Here's how to use it.

Format your paper. On each sheet of your notepaper, draw a vertical line, top to bottom, about 2 inches from the left edge of the paper. This line creates the cue column—the space to the left of the line. You can also find websites that allow you to print out pages in this format. Just do an Internet search using the key words *Cornell method pdf*.

Take notes, leaving the cue column blank. As you read an assignment or listen to a lecture, take notes on the right-hand side of the paper. Fill up this column with sentences, paragraphs, outlines, charts, or drawings. Do not write in the cue column. You'll use this space later, as you do the next steps.

Condense your notes in the cue column. Think of the notes you took on the right-hand side of the paper as a set of answers. In the cue column, list potential test questions that correspond to your notes. Write one question for each major term or point.

As an alternative to questions, you can list key words from your notes. Yet another option is to pretend that your notes are a series of articles on different topics. In the cue column, write a newspaper-style headline for each "article." In any case, be brief. If you cram the cue column full of words, you defeat its purpose—to reduce the number and length of your notes.

Write a summary. Pauk recommends that you reduce your notes even more by writing a brief summary at the bottom of each page. This step offers you another way to engage actively with the material.

Use the cue column to recite. Cover the right-hand side of your notes with a blank sheet of paper. Leave only the cue column showing. Then look at each item you wrote in the cue column and talk about it. If you wrote questions, answer each question. If you wrote key words, define each word and talk about why it's important. If you wrote headlines in the cue column, explain what each one means and offer supporting details. After reciting, uncover your notes and look for any important points you missed.

CUE COLUMN	NOTES
What are the 3 phases of Muscle Reading?	Phase 1: Before You Read Phase 2: While You Read Phase 3: After You Read
What are the steps in Phase 1?	1. Preview 2. Outline 3. Question
What are the steps in Phase 2?	4. Focus 5. Flag answers
What are the steps in Phase 3?	6. Recite 7. Review 8. Review Again
What's an acronym for Muscle Reading?	Pry Out Questions Focus Flag answers Recite Review Review again

SUMMARY: Muscle Reading includes 3 phases: before, during, and after reading. Each phase includes specific steps. Use the acronym to recall all the steps.

MIND MAPPING

Mind mapping, a system developed by Tony Buzan,[3] can be used in conjunction with the Cornell method to take notes. In some circumstances, you might want to use mind maps exclusively.

To understand mind maps, first review the features of traditional note taking. Outlines divide major topics into minor topics, which in turn are subdivided further. They organize information in a sequential, linear way.

The traditional outline reflects only a limited range of brain function—a point that is often made in discussions about "left-brain" and "right-brain" activities. People often use the term *right brain* when referring to creative, pattern-making, visual, intuitive brain activity. They use the term *left brain* when talking about orderly, logical, step-by-step characteristics of thought. Writing teacher Gabrielle Rico uses another metaphor. She refers to the left-brain mode as our "sign mind" (concerned with words) and the right-brain mode as our "design mind" (concerned with visuals).[4] A mind map uses both kinds of brain functions. Mind maps can contain lists and sequences and show relationships. They can also provide a picture of a subject. They work on both verbal and nonverbal levels.

One benefit of mind maps is that they quickly, vividly, and accurately show the relationships among ideas. Also, mind mapping helps you think from general to specific. By choosing a main topic, you focus first on the big picture, then zero in on subordinate details. And by using only key words, you can condense a large subject into a small area on a mind map. You can review more quickly by looking at the key words on a mind map than by reading notes word for word.

Give yourself plenty of room. To create a mind map, use blank paper that measures at least 11 by 17 inches. If that's not available, turn regular notebook paper on its side so that you can take notes in a horizontal (instead of vertical) format. If you use a computer in class to take notes, consider software that allows you to create digital mind maps that can include graphics, photos, and URL links.

Determine the main concept of the lecture, article, or chapter. As you listen to a lecture or read, figure out the main concept. Write it in the center of the paper and circle it, underline it, or highlight it with color. You can also write the concept in large letters. Record concepts related to the main concept on lines that radiate outward from the center. An alternative is to circle or box in these concepts.

Use key words only. Whenever possible, reduce each concept to a single word per line or circle or box in your mind map. Although this reduction might seem awkward at first, it prompts you to summarize and condense ideas to their essence. That means fewer words for

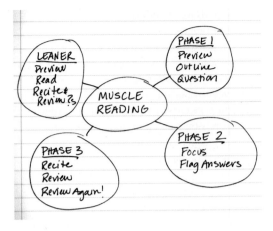

- In the second level of headings, record the key points that relate to each topic in the first-level headings.
- In the third level of headings, record specific facts and details that support or explain each of your second-level headings. Each additional level of subordinate heading supports the ideas in the previous level of heading.

Roman numerals offer one way to illustrate the difference between levels of headings. See the following examples:

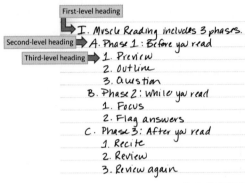

you to write now and fewer to review when it's time to prepare for tests. (Using shorthand symbols and abbreviations can help.) Key words are usually nouns and verbs that communicate the bulk of the speaker's ideas. Choose words that are rich in associations and that can help you recreate the lecture.

Create links. A single mind map doesn't have to include all of the ideas in a lecture, book, or article. Instead, you can link mind maps. For example, draw a mind map that sums up the five key points in a chapter, and then make a separate, more detailed mind map for each of those key points. Within each mind map, include references to the other mind maps. This technique helps explain and reinforce the relationships among many ideas. Some students pin several mind maps next to one another on a bulletin board or tape them to a wall. This allows for a dramatic—and effective—look at the big picture.

OUTLINING

A traditional outline shows the relationships among major points and supporting ideas. One benefit of taking notes in the outline format is that doing so can totally occupy your attention. You are recording ideas and also organizing them. This process can be an advantage if the material has been presented in a disorganized way.

By playing with variations, you can discover the power of outlining to reveal relationships among ideas. Technically, each word, phrase, or sentence that occupies a single line in an outline is called a *heading*. Headings are arranged in different levels:

- In the first, or top, level of headings, note the major topics presented in a lecture or reading assignment.

Distinguish levels with indentations only:

Muscle Reading includes 3 phases
　　Phase 1: Before you read
　　　　Preview

Distinguish levels with bullets and dashes:

— Muscle Reading includes 3 phases
　　• Phase 1: Before you read
　　　　- Preview

Distinguish levels by size:

MUSCLE READING INCLUDES 3 PHASES
Phase 1: Before you read
Preview

COMBINING FORMATS

Feel free to use different note-taking systems for different subjects and to combine formats. Do what works for you.

For example, combine mind maps along with the Cornell method. You can modify the

Cornell format by dividing your notepaper in half. Reserve one-half for mind maps and the other for linear information such as lists, graphs, and outlines, as well as equations, long explanations, and word-for-word definitions. You can incorporate a mind map into your paragraph-style notes whenever you feel one is appropriate. Minds maps are also useful for summarizing notes taken in the Cornell format.

John Sperry, a teacher at Utah Valley State College, developed a note-taking system that can include all of the formats discussed in this article:

- Fill up a three-ring binder with fresh paper. Open your notebook so that you see two blank pages—one on the left and one on the right. Plan to take notes across this entire two-page spread.

- During class or while reading, write your notes only on the left-hand page. Place a large dash next to each main topic or point. If your instructor skips a step or switches topics unexpectedly, just keep writing.

- Later, use the right-hand page to review and elaborate on the notes that you took earlier. This page is for anything you want. For example, add visuals such as mind maps. Write review questions, headlines, possible test questions, summaries, outlines, mnemonics, or analogies that link new concepts to your current knowledge.

- To keep ideas in sequence, place appropriate numbers on top of the dashes in your notes on the left-hand page. Even if concepts are presented out of order during class, they'll still be numbered correctly in your notes. ✖

REVIEW

The note-taking process flows

Think of reviewing as an integral part of note taking rather than an added task. To make new information useful, encode it in a way that connects it to your long-term memory. The key is reviewing.

Absodels/Getty Images

Review class notes promptly—within 24 hours of taking them. Better yet, review them right after class and once again on the same day. This note-taking technique might be the most powerful one you can use. Use it to save hours of review time later in the term.

Many students are surprised that they can remember the content of a lecture in the minutes and hours after class. They are even more surprised by how well they can read the sloppiest of notes at that time.

Unfortunately, short-term memory deteriorates quickly. The good news is that if you review your notes soon enough, you can move that information from short-term to long-term memory. And you can do it in just a few minutes—often 10 minutes or less.

practicing
CRITICAL
THINKING

17

Reflect on your review habits

Respond to the following statements by selecting "Always," "Often," "Sometimes," "Seldom," or "Never" after each.

I review my notes immediately after class.

_____ Always _____ Often _____ Sometimes

_____ Seldom _____ Never

I conduct weekly reviews of my notes.

_____ Always _____ Often _____ Sometimes

_____ Seldom _____ Never

I make summary sheets of my notes.

_____ Always _____ Often _____ Sometimes

_____ Seldom _____ Never

I edit my notes within 24 hours.

_____ Always _____ Often _____ Sometimes

_____ Seldom _____ Never

Before class, I conduct a brief review of the notes I took in the previous class.

_____ Always _____ Often _____ Sometimes

_____ Seldom _____ Never

The sooner you review your notes, the better, especially if the content is difficult. In fact, you can start reviewing during class. When your instructor pauses to set up the overhead display or erase the board, scan your notes. Dot the *i*'s, cross the *t*'s, and write out unclear abbreviations.

Another way to use this technique is to get to your next class as quickly as you can. Then use the four or five minutes before the lecture begins to review the notes you just took in the previous class. If you do not get to your notes immediately after class, you can still benefit by reviewing them later in the day. A review right before you go to sleep can also be valuable.

Think of the day's unreviewed notes as leaky faucets, constantly dripping and losing precious information until you shut them off with a quick review. Remember, it's possible to forget most of the material within 24 hours—unless you review.

Edit your notes. During your first review, fix words that are illegible. Write out abbreviated words that might be unclear to you later. Make sure you can read everything. If you can't read something or don't understand something you *can* read, mark it, and make a note to ask your instructor or another student about it. Check to see that your notes are labeled with the date and class and that the pages are numbered.

Fill in key words in the left-hand column. This task is important if you are to get the full benefit of using the Cornell method. Using the key word principles described earlier in this chapter, go through your notes and write key words or phrases in the left-hand column. These key words will speed up the review process later. As you read your notes, focus on extracting important concepts.

Use your key words as cues to recite. Cover your notes with a blank sheet of paper so that you can see only the key words in the left-hand margin. Take each key word in order, and recite as much as you can about the point. Then uncover your notes and look for any important points you missed.

Conduct short weekly review periods. Once a week, review all of your notes again. These review sessions don't need to take a lot of time. Even a 20-minute weekly review period is valuable. Some students find that a weekend review—say, on Sunday afternoon—helps them stay in continuous touch with the material. Scheduling regular review sessions on your calendar helps develop the habit.

As you review, step back to see the larger picture. In addition to reciting or repeating the material to yourself, ask questions about it: Does this relate to my goals? How does this compare to information I already know, in this field or another? Will I be tested on this material? What will I do with this material? How can I associate it with something that deeply interests me?

Consider typing your notes. Some students type up their handwritten notes on the computer. The argument for doing so is threefold. First, typed notes are easier to read. Second, they take up less space. Third, the process of typing them forces you to review the material.

Another alternative is to bypass handwriting altogether and take notes in class on a laptop. This solution has a potential drawback, though: Computer errors can wipe out your notes files. If you like using this method of taking notes, save your files frequently, and back up your work onto a jump drive, external hard drive, or online backup service.

Create summaries. Mind mapping is an excellent way to summarize large sections of your course notes or reading assignments. Create one map that shows all the main topics you want to remember. Then create another map about each main topic. After drawing your maps, look at your original notes, and fill in anything you missed. This system is fun and quick.

Another option is to create a "cheat sheet." There's only one guideline: Fit all your review notes on a single sheet of paper. Use any note-taking format that you want—mind map, outline, Cornell method, or a combination of all of them. The beauty of this technique is that it forces you to pick out main ideas and key details. There's not enough room for anything else!

If you're feeling adventurous, create your cheat sheet on a single index card. Start with the larger sizes (5 × 7 or 4 × 6) and then work down to a 3 × 5 card.

Some instructors might let you use a summary sheet during an exam. But even if you can't use it, you'll benefit from creating one while you study for the test. Summarizing is a powerful way to review.

Reducing your notes to summaries is a challenging task. Remember that you can do it in stages. Walter Pauk, creator of the Cornell method for note taking, suggests the following process. He calls it the *silver dollar system*:

1. Read through your notes while looking for important ideas. In the margin next to these ideas, write the letter *S*.

2. Next, read through only the notes that you marked with *S*'s. Some of these will be more important than others. Draw a vertical line through *S*'s that are next to those more important notes ($).

3. Finally, read only the notes marked with *$*'s. Mark the most important of these with another vertical line through the S ($).

In short, you are ranking your notes into three levels: important, *more* important, and *most* important. You might have only a handful of those most important notes. Be sure to include them in your summary.

While you're reviewing, evaluate your notes. Review sessions are excellent times to look beyond the *content* of your notes and reflect on your note-taking *process*. Remember these common goals of taking notes in the first place:

- *Reduce* course content to its essentials.
- *Organize* the content.
- Demonstrate that you *understand* the content.

If your notes consistently fall short on one of these points, then review this chapter for a strategy that can help. ✖

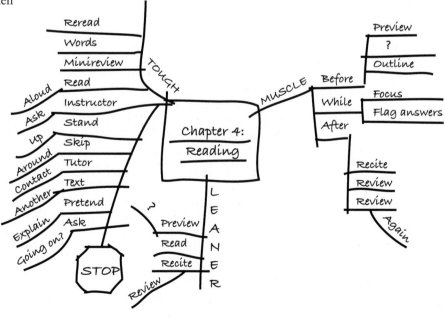

Turn PowerPoints into
POWERFUL NOTES

PowerPoint presentations are common. They can also be lethal for students who want to master course content or those who simply want to stay awake.

Some students stop taking notes during a PowerPoint presentation. This choice can be hazardous to your academic health for three major reasons:

- **PowerPoint presentations don't include everything.** Instructors and other speakers use PowerPoint to organize their presentations. Topics covered in the slides make up an outline of what your instructor considers important. Slides are created to flag the main points and signal transitions between points. However, speakers usually add examples and explanations that don't appear on the slides. In addition, slides will not contain any material from class discussion, including any answers that the instructor gives in response to questions.
- **You stop learning.** Taking notes forces you to capture ideas and information in your own words. Also, the act of writing things down helps you remember the material. If you stop writing and let your attention drift, you can quickly get lost.
- **You end up with major gaps in your notes.** When it's time to review your notes,

you'll find that material from PowerPoint presentations is missing. This can be a major pain at exam time.

To create value from PowerPoint presentations, take notes on them. Continue to observe, record, and review. See PowerPoint as a way to *guide* rather than to *replace* your own note taking. Even the slickest, smartest presentation is no substitute for your own thinking.

Experiment with the following suggestions. They include ideas about what to do before, during, and after a PowerPoint presentation.

BEFORE THE PRESENTATION

Sometimes instructors make PowerPoint slides available before a lecture. If you have computer access, download these files. Scan the slides, just as you would preview a reading assignment.

Consider printing out the slides and bringing them along to class. (If you own a copy of PowerPoint, then choose the "handouts" option when printing. This will save paper and ink.) You can take notes directly on the pages that you print out. Be sure to add the slide numbers if they are missing.

If you use a laptop computer for taking notes during class, then you might not want to bother with printing. Just open up the PowerPoint file and type your notes in the window that appears at the bottom of each slide. After class, you can print out the slides in note view. This will show the original slides plus any text that you added.

How Muscle Reading Works

- Phase 1 – Before You Read
  - ▪ Pry Out Questions

- Phase 2 – While You Read
  - ▪ Focus and Flag Answers

- Phase 3 – After You Read
  - ▪ Recite, Review, and Review Again

DURING THE PRESENTATION

In many cases, PowerPoint slides are presented visually by the instructor *only during class*. The slides are not provided as handouts, and they are not available online for students to print out.

This makes it even more important to take effective notes in class. Capture the main points and key details as you normally would. Use your preferred note-taking strategies.

Be selective in what you write down. Determine what kind of material is on each slide. Stay alert for new topics, main points, and important details. Taking too many notes makes it hard to keep up with a speaker and separate main points from minor details.

In any case, go *beyond* the slides. Record valuable questions and answers that come up during a discussion, even if they are not a planned part of the presentation.

AFTER THE PRESENTATION

If you printed out slides before class and took notes on those pages, then find a way to integrate them with the rest of your notes. For example, add references in your notebook to specific slides. Or create summary notes that include the major topics and points from readings, class meetings, and PowerPoint presentations.

Printouts of slides can make good review tools. Use them as cues to recite. Cover up your notes so that only the main image or words on each slide are visible. See whether you can remember what else appears on the slide, along with the key points from any notes you added.

Also consider editing the presentation. If you have the PowerPoint file on your computer, make another copy of it. Open up this copy, and see whether you can condense the presentation. Cut slides that don't include anything you want to remember. Also rearrange slides so that the order makes more sense to you. Remember that you can open up the original file later if you want to see exactly what your instructor presented.

When your instructor TALKS QUICKLY

Take more time to prepare for class. Familiarity with a subject increases your ability to pick up on key points. If an instructor lectures quickly or is difficult to understand, conduct a preview of the material to be covered.

Be willing to make choices. Focus your attention on key points. Instead of trying to write everything down, choose what you think is important. Occasionally, you will make a less than perfect choice or even neglect an important point. Don't worry. Stay with the lecture, write down key words, and revise your notes immediately after class.

Exchange photocopies of notes with classmates. Your fellow students might write down something you missed. At the same time, your notes might help them. Exchanging photocopies can fill in the gaps.

Leave large empty spaces in your notes. Leave plenty of room for filling in information you missed. Use a symbol that signals you've missed something, so you can remember to come back to it.

See the instructor after class. Take your class notes with you, and show the instructor what you missed.

Use an audio recorder. Recording a lecture gives you a chance to hear it again whenever you choose. Some audio recording software allows you to vary the speed of the recording. With this feature, you can perform magic and actually slow down the instructor's speech.

Before class, take notes on your reading assignment. You can take detailed notes on the text before class. Leave plenty of blank space.

Take these notes with you to class, and simply add your lecture notes to them.

Go to the lecture again. Many classes are taught in multiple sections. That gives you the chance to hear a lecture at least twice—once in your regular class and again in another section of the class.

Create abbreviations. Note-taking systems called *shorthand* were specifically designed for getting ideas down fast. Though these systems are dated, you can borrow the general idea. Invent your own shorthand—one- or two-letter abbreviations and symbols for common words and phrases.

A common way to abbreviate is to leave out vowels. For example, *said* becomes *sd, American* becomes *Amrcn.*

The trick is to define abbreviations clearly and use them consistently. When you use an abbreviation such as *comm*, you run the risk of not being able to remember whether you meant *committee, commission, common*, or *commit*. To prevent this problem, write a master key, or legend, that explains all your abbreviations.

Ask questions—even if you're totally lost. Many instructors allow a question session. This is the time to ask about the points you missed.

At times you might feel so lost that you can't even formulate a question. One option is to report this fact to the instructor. She can often guide you to a question. Another option is to ask a related question. Doing so might lead you to the question you really wanted to ask.

Ask the instructor to slow down. This solution is the most obvious. If asking the instructor to slow down doesn't work, ask him to repeat what you missed.

Take this article to work. See fast-talking instructors as people who are training you to take notes during meetings, conferences, and training sessions in the workplace. The ability to think clearly and write concisely under pressure will serve you for a lifetime. ✖

practicing
CRITICAL THINKING

18

Taking notes under pressure

With note taking, the more you practice, the better you become. You can use TV programs and videos to practice listening for key words, writing quickly, focusing your attention, and reviewing. Programs that feature speeches and panel discussions work well for this purpose. So do documentary films.

The next time you watch such a program, use pen and paper to jot down key words and information. If you fall behind, relax. Just leave a space in your notes and return your attention to the program. If a program includes commercial breaks, use them to review and revise your notes.

At the end of the program, spend five minutes reviewing your notes, and create a mind map based on them. Then sum up the main points of the program for a friend.

This exercise will help you develop an ear for key words. Because you can't ask questions or request that speakers slow down, you train yourself to stay totally in the moment.

Don't be discouraged if you miss a lot the first time around. Do this exercise several times, and observe how your mind works.

Another option is to record a program and then take notes. You can stop the recording at any point to review what you've written.

Ask a classmate to do this exercise with you. Compare your notes and look for any points that either of you missed.

Syda Productions/Shutterstock.com

Taking notes
WHILE READING

Taking notes on school- or work-related reading requires the same skills that apply to taking notes in class: observing, recording, and reviewing. Use these skills to take notes for review and for research.

REVIEW NOTES

Review notes will look like the notes you take in class. Take review notes when you want more detailed notes than writing in the margin of your text allows. You might want to single out a particularly difficult section of a text and make separate notes. Or make summaries of overlapping lecture and text material. Because you can't underline or make notes in library books, these sources require separate notes too. To take more effective review notes, use the following suggestions.

Set priorities. Single out a particularly difficult section of a text and make separate notes. Or make summaries of overlapping lecture and text material.

Use a variety of formats. Translate text into Cornell notes, mind maps, or outlines. Combine these formats to create your own. Translate diagrams, charts, and other visual elements into words. Then reverse the process by translating straight text into visual elements.

However, don't let the creation of formats get in your way. Even a simple list of key points and examples can become a powerful review tool. Another option is to close your book and just start writing. Write quickly about what you intend to remember from the text, and don't worry about following any format.

Condense a passage to key quotes. Authors embed their essential ideas in key sentences. As you read, continually ask yourself, "What's the point?" Then see whether you can point to a specific sentence on the page to answer your question. Look especially at headings, subheadings, and topic sentences of paragraphs. Write these key sentences word for word in your notes, and put them within quotation marks. Copy as few sentences as you can to still retain the core meaning of the passage.

Condense by paraphrasing. Pretend that you have to summarize a chapter, article, or book on a postcard. Limit yourself to a single para-

graph—or a single sentence— and use your own words. This is a great way to test your understanding of the material.

Take a cue from the table of contents. Look at the table of contents in your book. Write each major heading on a piece of paper, or key those headings into a word-processing file on your computer. Include page numbers. Next, see whether you can improve on the table of contents. Substitute your own headings for those that appear in the book. Turn single words or phrases into complete sentences, and use words that are meaningful to you.

Adapt to special cases. The style of your notes can vary according to the nature of the reading material. If you are assigned a short story or poem, for example, then read the entire work once without taking any notes. On your first reading, simply enjoy the piece. When you finish, write down your immediate impressions. Then go over the piece again. Make brief notes on characters, images, symbols, settings, plot, point of view, or other aspects of the work.

Note key concepts in math and science. When you read mathematical, scientific, or other technical materials, copy important formulas or equations. Recreate important diagrams, and draw your own visual representations of con-

cepts. Also write down data that might appear on an exam.

RESEARCH NOTES

Take research notes when preparing to write a paper or deliver a speech. One traditional method of research is to take notes on index cards. You write *one* idea, fact, or quotation per card, along with a

note about the source (where you found it). The advantage of limiting each card to one item is that you can easily arrange cards according to the sequence of ideas in your outline. If you change your outline, no problem. Just reorder your cards.

Taking notes on a computer offers the same

Note this information about your sources

Knowing how to organize and document your sources of information is a key skill for information literacy. Following are checklists of the information to record about various types of sources. Whenever possible, print out or make photocopies of each source. For books, include a copy of the title page and copyright page, both of which are found in the front matter. For magazines and scholarly journals, copy the table of contents.

For each BOOK you consult, record the following:
- Author
- Editor (if listed)
- Translator (if listed)
- Edition number (if listed)
- Full title, including the subtitle
- Name and location of the publisher
- Copyright date
- Specific page numbers for passages that you quote, summarize, or paraphrase

For each ARTICLE you consult, record the following:
- Author
- Editor (if listed)
- Translator (if listed)
- Full title, including the subtitle
- Name of the periodical
- Volume number
- Issue number
- Issue date
- Specific page numbers for passages that you quote, summarize, or paraphrase

For each ONLINE SOURCE you consult, record the following:
- Author
- Editor (if listed)
- Translator (if listed)
- Full title of the page or article, including the subtitle
- Name of the organization that posted the site or published the CD-ROM
- Dates when the page or other document was published and revised
- Date when you accessed the source
- URL for web pages (the uniform resource locator, or website address, which often starts with http://)
- Version number (for CD-ROMs)
- Volume, issue number, and date for online journals

Note: Computer-based sources may not list all this information. For web pages, at a minimum record the date you accessed the source and the URL.

For each INTERVIEW you conduct, record the following:
- Name of the person you interviewed
- Professional title of the person you interviewed
- Contact information for the person you interviewed—mailing address, phone number, email address
- Date of the interview

flexibility as index cards. Just include one idea, fact, or quotation per paragraph, along with the source. Think of each paragraph as a separate "card." When you're ready to create the first draft of your paper or presentation, just move paragraphs around so that they fit your outline.

Include your sources. No matter whether you use cards or a computer, be sure to *include a source for each note that you take*.

Say, for example, that you find a useful quotation from a book. You want to include that quotation in your paper. Copy the quotation word for word onto a card, or key the quotation into a computer file. Along with the quotation, note the book's author, title, date and place of publication, and publisher. You'll need such information later when you create a formal list of your sources—a bibliography or a list of endnotes or footnotes.

For guidelines on what information to record about each type of source, see the sidebar to this article as a place to start. Your instructors might have different preferences, so ask them for guidance as well.

Avoid plagiarism. When people take material from a source and fail to acknowledge that source, they are committing plagiarism. Even when plagiarism is accidental, the consequences can be harsh.

Many cases of plagiarism occur during the process of taking research notes.

To prevent this problem, remember that a major goal of taking research notes is to *clearly separate your own words and images from words and images created by someone else.* To meet this goal, develop the following habits:

- If you take a direct quote from one of your sources, then enclose those words in quotation marks, and note information about that source.
- If you take an image (photo, illustration, chart, or diagram) from one of your sources, then note information about that source.
- If you summarize or paraphrase *a specific passage* from one of your sources, then use your own words and note information about that source.
- If your notes include any idea that is closely identified with a particular person, then note information about the source.
- When you include one of your own ideas in your notes, then simply note the source as "me."

If you're taking notes on a computer and using Internet sources, be especially careful to avoid plagiarism. When you copy text or images from a website, separate those notes from your own ideas. Use a different font for copied material, or enclose it in quotation marks.

You do *not* need to note a source for these:

- Facts that are considered common knowledge ("The history of the

twentieth century includes two world wars").
- Facts that can be easily verified ("The United States Constitution includes a group of amendments known as the Bill of Rights").
- Your own opinion ("Hip-hop artists are the most important poets of our age").

The bottom line: Always present your own work—not materials that have been created or revised by someone else. If you're ever in doubt about what to do, then take the safest course: Cite a source. Give credit where credit is due.

Reflect on your notes. Schedule time to review all the information and ideas that your research has produced. By allowing time for rereading and reflecting on all the notes you've taken, you create the conditions for genuine understanding.

Start by summarizing major points of view on your topic. Note points of agreement and disagreement among your sources.

Also see whether you can find direct answers to the questions that you had when you started researching. These answers could become headings in your paper.

Look for connections in your material, including ideas, facts, and examples that occur in several sources. Also look for connections between your research and your life—ideas that you can verify based on personal experience. ✂

Visualize ideas with
CONCEPT MAPS

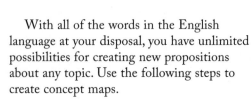

Like mind maps, concept maps let you form visual connections between ideas. Yet concept maps are slightly more formal. People who find mind maps too unstructured or messy may find concept maps more appealing.

Concept mapping is a tool pioneered by Joseph Novak and D. Bob Gowin.[5] These psychologists were deeply influenced by the work of a researcher named David Ausubel.

In *The Psychology of Meaningful Verbal Learning*, Ausubel wrote that the essence of learning a subject is integrating new concepts with concepts that we already know.[6] We do this by creating *propositions*—statements that link unfamiliar concepts to those that are familiar.

Concept maps express this process in visual form. The key elements are:

- A main concept written at the top of a page.
- Related concepts arranged in a hierarchy, with more general concepts toward the top of a page and more specific concepts toward the bottom.
- Links—lines with words that briefly explain the relationship between concepts.

When you combine concepts with their linking words, you'll often get complete sentences (or sets of coherent phrases). These are the propositions described by Ausubel.

With all of the words in the English language at your disposal, you have unlimited possibilities for creating new propositions about any topic. Use the following steps to create concept maps.

CHOOSE ONE CONCEPT AS A FOCUS

To begin, limit the scope of your concept map. Choose one general concept as a focus—the main topic of a chapter, article, or lecture. Express this concept in one to three words. Concept words are usually nouns and adjectives, including key terms and proper names. Circle your main concept.

LIST RELATED CONCEPTS

Next, brainstorm a list of concepts that are related to your main concept. Don't worry about putting these concepts in any order yet. Just list them—again, expressing each concept in a single word or short phrase. For ease in rearranging and ranking the concepts later, you might wish to write each one on a single index card, or on a single line in a word-processing file.

ARRANGE CONCEPTS IN A HIERARCHY

Rank concepts on a continuum from general to specific. Then create the body of your concept map by placing the main concept at the top and the most specific concepts at the bottom. Arrange the rest of the concepts in appropriate places throughout the middle. Again, circle each concept. Allow some time for this step, and be willing to shuffle concepts around until you're satisfied with the arrangement.

ADD LINKS

Draw lines that connect the concepts along with words that describe their relationships. Limit yourself to the fewest words needed to make accurate links. Linking words are often verbs, verb phrases, or prepositions.

REVISE YOUR MAP

Look for any concepts that are repeated in several places on the map. You can avoid these duplications by adding more links between concepts. Also add any missing concepts and see if you can clarify vague links.

Avoid "string maps"—concepts that flow in basically a straight line from top to bottom. String maps are often a signal to expand your understanding by adding concepts, links, or both. In this way you create a richer set of relationships between concepts.

EXAMPLES OF CONCEPT MAPS

Consider the following paragraph:

Muscle Reading consists of three phases. Phase 1 includes tasks to complete before reading. Phase 2 tasks take place during reading. Finally, Phase 3 includes tasks to complete after reading.

In this paragraph, the concepts are:

- *Muscle Reading*
- *Reading*
- *Phases*
- *Tasks*
- *Phase 1*
- *Phase 2*
- *Phase 3*

Links include:

- *Before*
- *During*
- *After*

A concept map of the previous paragraph is illustrated in Figure 5.1 Sample Concept Map on Muscle Reading:

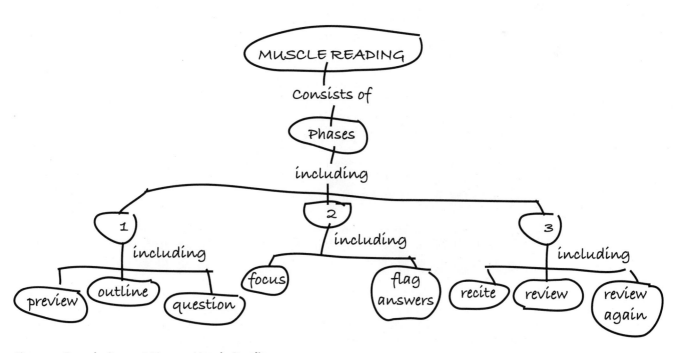

Figure 5.1 **Sample Concept Map on Muscle Reading**

You can often build a concept map from the headings within an article or a chapter of a book. For example, consider a textbook about nutrition that includes basic guidelines about how to eat well. This chapter includes the following headings:

Quantity

- Portion Sizes
- Watching Portion Sizes

Variety

- Eat Grains (Especially Whole Grains)
- Eat Water-Based Foods (Especially Fruits and Vegetables)

Figure 5.2 is a concept map based on these headings.

Figure 5.2 **Sample Concept Map on Nutrition**

BENEFITS OF CONCEPT MAPS

Concept mapping promotes critical thinking. It alerts you to missing concepts or faulty links between concepts.

Concept mapping is also "brain friendly." This technique for taking notes mirrors the way that your brain learns—that is, by linking new concepts to concepts that you already know. Links between concepts can be compared to the links between brain cells that start to form when you encounter new material. In short, concept maps are visual reminders of how your brain changes when you learn. ✖

Taking effective notes for ONLINE COURSEWORK

When you are taking an online course, or a course that is heavily supported by online materials, then get ready for new challenges to note taking. You can use a variety of strategies to succeed.

Manage time and tasks carefully. Courses that take place mostly or totally online can become invisible in your weekly academic schedule. This reinforces the temptation to put off dealing with these courses until late in the term.

Avoid this mistake! Consider the real possibility that an online course can take *more* time than a traditional, face-to-face lecture class. Online courses tend to embrace lots of activities—sending and receiving emails, joining discussion forums, commenting on blog posts, and more. New content might appear every day.

The biggest obstacle to online learning is procrastination. The solution is to keep up with the course through frequent contact and careful time management.

- Early in the term, create a detailed schedule for online courses. In your calendar, list a due date for each assignment. Break big assignments into smaller steps, and schedule a due date for each step.
- Schedule times in your calendar to complete online coursework. Give these scheduled sessions the same priority as regular classroom meetings. At these times, check for online announcements relating to assignments, tests, and other course events. Check for course-related emails daily.
- If the class includes discussion forums, check those daily as well. Look for new posts and add your replies. The point of these tools is to create a lively conversation that starts early and continues throughout the term.
- When you receive an online assignment, email any questions immediately. If you want to meet with an instructor in person, request an appointment several days in advance.
- Give online instructors plenty of time to respond. They are not always online. Many online

instructors have traditional courses to teach, along with administration and research duties.

- Download or print out online course materials as soon as they're posted on the class website. These materials might not be available later in the term.
- If possible, submit online assignments early. Staying ahead of the game will help you avoid an all-nighter at the computer during finals week.

If you still struggle with procrastination, remember a basic fact about human psychology. Emotions and behavior can operate independently. In other words, you can still engage with an online course even when you don't *feel* like doing it. Start with a simple task that you can do in five minutes or less. Following through on a small-scale commitment can help you overcome resistance.

Do a trial run with technology. Verify your access to course websites, including online tutorials, PowerPoint presentations, readings, quizzes, tests, assignments, bulletin boards, and chat rooms. Ask your instructors for website addresses, email addresses, and passwords. Work out any bugs when you start the course and well before that first assignment is due.

If you're planning to use a computer lab on campus, find one that meets course requirements. Remember that on-campus computer labs may not allow you to install all the software needed to access websites for your courses or textbooks.

Develop a contingency plan. Murphy's Law of Computer Crashes states that technology tends to

iStockphoto.com/Andrew Rich

break down at the moment of greatest inconvenience. You might not believe this piece of folklore, but it's still wise to prepare for it:

- Find a "technology buddy" in each of your classes—someone who can contact the instructor if you lose Internet access or experience other computer problems.
- Every day, make backup copies of files created for your courses.
- Keep extra printer supplies—paper and toner or ink cartridges—on hand at all times. Don't run out of necessary supplies on the day a paper is due.

Get actively involved with the course. Your online course will include a page that lists homework assignments and test dates. That's only the beginning. Look for ways to engage with the material by submitting questions, completing assignments, and interacting with the instructor and other students. Another way to stay involved is to find out whether your online courses offer apps for smartphones and tablets.

Take notes on course material. You can print out anything that appears on a computer screen. This includes online course materials—articles, books, email messages, chat-room sessions, and more.

The potential problem is that you might skip the note-taking process altogether. ("I can just print out everything!") You would then miss the chance to internalize a new idea by restating it in your own words—a principal

benefit of note taking. Result: Material passes from computer to printer without ever intersecting with your brain.

To prevent this problem, take notes in Cornell, mind map, concept map, or outline format. Write Discovery and Intention Statements to capture key insights from the materials and next actions to

---

Consider the real possibility that an online course can take more *time than a traditional, face-to-face lecture class. Online courses tend to embrace lots of activities—sending and receiving emails, joining discussion forums, commenting on blog posts, and more.*

---

take. Also talk about what you're learning. Recite key points out loud, and discuss what you find online with other students.

Of course, it's fine to print out online material. If you do, treat your printouts like mini-textbooks, and use reading techniques to extract meaning: Preview and outline them. Pose questions and

flag answers in the text. Then review and recite the material that you want to remember.

Another potential problem with online courses is the physical absence of the teacher. In a classroom, you get lots of visual and verbal clues to what kinds of questions will appear on a test. Those clues are often missing from an online course, which means that they could be missing from your notes. Ask your online instructor about what material she considers to be most important.

Set up folders and files for easy reference. Create a separate folder for each class on your computer's hard drive. Give each folder a meaningful name, such as *biology—spring2017*. Place all files related to a course in the appropriate folder. Doing this can save you from one of the main technology-related time wasters: searching for lost files.

Also name individual files with care. Avoid changing extensions that identify different types of files, such as .ppt for PowerPoint presentations or .pdf for files in the Adobe Reader portable document format. Changing extensions might lead to problems when you're looking for files later or sharing them with other users.

Take responsibility. If you register for an online course with no class meetings, you might miss the motivating presence of an instructor and classmates. Instead, manufacture your own motivation. Be clear about what you'll gain by doing well in the course. Relate course content to your major and career goals. Don't wait to be contacted by your classmates and instructor. Initiate that contact on your own.

Ask for help. If you feel confused about anything you're learning online, ask for help right away. This is especially important when you don't see the instructor face-to-face in class. Some students simply drop online courses rather than seek help. Email or call the instructor before you make that choice. If the instructor is on campus, you might be able to arrange for a meeting during office hours.

Focus your attention. Some students are used to visiting websites while watching television, listening to loud music, or instant messaging. When applied to online learning, these habits can reduce

your learning and imperil your grades. To succeed with technology, turn off the television, quit texting and online messaging, and turn down the music. Whenever you go online, stay in charge of your attention.

Ask for feedback. To get the most from online learning, request feedback from your instructor via email. When appropriate, also ask for conferences by phone or in person.

Sharing files offers another source of feedback. For example, Microsoft Word has a Track Changes feature that allows other people to insert comments into your documents and make suggested revisions. These edits are highlighted on the screen. Use such tools to get feedback on

your writing from instructors and peers.

Note: Be sure to check with your instructors to see how they want students enrolled in their online courses to address and label their emails. Many teachers ask their online students to use a standard format for the subject area so they can quickly recognize emails from them.

Contact other students. Make personal contact with at least one other student in each of your classes— especially classes that involve lots of online coursework. Create study groups to share notes, quiz each other, critique papers, and do other cooperative learning tasks. This kind of support can help you succeed as an online learner. ✠

Taking notes during meetings

In the workplace, notes matter. During meetings, people are hired, fired, and promoted. Problems are tackled. Negotiations are held. Decisions are made. Your job might depend on what you observe during meetings, what you record, and how you respond.

Consider adding the following topics—the four A's—to your notes on a meeting:

- *Attendance*—Start by observing who shows up. In many organizations, people expect meeting notes to include a list of attendees.
- *Agenda*—One path to more powerful meeting notes is observing the agenda. Think of it as a road map—a way to keep the discussion on track. Skilled planners often put an agenda in writing and distribute it in advance of a meeting. Record this agenda and use it to organize your notes. If there is no formal agenda, then create one in your notes, with separate headings for each major topic being discussed.

- *Agreements*—The purpose of most meetings is to reach an agreement about something—a policy, project, or plan. Record each agreement.
- *Actions*—During meetings, people often commit to take some type of action in the future. Record each follow-up action and who agreed to do it. This last A is especially important. Ask whether any of the points you included in your notes call for follow-up action on *your* part—perhaps a phone call to make, a fact to find, or another task to complete. Highlight such items in your notes. Then add them to your calendar or to-do list and follow through.

Follow-up action is often a make-or-break point for study groups and project teams. One mark of exceptional teams is that people make agreements about what they will do—and then keep those agreements. You can set a powerful example.

Note taking 2.0

Imagine how useful it would be to you anywhere, any time, from any digital device. Today there are digital tools—many of them free—for doing just that. Gain skills with them now while you're in school. Then transfer those skills to the workplace for taking notes on seminars, conferences, and training sessions.

Paula kc/Shutterstock.com

START WITH SOFTWARE YOU ALREADY OWN

One option is to create a plain text document for each of your courses and your personal journal. Key your notes into those documents.

Chances are that you already have software for creating plain text documents. Apple computers come loaded with TextEdit, and iPhones offer Notes. Windows users can use NotePad.

The documents you create with such software is called plain text because it's stripped of special formatting. The advantage is that almost any software can read plain text documents, and they consume little memory.

STORE YOUR NOTES IN THE "CLOUD"

To access your documents, store them in DropBox (**www.dropbox.com**), Google Drive (**drive.google.com**), OneDrive (**www.onedrive.live.com**), or another web-based service that backs up documents. Many of them will offer you several gigabytes of online storage for free. Sign up for the service, create a test document, and then edit it. Check to make sure that the edited version shows up correctly on all your devices.

CONSIDER ONLINE OUTLINERS AND MIND MAPPERS

A growing number of websites allow you to create outlines and mind maps. Just sign up for the service and create your first document. It will be available on any device with an Internet connection. And, your notes will remain private unless you choose to share them with specific people. For fun, start with these:

- WorkFlowy (**https://workflowy.com**) can be used with just a handful of keyboard shortcuts, allowing you to combine simplicity with speed.
- Checkvist (**https://checkvist.com**) offers options for exporting your outlines to other software.
- Online Outliner (**www.online-outliner.com**) is simple and free—no registration required.
- Fargo (**fargo.io**) is another free outliner that saves your outlines in Dropbox.
- The Outliner of Giants (**www.theoutlinerofgiants.com**) is an ideal choice for creating large scholarly documents that you can export to Microsoft Word.

- MindMeister (**www.mindmeister.com**) and Mindjet (**www.mindjet.com**) allow you to create mind maps that are stored online for free.
- TheBrain (**www.thebrain.com**), though not free, allows you to create multiple mind maps that link to one another, as well as links to websites and documents stored on your computer.

CONSIDER DEDICATED NOTE-TAKING SOFTWARE

Many note-taking applications offer features that go beyond plain text editing and online services.

- Simplenote (**http://simplenote.com**), which comes in free and paid versions, allows you to create text-based notes and store them online.
- Notational Velocity (**www.notational.net**, free and for Mac OSX only) stores text-based notes, searches them with blinding speed, and synchronizes with Simplenote.
- ResophNotes (**www.resoph.com**) brings the features of Notational Velocity to Windows-based computers.
- Evernote (**www.evernote.com**, free and paid versions) allows you to copy text and images from websites and add offline content, such as digital photos of business cards and receipts.
- Microsoft OneNote (**www.onenote.com**) overlaps with Evernote in features and integrates tightly with the Microsoft Office applications.

New tools are always under development. For more options, search the Web with the key words *note-taking software*. ✖

Courtesy of Prof. Teresa M. Amabile

Teresa Amabile

} *Professor of business administration, a director of research at Harvard Business School, and author of* The Progress Principle: Using Small Wins to Ignite Joy, Engagement, and Creativity at Work.

Nearly half of Americans (52%) are unhappy at work.

That's the conclusion of a 2014 job satisfaction survey by The Conference Board, a nonprofit research group.[7] Although job dissatisfaction reached its peak in 2010 after the Great Recession, the years since then have not brought much relief.

There are many possible reasons for workers' discontent. They worry about being laid off or replaced by robots or overseas workers. They talk about stagnant wages and higher health care costs.

Psychologist Teresa Amabile acknowledges these concerns. At the same time, she says, we can benefit by looking at another factor.

Amabile is fascinated by "inner work life"—how people respond emotionally to the daily events on the job. She says that workers often feel that they're falling behind no matter how hard they work. The struggle to keep up with email, meetings, and deadlines leaves many of us feeling that we spend ever more hours at work while accomplishing less and less. Instead of moving forward, we're standing still or even sliding backwards.

Progress is key to being happy at work, says Amabile. Her research points to "small wins"—daily movement toward meaningful goals—as the number one predictor of job satisfaction. She calls this the Progress Principle.

Amabile and her fellow researchers came to this conclusion after a study based on 12,000 daily journal entries from 238 people. When these people felt most engaged at work, she discovered, they were getting something done on a project that mattered to them. Even the smallest step toward a meaningful goal led workers to experience satisfaction.

During a 2012 conference sponsored by 99U (**99U.com**), Amabile said that anyone can use this strategy:[8]

Keeping a work diary can help you to celebrate the small wins that happen in your work—especially on a day that is so frustrating that it feels like you didn't get anything done on your most important work. You can usually find one thing where you did move forward. If you did, keep track of it. You can celebrate it this way.

Writing daily notes in this way helps you notice progress and remember it when it would be easier to focus on what you dislike about working.

In addition, reviewing your notes can remind you of days when you persisted on a task even when you felt distracted or discouraged. That in itself is motivating. "It can help you to cultivate patience because it can show you that in the past you have persevered and succeeded on days that might be even worse than whatever you're experiencing today," said Amabile.

Another way to experience the Progress Principle is to schedule periods during the work day when you can focus on an important project for at least 30 minutes. This sets up the conditions for you to experience "flow"—the deep satisfaction that comes with immersing yourself in a task for an extended time with no interruptions.

Some companies make this a policy by designating certain hours of the workday as "quiet time." For this period, no meetings or phone calls happen. In addition, there is no expectation that people reply to email. This is one of the simplest and most powerful tools that managers can use to increase employee engagement.

Amabile talks about one employee who spent a day working alone in a storage room filled with boxes. Freedom from the usual sources of distraction led this person to a highly satisfying day of work.

"Don't forget that small wins can accumulate to big breakthroughs," Amabile told the audience at 99U. "But unless you occasionally look back at where you've been, it can be hard to see where you're going."

Teresa Amabile's *research is about writing journal entries to monitor your daily progress in achieving goals. Making this a habit is one way to apply the Power Process: "I create it all" for experiencing more satisfaction at work.*

QUIZ

Chapter 5

1. The Power Process: "I create it all" is:
   a. An idea that you must believe in order to succeed in school
   b. A reminder that we ultimately control all of the events in our lives
   c. A reminder that you can choose your *response* to an event—even when the event itself is beyond your control
   d. None of the answer choices

2. According to the text, tools for note taking are worthless *unless* you:
   a. Participate as an energetic observer in class
   b. Review your notes *after* class
   c. Both a and b
   d. None of the answer choices

3. To "Be Here Now" when taking notes in class, remember to:
   a. Fight against daydreaming.
   b. Accept your wandering mind and refocus your attention.
   c. Hold imaginary debates with instructors whenever you disagree with them.
   d. Ignore the instructor's body language and avoid eye contact.

4. The suggested strategies for taking notes include *both* "postpone debate" and "think critically about what you hear."
   a. True
   b. False

5. The note-taking method that's based on using a cue column is called the _____ method.

6. To take effective notes, avoid combining mind mapping with any other note-taking method.
   a. True
   b. False

7. The suggested strategies for mind mapping include:
   a. Give yourself plenty of room.
   b. Use key words only.
   c. Put the main concept in the center.
   d. Create links.
   e. All of the answer choices.

8. Using roman numerals is only one way to create different levels of headings in an outline.
   a. True
   b. False

9. The notes that you take when preparing to write a paper are called:
   a. Review notes
   b. Research notes
   c. Combined notes
   d. None of the answer choices

10. The suggested strategies for taking notes during a meeting include recording the:
    a. Names of people who attended
    b. Agenda
    c. Agreements reached during the meeting
    d. Actions that people committed to take after the meeting
    e. All of the answer choices

SKILLS
snapshot

Take a snapshot of your note-taking skills as they exist today, after reading and doing this chapter. Begin by reflecting on some of your recent experiences with note taking. Then take the next step toward mastery by committing to a specific action in the near future.

Discovery

My score on the Notes section of the Discovery Wheel was . . .

If asked to rate the overall quality of the notes that I've taken in the last week, I would say that . . .

In general, I find my notes to be most useful when they . . .

Intention

I'll know that I've reached a new level of mastery with note taking when . . .

The idea from this chapter that could make the biggest difference in the quality of my notes is . . .

Action

The new note-taking habit that I plan to adopt is . . .

This habit can promote my success at work by . . .

By the time I finish this course, I would like my Notes score on the Discovery Wheel to be . . .

© Robert Kneschke/Shutterstock.com

Tests

why

Adopting a few simple techniques can make a major difference in how you feel about tests—and how you perform on them.

how

Think about how you want your experience of test taking to change. For example, you might want to walk into every test feeling well rested and thoroughly prepared. Next, preview this chapter to find at least three strategies to accomplish your goal.

what if...

I could let go of anxiety about tests—or anything else?

what is included . . .

202   Power Process: Detach

203   Think beyond the grade

204   What to do before the test

207   Ways to predict test questions

209   Cooperative learning: Studying in groups

211   What to do during the test

215   The high costs of cheating

216   Let go of test anxiety

218   Getting ready for math tests

222   Studying across the curriculum

224   The test isn't over until . . .

226   Celebrate mistakes

227   Notable failures

228   Master Student Profile: Lalita Booth

do you have a minute?

Write a study checklist for the next test in a course that you're taking right now. Include reading assignments and dates for class notes on which the test will be based.

POWER PROCESS

Detach

This Power Process helps you release the powerful, natural student within you. It is especially useful whenever negative emotions are getting in your way.

Attachments are addictions. When we are attached to something, we think we cannot live without it, just as a drug addict feels he cannot live without drugs. We believe our well-being depends on maintaining our attachments.

We can be attached to just about anything: beliefs, emotions, people, roles, objects. The list is endless.

One person, for example, might be so attached to his car that he takes an accident as a personal attack. Pity the poor unfortunate who backs into this person's car. He might as well have backed into the owner himself.

Another person might be attached to her job. Her identity and sense of well-being depend on it. She could become depressed if she got fired.

When we are attached and things don't go our way, we can feel angry, sad, afraid, or confused.

Suppose you are attached to getting an A on your physics test. You feel as though your success in life depends on getting that A. As the clock ticks away, you work harder on the test, getting more stuck. That voice in your head gets louder: "I must get an A. I *must* get an A. *I must get an A!*"

Now is a time to detach. See whether you can just *observe* what's going on, letting go of all your judgments. When you observe rather than react, you reach a quiet state above and beyond your usual thoughts. This is a place where you can be aware of being aware. It's a tranquil spot, apart from your emotions. From here, you can see yourself objectively, as if you were watching someone else.

That place of detachment might sound far away and hard to reach. You can get there in three ways.

First, pay attention to your thoughts and physical sensations. If you are confused and feeling stuck, tell yourself, "Here I am, confused and stuck." If your palms are sweaty and your stomach is one big knot, admit it.

Second, practice relaxation. Start by simply noticing your breathing. Then breathe more slowly and more deeply. See whether you can breathe the relaxing feeling into your whole body.

Third, practice seeing current events from a broader perspective. In your mind, zoom out to a bigger picture. Ask yourself how much today's test score will matter to you in one week, one month, one year, or one decade from today. You can apply this technique to any challenge in life.

Caution: Giving up an *attachment* to being an A student does not mean giving up *being* an A student. Giving up an attachment to a job doesn't mean giving up the job. When you detach, you get to keep your values and goals. However, you know that you will be okay even if you fail to achieve a goal.

Remember that you are more than your goals. You are more than your thoughts and feelings. These things come and go. Meanwhile, the part of you that can *just observe* is always there and always safe, no matter what happens.

Behind your attachments is a master student. Release that mastery. Detach. ✖

Tupungato/Getty Images

Think BEYOND *the grade*

On the surface, tests don't look dangerous. Maybe that's why we sometimes treat them as if they were land mines.

Suppose a stranger walked up to you on the street and asked, "Does a finite abelian P-group have a basis?" Would you break out in a cold sweat? Would your muscles tense up? Would your breathing become shallow?

Probably not. Even if you had never heard of a finite abelian P-group, you probably would remain coolly detached. However, if you find the same question on a test and you have never heard of a finite abelian P-group, your hands might get clammy.

Grades (A to F) are what we use to give power to tests. And there are lots of misconceptions about what grades are. Grades are not a measure of intelligence or creativity. They are not an indication of our ability to contribute to society. Grades are simply a measure of how well we do on tests.

Some people think that a test score measures what a student has accomplished in a course. This idea is false. A test score is a measure of what a student scored on a test. If you are anxious about a test and blank out, the grade cannot measure what you've learned. The reverse is also true: If you are a lucky guesser, the score won't be an accurate reflection of what you know.

Grades are not a measure of self-worth. Yet we tend to give test scores the power to determine how we feel about ourselves. Common thoughts include "If I fail a test, I am a failure" and "If I do badly on a test, I am a bad person." The truth is that if you do badly on a test, you are a person who did badly on a test. That's all. Carrying around misconceptions about tests and grades can put undue pressure on your performance.

If you experience test anxiety, you might feel that you're a victim of forces outside your control: cruel teachers, obscure textbooks, or trick questions. Another option is to ask yourself the following questions: What can *I* do to experience my next test differently? How can I study more effectively? How can I manage test-related stress? When you ask such questions, you start to take back your power.

It is easier to do well on exams if you don't put too much pressure on yourself. Don't give the test some magical power over your own worth as a human being. Academic tests are not a matter of life and death. Scoring low on important tests—standardized tests or medical school, bar exams, CPA exams—usually means only a delay.

Whether the chance of doing poorly is real or exaggerated, worrying about it can become paralyzing. The way to deal with tests is to keep them in perspective. ✕

What to do
BEFORE
the test

Students like to say that they plan to *study* for a test. There's a big problem with that term: It doesn't always have a clear definition. It might mean "read," "write," or "recite." It could mean all of those things—or something else entirely.

Philipp Nemenz/Cultura/Getty Images

Here's a solution: See each test as a performance. Studying for a test means rehearsing—or even better, *practicing*. Get ready for a test in the same way that an actor gets ready for opening night: Do the same things you'll be asked to do during the performance.

The goal is to define the information you'll want to remember and actively use it. Wire it firmly in your long-term memory circuits. Make it easy to retrieve at exam time.

You can prepare for a test in the same way that pilots prepare for a flight. Use a checklist. Before taking off, pilots physically mark off each item they need to check and adjust. A written list helps them to be sure they don't miss anything. Once they are in the air, it's too late.

Taking an exam is like flying a plane. Once the test begins, it's too late to memorize that one equation you forgot to use when practicing problem solving.

Make checklists that include exactly what you'll use to practice for a test. Your checklists will vary because they'll be geared to different subjects. For example, you can list:

- The date and time of the test, along with the name of the course and instructor
- Reading assignments by chapters or page numbers
- Dates of lecture notes
- Types of problems you will need to solve
- Major ideas, definitions, theories, formulas, and equations
- Other skills to master

Remember that a checklist is a to-do list. It contains two things. One is the briefest possible description of *what*

items you will use to practice. Second is a description of *how* you will use those items to practice. Here it's important to use active verbs other than *study* or *review*. For example, you can *outline* textbook chapters, *recite* key material based on your lecture notes, and *solve* sample problems.

FIND OR CREATE PRACTICE MATERIALS

Practice tests. Write your own questions based on course material. This is a good activity for study groups. Take your practice test several times before the actual exam. Type up this "test" so that it looks like the real thing. If possible, take your practice test in the same room where you will take the actual test. Consider testing yourself several times in preparation for an exam, using different practice tests. If this seems like a lot of effort, remember that informal self-testing is a learning strategy that's well supported by research.[1]

Copies of old exams. Copies of previous exams for the class might be available from the instructor, the instructor's department, the library, or the counseling office. Use these as practice tests.

Some cautions: If you rely on old tests exclusively, you might gloss over material the instructor has added since the last test. Also check your school's policy about making past tests available to students. Some schools might not allow it.

Mind map summary sheets. There are several ways to make a mind map as you practice for tests. Start by creating one totally from memory. You might be surprised by how much you already know. After you have gone as far as you can using recall alone, go over your notes and text, and fill in the rest of the map.

Another option is to go through your notes and write down key words as you pick them out. Then, without looking at your notes, create a mind map of everything you can recall about each key word. Go back to your notes and fill in material you left out.

Flash cards. Flash cards are like portable test questions. On one side of 3 × 5 cards, write questions. On the other side, write the answers. It's that simple.

Always carry a pack of flash cards with you and use them whenever you have a minute to spare. Use flash cards for formulas, definitions, theories, key words from your notes, axioms, dates, foreign language

phrases, hypotheses, and sample problems. Create flash cards regularly as the term progresses. Buy an inexpensive card file to keep your flash cards arranged by subject.

You can also create Web-based flash cards to use with your computer, smartphone, or tablet. Options include Quizlet (**www.quizlet.com**), StudyBlue (**www.studyblue.com**), and FlashCardMachine (**www. flashcardmachine.com**).

SCHEDULE YOUR PRACTICE SESSIONS

Many studies support the power of distributed learning.[2] This is opposite of cramming for a test. The goal is to spread (distribute) your learning across a whole term rather than trying to do it in a few marathon sessions.

Schedule specific times in your calendar for practice sessions before a test. Start focusing on key topics at least five days before you'll be tested on them. This allows plenty of time to find the answers to questions and close any gaps in your understanding.

Daily practice. Scan your lecture notes, and then cover them up and recite key points and details. Also practice with textbooks. Before reading a new assignment, scan your notes and the sections you underlined or highlighted in the previous assignment.

Concentrate daily practice on two kinds of material. One is new material from class meetings and your reading. Second is material that involves simple memorization—equations, formulas, dates, definitions. You can start practicing these within seconds after learning. During a lull in class,

HOW TO CRAM (EVEN THOUGH YOU "SHOULDN'T")

Know the limitations of cramming, and be aware of its costs. Cramming won't work if you've neglected all of the reading assignments or if you've skipped most of the lectures and daydreamed through the rest. The more courses you have to cram for, the less effective cramming will be. Also, cramming is not the same as learning: You won't remember what you cram.

If you *are* going to cram, however, then avoid telling yourself that you *should* have studied earlier, you *should* have read the assignments, or you *should* have been more conscientious. All those *shoulds* get you nowhere. Instead, write an Intention Statement about how you will change your study habits. Give yourself permission to be the fallible human being you are. Then make the best of the situation.

Make choices. Pick out *a few* of the most important elements of the course and learn them backward, forward, and upside down. For example, devote most of your attention to the topic sentences, tables, and charts in a long reading assignment.

Make a plan. After you've chosen what elements you want to study, determine how much time to spend on each one.

Recite and recite again. The key to cramming is repetition. Go over your material again and again.

for example, scan the notes you just took. Immediately after class, scan them again.

Each day that you practice for a test, assess what you have learned and what you still want to learn. See how many items you've covered from your checklist. This helps you evaluate your practice and alerts you to areas that still need attention.

Weekly practice. Practice for each subject at least once a week, allowing about one hour per subject. See if you can do most of the items on your checklist and cover them in more detail than you do in daily practice sessions. For example:

- Look over any summary sheets that you've written and then rewrite them from memory.
- Write answers to review questions in your textbooks.
- Solve problems from your textbooks.
- Recite the points in your notes that you want to remember.
- Rewrite your notes for greater precision and clarity.

Major practice sessions. These can be most helpful during the week before finals or other critical exams. They help you integrate concepts and deepen your understanding of material presented throughout the term.

For major practice sessions, schedule two to five hours at a stretch. Allow for breaks. Remember that the effectiveness of your session begins to drop after an hour or so unless you give yourself a short rest. After a certain point, short breaks every hour might not be enough to refresh you. That's when it's time to quit. Learn your limits by being conscious of the quality of your concentration.

During long sessions, focus on the most difficult subjects when you are the most alert: at the beginning of the session. ✘

Explore your feelings about tests

Complete the following sentences:

As exam time gets closer, one thing I notice that I do is . . .

When it comes to taking tests, I have trouble . . .

The night before a test, I usually feel . . .

The morning of a test, I usually feel . . .

During a test, I usually feel . . .

After a test, I usually feel . . .

When I learn a test score, I usually feel . . .

Ways to
PREDICT
test questions

Predicting test questions can do more than get you a better grade. It can also keep you focused on the purpose of a course and help you design your learning strategies. Making predictions can be fun too—especially when they turn out to be accurate.

Ask about the nature of the test. Eliminate as much guesswork as possible. Ask your instructor to describe upcoming tests. Do this early in the term so you can be alert for possible test questions throughout the course. Here are some questions to ask:

- What course material will the test cover: readings, lectures, lab sessions, or a combination?
- Will the test be cumulative, or will it cover just the most recent material you've studied?
- Will the test focus on facts and details or major themes and relationships?
- Will the test call on you to solve problems or apply concepts?
- Will you have choices about which questions to answer?
- What types of questions will be on the test: true/false, multiple choice, short answer, essay?

Note: In order to study appropriately for essay tests, find out how much detail the instructor wants in your answers. Ask how much time you'll be allowed for the test and about the length of essay answers (number of pages, blue books, or word limit). Having that information before you begin studying will help you gauge your depth for learning the material.

Put yourself in your instructor's shoes. If you were teaching the course, what kinds of questions would you put on an exam? You can also brainstorm test questions with other students—a great activity for study groups.

Look for possible test questions in your notes and readings. Have a separate section in your notebook labeled *Test Questions*. Add several questions to this section after every lecture and assignment. You can also create your own code or graphic signal—such as a T in a circle—to flag possible test questions in your notes. Use the same symbol to flag review questions and problems in your textbooks that could appear on a test.

Remember that textbook authors have many ways of pointing you to potential test items. Look for clues in chapter overviews and summaries, headings, lists of key words, and review questions. Some textbooks have related websites where you can take practice tests.

Look for clues to possible questions during class. During lectures, you can predict test questions by observing what an instructor says and how he or she says it. Instructors often give clues. They might repeat important points several times, write them on the board, or return to them in later classes.

Gestures can indicate critical points. For example, your instructor might pause, look at notes, or read passages word for word.

Notice whether your teacher has any strong points of view on certain issues. Questions on those issues are likely to appear on a test. Also pay attention to questions the instructor poses to students, and note questions that other students ask.

When material from reading assignments is covered extensively in class, it is likely to be on a test. For science courses and other courses involving problem solving, work on sample problems using different variables.

Save all quizzes, papers, lab sheets, and graded materials of any kind. Quiz questions have a way of reappearing, in slightly altered form, on final exams. If copies of previous exams and other graded materials are available, use them to predict test questions.

Apply your predictions. To get the most value from your predictions, use them to guide your review sessions.

Remember the obvious. Be on the lookout for these words: *This material will be on the test.* ✄

DISCOVERY STATEMENT/INTENTION STATEMENT

journal entry 14

Notice your excuses and let them go

Do a timed, four-minute brainstorm of all the reasons, rationalizations, justifications, and excuses you have used to avoid studying. Be creative. Write down your list of excuses.

Now, review your list. Then write a Discovery Statement about patterns that you see in your excuses.

I discovered that I . . .

Next, review your list, pick the excuse that you use the most, and circle it. Write an Intention Statement about what you will do to begin eliminating your favorite excuse. Make this Intention Statement one that you can keep, with a timeline and a reward.

I intend to . . .

Yellow Dog Productions/Lifesize/Jupiter Images

Cooperative learning: Studying in
GROUPS

Study groups can lift your mood on days when you just don't feel like working. If you skip a solo study session, no one else will know. If you declare your intention to study with others who are depending on you, your intention gains strength.

Study groups are especially important if going to school has thrown you into a new culture. Joining a study group with people you already know can help ease the transition.

To multiply the benefits of study groups, seek out people of other backgrounds, cultures, races, and ethnic groups. You can get a new perspective, along with some new friends.

None of us are born with these skills. Use study groups to start expanding your skills at collaboration. The time you invest now can advance your career in the future.

FORM A STUDY GROUP

Choose a focus for your group. Many students assume that the purpose of a study group is to help its members prepare for a test. That's one valid purpose—and there are others.

Through his research on cooperative learning,

psychologist Joe Cuseo has identified several kinds of study groups.[3] For instance, members of *test review* groups compare answers and help one another discover sources of errors. *Note-taking* groups focus on comparing and editing notes, often meeting directly after the day's class. Members of *research* groups meet to help one another find, evaluate, and take notes on background materials for papers and presentations. *Reading* groups can be useful for courses in which test questions are based largely on textbooks. Meet with classmates to compare the passages you underlined or highlighted and the notes you made in the margins of your books.

Look for dedicated students. Find people you are comfortable with and who share your academic goals. Look for students who pay attention, participate in class, and actively take notes. Invite them to join your group.

Of course, you can recruit members in other ways. One

way is to make an announcement during class. Another option is to post signs asking interested students to contact you. Or pass around a sign-up sheet before class. These methods can reach many people, but they do take more time to achieve results. And you have less control over who applies to join the group.

Limit groups to four people. Research on cooperative learning indicates that four people are an ideal group size.[4] Larger groups can be unwieldy.

Studying with friends is fine, but if your common interests are pizza and jokes, you might find it hard to focus.

Hold a planning session. Ask two or three people to get together for a snack and talk about group goals, meeting times, and other logistics. You don't have to make an immediate commitment.

As you brainstorm about places to meet, aim for a quiet meeting room with plenty of room to spread out materials. Your campus library probably has study rooms. Campus tutoring services might also have space and other resources for study groups.

Do a trial run. Test the group first by planning a one-time session. If that session works, plan another. After a few successful sessions, you can schedule regular meetings.

CONDUCT YOUR GROUP

Ask your instructor for guidelines on study group activities. Many instructors welcome and encourage study groups. However, they have different ideas about what kinds of collaboration are acceptable. Some activities—such as sharing test items or writing papers from a shared outline—are considered cheating and can have serious consequences. Let your instructor know that you're forming a group, and ask for clear guidelines.

Assign roles. To make the most of your time, ask one member to lead each group meeting. The leader's role is to keep the discussion focused on the agenda and ask for contributions from all members. Assign another person to act as recorder. This person will take notes on the meeting, recording possible test questions, answers, and main points from group discussions. Rotate both of these roles so that every group member takes a turn.

Cycle through learning styles. As you assign roles, think about the learning styles present in your group. Some people excel at raising questions and creating lots of ideas. Others prefer to gather information and think critically.

Some like to answer questions and make decisions, whereas others excel at taking action. To create an effective group, match people with their preferred activities. Also change roles periodically. This gives group members a chance to explore new learning styles.

Teach each other. Teaching is a great way to learn something. Turn the material you're studying into a list of topics, and assign a specific topic to each person, who will then teach it to the group. When you're done presenting your topic, ask for questions or comments. Prompt each other to explain ideas more clearly, find gaps in understanding, consider other points of view, and apply concepts to settings outside the classroom.

Test one another. During your meeting, take a practice test created from questions contributed by group members. When you're finished, compare answers. Or turn testing into a game by pretending you're on a television game show. Use sample test questions to quiz one another.

Compare notes. Make sure that all the group's members heard the same thing in class and that you all recorded the important information. Ask others to help explain material in your notes that is confusing to you.

Create wall-size mind maps or concept maps to summarize a textbook or series of lectures. Work on large sheets of butcher paper, or tape together pieces of construction paper. When creating a mind map, assign

one branch to each member of the study group. Use a different colored pen or marker for each branch of the mind map.

Monitor effectiveness. On your meeting agenda, include an occasional discussion about your group's effectiveness. Are you meeting consistently? Is the group helping members succeed in class?

Use this time to address any issues that are affecting the group as a whole. If certain members are routinely unprepared for study sessions, brainstorm ways to get them involved. If one person tends to dominate meetings, reel her in by reminding her that everyone's voice needs to be heard.

To resolve conflict among group members, keep the conversation constructive. Focus on solutions. Move from vague complaints ("You're never prepared") to specific requests ("Will you commit to bringing 10 sample test questions next time?"). Asking a "problem" member to lead the next meeting might make an immediate difference.

Ask about extending the focus of your group. If your group is going well, ask members whether they want to discuss problems with transportation, childcare, financial aid, and other issues that go beyond class work. Study groups can lead to lasting friendships that support long-term success in school.

Take this article to work. Joining a study group helps you to develop a number of skills for working on teams in the workplace. One of those skills is leading meetings.

When it's your turn to lead your study group, keep these ideas in mind as strategies you can also apply at work:

- **Schedule carefully.** Give people plenty of advance notice that you want to meet—at least one week.
- **Set clear starting and stopping times.** Experiment with scheduling less time for a group. If people know that a meeting will only last 60 minutes, they're more likely to show up on time.
- **Set a focused agenda.** At the beginning of each meeting, reach agreement on exactly what you intend to do. Then set a time limit for each agenda item. During the meeting, keep an eye on the clock to make sure that the group stays on schedule.
- **Make sure that necessary materials are available.** If you're planning to take a practice text, for example, make sure that everyone in the group will have a copy.
- **Monitor comprehension.** It's often easy to tell when people in the group are still struggling with a concept. Invite them to keep asking questions that help clarify concepts.

Answering those questions can reveal gaps in the group's understanding and suggest new issues to raise in class.

- **End each meeting with a to-do list.** Save the last 10 minutes of each meeting for appointing the next group leader and recorder. Also set a date, time, location, and agenda for your next meeting. If the group came up with questions that no one was able to answer, then assign someone to talk to an instructor about them and share answers with the group. ✖

What to do
DURING
the test

Prepare yourself for the test by arriving early. Being early often leaves time to do a relaxation exercise. While you're waiting for the test to begin and talking with classmates, avoid asking the question "How much did you study for the test?" This question might fuel anxious thoughts that you didn't study enough.

AS YOU BEGIN

Ask the teacher or test administrator whether you can use scratch paper during the test. (If you use a separate sheet of paper without permission, you might appear to be cheating.)

If you *do* get permission, use this paper to jot down memory aids, formulas, equations, definitions, facts, or other material you know you'll need and might forget. An alternative is to make quick notes in the margins of the test sheet.

Pay attention to verbal directions given as a test is distributed. Then scan the whole test immediately. Evaluate the importance of each section. Notice how many points each part of the test is worth; then estimate how much time you'll need for each section, using its point value as your guide. For example, don't budget 20 percent of your time for a section that is worth only 10 percent of the points.

Read the directions slowly. Then reread them. It can be agonizing to discover that you lost points on a test merely because you failed to follow the directions. When the directions are confusing, ask to have them clarified.

Now you are ready to begin the test. If necessary, allow yourself a minute or two of "panic" time. Notice any tension you feel, and apply one of the techniques explained in the article "Let Go of Test Anxiety" later in this chapter.

Answer the easiest, shortest questions first. This gives you the experience of success. It also stimulates associations and prepares you for more difficult questions. Pace yourself and watch the time. If you can't think of an answer, move on. Follow your time plan.

If you are unable to determine the answer to a test question, keep an eye out throughout the test for context clues that may remind you of the correct answer or provide you with evidence to eliminate wrong answers.

MULTIPLE-CHOICE QUESTIONS

- ***Answer each question in your head first.*** Do this step before you look at the possible answers. If you come up with an answer that you're confident is right, look for that answer in the list of choices.
- ***Read all possible answers before selecting one.*** Sometimes two answers will be similar and only one will be correct.
- ***Test each possible answer.*** Remember that multiple-choice questions consist of two parts: the stem (an incomplete statement or question at the beginning) and a list of possible answers. Each answer, when combined with the stem, makes a complete statement or question-and-answer pair that is either true or false. When you combine

---

Words to watch for in essay questions

The following words are commonly found in essay test questions. They give you precise directions about what to include in your answer. Get to know these words well. When you see them on a test, underline them. Also look for them in your notes. Locating such key words can help you predict test questions.

- ***Analyze:*** Break into separate parts and discuss, examine, or interpret each part. Then give your opinion.
- ***Compare:*** Examine two or more items. Identify similarities and differences.
- ***Contrast:*** Show differences. Set in opposition.
- ***Criticize:*** Make judgments about accuracy, quality, or both. Evaluate comparative worth. Criticism often involves analysis.

- ***Define:*** Explain the exact meaning—usually, a meaning specific to the course or subject. Definitions are usually short.
- ***Describe:*** Give a detailed account. Make a picture with words. List characteristics, qualities, and parts.
- ***Diagram:*** Create a drawing, chart, or other visual element. Label and explain key parts.
- ***Discuss:*** Consider and debate or argue the pros and cons of an issue. Write about any conflict. Compare and contrast.
- ***Enumerate:*** List the main parts or features in a meaningful order and briefly describe each one.
- ***Evaluate:*** Make judgments about accuracy, quality, or both (similar to *criticize*).
- ***Explain:*** Make an idea clear. Show logically how a concept is developed. Give the reasons for an event.

the stem with each possible answer, you are turning each multiple-choice question into a small series of true/false questions. Choose the answer that makes a true statement.

- **Eliminate incorrect answers.** Cross off the answers that are clearly not correct. The answer you cannot eliminate is probably the best choice.

TRUE/FALSE QUESTIONS

- **Read the entire question.** Separate the statement into its grammatical parts—individual clauses and phrases—and then test each part. If any part is false, the entire statement is false.
- **Look for qualifiers.** Qualifiers include words such as *all, most, sometimes,* or *rarely.* Absolute qualifiers such as *always* or *never* generally indicate a false statement.
- **Find the devil in the details.** Double-check each number, fact, and date in a true/false statement. Look for numbers that have been transposed or facts that have been slightly altered. These are signals of a false statement.
- **Watch for negatives.** Look for words such as *not* and *cannot.* Read the sentence without these words and see whether you come up with a true/false statement. Then reinsert the negative words and see whether the statement makes more sense. Watch especially for sentences with two negative words. As in math operations, two negatives cancel each other out: *We cannot say that Chekhov never succeeded at short story writing* means the same as *Chekhov succeeded at short story writing.*

COMPUTER-GRADED TESTS

- Make sure that the answer you mark corresponds to the question you are answering.
- Check the test booklet against the answer sheet whenever you switch sections and whenever you come to the top of a column.
- Watch for stray marks on the answer sheet; they can look like answers.
- If you change an answer, be sure to erase the wrong answer thoroughly, removing all pencil marks.

OPEN-BOOK TESTS

- Carefully organize your notes, readings, and any other materials you plan to consult when writing answers.

- **Illustrate:** Clarify an idea by giving examples of it. Read the test directions to see whether the question requires you to include an actual illustration (like a diagram).
- **Interpret:** Explain the meaning of a new idea or event by showing how it relates to more familiar ideas or events. Interpretation can involve evaluation.
- **List:** Write a series of concise statements (similar to *enumerate*).
- **Outline:** List the main topics, points, features, or events, and briefly describe each one. (This does not necessarily mean creating a traditional outline with roman numerals, numbers, and letters.)
- **Prove:** Support with facts, examples, and quotations from credible sources (especially those presented in class or in the text).
- **Relate:** Show the connections between ideas or events. Provide a larger context for seeing the big picture.

- **State:** Explain precisely and clearly.
- **Summarize:** Give a brief, condensed account of a longer text. Include only the overall main idea and major supporting points from the article or text you are summarizing. Do not include specific details or your personal opinion.
- **Trace:** Show the order of events or the progress of a subject or event.

Notice how these words differ. For example, *compare* asks you to do something different from *contrast*. Likewise, *criticize* and *explain* call for different responses.

If any of these terms are still unclear to you, look them up in an unabridged dictionary.

During a test, you might be allowed to ask for an explanation of a key word. Check with instructors for policies.

- Write down any formulas you will need on a separate sheet of paper.
- Bookmark the table of contents and index in each of your textbooks. Place sticky notes and stick-on tabs or paper clips on other important pages of books (pages with tables, for instance).
- Create an informal table of contents or index for the notes you took in class.
- Predict which material will be covered on the test, and highlight relevant sections in your readings and notes.

SHORT-ANSWER/FILL-IN-THE-BLANK TESTS

- Concentrate on key words and facts. Be brief.
- Overlearning material can really pay off. When you know a subject backward and forward, you can answer this type of question almost as fast as you can write.

MATCHING TESTS

- Begin by reading through each column, starting with the one with fewer items. Check the number of items in each column to see whether they're equal. If they're not, look for an item in one column that you can match with two or more items in the other column.
- Look for any items with similar wording, and make special note of the differences between these items.
- Match words that are similar grammatically. For example, match verbs with verbs and nouns with nouns.
- When matching individual words with phrases, first read a phrase. Then look for the word that logically completes the phrase.
- Cross out items in each column when you are through with them.

ESSAY QUESTIONS

Managing your time is crucial in answering essay questions. Note how many questions you have to answer, and monitor your progress during the test period. Writing shorter answers and completing all of the questions on an essay test will probably yield a better score than leaving some questions blank.

Find out what an essay question is asking—precisely. If a question asks you to *compare* the ideas of Sigmund Freud and Karl Marx, no matter how eloquently you *explain* them, you are on a one-way trip to No Credit City.

Before you write, make a quick outline. An outline can help speed up the writing of your detailed answer; you're less likely to leave out important facts; and if you don't have time to finish your answer, your outline could win you some points. To use test time efficiently, keep your outline brief. Focus on key words to use in your answer.

Introduce your answer by getting to the point. General statements such as "There are many interesting facets to this difficult question" can cause irritation to teachers grading dozens of tests.

One way to get to the point is to begin your answer with part of the question. Suppose the question is "Discuss how increasing the city police budget might or might not contribute to a decrease in street crime." Your first sentence might be this: "An increase in police expenditures will not have a significant effect on street crime for the following reasons." Your position is clear. You are on your way to an answer.

Then expand your answer with supporting ideas and facts. Start out with the most solid points. Be brief and avoid filler sentences.

Write legibly. Grading essay questions is in large part a subjective process. Sloppy, difficult-to-read handwriting might actually lower your grade.

Write on one side of the paper only. If you write on both sides of the paper, writing may show through and obscure the words on the other side. If necessary, use the blank side to add points you missed. Leave a generous left-hand margin and plenty of space between your answers, in case you want to add points that you missed later on.

Finally, if you have time, review your answers for grammar and spelling errors, clarity, and legibility. ✂

Lucky Business/Shutterstock.com

The high costs of
CHEATING

Cheating on tests can be a tempting strategy. It offers the chance to get a good grade without having to study.

Instead of studying, we could spend more time watching TV, partying, sleeping, or doing anything else that seems like more fun. Another benefit of cheating is that we could avoid the risk of doing poorly on a test—which could happen even if we *do* study.

Remember that cheating carries costs. Here are some consequences to consider.

We risk failing the course or getting expelled from college. The consequences for cheating are serious. Cheating can result in failing the assignment, failing the entire course, getting suspended, or getting expelled from college entirely.

Documentation of cheating may also prevent you from being accepted to other colleges.

We learn less. Although we might think that some courses offer little or no value, we can create value from any course. If we look deeply enough, we can discover some idea or acquire some skill to prepare us for future courses or a career after graduation.

We lose time and money. Getting an education costs a lot of money. It also calls for years of sustained effort. Cheating sabotages our purchase. We pay full tuition and invest our energy without getting full

value for it. We shortchange ourselves and possibly our future coworkers, customers, and clients. Think about it: You probably don't want a surgeon who cheated in medical school to operate on you.

Fear of getting caught promotes stress. When we're fully aware of our emotions about cheating, we might discover intense stress. Even if we're not fully aware of our emotions, we're likely to feel some level of discomfort about getting caught.

Violating our values promotes stress. Even if we don't get caught cheating, we

Perils of high-tech cheating

Digital technology offers many blessings, but it also expands the options for cheating during a test. For example, one student tried to read class notes from an iPhone. Another student dictated his class notes into files stored on his iPod and tried to listen to them. At one school, students used cell phones to take photos of test questions. They sent the photos to classmates outside the testing room, who responded by text-messaging the answers.[5]

All of these students were caught. Schools are becoming sophisticated about detecting high-tech cheating. Some

install cameras in exam rooms. Others use software that monitors the programs running on students' computers during tests. And some schools simply ban all digital devices during tests.

The bottom line: If you cheat on a test, you are more likely than ever before to get caught.

There's no need to learn the hard way—through painful consequences—about the high costs of high-tech cheating. Using the suggestions in this chapter can help you succeed on tests *and* preserve your academic integrity.

can feel stress about violating our own ethical standards. Stress can compromise our physical health and overall quality of life.

Cheating on tests can make it easier to violate our integrity again. Human beings become comfortable with behaviors that they repeat. Cheating is no exception.

Think about the first time you drove a car. You might have felt excited—even a little frightened. Now driving is probably second nature, and you don't give it much thought. Repeated experience with driving creates familiarity, which lessens the intense feelings you had during your first time at the wheel.

We can experience the same process with almost any behavior. Cheating once will make it easier to cheat again.

And if we become comfortable with compromising our integrity in one area of life, we might find it easier to compromise in other areas.

Cheating lowers our self-concept. Whether or not we are fully aware of it, cheating sends us the message that we are not smart enough or responsible enough to make it on our own. We deny ourselves the celebration and satisfaction of authentic success.

An alternative to cheating is to become a master student. Ways to do this are described on every page of this book. ✕

LET GO
of test anxiety

If you freeze during tests and flub questions when you know the answers, you might be dealing with test anxiety.

To perform gracefully under the pressure of exams, put as much effort into preventing test anxiety as you do into mastering the content of your courses. Think of test taking as the "silent subject" on your schedule, equal in importance to the rest of your courses.

A little tension before a test is fine. That tingly, butterflies-in-the-stomach feeling you get from extra adrenaline can sharpen your awareness and keep you alert. You can enjoy the benefits of a little tension while you stay confident and relaxed.

Chad McDermott/Shutterstock.com

If you notice that your mind is consumed with worries and fears—that your thoughts are spinning out of control—mentally yell, "Stop!" If you're in a situation that allows it, yell it out loud. This action can allow you to redirect your thoughts.

Once you've broken the cycle of worry or panic, you can use any of the following techniques.

ACCEPT YOUR FEELINGS

Telling someone who's anxious about a test to "just calm down" is like turning up the heat on a pan that's already boiling over: The "solution" simply worsens the problem. If you take such advice to heart, you can end up with two problems. First, there's your worry about the test. Second, there's your worry about the fact that you're worried!

There's a way to deal with both problems at the same time: Simply accept your feelings, whatever they are. Fear and anxiety tend to increase with resistance. The more you try to suppress them, the more intensity the feelings gain.

As an alternative, stop resisting. See anxiety as a cluster of thoughts and body sensations. Watch the thoughts as they pass through your mind. Observe the sensations as they wash over you. Let them arise, peak, and pass away. No feeling lasts forever. The moment you accept fear, you pave the way for its release.

DESCRIBE YOUR THOUGHTS IN WRITING

Certain thoughts tend to increase test anxiety. One way to defuse them is to simply acknowledge them. To get the full benefit of this technique, take the time to make a list. Write down what you think and feel about an upcoming test. Capture everything that's on your mind, and don't stop to edit. One study indicates that this technique can relieve anxiety and potentially raise your test score.[6]

DISPUTE YOUR THOUGHTS

You can take the previous technique one step further. Do some critical thinking. Remember that anxiety-creating thoughts about tests often boil down to this statement: *Getting a low grade on a test is a disaster.* Do the math, however: A four-year degree often involves taking about 32 courses (8 courses per year over four years for a full-time student). This means that your final grade on any one course amounts to about only 3 percent of your total grade point average. This is *not* an excuse to avoid studying. It is simply a reason to keep tests in perspective.

PRAISE YOURSELF

Many of us take the first opportunity to belittle ourselves: "Way to go, dummy! You don't even know the answer to the first question on the test." We wouldn't dream of treating a friend this way, yet we do it to ourselves. An alternative is to give yourself some encouragement. Treat yourself as if you are your own best friend. Prepare carefully for each test. Then remind yourself, "I am ready. I can do a great job on this test."

CONSIDER THE WORST

Rather than trying to put a stop to your worrying, consider the very worst thing that could happen. Take your fear to the limit of absurdity. Imagine the catastrophic problems that might occur if you were to fail the test. You might say to yourself, "Well, if I fail this test, I might fail the course, lose my financial aid, and get kicked out of school. Then I won't be able to get a job, so the bank will repossess my car, and I'll start drinking." Keep going until you see the absurdity of your predictions. After you stop chuckling, you can backtrack to discover a reasonable level of concern.

BREATHE

You can calm physical sensations within your body by focusing your attention on your breathing. Concentrate on the air going in and out of your lungs. Experience it as it passes through your nose and mouth. Do this exercise for two to five minutes. If you notice that you are taking short, shallow breaths, begin to take longer and deeper breaths. Imagine your lungs to be a pair of bagpipes. Expand your chest to bring in as much air as possible. Then listen to the plaintive chords as you slowly release the air.

OVER-PREPARE FOR TESTS

Performing artists know that stage fright can temporarily reduce their level of skill. That's

Have some FUN!

Contrary to popular belief, finals week does not have to be a drag. In fact, if you have used techniques in this chapter, exam week can be fun. You will have done most of your studying long before finals arrive.

When you are well prepared for tests, you can even use fun as a technique to enhance your performance. The day before a final, go for a run or play a game of basketball. Take in a movie or a concert. A relaxed brain is a more effective brain. If you have studied for a test, your mind will continue to prepare itself even while you're at the movies. Get plenty of rest too. There's no need to cram until 3 a.m. when you have reviewed material throughout the term.

why they often over-prepare for a performance. Musicians will rehearse a piece so many times that they can play it without thinking. Actors will go over their parts until they can recite lines in their sleep.

As you prepare for tests, you can apply the same principle. Read, recite, and review the content of each course until you know it cold. Then review again. For math courses, work most or all of the problems in your textbook, even problems that are not assigned. The idea is to create a margin of mastery that can survive even the most extreme feelings of anxiety.

CARE FOR YOUR BODY AS MUCH AS YOUR MIND

Being well rested and fed on exam day won't guarantee a higher test score. However, preparing for a test physically as well as mentally can reduce stress. Because sleep deprivation can affect memory, avoid all-nighters as a study strategy. Also moderate your use of mood-altering chemicals, including caffeine and alcohol.

TAKE THIS ARTICLE TO WORK

You are not necessarily done with tests, appraisals, or assessments once you graduate. People in many careers prepare for licensing tests and certification exams. You might even go back to school for another degree. Use the ideas presented to make peace with tests at any stage of your life.

In the workplace, performance reviews offer a test-like situation. These usually take place in a meeting with your direct supervisor at work. Reviews follow various formats, and organizations have their own systems for rating performance. To get the most from these meetings, focus on answering three questions: "What am I doing well? What could I do better? What skills are most important for me to develop right now?"

Also keep this in mind: The same techniques that help you manage test anxiety can also help you approach job interviews with confidence. If you feel nervous before an interview, experiment with disputing your thoughts, praising yourself, accepting the worst possible outcome, and yelling, "Stop!" when stressful thoughts arise. Also apply strategies for relaxing and dealing with emotions. ✖

Getting ready for MATH TESTS

Many students who could succeed in math shy away from the subject. Some had negative experiences in past courses. Others believe that math is only for gifted students.

At some level, however, math is open to all students. There's more to this subject than memorizing formulas and manipulating numbers. Imagination, creativity, and problem-solving skills are important, too.

iStockphoto.com/DNY59

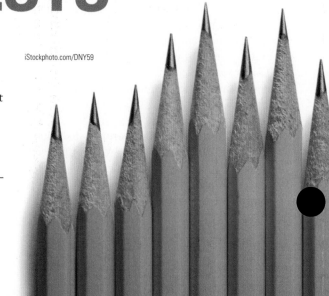

Consider a three-part program for math success. Begin with strategies for overcoming math anxiety. Next, boost your study skills. Finally, let your knowledge shine during tests.

OVERCOME MATH ANXIETY

Many schools offer courses in overcoming math anxiety. Ask your advisor about resources on your campus. Also experiment with the following suggestions.

Connect math to life. Think of the benefits of mastering math courses. You'll have more options for choosing a major and a career. Math skills can also put you at ease in everyday situations—calculating the tip for a waiter, balancing your checkbook, working with a spreadsheet on a computer. If you follow baseball statistics, cook, do construction work, or snap pictures with a camera, you'll use math. And speaking the language of math can help you feel at home in a world driven by technology.

Pause occasionally to get an overview of the branch of math that you're studying. What's it all about? What basic problems is it designed to solve? How do people apply this knowledge in daily life? For example, many architects, engineers, and space scientists use calculus daily.

Take a First Step. Math is cumulative. Concepts build upon each other in a certain order. If you struggled with algebra, you may have trouble with trigonometry or calculus.

To ensure that you have an adequate base of knowledge, tell the truth about your current level of knowledge and skill. Before you register for a math course, locate the assigned texts for any prerequisite courses. If the material in those books seems new or difficult for you, see the instructor. Ask for suggestions on ways to prepare for the course.

Notice your pictures about math. Sometimes what keeps people from succeeding at math is their mental picture of mathematicians. They see a man dressed in a baggy plaid shirt and brown wingtip shoes. He's got a calculator on his belt and six pencils jammed in his shirt pocket.

These pictures are far from realistic. Succeeding in math won't turn you into a nerd. Actually, you'll be able to enjoy school more, and your friends will still like you.

Mental pictures about math can be funny, but they can have serious effects. If math is seen as a field for white males, then women and people of color are likely to get excluded. Promoting math success for all students helps to overcome racism and sexism.

Change your conversation about math. When students fear math, they often say negative things to themselves about their abilities in this subject. Many times this self-talk includes statements such as *I'll never be fast enough at solving math problems* or *I'm good with words, so I can't be good with numbers.*

Get such statements out in the open, and apply some emergency critical thinking. You'll find two self-defeating assumptions lurking there: *Everybody else is better at math and science than I am* and *Because I don't understand a math concept right now, I'll never understand it.* Both of these statements are illogical.

Replace negative beliefs with logical, realistic statements that affirm your ability to succeed in math: *Any confusion I feel now can be resolved. I learn math without comparing myself to others.* And *I ask whatever questions are needed to aid my understanding.*

Choose your response to stress. Math anxiety is seldom just "in your head." It can also register as sweaty palms, shallow breathing, tightness in the chest, or a mild headache. Instead of trying to ignore these sensations, just notice them without judgment. Over time, simple awareness decreases their power. In addition, use stress management techniques.

No matter what you do, remember to breathe. You can relax in any moment just by making your breath slower and deeper. Practice doing this while you study math. It will come in handy at test time.

BOOST STUDY SKILLS FOR MATH

Choose teachers with care. Whenever possible, find a math teacher whose approach to math matches your learning style. Talk with several teachers until you find one you enjoy.

Another option is to ask around. Maybe your academic advisor can recommend math teachers. Also ask classmates to name their favorite math teachers—and to explain the reasons for their choices.

In some cases, only one teacher will be offering the math course you need. The suggestions that follow can be used to learn from a teacher regardless of his teaching style.

Take math courses back to back. Approach math in the same way that you learn a foreign language. If you take a year off in between Spanish I and Spanish II, you won't gain much fluency. To master a language, you take courses back to back. It works the same way with math, which is a language in itself.

Avoid short courses. Courses that you take during summer school or another shortened term are condensed. You might find yourself doing far more reading and homework each week than you do in longer courses. If you enjoy math, the extra intensity can provide a stimulus to learn. But if math is not your favorite subject, give yourself extra time. Enroll in courses spread out over more calendar days.

Form a study group. During the first week of each math course, organize a study group. Ask each member to bring five problems to group meetings, along with solutions. Also exchange contact information so that you can stay in touch via email, phone, and text messaging.

Make your text top priority. Math courses are often text driven. Budget for math textbooks and buy them as early as possible. Class activities closely follow the book. This fact underscores the importance of completing your reading assignments. Master one concept before going on to the next, and stay current with your reading. Be willing to read slowly and reread sections as needed.

Do homework consistently. Students who succeed in math do their homework daily—

from beginning to end, and from the easy problems all the way through the hard problems. If you do homework consistently, you're not likely to be surprised on a test.

When doing homework, use a common process to solve similar problems. There's comfort in rituals, and using familiar steps can help to reduce math anxiety.

Take notes that promote success in math. Though math courses are often text-driven, you might find that the content and organization of your notes makes a big difference as well. Take notes during every class and organize them by date. Also, number the pages of your notes. Create a table of contents or index for them so that you can locate key concepts quickly.

In addition, make separate notes to integrate material from class meetings and reading assignments. Paul Nolting, author of the *Math Study Skills Workbook*, suggests that you create a large table with three columns: Key Words/Rules, Examples, and Explanation.[7] Updating this table weekly is a way to review for tests, uncover questions, and monitor your understanding.

Participate in class. Success in math depends on your active involvement. Attend class regularly. Complete homework assignments *when they're due*—not just before the test. If you're confused, get help right away from an instructor, tutor, or study group. Instructors' office hours, free on-campus tutoring, and classmates are just a few of the resources available to you. Also support class participation by scheduling time for homework. Make daily contact with math.

Math tests often involve lists of problems to solve. Ask your instructor about what type of tests to expect. Then prepare for the tests, using strategies from this chapter.

Ask questions fearlessly. It's a cliché, and it's true: In math, there are no dumb questions. Ask whatever questions will aid your understanding. Keep a running list of them, and bring the list to class.

Read actively. To get the most out of your math texts, read with paper and pencil in hand. Work out examples. Copy diagrams, formulas, and equations. Use chapter summaries and introductory outlines to organize your learning. From time to time, stop, close your book, and mentally reconstruct the steps in solving a problem. Before you memorize a formula, understand the basic concepts behind it.

USE TESTS TO SHOW WHAT YOU KNOW

Practice problem solving. To get ready for math tests, work *lots* of problems. Find out whether practice problems or previous tests are on file in the library, in the math department, or with your math teacher.

Isolate the types of problems that you find the most difficult. Practice them more often. Be sure to get help with these kinds of problems *before* exhaustion or frustration sets in.

To prepare for tests, practice working problems fast. Time yourself. This activity is a great one for math study groups.

Approach problem solving with a three-step process, as shown in Figure 6.1. During each step, apply an appropriate strategy.

Practice test taking. In addition to solving problems, create practice tests:

- Print out a set of problems, and set a timer for the same length of time as your testing period.
- Whenever possible, work on these problems in the same room where you will take the actual test.
- Use only the kinds of supporting materials— such as scratch paper or lists of formulas— that will be allowed during the test.
- As you work problems, use deep breathing or another technique to enter a more relaxed state.

To get the most value from practice tests, use them to supplement—not replace—your daily homework.

1: Prepare	2: Compute	3: Check
• Read each problem two or three times, slowly and out loud whenever possible. • Consider creating a chart with three columns labeled *What I already know*, *What I want to find out*, and *What connects the two*. The third column is the place to record a formula that can help you solve the problem. • Determine which arithmetic operations (addition, subtraction, multiplication, division) or formulas you will use to solve the problem. • See if you can estimate the answer before you compute it.	• Reduce the number of unknowns as much as you can. Consider creating a separate equation to solve each unknown. • When solving equations, carry out the algebra as far as you can before plugging in the actual numbers. • Cancel and combine. For example, if the same term appears in both dividend and divisor, they will cancel each other out. • Remember that it's OK to make several attempts at solving the problem before you find an answer.	• Plug your answer back into the original equation or problem and see if it works out correctly. • Ask yourself if your answer seems likely when compared with your estimate. For example, if you're asked to apply a discount to an item, that item should cost less in your solution. • Perform opposite operations. If a problem involves multiplication, check your work by division; add, then subtract; factor, then multiply; find the square root, then the square; differentiate, then integrate. • Keep units of measurement clear. Say that you're calculating the velocity of an object. If you're measuring distance in meters and time in seconds, the final velocity should be in meters per second.

Figure 6.1 **Problem-Solving Process for Math Problems**

practicing
CRITICAL THINKING

19

Use learning styles for math success

Feel free to modify any of the suggested strategies for mastering math courses so that they work for you. Or invent new techniques of your own.

If you're a visual learner, for example, you might color-code your notes by writing key terms and formulas in red ink. If you like to learn by speaking and listening, consider reading key passages in your textbooks out loud. And if you're a kinesthetic learner, use "manipulatives," such as magnetic boards with letters and numbers, when you study math.

For more ideas, see the articles about learning styles in the First Steps chapter of this book. Commit to using at least one new strategy. Describe exactly what you will do.

Ask appropriate questions. If you don't understand a test item, ask for clarification. The worst that can happen is that an instructor or proctor will politely decline to answer your question.

Write legibly. Put yourself in the instructor's place. Imagine the prospect of grading stacks of illegible answer sheets. Make your answers easy to read. If you show your work, underline key sections and circle your answer.

Do your best. There are no secrets involved in getting ready for math tests. Master some stress management techniques, do your homework, get answers to your questions, and work sample problems. If you've done those things, you're ready for the test and deserve to do well. If you haven't done all those things, just do the best you can.

Remember that your personal best can vary from test to test, and even from day to day. Even if you don't answer all test questions correctly, you can demonstrate what you *do* know right now.

During the test, notice when solutions come easily. Savor the times when you feel relaxed and confident. If you ever feel math anxiety in the future, these are the times to remember.[8]

Studying across the
CURRICULUM

Think for a moment about the range of subjects that you're asked to study in higher education. Schools offer courses in everything from algebra to zoology, and you'll sample a variety of them. The challenge is to shift intellectual gears so that you can succeed in all those different subjects.

Some of the subjects you'll study in higher education share a single purpose—to *propose theories based on observations.* Physics, biology, and chemistry offer theories to explain and predict events in the natural world. Social sciences, such as psychology and sociology, offer theories to predict and explain events in the human world.

Other subjects go beyond theory to *define problems*

Subject Area	Strategies for Test Preparation
Humanities: English, literature, public speaking, history, religion, philosophy, fine arts	• Deepen your reading skills by previewing and reviewing each assignment. • Keep a dictionary handy, and create an updated list of new words and their definitions. • Experiment with several different formats for taking notes. • Keep a personal journal in which you practice writing and make connections between the authors and ideas that you're studying. • Take part in class discussions, and welcome chances to speak in front of groups.
Math and natural sciences: algebra, geometry, calculus, chemistry, biology, physics	• Before registering for a course, make sure that you are adequately prepared through prior course work. • In your notes, highlight basic principles—definitions, assumptions, and axioms. • Learn concepts in the sequence presented by your instructor. • If you feel confused, ask a question immediately. • Attend all classes, practice solving problems every day, and check your work carefully. • Translate word problems into images or symbols; translate images and symbols into words. • Balance abstract ideas with concrete experiences, including laboratory sessions and study groups. • Take math courses back to back so you can apply what you learn in one level of a math course immediately to the next level.
Social sciences: sociology, psychology, economics, political science, anthropology, geography	• Pay special attention to theories—statements that are used to explain relationships between observations and predict events. • Expect to encounter complex and contradictory theories, and ask your instructor about ways to resolve disagreements among experts in the field. • Ask your instructor to explain the scientific method and how it is used to arrive at theories in each of the social sciences. • Ask about current issues in the social sciences. • Ask for examples of a theory, and look for them in your daily life.
Foreign languages: learning to speak, read, and write any language that is new to you	• Pay special attention to the "rules"—principles of grammar, noun forms, and verb tenses. For each principle, list correct and incorrect examples. • Spend some time reading, writing, or speaking the language every day. • Welcome the opportunity to practice speaking in class, where you can get immediate feedback. • Start or join a study group in each of your language classes. • Spend time with people who are already skilled in speaking the language. • Travel to a country where the language is widely spoken. • Take your language courses back to back to ensure fluency.

*Figure 6.2 **Cross-Curriculum Study Strategies***

and offer solutions. Their subjects range from the abstract problems of pure mathematics to the practical problems of engineering and computer science.

Courses in the arts do not propose carefully reasoned theories. Nor do they focus on solving problems. Instead, they *teach through vicarious experience.* When you read a novel, see a play, or watch a film, you view the world through another human being's eyes. Just as you learn from your own experience, you can learn from the experience of others.

To deal with all those differences in subjects, pull out a full toolbox of strategies. When preparing for tests in specific subjects, consider the suggestions in Figure 6.2. Then create more strategies of your own. ✄

The test isn't over
UNTIL . . .

Many students believe that a test is over as soon as they turn in the answer sheet. Consider another point of view: You're not done with a test until you know the answer to any question that you missed—and why you missed it.

This point of view offers major benefits. Tests in many courses are cumulative. In other words, the content included on the first test is assumed to be working knowledge for the second test, midterm, or final exam. When you discover what questions you missed and understand the reasons for lost points, you learn something—and you greatly increase your odds of achieving better scores later in the course.

To get the most value from any test, take control of what you do at two critical points: the time immediately following the test and the time when the test is returned to you.

Immediately following the test. After finishing a test, your first thought might be to nap, snack, or go out with friends to celebrate. Restrain those impulses for a short while so that you can reflect on the test. The time you invest now carries the potential to raise your grades in the future.

To begin with, sit down in a quiet place. Take a few minutes to write some Discovery Statements related to your experience of taking the test. Describe how you felt about taking the test, how effective your review strategies were, and whether you accurately predicted the questions that appeared on the test.

Follow up with an Intention Statement or two. State what, if anything, you will do dif-ferently to prepare for the next test. The more specific you are, the better.

When the test is returned. When a returned test includes a teacher's comments, view this document as a treasure trove of intellectual gold.

First, make sure that the point totals add up correctly, and double-check for any other errors in grading. Even the best teachers make an occasional mistake.

Next, look at the test items that you missed. Ask these questions:

- On what material did the teacher base test questions—readings, lectures, discussions, or other class activities?
- What types of questions appeared in the test—objective (such as matching items, true/false questions, or multiple choice), short answer, or essay?
- What types of questions did you miss?
- Can you learn anything from the instructor's comments that will help you prepare for the next test?
- What strategies did you use to prepare for this test? What would you do differently to prepare for your next test?

Also see whether you can correct any answers that lost points. To do this, carefully analyze the source of your errors, and find a solution. Consult Figure 6.3 for help. ✖

Source of test error	Possible solutions
Study errors—studying material that was not included on the test, or spending too little time on material that *did* appear on the test	• Ask your teacher about specific topics that will be included on a test. • Practice predicting test questions. • Form a study group with class members to create mock tests.
Careless errors, such as skipping or misreading directions	• Read and follow directions more carefully—especially when tests are divided into several sections with different directions. • Set aside time during the next test to proofread your answers.
Concept errors—mistakes made when you do not understand the underlying principles needed to answer a question or solve a problem	• Look for patterns in the questions you missed. • Make sure that you complete all assigned readings, attend all lectures, and show up for laboratory sessions. • Ask your teacher for help with specific questions.
Application errors— mistakes made when you understand underlying principles but fail to apply them correctly	• Rewrite your answers correctly. • When studying, spend more time on solving sample problems. • Predict application questions that will appear in future tests, and practice answering them.
Test mechanics errors—missing more questions in certain parts of the test than others, changing correct answers to incorrect ones at the last minute, leaving items blank, miscopying answers from scratch paper to the answer sheet	• Set time limits for taking each section of a test, and stick to them. • Proofread your test answers carefully. • Look for patterns in the kind of answers you change at the last minute. • Change answers only if you can state a clear and compelling reason to do so.

Figure 6.3 **Test Errors and Possible Solutions**

F is for Feedback

When some students get an F on an assignment, they interpret that letter as a message: "You are a failure." That interpretation is not accurate. Getting an F means only that you failed a test—not that you failed your life.

From now on, imagine that the letter F when used as a grade represents another word: *feedback*. An F is an indication that you didn't understand the material well enough. It's a message to do something differently before the next test or assignment. If you interpret F as *failure*, you don't get to change anything. But if you interpret F as *feedback*, you can change your thinking and behavior in ways that promote your success. You can choose a new learning strategy or let go of an excuse about not having the time to study.

Getting prompt and meaningful feedback on your performance is a powerful strategy for learning *anything*. Tests are not the only source of feedback. Make a habit of asking for feedback from your instructors, advisors, classmates, coworkers, friends, family members, and anyone else who knows you. Just determine what you want to improve and ask, "How am I doing?"

Celebrate
MISTAKES

The title of this article is no mistake. And it is not a suggestion that you purposely set out to *make* mistakes. Rather, the goal is to shine a light on mistakes so that we can examine them and fix them. Mistakes that are hidden cannot be corrected and are often worth celebrating for the following reasons.

Mistakes are valuable feedback. Mistakes are part of the learning process. In fact, mistakes are often more interesting and more instructive than are successes.

Mistakes demonstrate that we're taking risks. People who play it safe make few mistakes. Making mistakes can be evidence that we're stretching to the limit of our abilities—growing, risking, and learning.

Celebrating mistakes gets them out into the open. When we celebrate a mistake, we remind ourselves that the person who made the mistake is not bad—just human. Everyone makes mistakes. And hiding mistakes takes a lot of energy that could be channeled into correcting errors. This is not a recommendation that you purposely set out to make mistakes. Mistakes are not an end in

yuris/Shutterstock.com

themselves. Rather, their value lies in what we learn from them. When we make a mistake, we can admit it and correct it.

Mistakes happen only when we're committed to making things work. Imagine a school where teachers usually come to class late. Residence halls are never cleaned, and scholarship checks are always late. The administration is in chronic debt, students seldom pay tuition on time, and no one cares. In this school, the word *mistake* would have little meaning. Mistakes become apparent only when people are committed to quality.

Celebrate mistakes at work. Recall a mistake you made at work and then write about it. In a Discovery Statement, describe what you did to create a result you didn't want ("I discovered that I tend to underestimate the number of hours projects take"). Then write an Intention Statement describing something you can do differently in the future ("I intend to keep track of my actual hours on each project so that I can give more accurate estimates"). Putting your insights and intentions in writing helps you gain perspective and draw powerful lessons from your experience. ✴

NOTABLE
failures

As you experiment with memory techniques, you may try a few that fail at crucial moments—such as during a test. Just remember that many people before you have failed miserably before succeeding brilliantly. Consider a few examples.

The first time **Jerry Seinfeld** walked onstage at a comedy club as a professional comic, he looked out at the audience and froze.

When **Lucille Ball** began studying to be an actress in 1927, she was told by the head instructor of the John Murray Anderson Drama School, "Try any other profession."

In high school, actor and comic **Robin Williams** was voted "Least Likely to Succeed."

Walt Disney was fired by a newspaper editor because "he lacked imagination and had no good ideas."

R. H. Macy failed seven times before his store in New York City caught on.

Emily Dickinson had only seven poems published in her lifetime.

Decca Records turned down a recording contract with the **Beatles** with an unprophetic evaluation: "We don't like their sound. Groups of guitars are on their way out."

In 1954, Jimmy Denny, manager of the Grand Ole Opry, fired **Elvis Presley** after one performance.

Babe Ruth is famous for his past home run record, but for decades he also held the record for strikeouts. **Mark McGwire** broke that record.

After **Carl Lewis** won the gold medal for the long jump in the 1996 Olympic Games, he was asked to what he attributed his longevity, having competed for almost 20 years. He said, "Remembering that you have both wins and losses along the way. I don't take either one too seriously."

Michael Jordan was cut from his high school basketball team. "I've missed more than 9,000 shots in my career," he later said. "I've lost almost 300 games. Twenty-six times I've been trusted to take the game-winning shot . . . and missed. I've failed over and over and over again in my life. That is why I succeed." ✄

Source: Adapted from "But They Did Not Give Up," Division of Educational Studies, Emory University, accessed February 24, 2016, from http://www.uky.edu/~eushe2/Pajares/OnFailingG.html.

---

practicing CRITICAL THINKING 20

20 things I like to do

One way to relieve tension is to mentally yell, "Stop!" and substitute a pleasant daydream for the stressful thoughts and emotions you are experiencing.

To create a supply of pleasant images to recall during times of stress, conduct an eight-minute brainstorm about things you like to do. Your goal is to generate at least 20 ideas. Time yourself, and write as fast as you can.

When you have completed your list, study it. Pick out two activities that seem especially pleasant, and elaborate on them by creating a mind map. Write down all of the memories you have about that activity.

You can use these images to calm yourself in stressful situations.

master student PROFILE

Lalita Booth }

Once homeless and a teenage mother, now CEO of a company that she co-founded.

At age 18, Lalita Booth was the mother of a baby boy, raising the child alone while her husband was away in the army.

"When my ex joined the military, I was responsible for taking care of myself with only a GED and no relevant job skills," Booth said during an interview with CBS news. By then she'd already experienced separation from her parents, sexual abuse by a family friend, and a period of homelessness.

Eventually she sent her son, Kieren, to stay with his father's parents. "I used to sleep with his little blue T-shirt and I would cry myself to sleep because I missed him so much," Booth said. (Since then she has reunited with Kieren.)

Soon afterward she decided "to start taking on things that I had though were impossible and proving myself wrong." This pattern of setting huge goals and pursuing them against all odds became a theme of her adult life.

Consider her decision at age 23 to move to Florida and enroll in Seminole Community College. As a high school dropout at age 16, she'd been out of school for seven years (and had missed fifth grade altogether). Yet she thrived in her new academic environment and graduated in 2006 with an associate degree in business administration.

From Seminole she transferred to a four-year school, the University of Central Florida. There she earned dual bachelor's degrees in accounting and finance. From there it was on to an MBA from Harvard Business School and a Master of Public Policy degree from Harvard University's Kennedy School of Government.

The idea of going from community college to graduate degrees from a prestigious university—all within six years—might seem impossible. Yet Booth did it. When she left Harvard, she had yet to prove herself wrong.

One big factor in achieving her goals was mastery of money. Booth financed her degrees with over a half-million dollars in scholarships from 20 different sources. While at Central Florida, she also founded a nonprofit organization called the Lighthouse for Dreams Financial Literacy Project, with a goal of "helping disadvantaged youth prepare for a sound financial future."

This passion of Booth's fueled her work as a professional speaker and consultant to organizations across the country. In addition, she found time to volunteer as an intern at the Florida House of Representatives and at the United States Congress. "I would like to run the Department of the Treasury's office of financial education," she said in 2010.

As sometimes happens with people who think big, Booth's career took a different turn. In 2013, she became an interim director of Exceptional Lives, a nonprofit dedicated to "helping families of children gain access to better services and supports." Booth and her cofounders from Harvard began this work knowing that there were already plenty of useful resources for these families. Even so, much of the available information was too general, and many of the existing services were hard to find.

Exceptional Lives aims to solve this problem through a website (**exceptionallives.org**) that offers free online guides for families of people with disabilities. These guides are aimed at Massachusetts residents and powered by software that customizes the guides based on answers to a series of questions. After 15 minutes online, people who use Exceptional Lives have a clear list of next steps to take in getting the best support for their loved ones.

Though still involved with Exceptional Lives as a volunteer, Booth's current position is chief executive officer of Navitome, a company based on Navitome Guidance Software. Navitome is a direct outgrowth of Exceptional Lives and had the same founders. Whereas Exceptional Lives offers guidance for people with disabilities and their families, Navitome helps companies develop step-by-step, interactive guides for their employees and customers.

In her personal statement on the Navitome website, Booth explains that many businesses and nonprofits think they have *people* problems, but what they really have is *process* problems: "Almost everyone is capable of doing extraordinary work when they're given a clear process to follow and the right set of tools to work with.

"My job is to take things that are complex and overwhelming and transform them into something easy and routine," she adds. "Who wouldn't love that?"

Lalita Booth *chooses to detach from beliefs about what is "impossible."*

QUIZ

Chapter 6

1. According to the Power Process in this chapter, detaching is not the same as giving up.
   a. True
   b. False

2. Strategies for detaching include:
   a. Pay attention to your thoughts and physical sensations
   b. Practice relaxation
   c. Zoom out to a bigger picture
   d. All of the answer choices

3. According to the text, test scores are accurate measures of what you actually learn in a course.
   a. True
   b. False

4. According to the text, saying that you plan to "study" for a test is a powerful intention.
   a. True
   b. False

5. A study checklist is:
   a. A mind map of key concepts
   b. An outline of key concepts
   c. A summary of key concepts written in short paragraphs
   d. A to-do list that includes exactly what you will use to practice for a test

6. It is not a good idea to ask instructors about what a future test will include.
   a. True
   b. False

7. One recommended strategy for answering a multiple-choice question is to read all of the possible answers *before* answering the question in your head.
   a. True
   b. False

8. The presence of absolute qualifiers—such as *always* or *never*—often indicates a false statement.
   a. True
   b. False

9. Suggestions for taking essay tests include:
   a. Find out what an essay question is asking—precisely.
   b. Make a quick outline before you write.
   c. Get to the point in the first paragraph of your answer.
   d. Write legibly.
   e. All of the answer choices

10. People who are skilled at stress management remember that:
    a. A little tension before a test is fine.
    b. The goal is to eliminate tension completely.
    c. You should never consider the worst thing that can possibly happen if you fail a test.
    d. It is unwise to over-prepare for tests.
    e. All of the answer choices

Take your discoveries and intentions about tests to the next level by completing the following sentences.

Discovery

My score on the Tests section of the Discovery Wheel was . . .

One strategy that really helps me with taking tests is . . .

If I feel stressed about a test, I respond by . . .

Intention

The thing that I would most like to change about my experience of tests is . . .

To make this change, I intend to . . .

Action

The specific new behavior that I will practice is . . .

My cue for doing this behavior is . . .

My reward for practicing this habit is . . .

Practicing this habit can add to my career skills by . . .

style-photography/Shutterstock.com

Thinking

why

The ability to think creatively and critically helps you succeed in any course—and any career.

how

Remember a time in your life when you felt unable to choose among several different solutions to a problem or struggled with making a decision. Then scan this chapter to find useful ideas for decision making, problem solving, and critical thinking.

what if...

I could solve problems more creatively and make decisions in every area of life with more confidence?

what is included . . .

232   Power Process: Embrace the new

233   Critical thinking: A survival skill

235   Six kinds of thinking

238   A process for critical thinking

243   Finding "aha!": Creativity fuels critical thinking

245   Ways to create ideas

250   Attitudes, affirmations, and visualizations

252   Don't fool yourself: 15 common mistakes in logic

256   Think critically about information on the Internet

257   Gaining skill at decision making

258   Four ways to solve problems

260   Asking questions: Learning through inquiry

263   Thinking about your major

265   Service-learning: Turn thinking into contribution

268   Master Student Profile: Irshad Manji

do you have a minute?

Do a one-minute mental exercise to explore the relationship between thinking and happiness:

1.   Think of a person in your life that you love or an activity that you deeply enjoy doing.
2.   Imagine what it would be like to lose this person or be unable to do the activity.
3.   Express your thanks that this person or activity is currently part of your life. Complete this sentence: *I am grateful that . . .*

Psychologists refer to what you've just done as *savoring*. If you experienced a benefit from this exercise, then consider making it a habit.

POWERPROCESS

Embrace the new

Heraclitus, the ancient Greek philosopher, said that you can never step into the same river twice. A river is dynamic—ever flowing, ever changing.

The same thing is true of you.

Right now, you are not the same person you were when you started reading this page. Nerve cells in your brain are firing messages and making connections that didn't exist a second ago. There is new breath in your lungs. Old cells in your body have been replaced by new ones.

What's true about your body is also true of your behavior. Think about all the activities that depend on embracing the new: going to school, gaining knowledge, acquiring skills, succeeding with technology, making friends, and falling in love.

Both creative thinking and critical thinking call on us to embrace the new. We can think critically about a new idea only if we're willing to *consider* it in the first place. And it's hard to create something original or change our behavior if we insist on sticking with what's already familiar to us. All the game-changing devices in human history—from the wheel to the iPhone—happened only because their inventors were willing to embrace the new.

Embracing the new is more than just a nice idea. It's an essential skill for anyone who wants to survive and thrive in the work world. Your next career might be one that doesn't exist today. Think about certain job titles—*information architect, social media director, content strategist*—that came to life only in the twenty-first century. There are many more opportunities just waiting to be created.

When learning to embrace the new, start with the way you speak. Notice comments such as these:

"That can't possibly be true."

"That idea will never work."

"We tried that last year and failed."

Those statements represent the sound of a closed mind snapping shut. Consider replacing them with:

"What if that *were* true?"

"How could we make that idea work?"

"What could we do differently this time?"

To get the most value from this suggestion, remember that it's about more than being open to ideas. You can embrace the new on many levels: be willing to think what you've never thought before, to say what you've never said before, to do what you've never done before. This is the essence of learning, and it's the heart of this book.

Also remember that embracing the new does *not* mean trashing the old. Adopting a new attitude does not mean giving up all your current attitudes. Adopting a new habit does not mean changing all your current habits. When you open up to unfamiliar ideas and experiences, you get to keep your core values. You can embrace change and still take a stand for what's important to you.

As you test new ideas and experiment with new strategies, keep those that work and let go of the rest. You might find that your current beliefs and behaviors work well with just a few tweaks and subtle changes. And in any case, you can go into the unknown with a known process—the cycle of discovery, intention, and action.

What's new is often going to stick around anyway. You have two basic options: resist it or embrace it. The former is a recipe for frustration. The latter offers a fresh possibility in every moment. ✄

Galyna Andrushko/Shutterstock.com

CRITICAL THINKING:

A survival skill

We have hundreds of choices about what to buy, where to go, and who to be. It's easy to lose our heads in the crosscurrent of competing options—unless we develop skills in critical thinking. When we think critically, we can make choices with open eyes.

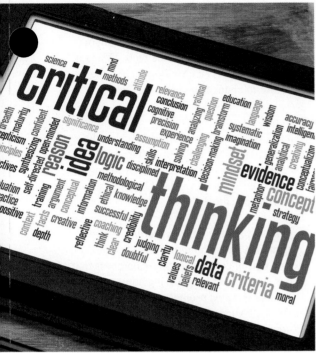

marekuliasz/Shutterstock.com

Society depends on persuasion. Advertisers want us to spend money on their products. Political candidates want us to "buy" their stands on the issues. Teachers want us to agree that their classes are vital to our success. Parents want us to accept their values. Authors want us to read their books. Broadcasters want us to spend our time in front of the radio or television, consuming their programs and not those of the competition. The business of persuasion has an impact on all of us.

A typical American sees thousands of television commercials each year, and TV is just one medium of communication. Add to that the writers and speakers who enter our lives through radio shows, magazines, books, billboards, brochures, Internet sites, and fundraising appeals—all with a product, service, cause, or opinion for us to embrace.

This flood of appeals leaves us with hundreds of choices about what to buy, where to go, and who to be. It's easy to lose our heads in the crosscurrent of competing ideas—unless we develop skills in critical thinking. When we think critically, we can make choices with open eyes.

It has been said that human beings are rational creatures. Yet no one is born an effective thinker. Critical thinking is a learned skill. This is one reason that you study so many subjects in higher education: math, science,

history, psychology, literature, and more. A broad base of courses helps you develop as a thinker. You see how people with different viewpoints arrive at conclusions, make decisions, and solve problems. This gives you a foundation for dealing with complex challenges in your career, your relationships, and your community.

Critical thinking frees us from nonsense. Novelist Ernest Hemingway once said that anyone who wants to be a great writer must have a built-in "crap" detector.[1] That inelegant comment points to a basic truth: as critical thinkers, we are constantly on the lookout for thinking that's inaccurate, sloppy, or misleading.

Critical thinking is a skill that will never go out of style. At various times in human history, nonsense has been taken for the truth. For example, people have believed the following:

- Illness results from an imbalance in the four vital fluids: blood, phlegm, black bile, and yellow bile.
- Racial integration of the armed forces will lead to destruction of soldiers' morale.
- Women are incapable of voting intelligently.
- We will never invent anything smaller than a transistor. (That was before the computer chip.)

The critical thinkers of history arose to challenge shortsighted ideas such as these. These courageous men and women held their peers to higher standards of critical thinking.

Even in mathematics and the hard sciences, the greatest advances take place when people re-examine age-old beliefs. Scientists continually uncover things that contradict everyday certainties. For example, physics presents us with a world where solid objects are made of atoms spinning around in empty space, where matter and energy are two forms of the same substance. At a moment's notice, the world can deviate from the "laws of nature." That is because those "laws" exist in our heads—not in the world.

Critical thinking frees us from self-deception.
Critical thinking is a path to freedom from half-truths and deception. You have the right to question everything that you see, hear, and read. Acquiring this ability is a major goal of a college education.

One of the reasons that critical thinking is so challenging—and so rewarding—is that we have a remarkable capacity to fool ourselves. Some of our ill-formed thoughts and half-truths have a source that hits a little close to home. That source is ourselves.

If you take a course in psychology, you might hear about the theory of cognitive dissonance.[2] This is a term for the tension we feel when we encounter a fact that contradicts our deeply held beliefs. To reduce the discomfort, we might deny the fact or explain it away with deceptive thinking.

For example, consider someone who stakes her identity on the fact that she is a valued employee. During a recession, she gets laid off. On her last day at work, she learns that her refusal to take part in on-the-job training sessions was the major reason that the company let her go. This brute fact contradicts her belief in her value. Her response: "I didn't need that training. I already knew that stuff anyway. Nobody at that company could teach me anything."

A skilled critical thinker would go beyond such self-justifying statements and ask questions instead: "What training sessions did I miss? Could I have learned something from them? Were there any signs that I was about to be laid off, and did I overlook them? What can I do to prevent this from happening again?"

Master students are willing to admit the truth when they discover that their thinking is fuzzy, lazy, based on a false assumption, or dishonest. These students value facts. When a solid fact contradicts a cherished belief, they are willing to change the belief.

More uses of critical thinking. Clear thinking promotes your success inside and outside the classroom. Any time that you are faced with a choice about what to believe or what to do, your thinking skills come in to play. Consider the following applications:

- *Critical thinking informs reading, writing, speaking, and listening.* These elements are the basis of communication—a process that occupies most of our waking hours.
- *Critical thinking promotes social change.* The institutions in any society—courts, governments, schools, businesses, nonprofit groups—are the products of cultural customs and trends. All social movements—from the American Revolution to the Civil Rights movement—come about through the work of engaged individuals who actively participated in their communities and questioned what was going on around them. As critical thinkers, we strive to understand and influence the institutions in our society.
- *Critical thinking uncovers bias and prejudice.* Working through our preconceived notions is a first step toward communicating with people of other races, ethnic backgrounds, and cultures.
- *Critical thinking reveals long-term consequences.* Crises occur when our thinking fails to keep pace with reality. An example is the world's ecological crisis, which arose when people polluted the earth, air, and water without considering the long-term consequences. Imagine how different our world would be if our leaders had thought like the first female chief of the Cherokees. Asked about the best advice her elders had given her, she replied, "Look forward. Turn what has been done into a better path. If you are a leader, think about the impact of your decision on seven generations into the future."

Critical thinking as thorough thinking. For some people, the term *critical thinking* has negative connotations. If you prefer, use *thorough* *thinking* instead. Both terms point to the same activities: sorting out conflicting claims, weighing the evidence, letting go of personal biases, and arriving at reasonable conclusions. These activities add up to an ongoing conversation: a constant process, not a final product.

We live in a culture that values quick answers and certainty. These concepts are often at odds with effective thinking. Thorough thinking is the ability to examine and re-examine ideas that might seem obvious. This kind of thinking takes time and the willingness to say three subversive words: *I don't know.*

Thorough thinking is also the willingness to change our opinions as we continue to examine a problem. This calls for courage and detachment. Just ask anyone who has given up a cherished point of view in light of new evidence.

Thorough thinking is the basis for much of what you do in school: reading, writing, speaking, listening, note taking, test taking, problem solving, and other forms of decision making.

Skilled students have strategies for accomplishing all these tasks. They distinguish between opinion and fact. They ask probing questions and make detailed observations. They uncover assumptions and define their terms. They make assertions carefully, basing them on sound logic and solid evidence. Almost everything that we call *knowledge* is a result of these activities. This means that critical thinking and learning are intimately linked.

Another kind of thorough thinking—planning—has the power to lift the quality of your daily life. When you plan, you are the equal of the greatest sculptor, painter, or playwright. More than creating a work of art, you are designing your life. *Becoming a Master Student* invites you to participate in this form of thinking by choosing your major, planning your career, and setting long-term goals.

Use the suggestions in this chapter to claim the thinking powers that are your birthright. The critical thinker is one aspect of the master student who lives inside you. ✳

SIX KINDS

of thinking

Thinking is a path to intellectual adventure. Although there are dozens of possible approaches to thinking well, the process boils down to *asking and answering questions*.

One quality of a master student is the ability to ask questions that lead to deeper learning. Your mind is an obedient servant. It will deliver answers at the same level as your questions. Becoming a critical thinker means being flexible and asking a wide range of questions.

A psychologist named Benjamin Bloom named six levels of thinking, as shown in Figure 7.1. He called them a *taxonomy of educational objectives*—basically, a list of different goals for learning.[3] Each level of thinking calls for asking and answering different kinds of questions.

Level 1: Remembering. At this level of thinking, the key question is *Can I recall the key terms, facts, or events?* To prompt level 1 thinking, an instructor might ask you to do the following:

- List the three parts of the master student process.
- Describe five qualities of a master student.
- Name the master student profiled in the first chapter of this book.

To study for a test with level 1 questions, you could create flash cards to review ideas from your readings and class notes. You could also read a book with a set of questions in mind and underline the answers to those questions in the text. Or you could memorize a list of definitions so that you can recite them exactly. These are just a few examples.

Although remembering is important, this is a relatively low level of learning. No critical or creative thinking is involved. You simply recognize or recall something that you've observed in the past.

Level 2: Understanding. At this level, the main question is *Can I explain this idea in my own words?* Often this means giving examples of an idea based on your own experience. The ability to summarize is also key to this level of thinking. Summarizing helps you to remember and understand.

Suppose that your instructor asks you to do the following:

- Explain the main point of the Power Process: "Ideas are tools."
- Write a summary of the steps involved in creating a PowerPoint presentation.
- Compare affirmations with visualizations, stating how they're alike and how they differ.

Other key words in level 2 questions are *discuss*, *estimate*, and *restate*. All of these are cues to go one step

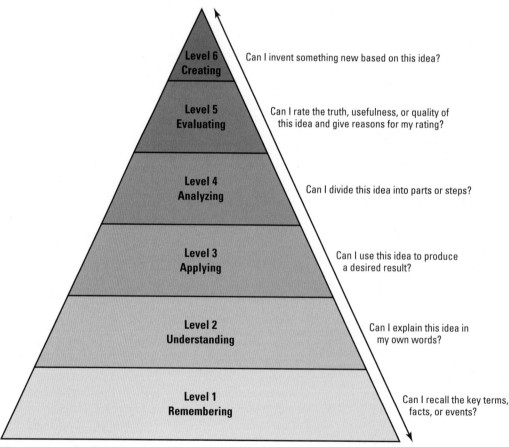

Figure 7.1 **Levels of Thinking**

- **Level 6 Creating** — Can I invent something new based on this idea?
- **Level 5 Evaluating** — Can I rate the truth, usefulness, or quality of this idea and give reasons for my rating?
- **Level 4 Analyzing** — Can I divide this idea into parts or steps?
- **Level 3 Applying** — Can I use this idea to produce a desired result?
- **Level 2 Understanding** — Can I explain this idea in my own words?
- **Level 1 Remembering** — Can I recall the key terms, facts, or events?

beyond remembering and to show that you truly *comprehend* an idea.

Level 3: Applying. Learning at level 3 means asking, *Can I use this idea to produce a desired result?* That result might include completing a task, meeting a goal, making a decision, or solving a problem.

Some examples of level 3 thinking are listed here:

- Write an affirmation about succeeding in school, based on the guidelines in this text.
- Use the guidelines in this text to write an effective goal for your career.
- Describe an action that you could take to demonstrate a professional work ethic.

Some key words in level 3 questions include *apply, solve, construct, plan, predict,* and *produce.*

Level 4: Analyzing. Questions at this level boil down to this: *Can I divide this idea into parts, groups, or steps?* For example, you could do the following:

- Divide a list of work skills into those that call for creative thinking, critical thinking, collaboration, or communication.
- Organize a list of 30 memory techniques into three different categories.
- Take a career goal and then list a series of actions you could take to achieve it by a specific date.

Other key words in level 4 questions are *classify, separate, distinguish,* and *outline.*

Level 5: Evaluating. Learning at level 5 means asking, *Can I rate the truth, usefulness, or quality of this idea and give reasons for my rating?* This is the level of thinking you would use to do the following:

- Judge the effectiveness of an Intention Statement.
- Recommend a method for taking lecture notes when an instructor talks fast.
- Rank the Power Processes in order of importance to you—from most useful to least useful.

Level 5 involves genuine critical thinking. At this level you agree with an idea, disagree with it, or suspend judgment until you get more information. In addition, you give reasons for your opinion and offer supporting evidence.

Some key words in level 5 questions are *critique, defend,* and *comment.*

Level 6: Creating. To think at this level, ask, *Can I invent something new based on this idea?* For instance, you might do the following:

- Invent your own format for taking lecture notes.
- Prepare a list of topics that you would cover if you were teaching a student success course.
- Imagine that you now have enough money to retire,

and then write goals you would like to accomplish with your extra time.
- Create a PowerPoint presentation based on ideas found in this chapter. Put the material in your own words, and use visual elements to enhance the points.

Creative thinking often involves analyzing an idea into parts and then combining those parts in a new way. Another source of creativity is taking several ideas and finding an unexpected connection among them. In either case, you are thinking at a very high level. You are going beyond agreement and disagreement to offer something unique— an original contribution of your own.

Questions for creative thinking often start with words such as *adapt, change, collaborate, compose, construct, create, design,* and *develop.* You might also notice phrases such as *What changes would you make . . . ? How could you improve . . . ? Can you think of another way to . . . ? What would happen if . . . ?*

FINDING ANSWERS
In each chapter of this book, you will find Practicing Critical Thinking exercises. As you complete them, you will answer questions at all six levels of Bloom's taxonomy. You'll get to solve specific problems and think through the kind of decisions you face in daily life. Approach each exercise as a way to awaken the master thinker inside you. ✄

A process for
CRITICAL THINKING

CHECK YOUR ATTITUDES

Be willing to find various points of view on any issue. Imagine George Bush, Cesar Chavez, and Barack Obama assembled in one room to debate the most desirable way to reshape our government. Picture Madonna, Oprah Winfrey, and Mark Zuckerberg leading a workshop on how to plan your career. When seeking out alternative points of view, let scenes like these unfold in your mind.

Dozens of viewpoints exist on every important issue: reducing crime, ending world hunger, educating our children, and countless other concerns. In fact, few problems have any single, permanent solution. Each generation produces its own answers to critical questions, based on current conditions. Our search for answers is a conversation that spans centuries. On each question, many voices are waiting to be heard. Add yours to the mix.

You can begin by seeking out alternative views with an open mind. When talking to another person, be willing to walk away with a new point of view—even if it's the one you brought to the table, supported with new evidence.

When asking questions, let go of the temptation to settle for just a single answer. Look for at least three. This is especially important when you're *sure* that you have the right answer to a complex question. Once you come up with a new possibility, say to yourself, "Yes, that is one answer. Now what's another?" Using this approach can lead to honest inquiry, creativity, and breakthroughs.

Be prepared: the world is complicated, and critical thinking is a complex business. Some of your answers might contradict others. Resist the temptation to have all of your ideas in a neat, orderly bundle.

Practice tolerance. Many ideas that are widely accepted in Western cultures—for example, civil liberties for people of color, and the right of women to vote—were once considered dangerous. Viewpoints that seem outlandish today might become widely accepted a century, a decade, or even a year from now. Remembering this idea can help us practice tolerance for differing beliefs. Doing this makes room for new ideas that can transform our lives.

Understand before criticizing. Notice that the six levels of thinking build on each other. Before you agree or disagree with an idea, make sure that you *remember* it accurately and truly *understand* it. Polished debaters make a habit of doing this. Often they can sum up their opponent's viewpoint better than anyone else can. This puts them in a much stronger position to *apply, analyze, evaluate,* and *create* ideas.

Effective understanding calls for reading and listening while suspending judgment. Enter another person's world by expressing her viewpoint in your own words. If you're conversing with that person, keep revising your summary until she agrees that you've stated her position accurately. If you're reading an article, write a short summary of it. Then scan the article again, checking to see whether your synopsis is on target.

Watch for hot spots. Many people have mental "hot spots"—topics that provoke strong opinions and feelings. Examples are abortion, homosexuality, gun control, and the death penalty.

To become more skilled at examining various points of view, notice your own particular hot spots. Make a clear intention to accept your feelings about these topics and to continue using critical thinking techniques in relation to them.

One way to cool down our hot spots is to remember that we can change or even give up our current opinions without giving up ourselves. We can remind ourselves that human beings are much more than the sum of their current opinions.

Also be sensitive to other people's hot spots. Demonstrate tolerance and respect before you start discussing highly personal issues.

Be willing to be uncertain. Some of the most profound thinkers have practiced the art of thinking by using a magic sentence: "I'm not sure yet."

It is courageous and unusual to take the time to pause, to look, to examine, to be thoughtful, to consider many points of view—and to be unsure. When a society adopts half-truths in a blind rush for certainty, a willingness to embrace uncertainty can move us forward.

CHECK FOR LOGIC

Logic is a branch of philosophy that seeks to distinguish between valid and invalid reasoning. Students of logic look at a series of related sentences to make sure that they are clear, consistent, and coherent.

Learning to think logically offers many benefits: when you think logically, you take your reading, writing, speaking, and listening skills to a higher level. You avoid costly mistakes in decision making. You can join discussions and debates with more confidence, cast your election votes with a clear head, and become a better-informed citizen.

The following suggestions will help you work with the building blocks of logical thinking: terms, assertions, arguments, assumptions.

It is courageous and unusual to take the time to pause, to look, to examine, to be thoughtful, to consider many points of view—and to be unsure.

Define key terms. A *term* is a word or phrase that refers to a clearly defined concept. Terms with several different meanings are ambiguous: fuzzy, vague, and unclear. One common goal of critical thinking is to remove ambiguous terms or define them clearly.

Conflicts of opinion can often be resolved—or at least clarified—when we define our key terms up front. This is especially true with abstract, emotion-laden terms such as *freedom, peace, progress,* or *justice.* Blood has been shed over the meaning of those words. Define them with care.

Your first task is to locate key terms. Skilled writers and speakers often draw attention to them. Even when they don't, you can use clues to spot them:

- Look or listen for words that are new to you.
- Be alert for words or phrases that are frequently repeated—especially in prominent places in a text or in a speech, such as an overview, introduction, summary, or conclusion.
- When reading, check the index for words or phrases that have many page references.

Also see whether the text includes a glossary. And look for words that are printed in *italics* or **boldface**.

As you look for clues, remember that several different words or phrases can stand for the same term. In this chapter, for example, *self-evident truth* and *assumption* are different words that refer to the same concept.

Look for assertions. A speaker or writer's key terms occur in a larger context called an *assertion*—a complete sentence that contains one or more key terms. The purpose of an assertion is to define a term or to state relationships between terms. These relationships are the essence of what we mean by the term *knowledge.*

To find a speaker or writer's assertions, listen or look for key sentences. These are sentences that make an important point or state a general conclusion.

Often speakers and writers will give you clues to their key sentences. Speakers will pause to emphasize these sentences or precede them with phrases such as "My point is that . . ." Writers may present key sentences in italics or boldface, or they may include them in summaries.

Look for arguments. Most of us think of argument as the process of disagreement or conflict. For specialists in logic, this term has a different meaning. For them, an *argument* is a series of related assertions.

There are two major types of reasoning used in building arguments—deductive and inductive.

Deductive reasoning builds arguments by starting with a general assertion and leading to a more specific one. Here's a classic example that you might hear in a beginning philosophy course. It involves Socrates, an ancient Greek philosopher:

- All men are mortal.
- Socrates is a man.
- Therefore, Socrates is mortal.

These three assertions make an argument that Socrates is mortal. Notice that in deductive reasoning, each assertion is like a link in a chain. A weakness or error in any link can break the entire chain.

With *inductive reasoning*, the chain of logic proceeds in the opposite direction—from specific to general. Suppose that you apply for a job and the interviewer says, "We hired two people from your school who did not work out well for us. When we found out where you're taking classes, our management team was concerned."

In this case, the interviewer began with specific examples ("We hired two people from your school"). From there he proceeded to a more general conclusion, which went unstated: *Therefore, students from your school do not make good employees.* This argument is a simple example of inductive reasoning.

As you can see, inductive reasoning can also contain errors. One is the error of *hasty generalization*—coming to a conclusion too quickly. For example, experience with two graduates does not offer enough evidence for judging the abilities of hundreds or even thousands of people who get degrees from your school.

Another possible error is the *false cause*. You will often observe one event that usually happens after another event. However, this does not mean that the first event *caused* the second event. It's true, for example, that children get more dental cavities as they develop a larger vocabulary. However, this does not mean that a large vocabulary causes cavities. Rather, a third factor is involved: children learn more words *and* get more cavities as they get older. Age is the key factor—not vocabulary.

Remember the power of assumptions.

Assumptions are beliefs that guide our thinking and behavior. Assumptions can be simple and ordinary. For example, when you drive a car, you assume that other drivers know the meaning of traffic signals and stop signs.

In other cases, assumptions are more complex and have larger effects. Scientists, for instance, assume that events in the world take place in a predictable way. Making this assumption makes it possible to develop the principles of biology, chemistry, and physics.

Despite their power to influence our speaking and action, assumptions are often unstated. People can remain unaware of their most basic and far-reaching assumptions—the very ideas that shape their lives. Heated conflict and hard feelings often result when people argue on the level of opinions and forget that the real conflict lies at the level of their assumptions.

Look for stated assumptions.

Sometimes you will find speakers and writers who are kind enough to state their assumptions directly. A famous example comes from the Declaration of Independence, adopted on July 4, 1776, by the 13 colonies that later developed into the United States. It included the "self-evident truths" that:

- All men are created equal.
- Men are born with rights to life, liberty, and happiness.
- Governments exist to secure these rights and deserve to be overthrown if they fail.

Over time, people change their minds about which assumptions are worth accepting. The men who wrote the Declaration of Independence did *not* assume that women or people of color are "endowed by their Creator with certain unalienable Rights." Later Americans passed amendments to the United States Constitution and a series of laws to widen the scope of their original "self-evident truths."

Look for unstated assumptions.

In many cases, assumptions are unstated and offered without evidence. They can sneak up on you in the middle of an argument and take you on a one-way trip to confusion.

In addition, people often hold many assumptions at the same time. And those assumptions might contradict each other. This makes uncovering assumptions a feat worthy of the greatest detective.

You can follow a two-step method for testing the validity of any argument. First, state the assumptions. Second, see whether you can find any exceptions to the assumptions.

Consider this statement: "My mother and father have a good marriage; after all, they're still together after 35 years." Behind this statement is an assumption: *If you've been married a long time, you must have a good relationship.* Yet there are possible exceptions. You might know married couples who have stayed together for decades even though they are unhappy in the relationship.

Uncovering assumptions and looking for exceptions can help you detect many errors in logic.

CHECK FOR EVIDENCE

In addition to testing arguments with the tools of logic, look carefully at the evidence used to support those arguments. Evidence comes in several forms, including facts, comments from recognized experts in a field, and examples.

To think critically about evidence, ask the following questions:

- Are all or most of the relevant facts presented?
- Are the facts consistent with each other?

- Are facts presented accurately?
- Are enough examples included to make a solid case for the assertion?
- Do the examples truly support the assertion?
- Are the examples typical? That is, could the author or speaker support the assertion with other examples that are similar?
- Is the expert credible—truly knowledgeable about the topic?
- Is the expert biased? For example, is the expert paid to represent the views of a corporation that is promoting a product or service?
- Is the expert quoted accurately?
- If the speaker or writer appeals to your emotions, is this done in a way that is also logical and based on evidence?

Answering these questions takes time and intellectual energy. It's worth it. You'll gain skills in critical thinking that will help you succeed in any class or career that you choose. ✘

practicing CRITICAL THINKING

21

Critical thinking scenarios

BUILDING A PORTFOLIO ON A BUDGET

Read the following scenario. Then write about which person in this scenario best demonstrates the attitudes of a master thinker. Give reasons for your choice.

John and Amir are both freshman and enrolled in a student success course. After class, they often walk to the student union for some coffee and conversation. Today they're talking about jobs.

"Our teacher is really big on job hunting," John says. "I get it, but we're only freshman. Isn't it a little early for this topic?"

"Not really," says Amir. "My whole reason for being in school is to get the job I want."

"That makes sense," John replies. "You worked full-time for a few years before coming here to school. You've got more of a career mindset than I do. I'm here straight out of high school."

Amir shrugs his shoulders. "It doesn't matter, man. It's never too early to start finding your place in the work world. It takes time to do that—for some people, years. Better start now."

John takes a moment to think about this before he responds. "Well, okay. So how are *you* doing it?"

"Well, I worked as a website designer. I'm still doing that on a freelance basis for 10 to 15 hours per week while I'm in school. In fact, I'm doing some work for nonprofit organizations in order to build a portfolio that I can use after I graduate. I'm discounting my hourly rate, so it's a big win for my clients."

John is stunned. "Man, are you kidding me? Why are you doing that? It doesn't make any sense! If they hire you, they should pay your full rate. You're letting yourself get ripped off."

"I can see why you might think that," Amir replies. "Keep in mind that I set clear limits. I will work up to 40 hours on a project at my discounted rate. After that, my full hourly rate kicks in. My clients know this up front and agree to it. It's right in the contract."

John shakes his head. "Last year I applied for a part-time job at a hardware store. They wanted to pay me at a lower rate while I was in training. After that, I'd get a raise. I couldn't believe they'd try to pull something like that. I just walked out of there and never looked back. My mind is totally made up on this topic: it's a cutthroat world. People always want to take advantage of you. You just can't let them do that."

BIBLIOGRAPHY BLUES

Read the following scenario. Then summarize each person's argument in two or three sentences. Reread the scenario to find the evidence offered for each argument. Who do you think makes a stronger case? List the reasons for your choice.

Maria enjoys writing. She expected to breeze through the required papers for her classes. Instead, her psychology course has turned into a nightmare.

The professor, Ms. Wright, assigned several research papers, and she's a stickler. She requires students to read at least five articles for each paper. And she wants those articles to be listed in a bibliography that follows a specific format: the one endorsed by the American Psychological Association (APA).

Maria likes writing the papers. But she finds keeping track of her sources and writing that bibliography to be a real pain. She's meeting with her professor to talk about this.

"Why do we even have to do a bibliography in the first place?" Maria asks. "It takes a lot of time. People can just do a Google search to find the original articles themselves. As long as I mention the title or the author in my paper, isn't that enough?"

Ms. Wright smiles. "You're not the first student to struggle with a bibliography," she says. "But there are good reasons to write one even though we have the Internet. For one thing, it shows readers that you're careful about documenting your sources. It also shows that you have evidence to back up your ideas. And the ability to write in APA style is a requirement for many jobs in psychology."

"But the whole field of psychology is changing," Maria says. "More and more articles are being published online. They include direct links to their sources. Anything that you want to find is just one click away."

"That's not always true," Ms. Wright says. "Many articles are still published only in print. And you have to pay a fee to access many articles that appear online. That's only fair, but it can also be tough for students to afford."

"This is all going to change," says Maria. "Look at how many newspapers and magazines you can now get online for free. All that content used to cost money. It's only a matter of time—maybe just months—before it's all free. Let's be part of the change. Let's get rid of bibliographies. They're pointless. They're so . . . *twentieth century.*"

WHY BOTHER WITH CAREER PLANNING?

Read the following scenario. Then write a short summary of Richard's argument. Reflect on his assumptions about career planning. What are they? Are they directly stated, implied, or both? Make a list of Richard's assumptions and also see whether you can list exceptions to any of them.

"I can't believe that we have to write a career plan for our student success class," says Richard. "There's a whole chapter in the textbook about it. What a pointless assignment."

"Why?" asks Ann, his girlfriend.

"Because career planning is pointless. How can you plan a career in today's economy? Just look at the job market. It changes all the time. The manufacturing jobs in this country are all going to China or being taken over by robots. Software companies in America are hiring people in India because they can cut labor costs. And computers are wiping out whole career fields. My mom says she used to call a travel agent to plan her vacation trips. Now she does it all online. Travel agents, bank tellers, tax preparers—jobs like those are all part of the past."

"Whoa!" Ann says. "Slow down. The last time I went into my bank—which was yesterday—there were still tellers. And my dad still hires a guy to do his taxes."

"Okay," Richard says. "Those jobs haven't quite disappeared *yet.* The main point is that planning makes sense only when you can predict events. And when it comes to the economy and jobs, you just can't predict anything. That's why I'm *not* going to plan my career. Any career that I choose now might not even *exist* by the time I graduate. I don't even care so much about getting a specific degree. While I'm in school, I'm just going to take courses I enjoy. I'll figure out the whole career thing after I graduate, when I'm actually in the work force full-time."

Ann frowns. "But isn't that kind of risky? I mean, you're paying a *lot* of money for classes. Are you really okay with leaving your career to chance? You might have a hard time finding a job. Besides, there are still a lot of people who need specific degrees to do the jobs they want. Like lawyers. And doctors. And veterinarians, and medical technicians, and . . ."

Richard raises his hand as if he's in class and says, "Hello, teacher, I'm not interested in *any* of those careers. After I graduate, I'll just get whatever job I can to make money. I'll probably work a lot of different jobs for a few years. That's the only way to find out what you like and what you don't. I just want to be spontaneous and forget about planning."

VLADGRIN/Shutterstock.com

Finding "aha!":
CREATIVITY
fuels critical thinking

This chapter offers you a chance to practice two types of thinking: convergent thinking and divergent thinking.

Convergent thinking *involves a narrowing-down process.* Out of all the possible solutions to a problem, you choose the one that is the most reasonable. This is the essence of *critical thinking*. Some people see convergent thinking and critical thinking as the same thing.

However, convergent thinking is just one part of critical thinking. Before you choose among viewpoints, generate as many of them as possible. Open up alternatives, and consider all of your options. Define problems in different ways. Keep asking questions and looking for answers.

This opening-up process is called divergent **thinking or creative thinking.** Creative thinking provides the basis for convergent thinking. In other words, one path toward having good ideas is to have *lots* of ideas. Then you can pick and choose from among them, combining and refining them as you see fit.

Remember that creative thinking and convergent thinking take place in a continuous cycle. After you've used convergent thinking to narrow down your options, you can return to creative thinking at any time to generate new ones.

Choose when to think creatively. The key is to make conscious choices about what kind of thinking to do in any given moment. Generally speaking, creative thinking is more appropriate in the early stages of planning and problem solving. Feel free to dwell in this domain for a while. If you narrow down your options too soon, you run the risk of missing an exciting solution or of neglecting a novel viewpoint.

Cultivate "aha!" Central to creative thinking is something called the "aha!" experience. Nineteenth-century poet Emily Dickinson described "aha!" this way: "If I feel physically as if the top of my head were taken off, I know that is poetry." "Aha!" is the burst of creative energy heralded by the arrival of a new, original idea. It is the sudden emergence of an unfamiliar pattern, a previously undetected relationship, or an unusual combination of familiar elements. It is an exhilarating experience.

Tangram

A tangram is an ancient Chinese puzzle game that stimulates the play instinct so critical to creative thinking. The cat figure here was created by rearranging seven sections of a square. Hundreds of images can be devised in this manner. Playing with tangrams allows us to see relationships we didn't notice before.

The rules of the game are simple: use these seven pieces to create something that wasn't there before. Be sure to use all seven. You might start by mixing up the pieces and seeing whether you can put them back together to form a square. Make your own tangram by cutting pieces like these out of poster board. When you come up with a pattern you like, trace around the outside edges of it, and see whether a friend can discover how you did it.

"Aha!" does not always result in a timeless poem or a Nobel Prize. It can be inspired by anything from playing a new riff on a guitar to figuring out why your car's fuel pump doesn't work. A nurse might notice a patient's symptom that everyone else missed. That's an "aha!" An accountant might discover a tax break for a client. That's an "aha!" A teacher might devise a way to reach a difficult student. *Aha!*

Follow through. The flip side of "aha!" is following through. Thinking is both fun and work. It is both effortless and uncomfortable. It's the result of luck and persistence. It involves spontaneity and step-by-step procedures, planning and action, convergent and creative thinking.

Companies that depend on developing new products and services need people who can find "aha!" and do something with it. The necessary skills include the ability to spot assumptions, weigh evidence, separate fact from opinion, organize thoughts, and avoid errors in logic. All these skills involve demanding work. Just as often, they can be energizing and fun. ✖

DISCOVERY STATEMENT

journal
entry 15

Use divergent thinking to brainstorm goals

Candy Chang, an artist and community activist, lived near an abandoned house in New Orleans. She got permission to turn one side of this house into a giant chalkboard and stenciled it with these words printed in big letters: *Before I die, I want to . . .* Anyone who passed by this house could pick up a piece of chalk and complete the sentence in their own way. Some of the answers were:

> *Before I die, I wvant to sing for millions.*
> *Before I die, I want to plant a tree.*
> *Before I die, I want to live off the grid.*
> *Before I die, I want to be completely myself.*[4]

This Journal Entry invites you to walk by that old house in your imagination and add your contribution. The purpose is not to dwell on death. Instead, it is to think creatively about how you want to be and what you want to do during the rest of your life. To do this, you'll draw on your skills in *divergent thinking*, which refers to opening up options and possibilities. Remember that this is an exercise in pure creativity. For best results, do not stop to censor or edit any of your ideas.

I discovered that before I die, I want to . . .

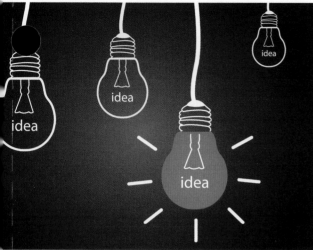

Ekapong/Shutterstock.com

Ways to create
IDEAS

Anyone can think creatively. Use the following techniques to generate ideas about anything—whether you're studying math problems, remodeling a house, or writing a best seller.

Conduct a brainstorm. Brainstorming is a technique for creating plans, finding solutions, and discovering new ideas. When you are stuck on a problem, brainstorming can break the logjam. For example, if you run out of money two days before payday every week, you can brainstorm ways to make your money last longer. You can brainstorm ways to pay for your education. You can brainstorm ways to find a job.

The overall purpose of brainstorming is to generate as many solutions as possible. Sometimes the craziest, most outlandish ideas, although unworkable in themselves, can lead to new ways to solve problems. Use the following steps to try out the brainstorming process:

- **Focus on a single problem or issue.** State your focus as a question. Open-ended questions that start with the words *what, how, who, where,* and *when* often make effective focusing questions. For example, "What is my ideal career?" "What is my ideal major?" "How can I raise the quality of relationships?"

"What is the single most important change I can make in my life right now?"

- **Relax.** Creativity is enhanced by a state of relaxed alertness. If you are tense or anxious, use relaxation techniques such as slow, deep breathing.
- **Set a quota or goal for the number of solutions you want to generate.** Goals give your subconscious mind something to aim for.
- **Set a time limit.** Use a clock to time it to the minute. Experiment with various lengths of time. Both short and long brainstorms can be powerful.
- **Allow all answers.** Brainstorming is based on attitudes of permissiveness and patience. Accept every idea. At this stage, there are no wrong answers. If it pops into your head, put it down on paper. Quantity, not quality, is the goal. Avoid making judgments and evaluations during the brainstorming session. If you get stuck, think of an outlandish idea, and write it down. One crazy

idea can unleash a flood of other, more workable solutions.

- **Brainstorm with others.** Group brainstorming is a powerful technique. Group brainstorms take on lives of their own. Assign one member of the group to write down solutions. Feed off the ideas of others, and remember to avoid evaluating or judging anyone's ideas during the brainstorm.

After your brainstorming session, evaluate the results. Toss out any truly nutty ideas but not before you give them a chance.

Also experiment with asking people to brainstorm individually, put their ideas in writing, and then bring their ideas to a larger group. This can lead to an even greater variety of options.

Focus and let go. Focusing and letting go are alternating parts of the same process. Intense focus taps the resources of your conscious mind. Letting go gives your subconscious mind time to work. When you focus for

---

INTENTION STATEMENT

Use convergent thinking to plan habits

When applied to goal setting, *convergent thinking* means turning a general idea into a specific plan of action. This kind of thinking is useful in goal setting. Our biggest dreams and desires can easily be forgotten *unless* we turn them into daily habits—physical, visible behaviors.

Say, for example, that before you die, you want to fill your life with loving relationships. That's a wonderful goal. Now turn it into an intention that affects what you do every day. Plan to adopt specific habits that align with your goal.

For more effective planning, take a cue from research in psychology and write a list of habits in the form of *implementation intentions.*[5] These intentions follow an "if-then" format. For example:

- *If* I feel angry, *then* I will take three deep breaths before saying anything.
- *If* I am listening to someone, *then* I will wait until they are finished speaking before I begin talking.
- *If* I feel grateful for what someone has done for me, *then* I will express my gratitude directly to that person.

Implementation intentions are useful examples of convergent thinking. They're practical because they link your planned habit to a specific cue that you can remember.

Experiment with convergent thinking now. Review your list of goals from the previous Journal Entry. Then choose one of them and complete the following sentence:

I intend to . . .

Next, create a list of habits to achieve this goal. Write each habit as an implementation intention, using an *If . . . then . . .* format.

intense periods and then let go for a while, the conscious and subconscious parts of your brain work in harmony.

Focusing attention means being in the here and now. To focus your attention on a project, notice when you pay attention and when your mind starts to wander. And involve all of your senses. For example, if you are having difficulty writing a paper at a computer, practice focusing by listening to the sounds as you type. Notice the feel of the keys as you strike them. When you know the sights, sounds, and sensations you associate with being truly in focus, you'll be able to repeat the experience and return to your paper more easily.

Be willing to recognize conflict, tension, and discomfort in yourself. Notice them and fully accept them rather than fighting against them. Look for the specific thoughts and body sensations that make up the discomfort. Allow them to come fully into your awareness, and then let them pass.

You might not be focused all of the time. Periods of inspiration might last only seconds. Be gentle with yourself when you notice that your concentration has lapsed. In fact, that might be a time to let go. *Letting go* means not forcing yourself to be creative. Practice focusing for short periods at first, and then give yourself a break. Play a board game. Go outside and look for shapes in the clouds. Switch to a new location. Take a nap when you are tired. Thomas Edison, the inventor, took frequent naps. Then the lightbulb clicked on.

Cultivate creative serendipity. The word *serendipity* was coined by the English author Horace Walpole from the title of an ancient Persian fairy tale, "The Three Princes of Serendip." The princes had a knack for making lucky discoveries. Serendipity is that knack, and it involves more than luck. It is the ability to see something valuable that you weren't looking for.

History is full of people who made serendipitous discoveries. Country doctor Edward Jenner noticed "by accident" that milkmaids seldom got smallpox. The result was his discovery that mild cases of cowpox immunized them. Penicillin was also discovered by accident. Scottish scientist Alexander Fleming was growing bacteria in a laboratory petri dish. A spore of *Penicillium notatum*, a kind of mold, blew in the window and landed in the dish, killing the bacteria. Fleming isolated the active ingredient. A few years later, during World War II, it saved thousands of lives. Had Fleming not been alert to the possibility, the discovery might never have been made.

Keep your eyes open. You might find a solution to an accounting problem in a Saturday morning cartoon. You might discover a topic for your term paper at the corner convenience store. Multiply your contacts with the world. Resolve to meet new people. Join a study or discussion group. Read. Go to plays, concerts, art shows, lectures, and movies. Watch television programs you normally wouldn't watch.

Also expect discoveries. One secret for success is being prepared to recognize "luck" when you see it.

Keep idea files. We all have ideas. People who treat their ideas with care are often labeled "creative." They not only recognize ideas but also record them and follow up on them.

One way to keep track of ideas is to write them down on 3 × 5 cards. Invent your own categories, and number the cards so you can cross-reference them. For example, if you have an idea about making a new kind of bookshelf, you might file a card under "Remodeling." A second card might also be filed under "Marketable Ideas." On the first card, you can write down your ideas, and on the second, you can write, "See card 321—Remodeling."

Include in your files powerful quotations, random insights, notes on your reading, and useful ideas that you encounter in class. Collect jokes too.

Keep a journal. Journals don't have to be exclusively about your own thoughts and feelings. You can record observations about the world around you, conversations with friends, important or offbeat ideas—anything.

To fuel your creativity, read voraciously, including newspapers, magazines, blogs, and other websites. Explore beyond mainstream journalism. Hundreds of low-circulation specialty magazines and online news journals cover almost any subject you can imagine. Keep letter-size file folders of important documents. Bookmark websites in your browser. Use an online service such as Evernote, Delicious, or Pinboard to save articles that you want to read and refer to later. Create idea files on your computer.

Safeguard your ideas, even if you're pressed for time. Jotting down four or five words is enough to capture the essence of an idea. You can write down one quotation in a minute or two. And if you carry 3 × 5 cards in a pocket or purse, you can record ideas while standing in line or sitting in a waiting room.

Review your files regularly. Some amusing thought that came to you in November might be the perfect solution to a problem in March.

Collect and play with data. Look from all sides at the data you collect. Switch your attention from one aspect to another. Examine each fact and avoid getting stuck on one particular part of a problem. Turn a problem upside down by picking a solution first and then working backward. Ask other people to look at the data. Solicit opinions.

Living with the problem invites a solution. Write down data, possible solutions, or a formulation of the problem on

Create on your feet

A popular trend in executive offices is the stand-up desk: a raised working surface at which you stand rather than sit.

Standing has advantages over sitting for long periods. You can stay more alert and creative when you're on your feet. One theory is that our problem-solving ability improves when we stand due to increased heart rate and blood flow to the brain.

Standing can ease lower-back pain too. Sitting for too long aggravates the spine and its supporting muscles.

Standing while working is a technique with tradition. If you search the Web for stand-up desks, you'll find models based on desks used by Thomas Jefferson, Winston Churchill, and writer Virginia Woolf. Consider setting your desk up on blocks or putting a box on top of your desk so that you can stand while writing, preparing speeches, or studying. Discover how long you can stand comfortably while working and whether this approach works for you.

courtesy of David Ellis

3 × 5 cards, and carry them with you. Look at them before you go to bed at night. Review them when you are waiting for the bus. Make them part of your life, and think about them frequently.

Look for the obvious solutions or the obvious "truths" about the problem—then toss them out. Ask yourself, "Well, I know X is true, but if X were *not* true, what would happen?" Or ask the reverse: "If that *were* true, what would follow next?"

Put unrelated facts next to each other and invent a relationship between them, even if it seems absurd at first. In *The Act of Creation*, novelist Arthur Koestler says that finding a context in which to combine opposites is the essence of creativity.[6]

Make imaginary pictures with the data. Condense it. Categorize it. Put it in chronological order. Put it in alphabetical order. Put it in random order. Order it from most to least complex. Reverse all of those orders. Look for opposites.

It has been said that there are no new ideas—only new ways to combine old ideas. Creativity is the ability to discover those new combinations.

Create while you sleep. A part of our mind works as we sleep. You've experienced this fact directly if you've ever fallen asleep with a problem on your mind and awakened the next morning with a solution. For some of us, the solution appears in a dream or just before we fall asleep or wake up.

You can experiment with this process. Ask yourself a question as you fall asleep. Keep pencil and paper or a recorder near your bed. The moment you wake up, begin writing or speaking, and see whether an answer to your question emerges.

Many of us have awakened from a dream with a great idea, only to fall asleep again and lose it forever. To capture your ideas, keep a notebook by your bed at all times. Put the notebook where you can find it easily.

There is a story about how Benjamin Franklin used this suggestion. Late in the

---

Genius resides in the follow-through— the application of perspiration to inspiration. One powerful tool you can use to follow through is the Discovery and Intention Journal Entry system.

---

evenings, as he was becoming drowsy, he would sit in his rocking chair with a rock in his right hand and a metal bucket on the floor beneath the rock. The moment he fell asleep, the rock would fall from his grip into the bottom of the bucket, making a loud noise that awakened him. Having placed a pen and paper nearby, he immediately wrote down what he was thinking. Experience taught him that his thoughts at

these moments were often insightful and creative.

Promote creative thinking in groups. Sometimes creative thinking dies in committee. People are afraid to disagree with a forceful leader and instead keep their mouths shut. Or a longstanding group ignores new members with new ideas. The result can be "group think," where no one questions the prevailing opinion. To stimulate creative thinking in groups, try these strategies:

- **Put your opinion on hold.** If you're leading a meeting, ask other people to speak up first. Then look for the potential value in *any* idea. Avoid nonverbal language that signals a negative reaction, such as frowning or rolling your eyes.
- **Rotate group leadership.** Ask group members to take turns. This strategy can work well in groups where people have a wide range of opinions.
- **Divide larger groups into several teams.** People might be more willing to share their ideas in a smaller group.
- **Assign a devil's advocate.** Give one person free permission to poke holes in any proposal.
- **Invite a guest expert.** A fresh perspective from someone outside the group can spark an "aha!"
- **Set up a suggestion box.** Let people submit ideas anonymously in writing.

Refine ideas and follow through. Many of us ignore the part of the creative process that involves refining ideas and following through. How many great moneymaking schemes have we had that we never pursued? How many good ideas have we had for short stories that we never wrote? How many times have we said to ourselves, "You know, what they ought to do is attach two handles to one of those things, paint it orange, and sell it to police departments. They'd make a fortune." And we never realize that *we* are "they."

Genius resides in the follow-through—the application of perspiration to inspiration. One powerful tool you can use to follow through is the Discovery and Intention Journal Entry system. First write down your idea in a Discovery Statement, and then write what you intend to do about it in an Intention Statement.

Another way to refine an idea is to simplify it. And if that doesn't work, mess it up. Make it more complex.

Finally, keep a separate file in your ideas folder for your own inspirations. Return to it regularly to see whether there is anything you can use. Today's defunct term paper idea could be next year's A in speech class.

Trust the process. Learn to trust the creative process, even when no answers are in sight. We are often reluctant to look at problems if no immediate solution is at hand. Trust that a solution will show up. Frustration and a feeling of being stuck are often signals that a solution is imminent.

Sometimes solutions break through in a giant *"aha!"* More often they come in a series of little "aha!s." Be aware of what your "aha!s" look, feel, and sound like. This understanding sets the stage for even more flights of creative thinking.

Take these ideas to work. A 2010 article from *Bloomberg Businessweek* ("What Chief Executives Really Want") makes the case for creative thinking in the workplace. This article reports the results of a survey: IBM's Institute for Business Value asked 1,500 chief executive officers to name the leadership skill they considered most important. The top answer was creativity.

Every suggestion in this article can help you create ideas for new products, services, and processes in your job. Use creative thinking to thrive in any career you choose. ✄

practicing
CRITICAL THINKING

22

Explore emotional reactions

Each of us has certain "hot spots"—issues that trigger strong emotional reactions. These topics may include abortion, gay and lesbian rights, capital punishment, and funding for welfare programs. There are many other examples, varying from person to person.

Examine your own hot spots by writing a word or short phrase summarizing each issue about which you feel very strongly. Then describe what you typically say or do when each issue comes up in conversation.

After you have completed your list, think about what you can do to become a more effective thinker when you encounter one of these issues. For example, you could breathe deeply and count to five before you offer your own point of view. Or you might preface your opinion with an objective statement such as: "There are many valid points of view on this issue. Here's the way I see it, and I'm open to your ideas."

Attitudes, affirmations, and
VISUALIZATIONS

"I have a bad attitude." Some of us say this as if we were talking about having the flu. An attitude is certainly as strong as the flu, but it isn't something we have to live with forever, any more than the flu is. You can change your attitudes through regular practice with affirmations and visualizations.

Ilaszlo/Shutterstock.com

Affirm it. An affirmation is a statement describing what you want. The most effective affirmations are:

- **Present tense.** Determine what you want. Then describe yourself as if you already have it. To get what you want from your education, you could write, "I am a master student. I take full responsibility for my education. I learn with joy. I use my experiences in each course to create the life that I want."
- **Detailed.** Use brand names, people's names, and your own name. Involve all of your senses—sight, sound, smell, taste, and touch.
- **Positive.** Avoid words such as *not, never*, and *can't*. Instead of saying "I will not make mistakes while playing music," say "I will play music with joy and ease."

Visualize it. This technique complements affirmations. It's a favorite among athletes and performance artists.

To begin, choose what you want to improve. Then describe in writing what it would look like, sound like, and feel like to experience that improvement in your life.

If you are learning to play the piano, write down briefly what you would see, hear, and feel if you were playing skillfully. If you want to improve your relationships with your children, write down what you would see, hear, and feel if you were communicating with them successfully.

Once you have a mental picture of successful behavior, practice it in your imagination. When you toss the basketball, it swishes through the net. When you invite someone out on a date, the person says "yes." Each test the teacher hands back to you is graded an A. Do your visualizations at least once a day. Then wait for the results to unfold in your life. ✄

I am willing to change!

I am responsible!

Be inquisitive, intuitive, optimistic.

Reprogram your attitude

Use this exercise to change your approach to any situation.

Step 1

Pick something in your life that you would like to change. It can be related to anything: relationships, work, money, or personal skills. Describe briefly what you choose to change.

Step 2

Add more details about the change you described in Step 1. Explain how you would like the change to come about. Be outlandish. Imagine that you are about to ask your fairy god-mother for a wish that you know she will grant. Be detailed in your description of your wish.

Step 3

Use affirmations and visualizations to start yourself on the path to creating exactly what you wrote about in Step 2. Provide at least two affirmations that describe your dream wish. Also, briefly outline a visualization that you can use to picture your wish. Be specific, detailed, and positive.

Step 4

Put your new attitudes to work. Set up a schedule to practice them. Let the first time you practice be right now. Then set up at least five other times and places where you intend to practice your affirmations and visualizations.

I intend to relax and practice my affirmations and visualizations for at least five minutes on the following dates and at the time(s) and location(s) given.

	Date	Time	Location
1.			
2.			
3.			
4.			
5.			

Step 5

Attitude change takes time. End this exercise by reflecting on your progress. Ask whether your practice of affirmations and visualization is actually changing the way that you speak and behave in daily life. You might want to change your affirmations and visualizations so that they're more detailed, positive, and vivid. Write down your revised versions.

Simple attitude replacements

You can use affirmations to replace a negative attitude with a positive one. There are no limitations other than your imagination and your willingness to practice. Here are some sample affirmations. Modify them to suit your individual hopes and dreams, and then practice them.

- "I have abundant energy and vitality throughout the day.
- I exercise regularly.
- I work effectively with many different kinds of people.
- I eat wisely.
- I plan my days and use time wisely.

- I have a powerful memory.
- I take tests calmly and confidently.
- I fall asleep quickly and sleep soundly.
- I have relationships that are mutually satisfying.
- I contribute to other people through my job.
- I make regular time to play and have fun.
- I focus my attention easily.
- I like myself.
- I have an income that far exceeds my expenses.
- I live my life in positive ways for the highest good of all people.

Don't fool yourself: 15 common MISTAKES in logic

Effective reasoning is not just an idle pastime for unemployed philosophers. Learning to think logically offers many benefits. When you think logically, you take your reading, writing, speaking, and listening skills to a higher level.

Dmitry Guzhanin/Shutterstock.com

With more logical thinking, you can avoid costly mistakes in decision making. You can join discussions with more confidence, cast your election votes with a clear head, and become a better-informed citizen. People have even improved their mental health by learning to dispute illogical beliefs.[7]

Students of logic look for valid steps in an argument, or a series of statements. The opening statements of the argument are the premises, and the final statement is the conclusion.

Over the last 2,500 years, specialists have listed some classic land mines on the path of coming to conclusions. These common mistakes in thinking are called *fallacies*. The study of fallacies could fill a yearlong course.

Following are 15 examples to get you started. Knowing about them before you string together a bunch of assertions can help you avoid getting fooled.

1 Jumping to conclusions.
Jumping to conclusions is the only exercise that some lazy thinkers get. This fallacy involves drawing conclusions without sufficient evidence. Take the bank officer who hears about a student's failing to pay back an education loan. After that, the officer turns down all loan applications from students. This person has formed a rigid opinion on the basis of hearsay. Jumping to conclusions—also called *hasty generalization*—is at work here.

Following are more examples of this fallacy:

- *When I went to Mexico for spring break, I felt sick the whole time. Mexican food makes people sick.*
- *All that Democrats want to do is tax and spend.*
- *All that Republicans want to do is cut taxes.*
- *During a recession, more people go to the movies. People just want to sit in the dark and forget about their money problems.*

Each item in this list includes two ideas, and the second idea does not necessarily follow from the first. More evidence is needed to make any possible connection.

2 Attacking the person.
The mistake of attacking the person is common at election time. An example is the candidate who claims that her opponent has failed to attend church regularly during the campaign. People who indulge in personal attacks

are attempting an intellectual sleight of hand to divert our attention away from the truly relevant issues.

3 Appealing to authority.

A professional athlete endorses a brand of breakfast cereal. A famous musician features a soft drink company's product in a rock video. The promotional brochure for an advertising agency lists all of the large companies that have used its services.

In each case, the people involved are trying to win your confidence—and your dollars—by citing authorities. The underlying assumption is usually this: *Famous people and organizations buy our product. Therefore, you should buy it too.* Or: *You should accept this idea merely because someone who's well known says it's true.*

Appealing to authority is usually a substitute for producing real evidence. It invites sloppy thinking. When our only evidence for a viewpoint is an appeal to authority, it's time to think more thoroughly.

4 Pointing to a false cause.

The fact that one event follows another does not necessarily mean that the two events have a cause-and-effect relationship. All we can actually say is that the events might be correlated. For example, as children's vocabularies improve, they can get more cavities. This does not mean that cavities are the result of an improved vocabulary. Instead, the increase in cavities is due to other factors such as physical maturation and changes in diet or personal care.

Suppose that you see this newspaper headline: "Student Tries to Commit Suicide After Failing to Pass Bar Exam." Seeing this headline, you might conclude that the student's failure to pass the exam lead to a depression that caused his suicide attempt. However, this is simply an assumption that can be stated in the following way: *When two events occur closely together in time, the first event is the cause of the second event.* Perhaps the student's depression was in fact caused by another traumatic event not mentioned in the headline, such as breaking up with a longtime girlfriend.

5 Thinking in all-or-nothing terms.

Consider these statements: *Doctors are greedy. You can't trust politicians. Students these days are in school just to get high-paying jobs; they lack idealism. Homeless people don't want to work.*

These opinions imply the word *all*. They gloss over individual differences, claiming that all members of a group are exactly alike. They also ignore key facts—for instance, that some doctors volunteer their time at free medical clinics and that many homeless people are children who are too young to work.

All-or-nothing thinking is one of the most common errors in logic. To avoid this fallacy, watch out for words such as *all, everyone, no one, none, always*, and *never*. Statements that include these words often make sweeping claims that require a lot of evidence. See whether words such as *usually, some, many,*

few, and *sometimes* lead to more accurate statements. Sometimes the words are implied. For example, the implication in the claim "Doctors are greedy" is that *all* doctors are greedy.

6 Basing arguments on emotion.

The politician who ends every campaign speech with flag waving and slides of his mother eating apple pie is staking his future on appeals to emotion. So is the candidate who paints a grim scenario of the disaster and ruination that will transpire unless she is elected. Get past the fluff and histrionics to see whether you can uncover any worthwhile ideas.

7 Using a faulty analogy.

An *analogy* states a similarity between two things or events. Some arguments rest on analogies that hide significant differences. Here is one you're likely to hear during a presidential election: *Running a country is like running a business. Therefore, the president should be someone with business experience.* Actually, there are many differences between running a country and running a business. For example, the chief executive of a business can hire people who share her vision and fire people who fail to meet their business objectives. In contrast, the chief executive of a country must work with members of Congress who are elected rather than hired or fired. Also, the purpose of a business depends on making a profit, whereas the purpose of a government is serving the interests of citizens.

8 Creating a straw man. The name of this fallacy comes from the scarecrows traditionally placed in gardens to ward off birds. A scarecrow works because it looks like a man. Likewise, a person can attack ideas that *sound like* his opponent's ideas but are actually absurd. For example, some legislators attacked the Equal Rights Amendment by describing it as a measure to abolish separate bathrooms for men and women. In fact, supporters of this amendment proposed no such thing.

9 Begging the question. Speakers and writers beg the question when their colorful language glosses over an idea that is unclear or unproven. Consider this statement: *Support the American tradition of individual liberty, and oppose mandatory seat belt laws!* Anyone who makes such a statement "begs" (fails to answer) a key question: Are laws that require drivers to use seat belts actually a violation of individual liberty?

10 Confusing fact and opinion. Facts are statements verified by direct observation or compelling evidence that creates widespread agreement. In recent years, some politicians argued for tax cuts on the grounds that the American economy needed to create more jobs. However, it's not a fact that tax cuts automatically create more jobs. This statement is almost impossible to verify by direct observation, and there's actually evidence against it.

11 Creating a red herring. When hunters want to throw a dog off a trail, they can drag a smoked red herring (or some other food with a strong odor) over the ground in the opposite direction. This distracts the dog, who is fooled into following a false trail. Likewise, people can send our thinking on false trails by raising irrelevant issues.

Case in point: At a party you meet someone who is fascinated by the history of World War II and has read many books about Hitler. As this person tells the story of Hitler's rise to power, someone walks up and says, "Why are you talking so much about Hitler? You must be anti-Semitic (prejudiced against Jewish people)." The red herring here is the accusation of prejudice. Merely being interested in the historical events surrounding Hitler is not the same as being anti-Semitic.

12 Appealing to tradition. Arguments based on an appeal to tradition take a classic form: *Our current beliefs and behaviors have a long history; therefore, they are correct.* This argument has been used to justify the divine right of kings, feudalism, witch burnings, slavery, child labor, and a host of other traditions that are now rejected

Cognitive biases: More ways we fool ourselves

Logical fallacies are isolated errors in reasoning. In contrast, cognitive biases are major blind spots in thinking. They can lead to *many* errors in decision making and problem solving.

For example, **confirmation bias** happens when we interact only with people who agree with us. **Post-purchase rationalization** happens when we justify an expense because we've already spent the money. **Negativity bias** leads us to pay more attention to news about disasters than positive events. And when we pay more attention to the latest reported information than earlier information, **recency bias** is at work.

These are just a few examples. To find out more, go online and search the Internet with the key words *cognitive bias*.

in most parts of the world. Appeals to tradition ignore the fact that unsound ideas can survive for centuries before human beings realize that they are being fooled.

13 Appealing to "the people."

Consider this statement: *Taylor Swift sells more albums than Kelly Clarkson; Taylor Swift must be better.* This is a perfect example of the *ad populum* fallacy. (In Latin, that phrase means "to the people.") The essential error is assuming that popularity, quality, and accuracy are the same.

Appealing to "the people" taps into our universal desire to be liked and to associate with a group of people who agree with us. No wonder this fallacy is also called "jumping on the bandwagon." Following are more examples:

- *Most people exaggerate their experience and qualifications on a résumé. It's just an accepted practice.*
- *Binge drinking is common among college students. It's just part of the experience of higher education.*
- *Same-sex marriages must be immoral. Most Americans think so.*

You can refute such statements by offering a single example: many Americans once believed that slavery was moral and that people of color should not be allowed to vote. That did not make either belief right.

14 Distracting from the real issue.

The fallacy of distracting from the real issue occurs when a speaker or writer makes an irrelevant statement and then draws a conclusion based on that statement. For example: *The most recent recession was caused by people who borrowed too much money and bankers who loaned too much money. Therefore, you should never borrow money to go to school.* This argument ignores the fact that a primary source of the recession was loans to finance housing—not loans to finance education. Two separate topics are mentioned, and statements about one do not necessarily apply to the other.

15 Sliding a slippery slope.

The fallacy of sliding a slippery slope implies that if one undesired event occurs, then other, far more serious events will follow:

- *If we restrict our right to own guns, then all of our rights will soon be taken away.*
- *If people keep downloading music for free, pretty soon they'll demand to get everything online for free.*
- *I notice that more independent bookstores are closing; it's just a matter of time before people stop reading.*

When people slide a slippery slope, they assume that different types of events have a single cause. They also assume that a particular cause will operate indefinitely. In reality, the world is far more complex. Grand predictions about the future often prove to be wrong.

Finding fallacies before they become a fatal flaw (bonus suggestions).

Human beings have a long history of fooling themselves. This article presents just a partial list of logical fallacies. You can prevent them and many more by following a few suggestions:

- When outlining a paper or speech, create a two-column chart. In one column, make a list of your main points. In the other column, summarize the evidence for each point. If you have no evidence for a point, a logical fallacy may be lurking in the wings.
- Go back to some of your recent writing—assigned papers, essay tests, Journal Entries, and anything else you can find. Look for examples of logical fallacies. Note any patterns, such as repetition of one particular fallacy. Write an Intention Statement about avoiding this fallacy.
- Be careful when making claims about people who disagree with you. One attitude of a critical thinker is treating everyone with fairness and respect. ✖

Think critically about information on the
INTERNET

La1n/Shutterstock.com

Sources of information on the Internet range from the reputable (such as the Library of Congress) to the flamboyant (such as the *National Enquirer*).

People are free to post *anything* on the Internet, including outdated facts as well as intentional misinformation.

Newspaper, magazine, and book publishers often employ fact checkers, editors, and lawyers to screen out errors and scrutinize questionable material before publication. Authors of web pages and other Internet sources might not have these resources or choose to use them.

Taking a few simple precautions when you surf the Internet can keep you from crashing onto the rocky shore of misinformation.

Distinguish between ideas and information. To think more powerfully about what you find on the Internet, remember the difference between information and ideas. For example, consider the following sentence: *Barack Obama was elected president of the United States in 2008.* That statement provides information about the United States. In contrast, the following sentence states an idea: *When Barack Obama was elected president, the United States entered a new era of politics.*

Information refers to facts that can be verified by independent observers. *Ideas* are interpretations or opinions based on facts. These include statements of opinion and value judgments. Several people with the same information might adopt different ideas based on that information.

People who speak of the Internet as the "information superhighway" often forget to make the distinction between information and ideas. Don't assume that an idea is more current, reasonable, or accurate just because you find it on the Internet. Apply your critical thinking skills to all published material—print and online.

Look for overall quality. Examine the features of a website in general. Notice the effectiveness of the text and visuals as a whole. Also note how well the site is organized and whether you can navigate the site's features with ease. Look for the date that crucial information was posted, and determine how often the site is updated.

Next, get an overview of the site's content. Examine several of the site's pages, and look for consistency of facts, quality of information, and competency with grammar and spelling. Are the links within the site easy to navigate?

Also evaluate the site's links to related web pages. Look for links to pages of reputable organizations. Click on a few of those links. If they lead you to dead ends, it might indicate that the site you're evaluating is not updated often—a clue that it's not a reliable source for late-breaking information.

Look at the source. Find a clear description of the person or organization responsible for the website. Many sites include this information in an "About" link.

The domain in the uniform resource locator (URL) for a website gives you clues about sources of information and possible bias. For example, distinguish among information from a for-profit commercial enterprise (URL ending in .com); a nonprofit organization (.org); a government agency (.gov); and a school, college, or university (.edu).

If the site asks you to subscribe or become a member, then find out what it does with the personal information that you provide. Look for a way to contact the site's publisher with questions and comments.

Look for documentation. When you encounter an assertion on a web page or some other Internet resource, note the types and quality of the evidence offered. Look for credible examples, quotations from authorities in the field, documented statistics, or summaries of scientific studies.

Remember that wikis (peer-edited sites) such as Wikipedia do not employ editors to screen out errors or scrutinize questionable material before publication. Do not rely on these sites when researching a paper or presentation. Also, be cautious about citing blogs, which often are not reviewed for accuracy.

Such sources may, however, provide you with key words and concepts that help lead you to scholarly research on your topic.

Set an example. In the midst of the Internet's chaotic growth, you can light a path of rationality. Whether you're sending a short email message or building a massive website, bring your own critical thinking skills into play. Every word and image that you send down the wires to the Web can display the hallmarks of critical thinking: sound logic, credible evidence, and respect for your audience. ✄

Gaining skill at
DECISION MAKING

We make decisions all the time, whether we realize it or not. Even avoiding decisions is a form of decision making. The student who puts off studying for a test until the last minute might really be saying, "I've decided this course is not important." In order to escape such a fate, decide right now to experiment with the following suggestions.

Recognize decisions. Decisions are more than wishes or desires. There's a world of difference between "I wish I could be a better student" and "I will take more powerful notes, read with greater retention, and review my class notes daily." Decisions are specific and lead to focused action. When we decide, we narrow down. We

give up actions that are inconsistent with our decision.

Establish priorities. Some decisions are trivial. No matter what the outcome, your life is not affected much. Other decisions can shape your circumstances for years. Devote more time and energy to the decisions with big outcomes.

Base your decisions on a life plan. The benefit of having long-term goals for our lives is that they provide a basis for many of our daily decisions. Being certain about what we want to accomplish this year and this month makes today's choices more clear.

Establish criteria. When making a decision, also define

what's most important for you to achieve. When buying a car, for example, your objective could be to save money, get better gas mileage, or maximize comfort. These are the criteria for your decisions. Choose the most important ones.

Balance learning styles in decision making. To make decisions more effectively, balance reflection with action. Take the time to think creatively and generate many options. Then think critically about the possible consequences of each option before choosing one. Remember, however, that thinking is no substitute for experience. Act on your chosen option, and notice what happens. If you're not getting the results that you want, then quickly return to creative thinking to invent new options.

Choose an overall strategy.

Every time you make a decision, you choose a strategy—even when you're not aware of it. Effective decision makers can articulate and choose from among several strategies. For example:

- *Find all of the available options, and choose one deliberately.* Save this strategy for times when you have a relatively small number of options, each of which leads to noticeably different results.
- *Find all of the available options, and choose one randomly.* This strategy can be risky. Save it for times when your options are basically similar and fairness is the main issue.

- *Limit the options, and then choose.* When deciding which search engine to use on the World Wide Web, visit many sites and then narrow the list down to two or three that you choose.

Use time as an ally. Sometimes we face dilemmas: situations in which any course of action leads to undesirable consequences. In such cases, consider putting a decision on hold. Wait it out. Do nothing until the circumstances change, making one alternative clearly preferable to another.

Use intuition. Some decisions seem to make themselves. A solution pops into your mind, and you gain newfound clarity. Using intuition is not the same as forgetting about the decision or refusing to make it. Intuitive decisions usually arrive after you've gathered

the relevant facts and faced a problem for some time.

Evaluate your decision. Hindsight is a source of insight. After you act on a decision, observe the consequences over time. Reflect on how well your decision worked and what you might have done differently.

Think choices. This final suggestion involves some creative thinking. Consider that the word *decide* derives from the same roots as *suicide* and *homicide*. In the spirit of those words, a decision forever "kills" all other options. That's kind of heavy. Instead, use the word *choice*, and see if it frees up your thinking. When you *choose*, you express a preference for one option over others. However, those options remain live possibilities for the future. Choose for today, knowing that as you gain more wisdom and experience, you can choose again. ✶

Four ways to solve PROBLEMS

Think of problem solving as a process with four P's: define the *problem*, generate *possibilities*, create a *plan*, and *perform* your plan.

Stone/Getty Images

1 DEFINE THE PROBLEM To define a problem effectively, understand what a problem is: a mismatch between what you want and what you have. Problem solving is all about reducing the gap between these two factors.

Tell the truth about what's present in your life right now, without shame or blame. For example: "I often get sleepy while reading my physics assignments, and after closing the book, I cannot remember what I just read."

Next, describe in detail what you want. Go for specifics: "I want to remain alert as I read about physics. I also want to accurately summarize each chapter I read."

Remember that when we define a problem in limiting ways, our solutions merely generate new problems. As Albert Einstein said, "The world we have made is a result of the level of thinking we have done thus far. We cannot solve problems at the same level at which we created them."[8]

This idea has many applications for success in school. An example is the student who struggles with note taking. The problem, she thinks, is that her notes are too sketchy. The logical solution, she decides, is to take more notes, and her new goal is to write down almost everything her instructors say. No matter how fast and furiously she writes, she cannot capture all of her instructors' comments.

Consider what happens when this student defines the problem in a new way. After more thought, she decides that her dilemma is not the *quantity* of her notes, but their *quality*. She adopts a new format for taking notes, dividing her notepaper into two columns. In the right-hand column, she writes down only the main points of each lecture. And in the left-hand column, she notes two or three supporting details for each point.

Over time, this student makes the joyous discovery that there are usually just three or four core ideas to remember from each lecture. She originally thought the solution was to take more notes. What really worked was taking notes in a new way.

One simple and powerful strategy for defining problems is simply to put them in writing. When you do this, you might find that potential solutions appear as well.

2 GENERATE POSSIBILITIES Now put on your creative thinking hat. Open up. Brain-storm as many possible solutions to the problem as you can. At this stage, quantity counts. As you generate possibilities, gather relevant facts. For example, when you're faced with a dilemma about what courses to take next term, get information on class times, locations, and instructors. If you haven't decided which summer job offer to accept, gather information on salary, benefits, and working conditions.

3 CREATE A PLAN After rereading your problem definition and list of possible solutions, choose the solution that seems most workable. Think about specific actions that will reduce the gap between what you have and what you want. Visualize the steps you will take to make this solution a reality, and arrange them in chronological order. To make your plan even more powerful, put it in writing.

4 PERFORM YOUR PLAN This step gets you off your chair and out into the world. Now you actually *do* what you have planned.

Ultimately, your skill in solving problems lies in how well you perform your plan. Through the quality of your actions, you become the architect of your own success.

Define the **problem.**	**What** is the problem?
Generate **possibilities.**	**What if** there are several possible solutions?
Create a **plan.**	**How** would this possible solution work?
Perform your plan.	**Why** is one solution more workable than another?

When facing problems, experiment with these four P's, and remember that the order of steps is not absolute. Also remember that any solution has the potential to create new problems. If that happens, cycle through the four P's of problem solving again. ✂

Asking questions: learning through
INQUIRY

© Robert Kneschke/Shutterstock.com

Thinking is born of questions. Questions wake us up. Questions alert us to hidden assumptions. Questions promote curiosity and create new distinctions. Questions open up options that otherwise go unexplored. Besides, teachers love questions.

There's a saying: "Tell me, and I forget; show me, and I remember; involve me, and I understand." Asking questions is a way to stay involved. One of the main reasons you are in school is to ask questions—a process called *inquiry-based learning*. This process takes you beyond memorizing facts and passing tests. Asking questions turns you into a lifelong learner.

One of the main reasons you are in school is to ask questions. This kind of learning goes beyond memorizing facts and passing tests. Educated people do more than answer questions. They also *ask* questions. They continually search for better questions, including questions that have never been asked before.

Questions have practical power. Asking for directions can shave hours off a trip.

Asking a librarian for help can save hours of research time. Asking your academic advisor a question can alter your entire education. Asking people about their career plans can alter *your* career plans.

Asking questions is also a way to improve relationships with friends and coworkers. When you ask a question, you offer a huge gift to people—an opportunity for them to speak their brilliance and for you to listen to their answers.

George Bernard Shaw, the playwright, knew the power of questions. *You see things; and you say, "Why?"* he wrote. *But I dream things that never were; and I say, "Why not?"*

Inquiry can take you into uncharted waters. Your questions can call forth possibilities that excite you, confuse you, and even scare you. Such feelings are milestones on the path of learning. They

are signs that you're asking questions that matter—the questions that other people forget to ask or fear to ask.

Students often say, "I don't know what to ask." If you have ever been at a loss for questions, here are some ways to discover them. Apply these strategies to any subject you study in school or to any area of your life that you choose to examine.

Ask questions that create possibilities. In Japan, there is a method of self-reflection called *Naikan* that is sometimes used in treating alcoholism. This program is based on asking three questions: "What have I received from others? What have I given to others? And what troubles and difficulties have I caused others?"[9] Taking the time to answer these questions in detail, and with rigorous honesty, can turn someone's life around.

Asking questions is also a way to help people release rigid, unrealistic beliefs: *Everyone should be kind to me. If I make a mistake, it's terrible. Children should always do what I say.* In her book *Loving What Is*, Byron Katie recommends that you ask four questions about such beliefs: Is it true? Can you absolutely know that it's true? How do you react when you believe that thought? And, who would you be *without* that thought?[10]

At any moment you can ask a question that opens up a new possibility for someone. Suppose a friend walks up to you and says, "People just never listen to me."

You listen carefully. Then you say, "Let me make sure I understand. Who, specifically, doesn't listen to you? And how do you know they're not listening?"

Another friend comes up to you and says, "I just lost my job to someone who has less experience. That should never happen."

"Wow, that's hard," you say. "I'm sorry you lost your job. Who can help you find another job?"

Then a relative seeks your advice. "My mother-in-law makes me mad," she says.

"You're having a hard time with this person," you say. "What does she say and do when you feel mad at her? And are there times when you *don't* get mad at her?"

These kinds of questions—asked with compassion and a sense of timing—can help people move from complaining about problems to solving them.

Ask questions for critical thinking. In their classic *How to Read a Book*, Mortimer Adler and Charles Van Doren list four different questions to sum up the whole task of thinking critically about any body of ideas:[11]

- **What is this piece of writing about as a whole?** To answer this question, state the main topic in one sentence. Then list the related subtopics.
- **What is being said in detail, and how?** List the main terms, assertions, and arguments. Also state what problems the writer or speaker is trying to solve.
- **Is it true?** Examine the logic and evidence behind the ideas. Look for missing information, faulty information, and errors in reasoning. Also determine which problems were solved and which remain unsolved.
- **What of it?** After answering the first three questions, prepare to change your thinking or behavior as a result of encountering new ideas.

Discover your own questions. Students sometimes say, "I don't know what questions to ask." Consider the following ways to create questions about any subject you want to study or about any area of your life that you want to change.

Let your pen start moving. Sometimes you can access a deeper level of knowledge by taking out your pen, putting it on a piece of paper, and writing down questions—even before you know what to write. Don't think. Just watch the pen move across the paper. Notice what appears. The results might be surprising.

15 questions to try on for size

1. What is the most important problem in my life to solve right now?
2. What am I willing to do to solve this problem?
3. How can I benefit from solving this problem?
4. Who can I ask for help?
5. What are the facts in this situation?
6. What are my options in this situation?
7. What can I learn from this situation?
8. What do I want?
9. What am I willing to do to get what I want?
10. What will be the consequences of my decision in one week? One month? One year?
11. What is the most important thing for me to accomplish today?
12. What's the best possible use of my time right now?
13. What am I grateful for?
14. Who loves me?
15. Whom do I love?

Ask about what's missing.
Another way to invent useful questions is to notice what's missing from your life and then ask how to supply it. For example, if you want to take better notes, you can write, "What's missing is skill in note taking. How can I gain more skill in taking notes?" If you always feel rushed, you can write, "What's missing is time. How do I create enough time in my day to actually do the things that I say I want to do?"

Pretend to be someone else. Another way to invent questions is first to think of someone you greatly respect. Then pretend you're that person. Ask the questions you think she would ask.

Begin a general question; then, brainstorm endings.
By starting with a general question and then brainstorming a long list of endings, you can invent a question that you've never asked before. For example:

- What can I do when . . . an instructor calls on me in class and I have no idea what to say? When a teacher doesn't show up for class on time? When

I feel overwhelmed with assignments?
- How can I . . . take the kind of courses that I want? Expand my career options? Become much more effective as a student, starting today?
- When do I . . . decide on a major? Transfer to another

When you ask a question, you offer a huge gift to people—an opportunity for them to speak their brilliance and for you to listen to their answers.

---

school? Meet with an instructor to discuss an upcoming term paper?
- What else do I want to know about . . . my academic plan? My career plan? My options for job hunting? My friends? My relatives? My spouse?

- Who can I ask about . . . my career options? My major? My love life? My values and purpose in life?

Ask questions to promote social change. If your friends are laughing at racist jokes, you have a right to ask why. If you're legally registered to vote and denied access to a voting booth, you have a right to ask for an explanation. Asking questions can advance justice.

Ask what else you want to know. Many times you can quickly generate questions by simply asking yourself, *What else do I want to know?* Ask this question immediately after you read a paragraph in a book or listen to someone speak.

Take these ideas to work.
When your team or coworkers meet, for example, start by brainstorming answers to key questions: Why are we doing this project? What would a successful outcome look like? How will we measure our results? What are the next actions to take? Who will take them? By when?

In any situation, start from the assumption that you are brilliant. Then ask questions to unlock your brilliance. ✖

Thinking about
YOUR MAJOR

M.Leheda/Shutterstock.com

One decision that troubles many students in higher education is the choice of a major or degree program. Weighing the benefits, costs, and outcomes of this choice is an intellectual challenge. This choice is an opportunity to apply your critical-thinking, decision-making, and problem-solving skills. The following suggestions will guide you through this seemingly overwhelming process.

1 DISCOVER OPTIONS

Follow the fun. Perhaps you look forward to attending one of your classes and even like completing the assignments. This is a clue to your choice of major.

See whether you can find lasting patterns in the subjects and extracurricular activities that you've enjoyed over the years. Look for a major that allows you to continue and expand on these experiences.

Also, sit down with a stack of 3 × 5 cards and brainstorm answers to the following questions:

- What do you enjoy doing most with your unscheduled time?
- Imagine that you're at a party and having a fascinating conversation. What is this conversation about?
- What kind of problems do you enjoy solving? Those that involve people? Products? Ideas?
- What interests are revealed by your choices of reading material, television shows, and other entertainment?
- What would an ideal day look like for you? Describe where you'd live, who would be with you, and what you'd do throughout the day. Do any of these visions suggest a possible major?

Questions like these can uncover a "fun factor" that energizes you to finish the work of completing a major.

Consider your abilities. In choosing a major, ability counts as much as interest. In addition to considering what you enjoy, think about times and places when you excelled. List the courses that you aced, the work assignments that you mastered, and the hobbies that led to rewards or recognition. Let your choice of a major reflect a discovery of your passions *and* potentials.

Use formal techniques for self-discovery. Explore questionnaires and inventories that are designed to correlate your interests with specific majors. Examples include the Strong Interest Inventory and the Self-Directed Search. Your academic advisor or someone in your school's career planning office can give you more details about these and related inventories. For some fun, take several of them and meet with an advisor to interpret the results. Remember inventories can help you gain self-knowledge, and other people can offer valuable perspectives. However, what you *do* with all this input is entirely up to you.

Link to long-term goals. Your choice of a major can fall into place once you determine what you want in life. Before you choose a major, back up to a bigger picture. List your core values, such as contributing to society, achieving financial security and professional recognition, enjoying good health, or making time for fun. Also write down specific goals that you want to accomplish 5 years, 10 years, or even 50 years from today.

Many students find that the prospect of getting what they want in life justifies all of the time, money, and day-to-day effort invested in going to school. Having a major gives you a powerful incentive for attending classes, taking part in discussions, reading textbooks, writing papers, and completing other assignments. When you see a clear connection between finishing school and creating the life of your dreams, the daily tasks of higher education become charged with meaning.

Ask other people. Key people in your life might have valuable suggestions about your choice of major. Ask for their ideas, and listen with an open mind. At the same time, distance yourself from any pressure to choose a major or career that fails to interest you. If you make a choice based solely on the expectations of other people, you could end up with a major or even a career you don't enjoy.

Gather information. Check your school's catalog or website for a list of available majors. Here is a gold mine of information. Take a quick glance, and highlight all the majors that interest you. Then talk to students who have declared them. Also read descriptions of courses required for these majors. Do you get excited about the chance to enroll in them? Pay attention to your "gut feelings."

Also chat with instructors who teach courses in a specific major. Ask for copies of their class syllabi. Go the bookstore and browse the required texts. Based on all this information, write a list of prospective majors. Discuss them with an academic advisor and someone at your school's career-planning center.

Invent a major. When choosing a major, you might not need to limit yourself to those listed in your school catalog. Many schools now have flexible programs that allow for independent study. Through such programs you might be able to combine two existing majors or invent an entirely new one of your own.

Consider a complementary minor. You can add flexibility to your academic program by choosing a minor to complement or contrast with your major. The student who wants to be a minister could opt for a minor in English; all of those courses in composition can help in writing sermons. Or the student with a major in psychology might choose a minor in business administration, with the idea of managing a counseling service some day. An effective choice of a minor can expand your skills and career options.

Think critically about the link between your major and your career. Your career goals might have a significant impact on your choice of major.

You might be able to pursue a rewarding career by choosing among *several* different majors. Even students planning to apply for law school or medical school have flexibility in their choice of majors. In addition, after graduation, many people are employed in jobs with little relationship to their major. And you might choose a career in the future that is unrelated to any currently available major.

2 MAKE A TRIAL CHOICE

Pretend that you have to choose a major today. Based on the options for a major that you've already discovered, write down the first three ideas that come to mind. Review the list for a few minutes, and then just choose one.

3 EVALUATE YOUR TRIAL CHOICE

When you've made a trial choice of major, take on the role of a scientist. Treat your choice as a hypothesis, and then design a series of experiments to evaluate and test it. For example:

- Schedule office meetings with instructors who teach courses in the major. Ask about required course work and career options in the field.
- Discuss your trial choice with an academic advisor or career counselor.

- Enroll in a course related to your possible major. Remember that introductory courses might not give you a realistic picture of the workloads involved in advanced courses. Also, you might not be able to register for certain courses until you've actually declared a related major.
- Find a volunteer experience, internship, part-time job, or service-learning experience related to the major.
- Interview students who have declared the same major. Ask them in detail about their experiences and suggestions for success.
- Interview people who work in a field related to the major and "shadow" them—that is, spend time with those people during their workday.
- Think about whether you can complete your major given the amount of time and money that you plan to invest in higher education.
- Consider whether declaring this major would require a transfer to another program or even another school.

If your "experiments" confirm your choice of major, celebrate that fact. If they result in choosing a new major, celebrate that outcome as well.

Also remember that higher education represents a safe place to test your choice of major—and to change your mind. As you sort through your options, help is always available from administrators, instructors, advisors, and peers.

4 CHOOSE AGAIN

Keep your choice of a major in perspective. There is probably no single "correct" choice. Your unique collection of skills is likely to provide the basis for majoring in several fields.

Odds are that you'll change your major at least once and that you'll change careers several times during your life. One benefit of higher education is mobility. You gain the general skills and knowledge that can help you move into a new major or career field at any time.

Viewing a major as a one-time choice that determines your entire future can raise your stress levels. Instead, look at choosing a major as the start of a continuing path that involves discovery, choice, and passionate action. ✖

SERVICE-LEARNING:

Turn thinking into contribution

As part of a service-learning project for a sociology course, students volunteer at a community center for older adults. For another service-learning project, history students interview people in veterans' hospitals about their war experiences. These students plan to share their interview results with a psychiatrist on the hospital staff.

Meanwhile, business students provide free tax-preparation help at a center for low-income people. Students in graphic arts classes create free promotional materials for charities. Other students staff a food cooperative and a community credit union.

These examples of actual projects from the National Service-Learning Clearinghouse demonstrate the working premise of service-learning: volunteer work and other forms of contributing can become a vehicle for higher education.

Fill yourself up and give it back. *Becoming a Master Student* is about filling yourself up, taking care of yourself, being selfish, and meeting your needs. The techniques and suggestions in these pages focus on ways to get what you want out of school, work, and the rest of your life.

One of the results of all this successful selfishness is the capacity to contribute. This means giving back to your community in ways that enhance the lives of other people.

People who are satisfied with life can share that satisfaction with others. It is hard to contribute to another person's joy until you experience joy yourself. The same is true for love. When people are filled with love, they can more easily contribute love to others. Contributing is what's left to do when your needs are met. It completes the circle of giving and receiving.

Service-learning is a form of contribution that allows you to create ideas for projects and turn those ideas into action. Use the following

suggestions to get the most from this process.

Understand the elements of service-learning. Service-learning generally includes three elements: meaningful community service, a formal academic curriculum, and time for students to reflect on what they learn from service. That reflection can include speeches, journal writing, and research papers.

Service-learning creates a win–win scenario. For one thing, students gain the satisfaction of contributing. They also gain experiences that can guide their career choices and help them develop job skills.

At the same time, service-learning adds to the community a resource with a handsome return on investment. For example, participants in the Learn and Serve America program (administered by the Corporation for National and Community Service) provided community services valued at four times the program cost.[12]

Find service-learning courses. Many schools offer service-learning programs. Look in the index of your school catalog under "service-learning," and search your school's website, using those key words. There might be a service-learning office on your campus.

Also turn to national organizations that keep track of service-learning opportunities. One is the Corporation for National and Community Service, a federal government agency (**www.nationalservice.gov**). You can also contact

the National Service-Learning Clearinghouse (**www.servicelearning.org**). These resources can lead you to others, including service-learning programs in your state.

GETTING THE MOST FROM SERVICE-LEARNING

When you design a service-learning project, consider the following suggestions.

Follow your interests. Think of the persistent problems in the world—illiteracy, hunger, obesity, addictions, unemployment, poverty, and more. Which of them generate the strongest feelings in you? Which of them link to your possible career plans and choice of major? The place where passion intersects with planning often creates a useful opportunity for service-learning.

Choose partners carefully. Work with a community organization that has experience with students. Make sure that the organization has liability insurance to cover volunteers.

Learn about the organization. Once you connect with a community organization, learn everything you can about it. Find its mission statement and explore its history. Find out what makes this organization unique. If the organization partners with others in the community, learn about those other organizations as well.

Handle logistics. Integrating service-learning into your schedule can call for detailed planning. If your volunteer work takes place off campus, arrange for transportation and allow for travel time.

Include ways to evaluate your project. From your Intention Statements, create action goals and outcome goals. *Action goals* state what you plan to do and how many people you intend to serve; for instance, "We plan to provide 100 hours of literacy tutoring to 10 people in the community." *Outcome goals* describe the actual impact that your project will have: "At the end of our project, 60 percent of the people we tutor will be able to write a résumé and fill out a job application." Build numbers into your goals whenever possible. That makes it easier to evaluate the success of your project.

Build long-term impact into your project. One potential pitfall of service-learning is that the programs are often short-lived. After students pack up and return to campus, programs can die. To avoid this outcome, make sure that other students or community members are willing to step in and take over for you when the semester ends.

Build transferable skills. Transferable skills are abilities that you can use in just about any job. Examples include writing, editing, note taking, researching, solving problems, supervising people, resolving conflict, and managing projects.

Keep a list of the transferable skills that you're developing through service-learning. It will come in handy when you write a résumé and fill out job applications. And before you plan to do another service-learning project, think about the skills you'd like to develop from that experience.

Make use of mistakes. If your project fails to meet its goals, then turn this result into an opportunity to learn. State—in writing—the obstacles you encountered and possible ways to overcome them. The solutions you offer will be worth gold to the people who follow in your footsteps. Sharing the lessons learned from mistakes is an act of service in itself.

Connect service learning to critical thinking. Remember that a *service* activity does not necessarily become a *service* attitude. Students can engage in service-learning merely to meet academic requirements and add a line to their résumé. Or students can engage in service-learning as a way to make long-term changes in their beliefs and behavior.

The idea behind service-learning is that community action is a strategy for academic achievement. This is what distinguishes service-learning from other forms of volunteer activity. A service-learning course combines work in the community with activities in the classroom. Contributing to others becomes a powerful and effective way to learn.

Turn to a tool you've used throughout this book: the Discovery and Intention Journal Entry system. Write Discovery Statements about what you gain from service-learning and how you feel about what you're doing. Follow up with Intention Statements about what you'll do differently for your next service-learning experience.

To think critically and creatively about your service-learning project, also ask questions such as these:

- What service did you perform?
- What roles did your service project include, and who filled those roles?
- What knowledge and skills did you bring to this project?
- After being involved in this project, what new knowledge and skills do you want to gain?
- What did you learn from this experience that can make another service-learning project more successful?
- Will this service-learning project affect your choice of a major? If so, how?
- Will this service-learning project affect your career plans? If so, how?

Service-learning provides an opportunity to combine theory and practice, reflection and action, "book learning" and "real-world" experience. Education takes place as we reflect on our experiences and turn them into new insights and intentions. Use service-learning as a way to take your thinking skills to a whole new level. ✱

Toronto Star/Getty Images

Irshad Manji }

Is director of the Moral Courage Project at New York University, executive producer of Moral Courage TV and author of The Trouble with Islam *and* Allah, Liberty and Love.

Irshad Manji knew that her first book, *The Trouble With Islam*, would outrage some of her fellow Muslims. She called the local police to ask about ways to protect herself. They suggested a security system and bulletproof windows for her Toronto home—and a personal bodyguard.[13]

Manji is a college teacher and journalist. She is a woman, openly lesbian. She is a critic of those who read sacred texts literally. And she is, on her own terms, a devout Muslim.

In an opinion piece for the *New York Times*, Manji explained how she reconciles these facets of her life. Without her religion, Manji wrote, "I could have become a runaway materialist, a robotic mall rat who resorts to retail therapy in pursuit of fulfillment." From Islam she draws core values, daily rituals, and an intellectual tension that "compels me to think and allows me to avoid fundamentalisms of my own."[14]

Manji draws on a progressive aspect of Islam that encourages critical thinking: *ijtihad*, Arabic for "effort." The term applies to a tradition within Islamic law that allows jurors to interpret sacred texts—the *Koran (Qur'ān)* and *Hadith*—in original ways based on reasoning and personal judgment. Although the Sunni sect in Islam rejected *ijtihad* during the Middle Ages, it still exists within Shiite courts.

In *The Trouble With Islam*, readers discover that Manji's personal form of *ijtihad* dates back to her childhood. When she was four years old, her family fled their native Uganda after General Idi Amin Dada directed death threats at the local Muslim community. Like many of her neighbors, Manji emigrated to the West. Her new home was Richmond, a suburb of Vancouver, British Columbia.

When her parents learned that the Rose of Sharon Baptist Church in Richmond offered free childcare, they sent Manji there. Bible study was part of the curriculum, and it was led by a South Asian lady who won Manji's respect.

"She made me believe my questions were worth asking," Manji recalls. "Where did Jesus come from? When did he live? What was his job? Who did he marry?"

At age eight Manji won the church's Most Promising Christian of the Year award. Her prize: a book titled *101 Bible Stories*.

"I look back now and thank God I wound up in a world where the *Koran* didn't have to be my first and only book, as if it's the lone richness that life offers to believers," Manji wrote.

"Lord I loved this society. I loved that it seemed perpetually unfinished, the final answers not yet known—if they ever would be. I loved that, in a world under constant renovation, the contributions of individuals mattered."

After she turned nine, Manji's father insisted that she switch schools. She started attending a local *madressa* (Islamic religious school). For the next five years she spent Saturdays there.

This new academic environment did not encourage critical thinking. Manji, however, was still full of questions.

One day she asked her teacher, Mr. Khaki, why women were not allowed to lead prayers at the mosque.

"Girls aren't permitted," he replied.

Manji asked why.

Mr. Khaki told her to read the *Koran*.

On another occasion she challenged Mr. Khaki to provide evidence of a Jewish conspiracy against Muslims.

He responded with an ultimatum: Believe. Or leave.

Manji stood up, left the room, and walked out of the madressa. She was 13 years old.

Yet this was not the end of her life as a Muslim. It was, in fact, a new beginning, as she explains in *The Trouble With Islam*:

The good news is I knew I lived in a part of the world that permitted me to explore. Thanks to the freedoms afforded me in the West—to think, search, speak, exchange, discuss, challenge, be challenged, and rethink—I was poised to judge my religion in a light that I couldn't have possibly conceived in the parochial Muslim microcosm of the madressa. No need to choose between Islam and the West. On the contrary, the West made it possible for to choose Islam, however tentatively.

Manji still believes that asking questions is a sign of respect, even for Muslims: "Dare to ask uncomfortable questions. When you do, you're showing faith in my capacity to think. You're also giving me an opportunity to deepen my relationship with Allah by remembering Him."[15]

Irshad Manji *demonstrates courage to embrace new ways of thinking about ancient beliefs and practices.*

QUIZ

Chapter 7

1. Level 1 thinking answers the question "Can I invent something new based on this idea?"
   a. True
   b. False

2. Level 2 thinking answers the question "Can I explain this idea in my own words?"
   a. True
   b. False

3. The process of narrowing down possible solutions to a problem is called _____ thinking.

4. The process of opening up alternatives and considering many options is called _____ thinking.

5. The categories of suggestions for critical thinking include:
   a. Check your attitudes.
   b. Check for logic.
   c. Check for evidence.
   d. All of the answer choices

6. The statement "doctors are greedy" is an example of:
   a. Thinking in all-or-nothing terms
   b. Creating a red herring
   c. Creating a straw man
   d. None of the answer choices

7. Creative thinking is only useful for artists—not people who run a company.
   a. True
   b. False

8. Learning through inquiry is based on asking questions.
   a. True
   b. False

9. The suggested strategies for making decisions do *not* include:
   a. Recognize decisions.
   b. Establish priorities.
   c. Balance learning styles.
   d. Make decisions immediately rather than putting them on hold.
   e. Use intuition.

10. The text suggests that you think of problem-solving as a process based on:
    a. Four "P's"—problem, possibilities, plan, perform
    b. Three "C's"—creating, considering, converging
    c. Three "A's"—asking, agreeing, acting
    d. None of the answer choices

SKILLS *snapshot*

Take a snapshot of your thinking skills as they exist today, after reading and completing the exercises in this chapter. Then take the next step toward mastery by committing to adopt new thinking strategies.

Discovery

My score on the Thinking section of the Discovery Wheel was . . .

When I face a major decision in my life, the way that I usually make that decision is . . .

One of the biggest problems I face right now is . . .

Mastery of critical and creative thinking could help my career by . . .

Intention

By the time I finish this course, I would like my *Thinking* score on the Discovery Wheel to be . . .

I'll know that I've reached a new level of mastery with thinking skills when I am able to . . .

The three suggestions from this chapter that will help me the most in reaching that level of mastery are . . .

Action

To put the suggestions I just listed into practice, the next actions I will take are . . .

Some possible obstacles to taking those actions are . . .

To overcome these obstacles, I will . . .

© Savageultralight/Shutterstock.com

Communicating

what is included . . .

272   Power Process: Employ your word

273   Communication: Keeping the channels open

274   Choosing to listen

278   Choosing to speak

282   Developing emotional intelligence

283   Communicating in teams: Getting things done as a group

287   Managing conflict

290   Five ways to say *no* . . . respectfully

292   Five steps to effective complaints

293   Communicating with instructors

295   Diversity is real—and valuable

297   Communicating across cultures

302   Communicating as a first-generation student

303   Staying safe on social networks

306   Three phases of effective writing

311   Academic integrity: Avoid plagiarism

313   Mastering public speaking

318   Master Student Profile: Chimamanda Adichie

why

Your communication abilities—including your skills in listening, speaking, and writing—are as important to your success as your technical skills.

how

Think of a time when you experienced an emotionally charged conflict with another person. Then scan this chapter for ideas that can help you get your feelings and ideas across more skillfully in similar situations.

what if...

I could consistently create the kind of relationships that I've always wanted?

do you have a minute?

It does not take long to plant the seeds of a positive relationship. As an experiment, take about 30 seconds today to talk to a friend or family member about the most positive event of your day. Ask the other person to do the same.

Do this every day for the next week and write a Discovery Statement about the impact of this exercise on your relationships. Follow up with an Intention Statement about turning this type of speaking and listening into a habit.

Employ your word

When you give your word, you are creating—literally. The person you are is, for the most part, a result of the agreements you make. Others know who you are by your words and your commitments. And you can learn who you are by observing which commitments you choose to keep and which ones you choose to avoid.

Relationships are built on agreements. When we break a promise to be faithful to a spouse, to help a friend move to a new apartment, or to pay a bill on time, relationships are strained.

The words we use to make agreements can be placed into six different levels. We can think of each level as one rung on a ladder—the ladder of powerful speaking. As we move up the ladder, our speaking becomes more effective.

The first and lowest rung on the ladder is *obligation*. Words used at this level include *I should, he ought to, someone had better, they need to, I must*, and *I had to*. Speaking this way implies that something other than ourselves is in control of our lives. When we live at the level of obligation, we speak as if we are victims.

The second rung is *possibility*. At this level, we examine new options. We play with new ideas, possible solutions, and alternative courses of action. As we

do, we learn that we can make choices that dramatically affect the quality of our lives. We are not the victims of circumstance. Phrases that signal this level include *I might, I could, I'll consider, I hope to*, and *maybe*.

From possibility, we can move up to the third level—*preference*. Here we begin the process of choice. The words *I prefer* signal that we're moving toward one set of possibilities over another, perhaps setting the stage for eventual action.

Above preference is a fourth rung called *passion*. Again, certain words signal this level: *I want to, I'm really excited to*, and *I can't wait to*.

Action comes with the fifth rung—*planning*. When people use phrases such as *I intend to, my goal is to, I plan to*, and *I'll try like mad to*, they're at the level of planning. The Intention Statements you write in this book are examples of planning.

The sixth and highest rung on the ladder is *promising*. This is where the power of your word really comes into play. At this level, it's common to use phrases such as these: *I will, I promise, I am committed*, and *you can count on it*. Promising is where we bridge from possibility and planning to action. Promising brings with it all of the rewards of employing your word. ✴

Your Design/Shutterstock.com

COMMUNICATION:
Keeping the channels open

In our daily contact with other people and the mass media, we are exposed to hundreds of messages. Yet the obstacles to receiving those messages accurately are numerous.

For one thing, only a small percentage of communication is verbal. We also send messages with our bodies and with the tone of our voices. Throw in a few other factors, such as a hot room or background noise, and it's a wonder we can communicate at all.

Written communication adds a whole other set of variables. When you speak, you supplement the meaning of your words with the power of body language and voice inflection. When you write, those nonverbal elements are absent. Instead, you depend on your skills at word choice, sentence construction, and punctuation to get your message across. The choices that you make in these areas can help—or hinder—communication.

In communication theory, the term *noise* refers to any factor that distorts meaning. When noise is present, the channels of communication start to close. Noise can be external (a lawn mower outside a classroom) or internal (the emotions of the sender or receiver, such as speech anxiety). To a large extent, skillful communication means reducing noise and keeping channels open.

One powerful technique for doing these crucial things is to separate the roles of sending and receiving. Communication channels get blocked when we try to send and receive messages at the same time. Instead, be aware of when you are the receiver and when you are the sender. If you are receiving (listening or reading), just receive; avoid switching into the sending (speaking or writing) mode. When you are sending, stick with it until you are finished.

Communication works best when each of us has plenty of time to receive what others send *and* the opportunity to send a complete message when it's our turn. Communication is a two-way street. When someone else talks, just listen. Then switch roles so that you can be the sender for a while. Keep this up until you do a reasonably complete job of creating shared meaning. ✂

practicing
CRITICAL THINKING

24

Practice sending or receiving

The purpose of this exercise is to help you slow down the pace of communication and clearly separate the roles of sending and receiving. Begin by applying the following steps to conversations on neutral topics. With some practice, you'll be ready to use this technique in situations that could escalate into an argument.

First, find a partner, and choose a topic for a conversation. Also set a time limit for doing this exercise. Then complete the following steps:

1. Get two 3 × 5 cards. Label one of them *sender*. Label the other *receiver*. Choose one card, and give the other one to your partner.

2. If you chose the *sender* card, then start speaking. If you chose the *receiver* card, then listen to your partner without saying a word.

3. When the sender is done speaking, exchange cards and switch roles. The person who listened in Step 2 now gets to speak. However, *do not exchange cards until the sender in Step 2 declares that she has expressed everything she wants to say*.

4. Keep switching cards and roles until your time is up.

After completing these steps, reflect on the experience. What has this exercise taught you about your current skills as a speaker and listener?

Choosing to
LISTEN

Observe a person in a conversation who is not talking. Is he listening? Maybe. Maybe not. Is he focusing on the speaker? Preparing his response? Daydreaming? Effective listening is not easy. It calls for concentration and energy. But it's worth the trouble. People love a good listener. The best salespeople, managers, coworkers, teachers, parents, and friends are the best listeners.

Champion Studio/Shutterstock.com

Through skilled listening, you can gain insight into other people and yourself. You can also promote your success in school through more powerful notes, more productive study groups, and better relationships with students and instructors.

To listen well, begin from a clear intention. *Choose* to listen well. Once you've made this choice, you can use the following techniques to be even more effective at listening.

Notice that these suggestions start with nonverbal listening, which involves remaining silent while another person talks. The second set of suggestions is about verbal listening, where you occasionally speak up to fully receive a speaker's message.

NONVERBAL LISTENING

Be quiet. Silence is more than staying quiet while someone is speaking. Allowing several seconds to pass before you begin to talk gives the speaker time to catch her breath and gather her thoughts. She might want to continue. Someone who talks nonstop might fear she will lose the floor if she pauses.

If the message being sent is complete, this short break gives you time to form your response and helps you avoid the biggest barrier to listening: listening with your answer running. If you make up a response before the person is finished, you might miss the end of the message, which is often the main point.

In some circumstances, pausing for several seconds

might be inappropriate. Ignore this suggestion completely, as you would in an emergency where immediate action is usually necessary.

Maintain eye contact. Look at the other person while he speaks. Maintaining eye contact demonstrates your attentiveness and helps keep your mind from wandering. Your eyes also let you observe the speaker's body language and behavior. If you avoid eye contact, you can fail to see *and* fail to listen.

This idea is not an absolute. Maintaining eye contact is valued more in some cultures than others. Also, some people learn primarily by hearing; they can listen more effectively by turning off the visual input once in a while.

Display openness. You can display openness through your facial expression and body position. Uncross your arms and legs. Sit up straight. Face the other person, and remove any physical barriers between you, such as a pile of books.

Send nonverbal acknowledgments. Let the speaker know periodically that you are still there. Nonverbal gestures of acknowledgment convey to the speaker that you are interested and that you are receiving his message without interrupting what the speaker is saying, such as with head nods.

These acknowledgments do not imply your agreement. When people tell you what they don't like about you, your head nod doesn't mean that you agree. It just indicates that you are listening.

Release distractions. Even when your intention is to listen, you might find your mind wandering. Thoughts about what *you* want to say or something you want to do later might claim your attention. There's a simple solution: Notice your wandering mind without judgment. Then bring your attention back to the act of listening.

You can also set up your immediate environment to release distractions. Turn off or silence your cell phone. Stash your laptop and other digital devices. Send the message that your sole intention in the moment is to listen.

Another option is to ask for a quick break so that you can make a written note about what's on your mind. Tell the speaker that you're writing so

that you can clear your mind and return to full listening.

Suspend judgments. Listening and agreeing are two different activities. As listeners, our goal is to fully receive another person's message. This does not mean that we're obligated to agree with the message. Once you're confident that you accurately understand a speaker's point of view, you are free to agree or disagree with it. The key to effective listening is understanding *before* evaluating.

VERBAL LISTENING

Send verbal acknowledgments. Similar to nonverbal acknowledgments, words such as "Um-hum," "Okay," and "Yes" also convey to the speaker that you are interested and that you are receiving his message.

Again, these acknowledgments do not imply your agreement. They just indicate that you are listening.

Choose when to speak. When we listen to another person, we often interrupt with our own stories, opinions, suggestions, and comments. Consider the following dialogue:

"Oh, I'm so excited! I just found out that I've been nominated to be in Who's Who in American Musicians.*"*
"Yeah, that's neat. My Uncle Elmer got into Who's Who in American Veterinarians. *He sure has an interesting job. One time I went along when he was treating a cow, and*

you'll never believe what happened next. . . ."

To avoid this kind of one-sided conversation, delay your verbal responses. This does not mean that you remain totally silent while listening. It means that you wait for an *appropriate* moment to respond.

Watch your nonverbal responses too. A look of "Good grief!" from you can deter the other person from finishing his message.

Feed back meaning. Sometimes you can help a speaker clarify her message by paraphrasing it. This does not mean parroting what she says. Instead, briefly summarize. Psychotherapist Carl Rogers referred to this technique as *reflection.*[1]

Feed back what you see as the essence of the person's message: "Let me see whether I understood what you said. . . ." or "What I'm hearing you say is . . ." Often, the other person will say, "No, that's not what I meant. What I said was . . ."

There will be no doubt when you get it right. The sender will say, "Yeah, that's it," and either continue with another message or stop sending when he knows you understand.

When you reflect on what the speaker has said, be concise. This is not a time to stop the other person by talking on and on about what you think you heard.

Notice verbal and nonverbal messages. You might point out that the speaker's body language seems to convey the exact opposite of what her words do. For example: "I noticed you said you are excited, but you look bored."

Keep in mind that the same nonverbal behavior can have various meanings across cultures. Someone who looks bored might simply be listening in a different way.

Listen for requests and intentions. An effective way to listen to complaints is to look for the request hidden in them. "This class is a waste of my time" can be heard as "Please tell me what I'll gain if I participate actively in class." "The instructor talks too fast" might be asking "What strategies can I use to take notes when the instructor covers material rapidly?"

We can even transform complaints into intentions. Take this complaint: "The parking lot by the dorms is so dark at night that I'm afraid to go to my car." This complaint can result in having a light installed in the parking lot.

Viewing complaints as requests gives us more choices. Rather than responding with defensiveness ("What does he know anyway?"), resignation ("It's always been this way and always will be"), or indifference ("It's not my job"), we can decide whether to grant the request (do what will alleviate the other's difficulty) or help the person translate his own complaint into an action plan.

Allow emotion. In the presence of full listening, some people will share things that they feel deeply about. They might shed a few tears, cry,

shake, or sob. If you feel uncomfortable when this happens, see whether you can accept the discomfort for a little while longer. Emotional release can bring relief and trigger unexpected insights.

Ask for more. Full listening with unconditional acceptance is a rare gift. Many people have never experienced it. They are used to being greeted with resistance, so they habitually stop short of saying what they truly think and feel. Help them shed this habit by routinely asking, "Is there anything more you want to say about that?" This question sends the speaker a message that you truly value what she has to say.

Be careful with questions and advice. Questions are directive. They can take conversations in a new direction, which may not be where the speaker wants to go. Ask questions only to clarify the speaker's message. Later, when it's your turn to speak, you can introduce any topic that you want.

Also be cautious about giving advice. Unsolicited advice can be taken as condescending or even insulting. Skilled listeners recognize that people are different, and they do not assume that they know what's best for someone else.

Take care of yourself. People seek good listeners, and there are times when you don't want to listen. You might be distracted with your own concerns. Be honest. Don't pretend to listen. You can say, "What you're telling me is important,

but I'm pressed for time right now. Can we set aside another time to talk about this?" It's okay not to listen.

STAY OPEN TO THE ADVENTURE OF LISTENING

Be willing to make the effort. To the untrained eye, listening looks passive. *I'm just going to listen while you talk*, we might say, *I'm not going to do anything.*

If you want to listen well, then experiment with the opposite idea. Think of listening as an active affair. See listening as something that you *do*. This alone can transform your experience of listening.

When you listen well, you actively send messages to another person: *You matter to me; and, what you say is worthwhile for me to hear.* People seldom get these messages. When they do, it can change them forever.

Deep listening takes time and energy. After listening at this level, you might feel that you've made significant effort, just as you would after doing physical labor. Just as exercise is a workout for the body, deep listening is a workout for the mind.

Be willing to put yourself on hold. Each of us looks out into the world through one set of eyes. We hear through one set of ears. We are each the star of our own movie, the center of our own world. We tend to judge every event by how it personally affects *us*.

When we listen deeply, we step out of that role. We move off center stage and step into another person's world. We ask: *What would it feel like to be this person? What is she thinking right now? What does he want? What does she fear? Who does he love? What experiences brought her to this point in her life?*

None of this means that you have to agree with everything that people say. It does mean remembering that your point of view is one of many.

Be willing to feel discomfort. When another person speaks, you might feel bored. You might feel afraid. You might feel angry or sad. When those feelings get strong, you might find it hard to listen.

When you listen, accept any feeling that comes up. Observe how it registers in your body. You might tense certain muscles and hold your breath. If that happens, just notice it. Then take a deep breath and return to the act of listening. Remind yourself that negative feelings can be a sign that you don't yet understand what the other person is saying.

Silence can be especially challenging. We want to fill the space by saying something—*anything*. Resist that urge. When we're willing to sit with the silence, we give people permission to go deeper and say things that they're holding back.

Be willing to change. Listening fully—truly opening yourself to the way another person sees the world—means taking risks. Your opinions may be challenged. You may be less certain or less comfortable than you were before. You might conclude that it's time

for you to change in a significant way.

When presented with a new idea, some of us take pride in being critics. We probe for weaknesses. We define ourselves by how we disagree with other people. When we listen, we continually ask: *What's wrong with this idea?*

Again, take the opposite approach. Ask yourself: *What if this idea is true?* This opens up all sorts of new possibilities. Recall the Power Process: "Ideas are tools." It reminds us to look for potential value in anything we see, hear, or read.

What sometimes stops us from doing this is a fear of letting "ridiculous" or "dangerous" ideas out in the open. Remember that during a genuine conversation, truly inaccurate and unworkable ideas can be exposed for what they are.

Experience the rewards. Along with the risks of listening come the benefits. Deep listening can take your relationships to a new depth and level of honesty. Deep listening can open up new possibilities for thinking, feeling, and behaving. Listening and learning are closely linked.

Listening creates community. When we listen, we make it possible for others to speak. And when you practice deep listening, other people are more likely to receive when it's your turn to send. ✦

FIVE WAYS TO SAY "I"

An "I" message can include any or all of the following five elements. Be careful when including the last two elements, though, because they can contain hidden judgments or threats.

Observations. Describe the facts—the indisputable, observable realities. Talk about what you—or anyone else—can see, hear, smell, taste, or touch. Avoid judgments, interpretations, or opinions. Instead of saying, "You're a slob," say, "Last night's lasagna pan was still on the stove this morning.'"

Feelings. Describe your own feelings. It is easier to listen to "I feel frustrated" than to "You never help me." Stating how you feel about another's actions can be valuable feedback for that person.

Wants. You are far more likely to get what you want if you say what you want. If someone doesn't know what you want, she doesn't have a chance to help you get it. Ask clearly. Avoid demanding or using the word *need*. Most people like to feel helpful, not obligated. Instead of saying, "Do the dishes when it's your turn, or else!" say, "I want to divide the housework fairly."

Thoughts. Communicate your thoughts, and use caution. Beginning your statement with the word "I" doesn't automatically make it an "I" message. "I think you are a slob" is a "you" judgment in disguise. Instead, say, "I'd have more time to study if I didn't have to clean up so often."

Intentions. The last part of an "I" message is a statement about what you intend to do. Have a plan that doesn't depend on the other person. For example, instead of "From now on, we're going to split the dishwashing evenly," you could say, "I intend to do my share of the housework and leave the rest."

Choosing to
SPEAK

HieroGraphic/Shutterstock.com

You have been talking with people for most of your life, and you usually manage to get your messages across. There are times, though, when you don't. Often, these times are emotionally charged.

We all have this problem. Sometimes we feel wonderful or rotten or sad or scared, and we want to express it. Emotions, though, can get in the way of the message. And although you can send almost any message through tears, laughter, fist pounding, or hugging, sometimes words are better. Begin with a sincere intention to reach common ground with your listener. Then experiment with the suggestions that follow.

Replace "you" messages with "I" messages. It can be difficult to disagree with someone without his becoming angry or your becoming upset. When conflict occurs, we often make statements about the other person, or "you" messages:

> "You are rude."
> "You make me mad."
> "You must be crazy."
> "You don't love me anymore."

This kind of communication results in defensiveness. The responses might be similar to these:

> "I am not rude."
> "I don't care."
> "No, *you* are crazy."
> "No, *you* don't love *me*!"

"You" messages are hard to listen to. They label, judge, blame, and assume things that may or may not be true. They demand rebuttal. Even praise can sometimes be an ineffective "you" message. "You" messages don't work.

Psychologist Thomas Gordon suggests that when communication is emotionally charged, consider limiting your statements to descriptions about yourself.[2] Replace "you" messages with "I" messages:

> "You are rude" might become "I feel upset."
> "You make me mad" could be "I feel angry."
> "You must be crazy" can be "I don't understand."
> "You don't love me anymore" could become "I'm afraid we're drifting apart."

Suppose a friend asks you to pick him up at the airport. You drive 20 miles and wait for the plane. No friend. You decide your friend missed her plane, so you wait three hours for the next flight. No friend. Perplexed and worried, you drive home. The next day, you see your friend downtown.

> "What happened?" you ask.
> "Oh, I caught an earlier flight."
> "You are a rude person," you reply.

Look for and talk about the facts—the observable behavior. Everyone will agree that your friend asked you to pick her up, that she did take an earlier flight, and that you did not receive a call from her. But the idea that she is rude is not a fact—it's a judgment.

She might go on to say, "I called your home, and no one answered. My mom had a stroke and was rushed to Valley View. I caught the earliest flight I could get." Your judgment no longer fits.

When you saw your friend, you might have said, "I waited and waited at the airport. I was worried about you. I didn't get a call. I feel angry and hurt. I don't want to waste my time. Next time, you can call me when your flight arrives, and I'll be happy to pick you up."

"I" messages don't judge, blame, criticize, or insult. They don't invite the other person to counterattack with more of the same. "I" messages are also more accurate. They report our own thoughts and feelings.

At first, "I" messages might feel uncomfortable or seem forced. That's okay. Your skill with using this technique will improve with practice.

Remember that questions are not always questions. You've heard these "questions" before. A parent asks, "Don't you want to look nice?" Translation: "I wish you'd cut your hair, lose the blue jeans, and put on a tie." Or how about this question from a spouse: "Honey, wouldn't you love to go to an exciting hockey game tonight?" Translation: "I've already bought tickets."

We use questions that aren't questions to sneak our opinions and requests into conversations. "Doesn't it upset you?" means "It upsets me," and "Shouldn't we hang the picture over here?" means "I want to hang the picture over here."

Communication improves when we say, "I'm upset" and "Let's hang the picture over here."

Choose your nonverbal messages. How you say something can be more important than what you say. Your tone of voice and gestures add up to a silent message that you send. This message can support, modify, or contradict your words. Your posture, the way you dress, how often you shower, and even the poster hanging on your wall can negate your words before you say them.

Most nonverbal behavior is unconscious. We can learn to be aware of it and choose our nonverbal messages. The key is to be clear about our intention and purpose. When we know what we want to say and are committed to getting it across, our inflections, gestures, and words work together and send a unified message.

Notice barriers to sending messages. Sometimes fear stops us from sending messages. We are afraid of other people's reactions, sometimes justifiably. Being truthful doesn't mean being insensitive to the impact that our messages have on others. Tact is a virtue; letting fear prevent communication is not.

Assumptions can also be used as excuses for not sending messages. "He already knows this," we tell ourselves.

Predictions of failure can be barriers to sending, too. "He won't listen," we assure ourselves. That statement might be inaccurate. Perhaps the other person senses that we're angry and listens in a guarded way. Or perhaps he is listening and sending nonverbal messages we don't understand.

Or we might predict, "He'll never do anything about it, even if I tell him." Again, making assumptions can defeat your message before you send it.

It's easy to make excuses for not communicating. If you have fear or some other concern about sending a message, be aware of it. Don't expect the concern to go away. Realize that you can communicate even with your concerns. You can choose to make them part of the message, "I am going to tell you how I feel, but I'm afraid that you will think it's stupid."

Talking to someone when you don't want to could be a matter of educational survival. Sometimes a short talk with an advisor, a teacher, a friend, or a family member can solve a problem that otherwise could jeopardize your education.

Speak candidly. When we brood on negative thoughts and refuse to speak them out loud, we lose perspective. And when we keep joys to ourselves, we diminish our satisfaction. A solution is to share regularly what we think and feel. Psychotherapist Sidney Jourard referred to such openness and honesty as *transparency* and wrote eloquently about how it can heal and deepen relationships.[3]

Sometimes candid speaking can save a life. For example, if you think a friend is addicted to drugs, telling her so in a supportive, non-judgmental way is a sign of friendship.

Imagine a community in which people freely and lovingly speak their minds—without fear or defensiveness. That can be your community.

This suggestion comes with a couple of caveats. First, there is a big difference between speaking candidly about your problems and griping about them. Gripers usually don't seek solutions. They just want everyone to know how unhappy they are. Instead, talk about problems as a way to start searching for solutions.

Second, avoid bragging. Other people are turned off by constant references to how much money you have, how great your partner is, how numerous your social successes are, or how much status your family enjoys. There is a difference between sharing excitement and being obnoxious.

Offer "feedforward." Giving people feedback about their past performance can be a powerful way to help them learn. Equally useful is "feedforward," which means exploring new options for the future.

Marshall Goldsmith, a management consultant, suggests a way to do this. First, talk about a specific, high-impact behavior that you'd like to change—for example, "I want to be a better listener." Then gather with a small group of trusted friends and ask for suggestions about ways to accomplish your goal. To make this process work, avoid any conversation about what's happened in the past. Focus instead on next actions you intend to take. Also listen to what others suggest without criticizing their ideas.[4]

Speak up! Look for opportunities to practice speaking strategies. Join class discussions, and keep a running list of questions and comments to share. Start conversations about topics that excite you. Ask for information and clarification. Ask for feedback on your skills.

Also speak up when you want support. Consider creating a team of people who help one another succeed. Such a team can develop naturally from a study group that works well. Ask members whether they would be willing to accept and receive support in achieving a wide range of academic and personal goals. Meet regularly to do goal-setting exercises from this book and brainstorm success strategies.

After you have a clear statement of your goals and a plan for achieving them, let family members and friends know. When appropriate, let them know how they can help. You may be surprised at how often people respond to a genuine request for support.

Take these ideas to work. In the workplace, you will regularly meet new coworkers, customers, and clients. One of the most practical communication skills you can develop is the ability to hold one-on-one conversations. The ability to put people at ease through "small talk" makes you valuable to an employer. This is a high-level skill that depends on the ability to listen closely and speak skillfully. Using "I" messages and the other suggestions in this article can help you thrive at work. ✖

practicing
CRITICAL THINKING

25

Write an "I" message

First, pick something about school that irritates you. Then pretend that you are talking to a person who is associated with this irritation. Write down what you would say to this person as a "you" message.

Now write the same complaint as an "I" message.

How do you think the conversation would go if you made the "you" message?

How would the conversation change if you used the "I" message instead?

Discover communication styles

The concept of *communication styles* can be useful when you want to discover sources of conflict with another person—or when you're in a conversation with someone from a different culture.

Consider the many ways in which people express themselves verbally. These characteristics can reflect an individual's preferred communication style:

- **Extroversion**—talking to others as a way to explore possibilities for taking action
- **Introversion**—thinking through possibilities alone before talking to others
- **Dialogue**—engaging in a discussion to hear many points of view before coming to a conclusion or decision
- **Debate**—arguing for a particular point of view from the outset of a discussion
- **Openness**—being ready to express personal thoughts and feelings early in a relationship
- **Reserve**—holding back on self-expression until a deeper friendship develops
- **A faster pace** of conversation—allowing people to speak quickly and forcefully while filling any gaps in conversation
- **A slower pace** of conversation—allowing people to speak slowly and quietly while taking time to formulate their thoughts

These are just a few examples of differences in communication styles. You might be able to think of others.

The point is that people with different communication styles can make negative assumptions about each other. For example, those who prefer fast-paced conversations might assume that people who talk slowly are indecisive. And people who prefer slower-paced conversations might assume that people who talk quickly are pushy and uninterested in anyone else's opinion.

Take this opportunity to think about your preferred communication styles and assumptions. Do they enhance or block your relationships with other people? Think back over the conversations you've had during the past week. Then complete the following sentences:

I discovered that I prefer conversations that allow me to . . .

I discovered that I usually feel uncomfortable in conversations when other people . . .

When people do the things listed in Item 2, I tend to make certain assumptions, such as . . .

As an alternative to making the assumptions listed in Item 3, I intend to . . .

Developing
EMOTIONAL
intelligence

In his book *Working with Emotional Intelligence*, Daniel Goleman defines emotional intelligence as a cluster of traits:

- **Self-awareness**—recognizing your full range of emotions and knowing your strengths and limitations
- **Self-regulation**—responding skillfully to strong emotions, practicing honesty and integrity, and staying open to new ideas
- **Motivation**—persisting to achieve goals and meet standards of excellence
- **Empathy**—sensing other people's emotions and taking an active interest in their concerns
- **Skill in relationships**—listening fully, speaking persuasively, resolving conflict, and leading people through times of change

Hlib Marderosiants/Shutterstock.com

Goleman concludes that "IQ washes out when it comes to predicting who among a talented pool of candidates *within* an intellectually demanding profession will become the strongest leader." At that point, emotional intelligence starts to become more important.[5]

If you're emotionally intelligent, you're probably described as someone with good "people skills." You're aware of your feelings. You act in thoughtful ways, show concern for others, resolve conflict, and make responsible decisions.

Your emotional intelligence skills will serve you in school and in the workplace, especially when you collaborate on project teams. You can deepen your skills with the following strategies.

RECOGNIZE THREE ELEMENTS OF EMOTION

Even the strongest emotion consists of just three elements: physical sensations, thoughts, and action. Usually they happen so fast that you can barely distinguish them. Separating them out is a first step toward emotional intelligence.

Imagine that you suddenly perceive a threat, such as a supervisor who's screaming at you. Immediately your heart starts beating more quickly and your stomach muscles clench (physical sensations). Then thoughts race through your head: *This is a disaster. She hates me. And everyone's watching.* Finally, you take action, which could mean staring at her, yelling back, or running away.

NAME YOUR EMOTIONS

Naming your emotions is a first step to going beyond the "fight or flight" reaction to any emotion. Naming gives you power. The second that you attach a word to an emotion, you start to gain perspective. People with emotional intelligence have a rich vocabulary to describe a wide range of emotions. For examples, do an Internet search with the key *words feeling list*. Read through the lists you find for examples of ways that you can name your feelings in the future.

ACCEPT YOUR EMOTIONS

Another step toward emotional intelligence is accepting your emotions—*all* of them. This can be challenging if you've been taught that some emotions are "good," whereas others are "bad." Experiment with another viewpoint; you do not choose your emotional reactions. However, you can choose what you *do* in response to any emotion.

EXPRESS YOUR EMOTIONS

One possible response to any emotion is expressing it. The key is to speak without blaming others. Use "I" messages to state what you observe, what you feel, and what you intend to do.

RESPOND RATHER THAN REACT

The heart of emotional intelligence is moving from mindless reaction to mindful action. See whether you can introduce an intentional gap between sensations and thoughts on the one hand and your next action on the other hand. To do this more often:

- **Run a "mood meter."** Check in with your moods several times each day. On a 3 × 5 card, note the time of day and your emotional state at that point. Rate your mood on a scale of 1 (relaxed and positive) to 10 (very angry, very sad, or very afraid).
- **Write Discovery Statements.** In your journal, write about situations in daily life that trigger strong emotions. Describe these events—and your usual responses to them—in detail.
- **Write Intention Statements.** After seeing patterns in your emotions, you can consciously choose to behave in new ways. Instead of yelling back at the angry supervisor, for example, make it your intention to simply remain silent and breathe deeply until he finishes. Then say, "I'll wait to respond until we've both had a chance to cool down."

MAKE DECISIONS WITH EMOTIONAL INTELLIGENCE

When considering a possible choice, ask yourself, *How am I likely to feel if I do this?* You can use "gut feelings" to tell when an action might violate your values or hurt someone.

Think of emotions as energy. Anger, sadness, and fear send currents of sensation through your whole body. Ask yourself how you can channel that energy into constructive action. ✳

Er Creatives Services Ltd/Iconica/Getty Images

Communicating in teams: Getting things done as a GROUP

Your experience in higher education will include group projects. These projects can be fun and rewarding. They can also fall flat and lead to frustration. To avoid the pitfalls that take teams down, develop some specific skills in communication.

START WITH AN ATTITUDE CHECK

Students come to group projects with a wide range of attitudes. Some people dread working with a team. They get good grades on their own and prefer to study alone. When forced to join a group, they fear getting paired with a dominating leader, or a slacker who does no work and still gets credit.

Those things can happen. And at the same time, group projects are here to stay. In the workplace, collaboration is the norm. Taking a project from a hazy idea to finished product requires the work of people with a variety of specialties and skills. Employers are looking for team players, not solo stars. If you can communicate well in groups, you're more likely to get the job you want and enjoy what you do.

There's a word that describes effective group work: *synergy*. Master students know about synergy firsthand. Groups of them experience it when they create results that none of them could achieve by working alone.

Your group is more likely to "synergize" when you see that teamwork presents two distinct issues. One is to produce a *result*, such as a paper or presentation. The second is to find a *process* of working together that leads to this result. Effective teams deal with both of these issues at their first meeting. They also deal with ongoing challenges in communication and take their group projects all the way to an effective conclusion.

MASTER YOUR FIRST MEETING

Following is a list of items to consider as you create the agenda for your first group meeting. For long and complex projects, you might need more than one meeting to get them done.

Introduce yourselves and share key information. Start with housekeeping details. Ask all group members to share their name and contact information: email address, phone number, and any other details that will help you stay in touch with each other. Also share the times that you're available for group meetings. Make sure that someone captures all this information, puts it in writing, and distributes it to everyone in your group.

Talk about your team experiences. You might get assigned to work with people you've never met before. To learn more about each other, talk about the group work you've done in other courses. Speak openly about what you liked and didn't like. Based on this discussion, create a list of what makes a successful team and ways to prevent any problems you've had with group work in the past.

Define your outcome. According to author Stephen Covey, one habit of successful people is that they begin with the end in mind.[6] In other words, they start a project by describing their desired result.

You can use the same strategy. Pose these questions to your group: How will you know that your group has succeeded? What would a successful outcome look like and sound like? How would you feel when you produced it?

Brainstorm a list of answers, and ask someone in the group to record them. Then combine the best words and phrases into a single sentence that expresses what you agree to produce. Check this sentence against the requirements of your assignment, and get feedback from your instructor.

Choose roles. Groups do their best work when the members agree on the roles that they'll play. For example, the group *leader* sends out the agenda for meetings, starts and ends meetings, monitors the group's overall progress, and keeps the instructor up to date on the group's activity. A *timer* watches the clock to ensure that the group stays on schedule and gets to each item on the agenda. A *recorder* takes notes during meetings and maintains copies of all group-related materials. Beyond these basic roles, add any others that seem useful.

Your instructor might assign people in your group to these roles. If not, ask members to volunteer based on their interests and experience. Also remember that you can rotate roles over the course of your project.

In addition to formal roles, group members take on informal roles based on their learning styles. For instance, some people focus on the group's purpose and ask, "*Why* are we doing this?" Others pose questions such as:

- *What* are we planning to do?
- *How* are we going to get this done?
- *What* if we did this a different way?

Welcome all these questions. They signal that your group is moving through a complete cycle of learning.

Plan tasks and timelines. Once your outcome and roles are clearly defined, create a step-by-step plan to actually get the work done. Answer these questions: *In order to produce our outcome, what's the very next action we need to take? What actions will follow that one? Who will take each action? By when?*

One handy way to record the results of this discussion is to create a four-column chart:

Action	Assigned to	Due Date	Done

List your planned actions in order, along with a due date and person responsible for each one. When an action is completed, your group leader can check it off in the "Done" column.

Distribute a draft of this chart to your group, and revise it until everyone agrees to it. Show the completed chart to your instructor as well, and ask for feedback.

A word to the wise about due dates: these are tricky. Students who are new to group work often underestimate the time they'll need to complete tasks. To prevent last-minute stress, start working on your project as soon as it's assigned. Also, plan to complete your group project several days before the assigned due date. This leaves your group with a cushion of extra time to deal with surprises and delays.

As you plan tasks and timelines, ask:

- Which tasks need to be handled by the whole group, and which can be done by individuals?
- Will we need specific applications, such as word-processing, spreadsheet, and presentation software?
- If our final outcome is a paper, who will write the first draft of each section? Who will revise the sections and assemble them into a final copy?
- If our outcome is a group presentation, then what format shall we use? For example, will we divide the presentation into sections and do them individually? What equipment will we need? When will we rehearse as a group before doing our final presentation in class?

Again, check with your instructor as you answer these questions.

Choose when and how to meet. End your first session by scheduling meetings for the rest of your project. Also choose how to stay in contact between meetings. Options include email, text, phone, and websites such as Google Drive (**drive.google.com**) that allow groups of people to share documents with one another.

Using technology to collaborate

When planning group projects, look for tools that allow you to create, edit, and share documents, spreadsheets, drawings, and presentations. Ideally, the technology that you choose will also allow team members to do the following:

- Update files in real time.
- Track changes or version history in shared documents.
- Share calendars and project-related action lists.
- Send instant messages.
- Set up video conferences.
- Create video and audio recordings of team meetings.
- Back up data online (in the "cloud").
- Use mobile devices to access project files.

You can find a growing list of applications for these purposes. Their capabilities and prices vary widely, though several are generous with features and some are also free. Some current options include Google+ Hangouts, AnyMeeting (www.anymeeting.com), Skype (www.skype.com), GoToMeeting (www.gotomeeting.com) and Zoho collaboration applications (www.zoho.com). For more ideas, do an Internet search with the key words *collaborate online*.

Equally important are "people skills." Whatever technology you use, set up a process to make sure that everyone's voice gets heard during a virtual meeting. People who get silenced will probably tune out.

Also function as a professional whenever you're online. Team members might get to know you mainly through emails and instant messages. Consider the impression you're making with your online presence. Avoid slang, idioms, sarcastic humor, and other expressions that can create misunderstandings. A small dose of civility can make a large difference in the quality of your virtual team experience.

DEAL WITH CHALLENGES

Groups take time to gel. Don't expect yours to function perfectly right away. If conflicts develop between group members, view them as opportunities to develop your communication skills. The following suggestions will help.

Get the most from meeting time. Nothing drains energy from a group more than meetings that crop up at the last minute and waste everyone's time. If you're leading the group, be sure to give plenty of notice before meetings, and write up an agenda for each one. Keep it to three items, tops. To focus everyone's thinking, state each agenda item as a question to answer. Instead of listing "project schedule," for example, write: "When is a realistic time for our next meeting?"

When scheduling meetings, also set clear starting and stopping times. Then stick to them.

End each meeting by updating your list of planned actions. Make sure that each action is assigned to a specific person, with a clear due date. You'll know that meetings are working when the energy level in the group stays high and when people have clear commitments to take planned action before the next meeting.

Reign in an overbearing member. A person who dominates the discussion in a meeting can prevent other group members from expressing their ideas. This is a common problem with group brainstorming. To prevent it, ask people to write up their ideas *before* a meeting. Gather these into one document and distribute it several days in advance. Then use this document to begin your discussion.

Resolve conflict. In an effective group, all ideas are welcome. Problems are freely admitted. Any item is open for discussion. Instead of automatically looking for what's wrong with a new idea, group members consider possible ways to use it. Even a proposal that seems outlandish at first might become workable with a few modifications.

Other ways to resolve conflict are listed here:

- **Allow emotions.** People can feel angry, hurt, or afraid for reasons that you don't understand. Don't judge them for it. If a group member gets emotional during a meeting, show that you noticed it and invite more details. Say something nonjudgmental, such as "You seem upset by what's happening here. Can you tell us what's not working for you?"
- **Listen fully.** When a group member speaks, give that person your complete attention. Don't think about your response while the person is talking: just focus on getting the message. Wait a few seconds after the person finishes speaking. Then invite more: "Thanks for talking. Is there anything more that you want to say?" Conflict can immediately be reduced when people feel that they're being heard.
- **Speak with I-messages.** When emotions run high, avoid criticizing others with statements such as "You're being totally unreasonable." Instead, share what *you* feel and want to do. For example: "I feel worried that we don't have enough information to write a paper. I suggest that we talk to our instructor and ask for more sources to check."
- **Focus on solutions.** When group members disagree, avoid arguments about who is right and who is wrong. Instead, restate the conflict as a question that invites a solution for everybody, such as "How can we even out the work load so that no one feels overwhelmed?"

PUT THE FINISHING TOUCHES ON YOUR PROJECT

Many groups come to a halt the moment they turn in their final project. This deprives the members of the chance to review their group experience, draw lessons from it, and develop continuing relationships. Instead, make it a habit to do the following:

- Send all group members an email thanking them for their work.
- Invite group members to get together socially after the course, if that seems appropriate.
- Keep your own copies of the materials that the group created and turned in to your instructor.
- Write Discovery Statements that describe what worked well in your group and what you'd like to improve.
- Write Intention Statements about what you'll do differently to make your next group project even more effective. ✖

Tiko Aramyan/Shutterstock.com

Managing
CONFLICT

Conflict management is one of the most practical skills you'll ever learn. Here are strategies that can help.

The first five strategies discussed are about dealing with the *content* of a conflict: defining the problem, exploring viewpoints, and discovering solutions. The remaining strategies are about finding a *process* for resolving any conflict, no matter what the content.

To bring these strategies to life, think of ways you would use them to manage a conflict you are facing right now.

FOCUS ON CONTENT

Back up to common ground. Conflict heightens the differences between people. When this happens, it's easy to forget how much we still agree with each other.

As a first step in managing conflict, back up to common ground. List all of the points on which you are *not* in conflict: "I know that we disagree about how much to spend on a new car, but we do agree that the old one needs to be replaced." Often, such comments put the problem in perspective and pave the way for a solution.

State the problem. Using "I" messages, as explained earlier in this chapter, state the problem. Tell people what you observe, feel, think, want, and intend to do. Allow the other people in a particular conflict to do the same.

Each person might have a different perception of the problem. That's fine. Let the conflict come into clear focus. It's hard to fix something unless people agree on what's broken.

Remember that the way you state the problem largely determines the solution. Defining the problem in a new way can open up a world of possibilities. For example, "I need a new roommate" is a problem statement that dictates one solution. "We could use some agreements about who cleans the apartment" opens up more options, such as resolving a conflict about who will wash the dishes tonight.

State all points of view. If you want to defuse tension or defensiveness, set aside your opinions for a moment. Take the time to understand the other points of view. Sum up those viewpoints in words that the other parties can accept. When people feel that they've been heard, they're often more willing to listen.

Ask for complete communication. In times of conflict, we often say one thing and mean another. So before responding to what the other person says, use active listen-

ing. Check to see whether you have correctly received that person's message by saying, "What I'm hearing you say is . . . Did I get it correctly?"

Focus on solutions. After stating the problem, dream up as many solutions as you can. Be outrageous. Don't hold back. Quantity—not quality—is the key. If you get stuck, restate the problem and continue brainstorming.

Next, evaluate the solutions you brainstormed. Discard the unacceptable ones. Talk about which solutions will work and how difficult they will be to implement. You might hit upon a totally new solution.

Choose one solution that is most acceptable to everyone involved, and implement it. Agree on who is going to do what by when. Then keep your agreements.

Finally, evaluate the effectiveness of your solution. If it works, pat yourselves on the back. If not, make changes or implement a new solution.

Focus on the future. Instead of rehashing the past, talk about new possibilities. Think about what you can do to prevent problems in the future. State how you intend to change, and ask others for their contributions to the solution.

FOCUS ON PROCESS

Commit to the relationship.
The thorniest conflicts usually arise between people who genuinely care for each other. Begin by affirming your commitment to the other person: "I care about you, and I want this relationship to last. So I'm willing to do whatever it takes to resolve this problem." Also ask the other person for a similar commitment.

Allow strong feelings. Permitting conflict can also mean permitting emotion. Being upset is all right. Feeling angry is often appropriate. Crying is okay. Allowing other people to see the strength of our feelings can help resolve the conflict. This suggestion can be especially useful during times when differences are so extreme that reaching common ground seems impossible.

Expressing the full range of your feelings can transform the conflict. Often what's on the far side of anger is love. When we express and release resentment, we might discover genuine compassion in its place.

Notice your need to be "right." Some people approach conflict as a situation where only one person wins. That person has the "right" point of view. Everyone else loses.

When this happens, step back. See whether you can approach the situation in a neutral way. Define the conflict as a problem to be solved, not as a contest to be won. Explore the possibility that you might be mistaken. There might be more than one acceptable solution. The other person might simply have a different learning style than yours. Let go of being "right," and aim for being effective at resolving conflict instead.

Sometimes this means apologizing. Conflict sometimes arises from our own errors. Others might move quickly to end the conflict when we acknowledge this fact and ask for forgiveness.

Slow down the communication. In times of great conflict, people often talk all at once. Words fly like speeding bullets, and no one listens. Chances for resolving the conflict take a nosedive.

When everyone is talking at once, choose either to listen or to talk—not both at the same time. Just send your message. Or just receive the other person's message. Usually, this technique slows down the pace and allows everyone to become more levelheaded.

To slow down the communication even more, take a break. Depending on the level of conflict, this might mean anything from a few minutes to a few days.

A related suggestion is to do something nonthreatening together. Share an activity with the others involved that's not a source of conflict.

Communicate in writing. What can be difficult to say to another person face-to-face might be effectively communicated in writing. When people in conflict write letters or emails to each other, they automatically apply many of the suggestions in this article. Writing is a way to slow down the communication and ensure that only one person at a time is sending a message.

There is a drawback to this tactic, though: it's possible for people to misunderstand what you say in a letter or email. To avoid further problems, make clear what you are *not* saying: "I am saying that I want to be alone for a few days. I am *not* saying that I want you to stay away forever." Saying what you are *not* saying is often useful in face-to-face communication as well.

Before you send your letter or email, put yourself in the shoes of the person who will receive it. Imagine how your comments could be misinterpreted. Then rewrite your note, correcting any wording that might be open to misinterpretation.

There's another way to get the problem off your chest, especially when strong, negative feelings are involved: write the nastiest, meanest email response you can imagine, leaving off the address of the recipient so you don't accidentally send it. Let all of your frustration, anger, and venom flow onto the page. Be as mean and blaming as possible. When you have cooled off, see whether there is anything else you want to add.

Then destroy the letter or delete the email. Your writing has served its purpose. Chances are that you've calmed down and are ready to engage in skillful conflict management.

Get an objective viewpoint. With the agreement of everyone involved, set up a video camera and record a conversation about the conflict. In the midst of a raging argument, when emotions run high, it's almost impossible to see ourselves objectively. Let the camera be your unbiased observer. Another way to get an objective viewpoint is to use a mediator: an objective, unbiased third party. Even an untrained mediator—as long as he or she is someone who is not a party to the conflict—can do much to decrease tension. Mediators can help everyone get their point of view across. The mediator's role is not to give advice, but to keep the discussion on track and moving toward a solution.

Allow for cultural differences. People respond to conflict in different ways, depending on their cultural background. Some stand close, speak loudly, and make direct eye contact. Other people avert their eyes, mute their voices, and increase physical distance.

When it seems to you that other people are sidestepping or escalating a conflict, consider whether your reaction is based on cultural bias.

Agree to disagree. Sometimes we say all we have to say on an issue. We do all of the problem solving we can do. We get all points of view across. And the conflict still remains, staring us right in the face.

What's left is to recognize that honest disagreement is a fact of life. We can peacefully coexist with and respect other people, even if we don't agree on fundamental issues. Conflict can be accepted even when it is not resolved.

See the conflict within you. Sometimes the turmoil we see in the outside world has its source in our own inner world. A cofounder of Alcoholics Anonymous put it this way: "It is a spiritual axiom that every time we are disturbed, no matter what the cause, there is something awry with us."

When we're angry or upset, we can take a minute to look inside. Perhaps we are

ready to take offense—waiting to pounce on something the other person said. Perhaps, without realizing it, we did something to create the conflict. Or maybe the other person is simply saying what we don't want to admit is true.

When these things happen, we can shine a light on our own thinking. A simple spot check might help the conflict disappear right before our eyes.

Take these ideas to work. If you get into a personal conflict on the job, choose a suggestion from this article and use it. For example, slow down the communication during a conflict by asking people to put their viewpoints in writing. Doing this can immediately lower the tension of conflicts with supervisors, clients, customers, and employees. ✖

DISCOVERY/INTENTION STATEMENT

journal entry **18**

Recreate a relationship

Think about one of your relationships for a few minutes. It can involve a parent, sibling, spouse, child, friend, hairdresser, or anyone else. Write down some things that are not working in the relationship. What bugs you? What do you find irritating or unsatisfying?

I discovered that ...

Now think for a moment about what you want from this relationship. More attention? Less nagging? More openness, trust, financial security, or freedom? Choose a suggestion from this chapter, and describe how you could use it to make the relationship work.

I intend to ...

Five ways to say
NO . . .
respectfully

All your study plans can go down the drain when a friend says, "Time to party!" Sometimes, succeeding in school means replying with a graceful and firm *no*.

© simonox/Shutterstock.com

Students in higher education tend to have many commitments. Saying no helps you to prevent an overloaded schedule that compromises your health and grade point average. You can use the following five strategies to respectfully and gracefully say "no."

Think critically about your assumptions. An inability to say no can spring from the assumption that you'll lose friends if you state what you really want. But consider this: if you cannot say no, then you are not in charge of your time. You've given that right to whoever wants to interrupt you. This is not a friendship based on equality. True friends will respect your wishes.

Plan your refusal. You might find it easier to say no when you don't have to grasp for words. Choose some key words and phrases in advance, for example, "I'd love to, but not today," or, "Thanks for asking. I have a huge test tomorrow and want to study," or, "I'd prefer not to do anything tonight; do you want to grab lunch tomorrow instead?"

When you refuse, align your verbal and nonverbal messages. Reinforce your words with a firm voice and a posture that communicates confidence.

Avoid apologies or qualifiers. People give away their power when they couch their no's in phrases such as "I'm sorry, but I just don't know whether I want to" or "Would you get upset if I said no?"

You don't have to apologize for being in charge of your life. It's okay to say no. Give up the need for excuses. Don't assume that you have to explain or defend your response. Saying no for your own reasons is often enough.

Wait for the request. People who worry about saying no often give in to a request before it's actually been made. Wait until you hear a question. "Time to party!" is not a question. Nor is it a call to action. Save your response until you hear a specific request, such as "Would you go to a party with me?"

Remember that one no leads to another yes. *Yes* and *no* are complementary, not contradictory. Saying no to one activity allows you to say yes to something that's more important right now. Saying no to a movie allows you to say yes to outlining a paper or reading a textbook chapter. You can say an unqualified yes to the next social activity—and enjoy it more—after you've completed some key tasks on your to-do list. ✕

CRITICAL THINKING

26

VIPs (very important persons)

Step 1

Under the column titled "Name," write the names of at least seven people who have positively influenced your life. They might be relatives, friends, teachers, or perhaps persons you have never met. (Complete each step before moving on.)

Step 2

In the next column, rate your gratitude for this person's influence (from 1 to 5, with 1 being "a little grateful" and 5 being "extremely grateful").

Step 3

In the third column, rate how fully you have communicated your appreciation to this person (again, 1 to 5, with 1 being "not communicated" and 5 being "fully communicated").

Step 4

In the final column, put a U to indicate the persons with whom you have unfinished business (such as an important communication that you have not yet sent).

Name	Grateful (1–5)	Communicated (1–5)	U
1.			
2.			
3.			
4.			
5.			
6.			
7.			

Step 5

Now select two persons with U's beside their names, and write each of them a letter. Express the love, tenderness, and joy you feel toward them. Tell them exactly how they have helped change your life and how glad you are that they did.

Step 6

You also have an impact on others. Write the names of people whose lives you have influenced. Consider sharing with these people why you enjoy being a part of their lives.

Five steps to
EFFECTIVE
complaints

Sometimes relationship building means making a complaint. Whining, blaming, pouting, screaming, and yelling insults usually don't get results. Consider the following suggestions instead.

1 Go to the source. Start with the person who is most directly involved with the problem. When you're in school, that person is usually an instructor. Give this person the first chance to resolve an issue. Instructors usually appreciate feedback, and they can't always read a student's mind to know when a problem occurs.

2 Present the facts without blaming anyone. Consider how it might feel to receive complaints like these: "I put a lot of work into this project, but you gave me a C." "Your class is boring." "I just can't trust you."

Your complaint will carry more weight if you document the facts instead. Keep track of names and dates. Note what actions were promised and what results actually occurred.

3 Learn about other options. Schools have policies and procedures related to student complaints. Look for them in your school's catalog and website. Student government is also a potential resource. At many schools you can talk to a student or staff ombudsman—someone who is trained to help resolve conflicts between students and instructors.

4 Ask for commitments. When you find someone who is willing to solve your problem, get him to say exactly what he is going to do, and when.

5 Persist. Assume that others are on your team. Many people are out there to help you. State what you intend to do, and ask for their partnership.

Today, many companies shield themselves from complaints with a voice mail maze and lengthy "hold" times. This calls for patience and persistence. It's worth it. Your complaint deserves to be heard. ✈

Criticism is constructive

Although receiving criticism is rarely fun, it is often educational. Here are some ways to get the most value from it.

Avoid finding fault. When your mind is occupied with finding fault in others, you aren't open to hearing constructive comments about yourself.

Take criticism seriously. Some people laugh or joke to cover up their anger or embarrassment at being criticized. A humorous reaction on your part can be mistaken for a lack of concern.

React to criticism with acceptance. Most people don't enjoy pointing out another's faults. Your denial, argument, or joking makes it more difficult for them to give honest feedback. You can disagree with criticism and still accept it calmly. Keep criticism in perspective. Avoid blowing the criticism out of proportion. The purpose of criticism is to generate positive change and self-improvement. There's no need to overreact to it.

Listen without defensiveness. You can't hear the criticism if you're busy framing your rebuttal.

Communicating with
INSTRUCTORS

Thinkstock/Comstock/Thinkstock

Faced with an instructor you don't like, you have two basic choices. One is to label the instructor a "dud" and let it go at that. When you make this choice, you endure the class and complain to other students. The other option is take responsibility for your education, no matter who teaches your classes.

Usually we think of students as the people who enroll in school. Turn this idea on its head. See whether you can enroll instructors as partners in getting what you want from higher education. The key is communicating effectively.

Research the instructor. When deciding what classes to take, you can look for formal and informal sources of information about instructors. One source is the school catalog. Alumni magazines or newsletters or the school newspaper might run articles on teachers. Also talk to students who have taken courses from the instructor you're researching.

Also introduce yourself to the instructor and ask about the course. This conversation can help you get the flavor of a class and the instructor's teaching style. Other clues to an instructor's style include the *types* of material he presents (ranging from theory or fact) and the *ways* that the material is presented (ranging from lectures to discussion and other in-class activities). Ask for syllabi from the instructor's past courses, and take a look at the instructor's website.

Show interest during class. Participate fully. Take notes and join in discussions. Turn off your cell phone or any other electronic device unless you need it for class.

Consider that sleeping or texting in class, or doing work for one class while you're in another, is a waste of your time and money. Instructors notice distracting activities and take them as a sign of your lack of interest and commitment. So do employers.

Before packing up your notebooks and other materials, wait until class has been dismissed. Instructors often give assignments or make a key point at the end of a class period. Be there when it happens.

Interest gets communicated in the smallest details. For instance, avoid making distracting noises, and cover your mouth if you yawn or cough. Also avoid wearing inappropriate or revealing clothing. And even if you meet your future spouse in class, refrain from public displays of affection. Save that for after-class time.

Engage with "boring" instructors. During class, students give instructors moment-by-moment feedback. That feedback comes through posture, eye contact, responses to questions, and participation in class discussions.

If you find a class boring, then change your experience with the instructor. You can do this through a massive display of interest. Ask lots of questions. Sit up straight, make eye contact, and take detailed notes. Your enthusiasm might enliven your instructor. If not, you are still creating a more enjoyable class for yourself.

Also remember that instructors who seem boring in class can be fascinating in person. Schedule times to meet with them during their office hours.

Release judgments. Maybe your instructor reminds you of someone you don't like: your annoying Aunt Edna, a rude store clerk, or the fifth-grade teacher who kept you after school. Your attitudes are in your own head and beyond the instructor's control.

Likewise, an instructor's beliefs about subjects like politics, religion, or feminism are not related to teaching ability. Being aware of such things can help you let go of negative judgments.

Separate liking from learning. You don't have to like an instructor to learn from her. See whether you can focus on content instead of

form. *Form* is the way something is organized or presented. If you are irritated at the sound of an instructor's voice, you're focusing on form. When you put aside your concern about her voice and turn your attention to the points she's making, you're focusing on *content*.

Form your own opinion about each instructor. You might hear conflicting reports about teachers from other students. The same instructor could be described by two different students as a riveting speaker and as completely lacking in charisma. Decide for yourself what descriptions are accurate.

Seek alternatives. You might feel more comfortable with another teacher's style or method of organizing course materials. Consider changing teachers, asking another teacher for help outside class, or attending an additional section taught by a different instructor.

Communicating respect for your instructors

Communicate respect by showing up. In a school setting, communicating respect is called *classroom civility*. Show up for classes on time. If you arrive late, do not disrupt class. Close the door quietly and take a seat.

If you know that you're going to miss a class or be late, then let your instructor know ahead of time. Take the initiative to ask your instructor or another student about what you missed.

When you know that you will have to leave class early, tell your instructor before class begins, and sit near an exit. If you leave class to use the restroom or handle an emergency, do so quietly.

Communicate respect through your words. When you speak in class, begin by addressing your instructor as *Ms., Mrs., Mr., Dr., Professor*, or whatever the teacher prefers.

Discussions gain value when everyone gets a chance to speak. Show respect for others by not monopolizing class discussions. Refrain from side conversations and profanity. When presenting viewpoints that conflict with those of classmates or your instructor, combine the passion for your opinion with respect for the opinions of others.

Ask instructors how to contact them outside of class. If they take phone calls, leave a voice mail message that includes your first and last name, course name, section, and phone number. If your instructor encourages contact via email, then craft your messages with care. Start by including your name, course title, and section number in the subject line. Keep the body of your message brief and get to the point immediately.

Meet with instructors. Meeting with instructors outside class can save hours of study time and lead to rewarding relationships. Students who do well in higher education often get to know at least one instructor outside of class. In some cases, these instructors become mentors and informal advisors.

Schedule a meeting time during the instructor's office hours. If you need to cancel or reschedule, let your instructor know well in advance. Prepare for the meeting with a list of questions to ask and any materials you'll need. Avoid questions that might offend your instructor, such as "I missed class on Monday. Did we do anything important?"

Avoid excuses. Instructors know them all. They won't be fooled. Accept responsibility for your own mistakes, and avoid thinking that you can fool the teacher.

Submit professional work. Prepare papers and projects as if you were submitting them to an employer. Imagine that your work will determine whether you get a promotion and raise. Instructors often grade hundreds of papers during a term. Your neat, orderly, well-organized paper can stand out and lift a teacher's spirits, ultimately helping you.

Accept criticism. Learn from your teachers' comments about your work. It is a teacher's job to give feedback so that you can improve. Don't take it personally. Just work harder and do better next time.

If you disagree with a class requirement or grade you received, then talk to your instructor about it after class in a respectful way. In a private setting, your ideas will get more attention.

Use course evaluations. In many classes, you'll have an opportunity to evaluate the instructor. Respond honestly. Write about the aspects of the class that did not work well for you. Offer specific ideas for improvement. Also note what *did* work well. Keep it positive, remembering that you might have this instructor again for another class.

Take further steps, if appropriate. If you're in conflict with an instructor, do not try to resolve the situation during a few minutes before or after class. Instead, schedule a time during the instructor's office hours to meet with her in person. During this meeting, be specific. State the facts about the problem. Also be positive. Offer possible solutions, and state what you're willing to do to resolve the conflict.

If this meeting does not lead to a solution, then find out your school's grievance procedures. You are a consumer of education and have a right to fair treatment. ✳

Brand New Images/Lifesize/Getty Images

DIVERSITY
is real—and valuable

A typical American citizen awakens in a bed (an invention from the Near East). After dressing in clothes (possibly designed in Italy), she slices a banana (grown in Honduras) on her bowl (made in China) of cereal, and then brews coffee (shipped from Nicaragua).

After breakfast, she reads the morning newspaper (printed by a process invented in Germany, on paper, which was first made in China). Then she turns on her portable media player (made in Taiwan) and listens to music (possibly by a band from Cuba).

The United States has a rich tradition of cultural diversity. The things we eat, the tools we use, and the words we speak are a cultural tapestry woven by many different peoples.

Consider the many meanings of culture. The word *culture* embraces many kinds of differences. We can speak of the culture of large corporations and the culture of the fine arts. There are the cultures of men and women; heterosexual, homosexual, and bisexual people; and older and younger people.

There are also the cultures of urban and rural dwellers, the cultures of able-bodied people and people with disabilities, and the cultures of two-parent families and single-parent families. There are cultures defined by differences in standards of living and differences in religion.

Recognize the many shades of discrimination. Hate crimes, hate speech, and harassment are obvious examples of intolerance. These are never acceptable. Yet racism, homophobia, religious stereotyping, and other forms of discrimination can exist in ways that are subtle and still harmful. For example:

- Members of a sociology class are debating the merits of reforming the state's welfare system. The instructor calls on a student who grew up on a reservation and says, "Tell us: What's the Native American perspective on this issue?" Here the student is being typecast as a spokesperson for her entire ethnic group.
- Students in a mass media communications class are discussing a situation comedy set in an urban,

high-rise apartment building with mostly African American residents. "Man, they really whitewashed that show," says one student. "It's mostly about inner-city black people, but they didn't show anybody on welfare, doing drugs, or joining gangs." The student's comment perpetuates racial stereotypes.

- On the first day of the term, students taking English Composition enter a class taught by a professor from Puerto Rico. One of the students asks the professor, "Am I in the right class? Maybe there's been a mistake. I thought this was supposed to be an English class, not a Spanish class." The student assumed that only white people are qualified to teach English courses.
- Two students are talking about a classmate named Ari Singh. "Ari's a nice guy," says one of the students, "but why doesn't he get a haircut and lose the turban? Someone's going to think that he's a radical Muslim." Yet Ari is actually a Sikh whose religion requires both men and women to cover their hair. These students assumed that Ari was Muslim. Even if Ari *were* Muslim, the assumption that he's radical is another stereotype.

Recognize the value of diversity. Immigration is a case in point. Politicians might point to immigrants as

"freeloaders" who steal jobs and drag down the economy. They forget about Steve Jobs, the son of a Syrian immigrant, who founded a company that employs thousands of people—Apple Computers. They also forget about Sergey Brin, who emigrated with his parents from Russia and became a founder of Google.

Research indicates that immigrants boost the labor force, increase the demand for goods and services, and raise employment by starting companies.[7] In addition, companies that value diversity can recruit more qualified employees, increase their revenue, and reduce employee turnover.[8]

Seize the opportunity. Going to school brings you into one of the most diverse environments that you will ever encounter. Your fellow students could come from many ethnic groups and countries. In addition, consider faculty members, staff members, alumni, donors, and their families. Think of all the possible differences in their family backgrounds, education, job experiences, religion, marital status, sexual orientation, and political viewpoints.

Higher education offers an opportunity to move past discrimination in all its forms. Schools can become cultural laboratories—places where people of many cultures meet with the shared purpose of education. Learning to thrive with diversity will help you succeed in classrooms and workplaces that become more diverse each year. ✄

Communicating across
CULTURES

Rawpixel.com/Shutterstock.com

Communicating with people from other races, ethnic groups, and cultures starts with a commitment to create understanding. When you truly value diversity, you can discover ways to build bridges between people. Begin with the following suggestions and invent more of your own.

See the world through a different set of eyes. One step to developing diversity skills is to intentionally switch lenses. Make it your intention to look at familiar events in a new way.

For example, think of an emotionally charged conflict that you had with another person. Ask yourself how you would view this situation if you were that person.

Go deeper by asking more questions. How would you experience this conflict if you were a person of the opposite gender? Of a different racial or ethnic group? If you were older or younger?

Do this exercise consistently and you'll discover that we live in a world of multiple realities. There are many different ways to interpret any event, and just as many ways to respond, given our individual differences.

Reflect on experiences of privilege and prejudice. For example, someone might tell you that he's more likely to be promoted at work because he's white and male—*and* that he's been called "white trash" because he lives in a trailer park.

See whether you can recall incidents such as these from your own life. Think of times when you were favored because of your gender, race, or age, and times when you were excluded or ridiculed based on one of those same characteristics. In doing this, you'll discover ways to identify with a wider range of people.

Look for differences between individualist and collectivist cultures. *Individualist* cultures flourish in the United States, Canada, and Western Europe. If your family has deep roots in one of these areas, you were probably raised to value personal fulfillment and personal success. You received recognition or rewards when you stood out from your peers by earning the highest grades in your class, scoring the most points during a basketball season, or demonstrating another form of individual achievement.

In contrast, *collectivist* cultures value cooperation over competition. Group progress is more important than individual success. Credit for an achievement is widely shared. If you were raised in such a culture, you probably place a high value on your family and were taught to respect your elders. Collectivist cultures dominate Asia, Africa, and Latin America.

In short, individualist cultures often emphasize "I." Collectivist cultures tend to emphasize "we." Forgetting about the differences between them can strain a friendship or wreck an international business deal.

If you were raised in an individualist culture:

- *Remember that someone from a collectivist culture may place a high value on "saving face."* This idea involves more than simply avoiding embarrassment. This person may *not* want to be singled out from other members of a group, even for a positive achievement. If you have a direct request for this person or want to share something that could be taken as a personal criticism, save it for a private conversation.

- *Respect titles and last names.* Although Americans often like to use first names immediately after meeting someone, in some cultures this practice is acceptable only among family members. Especially in work settings, use last names and job titles during your first meetings. Allow time for informal relationships to develop.
- *Put messages in context.* For members of collectivist cultures, words convey only part of an intended message. Notice gestures and other nonverbal communication as well.

If you were raised in a collectivist culture, you can creatively "reverse" this list. Keep in mind that direct questions from an American student or coworker are meant not to offend, but only to clarify, an idea. Don't be surprised if you are called by a nickname, if no one asks about your family, or if you are rewarded for a personal achievement. In social situations, remember that indirect cues might not get another person's attention. Practice asking clearly and directly for what you want.

Look for common ground. Students in higher education often find that they worry about many of the same things, including tuition bills, the quality of dormitory food, and the shortage of on-campus parking spaces. More important, our fundamental goals as human beings—such as health, physical safety, and economic security—cross culture lines.

The key is to honor the differences among people while remembering what we have in common. Diversity is not just about our differences; it's also about our similarities. On a biological level, less than 1 percent of the human genome accounts for visible characteristics such as skin color. In terms of our genetic blueprint, we are more than 99 percent the same.[9]

Speak and listen with cultural sensitivity. After first speaking with someone from another culture, don't assume that you've been understood or that you fully understand the other person. The same action can have different meanings at different times, even for members of the same culture. Check it out. Verify what you think you have heard. Listen to see whether what you spoke is what the other person received.

If you're speaking with someone who doesn't understand English well:

- Speak slowly, distinctly, and patiently.
- To clarify your statement, don't repeat individual words over and over again. Restate your entire message with simple, direct language and short sentences.
- Avoid slang and figures of speech.
- Use gestures to accompany your words.
- Remember that English courses for non-native speakers often emphasize written English, so write down what you're saying. Print your message in capital letters.
- Stay calm and avoid sending nonverbal messages that you're frustrated.

Look for individuals, not group representatives. Sometimes the way we speak glosses over differences among individuals and reinforces stereotypes. For example, a student worried about her grade in math expresses concern over "all those Asian students who are skewing the class curve." Or a white music major assumes that her black classmate knows a lot about jazz or hip-hop music. We can avoid such errors by seeing people as individuals—not spokespersons for an entire group.

Find a translator, mediator, or model. People who move with ease in two or more cultures can help us greatly. Diane de Anda, a professor at the University of California, Los Angeles, speaks of three kinds of people who can communicate across cultures. She calls them *translators*, *mediators*, and *models*.[10]

A *translator* is someone who is truly bicultural: a person who relates naturally to both people in a mainstream culture and people from a contrasting culture. This person can share her own experiences in overcoming discrimination, learning another language or dialect, and coping with stress.

Mediators are people who belong to the dominant or mainstream culture. Unlike translators, they might not be bicultural. However, mediators value diversity and are committed to cultural understanding. Often they are teachers, counselors, tutors, mentors, or social workers.

Models are members of a culture who are positive examples. Models include students from any racial or cultural group who participate in class and demonstrate effective study habits. Models can also include entertainers, athletes, and community leaders.

Your school might have people who serve these functions, even if they're not labeled translators, mediators, or models. Some schools have mentor or "bridge" programs that pair new students with teachers of the same race or culture. Ask your student counseling service about such programs.

Develop support systems. Many students find that their social adjustment affects their academic performance. Students with strong support systems—such as families, friends, churches, self-help groups, and mentors—are using a powerful strategy for success in school. As an exercise, list the support systems that you rely on right now. Also list new support systems you could develop.

Support systems can help you bridge culture gaps. With a strong base of support in your own group, you can feel more confident in meeting people outside that group.

Be willing to accept feedback. Members of another culture might let you know that some of your words or actions had a meaning other than what you intended. For example, perhaps a comment that seems harmless to you is offensive to them. And they may tell you directly about it.

Students with disabilities: Ask for what you want

Learn about services. Visit the disability services office and student health center at your school. Ask about:

- Permits that allow you to park a car closer to classrooms
- Lecture transcriptions
- Textbook-reading services
- Assistants for laboratory courses in science
- Shuttle buses for transportation between classes
- Closed captioning for instructional television programs
- Interpreters for the hearing impaired
- Books and other course materials in braille or on audio

Learn about the laws that apply to you. Equal opportunity for people with disabilities is the law. In the United States, both the Civil Rights Act of 1964 and the Rehabilitation Act of 1973 offer legal protection. The Americans with Disabilities Act (ADA) of 1990 extends earlier legislation.

Almost every school has a person who monitors compliance with disability laws. This person is often called the Section 504 coordinator, ADA coordinator, or disability services coordinator. If you think a school is discriminating against you because of your disability, this is the person to contact.

Ask for adjustments. You do not have to reveal that you have a disability. If you want an adjustment in course requirement or choose to use disability services, however, then you will need to disclose the facts about your condition. To get what you want, describe the challenges that your disability has created in the past. Help instructors and administrators understand how your education has been affected. Also describe possible solutions. Be specific and make your request as early as possible.

Take care of yourself. Many students with chronic illnesses or disabilities find that rest breaks are essential. If this is true for you, write such breaks into your daily or weekly plan.

Treat yourself with respect. If your health changes in a way that you don't like, avoid berating yourself. Focus on finding an effective medical treatment or other solution.

It's important to accept compliments and periodically review your accomplishments in school. Fill yourself with affirmation. As you educate yourself, you are attaining mastery.

Avoid responding to such feedback with comments such as "Don't get me wrong," "You're taking this way too seriously," or "You're too sensitive." Instead, listen without resistance. Open yourself to what others have to say. Remember to distinguish between the *intention* of your behavior and its actual *impact* on other people. Then take the feedback you receive and ask yourself how you can use it to communicate more effectively in the future.

You can also interpret such feedback positively: a sign that others believe you can change and that they see the possibility of a better relationship with you.

If you are new at responding to diversity, expect to make some mistakes along the way. As long as you approach people in a spirit of tolerance, your words and actions can always be changed.

Speak up against discrimination. You might find yourself in the presence of someone who tells a racist joke, makes a homophobic comment, or utters an ethnic slur. When this happens, you have a right to state what you observe, share what you think, and communicate how you feel. You might say, "That's a stereotype, and we don't have to fall for it." Or, "Other people are going to take offense at that. Let's tell jokes that don't put people down."

This kind of speaking may be the most difficult communicating you ever do. However, if you *don't* do it, you give the impression that you agree with biased speech.

In response to your candid comments, many people will apologize and express their willingness to change. Even if they don't, you can still know that you practiced integrity by aligning your words with your values.

Change the institution. None of us lives in isolation. We all live in systems, and these systems do not always tolerate diversity. As a student, you might see people of color ignored in class. You might see people of a certain ethnic group passed over in job hiring or underrepresented in school organizations. And you might see gay and lesbian students ridiculed or even threatened with violence.

One way to stop these actions is to point them out. You can speak more effectively about what you believe by making some key distinctions:

- *Stereotypes* are errors in thinking—inaccurate ideas about members of another culture.
- *Prejudice* refers to positive or negative feelings about others, which are often based on stereotypes.
- *Discrimination* takes places when stereotypes or prejudice gets expressed in policies and laws that undermine equal opportunities for all cultures.

If your school receives federal aid, it must set up procedures that protect students against discrimination. Ask your advisor about the civil rights laws and policies that apply at your school. Claim your power to communicate across cultures. ✂

You deserve compliments

Some people find it more difficult to accept compliments than criticisms. Here are some hints for handling compliments.

Accept the compliment. People sometimes respond to praise with "Oh, it's really nothing" or "This old thing? I've had it for years." This type of response undermines both you and the person who sent the compliment.

Choose another time to deliver your own compliments. Automatically returning a compliment can appear suspiciously polite and insincere.

Let the compliment stand. "Do you really think so?" questions the integrity of the message. It can also sound as if you're fishing for more compliments.

Accepting compliments is not the same as being conceited. If you're in doubt about how to respond, just smile and say, "Thank you!" This simple response affirms the compliment along with the person who delivered it.

You are worthy and capable. Allow people to acknowledge that fact.

practicing
CRITICAL THINKING

27

Becoming a culture learner

To learn about other cultures in depth, actively move through the cycle of learning. This exercise, which has three parts, illustrates one way to apply the cycle of learning.

Part 1: Concrete experience

Think of a specific way to interact with people from a culture different from your own. For example, attend a meeting for a campus group that you normally would not attend. Or sit in a campus cafeteria with a new group of people.

Describe what you will do to create your experience of a different culture.

Part 2: Reflective observation

Describe the experience you had while doing Part 1 of this exercise. Be sure to separate your observations—what you saw, heard, or did—from your interpretations. In addition, see whether you can think of other ways to interpret each of your observations.

Use the table here for this part of the exercise. An example is included to get you started.

Observation	Your Initial Interpretation	Other Possible Interpretations
For 30 minutes starting at noon on Tuesday, I sat alone in the northeast section of the cafeteria in our student union. During this time, all of the conversations I overheard were conducted in Spanish.	I sat alone because the Spanish-speaking students did not want to talk to me. They are unfriendly.	The Spanish-speaking students are actually friendly. They were just not sure how to start a conversation with me. Perhaps they thought I wanted to eat alone or study. Also, I could have taken the initiative to start a conversation.

Part 3: Abstract conceptualization

Next, see whether you can refine your initial interpretations and develop them into some informed conclusions about your experience in Part 1. Do some research about other cultures, looking specifically for information that can help you understand the experience. (Your instructor and a librarian can suggest ways to find such information.) Whenever possible, speak directly to people of various cultures. Share your observations from Part 1, and ask for *their* interpretations.

Reflect on the information you gather. Does it reinforce any of the interpretations you listed in Part 2? Does it call for a change in your thinking? Summarize your conclusions.

Communicating as a FIRST-GENERATION STUDENT

XiXinXing/Shutterstock.com

One lesson of American history is that people who are the first in their family to enter higher education can succeed. Think about the former slaves who enrolled in the country's first African American colleges. Remember the ex-soldiers who used the GI Bill to earn advanced degrees. From their experiences, you can take some life-changing lessons about communicating with family members, friends, instructors, and fellow students.

ASK FOR ACADEMIC SUPPORT

You don't have to go it alone. Your tuition buys access to many services: academic advising, dormitory advising, career services, financial aid, multicultural programs, tutoring, counseling, and more. Explore these sources of support. Also ask about specific programs for first-generation students.

Schedule a meeting with your academic advisor after every term. Share your successes and ask for help in solving problems.

The key is to ask for help right away. Do this as soon as you feel stuck in class or confused about how to complete the next step in your education.

ASK FOR EMOTIONAL SUPPORT

Keep a list of every person who stands behind you: relatives, friends, instructors, advisors, and employers. Check in with these people regularly via phone, email, and personal visits. Remind yourself that you are surrounded by people who want you to succeed.

RESOLVE CONFLICT WITH FAMILY MEMBERS

When you walked into your first class in higher education, you brought along the expectations of your family members. Those people might assume that you'll return home and be the same person you were last year.

The reality is that you will change while you're in school. Your attitudes, your friends, and your career goals may all shift. You might think that some of the people back home have limited ideas. In turn, they might criticize you.

This kind of conflict is normal in families with first-generation students. Maintain your relationships with loved ones, and give them time to understand your world. Talk about what you're learning and how it will help you succeed. Also apply the suggestions in this book for resolving conflict.

BUILD RELATIONSHIPS WITH INSTRUCTORS

Long-term relationships with your favorite instructors offer many benefits. Over the years, instructors can turn into mentors, colleagues, and even friends.

In particular, seek out instructors who were first-generation students. Ask them to put you in contact with other first-generation students and alumni. They can become part of your personal and professional networks.

When you have instructors that you like, stay in contact with them after their courses end. Visit these instructors during office hours at least once per term until you graduate. Talk about your current experiences, and thank them for their contribution to your life. If you do well in their classes, ask instructors if they'd be willing to write a recommendation for you in the future.

RESPOND TO PREJUDICE

Bias and discrimination can exist on any campus. Just ask students of color, gay and lesbian students, immigrants, and students from working-class or poor families. You might discover some common ground with all of them.

Remember that the law is on your side. Every school has antidiscrimination policies based on state and federal rules. Search your school's website to find out exactly what those policies are and whom to contact if you experience discrimination.

In addition, speak up if someone makes a negative comment or joke at your expense. Sometimes people have no idea how they affect you. Respond with I messages: "I realize that you don't mean to offend anybody, but I feel hurt and angry about what you just said." Or, "What you're saying is not accurate. It's based on a stereotype, not the facts about me."

SHARE YOUR EXPERIENCES

Return to your high school and talk to students about your experiences as a first-generation student. Invite students who are considering college to visit you on campus. Also thank the teachers and mentors who encouraged you to enter higher education.

Remember that you can contribute to other students simply by sharing how you got to higher education.

Did you grow up in a family that struggled to make ends meet financially? Then you know about how to live on a tight budget.

Did you work to support your family while you were in high school? Then you know about managing your time to balance major commitments.

Did you grow up in a neighborhood with people of many races, religions, and levels of income? Then you know about how to thrive with diversity.

Talking about your strengths can lead to a conversation that changes lives—including your own. ✖

Staying
SAFE
on social networks

Social networks create value. Websites such as Facebook, Twitter, Google+, and LinkedIn are known as places to share news, photos, and personal profiles. You can also use such sites to form study groups, promote special events, and make job contacts.

Activity in online communities can also have unexpected consequences. For some students, social networking takes time away from studying and other activities that contribute to long-term goals. Other students get involved in cyberbullying—hate speech or threats of violence. And some students find that embarrassing details from their online profiles come back to haunt them years later, especially when they're looking for a job.

You can use simple strategies to stay in charge of your safety, reputation, and integrity any time you connect with people online.

Post only what you want made public and permanent. The Internet as a whole is a public medium. This is true of its online communities as well. Avoid over-sharing. Post only the kind of information about yourself that you *want* to be made public—forever.

Friends, relatives, university administrators, potential employers, and police officers might be able to access your online profile. Don't post anything that could embarrass you later. (This is a good reason to avoid social networking if you're under the influence of alcohol or other drugs.) Act today to protect the person that you want to be four or five years from now.

Remember that there is no delete key for the Internet. Anything you post online will *stay* online for a long time. And anyone with Internet access can take your words and images and post them on a website or distribute them via email to damage your reputation. In the virtual world, you never know who's following you.

To avoid unwanted encounters with members of online communities, also avoid posting the following:

- Your home address
- Your school address
- Your phone number
- Your birth date
- Your class schedule
- Your financial information, such as bank account numbers, credit card numbers, your social security number, or information about an eBay or PayPal account
- Information about places that you regularly go to at certain times of the day
- Information about places you plan to visit in the future
- Provocative pictures or messages with sexual innuendos
- Pictures of yourself at school or at work
- Plans for vacation or out-of-town visits

To further protect your safety, don't add strangers to your list of online friends.

Use similar caution and common sense when joining groups. Signing up for a group with a name like *Binge Drinking Forever* can have consequences for years to come.

Also avoid flirting while you're online. People may not be who they say they are.

Use privacy features. Many online communities offer options for restricting how many people can access your updates and profile. When in doubt, use the most restrictive settings possible. Also consider creating both private and public profiles. For specific instructions, look for a link on each site titled "Help," "Frequently Asked Questions," "Security Features," "Account Settings," or "Privacy Settings." For further protection:

- Review and update your list of followers or friends on a regular basis.
- Find out which third-party applications have permission to access and post on your profile. If you're not familiar with an application or unsure about its privacy policies, revoke its access.
- Protect your profile with a secure password and change it frequently.
- Adjust your profile settings to reduce the number of email notifications and alerts that you get.
- Restrict the number of people that you "friend" or follow. Think twice about connecting with coworkers and supervisors.
- Check the address bar of your browser whenever you use a social networking site. Make sure the site address begins with *https*. This means that the site has built in an extra level of privacy and security.

Monitor your online presence. Use Google or another popular search engine to key in your name. This will reveal what another person, such as a potential employer, might see when he or she goes online to learn about you. If someone else has posted a fake profile in your name, this is one way to find out. Contact your school's information technology department or computer help desk for help in deleting such profiles.

Respect the privacy of others. Post photos of other people only with their permission. Also take care not to reveal confidential or potentially embarrassing information about the people in your network.

"Friend" people with care. You do not have to accept every friend request or "follow" every person who chooses to follow you. Remember that many instructors will not connect with students in social networks, and some schools have policies to discourage this. Networks such as Facebook are by definition social websites. The relationship between students and instructors is professional—not social.

Be cautious about meeting community members in person. Because people can give misleading or false information about themselves online, avoid meeting someone you only know online in person. If you do opt for a face-to-face meeting, choose a public place, and bring along a friend you trust.

Report malicious content. If you find online content that you consider offensive or dangerous, report it to site administrators. In many online communities, you can do this anonymously. You can help to prevent online forms of intolerance, prejudice, and discrimination. Set a positive counterexample by posting messages that demonstrate acceptance of diversity.

Remember netiquette. The word *etiquette* refers to common courtesy in interpersonal relationships. Its online equivalent is called *netiquette*—a set of guidelines for using computers, cell phones, or any other form of technology. Certain kinds of exchanges can send the tone of online communications—including social networking, email messages, and blog postings— into the gutter. To promote a cordial online community, abide by the following guidelines:

- **Respect others' time.** People often turn to the Internet with the hope of saving time— not wasting it. You can accommodate their desires by typing concise messages. Adopt the habit of getting to your point, sticking to it, and getting to the end.
- **Fine-tune the mechanics.** Proofread your message for spelling and grammar—just as you would a printed message. Some email programs have built-in spelling checkers as an optional tool. Give your readers the gift of clarity and precision. Use electronic communications as a chance to hone your writing skills.
- **Avoid typing passages in ALL UPPERCASE LETTERS.** This is the online equivalent of shouting.
- **Design your messages for fast retrieval.** Avoid graphics and attachments that take a long time to download, tying up your recipient's computer.
- **Remember that the message is missing the emotion.** When you communicate online, the people who receive your email will miss out on voice inflection and nonverbal cues that are present in face-to-face communication. Without these cues, words can be easily misinterpreted. Reread your message before sending it, to be sure you have clarified what you want to say and how you feel.
- **Avoid writing and then immediately sending emails, text messages, and status updates when you feel angry.** Instead, write a rough draft of what you want to say, and let it sit for 24 hours. Then reread and revise your message when you feel calmer. Waiting before you click "Send" is a sign of emotional intelligence.
- **Mind the details in text messages.** Small changes in spelling and punctuation can convey big differences in attitudes. *OK* is usually acceptable. If you shorten that to a single letter—K—the receiver might conclude that you don't have time for her. Keep it friendly by texting whole words, spelling them correctly, and adding a pleasant emoji or exclamation mark (!) for goodwill.
- **Keep the context in mind.** Whenever you're online for job-related or academic purposes, edit and proofread your updates and posts with special attention. Write with a more formal voice—the same style that you would use for a research paper.

The cornerstone of netiquette is to remember that the recipient on the other end is a human being. Whenever you're at a keyboard or cell phone typing up messages, ask yourself one question: "Would I say this to the person's face?" ✕

Three phases of
EFFECTIVE WRITING

© iStockphoto.com/boboling

Effective writing is essential to your success. Papers, presentations, essay tests, email, social networking sites—and even the occasional text message—call for your ability to communicate ideas with force and clarity.

This is another article that you can take to work. The ability to write is in demand. To verify this, scan job postings and notice how many of them call for the skill of writing.

Most new products and services, especially those that involve high budgets, begin with a written proposal. Reports, email messages, web pages, and other documents are essential to the flow of ideas and information.

People without writing skills can only influence people through direct contact. If you can write a persuasive memo, however, your ideas can spread to hundreds of people.

This chapter outlines a three-phase process for writing anything:

1. Getting ready to write
2. Writing a first draft
3. Revising your draft

PHASE 1: GETTING READY TO WRITE

Schedule and list writing tasks. You can divide the ultimate goal—a finished paper—into smaller steps that you can tackle right away. Estimate how long it will take to complete each step. Start with the date your paper is due, and work backward to the present. Say that the due date is December 1, and you have about three months to write the paper. To give yourself a cushion, schedule November 20 as your targeted completion date. Plan what you want to get done by November 1, and then list what you want to get done by October 1.

Choose a topic. It's easy to put off writing if you have a hard time choosing a topic. However, it is almost impossible to make a wrong choice of topic at this stage. You can choose a different topic later if you find the one you've chosen isn't working out.

Using your instructor's guidelines for the paper or speech, write down the list of possible topics that you created earlier. Then choose one. If you can't decide, use scissors to cut your list into single items, put them in a box, and pull one out. To avoid getting stuck on this step, set a precise timeline: "I will choose a topic by 4:00 p.m. on Wednesday."

There's no need to brainstorm topics in isolation. You can harness the energy and the natural creative power of a group to assist you in creating topics for your paper.

Narrow your topic. The most common pitfall is selecting a topic that's too broad. "Harriet Tubman" is not a useful topic for your American history paper because it's too broad. Covering that topic would take hundreds of pages. Instead, consider "Harriet Tubman's activities as a Union spy during the Civil War." Your topic statement can function as a working title.

Write a thesis statement. Clarify what you want to say by summarizing it in one concise sentence. This sentence, called a *thesis statement*, refines your working title. It also helps in making a preliminary outline.

You might write a thesis statement such as "Harriet Tubman's activities with the Underground Railroad led to a relationship with the Union army during the Civil War." A thesis statement that's clear and to the point can make your paper easier to write. Remember, you can always rewrite your thesis statement as you learn more about your topic.

A thesis statement is different from a topic. Like newspaper headlines, a thesis statement makes an assertion or describes an action. It is expressed in a complete sentence including a verb.

"Diversity" is a topic. "Cultural diversity is valuable" is a thesis statement.

Consider your purpose. Effective writing flows from a purpose. Discuss the purpose of your assignment with your instructor. Also think about how you'd like your reader or listener to respond after considering your ideas. Do you want your audience to think differently, to feel differently, or to take a certain action?

How you answer these questions greatly affects your writing strategy. If you want someone to think differently, make your writing clear and logical. Support your assertions with evidence. If you want someone to feel differently, consider crafting a story. Write about a character your audience can empathize with, and tell how that character resolves a problem that the audience can relate to. And if your purpose is to move the reader into action, explain exactly what steps to take, and offer solid benefits for doing so.

To clarify your purpose, state it in one sentence, for example, "I will define the term *success* in such a clear and convincing way that I win a scholarship from the publisher of this textbook."

Do initial research. At the initial stage, the objective of your research is not to uncover specific facts about your topic.

That comes later. First, you want to gain an overview of the subject. Discover the structure of your topic: its major divisions and branches.

Say that you want to persuade the reader to vote for a certain candidate. You must first learn enough about this person to summarize her background and state her stands on key issues.

Outline. An outline is a kind of map. When you follow a map, you avoid getting lost. Likewise, an outline keeps you from wandering off the topic.

To start an outline, gather a stack of 3×5 cards. Brainstorm ideas you want to include in your paper. Write

Writing for online readers

Much of your writing may take the form of email messages and text for websites. Your readers will be pressed for time and impatient. Do them a favor by getting to the point without taking detours.

Write email that gets results. Be conscious of the amount of email that busy people receive. Send email messages only to the people who need them, and only when necessary.

Start by using a professional email address. Avoid anything that resembles *iliketoparty@yahoo.com*.

Keep the "To" line blank until you've reread and revised your message. That way you'll avoid the main email pitfall: accidentally hitting "Send" too soon. This is especially important for work-related messages and sensitive personal messages.

Next, write an informative subject line. Rather than offering a generic description of your message, include a capsule summary—a complete sentence with the main point of your message.

Write the body of your message in complete, grammatically correct sentences. Highlight important items such as meeting dates and times.

After drafting your message, look at it again to see if you can make it shorter. Overly long emails are almost begging to be ignored or trashed.

Use the "Reply All" feature only when everyone who received a message truly needs to know your response. People will appreciate your help in keeping their incoming messages to a minimum.

Write for website readers. Jakob Nielsen, author of *Designing Web Usability: The Practice of Simplicity*, suggests that effectively written web pages have these attributes:

- *Concise*: free of needless words and organized so that the main point of each section and paragraph comes at the beginning
- *Scannable*: prepared with subheadings and visuals that allow readers to skim and quickly find what they need
- *Objective*: packed with credible facts and free of "hype," that is, vague or exaggerated claims presented without evidence[13]

Following these guidelines can assist you in *all* forms of business writing.

one phrase or sentence per card. Then experiment with the cards. Group them into separate stacks, each stack representing one major category. After that, arrange the stacks in order. Finally, arrange the cards within each stack in a logical order. Rearrange them until you discover an organization that you like. If you write on a computer, consider using the outlining feature of your word-processing software.

The main thing is to keep it simple. Traditional outlines sometimes include many levels: a main topic, subtopics, and *sub*-subtopics. This kind of outline can make your head explode when it's time to write your first draft.

Instead, keep your outline "flat." Include a title for your paper that captures the main topic. Then add a series of subheadings, one for each main subtopic, in a bulleted list. For example:

TITLE: Creating an Effective Study Group
- Finding Members
- Scheduling Your First Meeting
- Choosing a Format for Your Group
- Common Problems with Study Groups—and Solutions

PHASE 2: WRITING A FIRST DRAFT

Gather your notes and outline. If you've planned your writing project and completed your research, you've already done much of the hard work. Now you can relax into writing your first draft. To create your draft, gather your notes and arrange them to follow your outline. Then write about the ideas in your notes. Write in paragraphs, with one idea per paragraph. If you have organized your notes logically, related facts will appear close to one another.

Ease into it. Some people find that it works well to forget the word *writing*. Instead, they ease into the task with activities that help generate ideas. You can free associate, cluster, meditate, daydream, doodle, draw diagrams, visualize the event you want to describe, talk into a voice recorder— anything that gets you started.

Remember that the first draft is not for keeps. You can worry about quality later, when you revise. Your goal at this point is simply to generate lots of material. Later, during phase 3, you can revise and polish it.

Speak it. To get ideas flowing, start talking. Admit your confusion or lack of clear ideas. Then just speak. By putting your thoughts into words, you'll start thinking more clearly. Novelist E. M. Forster said, "'Speak before you think' is creation's motto."[11]

Use free writing. Free writing, a technique championed by writing teacher Peter Elbow, sends a depth probe into your creative mind.[12] There's only one rule in free writing: Write without stopping. Set a time limit— say, 10 minutes—and keep your pencil in motion or your fingers dancing across the keyboard the whole time. Give

Befriend your word processor

Knowing how to use some common features of Microsoft Word will help you get up to speed with almost any word-processing software. To get a current list of Word commands, go online to **office.microsoft.com**, find a search box, and enter *keyboard shortcuts microsoft word*. Find out how to open documents, create documents, apply templates, track changes, insert comments, print documents, and save your work. (That last command is the most important one you will ever learn.)

Other companies offer free or low-cost word-processing software with commands and features similar to Word.

Examples are Google Docs (**drive.google.com**) and Zoho Docs (**www.zoho.com/docs**).

Another option is to use plain text editors. Though they offer fewer features than Word, plain text editors are far less expensive, handle many common writing tasks, and are compatible with most other software. NotePad is a text editor that comes free with the Windows operating system, and TextEdit is bundled with Mac OSX.

In any case, check with your instructors to find out which software and document formats they will accept.

yourself permission to keep writing. Ignore the urge to stop and rewrite, even if you think what you've written isn't very good. There's no need to worry about spelling, punctuation, or grammar. It's okay if you stray from the initial subject. Just keep writing, and let the ideas flow. Experiment with free writing as soon as your instructor assigns a paper.

Make writing a habit. The word *inspiration* is not in the working vocabulary for many professional writers. Instead of waiting for inspiration to strike, they simply make a habit of writing at a certain time each day. You can use the same strategy. Schedule a block of time to write your first draft. The very act of writing can breed inspiration.

Respect your deep mind. Part of the process of writing takes place outside our awareness. There's nothing mysterious about this process. Many people report that ideas come to them while they're doing something totally unrelated to writing. Often this happens after they've been grappling with a question and have reached a point where they feel stuck. It's like the composer who said, "There I was, sitting and eating a sandwich, and all of a sudden this darn tune pops into my head." You can trust your deep mind. It's writing while you eat, sleep, and brush your teeth.

Get physical. Writing, like jogging or playing tennis, is a physical activity. You can move your body in ways that are in tune with the flow of your ideas. While working on the first draft, take breaks. Go for a walk. Speak or sing your

ideas out loud. From time to time, practice relaxation techniques and breathe deeply.

PHASE 3: REVISING YOUR DRAFT

Plan to revise a paper two or three times. Make a clean copy of each revision, and then let the last revised draft sit for at least three or four days.

Schedule time for rewrites before you begin, and schedule at least one day between revisions so that you can let the material sit. On Tuesday night, you might think your writing sings the song of beautiful language. On Wednesday, you will see that those same words, such as the phrase "sings the song of beautiful language," belong in the trash basket.

Keep in mind the saying "Write in haste; revise at leisure." When you edit and revise, slow down and take a microscope to your work. One guideline is to allow 50 percent of writing time for planning, researching, and writing the first draft. Then give the remaining 50 percent to revising.

While you're in the revising phase, consider making an appointment to see your instructor during office hours. Bring along a current draft of your paper. Be willing to share your thesis and outline. Ask for revision tips. If your school has a writing assistance center, see someone there as well.

One effective way to revise your paper is to read it out loud. The eyes tend to fill in the blanks in our own writing. The combination of voice and ears forces us to pay attention to the details.

Another technique is to ask other people to review your paper. If you do this in class,

it's called peer editing. This is never a substitute for your own review, but other people can often see mistakes you miss. Remember, when other people criticize or review your work, they're not attacking you. They're just commenting on your paper. With a little practice, you can actually learn to welcome feedback.

When it's your turn to edit someone else's writing, remember two guidelines: First, be positive. Find something that you like about the paper and talk about that. Second, offer a specific suggestion. Begin this statement with words such as: "I think your paper would be even stronger if . . ."

After getting feedback on your draft, revise it while keeping the following suggestions in mind.

Cut. Look for excess baggage. Avoid at all costs and at all times the really, really terrible mistake of using way too many unnecessary words, a mistake that some student writers often make when they sit down to write papers for the various courses in which they participate at the fine institutions of higher learning that they are fortunate enough to attend. (Example: The previous sentence could be edited to "Avoid unnecessary words.")

Approach your rough draft as if it were a chunk of granite from which you will chisel the final product. In the end, much of your first draft will be lying on the floor. What is left will be the clean, clear, polished product. Sometimes the revisions are painful. Sooner or later, every writer invents a phrase that is truly clever but makes no contribution to the purpose of the paper. Grit your teeth and let it go.

Note: For maximum efficiency, make the larger cuts first: sections, chapters, pages. Then go for the smaller cuts: paragraphs, sentences, phrases, words. Stay within the word limit that your instructor assigns.

Paste. In deleting both larger and smaller passages in your first draft, you've probably removed some of the original transitions and connecting ideas. The next task is to rearrange what's left of your paper or speech so that it flows logically. Look for consistency within paragraphs and for transitions from paragraph to paragraph and section to section.

If all or part of your draft doesn't hang together, reorder your ideas. Imagine yourself with scissors and glue, cutting the paper into scraps— one scrap for each point. Then paste these points down in a new, more logical order.

Fix. Now it's time to look at individual words and phrases. Define any terms that the reader might not know, putting them in plain English whenever you can. Scan your paper for any passages that are written in the language of texting or instant messaging. Rewrite those into full sentences.

In general, rely on vivid nouns and verbs. Using too many adjectives and adverbs weakens your message and adds unnecessary bulk to your writing. Write about the details, and be specific. Also, use active rather than passive verbs.

Instead of writing in the passive voice:
A project was initiated.

You can use the active voice:
The research team began a project.

Instead of writing verbosely:
After making a timely arrival and perspicaciously observing the unfolding events, I emerged totally and gloriously victorious.

You can write to the point, as Julius Caesar did:
I came. I saw. I conquered.

Instead of writing vaguely:
The speaker made effective use of the television medium, asking in no uncertain terms that we change our belief systems.

You can write specifically:
The reformed criminal stared straight into the television camera and shouted, "Take a good look at what you're doing! Will it get you what you really want?"

Prepare. In a sense, any paper is a sales effort. If you hand in a paper that is wearing wrinkled jeans, its hair tangled and unwashed and its shoes untied, your instructor is less likely to buy it. To avoid this situation, format your paper following accepted standards for margin widths, endnotes, title pages, and other details.

Ask your instructor for specific instructions on how to cite the sources used in writing your paper. You can find useful guidelines in the *MLA Handbook for Writers of Research Papers*, a book from the Modern Language Association. Also visit the MLA website at **www.mla.org/style**.

If you cut and paste material from a web page directly into your paper, be sure to place that material in quotation marks and cite the source. And before referencing an email message, verify the sender's identity. Remember that anyone sending email can pretend to be someone else.

Use quality paper for your final version. For an even more professional appearance, bind your paper with a plastic or paper cover.

Proof. As you ease down the homestretch, read your revised paper one more time. This time, go for the big picture, and look for the following:

- A clear thesis statement
- Sentences that introduce your topic, guide the reader through the major sections of your paper, and summarize your conclusions
- Details—such as quotations, examples, and statistics—that support your conclusions
- Lean sentences that have been purged of needless words
- Plenty of action verbs and concrete, specific nouns

Finally, look over your paper with an eye for spelling and grammar mistakes. If you're writing with software that checks for such errors, take advantage of this feature. Also keep in mind that even the best software will miss some mistakes. Computers still cannot replace a skilled human proofreader.

When you're through proofreading, take a minute to savor the result. You've just witnessed something of a miracle—the mind attaining clarity and resolution. That's the "aha!" in writing. ✖

Academic integrity: Avoid
PLAGIARISM

'YOU'VE COPIED ALL THIS OFF
THE INTERNET...'

Grizelda/CartoonStock

Using another person's words, images, or other original creations without giving proper credit is called *plagiarism*. Plagiarism amounts to taking someone else's work and presenting it as your own—the equivalent of cheating on a test.

Higher education consists of a community of scholars who trust one another to speak and write with integrity. Plagiarism undermines this trust. The consequences of plagiarism can range from a failing grade to expulsion from school.

Plagiarism can be unintentional. Some students don't understand the research process. Sometimes they leave writing until the last minute and don't take the time to organize their sources of information.

Students raised in cultures where identity is based on group membership rather than individual achievement may find it hard to understand how an individual can own creative work. Remember, however, that even accidental plagiarism can lead to penalties.

To avoid plagiarism, ask an instructor where you can find your school's written policy on this issue. Read this document carefully, and ask questions about *anything* you don't understand.

The basic guideline for preventing plagiarism is to cite a source for any fact or idea that is new to you. These include words and images created by another person. The overall goal is to clearly distinguish your own work from the work of others. A secondary goal is to give enough information about your sources so that they are easy for other people to find and use for themselves. There are several ways to ensure that you meet both of these goals consistently.

Know the perils of "paper mills." A big part of the problem is misuse of the Internet. Anyone with a computer can access thousands of web pages on a given topic. Images and text from those sources are easily copied and pasted into another document. Technology makes it easy to forget that some information is free for the taking, and some is privately owned.

Plagiarism is a now a growth industry. A quick web search will uncover hundreds of online businesses that sell term papers, essays, and book reports. These businesses are often called "paper mills." Some of them offer to customize their products for an additional fee. Even so, these services are based on plagiarism.

Students who use these services might answer, "When I buy a paper online, it's not plagiarism. I paid for those words, so now they're mine." But in fact, those words were still created by someone else. Plagiarism is more than merely copying words from another source: it's turning in work that you did not produce.

Also remember that plagiarism includes turning in a paper—or portions of a paper—that you have already written for another class. If you want to draw on prior research, talk to your instructor first.

Identify direct quotes. If you use a direct quote from another writer or speaker, put that person's words in quotation marks. If you do research online, you might find yourself copying sentences or paragraphs from a web page and pasting them directly into your notes. *This is the same as taking direct quotes from your source.* To avoid plagiarism, identify such passages in an obvious way. Besides enclosing them in quotation marks, you could format them in a different font or color.

Paraphrase carefully. Instead of using a direct quote, you might choose to paraphrase an author's words. Paraphrasing means restating the original passage in your own words, usually making it shorter and simpler. Students who copy a passage word for word and then just rearrange or delete a few phrases are running a serious risk of plagiarism. Consider this paragraph:

Higher education also offers you the chance to learn how to learn. In fact, that's the subject of this book. Employers value the person who is a "quick study" when it comes to learning a new job. That makes your ability to learn a marketable skill.

Following is an improper paraphrase of that passage:

With higher education comes the chance to learn how to learn. Employers value the person who is a "quick study" when it comes to learning a new job. Your ability to learn is a marketable skill.

A better paraphrase of the same passage would be this one:

The author notes that when we learn how to learn, we gain a skill that is valued by employers.

Remember to cite a source for paraphrases, just as you do for direct quotes.

When you use the same sequence of ideas as one of your sources—even if you have not paraphrased or directly quoted—cite that source.

Summarize carefully. For some of your notes, you may simply want to summarize your source in a few sentences or paragraphs. To do this effectively:

- Read your source several times for understanding.
- Put your source away; then write a summary in your own words.
- In your summary, include only the author's major points.
- Check your summary against your source for accuracy.

Identify distinctive terms and phrases. Some ideas are closely identified with their individual creators. Students who present such ideas with-

out mentioning the individual are plagiarizing. This is true even if they do not copy words, sentence structure, or overall organization of ideas.

For example, the phrase "seven habits of highly effective people" is closely linked to Stephen Covey, author of several books based on this idea. A student might write a paper titled "Habits of Effective People," using words, sentences, and a list of habits that differ completely from Covey's. However, the originality of this student's thinking could still be called into question. This student would be wise to directly mention Covey in the paper and acknowledge Covey's idea that effectiveness and habits are closely linked.

Note details about each source. Identify the source of any material that you quote, paraphrase, or summarize. For books, details about each source include the author, title, publisher, publication date, location of publisher, and page number. For articles from print sources, record the article title and the name of the magazine or journal as well. If you found the article in an academic or technical journal, also record the volume and number of the publication, and inclusive page numbers for the article as well as the page number for the quote. A librarian can help identify these details.

If your source is a web page, record as many identifying details as you can find—author, title, sponsoring organization, URL, publication date, and revision date. In addition, list the date that you accessed the page.

Cite your sources as endnotes or footnotes to your paper. Ask your instructor for examples of the format to use.

Submit only your own work. Turning in materials that have been written or revised by someone else puts your education at risk.

Allow time to digest your research. If you view research as a task that you can squeeze into a few hours, then you may end up more confused than enlightened. Instead, allow for time to reread and reflect on the facts you gather. This creates conditions for genuine understanding and original thinking.

In particular, take the time to:

- Read over all your notes without feeling immediate pressure to write.

- Summarize major points of view on your topic, noting points of agreement and disagreement.
- Look for connections in your material: ideas, facts, and examples that occur in several sources.
- Note direct answers to your main and supporting research.

- Revise your thesis statement, based on discoveries from your research.
- Put all your notes away and write informally about what you want to say about your topic.
- Look for connections between your research and your life—ideas that you can verify based on personal experience. ✄

Mastering public SPEAKING

Some people tune out during a speech. Just think of all the times you have listened to instructors, lecturers, and politicians. Remember all the wonderful daydreams you had during their speeches.

Nick Bland/Laurie Smale

Your audiences are like you. The way you plan and present your speech can determine the number of audience members who will stay with you until the end. Polishing your speaking and presentation skills can also help you think on your feet and communicate clearly. You can use these skills in any course, and they'll help you advance in your career as well.

Doing a presentation is much like writing a paper. Divide the project into three phases:

1. Preparing your presentation
2. Delivering your presentation
3. Reflecting on your presentation

PHASE 1: PREPARING YOUR PRESENTATION

Start from your passions. If your instructor allows you to choose the topic of presenta-

tion, then choose one that you find interesting. Imagine that the first words in your presentation will be: "I'm here to talk to you because I feel passionately about . . ." How would you complete the sentence? Turn your answer into your main topic.

Consider a "process speech." In this type of presentation, your purpose is to explain a way to do or make something. Examples are changing a tire, planting asparagus, or preparing a healthy meal in 15 minutes. Choose a short, step-by-step process with a concrete outcome. This makes it easier to organize, practice, and deliver your first presentation.

In the introduction to your process speech, get the audience's attention and establish rapport. State the topic and purpose of your speech. Relate the topic to something that audience members care about. During the body of your speech, explain each step in the process, following a logical order. To conclude, quickly summarize the process, and remind your audience of its usefulness.

Analyze your audience. Developing a speech is similar to writing a paper. Begin by writing out your topic, purpose, and thesis statement. Then carefully analyze your audience by using the strategies in Table 8.1.

Table 8.1 *Tailor Your Topic to Your Audience*

If your topic is new to listeners . . .	☐ Explain why your topic matters to them. ☐ Relate the topic to something that listeners already know and care about. ☐ Define any terms that listeners might not know.
If listeners already know about your topic . . .	☐ Acknowledge this fact at the beginning of your speech. ☐ Find a narrow aspect of the topic that may be new to listeners. ☐ Offer a new perspective on the topic, or connect it to an unfamiliar topic.
If listeners disagree with your thesis . . .	☐ Tactfully admit your differences of opinion. Reinforce points on which you and your audience agree. ☐ Build credibility by explaining your qualifications to speak on your topic. ☐ Quote expert figures that agree with your thesis—people whom your audience is likely to admire. ☐ Explain that their current viewpoint has costs for them, and that a slight adjustment in their thinking will bring significant benefits.
If listeners may be uninterested in your topic . . .	☐ Explain how listening to your speech can help them gain something that matters deeply to them. ☐ Explain ways to apply your ideas in daily life.

Remember that audiences want to know that your presentation relates to their needs and desires. To convince people that you have something worthwhile to say, write down your main point. Then see whether you can complete this sentence: *I'm telling you this because . . .*

Organize your presentation. List three to five questions that your audience members are likely to ask about your topic. Put those questions in logical order. Organize your presentation so that it directly answers those questions.

Also consider the length of your presentation. As a general guideline, plan on delivering about a hundred words per minute. Remember that you could lose points if your presentation goes over the assigned time limit.

Aim for a lean presentation—enough words to make your point but not so many as to make your audience restless. Leave your listeners wanting more. When you speak, be brief and then be seated.

Speeches are usually organized in three main parts: the introduction, the main body, and the conclusion.

Write the introduction. Rambling speeches with no clear point or organization put audiences to sleep. Solve this problem with your introduction. The following introduction, for example, reveals the thesis and exactly what's coming. It reveals that the speech will have three distinct parts, each in logical order:

> *Dog fighting is a cruel sport. I intend to describe exactly what happens to the animals, tell you who is doing this, and show you how you can stop this inhumane practice.*

Whenever possible, talk about things that hold your interest. Include your personal experiences, and start with a bang. Consider this introduction to a speech on the subject of world hunger:

> *I'm very honored to be here with you today. I intend to talk about malnutrition and starvation. First, I want to outline the extent of these problems; then I will discuss some basic assumptions concerning world hunger; and finally I will propose some solutions.*

You can almost hear the snores from the audience. Following is a rewrite:

> *More people have died from hunger in the past 5 years than have been killed in all of the wars, revolutions, and murders in the past 750 years. Yet there is enough food to go around. I'm honored to be here with you today to discuss solutions to this problem.*

Some members of an audience will begin to drift during any speech, but most people pay attention for at least the first few seconds. Highlight your main points in the beginning sentences of your speech.

A related option is to simply announce the questions you intend to answer. You can number these questions and write them on a flip chart. Or create an overview slide with the list of questions.

People might tell you to start your introduction with a joke. Humor is tricky. You run the risk of falling flat or offending somebody. Save jokes until you have plenty of experience with public speaking and know your audiences well.

Also avoid long, flowery introductions in which you tell people how much you like them, how thrilled you are to address them, and how humble you feel standing in front of them. If you lay it on too thick, your audience won't believe a word of it.

Draft your introduction, and then come back to it after you've written the rest of your speech. In the process of creating the main body and conclusion, your thoughts about the purpose and main points of your speech might change. You might even want to write the introduction last.

Write the main body. The main body of your speech is the content, which accounts for 70 to 90 percent of most speeches. In the main body, you develop your ideas in much the same way that you develop a written paper. If you raised questions in your introduction, be sure to directly answer them.

Transitions are especially important. Give your audience a signal when you change points. Do so by using meaningful pauses and verbal emphasis as well as transitional phrases: "On the other hand, until the public realizes what is happening to children in these countries . . ." or "The second reason hunger persists is . . ."

In long speeches, recap from time to time. Also preview what's to come. Hold your audience's attention by using facts, descriptions, expert opinions, and statistics.

Write the conclusion. At the end of the speech, summarize your points and draw your conclusion. You started with a bang; now finish with drama. The first and last parts of a speech are the most important. Make it clear to your audience when you've reached the end. Avoid endings such as "This is the end of my speech." A simple standby is "So in conclusion, I want to reiterate three points: First, . . ." When you are finished, stop talking.

Create speaking notes. Some professional speakers recommend writing out your speech in full, and then putting key words or main points on a few 3 × 5 cards. Number the cards so that if you drop them, you can quickly put them in order again. As you finish the information on each card, move it to the back of the pile. Write information clearly and in letters large enough to be seen from a distance.

The disadvantage of the 3 × 5 card system is that it involves card shuffling. Some speakers prefer to use standard outlined notes. Another option is mind mapping. Even an hour-long speech can be mapped on one sheet of paper. You can also use memory techniques to memorize the outline of your speech.

Create supporting visuals. Presentations often include visuals such as PowerPoint slides and posters. With PowerPoint, you can also add video clips from your computer or cell phone. These visuals can reinforce your main points and help your audience understand how your presentation is organized.

Use visuals to *complement* rather than *replace* your speaking. If you use too many visuals—or visuals that are too complex—your audience might focus on them and forget about you. To prevent this:

- Ask your instructor whether it's acceptable to use technology in your presentation.
- Ask yourself whether slides will actually benefit your presentation. If you use PowerPoint simply because you *can*, you run the risk of letting the technology overshadow your message.
- Use fewer slides rather than more. For a 15-minute presentation, 10 slides are enough.
- Use slides to *show* rather than *tell*. Save them for illustrations, photos, charts, and concepts that are hard to express in words. Don't expect your audience to read a lot of text.
- Limit the amount of text on each visual. Stick to key words presented in short sentences or phrases.
- Use a consistent set of plain fonts that are large enough for all audience members to see. Avoid using more than two fonts, and avoid UPPERCASE letters.
- Stick with a simple, consistent color scheme. Use dark text on a light background. Keep backgrounds consistent, and avoid colors that compete with each other.

The most popular application for creating presentations is PowerPoint. To learn about it, go online to **office.microsoft.com**, find a search box, and enter *keyboard shortcuts powerpoint*. Find out how to open a presentation, create a presentation, apply a template, insert a new slide, add visuals to slides, view a slide show, print a presentation, and save a presentation. (Knowing and using the last command often will save you much time and stage fright.)

Also make backup copies of your presentation. At the very least, attach your PowerPoint file to an email message and send it to yourself.

You might enjoy exploring some of PowerPoint's competitors as well. These include Prezi, Jing, and Animoto as well as Keynote for Mac OSX. Also experiment with Zoho Docs (**www.zoho.com/docs**).

Overcome fear of public speaking. Even skilled speakers can panic at the thought of getting up in front of an audience, so try not to stress if you feel fear. Instead, you can take three steps to reduce and manage it.

First, prepare thoroughly. Research your topic thoroughly. Knowing your topic inside and out can create a baseline of confidence. To make a strong start, memorize the first four sentences that you plan to deliver, and practice them many times. Delivering them flawlessly when you're in front of an audience can build your confidence for the rest of your speech.

Second, accept your physical sensations. You've probably experienced physical sensations that are commonly associated with stage fright: dry mouth, a pounding heart, sweaty hands, muscle jitters, shortness of breath, and a shaky voice. One immediate way to deal with such sensations is to simply notice them. Tell yourself, "Yes, my hands are clammy. Yes, my stomach is upset. Also, my face feels numb." Trying to deny or ignore such facts can increase your fear. When you fully accept sensations, however, they start to lose power.

Third, focus on content, not delivery. Michael Motley, a professor at the University of California–Davis, distinguishes between two orientations to speaking. People with a *performance orientation* believe that the speaker must captivate the audience by using formal techniques that differ from normal conversation. In contrast, speakers with a *communication orientation* see public speaking simply as an extension of one-to-one conversation. The goal is not to perform, but to communicate your ideas to an audience in the same ways that you would explain them to a friend.[14]

Adopting a communication orientation can reduce your fear of public speaking. Instead of thinking about yourself, focus on your message. Your audience is more interested in *what* you have to say than *how* you say it. Forget about giving a "speech." Just give people valuable ideas and information that they can use.

Practice your presentation. The key to successful public speaking is practice. Do this with your "speaker's voice." Your voice sounds different when you talk loudly, and this fact can be unnerving. Get used to it early on.

Several days before you deliver your presentation, start practicing it. If possible, do this in the room where you will actually face your audience. Keep an eye on the time, to make sure that you stay within the limit.

Hear what your voice sounds like over a sound system. If you can't practice your speech in the actual room, at least visit the site ahead of time. Also make sure that the materials you will need for your speech, including any audiovisual equipment, will be available when you want them.

Whenever possible, make a recording. Many schools have video-recording equipment available for student use. Use it while you practice. Then view the finished recording to evaluate your presentation.

Listen for repeated words and phrases. Examples include *you know, kind of,* and *really,* plus any little *uh's, umm's,* and *ah's.* To get rid of them, tell yourself that you intend to notice every time they pop up in your daily speech. When you hear them, remind yourself that you don't use those words anymore.

Keep practicing. Avoid speaking word for word, as if you were reading a script. When you know your material well, you can deliver it in a natural way. Practice your presentation until you could deliver it in your sleep. Then run through it a few more times.

PHASE 2: DELIVERING YOUR PRESENTATION

Before you begin, get the audience's attention. If people are still filing into the room or adjusting their seats, they're not ready to listen. When all eyes are on you, then begin.

Dress for the occasion. The clothing you choose to wear on the day of your speech delivers a message that's as loud as your words. Consider how your audience will be dressed, and then choose a wardrobe based on the impression you want to make.

Project your voice. When you speak, talk loudly enough to be heard. Avoid leaning over your notes or the podium.

Maintain eye contact. When you look at people, they become less frightening. Also, remember that it is easier for the audience to listen to someone when that person is looking at them. Find a few friendly faces around the room, and imagine that you are talking to each of these people individually.

Notice your nonverbal communication. Be aware of what your body is telling your audience. Contrived or staged gestures will look dishonest. Be natural. If you don't know what to do with your hands, notice that. Then don't do anything with them.

Notice the time. You can increase the impact of your words by keeping track of the time during your speech. It's better to end early than to run late.

Pause when appropriate. Beginners sometimes feel that they have to fill every moment with the sound of their voice. Release that expectation. Give your listeners a chance to make notes and absorb what you say.

Have fun. Chances are that if you lighten up and enjoy your presentation, so will your listeners.

PHASE 3: REFLECTING ON YOUR PRESENTATION

Many students are tempted to sigh with relief when their presentation is done, and put the event behind them. Resist this temptation. If you want to get better at making presentations, then take time to reflect on each performance. Did you finish on time? Did you cover all of the points you intended to cover? Was the audience attentive? Did you handle any nervousness effectively?

Write Journal Entries about what you discovered and intend to do differently for your next presentation. Remember to be as kind to yourself as you would be to someone else after a presentation. In addition to noting areas for improvement, note what you did well. Congratulate yourself on getting up in front of an audience and completing your presentation.

Also welcome feedback from others. Most of us find it difficult to hear criticism about our speaking. Be aware of resisting such criticism, and then let go of your resistance. Listening to feedback will increase your skill. ✄

Making the grade in group presentations

When preparing group presentations, you can use three strategies for making a memorable impression.

Get organized. As soon as you get the assignment, select a group leader and exchange contact information. Schedule specific times and places for planning, researching, writing, and practicing your presentation.

At your first meeting, write a to-do list that includes all of the tasks involved in completing the assignment. Distribute tasks fairly, paying attention to the strengths of individuals in your group. For example, some people excel at brainstorming, whereas others prefer researching.

One powerful way to get started is to define clearly the topic and thesis, or main point, of your presentation. Then support your thesis by looking for the most powerful facts, quotations, and anecdotes you can find.

As you get organized, remember how your presentation will be evaluated. If the instructor doesn't give grading criteria, create your own.

Get coordinated. Get together several times to practice your presentation before it's scheduled to be given in class. Develop smooth, short transitions between individual speakers. Keep track of the time so that you stay within the guidelines for the assignment.

Also practice using visuals such as flip charts, posters, DVDs, videotapes, or slides. To give visuals their full impact, make them appropriate for the room where you will present. Make sure that text is large enough to be seen from the back of the room. For bigger rooms, consider using presentation software or making overhead transparencies.

Get cooperation. Presentations that get top scores take teamwork and planning—not egos. Communicate with group members in an open and sensitive way. Contribute your ideas, and be responsive to the viewpoints of other members. When you cooperate, your group is on the way to an effective presentation.

Chimamanda Adichie }

Was born in Nigeria, earned graduate degrees from Johns Hopkins and Yale. Her novels include **Purple Hibiscus** *and* **Half of a Yellow Sun.**

When Chimamanda Adichie left her native Nigeria to attend college in the United States, her first roommate was American. She was surprised that Adichie spoke English so well.

Adichie told her that the official language of Nigeria is English.

Her roommate asked to listen to some of Adichie's "tribal music."

Adichie pulled out a tape of Mariah Carey songs.

The roommate also assumed that Adichie did not how to use a stove.

In reality, Adichie's father was a professor at the University of Nigeria, and her mother worked there as an administrator. Their family could afford live-in, domestic help. Chinua Achebe—one of Africa's most famous writers—had once lived in their house.

During a TED Talk in 2009, Adichie recalled this conversation. "My roommate had a single story of Africa: a single story of catastrophe. In this single story there was no possibility of Africans being similar to her in any way, no possibility of feelings more complex than pity, no possibility of a connection as human equals."

Adichie also recalled that she learned to read before age five, devouring British and American children's books. By age seven, she was writing stories with crayon illustrations. Her characters were white. They ate apples. They enjoyed playing in the snow and talking about the weather, especially when the sun finally emerged from cloudy skies.

Yet she was living in Nigeria, a land of constant sun and no snow. She ate mangoes, not apples. And her friends never discussed the weather.

To Adichie, this conflict between life and literature demonstrates the danger of a single story.

Things changed when she discovered books from African writers such as Achebe and Camara Laye: "I realized that people like me, girls with skin the color of chocolate, whose kinky hair could not form ponytails, could also exist in literature." She learned that books can tell more than one story and that any event can be described from more than one viewpoint.

This is a theme that Adichie explores in much of her writing. Her novel *Half of the Yellow Sun*, for example, is told from the perspective of three characters: a teenage Nigerian boy; a rich, young Nigerian woman; and a white man from England.

"Generalizations are always reductive, I think, because they shrink you from a whole to a mere part," Adichie says. "I am Nigerian, feminist, Black, Igbo [an ethnic group in southeastern Nigeria], and more, but when I am categorized as one, it makes it almost impossible to be seen as all of the others, and I find this limiting."

Adichie says that storytelling and power are closely linked. When anyone can tell a single story about us and make it the *only* story, that person dominates us.

This is why novelists and other storytellers are so important in our multinational world. They can tell many stories about any person or place. They open our eyes to complexity and diversity. And in embracing those varied stories, Adichie says, "we regain a kind of paradise."

Chimamanda Adichie *employs her word to embrace diversity in thinking.*

QUIZ

Chapter 8

1. The Power Process: "Employ your word" refers to the ladder of powerful speaking. The characteristic that distinguishes the bottom rung of this ladder from the upper five rungs is:
   a. Possibility
   b. Preference
   c. Planning
   d. Obligation

2. You can listen skillfully to a speaker even when you disagree with that person's viewpoint.
   a. True
   b. False

3. "You always interrupt when I talk" is a complaint. An effective way to restate this as a request is:
   a. "You almost always interrupt when I talk."
   b. "You sometimes interrupt when I talk."
   c. "Please let me finish speaking before you talk."
   d. "Why do you interrupt me?"

4. According to the text, the most effective listeners remain totally silent while another person speaks.
   a. True
   b. False

5. In contrast to verbal messages, _____ messages include your posture, gestures, and style of clothing.

6. According to the text, people who master public speaking are able to eliminate their fear of getting up in front of an audience.
   a. True
   b. False

7. Effective "I" messages include:
   a. Your observations
   b. A description of your feelings
   c. A statement about what you want
   d. A statement about what you intend to do
   e. Any or all of the answer choices

8. Skilled writers assume that people will read every word in your message when it appears online.
   a. True
   b. False

9. From the list below, choose effective examples of an "I" message:
   a. "I think that you are sometimes rude."
   b. "I feel that you don't love me any more."
   c. "When you come home late, I feel worried."
   d. "I'm afraid we're drifting apart."
   e. Both c and d.

10. Which of the following is an example of an effective thesis statement?
    a. Student success
    b. Student success depends on strategies that can be learned
    c. Student success and learning
    d. Strategies, student success, and learning

Take a minute to reflect on how you can use this chapter to make a lasting, positive difference in the way that you communicate. First, take a snapshot of your current skills in this area of your life. Then create a clear intention for taking action to develop more mastery.

Discovery

My score on the Communicating section of the Discovery Wheel was . . .

When I feel angry with people, the way I usually express it is . . .

I would describe my current level of emotional intelligence as . . .

Intention

The suggestion from this chapter that can help me most with listening is . . .

The suggestion from this chapter that can help me most with speaking is . . .

The suggestion from this chapter that can help me most with writing is . . .

Using these suggestions can make me more effective in my career by . . .

Action

To take the suggestions that I just listed and put them into practice, the three new habits that I will adopt next are . . .

Singkham/Shutterstock.com

Money

why

Money can stop being a barrier to getting what you want from school—and from your life.

how

Scan this chapter with an eye for strategies that could help you increase your income, decrease your expenses, or both. Note three money strategies that you'd like to use right away.

what if...

I could adopt habits that would free me from money worries for the rest of my life?

what is included . . .

322   Power Process: Risk being a fool

323   The end of money worries

329   Make more money

333   Spend less money

336   Managing money during tough times

338   Take charge of your credit

343   Education pays off—and you can pay for it

345   Money for the future

349   Use tools to tame your money

351   Your money and your values

352   Master Student Profile: Leo Babauta

do you have a minute?

Take a minute right now to search your school's website for the location, phone, number, and email address of the financial aid office. If you have a few seconds to spare, also make an appointment to meet with someone in that office.

Risk being a fool

A master student has the courage to take risks. And taking risks means being willing to fail sometimes—even being willing to be a fool. This idea can work for you because you already are a fool.

Don't be upset. All of us are fools at one time or another. There are no exceptions. If you doubt it, think back to that stupid thing you did just a few days ago. You know the one. Yes . . . *that* one. It was embarrassing, and you tried to hide it. You pretended you weren't a fool. This happens to everyone.

We are all fallible human beings. Most of us, however, spend too much time and energy trying to hide our foolishness. No one is really tricked by this—not even ourselves. It's okay to look ridiculous while dancing. It's all right to sound silly when singing to your kids. Sometimes it's okay to be absurd. It comes with taking risks.

This Power Process comes with a warning label: Taking risks does *not* mean escaping responsibility for our actions. "Risk being a fool" is not a suggestion to get drunk at a party and make a fool of yourself. It is not a suggestion to fool around or do things badly. Mediocrity is not the goal.

The point is that mastery in most activities calls for the willingness to do something new, to fail, to make corrections, to fail again, and so on.

Take money, for example. This chapter asks you to consider an outrageous idea: that you can end money worries. If you share this idea with your friends, they might think you've fallen for some get-rich-quick scheme. Someone might even call you a fool. If you're okay with those reactions, then nobody's criticism will stop you. You're free to explore any idea and even make a few mistakes. In the process, you could learn something that changes your whole experience of money.

"Risk being a fool" means that foolishness—along with courage, cowardice, grace, and clumsiness—is a human characteristic. We all share it. You might as well risk being a fool because you already are one, and nothing in the world can change that. Why not enjoy it once in a while?

There's one sure-fire way to avoid any risk of being a fool, and that's to avoid life. The writer who never finishes a book will never have to worry about getting negative reviews. The center fielder who sits out every game is safe from making any errors. And the comedian who never performs in front of an audience is certain to avoid telling jokes that fall flat. The possibility of succeeding at any venture increases when we're comfortable with making mistakes—that is, with the risk of being a fool. ◼

THE END
of money worries

Most money problems result from spending more than is available. It's that simple even though we often do everything we can to make the problem much more complicated.

Image Source/Corbis

The solution also is simple: *Don't spend more than you have.* If you are spending more than you have, then increase your income, decrease your spending, or do both. This idea has never won a Nobel Prize in Economics, but you won't go broke applying it to your life.

Money produces more unnecessary conflict and worry than almost anything else. And it doesn't seem to matter how much money a person has. People who earn $10,000 a year never have enough. People who earn $100,000 a year might also say that they never have enough.

Let's say they earned $1 million a year. Then they'd have enough, right? Not necessarily. Money worries can upset people no matter how much they have, especially when the economy dips into recession.

Money management may be based on a simple idea, but there is a big incentive for us to make it seem more complicated and scarier than it really is. If we don't understand money, then we don't have to be responsible for it. After all, if you don't know how to change a flat tire, then you don't have to be the one responsible for fixing it.

"I can't afford it" is a common reason that students give for dropping out of school. Actually, "I don't know how to pay for it" or "I don't think it's worth it" are probably more accurate ways to state the problem.

Using the strategies in this chapter could help you create financial peace of mind. That's a bold statement—perhaps even an outrageous one. But what if it's true? Approach this idea as a possibility. Then experiment with it, using your own life as the laboratory.

This chapter can benefit you even during a recession. Although the state of the overall economy matters as well, your financial fate depends far more on the small choices you make every day about spending and earning money.

The strategies you're about to learn are not complicated. In fact, they're not even new. The strategies are all based on the cycle of discovery, intention, and action that you've already practiced with the Journal Entries in this book. With these strategies—and the abilities to add and subtract—you have everything you need to manage your money.

There are three main steps in money management:

- Tell the truth about how much money you have and how much you spend (discovery).
- Commit to live within your means by spending less than you earn (intention).
- Experiment with suggestions for earning more money, spending less money, or both (action).

If you do these three things consistently, you can eventually say goodbye to most money worries. For example, the single habit of paying off your entire credit card balance each month might be enough to transform your financial life.

This chapter about money does not tell you how to become a millionaire, though you can certainly adopt that as a goal if you choose. Instead, the following pages reveal what many millionaires know: ways to control money instead of letting money control you. ✖

The Money Monitor/Money Plan

Many of us find it easy to lose track of money. It likes to escape when no one is looking. And usually, no one *is* looking. That's why the simple act of noticing the details about money can be so useful—even if this is the only idea from the chapter that you ever apply.

Use this exercise as a chance to discover how money flows into and out of your life. The goal is to record all the money you receive and spend over the course of one month. This sounds like a big task, but it's simpler than you might think. Besides, there's a big payoff for this action. With increased awareness of income and expenses, you can make choices about money that will change your life. Here's how to begin.

> **Step 1. Review Figure 9.1 and save copies of Figure 9.2, the Money Monitor/Money Plan form.**

Make photocopies of Figure 9.2 to use each month. This form helps you do two things. One is to get a big picture of the money that flows in and out of your life. The other is to plan specific and immediate changes in how you earn and spend money.

> **Step 2. Keep track of your income and expenses.**

Use your creativity to figure out how you want to carry out this step. The goal is to create a record of exactly how much you earn and spend each month. Use any method that works for you. And keep it simple. Following are some options:

- **Save all receipts and file them.** Every time you buy something, ask for a receipt. Then stick it in your wallet, purse, or pocket. When you get home, make notes about the purchase on the receipt. Then file the receipts in a folder labeled with the current month and year (e.g., January 2018). Every time you get a paycheck during that month, also save the stub and add it to the folder. If

you do not get a receipt or record of payment, then create one of your own. Detailed receipts will help you later on when you file taxes, categorize expenses (such as food and entertainment), and check your purchases against credit card statements.

- **Use money apps for your smartphone.** If you always carry a smartphone, then you have a device for recording income and expenses. To find current apps for this purpose, do an Internet search with the key words *money trackers Android* or *money trackers iOS*.
- **Use personal finance software.** Learn to use Quicken or a similar product that allows you to record income and expenses on your computer and to sort them into categories.
- **Use online banking services.** If you have a checking account that offers online services, take advantage of the records that the bank is already keeping for you. Every time you write a check, use a debit card, or make a deposit, the transaction will show up online. You can use a computer to log in to your account and view these transactions at any time. Some bank websites even allow you to set up categories for your income and expenses and tag transactions with one of these categories. If you're unclear about how to use online banking, go in to your bank and ask for help.
- **Experiment with several of the provided options.** Settle into one that feels most comfortable to you. Or create a method of your own. Anything will work, as long as you end each month with an *exact and accurate* record of your income and expenses.

> **Step 3. On the last day of the month, fill out your Money Monitor/Money Plan.**

Pull out a blank Money Monitor/Money Plan from Figure 9.2. Label it with the current month and year. Fill out this form, using the records of your income and expenses for the month.

DISCOVERY/

INTENTION STATEMENT

Reflect on your experience of money

List any statements you've made about your financial life recently—anything from "I never have enough" to "I have some extra money to invest, and I'm wondering where to put it." Write your statements here.

When speaking about my money life, I discovered that I . . .

Now scan this chapter with an eye for articles that align with any of the statements you just wrote, or state a differing point of view. Make a note of these articles and plan to read them in detail.

I intend to . . .

Notice that the far left column of the Money Monitor/Money Plan includes categories of income and expenses. (You can use the blank rows for categories of income and expenses that are not already included.) Write your total for each category in the middle column.

For example, if you spent $300 at the grocery store this month, write that amount in the middle column next to *Groceries*. If you work a part-time job and received two paychecks for the month, write the total in the middle column next to *Employment*. See Figure 9.1, the sample Money Monitor/Money Plan on the next page for more examples.

Remember to split expenses when necessary. For example, you might write one check each month to pay the balance due on your credit card. The purchases listed on your credit card bill might fall into several categories. Total up your expenses in each category, and list them separately.

Suppose that you used your credit card to buy music online, purchase a sweater, pay for three restaurant meals, and buy two tanks of gas for your car. Write the online music expense next to *Entertainment*. Write the amount you paid for the sweater next to *Clothes*. Write the total you spent at the restaurants next to *Eating Out*. Finally, write the total for your gas stops next to *Gas*.

Now look at the column on the far right of the Money Monitor/Money Plan. This column is where the magic happens. Review each category of income and expense. If you plan to reduce your spending in a certain category during the next month, write a minus sign (−) in the far right column. If you plan a spending increase in any category next month, write a plus sign (+) in the far right column. If you think that a category of income or expense will remain the same next month, leave the column blank.

Look again at Figure 9.1, the sample Money Monitor/Money Plan. This student plans to reduce her spending for eating out and entertainment (which for her includes movies and DVD rentals). She plans to increase the total she spends on groceries. She figures that even so, she'll save money by cooking more food at home and eating out less.

Step 4. After you've filled out your first Money Monitor/Money Plan, take a moment to congratulate yourself.

You have actively collected and analyzed the data needed to take charge of your financial life. No matter how the numbers add up, you are now in conscious control of your money. Repeat this exercise every month. It will keep you on a steady path to financial freedom.

Sample Money Monitor/Money Plan

Income	This Month	Next Month
Employment	500	
Grants	100	
Interest from Savings		
Loans	300	
Scholarships	100	
Total Income	1000	

Expenses	This Month	Next Month
Books and Supplies		
Car Maintenance		
Car Payment		
Clothes		
Deposits into Savings Account		
Eating Out	50	–
Entertainment	50	–
Gas	100	
Groceries	300	+
Insurance (Car, Life, Health, Home)		
Laundry	20	
Phone	55	
Rent/Mortgage Payment	400	
Tuition and Fees		
Utilities	50	
Total Expenses	1025	–

Figure 9.1 **Sample Money Monitor/Money Plan**

Money Monitor/Money Plan
Month_____ Year____

Income	This Month	Next Month
Employment		
Grants		
Interest from Savings		
Loan		
Scholarships		
Total Income		

Expenses	This Month	Next Month
Books and Supplies		
Car Maintenance		
Car Payment		
Clothes		
Deposits into Savings Account		
Eating Out		
Entertainment		
Gas		
Groceries		
Insurance (Car, Life, Health, Home)		
Laundry		
Phone		
Rent/Mortgage Payment		
Tuition and Fees		
Utilities		
Total Expenses		

Figure 9.2 **Money Monitor/Money Plan**

Money Monitor/Money Plan
Month_____ Year____

Income	This Month	Next Month	Expenses	This Month	Next Month
Employment			Books and Supplies		
Grants			Car Maintenance		
Interest from Savings			Car Payment		
Loan			Clothes		
Scholarships			Deposits into Savings Account		
			Eating Out		
			Entertainment		
			Gas		
			Groceries		
			Insurance (Car, Life, Health, Home)		
			Laundry		
			Phone		
			Rent/Mortgage Payment		
			Tuition and Fees		
			Utilities		
Total Income			Total Expenses		

Figure 9.2 **(Continued)**

Dragon Images/Shutterstock.com

Make more
MONEY

Along with controlling your expenses, making more money is a powerful way to build wealth. Skipping daily visits to the coffee shop might save you a couple hundred dollars this year. Negotiating a raise or finding a better-paying job could put thousands of extra dollars in your pocket in the short term—and many times that over the long term. Although there are limits to how much money you can save, your ability to earn is practically unlimited.

There are differences between the psychology involved in spending less and earning more. Reducing expenses is often about saying *no* to spending, which can feel like self-denial. Earning more allows you to say *yes* to purchases that align with your values while avoiding financial problems in the future.

Among the ways to make more money are these:

- Get financial aid
- Work at a job while you're in school
- Ask for a raise
- Start a business on the side
- Be a high performer
- Be a lifetime learner

GET FINANCIAL AID
Student grants, scholarships, and low-interest loans can play a major role in your college success by freeing you up from having to work full-time or even part-time. Many students assume they don't qualify for financial aid. That assumption could cost you thousands of dollars. Visit the financial aid office at your school to discover your options.

WORK AT A JOB WHILE YOU'RE IN SCHOOL
If you work while you're in school, you earn more than money. You gain experience, establish references, interact with a variety of people, and make contact with people who might hire you in the future. Also, regular income in any amount can make a difference in your monthly cash flow.

Many students work full-time or part-time jobs. Work and school don't have to conflict, especially if you plan your week carefully and ask for your employer's support. See the Time chapter for ways to manage your schedule.

On most campuses, the financial aid office employs a person whose job it is to help students find work while they're in school. See that person. Some jobs are just made for students. Serving or delivering food may not be glamorous, but the tips can really add up. Other jobs, such as working the reference desk at the campus library or monitoring the front desk in a dorm, offer quiet times that are ideal for studying.

See whether you can find a job related to your chosen career. Even an entry-level job in your field can provide valuable experience. Once you've been in such a job for a while, find out how to get promoted.

ASK FOR A RAISE
There are two situations in which you could ask for a raise. One is while you're interviewing for a job that you want to get. Another is during a performance review with your supervisor in a job that you already have. The suggestions in this section can apply in either case.

Consider the potential rewards. Effective salary discussion can make a huge difference in your financial well-being. Consider the long-term impact of making just an extra $1,000 per year. Over the next decade, that's an extra $10,000 dollars in pretax income, even if you get no other raises. Now imagine the long-term impact of an even bigger raise—$2,000, $3,000, $5,000, $10,000, or even more per year.

Put the numbers in a bigger context. Write a Discovery Statement about the benefits of getting a raise that go beyond money. For example: *I discovered that I could . . .*

- *Enjoy the peace of mind that comes with paying down my debt.*

- *Deepen my relationships with friends and family members by taking a trip with them that we'd all enjoy.*
- *Enjoy work more by knowing that I'm getting paid what I deserve.*
- *Enjoy being recognized for the quality of work that I do.*
- *Allow my friends and family members to feel happy for me.*
- *Earn my boss's respect by sticking up for myself.*

Think about your thinking. Before you ask for a raise, take some time to look for any hidden beliefs that could work against you. Some possible examples are:

- *My boss will just say that there's no money in the budget for a raise.*

- *I'm just lucky to have a job in this economy.*
- *I'm lousy at asking for what I want, especially when it comes to money.*
- *Only my boss's favorites get raises. The rest of us are just out of luck.*
- *If I ask for a raise and don't get it, that means I'm a real loser.*
- *Asking for a raise has never worked for me, and it never will.*

Going into a meeting with any of these thoughts running through your head makes it tough to talk about money.

Remember that many interviewers and supervisors use a standard negotiating tactic, regardless of the state of the economy: They come to the interview with a salary

Reflect on your Money Monitor/Money Plan

Now that you've experimented with the Money Monitor/Money Plan process, reflect on what you're learning. To start creating a new future with money, complete the following statements:

After monitoring my income and expenses for one month, I was surprised to discover that . . .

When it comes to money, I am skilled at . . .

When it comes to money, I am *not* so skilled at . . .

I could increase my income by . . .

I could spend less money on . . .

After thinking about the most powerful step I can take right now to improve my finances, I intend to . . .

range in mind. Then they offer a starting salary at the lower end of that range.

There's an important message here: Salaries are often flexible. You do not have to accept the first offer.

Also keep in mind that salary negotiation is a skill that anyone can learn. To learn more, keep reading.

Find out the salary range for the job you have or want. With this information in mind, you'll be able to tell whether a job interviewer or supervisor is offering a salary that's unreasonably low.

Start your research online. One place to begin is America's Career InfoNet at **www. careerinfonet.org**; click on *Occupation Information.* Also go to your favorite Internet search engine, and key in the term *salary ranges.*

In addition, talk to friends who work in your field, and do informational interviews with people who are already employed in the kind of job you want.

Keep in mind that salaries for a given position can vary based on location: big city versus smaller city, urban versus rural.

Know how much money you want. Figure out how much money you need to maintain your desired standard of living. Then add some margin for comfort. If you're working a job that's comparable to the one you're applying for, consider adding 10 percent to your current salary.

As you do this, take into account the value of any benefits the employer provides. Also be prepared to

state a desired salary range rather than a fixed figure.

Save the discussion for an ideal time. If you're applying for a job, then avoid talking about salary too early. Wait until the interviewer is ready to offer you a job. This often takes place during a second or even third interview. At this point the company might be willing to part with some more money—especially if you're well qualified and they fear losing you to another employer.

If you're asking for a raise in your current job, then see if you can have this discussion when you've recently made a visible and notable contribution at work.

Let the other person name a figure first. When the topic of salary comes up, the person on the other side of the desk will probably start by asking a question: *What figure did you have in mind?*

Be careful. This is a tricky question. Naming a figure that's too high could get you screened out. Naming a figure that's too low could undermine your credibility and lock you into in a smaller paycheck for a long time.

You are under no obligation to answer this question right away. Instead of naming a figure at this point, say something like: *I am open to discussion. What figure did you have in mind?*

The other person's first answer is likely to be in the lower end of the range that they're prepared to offer. If their figure is within your desired range, then say: *I think we're within range. What would*

it take to get to . . . ? End the sentence with a number that's toward the high end of your desired range. This gives you room to negotiate. It also prompts interviewers and supervisors to clarify what they expect from you.

Request a performance review. Ask to schedule a date, and put it in writing. This request sets you apart from other applicants and employees. It sends a couple of messages: First, you're confident that you can create value for your employer. Second, you're willing to meet at a specific date in the future to evaluate what you've done.

Talk about benefits. Salary negotiation often gives you an opening to ask about benefits. Depending on the company and the job involved, these might include health insurance, life insurance, disability plans, use of a company car, reimbursement for travel expenses, retirement plans, and tuition reimbursement.

START A BUSINESS ON THE SIDE

Another way to make more money is to start your own business. Consider a service you could offer on a part-time basis—anything from lawn mowing to computer consulting. Students can boost their income in many other ways, such as running errands, giving guitar lessons, tutoring, designing websites, walking pets, detailing cars, and house sitting. Charge reasonable rates, provide impeccable service, and ask your clients for referrals. Earning even a couple of hundred more dollars each month can make a difference in your experience of money.

Ask someone in the financial aid office about jobs that can be done from home with an Internet connection. A growing number of companies hire people who work online to handle their customer service, and many consultants work this way.

There's an old saying: *Profit comes from creating value.* To increase your chances of running a successful business, think hard about what your potential customers or clients want. What problems do they want to solve? What do they worry about? What benefits do they want to experience? Offer your product or service as a way to satisfy these desires.

This is a more powerful approach than simply approaching people with a laundry list of your skills and asking them if they'll hire you to do something. Instead, make it easier for people to part with their money: State the value that you can create *before* you mention your skills. For example: *I can help you get more online traffic by creating a professional-looking website.*

Or: *I can help you get more sales by writing emails with a compelling subject line and a clear call to action.*

You might find yourself testing several business ideas before you find one that works. This is a priceless way to discover what people value and are willing to buy.

BE A HIGH PERFORMER

Once you get a job or start a business, make it your intention to excel at what you do. A positive work experience can pay off for years by leading to other jobs, recommendations, and contacts.

Make yourself indispensable. Look for ways to excel at your job by building relationships, becoming a rock-star collaborator, and consistently delivering results. Whenever possible, exceed your work-related goals. Suggest ideas that can increase revenue, decrease costs, solve problems, and make processes more efficient. Then ask to get assigned to the teams that implement your ideas.

Finally, keep things in perspective. If your job is lucrative and rewarding,

great. If not, remember that almost any job can support you in becoming a master student and reaching your educational goals.

BE A LIFETIME LEARNER

To maximize your earning power, keep honing your job-hunting skills. The career office at your school can help. Also see the articles about careers and job hunting in the next chapter of this book.

You can use your education to develop knowledge, experience, and skills that create income for the rest of your life. According to the US Department of Labor, the median weekly earning for people with a bachelor's degree is $1,101, compared to $668 for people with only a high school diploma. In addition, people with a bachelor's degree are less likely to be unemployed.[1]

Once you graduate and land a job in your chosen field, continue your education. Look for ways to gain additional skills or certifications that lead to higher earnings and more fulfilling work assignments. ◗

No budgeting required

Notice one more thing about the Money Monitor/ Money Plan: It does not require you to create a budget. Budgets—like diets—often fail. Many people cringe at the mere mention of the word *budget*. To them it is associated with scarcity, drudgery, and guilt. The idea of creating a budget conjures up images of a penny-pinching Ebenezer Scrooge shaking a bony, wrinkled finger at them and screaming, "You spent too much, you loser!"

That's not the idea behind the Money Monitor/Money Plan. In fact, there is no budget worksheet for you to complete each month. And no one is pointing a finger at you. Instead of budgeting, you simply write a plus sign or a minus sign next to each expense or income category that you *freely choose* to increase or decrease next month. There's no extra paperwork, no shame, and no blame.

Dragon Images/Shutterstock.com

Spend less
MONEY

Controlling your expenses is something you can do right away. Use ideas from the following list, and invent more of your own.

Look to big-ticket items. When you look for places to cut expenses, start with the items that cost the most. Choices about where to live, for example, can save you thousands of dollars. Sometimes a place a little farther from campus, or a smaller house or apartment, will be much less expensive. You can also keep your housing costs down by finding a roommate. Offer to do repairs or maintenance in exchange for reduced rent. Pay your rent on time, and treat property with respect.

Another high-ticket item is a car. Take the cost of buying or leasing and then add expenses for parking, insurance, repairs, gas, maintenance, and tires. You might find that it makes more sense to walk, bike, use public transportation, ride a campus shuttle, and call for an occasional taxi ride. Or carpool. Find friends with a car, and chip in for gas.

Track your expenses to discover the main drains on your finances. Then focus on one or two areas where you can reduce spending while continuing to pay your fixed monthly bills such as rent and tuition.

Look to small-ticket items. Reducing or eliminating the money you spend on low-cost purchases can make the difference between saving money or going into debt. For example, $3 spent at the coffee shop every day adds up to $1,095 over a year. That kind of spending can give anyone the jitters.

Do comparison shopping. Prices vary dramatically. Shop around, wait for off-season sales, and use coupons. Check out secondhand stores, thrift stores, and garage sales. Before plunking down the full retail price for a new item, consider whether you could buy it used. You can find "pre-owned" clothes, CDs, furniture, sports equipment, audio equipment, and computer hardware in retail stores and on the Internet.

Also go online to find websites that will compare prices for you. Examples include Yahoo! Shopping (**http://shopping.yahoo.com**) and Google Product Search (**www.google.com/prdhp**).

Ask for student discounts. Movie theaters, restaurants, bars, shopping centers, and other businesses sometimes discount prices for students. Also see if your college bookstore sells software at reduced rates. In addition, ask your bank whether you can open a student checking and savings account with online banking. The fees and minimum required amounts could be lower. Go online to check your balances weekly so that you avoid overdraft fees.

Be aware of quality. The cheapest product is not always the least expensive over the long run. Sometimes, a slightly more expensive item is the best buy because it will last longer. Remember, there is no correlation between the value of something and the amount of money spent to advertise it. Carefully inspect things you are considering to buy to see whether they are well made.

Save money on eating and drinking. This single suggestion could significantly lower your expenses. Instead of hitting a restaurant or bar, head to the grocery store. In addition, clip food coupons. Sign up for a shopper's discount card.

Cooking for yourself doesn't need to take much time if you do a little menu planning. Create a list of your five favorite home-cooked meals. Learn how to prepare them. Then keep ingredients for these meals always on hand. To reduce grocery bills, buy these ingredients in bulk.

If you live in a dorm, review the different meal plans you can buy. Some schools offer meal plans for students who live off campus. These plans might be cheaper than eating in restaurants while you're on campus.

More deals are online. Find coupons at websites such as Groupon (**groupon. com**) and Living Social (**livingsocial.com**).

Lower your phone bills. If you use a cell phone, pull out a copy of your latest bill. Review how many minutes you used last month. Perhaps you could get by with a less expensive phone, fewer minutes, fewer text messages, and a cheaper plan.

Do an Internet search on *cell phone plan comparison*, and see whether you could save money by switching providers. Also consider a family calling plan, which might cost less than a separate plan for each person. In addition, consider whether you need a home phone (a land line) *and* a cell phone. Dropping the home phone could save you money right away.

Keep an eye on Web-based options for turning your voice into a digital signal that travels over the Internet. This technology is called Voice over Internet Protocol (VoIP), and Skype (**www.skype.com**) is just one example of it. Using VoIP can be cheaper than making international phone calls.

Go "green." To conserve energy and save money on utility bills, turn out the lights when you leave a room. Keep windows and doors closed in winter. In summer, keep windows open early in the day to invite lots of cool air into your living space. Then close up the apartment or house to keep it cool during the hotter hours of the day. Leave air-conditioning set at 72 degrees or above. In cool weather, dress warmly and keep the house at 68 degrees or less. In hot weather, take shorter, cooler showers.

Unplug any electric appliances that are not in use. Appliances like microwaves, audio systems, and cell phone chargers use energy when plugged in, even when they're not in use. Also, plug computer equipment into power strips that you can turn off while you sleep.

Explore budget plans for monthly payments that fluctuate, such as those for heating your home. These plans average your yearly expenses, so you pay the same amount each month.

Pay cash. To avoid interest charges, deal in cash. If you don't have the cash, don't buy. Buying on credit makes it more

Free fun

Sometimes it seems that the only way to have fun is to spend money. Not true. Search out free entertainment on campus and in your community. Beyond this, your imagination is the only limit. Some suggestions are listed here. If you think they're silly or boring, create better ideas of your own.

Browse a bookstore.
Volunteer at a childcare center.
Draw or color.
Exercise.
Find other people who share your hobby, and start a club.
Give a massage.
Do yoga with a friend.
Play Frisbee golf.
Make dinner for your date.
Picnic in the park.
Take a long walk.
Ride your bike.
Listen to music that you already own but haven't heard for a while.
Take a candlelight bath.
Play board games.
Have an egg toss.
Test-drive new cars.
Donate blood.
Make yourself breakfast in bed.

difficult to monitor spending. You can easily bust next month's money plan with this month's credit card purchases.

Postpone purchases. If you plan to buy something, leave your checkbook or credit card at home when you first go shopping. Look at all the possibilities. Then go home and make your decision when you don't feel pressured. When you are ready to buy, wait a week, even if the salesperson pressures you. What seems like a necessity today may not even cross your mind the day after tomorrow.

Notice what you spend on "fun." Blowing your money on fun is fun. It is also a fast way to burn through your savings. When you spend money on entertainment, ask yourself what the benefits will be and whether you could get the same benefits for less money. You can read magazines for free at the library, for example. Most libraries also loan CDs and DVDs for free.

Use the envelope system. After reviewing your monthly income and expenses, put a certain amount of cash each week in an envelope labeled *Entertainment/Eating Out.* When the envelope is empty, stop spending money on these items for the rest of the week. If you use online banking, see whether you can create separate accounts for various spending categories. Then deposit a fixed amount of money into each of those accounts. This is an electronic version of the envelope system.

Don't compete with big spenders. When you watch other people spend their money, remember that you don't know the whole story. Some students have parents with deep pockets. Others head to Mexico every year for spring break but finance the trips with high-interest credit cards. If you find yourself feeling pressured to spend money so that you can keep up with other people, stop to think about how much it will cost over the long run. Maybe it's time to shop around for some new friends.

Use the money you save to prepare for emergencies and reduce debt. If you apply strategies such as those listed here, you might see your savings account swell nicely. Congratulate yourself. Then choose what to do with the extra money. To protect yourself during tough times, create an emergency fund. Then reduce your debt by paying more than the minimum on credit card bills and loan payments.

Spend less and feel the power. Cutting your spending might be challenging at first. Give it time. Spending less is not about sacrificing pleasure. It's about something that money can't buy—the satisfaction of choosing exactly where your money goes and building a secure financial future. Every dollar that you save on a frivolous expense is a dollar you can invest in something that truly matters to you. ✕

practicing CRITICAL THINKING 29

Show me the money

See whether you can use *Becoming a Master Student* to create a financial gain that is many times more than the cost of the book. Scan the entire text, and look for suggestions that could help you save money or increase income in significant ways:

- Use suggestions for career planning and job hunting to find your next job more quickly, and start earning money sooner.
- Use suggestions for résumé writing and job interviewing to get a higher-paying job.
- Use suggestions from this chapter to reduce your monthly expenses and fatten up your savings account.

Write down your ideas for creating more money from your experience of this book.

Managing money during
TOUGH TIMES

A short-term crisis in the overall economy can reduce your income and increase your expenses. So can the decision to go back to school.

© zimmytws/Shutterstock.com

The biggest factor in your long-term financial well-being, though, is your daily behavior. Habits that help you survive during tough times will also help you prosper after you graduate and when the economy rebounds.

If the economy tanks, we can benefit by telling the truth about it and ourselves. It's one thing to condemn the dishonesty of mortgage bankers and hedge fund managers. It's another thing to have an unpaid credit card or wipe out a savings account and still believe that we are in charge of our money.

The first step to changing such behaviors is simply to admit that they don't work. Taking informed action is a way to cut through financial confusion and move beyond fear. Start by collecting the details about what you're spending and earning right now. With that knowledge, you can choose your next strategy from among the following.

SPEND LESS AND SAVE MORE
The less you spend, the more money you'll have on hand. Use that money to pay your monthly bills, pay off your credit cards, and create an emergency fund to use in case you lose your job or a source of financial aid.

Author Suze Orman recommends three actions to show that you can reduce spending at any time: (1) Do not spend money for one day; (2) do not use your credit card for one week; and (3) do not eat out for one month. Success

with any of these strategies can open up your mind to other possibilities for spending less and saving more.[2]

MAKE SURE THAT YOUR SAVINGS ARE PROTECTED
The Federal Deposit Insurance Corporation (FDIC) backs individual saving accounts. The National Credit Union Administration (NCUA) offers similar protection for credit union members. If your savings are protected by these programs, every penny you deposit is safe. Check your statements to find out, or go online to **www.fdic.gov/edie/index.html**.

PAY OFF YOUR CREDIT CARDS
If you have more than one credit card with an outstanding balance, then find out which one has the highest interest rate. Put as much money as you can toward paying off that balance while making the minimum payment on the other cards. Repeat this process until all unpaid balances are erased.

INVEST ONLY AFTER SAVING
The stock market is only for money that you can afford to lose. Before you speculate, first save enough money to live on for at least six months in case you're unemployed. Then consider what you'll need over the next five years to finish your schooling and handle other major expenses. Save for these expenses before taking any risks with your money.

DO STELLAR WORK AT YOUR CURRENT JOB

The threat of layoffs increases during a recession. However, companies will hesitate to shed their star employees. If you're working right now, then think about ways to become indispensable. Gain skills and experience that will make you more valuable to your employer.

No matter what job you have, be as productive as possible. Look for ways to boost sales, increase quality, or accomplish tasks in less time. Ask yourself every day how you can create extra value by solving a problem, reducing costs, improving service, or attracting new clients or customers.

THINK ABOUT YOUR NEXT JOB

Create a career plan that describes the next job you want, the skills that you'll develop to get it, and the next steps you'll take to gain those skills. Stay informed about the latest developments in your field. Find people who are already working in this area, and contact them for informational interviews.

You might want to start an active job hunt now, even if you have a job. Find time to build your network, go to job-related conferences, and stay on top of current job openings in your field.

Remember that even during a recession, the state of the economy at large does not determine your individual prospects for finding a job. When people say, "There are no jobs," maybe what they really mean is "My current job hunting method is not working." There's a world of difference between those statements. The first one kills options. The second one *creates* options. Go to your school's career planning office to learn new strategies for job hunting.

RESEARCH UNEMPLOYMENT BENEFITS

Unemployment benefits have limits and may not replace your lost wages. However, they can cushion the blow of losing a job while you put other strategies in place. To learn about the benefits offered in your state, go online to **www .servicelocator.org**. Click "Unemployment Benefits." Then enter your state.

GET HEALTH INSURANCE

A sudden illness or lengthy hospital stay can drain your savings. Health insurance can pick up all or most of the costs instead. If possible, get health insurance through your school or employer.

Another option is private health insurance. This can be cheaper than extending an employer's policy if you lose your job. To find coverage, go online to **healthcare.gov** and search for your state's health insurance exchange under the Affordable Care Act. Also do an Internet search for health insurance brokers in your area. Their services are usually free to clients, but ask to be sure.

GET HELP THAT YOU CAN TRUST

Avoid debt consolidators that offer schemes to wipe out your debt. What they don't tell you is that their fees are high, and that using them can lower your credit rating. Turn instead to the National Foundation for Credit Counseling (**www.nfcc.org**). Find a credit counselor that is accredited by this organization. Work with someone who is open about fees and willing to work with all your creditors. Don't pay any fees up front before you actually get help.

PUT YOUR PLAN IN WRITING

List the specific ways that you will reduce spending and increase income. If you have a family, consider posting this list for everyone to see. The act of putting your plan in writing can help you feel in control of your money. Review your plan regularly to make sure that it's working and that everyone who's affected is on board.

COPE WITH STRESS IN POSITIVE WAYS

When times get tough, some people are tempted to reduce stress with unhealthy behaviors like smoking, drinking, and overeating. Find better ways to cope. Exercise, meditation, and a sound sleep can do wonders.

Social support is one of the best stress busters. If you're unemployed or worried about money, connect with family members and friends often. Turn healthy habits such as exercising and preparing healthy meals into social affairs.

CHOOSE YOUR MONEY CONVERSATIONS

When the economy tanks, the news is filled with gloomy reports and dire predictions. Remember that reporters are constantly competing for your attention. Sometimes they use gloom-and-doom headlines to boost their ratings.

Keep financial news in perspective. Recessions can be painful. And they eventually end. The mortgage credit crisis in recent years was due to speculation, not to a lack of innovation. Our economy will continue to reward people who create valuable new products and services.

To manage stress, limit how much attention you pay to fear-based articles and programs. You can do this even while staying informed about news. Avoid conversations that focus on problems. Instead, talk about ways to take charge of your money and open up job prospects. Even when the economy takes a nosedive, there is always at least one more thing you can do to manage stress and get on a firmer financial footing.

Talk about what gives your life meaning beyond spending money. Eating at home instead of going out can bring your family closer together and save you money weekly, monthly, and annually. Avoiding loud bars and making time for quiet conversation can deepen your friendships. Finding free sources of entertainment can lead you to unexpected sources of pleasure. Letting go of an expensive vacation can allow you to pay down your debts and find time for a fun hobby. Keeping your old car for another year might allow you to invest in extra skills training.

When tough times happen, use them as a chance to embrace the truth about your money life rather than resist it. Live from conscious choice rather than unconscious habit. Learning to live within your means is a skill that can bring financial peace of mind for the rest of your life. ✖

Take charge of your CREDIT

© iStockphoto.com/Laurent davoust/daboost

A credit card is compact and convenient. That piece of plastic seems to promise peace of mind. Low on cash this month? Just whip out your credit card, slide it across the counter, and relax. Your worries are over—that is, until you get the bill. Credit cards often come with a hefty interest rate, sometimes as high as 30 percent.

On average, families in the United States with debt owe $15,355 on credit cards. Each year they pay $6,658 *in interest charges alone*—about 9 percent of average household income.[3]

When faced with high credit card balances and soaring interest rates, some people make late payments or skip them altogether. The result is a poor credit score.

A high credit score will serve you for a lifetime. With this asset, you'll be able to borrow money any time you need it. A low credit score, however, can keep you from getting a car or a house in the future. You might also have to pay higher insurance rates, and you could even be turned down for a job.

To take charge of your credit, borrow money only when truly necessary. If you do borrow, make all of your payments, and make them on time. These are strategies you can use for managing student loans as well as credit cards.

TAKE CONTROL OF YOUR CREDIT CARDS

Balance the benefits with the real costs. Credit cards do offer potential benefits, of course. Having one means that you don't have to carry around a checkbook or large amounts of cash, and they're pretty handy in emergencies. Getting a card is one way to establish a credit record. Some cards offer rewards, such as frequent flier miles and car rental discounts.

Used unwisely, however, credit cards can create a debt that takes decades to repay. Here's an example published by the Federal Trade Commission. Suppose that you make a $1,500 purchase with a credit card with a 19 percent interest rate. Also suppose that you pay only the minimum balance on that card every month. It will take you 106 months to pay off this purchase, and you will pay $889 in interest. This will be true even if you never use the card again and pay no late fees.[4]

Credit card debt can seriously delay other goals— paying off student loans, financing a new car, buying a home, or saving for retirement.

Pay off the balance each month. An unpaid credit card balance is a sure sign that you are spending more money than you have. To avoid this outcome, keep track of how much you spend with credit cards each month. Pay off the card balance each month, on time, and avoid finance or late charges.

If you do accumulate a large credit card balance, go to your bank and ask about ways to get a loan with a lower interest rate. Use this loan to pay off your credit cards. Then promise yourself never to accumulate credit card debt again.

Scrutinize credit card offers. Finding a card with a lower interest rate can make a dramatic difference. Suppose that you have an $8,000 balance on a card with a 16 percent APR. Your interest charges would be $1,280 per year. If you have the same balance on a card with a 4.9 percent APR, your annual interest charges would be $392. It pays to shop around.[5]

However, look carefully at credit card offers. Low rates might be temporary. After a few months, they could double or even triple. Also look for annual fees, late fees, and other charges buried in the fine print.

Be especially wary of credit card offers made to students. Remember that the companies who willingly dispense cards on campus are not there to offer an educational service. They are in business to make money by charging you interest.

Avoid cash advances. Due to their high interest rates and fees, credit cards are not a great source of spare cash. Even when you get cash advances on these cards from an ATM, it's still borrowed money. As an alternative, get a debit card tied to a checking account, and use that card when you need cash on the go.

Check statements against your records. File your credit card receipts each month. When you get the bill for each card, check it against your receipts for accuracy. Mistakes in billing are rare, but they can happen. In addition, checking your statement reveals the interest rate and fees that are being applied to your account.

Credit card companies can change the terms of your agreement with little or no warning. Check bills carefully for any changes in late fees, service charges, and credit limits. When you get letters about changes in your credit card policies, read them carefully. Cancel cards from companies that routinely raise fees.

Use just one credit card. To simplify your financial life and take charge of your credit, consider using only one card. Choose one with no annual fee and the lowest interest rate. Consider the bottom line, and be selective. If you do have more than one credit card, pay off the one with the highest interest rate first. Then consider cancelling that card.

Get a copy of your credit report. A credit report is a record of your payment history and other credit-related items. You are entitled to get a free copy each year. Go to your bank and ask someone there how to do this. You can also request a copy of your credit report online at **https://www .annualcreditreport.com**.

This site was created by three nationwide consumer credit-reporting companies—Equifax, Experian, and TransUnion. Check your report carefully for errors or accounts that you did not open. Do this now, before you're in financial trouble.

Protect your credit score. Whenever you apply for a loan, the first thing a lender will do is check your credit score. The higher your score, the more money you can borrow at lower interest rates. To protect your credit score:

- Pay all your bills on time.
- Hold on to credit cards that you've had for a while. Avoid applying for new credit cards.
- Pay off your credit card balance every month—especially for the cards that you've had the longest.
- If you can't pay off the entire balance, then pay as much as you can above the minimum monthly payment.
- Never charge more than your limit.
- Avoid using a credit card as a source of cash.
- Avoid any actions that could lead a credit card company to reduce your credit limit.

Common credit terms

annual fee—a yearly charge for using a credit card, sometimes called a *membership fee* or *participation fee*.

annual percentage rate (APR)—the interest that you owe on unpaid balances in your account. The APR equals the periodic rate times the number of billing periods in a year.

balance due—the remaining amount of money that you owe a credit card company or other lender.

balance transfer—the process of moving an unpaid debt from one lender to another lender.

bankruptcy—a legal process that allows borrowers to declare their inability to pay their debts. People who declare bankruptcy transfer all their assets to a court-appointed trustee and create a plan to repay some or all of their borrowed money. Bankruptcy protects people from harassment by their creditors but lowers their credit scores.

credit score—a three-digit number that reflects your history of repaying borrowed money and paying other bills on time (also called a *FICO score*—an acronym for the Fair Isaac Corporation, which was the first company to create credit ratings). This number ranges from 300 to 850. The higher the number, the better your credit rating.

default—state of a loan when the borrower fails to make required payments or otherwise violates the terms of the agreement. Default may prompt the creditor to turn the loan over to a collection agency, which can severely harm the borrower's credit score.

finance charge—the total fee for using a credit card, which includes the interest rate, periodic rate, and other fees. Finance charges for cash advances and balance transfers can be different from finance charges for unpaid balances.

grace period—for a credit card user who pays off the entire balance due, a period of time when no interest is charged on a purchase. When there is no grace period, finance charges apply immediately to a purchase.

interest rate—an annual fee that borrowers pay to use someone else's money, normally a percentage of the balance due.

minimum payment—the amount you must pay to keep from defaulting on an account; usually 2 percent of the unpaid balance due.

payment due date—the day that a lender must receive your payment—*not* the postmarked date or the date you make a payment online. Check your statements carefully, as credit card companies sometimes change the due dates.

periodic rate—an interest rate based on a certain period of time, such as a day or a month.

MANAGE STUDENT LOANS

A college degree is one of the best investments you can make. But you don't have to go broke to get that education. You can make that investment with the lowest debt possible.

Choose schools with costs in mind. If you decide to transfer to another school, you can save thousands of dollars the moment you sign your application for admission. In addition to choosing schools on the basis of reputation, consider how much they cost and the financial aid packages that they offer.

Avoid debt when possible. The surest way to manage debt is to avoid it altogether. If you do take out loans, borrow only the amount that you cannot get from other sources—scholarships, grants, employment, gifts from relatives, and personal savings. Predict what your income will be when the first loan payments are due and whether you'll make enough money to manage continuing payments.

Also set a target date for graduation, and stick to it. The fewer years you go to school, the lower your debt.

Shop carefully for loans. Go to the financial aid office and ask whether you can get a Stafford loan. These are fixed-rate, low-interest loans from the federal government. If you qualify for a subsidized Stafford loan, the government pays the interest due while you're in school. Unsubsidized Stafford loans do not offer this benefit, but they are still one of the cheapest student loans you can get. Remember that *anyone* can apply for a Stafford loan. Take full advantage of this program before you look into other loans. For more information on the loans that are available to you, visit **www.studentaid.ed.gov**.

If your parents are helping to pay for your education, they can apply for a PLUS loan. There is no income limit, and parents can borrow

---

A college degree is one of the best investments you can make. But you don't have to go broke to get that education. You can make that investment with the lowest debt possible.

---

up to the total cost of their children's education. With these loans, your parents—not you—are the borrowers. A new option allows borrowers to defer repayment until after you graduate.

If at all possible, avoid loans from privately owned companies. These companies often charge higher interest rates and impose terms that are less favorable to students. Unfortunately, there are loan companies that prey on students. To avoid them, calculate the total amount of interest that you'll be charged over the life of a loan. You can do this with online tools such as SallieMae's Student Loan Repayment Calculator (**http://smartoption.salliemae.com/Entry.aspx**).

While you're shopping around, ask about options for repaying your loans. Lenders might allow you to extend the payments over a longer period or adjust the amount of your monthly payment based on your income.

Some lenders will forgive part of a student loan if you agree to take a certain type of job for a few years—for example, teaching in a public school in a low-income neighborhood or working as a nurse in a rural community.

Repay your loans. If you take out student loans, find out exactly when the first payment is due on each of them. Make all your payments, and make them on time. Don't assume that you can wait to start repayment until you find a job. Any bill payments that you miss will hammer your credit score.

Also ask your financial aid office about whether you can consolidate your loans. This means that you lump them all together and owe just one payment every month. Loan consolidation makes it easier to stay on top of your payments and protect your credit score. ✴

Create a new experience of money

You can change the way that you experience money. And you can do it now. This is true even if you are in debt and living in a dorm on a diet of macaroni. If you're not convinced, then read on.

Remember that when it comes to money, you can declare two different types of intention. Either can lead to profound changes in your personal finances.

One is an intention to create new **outcomes.** Here are some examples:

- Saving $2,000 to buy a new computer by December 31 of this year
- Saving $5,000 for a car down payment by January 1, 2020.
- Saving $10,000 for a house down payment by July 1, 2025

Second is an intention to create new **habits** related to money. These intentions are not tied to a particular outcome such as having a specific amount of money in hand by a certain date. Instead, habits are things that you intend to do on a daily, weekly, or monthly basis.

Some examples of habits related to money are listed here:

- Saving 5 percent of every paycheck received and depositing it in a savings account to use for emergency expenses.
- Reducing restaurant expenses by splitting meals and skipping desserts.
- Reducing entertainment expenses by streaming movies with a computer rather than going to a theater.

Outcome goals can involve large amounts of money and often depend on your having a certain level of income.

In contrast, habits can involve any amount of money, and they are not tied to any income level. You can set a goal to save 5 percent of every paycheck, whether that amount is $5, $50, or $500. Such habits might produce only modest results in the near future. When sustained over decades, however, they can make a major difference in your net worth.

Write at least three intentions. Clearly label each one as an outcome or habit. If your intention is to create a new habit, then be sure to describe an observable behavior.

I intend to . . .

I intend to . . .

I intend to . . .

If you get into trouble . . .

You might face obstacles to meeting your financial goals. Money problems are common. Solve them in ways that protect you for the future.

Get specific data. Gather all your receipts and bank account statements for the past several months. Determine the exact amount of money that flowed into your life during that period and the amount that flowed out. See if you can spot the exact points when you got into trouble with money.

Be honest with creditors. Determine the amount that you are sure you can repay each month, and ask the creditor whether that would work for your case.

Go for credit counseling. Most cities have agencies with professional advisors who can help straighten out your financial problems.

Change your spending patterns. If you have a history of overspending (or underearning), change *is* possible. This chapter is full of suggestions.

Keep your money secure. To prevent other security breaches when managing money, regularly monitor online bank accounts. Use websites with an address (URL) that begins with *https://* rather than *http://*. The extra *s* stands for *secure*, meaning that any data you send will be encrypted.

EDUCATION
pays off—and you can pay for it

cigdem/Shutterstock.com

Education is one of the few things you can buy that will last a lifetime. It can't rust, corrode, break down, or wear out. It can't be stolen, burned, repossessed, or destroyed. Once you have a degree, no one can take it away. That makes your education a safer investment than real estate, gold, oil, diamonds, or stocks.

Higher levels of education are associated with the following:[6]

- Greater likelihood of being employed
- Greater likelihood of having health insurance
- Higher income
- Higher job satisfaction
- Higher tax revenues for governments, which fund libraries, schools, parks, and other public goods
- Lower dependence on income support services, such as food stamps
- Higher involvement in volunteer activities

In short, education is a good deal for you and for society. It's worth investing in it periodically to update your skills, reach your goals, and get more of what you want in life.

Millions of dollars are waiting for people who take part in higher education. The funds flow to students who know how to find them.

There are many ways to pay for school. The kind of help you get depends on your financial need. In general, *financial need* equals the cost of your schooling minus what you can reasonably be expected to pay.

A financial aid package includes three major types of assistance:

- Money you do not pay back (grants and scholarships)
- Money you *do* pay back (loans)
- Work-study programs

Many students who get financial aid receive a package that includes all of the listed elements.

To find out more, visit your school's financial aid office on a regular basis. Also go online. Start with Student Aid on the Web at **http://studentaid.ed.gov.**

Remember to keep applying for financial aid every academic year, even if you didn't get any for the previous year. Finding ways to pay for your education allows you to practice many of the skills presented in this text. ✄

practicing CRITICAL THINKING

Education by the hour

Determine exactly what it costs you to go to school. Fill in the blanks using totals for a semester, quarter, or whatever term system your school uses.

Note: Include only the costs that relate directly to going to school. For example, under "Transportation," list only the amount that you pay for gas to drive back and forth to school, not the total amount you spend on gas for a semester.

Tuition	$_____
Books	$_____
Fees	$_____
Transportation	$_____
Clothing	$_____
Food	$_____
Housing	$_____
Entertainment	$_____
Other expenses (such as insurance, medical costs, and childcare)	$_____
Subtotal	$_____
Salary you could earn per term if you weren't in school	$_____
Total (A)	$_____

Now figure out how many classes you attend in one term. This is the number of your scheduled class periods per week

Diamond Sky Images/Digital Vision/Getty Images

multiplied by the number of weeks in your school term. Put that figure here:

Total (B)_____ $____

Divide **Total (A)** by **Total (B)**, and put that amount here: $_____

This is what it costs you to go to one class one time.

Now, describe your responses to discovering this figure. Also list anything you will do differently as a result of knowing the hourly cost of your education.

Money for the FUTURE

SAVE FOR AN EMERGENCY FUND

Take some percentage of every paycheck you receive, and immediately deposit that amount into a savings account. Start by saving 5 to 10 percent of your income. Then see if you can increase that amount over time.

One big purpose of this savings account is to have money on hand for surprises and emergencies—anything from a big car repair bill or medical expense to a sudden job loss. For peace of mind, have an emergency fund equal to at least six months of living expenses. Keep in mind that your living expenses might increase as you get older. This means that it's wise to add to your emergency fund over time.

To begin saving, deposit your money into a savings account. This type of account offers several benefits. One is that your money is *liquid*. This means that you can withdraw all or part of the money at any time and get your hands on the cash immediately. In addition, interest rates on savings accounts are usually higher than checking accounts.

Be sure to choose an account from a bank that belongs to the Federal Deposit Insurance Corporation (FDIC). This means that balances up to $250,000 are insured by the federal government. Even if the bank fails, your money is safe.

Keep in mind that interest rates, minimum balances, and transaction fees can vary drastically between banks. Research your options carefully.

SAVE FOR LONG-TERM GOALS

Once you have an emergency fund in place, start saving for long-term goals such as your retirement or a child's college education. Consider putting your money in certificates of deposit, savings bonds, and Treasury securities (bills, notes, and bonds backed by the federal government). These are not as liquid as a savings account. However, they are low-risk ways to save for long-term goals and often yield higher interest than a savings account.

SAVE FOR THE LAST DECADES OF YOUR LIFE

It's never too early to start thinking about your retirement. Imagine yourself at age 65. In an ideal world, what will you be doing? Working full-time or part-time? Taking classes? Relaxing? Traveling? Starting a new career? Over time you might pursue some or all of these options.

Once you have a vision for your last decades of life, think about how to pay for it.

If you work for an employer who offers a 401(k) or other retirement plan and will match your contributions, then contribute as much as you can. If not, then set up your own retirement plan and contribute to it every month. When creating this plan, talk to an independent, certified financial planner or someone else who is not tied to a specific company or product.

Nattapol Sritongcom/Shutterstock.com

practicing CRITICAL THINKING

31

Plan to pay for your degree

The purpose of this exercise is to ensure that you will have enough money to pay for your entire degree. To do this, you will estimate your income and expenses for each term that you plan to be in school. The goal is to spot possible shortfalls in funding well *before* they happen. By thinking ahead, you can plan to persist to graduation without financial setbacks. To get the most benefit from this exercise, keep the following points in mind.

Complete the Money Monitor/Money Plan exercise first. You'll need data from that exercise to complete this one.

Make copies of the blank worksheet that follows. Your income, expenses, and schedule of courses can change from one term to another. No problem. Keep blank copies of the worksheet on hand so that you can update them with the most recent information you have.

Complete the worksheet. Start by setting a date that you plan to graduate. This step alone will help you create value from this exercise. Then fill out the table:

- **Use the figures from your most recent Money Monitor/Money Plan as a starting point.** If a quarter lasts three months, for example, then take the total income and total expenses from your Money Monitor/Money Plan and multiply them by three.

- **Fine-tune those figures.** Predict term-by-term changes in your financial state. For estimated income, consider scholarships, loans, grants, work-study assignments, and contributions from parents that might increase or decrease before you graduate. Do the same for expenses. If you plan to replace a car or move to a more expensive apartment during a certain term, for instance, then adjust your estimated expenses for that term.

- **Note surpluses and deficits.** If you predict that your income will exceed your expenses for a term, you'll have a surplus. Note this with a plus sign followed by the amount of the surplus for that term. If your expenses will exceed income, then you'll have a deficit. Note this amount with a minus sign.

- **Write discoveries and intentions.** If you predict that you could have a deficit during a certain term, put that discovery in writing. Then brainstorm possible solutions. Think of ways to increase your income, reduce your expenses, or do both. Review this chapter for specific suggestions and write Intention Statements to describe what you'll do. Translate those intentions into specific actions, and add them to your to-do list or calendar.

Share the results of this exercise. When you meet with family members or staff members at the financial aid office, have filled-in and blank copies of your worksheet on hand. This will give you a clear and specific framework to talk about your current finances and make plans for the future.

Graduation Date_____

Term	Estimated Income	Estimated Expenses	Surplus or Deficit
Fall Semester 2019	3000	3500	– 500
Spring Semester 2019	3000	3250	+ 250
Fall Semester 2020	3300	3250	+ 50
Spring Semester 2020	3300	4000	–700

Graduation Date_____

Term	Estimated Income	Estimated Expenses	Surplus or Deficit

I discovered that . . .

I intend to . . .

INVEST CAREFULLY

Investing in individual stocks, corporate bonds, or mutual funds is risky. Do this only if you regularly save money, pay off the full balance on your credit cards each month, and have plenty of time to monitor your investments. Even then, only invest money that you can afford to lose. Keep the grocery money.

When you bring up the subject of investing, some people will offer hot tips for what to do with your money. Regard these tips with extreme skepticism. Even professionals who manage mutual funds and hedge funds have a hard time "beating the market" on a consistent basis.

One option for safer investing is an *index fund*. These funds have relatively low fees and simply aim to match the returns of a stock market index such as the Standard & Poor's (S&P) 500. The people who manage these funds do not try to score big wins. Instead, their goal is simply to deliver consistent returns over the long term.

If you choose to invest, then put time on your side. Invest as early as you can. This gives you the power of long-term compound interest. Say that you invest $500 in an account that earns 8 percent interest. In 30 years, that investment will grow to $5,031. Given the same interest rate and number of years, a $1,000 investment will grow to $10,063.

CONSIDER HOME OWNERSHIP CAREFULLY

The traditional American dream includes owning a house. Yet home ownership can turn into a nightmare if you can't really afford it. During the most recent recession, many home-owners found themselves saddled with debt they could not afford to repay. Some of them owed more money on their mortgage than their houses were worth on the market.

Houses can be an unwise investment if you pay for one by borrowing lots of money. Buy a home only if you can make the down payment in cash and afford the monthly mortgage payments with room to spare.

BE A WISE CAR-SHOPPER

Though cars offer many benefits, they are not always the wisest investment. The minute that you drive a car off the dealer's lot, it loses value. The trade-in value on a car is often not enough to pay off a car loan.

If you borrow money to buy a car, then keep the costs as low as possible. Reduce

interest by sticking to a three-year loan rather than four or five years.

Also check into certified, pre-owned cars. These come with a warranty from the manufacturer rather than the car dealer.

Buy a car with loans rather than leasing. Once you pay off a three-year loan, you own the car and can keep driving it with no monthly payments. If you lease a car for three years, then you don't own it. And, you might also be tempted to turn around and start leasing another car.

BE CAREFUL WITH CONTRACTS

Before you sign anything, read the fine print. If you are confused, ask questions. Keep asking until you are no longer confused.

Be leery of someone who says anything like this: "Oh, this is just the standard lease agreement. I wouldn't try to pull the wool over your eyes. You look too smart for that."

After you sign a contract or lease, read the whole thing again. If you think you signed something that you will regret, see if you can back out. Sometimes you can do this if you act quickly. If so, get your release in writing.

If you can't get out, then consider getting legal help. Search your school's website to see if legal services for students are available. Another option is legal aid from attorneys who offer free or low-cost assistance to people who meet certain income guidelines.

Be particularly careful with long-term purchase agreements. That beautiful cookware might only cost you 72 cents a day. If you make payments for three years, however, your total cost will be $78. Before you sign on the dotted line, know the total cost up front.

SAVE ON INSURANCE

Protect your financial future by insuring your car, home, health, and life. If you live in an apartment, also consider getting renter's insurance to protect your possessions in case of fire or theft.

Life insurance is especially important if you have a spouse, children, or anyone else who depends on your income. There are basically two kinds of life insurance: term and whole life. Term insurance is the least expensive. It pays if you die, and that's it.

Whole life insurance is more expensive. It pays if you die and also accumulates money like a savings plan does. You might get a higher return on your money if you buy the lower-priced term insurance instead and save or invest the extra dollars.[7] Policies vary widely, however, so study each one carefully.

If you drive at all, car insurance is a must. Premiums vary considerably, so shop around. Ask about discounts for good students and safe drivers.

Find an independent insurance agent or broker who can help you with all these policies. See if you can get discounts for buying more than one policy from the same insurance company. Also ask if you can lower your insurance premiums by choosing higher deductibles. Raise questions about anything you don't understand. If the agent can't answer your questions, then get another agent.

Some schools offer health insurance for students at bargain rates. Find out what's available at your campus. Also check to see what's available from your employer and under the Affordable Care Act (**healthcare.gov**). Again, if you're confused by the options, then talk to an independent insurance broker who knows the policies that are available in your state. Insurance brokers' services are usually free to their clients. To make sure, ask about this up front.

Anyone can develop an illness or sustain an injury that calls for major medical care. Health insurance is a way to be prepared and protect more of your money for the future. ✄

© Christos Georghiou/Shutterstock.com

USE TOOLS
to tame your money

You can use technology to track the details of your money life and gain more financial peace of mind. The following tools—both digital and paper-based—offer ways to begin.

LEARN SPREADSHEET SOFTWARE

With spreadsheet programs such as Microsoft Excel, you can enter data into a chart with rows and columns and then apply various formulas.

You can use Excel to create budgets, income reports, expense records, and investment projections. Many organizations use spreadsheets to track their finances. Master this software now and you'll have a marketable skill to add to your résumé.

To get a current list of Excel commands, go online to **support.microsoft.com**, find a search box, and enter *keyboard shortcuts Excel*. Find out how to apply templates, enter data into a spreadsheet, sort these data, apply formulas, print a spreadsheet, and save your spreadsheets.

Other companies offer free or low-cost spreadsheet software with commands and features similar to Excel. An example is Zoho Docs (**www.zoho.com/docs**).

EXPLORE OTHER APPLICATIONS

Most Web-based applications allow you to download transactions from your checking and savings accounts, sort those transactions into categories, create budgets and projections, and keep other financial records. Examples are Buxfer (**www.buxfer.com**) and Mint (**www.mint.com**). Note that there's a monthly fee for some of these services.

Instead of going online, you might prefer to download an application to your computer, smartphone, or tablet. For example, Mint also comes in a desktop version. Another popular application is Quicken.

ORGANIZE YOUR MONEY FILES

You probably use notebooks and folders to organize your coursework. Treat your money information with the same level of care. Doing this will help you pay bills on time and promote financial peace of mind.

You can use a paper-based filing system or create money-related folders on a computer. Start with the following folders and then change them to meet your individual needs:

- *Bank statements* for your checking and savings accounts
- *Bills* due this month (check this folder once per week)
- *Financial aid*—copies of your applications; records of scholarships, grants, and work-study income; records of loan repayments; notes on your conversations with people in the financial aid office

- *Insurance*—copies of life, health, car, and renter's policies
- *Major purchases*—receipts and warranties related to major expenses, such as appliances and cars
- *School*—copies of transcripts and other records of courses completed, credits earned, and grades received
- *Taxes*—W-2 forms, paycheck stubs, and copies of tax returns

You'll probably have some money documents—such as records of bills paid and receipts for smaller purchases—that don't fit into any of the given categories. File these documents in folders labeled by month and year. The Internal Revenue Service recommends that you keep these records for seven years.

AUTOMATE YOUR PERSONAL FINANCES

Think of your checking account as a kind of inbox. It's the point where you first deposit your salary or self-employment income. From that account, you can transfer money to a savings account, retirement account, and an account for major upcoming expenses, such as a new car.

Make an appointment with a personal banker to find out how you can make these transfers happen automatically on a specific day each month.

Add an option to protect your checking account from overdrafts as well.

PROTECT YOUR MONEY

Guard your private information, including your social security number and bank account numbers. People who steal this information might be able to access your money and even pretend to *be* you (something that's called *identity theft*):

- Give your private information only to people and organizations you trust, such as a tax preparer, accountant, or employer you know personally.
- Delete any emails or text messages that ask you for private information.
- Share private information online only via a secure website from an organization that you trust.
- Use strong passwords for financial websites, and change those passwords at least once per year.
- Shred any paper-based financial records more than seven years old.
- Check your credit card and bank account statements to make sure they include only purchases that you made.
- If you check your statements and see purchases you did *not* make, call your bank immediately. In case of major theft, notify the police. ✄

Your money and your VALUES

Want a clue to your values? Look at the way you handle money.

You might not think about values when you pull out a credit card or put cash on the counter. Even so, your values are at work.

For example, the amount you spend on fast food shows how much you value convenience. The amount you spend on clothes shows how much you value appearance. And the amount you spend on tuition shows how much you value education.

Think of any value as having two aspects. One is invisible, and the other is visible.

The *invisible* aspect is a belief about what matters most in life. You can define this belief by naming something you want and asking, "*Why* do I want that?" Keep asking until you reach a point where the question no longer makes sense. At that point, you'll bump into one of your values.

Suppose that you want to start dating. Why do you want that? Perhaps you want to find someone who will really listen to you and also share his deepest feelings. Why do you want *that*? Perhaps because you want to love and be loved. If someone asks why you want *that*, you might say, "I want that because . . . well, I just want it." At that point, the *why?* question no longer applies. To you, love is an end in itself. You desire love simply for its own sake. Love is one of your values.

The *visible* aspect of any value is a behavior. If you value love, you will take action to meet new people. You'll develop close friendships. You'll look for a spouse or life partner and build a long-term relationship. These behaviors are visible signs that you value love.

We experience peace of mind when our behaviors align with our values. However, this is not always the case. If you ever suspect that there's a conflict between your values and your behavior, then look at your money life for clues.

For example, someone says that he values health. After monitoring his expenses, he discovers that he spent $200 last month on fast food. He's discovered a clear source of conflict. He can resolve that conflict by redefining his values or changing his behavior. We sometimes work to buy more things that we have no time to enjoy . . . because we work so much. This can be a vicious cycle.

Sometimes we live values that are not our own. Values creep into our lives due to peer pressure or advertising. Movies, TV, and magazines pump us full of images about the value of owning more *stuff*—bigger houses, bigger cars, better clothes. All that stuff costs a lot of money. The process of acquiring it can drive us into debt—and into jobs that pay well but deny our values.

Money gives us plenty of opportunities for critical thinking. For example, think about the wisdom of choosing to spend money on the latest video game or digital gadget rather than a textbook or other resource needed for your education. Games and gadgets can deliver many hours of entertainment before they break down. Compare that to the value of doing well in a course, graduating with better grades, and acquiring skills that increase your earning power for the rest of your career.

One way to align your behaviors with your beliefs is to ask one question whenever you spend money: *Is this expense consistent with my values?* Over time, this question can lead to daily changes in your behavior that make a big difference in your peace of mind.

Keeping track of your income and expenses allows you to make choices about money with your eyes open. It's all about handling money on purpose and living with integrity. With the financial facts at hand, you can spend and earn money in ways that demonstrate your values. ✖

Leo Babauta

Leo Babauta }

Started the website Zen Habits (zenhabits.net) in 2007. With over a million monthly readers, it is consistently ranked as one of the top 25 blogs.

I started my own business at a late age—by the time I made Zen Habits into a business in 2007, I was in my mid-30s and had toiled through various jobs for 17 years.

So when I started out, I didn't know what I was doing (and still don't, but less so now). I tried everything to make money, to make my site more popular (which I thought was important). Some of it worked, some [of it] didn't.

Through this trial and error, I learned some principles that work for me. I don't share them here to show that I'm superior to anyone but to show an example of what might work for you. To show that doing things that feel right can make a business succeed.

Here's how I conduct my business:

Readers first. This is my No. 1 rule, and it has served me extremely well. When I have a question ("should I promote X or not?") the answer is always, "What would my readers want? What would help them most?" When the choice is between making some extra money or my readers' interest, the choice is obvious. There is no choice.

Trust is everything. The most valuable assets I have are my readers' trust and attention. And the attention will go really fast if they stop trusting me. Everything else in this list is based around these first two principles.

Make money by helping. I put out products and courses that I think will really help people, and that's how I make money. This works really well for me. People are happy because their lives are better, and I'm happy because the revenue I make is entirely coming from making people's lives better. We both win; our lives are all enriched.

Just the text—no social media buttons, pop-ups, drop-downs, or anything else that annoys or distracts. This goes back to trust—people come to my site to read something that will add value to their lives. Not to be pushed to share something on social media, or like something, or subscribe to my email newsletter. Yes, I have a thing at the bottom to

subscribe, but it's not pushy, and I don't promise any gimmicky downloads. When your site has a pop-up or dropdown that asks people to subscribe, it's annoying.

No ads, affiliate marketing. These are both the same, really. When you market someone else's product as an affiliate, it's just a hidden form of advertising. I should note that I had ads and did affiliate marketing for a couple years before giving it up. Why'd I give it up? Well, I realized (through experimentation) that the return on this kind of business model is very bad. You get very little revenue, and erode trust. That's a bad formula for making money.

Admit mistakes. I've been overly promotional, I've done affiliate marketing (just a couple of times), I had advertising, I asked people to share my work, I asked for votes. Those were mistakes, but I learned from them and try my best not to repeat them.

Don't front. I'm not the world's leading anything. I am just a guy who has a wife and six kids, who has changed his life by making small habit changes, one at a time. When you only try to be yourself, you can't fail.

Forget about stats; focus on helping. In the early days, I was obsessed about site statistics. I would check my stats counter several times a day, look at where all the traffic was coming from, try to get my numbers up. Here's the thing: You can't do anything with those stats. The stats just make you obsessive. About three years ago, I removed all stats trackers from my site and now am freed from that worry. Now I focus on what really matters: helping people as best I can.

Leo Babauta *took the risk of looking foolish to adopt some unusual—and effective—business practices.*

Source: Adapted from "How I Conduct My Business," http://zenhabits.net/conduct/, accessed February 2, 2015.

QUIZ

Chapter 9

1. The main steps for money management suggested in this chapter include:
   a. Focus on increasing your income, and spend as much as you want.
   b. Focus on decreasing your expenses, and don't worry about how much you earn.
   c. Increase your income, decrease your expenses, or do both.
   d. None of the answer choices

2. According to the text, what is the biggest factor in your long-term financial well-being?
   a. The state of the overall economy
   b. The interest rates on your credit cards
   c. The federal deficit
   d. Your daily behavior
   e. None of the answer choices

3. Privately-owned companies generally offer better student loans than the federal government.
   a. True
   b. False

4. The main point of the Power Process: "Risk being a fool" is that mastery in most activities calls for the willingness to do something new, to fail, to make corrections, to fail again.
   a. True
   b. False

5. The three major types of financial aid do *not* include:
   a. Money that you don't have to pay back
   b. Money that you *do* have to pay back
   c. Work-study assignments
   d. Full-ride scholarships

6. Strategies for using credit cards effectively do *not* include:
   a. Choosing cards with no annual fees and lower interest rates
   b. Paying off the full balance due each month
   c. Avoiding cash advances
   d. Using several credit cards so that you can spread around your unpaid balances
   e. All of the answer choices

7. The text recommends that you save for long-term goals such as retirement *before* you have an emergency fund in place.
   a. True
   b. False

8. According to the text, students who drop out of school for financial reasons can often benefit by stating the problem as:
   a. "I can't afford it."
   b. "I don't know how to pay for it."
   c. "I don't think it's worth it."
   d. Both a and c.
   e. Both b and c.

9. The text suggests that you manage money based on the belief that there are limits to how much money you can earn.
   a. True
   b. False

10. According to the text, the best way to begin cutting expenses is to look at how much you spend on "small ticket" (low-cost) items over the course of an entire year.
    a. True
    b. False

SKILLS
snapshot

Now that you've reflected on the ideas in this chapter and experimented with some new strategies, reflect on your money skills. Then think about the most powerful action you could take in the near future to gain more financial mastery.

Discovery
My score on the Money section of the Discovery Wheel was . . .

Right now my main sources of income are . . .

My three biggest expenses each month are . . .

Intention
I plan to graduate by (month and year) . . .

I plan to pay for my education next year by . . .

Mastery with money will enhance my career by . . .

Action
To reach that level of mastery, the most important habit I can adopt is . . .

My cue for remembering to practice this habit is . . .

My reward for practicing this habit will be . . .

HxdbzxУ/Shutterstock.com

Next Steps

what is included . . .

356 Power Process: Persist

357 Jump-start your education with transferable skills

364 Taking the road to graduation

367 Transferring to a new school

369 Start creating your career

372 Start creating your résumé

373 Discover the hidden job market

376 Develop interviewing skills

378 Join a diverse workplace

380 Put your health to work

381 Persist on the path of mastery

386 Tools for lifelong learning

388 The Discovery Wheel: Coming full circle

396 Master Student Profile: Ben Barry

do you have a minute?

Seize this moment to do something that will create a positive future for yourself. For example:

- Go online to your school's website and look for information about the career center.
- Make an appointment with your academic advisor to talk about the procedure for declaring a major.
- Brainstorm a list of ideas for a business that you could start now or after you graduate.

why

You can use the techniques introduced in this book to set a course to graduation and lifelong learning.

how

Visualize yourself at a commencement ceremony, walking up to the front of the room and receiving the diploma for your degree. Also imagine what you'd most like to do during the year after you graduate. Preview this chapter for strategies that can help you turn these visions into realities.

what if...

I could gain any skill or master any subject I wanted—at any point in my life?

Persist

Most students enter school with the desire to graduate. Ask them what it takes to succeed and you'll get a lot of great ideas. What students sometimes forget is the power of persistence—doing the gritty and unglamorous things that really work, day after day.

This is how habits pay off. For instance, exercising for better health is a great idea. And exercising is bound to fail if you only go to the gym once. Networking is highly recommended for finding a job. And it's pointless if you stop after talking to one person. These are just a couple of examples. The point is that the power of any strategy or habit emerges only when you persist.

Research indicates that it takes about 10,000 hours of deliberate practice for athletes, musicians, and other performers to win international competitions.[1] Look into the biographies of Master Students profiled in this book and you'll find many examples of deliberate practice—a fancy term for persistence.

One such example is Abraham Lincoln, who failed in business in 1831 and 1833. He was also defeated while running for elected seats in 1832, 1838, 1840, 1843, 1855, 1856, and 1858. In 1860, Lincoln was elected president of the United States.

More recently, the manuscripts for the Harry Potter books were rejected by multiple editors. Author J. K. Rowling persisted until she eventually found a publisher. She went on to sell 450 million books.

In 2006, a young student named Stefani Germanotta signed a deal with Def Jam Records. In three months, the company decided that her style was not a good fit and cancelled the contract. After that, Germanotta spent a couple years playing in small clubs, making little money, and crafting her performance skills. People noticed. Finally there was another record deal and a new name for her act: Lady Gaga.

The willingness to persist unleashes many qualities of a master student: competence, courage, self-direction, and more. To make this Power Process work, remember four things.

First, persistence is not about positive thinking or mental cheerleading. Persistence works better when you tell the truth about your current abilities. Accepting who you are—with all your strengths and weaknesses—makes it easier to take setbacks in stride, learn from mistakes, and move back into action.

Second, persistence is not about blind determination. If a strategy fails to produce the results that you want, then feel free to give it up and choose a new one. Keep your eyes on the prize—your goal—and stay flexible about ways to achieve it. If plan A fizzles out, then move on to plan B or C.

Third, persistence is not about going it alone. In life, there are no solos. We are social creatures and find strength in community. One key to persistence is finding people who have already achieved what you want. Seek out these people. Spend time with them. Ask them for guidance. They are living reminders that getting what you want is possible—if you persist.

Finally, persistence calls on you to give up the constant desire for instant gratification. This can be tough to remember when we see advertisements for drugs that promise quick relief; when we see self-help books telling us that we can turn our lives around in a few weeks, a few days, or even a few hours; when we see movies about people who overcome tremendous obstacles in 90 minutes.

Master students harness their critical thinking skills to cut through all the hype. They know that they are in the game for the long haul and that there are no quick fixes. They know that getting a degree is like training for a marathon. They remember that every class attended and every assignment completed is one small win on the way to a big victory.

Becoming a Master Student is about getting what you ultimately want. There's nothing mysterious about the process of doing this: Discover the outcomes that you want to achieve. Make it your intention to do what it takes to produce those outcomes. Then act on your intentions.

And persist. ➤

Fotolia/Shutterstock.com

Jump-start your education with
TRANSFERABLE SKILLS

When meeting with an academic advisor, you may be tempted to say, "I've just been taking general education and liberal arts courses. I don't have any marketable skills." Think again.

Few words are as widely misunderstood as skill. Defining it carefully can have an immediate and positive impact on your career planning. One dictionary defines *skill* as "the ability to do something well, usually gained by training or experience."

Work-content skills *are acquired through formal schooling, on-the-job training, or both.* For instance, the ability to repair fiber-optic cables or do brain surgery is considered a work-content skill.

However, **transferable skills** *are skills that we develop through experiences both inside and outside the classroom.* These are abilities that help people thrive in any job—no matter what work-content skills they have. You start developing these skills even before you take your first job.

Perhaps you've heard someone described this way: "She's really smart and knows what she's doing, but she's got lousy people skills." People skills, such as *listening* and *negotiating*, are prime examples of transferable skills.

SUCCEED IN MANY SITUATIONS

Transferable skills are often invisible to us. The problem begins when we assume that a given skill can be used in only one context, such as being in school or working at a particular job. Thinking in this way places an artificial limit on our possibilities.

As an alternative, think about the things you routinely do to succeed in school. Analyze your activities to isolate specific skills. Then brainstorm a list of jobs where you could use the same skills.

wavebreakmedia/Shutterstock.com

Consider the task of writing a research paper. This calls for the following skills:

- **Planning**, including setting goals for completing your outline, first draft, second draft, and final draft
- **Managing time** to meet your writing goals
- **Interviewing** people who know a lot about the topic of your paper
- **Researching** using the Internet and campus library to discover key facts and ideas to include in your paper
- **Writing** to present those facts and ideas in an original way
- **Editing** your drafts for clarity and correctness

Now consider the kinds of jobs that draw on these skills.

For example, you could transfer your skill at writing papers to a possible career in journalism, technical writing, or advertising copywriting.

You could use your editing skills to work in the field of publishing as a magazine or book editor.

Interviewing and research skills could help you enter the field of market research. And the abilities to plan, manage time, and meet deadlines will help you succeed in all the jobs mentioned so far.

Use the same kind of analysis to think about transferring skills from one job to another. Say that you work part-time as an administrative assistant at a computer dealer that sells a variety of hardware and software. You take phone calls from potential customers, help current customers solve problems using their computers, and attend meetings where your coworkers plan ways to market new products. You are developing skills at *selling, serving customers,* and *working on teams.* These skills could help you land a job as a sales representative for a computer manufacturer or software developer.

The basic idea is to take a cue from the word *transferable.* Almost any skill you use to succeed in one situation can *transfer* to success in another situation.

The concept of transferable skills creates a powerful link between higher education and the work world. Skills are the core elements of any job. While taking any course, list the specific skills you are developing and how you can transfer them to the work world. Almost everything you do in school can be applied to your career—if you consistently pursue this line of thought.

FOCUS ON THE "4 C'S"

There are hundreds of transferable skills. To develop skills that promote your success, think in terms of four categories of skills. Conveniently, each category starts with the letter C:

- **Creative thinking**—Companies value people who can create ideas for new products and services and turn those ideas into reality.
- **Critical thinking**—People with this skill can state questions precisely, consider a variety of possible answers, and test them for logic and evidence. Critical thinkers excel at making decisions and solving problems.
- **Communication**—No matter where you work, you'll benefit from excellence at speaking, listening, writing, and reading. This means knowing your purpose for communicating and finding ways to achieve that purpose with a variety of audiences.

- **Collaboration**—Projects get done by teams. If you can work with a diverse group of people, set goals and achieve them, you'll have another skill that employers value.

The Thinking and Communicating chapters are filled with strategies for learning the "4 C's."

THINK OF CHARACTER AS A SKILL

Character takes other skills and embeds them in a larger context. This is a fifth "C" that refers to master student qualities: commitment, flexibility, willingness to learn, caring about people, and more.

When employers talk about a "professional work ethic," they're referring to character. People without character skills perform just up to minimum requirements without much energy, enthusiasm, or commitment. Their verbal and nonverbal behavior often conveys a single message: *I'd really rather be somewhere else.*

If you want to prosper in your next job and open up new career options for the future, then develop character skills. Start with simple behaviors to enhance your relationships and build a positive reputation.

Smile. The power of a smile is obvious and often forgotten. When combined with eye contact and a relaxed, receptive posture, it sends an unmistakable message to the people you meet: *I'm glad that you're here. I care about what you have to say.*

Shake hands. You already know how to give firm, friendly handshakes. The key is to offer them consistently in the workplace, even with people you don't know well or even like all that much. The simple human connection that comes through touch can lower people's defenses just enough for a constructive dialogue to begin.

Make small talk. Meeting new clients, customers, and coworkers often means making small talk. Remember that people often enjoy talking about themselves. If you're meeting someone for the first time and you both work for the same organization, that's a place to start. Ask about how his or her career path led this person to this point. Then just relax, ask more questions, and let people talk.

Be social. If your employer, clients, or customers invite you to a social event, make it a

practicing
CRITICAL THINKING

32

Recognize your skills

This exercise about discovering your skills includes three steps. Allow about one hour to complete the exercise.

Step 1: List recent activities

Recall your activities during the past week or month. Write down as many of these activities as you can. Include work-related activities, school activities, and hobbies. Spend at least 10 minutes on this step.

Step 2: List rewards and recognitions

Next, list any rewards you've received, or other recognition of your achievements, during the past year. Examples include scholarship awards, athletic awards, or recognitions for volunteer work. Allow at least 10 minutes for this step as well.

Step 3: List work-content skills

Now review the two lists you just created. Then take another 10 minutes to list any specialized areas of knowledge needed to do those activities, win those awards, and receive those recognitions. These areas of knowledge indicate your *work-content skills*. For example, tutoring a French class requires a working knowledge of that language. List all of your skills that fall into this category, labeling each one as "work-content."

Step 4: List transferable skills

Go over your list of activities one more time. Spend 10 minutes looking for examples of *transferable skills*—those that can be applied to a variety of situations. For instance, giving a speech or working as a salesperson in a computer store requires the ability to persuade people. Tuning a car means that you can attend to details and troubleshoot. List all your skills that fall into this category. Label each one as "transferable."

Step 5: Review and plan

You now have a detailed picture of your skills. Review all the lists you created in the previous steps. See whether you can add any new items that occur to you. Plan to update your lists of work-content and transferable skills at least once each year. These lists will come in handy for writing your résumé, preparing for job interviews, and doing other career-planning tasks.

point to attend. You can do this even if you feel uncomfortable in social settings. See them as opportunities to practice new habits.

To develop deeper relationships, go beyond regularly scheduled events. Also, invite people to coffee, lunch, or dinner. Seek opportunities for informal contact with coworkers, but maintain a professional tone.

Build on areas of agreement. When someone expresses an opinion that differs from yours, you might feel an urge to say something like:

- I disagree completely.
- I tried that once and it flopped.
- That idea will never work.

None of these statements open a door to understanding or even constructive disagreement.

Practice replacing them with sentences that invite people to find areas of agreement. Here are some examples:

- I can see where that could work because . . .
- I like that idea because . . .
- Would you also consider . . .

This does not mean that you have to agree with everything that other people say. It *does* mean that you search for common ground first. Build a level of trust that helps people feel safe with disagreement.

Help other people get what they want. In his book *Give and Take: A Revolutionary Approach to Success*, Adam Grant explains the differences between two approaches to relationships in the workplace:[2]

65 transferrable skills

There are hundreds of transferable skills. To learn more, check out O*NET OnLine, a website from the federal government at **www.onetonline.org**. There you'll find tools for discovering your skills and matching them to specific occupations. Additional information on careers and job hunting is available through CareerOneStop (**www.careeronestop.org**).

As you read through the following list of transferable skills, notice how many of them are addressed in this book. Underline or highlight those that are most essential to the career that you want.

Self-Discovery and Self-Management Skills
1. Assessing your current knowledge and skills
2. Seeking out opportunities to acquire new knowledge and skills
3. Choosing and applying learning strategies
4. Showing flexibility by adopting new attitudes and behaviors

Time-Management Skills
5. Scheduling due dates for project outcomes
6. Scheduling time for goal-related tasks
7. Choosing technology and applying it to goal-related tasks
8. Choosing materials and facilities needed to meet goals
9. Designing other processes, procedures, or systems to meet goals

10. Working independently to meet goals
11. Planning projects for teams
12. Managing multiple projects at the same time
13. Monitoring progress toward goals
14. Persisting in order to meet goals
15. Delivering projects and outcomes on schedule

Reading Skills
16. Reading for key ideas and major themes
17. Reading for detail
18. Reading to synthesize ideas and information from several sources
19. Reading to discover strategies for solving problems or meeting goals
20. Reading to understand and follow instructions

Note-Taking Skills
21. Taking notes on material presented verbally, in print, or online
22. Creating pictures, graphs, and other visuals to summarize and clarify information
23. Organizing information and ideas in digital and paper-based forms
24. Researching by finding information online or in the library
25. Gathering data through field research or working with primary sources

- *Takers* tend to put competition first. They're likely to say that we live in a "dog-eat-dog" world. Their primary concerns in the workplace are to get promoted and to get plenty of credit for their accomplishments.
- *Givers* share ideas, resources, and contacts. They're as likely to give credit as take it. They get energy from mentoring and encouraging others. Over the long term, these qualities help givers succeed and rise to the top levels of their organizations.

By the way, helping people get what they want does not usually include giving them advice. If you give advice without being asked for it, you run the risk of seeming arrogant and rude.

As an alternative to advice, consider coaching. Conversations that lead to effective coaching are built on four questions. You can remember them with the acronym GROW:

- What is your **g**oal: Where do you want to be?
- What is the **r**eality: Where are you right now?
- What are your **o**ptions: How can you bridge the gap between where you are and where you want to be?
- What's the **w**ay forward: What option will you act on next, and what specifically will you do?

Express appreciation. There's a powerful way to boost morale at work that's both simple and free: Tell people that you appreciate them.

Many of us remember to express appreciation when people succeed in big ways. It's just as important to celebrate small victories: the meeting that was masterfully conducted, the

Test-Taking and Related Skills
26. Assessing personal performance at school or at work
27. Using test results and other assessments to improve performance
28. Working cooperatively in study groups and project teams
29. Managing stress
30. Applying scientific findings and methods to solve problems
31. Using mathematics to do basic computations and solve problems

Thinking Skills
32. Thinking to create new ideas, products, or services
33. Thinking to evaluate ideas, products, or services
34. Evaluating material presented verbally, in print, or online
35. Thinking of ways to improve products, services, or programs
36. Choosing appropriate strategies for making decisions
37. Choosing ethical behaviors
38. Stating problems accurately
39. Diagnosing the sources of problems
40. Generating possible solutions to problems
41. Weighing benefits and costs of potential solutions
42. Choosing and implementing solutions
43. Interpreting information needed for problem solving or decision making

Communication Skills
44. Assigning and delegating tasks
45. Coaching
46. Consulting
47. Counseling
48. Editing publications
49. Giving people feedback about the quality of their performance
50. Interpreting and responding to nonverbal messages
51. Interviewing people
52. Leading meetings
53. Leading project teams
54. Listening fully (without judgment or distraction)
55. Preventing conflicts (defusing a tense situation)
56. Resolving conflicts
57. Responding to complaints
58. Speaking to diverse audiences
59. Writing
60. Editing

Money Skills
61. Monitoring income and expenses
62. Raising funds
63. Decreasing expenses
64. Estimating costs
65. Preparing budgets

email that was gracefully written, the sale that was successfully closed.

When such things happen, express appreciation. Also describe the specific behavior that you appreciate, and do this in the presence of your coworkers. People will remember it.

LEARN TO DEVELOP NEW SKILLS

The ability to learn new skills over the course of your entire life is a skill all in itself. Josh Kaufman, author of *The First 20 Hours: How to Learn Anything . . . Fast!*, suggests ways to make learning efficient and more rewarding.[3]

Define the skill. State what you will be able to do when you've acquired the new skill. Be specific. For example, *use Wordpress.org to build a basic self-hosted website with a blog* is better than *build websites*. Also focus on learning one new skill at a time. You can develop other skills later.

In addition, define your *target performance level*. Rather than trying to be a world-class performer at the new skill you want to learn, set a goal that you can reach in a relatively short time. To gain skill at writing, for instance, your first performance target might be to write a series of 400-word blog posts that drive more traffic to your website. Once you reach that level of skill in writing, you can aim for writing longer posts and even a short book.

Define the key sub-skills. Big skills, such as playing music, writing well, and public speaking, can be broken down into many smaller skills, or *sub-skills*. Playing the guitar, for example, consists of:

- Holding the instrument
- Tuning the strings
- Placing your fingers on the neck to form different chords
- Strumming or plucking the strings in different combinations

Once you isolate sub-skills, you can learn them one at a time.

Remember that some sub-skills matter more than others. A few will be critical to achieving the outcome you want. The rest are optional. To tell the difference, do some research. Skim a few articles, books, and websites about the skill you want to learn. If possible, also talk to people who have already mastered the skill.

After a few hours of research, you'll discover that certain sub-skills are mentioned more than others. Those are the ones you want to study in detail. Break each sub-skill down into a series of "baby steps," and arrange them in a sequence that makes sense.

Although it's important to gather information, don't linger on this step. Learn enough about each sub-skill to determine how to practice and when to self-correct when you make errors. Start practicing as soon as possible.

Make time to practice. You'll need a critical mass of practice time to make visible and lasting progress. Kaufman recommends 20 hours (about 40 minutes of practice per day for 30 days). Use this figure as a starting point and adjust it as needed.

Pull out your calendar and schedule daily practice time over the next month. This might call for eliminating some activities or postponing them. If you are not willing to do these things, then simply tell the truth about that. Perhaps the skill is not a priority for you right now.

Make it easy to practice. When learning a new skill, set yourself up to succeed. Design your environment so that it's easy to practice. If you want to practice playing the guitar, then put it in a place where you can easily reach for it. If you want to build a website, then print out a list of step-by-step instructions, and place it next to your computer.

Also eliminate sources of distraction. Find a quiet place where you can focus your attention. Shut down your mobile phone, Internet connection, and TV (unless you need them to practice).

Practice. Start with the first sub-skill you want to learn. Whenever possible, practice it in context. If you want to start a yoga practice, for instance, then spend as much time on the mat as possible. If you want to master a tennis serve, then head to the court.

If possible, get a coach. By observing you and offering immediate feedback, this person can speed your progress.

The early hours of practicing can be the most frustrating. Just ask people about their early experiences in playing a musical instrument or speaking a new language. They'll tell you about a string of missed notes and mistakes on the way to mastery.

Accept the discomfort that comes with learning something new. Persist until you experience the rewards you desire. ✖

practicing
CRITICAL THINKING

33

Plan to develop a new skill

This is an exercise based on one of the six levels of thinking in Bloom's taxonomy of educational objectives—*analyzing*. You will describe a skill that you'd like to learn, break it down into smaller behaviors, and create a plan to practice those behaviors. To prepare for this exercise, read the article about transferable skills first.

Step 1: Define the skill you want to learn

Think of something new that you want to able to do. Be specific and keep it focused. Choose a skill that you could realistically acquire in about 20 hours of concentrated practice. Examples might include learning how to:

- Touch-type
- Serve a tennis ball
- Cook five delicious meals, preparing each one in 20 minutes or less with a short list of common ingredients
- Use Adobe Photoshop to edit images
- Do a 20-minute series of yoga poses that stretch and strengthen muscles throughout the body
- Speak enough Spanish to book a hotel, order meals, and shop in Mexico City during a spring break trip

Describe your skill here:

Step 2: Define the key sub-skills

Next, analyze the skill that you just described. Break it down into a series of simpler behaviors, or *sub-skills*. Cooking a meal, for example, includes sub-skills such as choosing ingredients and combining them in specific ways. Learning to peel, chop, slice, dice, boil, broil, bake, sauté, or fry ingredients might also be important.

List the sub-skills that you intend to learn. Arrange them in a logical sequence, proceeding from simpler to more complex. If possible, find a coach or tutor who can observe you and offer immediate feedback as you practice the sub-skills.

Note: You might need a few hours of research to complete this step. If so, then schedule a time to do that research. Also schedule a time to come back to this exercise and complete the remaining steps.

Step 3: Make time to practice

Review your calendar for the next month (or a specific month in the future). Schedule 45 to 60 minutes each day to practice the sub-skills you just listed.

Step 4: Make it easy to practice

Set up your environment so that practicing becomes convenient. If you're planning to prepare new meals, for instance, then make sure that you have the pots, pans, utensils, and ingredients you'll need.

Step 5: Practice

When your scheduled practice time begins, start with the first sub-skill on your list. Repeat that behavior, correcting errors along the way until you can do the sub-skill proficiently. Then proceed through the other sub-skills on your list. If you have a coach or tutor, invite that person to some of your practice sessions.

Step 6: Reflect on your experience with learning a new skill

After about 20 hours of practicing your new skill, think creatively and critically about what you learned from the experience. Are you satisfied with your performance? Was the skill too challenging to learn in 20 hours? Were you able to define and sequence the sub-skills? Do you have ideas about how to practice more efficiently? Write Discovery Statements to summarize the major insights you got from this exercise. Then write Intention Statements to describe how you will apply those insights to learning new skills in the future.

Taking the road to
GRADUATION

People go to school with many different definitions of success. For most students, that definition includes getting a degree. Every chapter in *Becoming a Master Student* offers a set of strategies that you can use for this purpose. Following are some additional suggestions for persisting to the day you graduate.

Alex Slobodkin/E+/Getty Images

DISCOVER WHAT YOUR ACADEMIC GOALS MEAN FOR TODAY

One key to persistence is knowing exactly what you want from your education. Some students enter higher education with only a vague idea of their goals. These students can find it easy to disengage from school and let other activities take over.

This is where the master student process can make the difference between staying in school and dropping out. As you plan your week, write a Discovery Statement to complete these sentences:

- *What I most want from school is . . .*
- *What I also want is . . .*
- *To get what I want from school, the main goals for me to achieve this term are . . .*

This writing will give you the big picture of your priorities. Now zoom in for a close-up view. Create Intention Statements by completing the following sentences at least once each month:

- *To achieve my main goal for this term, the things that I intend to accomplish this month are . . .*
- *To meet my goals for this month, the things I intend to do this week are . . .*

Your answers to the last sentence will be tasks that you can add to a daily to-do list or enter in your calendar.

Persistence depends on planning. Goals become real only when they dictate what we do in the present moment. Take the goal of graduation and ask yourself: What does that goal mean for *today*?

CONNECT WITH SERVICES

After you finish this course, you never have to feel that you're alone and unsupported. A whole catalog of student services awaits you. Any of them can help you succeed in school, and many of them are free.

Name a problem that you're facing right now: financial problems, the need for childcare, conflict with a teacher, or anything else that seems like an obstacle to getting your degree. Chances are that a school service can help you solve that problem.

Start with academic advising. You've already been encouraged to visit with your academic advisor. If you want to graduate on time, then be sure to *stay* in contact with this person until you graduate. Your academic advisor is there to help you adapt to the culture of higher education, choose a major, and select the courses needed to complete your degree.

Schedule a meeting with your advisor early during your first term. Then meet with this person at least once per term as long as you're in school. Prepare carefully for each meeting by writing down your questions and listing courses you're interested in taking.

Following are examples of other student services that your college may offer:

- Childcare
- Fitness and athletic centers
- Computer labs and help desks
- Counseling services
- Career planning services
- Financial aid
- Legal aid services
- Security and safety services
- Special needs and disability services
- Student health clinics
- Tutoring
- Student organizations and extracurricular activities

Check your school website for the specific options available to you. Also remember that you can connect with many services online as well as in person.

The key is to seek services the moment when you need help. Do this right away, before a small problem grows into a barrier to getting your degree.

CONNECT WITH PEOPLE

School can be a frightening place for new students. Older students, people from different backgrounds and cultures, commuter students, and people with disabilities can feel excluded. Some people attend classes for months and still feel they're standing on the outside, looking in.

Students who overcome isolation increase their chances of staying in school and getting to graduation. Begin by planning to meet people. Write an Intention Statement promising to meet three new people each week. Name specific people, and describe how you intend to meet them. For example, introduce yourself to classmates. Get to class early and break the ice by discussing the previous assignment, or stay late and talk about the lecture.

Your instructors are people, too! Meet with your instructors outside of class. You will discover human beings who want you to succeed. Students who persist to graduation tend to develop long-term relationships with instructors who act as mentors, advisors, and coaches. These instructors can assist you by writing letters of recommendation and becoming part of your job-hunting network.

LIGHT THE PATH WITH LOTS OF REWARDS

One key to persistence is filling the long road to graduation with lots of small "wins." These are rewards that you enjoy on a regular basis—even on days when money is tight, the kids are crabby, or a schedule crammed with work and classes leaves you feeling exhausted.

According to Teresa Amabile and Steven Kramer, authors of *The Progress Principle: Using Small Wins to Ignite Joy, Engagement, and Creativity at Work*, the single most

practicing
CRITICAL
THINKING 34

Make a trial choice of a major

Step 1: Discover options

Look at your school's catalog or website for a list of majors. Make a photocopy of that list or print it out. Spend at least five minutes reading through all the majors that your school offers.

Step 2: Make a trial choice

Next, cross out all of the majors that you already know are not right for you. You will probably eliminate well over half the list. Scan the remaining majors. Next to the ones that definitely interest you, write "yes." Next to majors that you're willing to consider and are still unsure about, write "maybe."

Now, focus on your "yes" choices. See whether you can narrow them down to three majors. List those here:

Finally, put an asterisk next to the major that interests you most right now. *This is your trial choice of major.*

Step 3: Evaluate your trial choice

Congratulations on making your choice! Now take a few minutes to reflect on it. Does it align with your interests, skills, and career plans? Set a goal to test your choice of major with out-of-classroom experience. Examples are internships, field experiences, study abroad programs, and work-study assignments. Note that this experience might confirm your trial choice—or lead to a new choice of major.

important source of motivation is making daily progress on meaningful work.[4] This idea applies to students. Keep a record of your academic successes, no matter how small. Take one minute each day to notice something that you've done well: a perfect score on a pop quiz, a well-written essay, a presentation where you connect with your audience, or anything else that you feel good about.

Whenever you successfully complete a task that brings you closer to graduation, pause to reflect on and remember it. Also tell someone—a family member or friend—about it. Accept compliments from others, and from yourself.

Notice that this suggestion differs from the typical problem-solving approach, where you look for something that's wrong and find ways to fix it. To apply the progress principle, you look for something that's right and find ways to celebrate it.

In your journal, also write Discovery Statements in response to these questions:

- What was it about getting a degree that originally excited you?
- When have you felt enthusiastic about going to school?
- When have you felt proud of the work you're doing in school?
- What parts of going to school do you find motivating and fun?

Staying in touch with your original reasons for going to school can rekindle your enthusiasm for persisting to graduation.

FIND THE TIME AND THE MONEY

Make careful choices about balancing school with work. If you're a full-time student, think of this commitment as on par with a 40-hour-per-week job. (If you study two

Persistence depends on planning. Goals become real only when they dictate what we do in the present moment.

hours for every hour that you spend in class, you might even spend *more* than 40 hours per week on school.) This places obvious limits on the number of hours per week that you can work.

Also create a complete plan for funding your education. Get to know the staff at your school's financial aid office. Meet with them regularly to discuss work-study programs, grants, loans, scholarships, and other financial resources. Make sure that you know

how you're going to fund each term from now until the day you graduate.

REVISIT YOUR STRATEGIES

Becoming a Master Student comes with a guarantee. The strategies explained in this book are guaranteed to work—except when they don't. A technique that works in one class with one instructor might fail in another class with a different instructor. When that happens, it's time to modify the technique or find a new one.

Here is where your skills in creative and critical thinking come into play. Taking the road to graduation is about consistently asking two questions: *What kind of results am I getting right now in my academic life? And what can I do differently to get better results?*

One way to answer these questions is to learn from the people around you. When you meet excellent students, observe them. Isolate specific things they do and say to promote their mastery. Then adopt one of these behaviors and see if it works for you. Also look for self-defeating habits you see in other students and draw lessons from them on what to avoid.

In addition, observe yourself during the times you're "on" as a student—times when learning is effortless and joyful. Notice the attitudes and actions that create such moments of success. These are more clues to your next steps on the road to graduation. ✖

Steve Debenport/E+/Getty Images

Transferring to a new
SCHOOL

If you ever choose to change schools, you won't be alone. The *New York Times* reports that about 60 percent of students graduating from college attend more than one school.[5]

The way that you choose a new school will have a major impact on your education. This is true whether you're transferring from a community or technical college to a four-year school or you're choosing a graduate school.

Even if you don't plan to go through the process of choosing schools again, you can use the following ideas to evaluate your current school.

KNOW KEY TERMS

As you begin researching schools, take a few minutes to review some key terms:

Accreditation is a process used in judging the merits of the programs offered by a school. An accredited school is recognized as meeting standards set by a professional organization such as the American Bar Association.

Articulation agreements are official documents that spell out the course equivalents that a school accepts.

Attrition refers to the number of students who drop out of a school or a program offered by that school during a certain period of time.

An *associate of arts (AA)* or *associate of science (AS)* is the degree title conferred by many two-year colleges. Having a degree from a two-year

college can make it easier to change schools than transferring without a degree.

CLEP is an acronym for *College Level Examination Program*. Passing a CLEP test might allow you to earn college credit for skills and knowledge you already have.

Course equivalents are courses you've already taken that another school will accept as meeting its requirements for graduation.

Prerequisites are courses or skills that a school requires students to complete or have before they enter college, take certain classes, or even graduate. In contrast, a *corequisite* is a course that you're required (or allowed) to take at the same time as a another course.

GATHER INFORMATION

To research schools, start with publications. These include print sources, such as school catalogs and school websites. Next, contact people: academic advisors, counselors, other school staff members, and current or former students from the schools you're considering. Contact the advisor at the new school to find out what the acceptance and graduation requirements are.

Use your research to dig up key facts such as these about each school you're considering:

- Location
- Number of students
- Class sizes
- Possibilities for contact with instructors outside class
- Percentage of full-time faculty members
- Admissions criteria
- Availability of degrees that interest you
- Tuition and fees
- Housing plans
- Financial aid programs
- Religious affiliation
- Diversity of students and staff
- Course requirements
- Retention rates (how many students come back to school after their freshman year)

To learn the most about a school, go beyond the first statistics you see. For example, a statement that "30 percent of our students are persons of color" doesn't tell you much about the numbers of people from specific ethnic or racial groups.

Also, you could transfer to a school that advertises student–instructor ratios of 15 to 1 and then find yourself in classes with 100 people.

Remember that any statement about average class size is just that—an average. To gain more details, ask how often you can expect to enroll in smaller classes, especially during your final terms.

VISIT SCHOOLS

Take trips to the two or three schools that interest you most. Ask for a campus tour and a chance to sit in on classes. Take a thorough tour of the campus: the classrooms, laboratories, residence halls, bookstores, cafeterias, library, sports facilities, and student center. Also ask about sources of entertainment, such as restaurants, theaters, galleries, and concert halls. When you're done with the "official" tour, just walk around and observe the school grounds. To learn even more, work in the surrounding community for a summer or take a course at the school before you transfer.

In addition, gather facts about your current academic profile. Include your grades, courses completed, degrees attained, and grade point average (GPA). Standardized test scores are important. They include your scores on the Scholastic Assessment Test (SAT), American College Test (ACT), Graduate Record Examinations (GRE), and any advanced placement (AP) tests you've taken.

CHOOSE YOUR NEW SCHOOL

As you sort through all this information, remember that your impressions of a school will go beyond a list of dry facts. Also pay attention to your instincts and intuitions—your "gut feelings" of attraction to one school or hesitation about another. These impressions can be important to your choice.

Allow time for such feelings to emerge. You can also benefit from putting your choice of schools in a bigger context. Consider the purposes, values, and long-term goals you've generated by doing the exercises and Journal Entries in this book. Consider which school is most likely to support the body of discoveries and intentions that you've created.

As you choose your new school, consider the needs and wishes of your family members and friends. Ask for their guidance and support. If you involve them in the decision, they'll have more of a stake in your success.

At some point, you'll just choose a school. Remember that there is no one "right" choice. You could probably thrive at many schools—perhaps even at your current one. Use the suggestions in this book to practice self-responsibility. Take charge of your education no matter which school you attend.

SUCCEED AT YOUR NEW SCHOOL

Be willing to begin again. Some students approach a transfer with a "been there, done that" attitude. Having enrolled in higher education before, they assume that they don't need the orientation, advising, or other student services available at their new school.

Consider an alternative. Because your tuition and fees cover all these services, you might as well take advantage of them. By doing so, you could uncover opportunities that you missed while researching schools. At the very least, you'll meet people who will support your transition.

Your prior experience in higher education gives you strengths. Acknowledge them, even as you begin again at your new school. While celebrating your past accomplishments, you can explore new paths to student success.

Connect to people. At your new school, you'll be in classes with people who have already developed social networks. To avoid feeling left out, seek out chances to meet people. Join study groups, check out extracurricular activities, and consider volunteering for student organizations. Making social connections can ease your transition to a new academic environment.

Check credits. If you plan to transfer, meet with an advisor at your new school as soon as possible. Talk about how the credits that you've already earned will transfer to that school. This can save you a lot of tuition money. Find out whether you can get credit for prior learning in the workplace or military service. If you have results from College Level Examination Programs (CLEPs) or certification from massive open online courses (MOOCs), ask about credit for those as well.

No two schools offer the same sets of courses, so determining credits is often a matter of interpretation. In some cases, you might be able to persuade a registrar or the admissions office to accept some of your previous courses. Keep a folder of syllabuses from your courses for this purpose. Ask your academic advisor for help. Taking care of these details can help you graduate from your new school on time, with the education that you want. ✂

Start creating your CAREER

Many people approach career planning as if they were panning for gold. They keep sifting through the dirt, clearing dust, and throwing out rocks. They hope to strike it rich and discover the perfect career.

Maridav/Shutterstock.com

Instead of seeing a career as something you discover, you can see it as something you choose. You don't *find* the right career. You *create* it.

There's a big difference between these two approaches. Thinking that there's only one "correct" choice for your career can lead to a lot of anxiety: "Did I choose the right one?" "What if I made a mistake?"

Viewing your career as your creation helps you relax. Instead of anguishing over finding the right career, you can stay open to possibilities. Choose one career today, knowing that you can choose again later.

When you adopt this point of view, you stop thinking of your career as a once-in-a-lifetime choice and start seeing it as a series of experiments. The rewards are lifelong learning and long-term satisfaction.

RETHINK THE ROLE OF PASSION

One common piece of career advice is to "follow your passion." In other words, choose a career based on what you *love* to do.

Enjoying your work is important. Yet the advice to follow your passion has some problems. Many people don't have a clear passion. Also, passion doesn't always come first. You might find that your enjoyment of a task grows *after* you begin to master the skills that it requires.

In a competitive job market, you can benefit by considering two factors beyond passion. First is your level of *skill*. For example, someone can enjoy playing the guitar and never do it well enough to make a living as a musician. Feeling passion for your work is not the same as being skilled enough to earn money at it.

The second factor is *market demand*. In addition to thinking about what you love to do, ask yourself: What skills are rewarded in the work world? What can I do that solves a problem or otherwise creates clear value to employers, clients, or customers?

Keep looking for connections between your passion, your skills, and market demand. There's probably more than one career that can give you a satisfying career.

THINK LIKE AN ENTREPRENEUR

An *entrepreneur* is someone who owns a business. An entrepreneur's goals include making a profit. This usually means taking a risk—creating products or services (or both) and working hard to make sure that people buy them.

Maybe you don't see yourself as an entrepreneur. Perhaps you'd rather find a steady job with a regular paycheck and benefits that you can have for the rest of your life. Although this is a traditional career goal, you might find it difficult to achieve. Jobs that offer long-term security and generous benefits are harder to find than they were in the past.

One solution is to *think* like an entrepreneur, even if you don't intend to be one. Rather than depending on your current employer, take charge of your career by:

DISCOVERY STATEMENT

Plan a career by naming names

Experiment with career planning, starting now. See your response to this Journal Entry as a statement of a career direction rather than a detailed career plan. Also remember that a key part of career planning is changing your direction as you learn more about your skills, your interests, and the job market.

Of course, there are many possible ways to capture your career-related discoveries and intentions. For now, experiment with career planning by "naming names."

Note: To prepare for this writing, you might want to review a list of careers and related job titles such as the *Occupational Outlook Handbook* (**http://bls.gov/ooh**).

Name your skills

List the skills that you've enjoyed using in school and in past work or volunteer experiences.

Name your job

Now, list the kinds of jobs that draw on the skills you just listed. What are those jobs called?

Name your company

Perhaps you know of some businesses or non-profit organizations that you'd like to work for. List them.

If you prefer to be self-employed or start your own business instead, then name the products or services that you'd like to sell. Also list some possible names for your business.

Name the people in your network

Finally, begin listing the names of people in your network. Include *anyone* who could help you find a job that interests you. Possibilities include former employers, your current employer, roommates, classmates, teachers, friends, relatives, people in your school's career planning office, and people who've graduated from your school and are now working in jobs similar to those you listed previously.

Finally, plan to meet with five people in your network for an informational interview.

I will contact . . .

1. _____
2. _____
3. _____
4. _____
5. _____

- Mastering skills that are valued in the marketplace
- Becoming a top performer in your field
- Building a strong network of people who can help you find a new job
- Managing your own benefits by saving money for emergencies, health care, and retirement
- Brainstorming ideas for products or services that you could sell
- Testing those ideas with a part-time job or projects that you pursue outside of your regular work hours

USE CAREER SERVICES TO EXPLORE YOUR OPTIONS

Visit the career center on your campus. The staff members can help you explore possibilities as you seek your niche in the work world. Take career-planning workshops and go to career fairs.

Also ask about assessments that can help you discover more about your skills and identify jobs that call for those skills. These have several names, including *interest assessments, vocational aptitude tests*, or *skill inventories*. Although assessments cannot offer the final word on what kind of work is best for you, they can yield ideas that might not otherwise occur to you and suggest useful ways to follow up.

DESCRIBE YOUR IDEAL LIFESTYLE

In addition to choosing the content of your career, you have many options for integrating work into the context of your life. You can work full-time. You can work part-time. You can commute to a cubicle in a major corporation. Or you can work at home and take the 30-second commute from your bedroom to your desk.

Close your eyes. Visualize an ideal day in your life after graduation. Vividly imagine the following:

- Your work setting
- Your coworkers
- Your appointments and to-do list for that day
- Other sights and sounds in your work environment

The point is that it's important to find a match between your career and your lifestyle preferences. These include the amount of flexibility in your schedule, the number of people you see each day, the variety in your tasks, and the ways that you balance work with other activities.

TEST YOUR CAREER CHOICE AND BE WILLING TO CHANGE

Once you have a career choice, translate it into workplace experience. For example:

- Contact people who are actually doing the job you're researching, and ask them a lot of questions about what it's like (an *informational interview*).
- Choose an internship or volunteer position in a field that interests you.
- Get a part-time or summer job in your career field.

If you find that you enjoy such experiences, you've probably made a wise career choice. And the people you meet are possible sources of recommendations, referrals, and employment in the future.

If you did *not* enjoy your experiences, celebrate what you learned about yourself. Now you're free to refine your initial career choice or go in a new direction. ✖

Another option: Don't plan your career

When they hear the term *career plan*, some people envision a long document that lists goals with due dates and action steps. This is one type of career plan, and it can be useful for people with careers in stable industries. However, there are few of those left anymore.

Consider another approach: Don't plan your career—at least in the conventional way. In an economy that's constantly shedding jobs and adding new ones, you can gain stability with an alternative approach.

Choose your direction rather than your destination. Instead of listing specific jobs that you'd like to have in the years to come, get in touch with your values. Determine what matters to you most about working. Ask yourself these questions:

- Do you want to work primarily with people? Ideas? Specific products or materials?
- Do you want to manage people, or answer only to yourself and a handful of clients?
- What's the one thing that you do best—and enjoy doing—that creates value for people?

Put your answers in writing and revise them at least once each year.

Take one new step in that direction. Determine the very next action you will take to move in your chosen direction. Create an intention that you can act on immediately. If you

want to become self-employed, for instance, then contact one person who started a successful business, and ask for an informational interview.

Reflect on what you learn and choose your next step. Write Discovery Statements about the results of acting on your intention. What did you learn? In light of those lessons, what is the *next* step you'll take to move in your desired career direction?

The key is to take frequent action and reflect on the results. You'll gain a flexible and stable direction for your career, no matter what happens to the economy.

Be honest about what you do *not* want to do. Some of the steps you take might lead to a job that you hate. That's valuable information. Write Discovery Statements about the specific aspects of the job that you dislike. Follow up with Intention Statements about the kind of work you will avoid in the future.

Stay open to surprise. Set aside a day to do something you normally wouldn't do, such as reading a book you wouldn't normally read or go to a presentation you normally wouldn't attend. Take a course in a subject that's completely outside your major. Go out to lunch with someone with a different major. Invite two friends to dinner and ask each of them to invite a person you don't know. Experiences such as these can lead to career directions that would otherwise never occur to you.

Start creating your RÉSUMÉ

You can gain a lot from writing a résumé now, even if you don't plan to apply for a job in the near future. Start *building* your résumé now and update it each term that you're in school.

NPFire/Shutterstock.com

START BUILDING SKILLS FOR YOUR IDEAL RÉSUMÉ

To get the most from your education, think about the résumé you want to have when you graduate. With that vision of the person you want to be, choose the skills that you want to gain.

Write goals to develop specific skills. Then list the actions you will take to develop those skills. Add reminders of these actions to your to-do list and calendar so that you can actually achieve your goals.

Many of your plans will involve taking courses. In addition, look for ways to gain and use skills outside the classroom. Sign up for internships and service learning projects related to your major. Find part-time jobs related to your career plan. Seize every opportunity to take theories and test them in the work world. These experiences will help you develop an expertise, build a job network, and make a seamless transition to your next career.

REMEMBER THE REASON FOR A RÉSUMÉ

For an employer, a résumé has one main purpose: choosing which people to contact for a job interview. In response, include just enough detail about yourself to make a potential employer say, "This person sounds interesting. Let's meet him in person so that we can find out more."

An effective résumé states how you can benefit a potential employer. It also offers evidence that you can deliver those benefits. Make every word in your résumé serve these goals.

To write an effective résumé, consider your audience. Picture a person who has a several

hundred résumés to plow through and almost no time for that task. She may spend only 20 seconds scanning each résumé before making a decision about whom to call for interviews so remember to be concise. Employers will not read long résumés with attachments and pages of details.

Your goal is to get past this first cut. Neatness, organization, and correct grammar and punctuation are essential. Meet these goals, and then make an even stronger impression with the following strategies.

Ask yourself: *From an employer's perspective, what kind of person would make an ideal candidate for this job?* Then write your résumé to answer this question directly.

CUT THE FLUFF

Write one page. Period. A longer résumé sends a message that the writer has trouble communicating the big picture of her work life.

Besides, the people who screen your résumé are pressed for time. They'll spend only a few seconds scanning it. For this reason, avoid writing in full sentences and paragraphs. Bulleted lists work better. If you're applying for a specific position, be sure to include key words from the job listing.

The body of a résumé usually includes a section titled *Experience*. Here is where you give a few relevant details about your past jobs, listed in chronological order starting with your most recent position.

This is also where many résumé writers go off track. To avoid common mistakes, remember to focus the body of your résumé on what you *accomplished*—not just on what you *did*.

Whenever possible, use phrases that start with an active verb: "*supervised* three people," "*generated* leads for sales calls," "*wrote* speeches and *edited* annual reports," "*designed* a process that reduced production expenses by 20 percent."

Active verbs refer directly to your skills. Make them relevant to the job you're seeking, and be prepared to discuss them in more detail during a job interview.

Avoid boilerplate language—stock wording or vague phrases such as "proven success in a high-stress environment," "highly motivated self-starter," or "a demonstrated capacity for strategic thinking." These can eliminate you from the hiring process and send your résumé straight to the trash.

The same focus on accomplishment applies to the *Education* section of your résumé. List any degree that you attained beyond high school. Also mention honors and awards. If you have a decent grade point average, include it.

If you are currently enrolled in classes, note that as well. Include your planned degree and date of graduation.

GET FEEDBACK

Plan to write many drafts of your résumé. Ask friends and family members if your résumé is persuasive and easy to understand. Also ask them to check for grammar and spelling errors.

In addition, get feedback from people at your school's career center. Revise your résumé based on their comments. Then revise some more. ✖

Discover the
HIDDEN
job market

When people say "There are no jobs," maybe what they really mean is "My current job hunting method is not working." There's a world of difference between those statements. The first one kills options. The second one *creates* options.

Santiago Cornejo/Shutterstock.com

One of those options is networking—a powerful way to tap the hidden job market. By networking skills, you can discover job openings *before* they are advertised. (Many never are.)

Some people hear the word *networking* and wince. They think of it as sleazy or a waste of time. In reality, networking can be effective and fun. And when you give something back to the people you meet, such as useful information or an introduction to someone else, you add value to their lives as well as yours.

THINK LIKE AN EMPLOYER

Imagine that you're the hiring manager for a small business or head of human resources for a larger company. Your organization has a job opening, and your task is to fill it as soon as possible. You'd prefer to hire someone you already know. If you don't know anyone with appropriate qualifications, however, then your preferred hiring process will probably include:

- Asking other members of your network to recommend a person for the job
- Talking to people who contact you directly and demonstrate that they have the appropriate qualifications
- Posting help-wanted ads and turning to employment agencies only as a last resort

Now consider the traditional process that people use to *find* a job. It often relies on:

- Responding blindly to help-wanted ads and online job boards
- Sending out a generic résumé and cover letter
- Contacting employment agencies

Take a minute to compare these two processes. *They are essentially opposites.* It's no wonder that people find the process of hiring and getting hired to be so frustrating.

The lesson here is to think like an employer. Activate your network—the people you know.

DISCOVER YOUR NETWORK

You might not believe that you have a network. If so, then just notice that thought and gently let it go. *Everyone* has a network. The key is to discover and develop it.

Begin by listing contacts. These include any person who can help you find a job. Contacts can include roommates, classmates, teachers, friends, relatives, and their friends. Also list former employers and current employers.

In addition, go to your school's alumni office and see if you can get contact information for past graduates, especially people who are working in your career field. This is a rich source of contacts that many students ignore.

Start your contact list now. Record each person's name, phone number, and email address on a separate 3 × 5 card or Rolodex card. Another option is to keep your list on a computer, using word processing, database, contact management software, or an app on your smartphone.

CONTACT PEOPLE IN YOUR NETWORK

Next, send a short email to a person on your list: someone who's doing the kind of work that you'd love to do. Invite that person to coffee or lunch. If that's not feasible, then ask for a time to make a phone call. Explain that you'd like to have a 20-minute conversation to learn more about what these people do. In other words, you're asking for an *informational interview* rather than a job interview. Whenever possible, make this contact after getting an introduction from someone that both of you know.

Before you meet with your contacts in person or over the phone, create a short list of questions to ask. Plan to ask them how they chose their career and found their job. Ask about what they enjoy, what they find challenging, and what trends are shaping their work. Find out what kind of work they'd like to be doing in a year, five years, and even ten years from today. In particular, ask about how people find jobs in their field, and if there is anyone else you could meet with for more information.

During the actual interview, listen closely to what people say. Take notes and highlight any follow-up actions that you'd like to take. Keep the focus of the conversation on the other person rather than you. Do not ask for a job at this point.

Keep in mind that people are busy. Stick to your agreed time limit for the conversation, unless it's clear that both of you want to continue. When you're done, say thank you. If you met in person for coffee or a meal, then offer to pay the bill.

After the interview, send a thank-you note. Refer to a specific topic or point from your conversation. If the person made a suggestion and you acted on it, then be sure to mention this.

EXTEND YOUR NETWORK

Through your job research and informational interviews, you'll learn about many people in your career field. Some of them might be people who fall outside your current network. You can reach out to them anyway.

Tap the power of the Internet. Get the name of the person that you'd like to meet and key it into your favorite search engine. You might be able to find contact information through a website such as pipl (**pipl.com**) or PeekYou (**peekyou.com**) as well. In addition, LinkedIn (**linkedin .com**) offers many ways to learn about and connect with people in your career field. Scan the search results to find out whether this person has a website, blog, or both. Also look for their presence on social networks such as Facebook, Twitter, and LinkedIn. With this information you can do many things to connect. For example:

- Comment on a blog post that the person wrote.
- Join Twitter and post an update about this person or "retweet" one of their updates.
- Create your own website, add a blog, and write a post about this person.
- Send a short email—or handwritten note—that expresses your appreciation for their work.

In any case, do not ask anything of people at this stage. Your goal is simply to show up on their personal "radar." Over time, they might initiate a contact with you. Then you can feel free to respond and suggest an informational interview.

BE SPECIFIC ABOUT THE JOB YOU WANT—AND WHY YOU CAN DO IT

After doing some informational interviews, you'll learn more about the language used by people in your career field.

Listen closely for common job titles. When you find one that matches the kind of work that you want to do, make a habit of using that title.

Don't worry about limiting your options by focusing on just one specific job title or career option for now. If your current choice doesn't work out, you can choose another one later.

When you're actually in a job interview with a person who can hire you, be prepared to answer a common question: *Why should I hire you?* Answers such as *Because I can make a contribution to this company* or *Because I'm well qualified* are too general. Don't worry about being the best-qualified person for the position. Just give specific reasons why you'd be a good "hire."

This evidence can take various forms, depending on the job that you want. It might be a list of measurable outcomes that you achieved on a previous job. It might also be something tangible that you've just created, such as a website with a blog that you update regularly.

PITCH IDEAS AND OFFER TO IMPLEMENT THEM

Make direct contact with people who have the power to hire you. Do this even when their organization does not have an advertised job opening.

This means doing research. Find out what problems the company wants to solve. Discover what kind of services and products they want to offer. Then propose ideas that create value for the company.

You might send an email that goes something like this: "I have some specific

ideas for the home page of your company's website that could increase the number of customer responses and raise its ranking on Google and other search engines. Over the next two weeks, I will develop some prototypes for a new home page. If you like my ideas, then I'd like to meet with you."

OFFER A LIMITED AMOUNT OF WORK FOR FREE

If you really want to get a potential employer's attention, then offer to work for free. This is not a joke. When done with care, working for free offers a low-risk way for you and an employer to get to know each other. Just be sure to set a limit on how long you're willing to do this, and put this limit in writing.

Working for free can have several outcomes. You could get hired as an employee or regular contractor. Or you might part with a company on friendly terms and agree to stay in contact for the future. In any case, you're growing your network. ✖

Develop
INTERVIEWING SKILLS

Job interviews are times for an employer to size up applicants and screen most of them out. The reverse is also true: Interviews offer *you* a chance to size up potential employers. Careful preparation and follow-up can help you get the information—and the job—that you want.

BEFORE YOU GO TO THE INTERVIEW

To get the most from your interviews, also learn everything you can about each organization that interests you. Start by searching the Internet. Then head to your campus and public libraries. Tell a reference librarian that you're researching specific companies in preparation for a job interview, and ask for good sources of information.

Next, prepare to answer common questions. Many interviewers have the following questions on their mind, even if they don't ask them directly:

- How did you find out about us?
- Will we be comfortable working with you?
- How can you help us?
- Will you learn this job quickly?
- What makes you different from other people applying for this job?

Write out brief answers to those questions. Summarize the main points you want to make on a single sheet of paper. Then practice delivering them verbally to the point where you barely refer to the sheet. Your goal is to sound prepared without delivering canned answers.

DURING THE INTERVIEW

Plan to arrive early for your interview. While you're waiting, observe the workplace. Notice what people are saying and doing. See whether you can "read" the company culture by making informal observations.

Andrey_Popov/Shutterstock.com

When you meet the interviewer, do three things right away: Smile, make eye contact, and give a firm handshake. Nonverbal communication creates a lasting impression.

After making small talk, the interviewer will start asking questions. Draw on the answers you've prepared. At the same time, respond to the *exact* questions that you're asked. Speak naturally and avoid the impression that you're making a speech or avoiding a question.

Stay aware of how much you talk. Avoid answers that are too brief or too long. Respond to each question for a minute or two. If you have more to say, end your answer by saying, "Those are the basics. I can add more if you want."

Save questions about benefits, salary, and vacation days for the second interview. When you get to that point, you know that the employer is interested in you. You might have leverage to negotiate.

Be sure to find out the next step in the hiring process and when it will take place. Also ask interviewers for their business cards and how they want you to follow up. Some people

CRITICAL THINKING

35

Plan to explore your career

Many students say that their purpose for being in school is to find a good job after graduation and create a fulfilling career beyond that. If this is true for you, then get specific. Declare exactly what you will do each term to explore your options and move closer to the career of your dreams.

Use the following worksheet to stimulate your thinking. It lists examples of activities that can be useful in exploring your career. Use the blank spaces to add more activities of your own. For purposes of this exercise, include only the activities that are most directly related to your career choices.

Notice that the worksheet includes a column for reflections. This is a place to note how useful the activity was for you, along with the key discoveries and intentions that resulted.

Make copies of this page before writing on it so that you can redo this exercise in the future. Update the worksheet every term or as your planned activities change.

Keep copies of your completed worksheet for each term. You'll find them useful when creating your résumé and applying for jobs, internships, or graduate school.

ACTIVITY	DATES	REFLECTIONS
Internship Working at the help desk for students at the campus computer center	6/1/19 to 8/30/19 (completed)	I discovered that this job calls for patience and the ability to listen! I intend to develop the habit of defining problems exactly *before* recommending solutions. When I do that, the solutions tend to be more effective and easier to explain.
Employment Apply for a part-time job staffing a help desk for computer users at a local business off-campus	6/1/20 to 8/30/20 (planned for next summer)	

ACTIVITY	DATES	REFLECTIONS
Internship		
Employment		
Courses		
Campus activities		
Workshops		
Career Center Services		
Books to read		
Other		
Other		
Other		
Other		
Other		
Other		

are fine with a phone call, fax, email, or other form of online communication. Others prefer a good, old-fashioned letter.

If you're truly interested in the job and feel comfortable with the interviewer, ask one more question: "Do you have any concerns about hiring me?" Listen carefully to the reply. Then respond to each concern in a polite way.

AFTER THE INTERVIEW

Now comes follow-up. This step can give you the edge that leads to a job offer.

Pull out the business cards from the people who interviewed you. Write them thank-you notes, following each person's preference for paper-based or online contact. Do this within two business days after the interview.

If you talked to several people at the same company, then write a different note to each one. Besides thanking each person for an interview, mention something that you discussed. Also alert your references that they might get a contact from the interviewers.

Within five business days, find a reason to contact the interviewer again. For example, email a link to an interesting article and explain how it might be useful. If you have a website with a blog, let the interviewer know about a recent post. Reinforce the value you will bring to the company team.

If you get turned down for the job after your interview, don't take it personally. Every interview is a source of feedback about what works—and what doesn't work—in contacting employers. Use that feedback to interview more effectively next time.

Also remember that each person you talked to is now a member of your network. This is true even if you do not get a job offer. Follow up by asking interviewers to keep you in mind for future job openings. Using this approach, you gain from every interview, no matter what the outcome. ✖

Join a diverse WORKPLACE

Rawpixel.com/Shutterstock.com

As companies look for ways to gain overseas market share, they will hire people who can enter a global environment with ease. To develop this quality of a master employee, experiment with the following strategies.

EXPECT DIFFERENCES

People differ. This fact is obvious. It's also easy to forget. Most of us unconsciously judge others by a single set of standards: our own. That can lead to communication breakdown. Consider some possible examples:

- A man in Costa Rica works for a multinational company. He turns down a promotion that would take his family to California.

This choice mystifies the company's executives. Yet the man has grandparents who are in ill health, and leaving them behind would be taboo in his culture.

- A Native American woman avoids eye contact with her superiors. Her coworkers see her as aloof. However, she comes from a culture where people seldom make eye contact with their superiors.

- A Caucasian woman from Ohio travels to Mexico City on business. She shows up promptly for a 9:00 a.m. meeting, and finds that it starts 30 minutes late and goes an hour beyond its scheduled ending time. She's entered a culture with a flexible sense of time.

To prevent misunderstandings, remember that culture touches every aspect of human behavior, ranging from the ways people greet one another to the ways they resolve conflict. Differences in culture could affect any encounter you have with coworkers. Expecting differences up front helps you keep an open mind.

MIND THE DETAILS

Pay attention to details that people from a given culture will use to form first impressions of you. Lydia Ramsey, author of *Manners that Sell: Adding the Polish That Builds Profits*, suggests these strategies:[6]

- **Shake hands appropriately.** Although the handshake is a near-universal form of greeting, people do it differently across the world. You might have been coached to take a firm grip, make eye contact, pump twice, and then let go. In other countries, however, people might prefer a lighter grip or longer contact. When traveling to the Middle East, you might even be greeted with a kiss or hug. Observe closely to discover the norm.

- **When in doubt, dress up.** Americans are relatively informal about workplace fashion. In many cultures, there are no "casual days." Formal business wear is expected every day. Dress up unless it's clearly okay to do otherwise.

- **Treat business cards carefully.** In many cultures, the way that you exchange cards conveys your respect for others. When someone gives you a card, take a second to look at it. Then offer your thanks and place the card in a folder or briefcase with other work-related documents. Don't stash it quickly in a pocket or purse.

- **Respect titles and names.** Though Americans like to do business on a first-name basis, this is acceptable in some cultures only among family members. Avoid misunderstandings by using last names and job titles when you greet people in work settings.

PUT MESSAGES IN CONTEXT

When speaking to people of another culture, you might find that words carry only part of an intended message. In many countries, strong networks of shared assumptions form a context for communication.

As an example, people from some Asian and Arabic countries might not include every detail of an agreement in a written contract. These people often place a high value on keeping verbal promises. Spelling out all the details in writing might be considered an insult. Knowing such facts can help you prevent and resolve conflicts in the workplace.

BE WILLING TO BRIDGE GAPS

Simply being *willing* to change your behavior can be just as crucial as knowing about another group's customs or learning their language. People from other cultures might sense your attitude and reach out to you.

Begin by displaying some key attributes of a critical thinker. Be open-minded and willing to suspend judgment. Notice when you make assumptions based on another person's accent, race, religion, sexual orientation, or gender. Become willing to discover your own biases, listen fully to people with many points of view, enter new territory, and even feel uncomfortable at times.

It's worth it. Joining a diverse workplace gives you opportunities to learn, make friends, and expand your career options. ✖

Put your
HEALTH
to work

Few students want another lecture about the health risks of drug dependence, unprotected sex, sleep deprivation, and a high-fat diet.

© iStockphoto.com/AlbanyPictures

You already know about that. What students might forget, however, is that poor health can hurt their chances for getting a job, keeping a job, and earning more money.

One quality of a master student—and master employee—is a strong work ethic. This includes showing up for work, staying alert, and tackling tasks with energy. Employers hire people with these characteristics and reward them with more opportunities and higher salaries. Use the following strategies to gain those benefits.

Manage your overall health. Losing sleep, skipping exercise, and eating poorly can take a toll on your ability to work. Getting more rest, physical activity, and nutritious food can lift your mood during difficult projects and boost your stamina for long days on the job.

Manage your energy levels at work. Once you've got a job, give it your best. Whenever possible, save demanding tasks for times when your physical and mental energy peaks.

Take advantage of scheduled breaks and meal times. Rather than heading to the lounge to guzzle coffee or fill up on sweets, consider going outside for a walk and breath of fresh air.

If you sit for long hours at a computer, prevent eyestrain. Turn away from the screen and rest your eyes from time to time. Looking out a window or at a distant object can help.

In addition, pay attention to your posture. Adjust your chair so that you can sit comfortably, with your back relaxed and your spine erect. Place a pillow or small cushion behind your lower back. Also remember that crossing your legs while sitting can reduce circulation and leave you with sore muscles.

Manage your projects. According to David Allen, consultant and author of *Getting Things Done: The Art of Stress-Free Productivity*, most professionals are working on anywhere from 30 to 100 projects at any given time.[7] This can be a major source of stress. To stay on top of your workload, Allen suggests that you make two lists.

The first is a list of all your active projects. This step might sound obvious, and it's easy to forget when your workload gets heavy. With a projects list in hand, you know exactly what you've agreed to complete. You might also discover that there are more projects than you can possibly do. If so, see if you can delegate projects to other people and say no to any new projects.

The second is a list of the *very next action* that you will take to move each project forward. Including only next actions will make this list shorter and help you focus on the most important tasks.

After making these two lists, you might be surprised by all the details you were trying to remember. Getting projects and next actions out of your head and onto lists is a way to keep your mind clear and reduce stress.

Manage stress during a job search. Job hunting can raise anyone's anxiety level. If you face this challenge, discover any stress-inducing thoughts and think critically about them. Despite what people say, for example, it is never true that "there are no jobs out there." Jobs are always opening up as people retire, find new jobs in their career field, or change careers. Even in January 2009, during the height of a recession, 4,300,000 people in the United States found new jobs. In addition, 3,000,000 jobs went unfilled.[8]

Also be willing to change your behavior. When the economy contracts, competition for jobs increases. People who are persistent and flexible in their strategies will gain an edge. If one approach to job hunting fails, then use another one. Reading help-wanted ads and sending out résumés are just a few possibilities. Others are networking, going to state and federal employment agencies, working temporary jobs, volunteering, taking a part-time job while looking for a full-time position, starting a business, and directly approaching companies that interest you.

Take full advantage of health benefits. Your employee health benefits might include screenings for a variety of conditions, paid time off for medical appointments, and discounts for health club memberships. Set up a meeting with someone at work who can explain all the options available to you. ✖

PERSIST

on the path of mastery

iStockphoto.com/Esolla

You are on the edge of a universe so miraculous and full of wonder that your imagination, even at its most creative moment, cannot encompass it Paths are open to lead you to worlds beyond your wildest dreams.

If this sounds like a pitch for the latest recreational drug, it might be. That "drug" is enthusiasm. It is automatically generated by your body when you are learning, planning, taking risks, achieving goals, and discovering new worlds inside and outside your skin. This is a path of mastery that you can travel for the rest of your life.

Consider the possibility that you can create the life of your dreams. Your responses to any of the ideas, exercises, and Journal Entries in this book can lead you to think new thoughts, say new things, and do what you never believed you could do. If you're willing to master new ways to learn, the possibilities are endless.

The key is to continue the cycle of discovery, intention, and action that's included in every chapter of this book. In other words, persist with the master student process.

If you used this book fully—if you actively participated in reading the content, writing the Journal Entries and Practicing Critical Thinking exercises, and putting the suggestions to work—you have had quite a journey.

Recall some high points of that journey. The first half of this book is about the nuts and bolts of education—the business of acquiring knowledge. All of this activity prepares you for another goal of education—generating new knowledge. Meeting this goal leads you to the topics in the second half of this book: thinking for yourself, enhancing your communication skills, and creating a unique place for yourself in the world. All are steps on the path of becoming a master student.

Now what? What's your next step? Start with the following answers. Then create more of your own.

Keep a journal. Psycho-therapist Ira Progoff based his Intensive Journal System on the idea that regular journaling can be a path to life-changing insights.[9] To begin journaling, consider buying a bound notebook in which to record your private reflections and dreams for the future. Get a notebook that will be worthy of your personal discoveries and intentions. Or keep an electronic journal on your computer. Write or type in your journal daily. Record what you are learning about yourself and the world.

Write about your hopes, wishes, and goals. Keep a record of significant events. Consider using the format of Discovery Statements and Intention Statements that you learned in this book.

Take a workshop. Schooling doesn't have to stop at graduation, and it doesn't have to take place on a campus. In most

cities, a variety of organizations sponsor ongoing workshops covering topics from cosmetology to cosmology.

Take workshops to learn skills, understand the world, and discover yourself. You can be trained in cardiopulmonary resuscitation (CPR), attend a lecture on developing nations, or take a course on assertiveness training.

Take an unrelated class. Sign up for a class that is totally unrelated to your major. If you are studying economics, take a physics course. If you

_____

If you didn't get everything you wanted from this book, it's not too late. You can read part of it, or all of it, again at any time.

_____

are planning to be a doctor, take an accounting course. Take a course that will help you develop new computer skills and expand your possibilities for online learning.

You can discover a lot about yourself and your intended future when you step out of old patterns. In addition to formal courses offered at your school, check out local community education courses. They offer a low-cost alternative that poses no threat to your grade point average.

Travel. See the world. Visit new neighborhoods. Travel to other countries. Explore. Find out what it looks like inside buildings that you normally have no reason to enter, museums that you never found interesting before, cities that are out of the way, forests and mountains that lie beyond your old boundaries, and far-off places that require planning and saving to reach.

Get counseling. Solving emotional problems is not the only reason to visit a counselor, therapist, or psychologist. These people are excellent resources for personal growth. You can use counseling to look at and talk about yourself in ways that might be uncomfortable for anyone except a trained professional. Counseling offers a chance to focus exclusively on yourself—something that is usually not possible in normal social settings.

Form a support group. Just as a well-organized study group can promote your success in school, an organized support group can help you reach goals in other areas of your life.

Today, people in support groups help one another lose weight, stay sober, cope with chronic illness, recover from emotional trauma, and overcome drug addiction.

Groups can also brainstorm possibilities for job hunting, career planning, parenting, solving problems in relationships, promoting spiritual growth—strategies for reaching almost any goal you choose.

Find a mentor or become one. A mentor relationship can bridge the boundaries of age, race, and culture. Seek coaching from experienced people whom you respect and admire. Use them as role models. If they are willing, ask them to be sounding boards for your plans and ideas. You'll find people who are flattered to be asked and happy to mentor you for free. Skilled mentors often find that the joy of working with people is all the reward that they need.

You can get just as much value out of being a mentor as you can by having one. If you want to perfect your skills as a master student, for example, teach them to someone else. Offer to coach another student in taking notes, predicting test questions, or writing papers. Assist people to gain skills that support success in school and in the workforce. If they object to being mentored for free, then offer your services in exchange for childcare, free lunches, or something else you value.

Make a habit of asking powerful questions. You can also mentor yourself. The key is asking questions that stretch your thinking. Powerful questions invite more than one answer. They start from the assumption that you can choose your response to any circumstance, no matter how challenging. And they invite action.

As you pose questions, take a cue from the key words at the beginning of this chapter. For example, ask: *Why* am I in school? *What* new outcomes in life do I want? *How* can I produce that outcome? *What if* I could be relaxed and productive as I achieve my goals?

Consider further education and training. Your career plan might call for continuing education, additional certifications, or an advanced degree. Remember that the strategies in this book can help you gain new knowledge and skills at any point in your life.

Redo this book. If you didn't get everything you wanted from this book, it's not too late. You can read part of it, or all of it, again at any time.

Also redo portions of the book that you found valuable. Redo the quizzes to test your ability to recall certain information. Redo the exercises that were particularly effective for you. They can work again. Many of the exercises in this book can produce a different result after a few months. You are changing and your responses change too.

You can also redo any of the Journal Entries in this book. Use them as a springboard for creating a journal that you keep for the rest of your life.

As you redo this book or any part of it, reconsider techniques that you skimmed over or skipped before. They might work for you now. Modify the suggestions, or add new ones. Redoing this book can refresh and fine-tune your study habits.

Another way to redo this book is to retake your student success course. People who do this often say that the second time is much different from the first. They pick up ideas and techniques that they missed the first time around and gain deeper insight into things they already know. ◗

practicing
CRITICAL THINKING

36

Plan to persist with an academic plan

One powerful tool for persisting in school until you graduate is an academic plan. (At some schools, it is called a *degree plan* instead.) This document is basically a list of all the courses you plan to take and *when* you plan to take each one. Use it to chart your term-by-term progress in completing your degree.

An academic plan is much more than a list. You can use it to create a life-changing conversation about what you want from school and how you intend to get it.

Use the following instructions to do this exercise:

- To begin, note the term you plan to take each course (e.g., *Spring 2016*). Be sure to check your college catalog for course prerequisites or corequisites.
- In the first column of the table, list the name of each course you plan to take that term.
- Use the second column to write the number of credits for each course.
- In the third column, list the grade you receive in each course.

- The final column is for brief notes about each course. Designate it as a general education requirement, major requirement, elective, or course that does not count toward a degree.

Below the table are places to record your grade point average (GPA) for each individual term ("this term") and for all the terms you've completed so far ("cumulative"). Check your school's policies on calculating a GPA. The school website might include an online GPA calculator.

Finally, check your rough academic plan to see that it:

- Gives you the total number of credits you need to graduate
- Meets your school's requirements for general education
- Meets the requirements for your major, your minor, or both

After completing this exercise, reach out to your instructors, academic advisor, and counselor for help in creating a more formal academic plan. Be sure to update that plan at least once each term to reflect any changes in your declared major and course schedule.

TERM: _____

Course	Credits	Grade	Notes

GPA (this term): _____

GPA: (cumulative): _____

TERM: _____

Course	Credits	Grade	Notes

GPA (this term): _____

GPA: (cumulative): _____

TERM: _____

Course	Credits	Grade	Notes

GPA (this term): _____

GPA: (cumulative): _____

TERM: _____

Course	Credits	Grade	Notes

GPA (this term): _____

GPA: (cumulative): _____

Tools for lifelong
LEARNING

Going back to school is one way to gain knowledge, skills, and certifications for a new job. Another option is to teach yourself. To build financial security and career opportunities, develop a habit of lifelong learning. Get started with the following tools.

Jamie Grill/Blend Images/Getty Images

MAKE TIME TO LEARN

Yes, it is possible to further your education even if you have a full-time job and family. Look for holes in your daily schedule and devote them to learning something. Reduce time on social media and aimless web surfing. Listen to podcasts or audio books while commuting to work. Spend 15 minutes over your lunch break reading a book. Take time every day to learn something. Also keep a "to-learn" list with ideas for skills you want to develop in the future. It can become as important as your to-do list.

GO ONLINE

Begin by doing an Internet search on any topic that interests you. To get ideas, go online to Alltop (**alltop.com**), a site that links to articles and blog posts from many popular websites. Also look for websites related to your courses, including blogs by your instructors and the authors of your textbooks.

Some websites are devoted to lifelong learning. Examples are:

- Mind Tools (**www.mindtools.com**)
- LearnOutLoud.com (**www.learnoutloud.com**)
- About.com (**www.about.com**)
- Instructional videos on YouTube (**www.youtube.com**)
- Open Culture (**www.openculture.com**), a growing collection of links to free ebooks, audio books, films, videos, and online courses.

- Lynda (**www.lynda.com**) and Treehouse (**https://teamtreehouse.com**)—video courses about developing software and building apps
- Codecademy (**www.codecademy.com**), Coursera (**www.coursera.org**), and Khan Academy (**www.khanacademy.org**)—online courses on a growing list of topics

For additional ways to learn online, do an Internet search using key words such as *online education, virtual education, instructional websites,* and *distance learning.* If you're an iTunes user, also check the offerings from iTunes U. Make the Internet your classroom.

LEARN AT WORK

Ask your supervisor for projects that will help you master new skills. If your company offers training during work hours, sign up. Also ask your coworkers about what they do and how they learned to do it. Seize opportunities to join new teams, tackle new tasks, and build your résumé.

LAUNCH SIDE PROJECTS

Many companies start as part-time projects that expand to full-time enterprises. Brainstorm a list of businesses that you could build outside of work hours. Search the Internet for information about how to develop and market them. Ask a reference librarian to help you find related books.

As you have a minimum viable product or service, start selling it. Ask your customers and clients how to make it better. If your first ideas fail, view that as feedback. You're learning about what people really want and are willing to buy.

MEET PEOPLE

Conversation still offers one of the richest and most natural ways to learn. Start now by meeting with fellow students and instructors outside of class. You could develop friendships that last a lifetime.

Informal classes and workshops offer another way to meet people interested in learning something. Check your local library's calendar for upcoming events that will take place on campus and in your larger community. ✱

practicing
CRITICAL THINKING

37

This book shouts, "Use me!"

Becoming a Master Student is designed to be used for years. The success strategies presented here are not likely to become habits overnight. There are more suggestions than can be put into action immediately. Some of what is discussed might not apply to your life right now but might be just what you could use in a few months.

Plan to keep this book and use it again. Imagine that your book has a mouth. (Visualize the mouth.) Also imagine that it has arms and legs. (Visualize them.)

Now picture your book sitting on a shelf or table that you see every day. Imagine a time when you are having trouble in school and struggling to be successful as a student. Visualize your book jumping up and down, shouting, "Use me! Read me! I might have the solution to your problem, and I know I can help you solve it."

This is a memory technique to remind you to use a resource. Sometimes when you are stuck, all you need is a small push or a list of possible actions. At those times, hear your book shout, "Use me!"

The Discovery Wheel: Coming full circle

This book doesn't work. It is worthless. Only you can work. Only you can make a difference and use this book to become a more effective student.

The purpose of this book is to give you the opportunity to change your behavior. This exercise gives you a chance to see what behaviors you have actually changed on your journey toward becoming a master student. If there are some gaps between your intentions and actions, this is your chance to tell the truth about that and choose what to do about it.

Answer each item in this exercise quickly and honestly. Then record your results on the Discovery Wheel in Figure 10.1. The scores on this Discovery Wheel indicate your current strengths and weaknesses on your path toward becoming a master student.

If you completed the earlier Discovery Wheel in this book, then you can also compare the two sets of scores. Keep in mind that your commitment to change allows you to become a master student. *Your scores might be lower here than on your earlier Discovery Wheel.* That's okay. Lower scores might result from increased self-awareness and honesty as well as other valuable assets. The Skills Snapshot that follows this exercise provides an opportunity to update your intentions in light of what you've discovered.

Note: If you did your previous Discovery Wheel online, do it online again. This will help you compare your two sets of responses more accurately.

5 points	This statement is always or almost always true of me.
4 points	This statement is often true of me.
3 points	This statement is true of me about half the time.
2 points	This statement is seldom true of me.
1 point	This statement is never or almost never true of me.

1 Attitude

_____ I enjoy learning.

_____ I understand and apply the concept of multiple intelligences.

_____ I connect my courses to my purpose for being in school.

_____ I make a habit of assessing my personal strengths and areas for improvement.

_____ I am satisfied with how I am progressing toward achieving my goals.

_____ I use my knowledge of learning styles to support my success in school.

_____ I am willing to consider any idea that can help me succeed in school.

_____ I regularly remind myself of the benefits I intend to get from my education.

_____ **Total Score: Attitude**

2 Time

_____ I set long-term goals and periodically review them.

_____ I set short-term goals to support my long-term goals.

_____ I write a plan for each day and each week.

_____ I assign priorities to what I choose to do each day.

_____ I plan review time so I don't have to cram before tests.

_____ I plan regular recreation time.

_____ I adjust my study time to meet the demands of individual courses.

_____ I have adequate time each day to accomplish what I plan.

_____ **Total Score: Time**

3 Memory

_____ I am confident of my ability to remember.

_____ I can remember people's names.

_____ At the end of a lecture, I can summarize what was presented.

_____ I apply techniques that enhance my memory skills.

_____ I can recall information when I'm under pressure.

_____ I remember important information clearly and easily.

_____ I can jog my memory when I have difficulty recalling.

_____ I can relate new information to what I've already learned.

_____ **Total Score: Memory**

4 Reading

_____ I preview and review reading assignments.

_____ When reading, I ask myself questions about the material.

_____ I underline or highlight important passages when reading.

_____ When I read textbooks, I am alert and awake.

_____ I relate what I read to my life.

_____ I select a reading strategy to fit the type of material I'm reading.

_____ I take effective notes when I read.

_____ When I don't understand what I'm reading, I note my questions and find answers.

_____ **Total Score: Reading**

5 Notes

_____ When I am in class, I focus my attention.

_____ I take notes in class.

_____ I know about many methods for taking notes and choose those that work best for me.

_____ I distinguish important material and note key phrases in a lecture.

_____ I copy down material that the instructor writes on the board or overhead display.

_____ I can put important concepts into my own words.

_____ My notes are valuable for review.

_____ I review class notes within 24 hours.

_____ **Total Score: Notes**

6 Tests

_____ I use techniques to manage stress related to exams.

_____ I manage my time during exams and am able to complete them.

_____ I am able to predict test questions.

_____ I adapt my test-taking strategy to the kind of test I'm taking.

_____ I understand what essay questions ask and can answer them completely and accurately.

_____ I start reviewing for tests at the beginning of the term.

_____ I continue reviewing for tests throughout the term.

_____ My sense of personal worth is independent of my test scores.

_____ **Total Score: Tests**

7 Thinking

_____ I have flashes of insight and think of solutions to problems at unusual times.

_____ I use brainstorming to generate solutions to a variety of problems.

_____ When I get stuck on a creative project, I use specific methods to get unstuck.

_____ I learn by thinking about ways to contribute to the lives of other people.

_____ I am willing to consider different points of view and alternative solutions.

_____ I can detect common errors in logic.

_____ I construct viewpoints by drawing on information and ideas from many sources.

_____ As I share my viewpoints with others, I am open to their feedback.

_____ **Total Score: Thinking**

8 Communicating

_____ I am honest with others about who I am, what I feel, and what I want.

_____ Other people tell me that I am a good listener.

_____ I can communicate my upset and anger without blaming others.

_____ I can make friends and create valuable relationships in a new setting.

_____ I am open to being with people I don't especially like in order to learn from them.

_____ I can effectively plan and research a large writing assignment.

_____ I create first drafts without criticizing my writing, then edit later for clarity, accuracy, and coherence.

_____ I know ways to prepare and deliver effective speeches.

_____ **Total Score: Communicating**

9 Money

_____ I am in control of my personal finances.

_____ I can access a variety of resources to finance my education.

_____ I am confident that I will have enough money to complete my education.

_____ I take on debts carefully and repay them on time.

_____ I have long-range financial goals and a plan to meet them.

_____ I make regular deposits to a savings account.

_____ I pay off the balance on credit card accounts each month.

_____ I can have fun without spending money.

_____ **Total Score: Money**

10 Purpose

_____ I see learning as a lifelong process.

_____ I relate school to what I plan to do for the rest of my life.

_____ I see problems and tough choices as opportunities for learning and personal growth.

_____ I use technology in a way that enriches my life and supports my success.

_____ I am developing skills that will be useful in the workplace.

_____ I take responsibility for the quality of my education—and my life.

_____ I live by a set of values that translates into daily actions.

_____ I am willing to accept challenges even when I'm not sure how to meet them.

_____ **Total Score: Purpose**

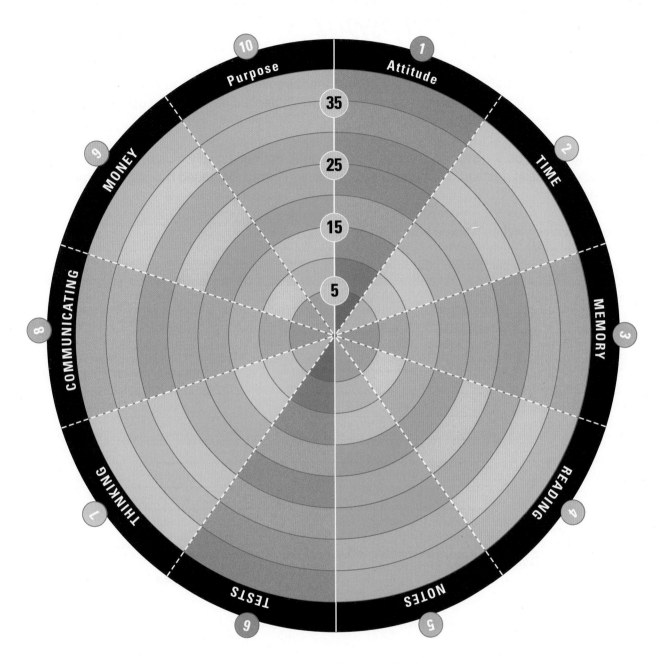

Figure 10.1 *Your Discovery Wheel.*

Filling in Your Discovery Wheel

Using the total score from each category, shade in each corresponding wedge of the Discovery Wheel in Figure 10.1.
Use different colors, if you want. For example, you could use green to denote areas you want to work on.
When you have finished, complete the Skills Snapshot that follows.

The purpose of this exercise is to (1) review both of the Discovery Wheels you completed in this book, (2) summarize your insights from doing them, and (3) declare how you will use these insights to promote your continued success in school.

Again, a lower score on the second Discovery Wheel does not necessarily indicate decreased personal effectiveness. Instead, the lower score could result from increased honesty and greater self-awareness.

Enter your Discovery Wheel scores from both chapters.

	Earlier Chapter	This Chapter
Attitude	_____	_____
Time	_____	_____
Memory	_____	_____
Reading	_____	_____
Notes	_____	_____
Tests	_____	_____
Thinking	_____	_____
Communicating	_____	_____
Money	_____	_____
Purpose	_____	_____

Comparing the Discovery Wheel in this chapter with the Discovery Wheel in the earlier chapter, I discovered that I . . .

In the next six months, I intend to review the following articles from this book for additional suggestions I could use:

Celebrate your gains, clarify your intentions

This Journal Entry invites you to step back from your daily routine and reflect on what you've gained from your student success course. If you've fully participated with this book, then you've made discoveries and created intentions that can make a huge difference in the continuing quality of your life. Don't let this work go to waste. Capture the high points of your learning now, before they fade into distant memories.

There are at least two major reasons for doing a Journal Entry such as this one. The first is to celebrate your progress. Believe it or not, success is something that's easy to overlook. Our shortcomings and failures have a magnetic pull on our attention. Many students find it easy to focus on what's *not* working in their lives rather than what *is* working. Do yourself a favor by taking the time to shift your attention and choose a new conversation. Noticing any evidence of progress, no matter how small, can be tremendously motivating.

Second, you can turn your mistakes into your most powerful teachers. Every mistake has a lesson to offer us *if* we take the time to find it.

Set aside about one hour to complete the following sentences. This could be one of the most productive hours that you spend this term.

In preparation, you might find that it helps to quickly look through this book and glance over your responses to previous Journal Entries and exercises. When you're done, immediately begin writing.

Discovery

In reflecting on my experience with this course, I discovered that my biggest gain was . . .

The most useful thing I learned was . . .

The smartest decision I made was . . .

The biggest risk I took was . . .

My biggest surprise was . . .

The biggest compliment that I received was . . .

The biggest compliment that I gave was . . .

If I could repeat this course, the most important thing I would do differently is . . .

Intention

After reviewing my Discovery Statements, the goal that I would be most excited to achieve this year is . . .

Another goal that excites me is . . .

The people that I am most committed to loving are . . .

Action

As I reflect on my intention to complete my degree, the most important new habit I will adopt is . . .

Another important habit that I will develop is . . .

practicing CRITICAL THINKING

38

Are you getting there?

It's easy to set long-term goals and then forget about them because they seem so distant. The purpose of this exercise is for you to take those goals out of the closet, dust them off, and determine whether you are actually on the way to meeting them. Make this your first step toward a lifelong habit of monitoring your progress on the things that matter most to you.

To begin, remember that big goals—such as changing your career or starting a business—are achieved by stringing together dozens or even hundreds of daily tasks. On the way to meeting these goals you might also reach some milestones, or short-term goals. Say that your long-term goal is to finish school in four years. Your short-term goals could include completing a certain number of course credits each year between today and your projected graduation date.

Use the following steps to shine a light on your dreams and make them come alive again. Start by reviewing just one of your long-term goals. Then apply the same steps to the rest of them.

Step 1

Review your responses to the Journal Entries, Practicing Critical Thinking exercises, and Skills Snapshots in this book. Look for long-term goals: those that will take 5 or more years to achieve. Gather all those goals into a single list.

Step 2

Now choose one of the most important long-term goals from your list. Write it down in the space below:

Step 3

Think about whether you are still committed to reaching this goal. Does it still excite you? Does it connect with your heart as well as your head? If not, then rewrite it here. Or simply let go of it and replace it with another long-term goal that you truly want to achieve.

Step 4

Next, consider setting some short-term goals that will help you meet the long-term goal that you just identified. List those short-term goals here along with a target date for meeting each one.

Step 5

Now go to the Time chapter of this book and look at your completed Time Monitor/Time Plan. Identify everything you did that brought you closer to achieving the long-term goal or any of the related short-term goals you listed above. Then fill in the table on next page by listing those activities and the amount of time that you spent on them.

Activities	Time spent

Step 6

The final step is to reflect on the data that you just collected. Write this in the form of Discovery and Intention Statements.

When looking at my daily activities in light of my goals, I discovered that . . .

To align my activities with my goals, I intend to . . .

Ben Barry }

Now self-employed and living in San Francisco, worked for Facebook as one of the company's first communication designers.

Ben Barry was on Facebook one day in 2008 and clicked on a link about job openings. He discovered that the social network was starting to hire designers—the occupation listed on his profile. He applied.

Soon Barry was in Silicon Valley to interview with a team of people at Facebook. They offered him a job and he took it.

Over the next six years Barry worked on a series of highly visible projects, including the design of Facebook's new campus in Menlo Park, California and the visual side of the company's brand.

It was a role that allowed him to dwell in two worlds at once. As a "digital native," Barry likes to build websites and code software. In addition, he enjoys being offline and getting his hands dirty while drawing, binding books, and silk-screening posters. As a side project, he spent a string of nights and weekends setting up an old-fashioned print shop in a warehouse on the Facebook campus. Over time this personal passion expanded to become the Facebook Analog Research Laboratory, an art program that's popular with employees.

"As the company of Facebook grew, we faced a lot of challenges," Barry notes on **benbarry.com**. "Over the years, a lot of formative company discussions and debates had happened in Facebook Groups, over email, or in person. Those who had been present at the time had context, but for new employees that information was difficult to find, even if you knew what you were looking for."

Barry's solution was the "little red book"—a printed and bound collection of images and text that captures Facebook's history, mission, and culture. It includes slogans such as these:

- *Facebook was not originally created in order to be a company. It was built to accomplish a social mission—to make the world more open and connected.*
- *Changing how people communicate will always change the world.*
- *Greatness and comfort rarely coexist.*
- *We don't build services to make money; we make money to build better services.*

Barry admires people who know how to make art *and* make money—who can think creatively *and* meet deadlines. In recent interviews he shared insights for anyone who wants to thrive in the job market of the twenty-first century.

Block out periods of time for distraction-free work. The conditions of the modern office make it hard to focus our attention, much less get anything done. Anyone with access to a computer is only one click away from email, social networks, and web surfing. Then there's the fact of meetings, which can eat up large chunks of the workday.

While at Facebook, Barry responded to these challenges by guarding his calendar. "I kept a schedule where Monday and Friday I was available for meetings, and Friday morning I had open office hours," he said. "Tuesday and Thursday I was in the office, but my calendar was blocked off so I could work on whatever I needed to, and Wednesdays I worked from my desk at home so I could be in a distraction free environment."[10]

Learn to sell your ideas. While he was studying design at the North Texas State University, Barry's teachers stressed the need to do good work. Although this is obviously crucial, he says, it's not enough. Dealing with budgets and satisfying clients are just as important.

"When you come out of school, you have to convince people that you have good ideas so they will give you money to do stuff," Barry said. "A big part of this is knowing your own weaknesses and then identifying and partnering with people that can help you accomplish your goals."[11]

Finish! Barry talks about friends who are talented designers but fail to follow through. They propose big ideas and ambitious plans. Then they get derailed by boredom, distraction, and perfectionism.

In response, Barry quotes an old line: "Done is better than perfect." This does not mean submitting sloppy work. Instead, deliver the best product or service that you can while also meeting your due dates.

In the new economy, this quality will give you a competitive edge, says Barry. "I think if you follow through on projects and just put the tiniest little effort into promoting yourself and have the tiniest bit of self-confidence, you can get the job you want."[12]

Ben Barry *demonstrates the power of persisting through all phases of a project—from brainstorming ideas to delivering a finished product.*

QUIZ

Chapter 10

1. According to the text, employers have one main purpose for reviewing résumés—choosing which people to contact for a job interview.
   a. True
   b. False

2. The main point of "Another option: Don't plan your career" is to:
   a. Forget about career planning totally
   b. Plan your career only when absolutely necessary
   c. Choose a direction, take one new step in that direction, reflect on what you learn, and choose your next step
   d. Never write a cover letter or résumé

3. The _____ job market is a group of job openings that have not been advertised.

4. According to the text, job interviewers often have certain questions in mind—even if they don't directly *ask* them. These questions include:
   a. How did you find out about us?
   b. Will we be comfortable working with you?
   c. Will you learn this job quickly?
   d. What makes you different from other applicants?
   e. All of the answer choices

5. According to the text, the best strategy for career planning is to follow your passion above all.
   a. True
   b. False

6. Examples of transferable skills include:
   a. Accounting
   b. Listening
   c. Speaking
   d. Both listening and speaking
   e. Both accounting and speaking

7. An *entrepreneur* is someone:
   a. Who owns a business
   b. Whose goals include making money
   c. Who takes a risk by creating products, services, or both
   d. Works hard to make sure that people buy products, services, or both
   e. All of the answer choices

8. The text suggests that you *think* like an entrepreneur even if you are currently an employee.
   a. True
   b. False

9. According to the text, offering a limited amount of work for free is never a recommended strategy for getting hired.
   a. True
   b. False

10. The text suggests that both employers and job applicants struggle with the hiring process because:
    a. There are too many laws and regulations that apply to this process.
    b. Employers are usually in a hurry to hire someone and don't take the time to make careful decisions.
    c. An employer's process for hiring is often the *opposite* of an applicant's process for getting hired.
    d. None of the answer choices

SKILLS *snapshot*

If you fully participated with this chapter, then you've got a lot of ideas about staying on the path of mastery that you began with this book and with this course. Now take a few minutes to clarify your intentions about continuing on this path.

Discovery

My scores on the Purpose section on the first and second Discovery Wheel were . . .

What I now want most from my education is . . .

What I now want most from any career is . . .

Intention

The most important work-content skills that I intend to develop are . . .

The most important transferable skills that I intend to develop are . . .

I intend to use these skills to succeed in the workplace by . . .

Action

The very next thing that I will do to develop the work-content skills I just listed is . . .

The very next thing that I will do to develop the transferable skills I just listed is . . .

The
MASTER GUIDE
to Becoming a Master Student

It is impossible to summarize every strategy from *Becoming a Master Student* in two pages. However, it is possible to summarize the process that inspired all those strategies.

Robert Churchill/E+/Getty Images

You can use the **master student process** to create your own strategies for success in any area of life:

- **Discovery.** Tell the truth about your current thoughts, feelings, behaviors, and circumstances. Record the specifics in writing. Be honest and let go of self-judgment. Another name for this is taking a **First Step**.
- **Intention.** Based on your discoveries, commit to make specific changes in your behavior. As with discoveries, put your intentions in writing. Add them to your list of goals, your to-do list, or your calendar.
- **Action.** Translate your intentions into real changes in behavior. Successful people are those who consistently produce the results that they want. The secret is sustained action.

This process is a cycle. First, you write Discovery Statements about where you are now. Next, you write Intention Statements about where you want to be and the specific steps you will take to get there. Follow up with action—the sooner, the better.

A **master student** is someone who uses this process so often and so well that it becomes second nature. **Mastery** is a level of skill that goes beyond technique and beyond explanation.

ABOUT SUCCESS

Success means setting and achieving goals based on your values.

A **value** is something that you desire for its own sake—something you'd like to *be*. For example, you might want to be happy, healthy, loving, and competent. Values shape your goals and strategies.

A **goal** is any outcome or result that you desire. Goals lead to changes in what you *have* (such as more money or higher grades), in what you *do* (such as gaining a new skill), or both.

A **strategy** is any action that you take consistently over time in order to achieve a goal. Strategies might also be called *habits, tools, tips, techniques, methods, processes, procedures, skills,* or *suggestions.*

Becoming a Master Student is a catalog of success strategies. You can use these strategies to achieve any goal, including goals related to your success in school.

Adopt strategies in "baby steps." Start with small changes in behavior that you can do immediately—even when you don't feel motivated. Link each new behavior to a specific trigger, or cue. Then reward yourself each time that you practice the new behavior.

THE POWER PROCESSES

Students consistently find that certain strategies presented in this book are especially useful in achieving their goals. These "super strategies" are called **Power Processes**. They include the following:

Discover what you want. To more consistently get the results that you desire, carefully define your values and goals.

Ideas are tools. Rather than looking for what's wrong with a new idea, see whether you can find something in it that's potentially valuable.

Be here now. To do anything more effectively, give it your full attention.

Love your problems. To solve a problem, move beyond denial and resistance to acceptance and action.

Notice your pictures and let them go. To release frustration and take effective action, be willing to release rigid beliefs about the way things "ought" to be.

I create it all. When you experience a problem, ask whether it results from any of your own beliefs or behaviors.

Detach. Discover a source of serenity that does not depend on achieving any goal.

Embrace the new. Be willing to think what you've never thought before, to say what you've never said before, and to do what you've never done before.

Employ your word. Speak about your possibilities, preferences, passions, plans, and promises as a way to direct your behavior.

Risk being a fool. Remember that mastery calls for the courage to do something new, fail, make corrections, and fail again before succeeding.

Persist. Success is often about doing the gritty and unglamorous things that really work, day after day.

DISCOVERING YOURSELF

Move through a complete cycle of learning by asking:

- *Why?* Your answer to this question helps you discover a reason for learning (Mode 1).
- *What?* Your answer to this question helps you gather relevant information (Mode 2).
- *How?* Your answer to this question helps you experiment with ways to apply what you're learning (Mode 3).
- *What if?* Your answer to this question helps you integrate new knowledge and skills into your day-to-day life (Mode 4).

TIME

Use the Discovery–Intention–Action cycle to:

- Monitor your activities, and use the data you collect to make informed choices about how to spend your time.
- Use a monthly or yearly calendar to anticipate heavy demands on your time.
- Restate your wants as goals—specific outcomes with clear due dates.
- List the actions you'll take to achieve your goals on your to-do list and calendar.
- Overcome procrastination, accept feelings of discomfort about a task, and then move into action.

MEMORY

Use the Discovery–Intention–Action cycle to:

- Organize new material so that it is easier to remember.
- Change studying from a passive affair to an active process that involves all your senses.
- Engage your emotions, take advantage of your peak energy periods, and elaborate on new information.
- Review important ideas and information on a regular basis and recall them whenever you want.
- Experiment with a variety of memory strategies, including mnemonics.

READING

Use the Discovery–Intention–Action cycle to:

- Experiment with Muscle Reading, a process that includes previewing a text, reading to answer specific questions, and reviewing the answers.
- Monitor your understanding of a text and get past confusion.
- Adjust your reading rate to your purpose and the nature of the material.
- Expand your vocabulary.
- Develop information literacy—the ability to find information in appropriate sources, evaluate the information, and use it to achieve a purpose.
- Stay on top of your reading load in the midst of a busy life.

NOTES

Use the Discovery–Intention–Action cycle to:

- Get the most value from note taking by carefully observing what happens in class, recording the material that matters, and reviewing what you record.
- Experiment with variety of note-taking formats, such as the Cornell method, mind maps, outlines, and concept maps.
- Take effective notes on reading material.
- Continue taking effective notes even when you feel confused.
- Take effective notes for online coursework.

TESTS

Use the Discovery–Intention–Action cycle to:

- Predict test questions.
- Review important material several times before a test.
- Create study groups that promote your success.
- Manage your time effectively during a test and respond to questions in a variety of formats, such as multiple choice, true/false, and essay questions.
- Learn from tests after they are scored and returned to you.
- Manage test-related anxiety.

THINKING

Use the Discovery–Intention–Action cycle to:

- Think flexibly by moving freely through all the levels of Bloom's taxonomy (remembering, understanding, applying, analyzing, evaluating, and creating).

- Detect logical fallacies.
- Uncover assumptions.
- Make decisions in a way that balances creative and critical thinking.
- Define problems, create possible solutions, implement solutions, and evaluate them.
- Ask questions that deepen your thinking.
- Gain life-changing lessons from service-learning experiences.

COMMUNICATING

Use the Discovery–Intention–Action cycle to:

- Listen fully while another person speaks and respond in ways that deepen your relationship.
- Speak honestly about your thoughts and feelings without judging or blaming other people.
- Develop an emotional intelligence that makes you an effective team member.
- Manage conflict in a way that respects the views of all people involved.
- Write to achieve a specific purpose, complete a quick first draft, and allow time for revision.
- Create presentations that are organized, memorable, and designed for your audience.

MONEY

Use the Discovery–Intention–Action cycle to:

- Monitor how much money you earn and spend each month.
- Live within your means by increasing income.
- Live within your means by decreasing expenses.
- Use credit cards with caution.
- Borrow as little money as possible and select loans carefully.
- Plan to fund your education from now until graduation.

NEXT STEPS

Use the Discovery–Intention–Action cycle to:

- Develop work-content skills and transferable skills that are valued in the job market.
- Connect with people and services that can help you persist in school through graduation.
- Translate academic goals into daily tasks and celebrate when you complete them.
- Set and achieve career goals throughout your working life.
- Test your career choices through internships and other work experiences.
- Tap the hidden job market through a network of friends, relatives, coworkers, and fellow students.
- Create a résumé that is easy to scan and documents specific accomplishments in your education and work experience.
- Prepare for job interviews by practicing your answers to the common questions.
- Enhance your personal growth with tools such as continuing education, counseling, coaching, mentoring, and support groups. ✈

Endnotes

INTRODUCTION

1. A. H. Maslow, *The Farther Reaches of Human Nature* (New York: Viking Compass, 1972), 41–52.

2. Brad Isaac, "Jerry Seinfeld's Productivity Secret," Lifehacker, July 24, 2007, accessed February 12, 2016, from http://lifehacker.com/281626/jerry-seinfelds-productivity-secret.

3. Charles Duhigg, *The Power of Habit: Why We Do What We Do in Life and Business* (New York: Random House, 2012), 276–86.

CHAPTER 1

1. David A. Kolb, *Experiential Learning: Experience as the Source of Learning and Development* (Englewood Cliffs, NJ: Prentice Hall, 1984).

2. Douglas A. Bernstein, Louis A. Penner, Alison Clarke-Stewart, and Edward J. Roy, *Psychology* (Boston: Houghton Mifflin, 2006), 368–9.

3. Howard Gardner, *Frames of Mind: The Theory of Multiple Intelligences* (New York: Basic Books, 1993).

4. "VARK—a guide to learning styles," 2016, accessed February 12, 2016 from http://vark-learn.com.

CHAPTER 2

1. Stephen R. Covey, *The Seven Habits of Highly Effective People: Restoring the Character Ethic* (New York: Simon & Schuster, 1990), 150–4.

2. Mei-Ching Lien, Eric Ruthruff, and James C. Johnston, "Attentional Limitations in Doing Two Tasks at Once: The Search for Exceptions," *Current Directions in Psychological Science* 15, no. 2 (2005): 89–93.

3. Alan Lakein, *How to Get Control of Your Time and Your Life* (New York: New American Library, 1973; reissue 1996).

4. Stephen Chew, "How to Get the Most Out of Studying," accessed February 12, 2016, from http://www.samford.edu/departments/academic-success-center/how-to-study.

5. David Allen, *Getting Things Done: The Art of Stress-Free Productivity* (New York: Penguin, 2001), 46–7.

6. Linda Sapadin, with Jack Maguire, *It's About Time! The Six Styles of Procrastination and How to Overcome Them* (New York: Penguin, 1997).

7. Michael Pollan, "Unhappy Meals," *New York Times*, January 28, 2007, accessed February 12, 2016, from http://michaelpollan.com/articles-archive/unhappy-meals/.

8. Tom Rath, *Eat Move Sleep: How Small Choices Lead to Big Changes* (Arlington, VA: Missionday, 2013).

9. Ramit Sethi, "Top 5 Productivity Mistakes," 2016, accessed February 12, 2016, from http://www.iwillteachyoutoberich.com/special/top-5-productivity-mistakes/.

CHAPTER 3

1. Donald Hebb, quoted in D. J. Siegel, "Memory: An Overview," *Journal of the American Academy of Child and Adolescent Psychiatry* 40, no. 9 (2001): 997–1011.

2. "Brain Health," Alzheimer's Association, accessed February 12, 2016, from http://www.alz.org/we_can_help_brain_health_maintain_your_brain.asp.

3. Siegel, "Memory: An Overview."

4. Daniel L. Schacter, *The Seven Sins of Memory: How the Mind Forgets and Remembers* (Boston: Houghton Mifflin, 2001), 13–15.

5. Siegel, "Memory: An Overview."

6. Jocelyn K. Glei, "Maria Popova: Staying Present and Grounded in the Age of Information Overload," accessed February 12, 2016, from http://99u.com/articles/29651/maria-popova-staying-present-and-grounded-in-the-age-of-information-overload.

CHAPTER 4

1. "To Read or Not to Read: A Question of National Consequence," National Endowment for the Arts, November 7, 2007, accessed February 12, 2016, from https://www.arts.gov/sites/default/files/ToRead.pdf.

2. Jeffrey D. Karpicke and Janell R. Blunt, "Retrieval Practice Produces More Learning than Elaborative Studying with Concept Mapping," *Science* 20 (January 2011), accessed March 6, 2013, from www.sciencemag.org/content/331/6018/772.abstract.

3. O. Pineño and R. R. Miller, "Primacy and Recency Effects in Extinction and Latent Inhibition: A Selective Review with Implications for Models of Learning," *Behavioural Processes* 69 (2005): 223–235.

4. Keith Rayner, Elizabeth R. Schotter, Michael E. J. Masson et al, "So Much to Read, So Little Time: How Do We Read, and Can Speed Reading Help?" accessed February 12, 2016, from http://www.psychologicalscience.org/index.php/publications/speed_reading.html.

5. Cal Newport, "Monday Master Class: The Art of Pseudo-Skimming," February 25, 2008, accessed February 12, 2016, from http://calnewport.com/blog/2008/02/25/monday-master-class-the-art-of-pseudo-skimming/.

CHAPTER 5

1. Gayle A. Brazeau, "Handouts in the Classroom: Is Note Taking a Lost Skill?" *American Journal of Pharmaceutical Education* 70, no. 2 (April 15, 2006): 38.

2. Walter Pauk and Ross J. Q. Owens, *How to Study in College*, 10th ed. (Boston: Cengage Learning, 2011).

3. Tony Buzan, *Use Both Sides of Your Brain* (New York: Dutton, 1991).

4. Gabrielle Rico, *Writing the Natural Way* (New York: Penguin, 2000).

5. Joseph Novak and D. Bob Gowin, *Learning How to Learn* (New York: Cambridge University Press, 1984).

6. David Ausubel, *The Psychology of Meaningful Verbal Learning* (New York: Grune & Stratton, 1963).

7. The Conference Board, "Job Satisfaction: 2014 Edition," June 2014, accessed February 12, 2016, from https://www.conference-board .org/publications/publicationdetail.cfm?publicationid=2785.

8. "Teresa Amabile: Track Your Small Wins to Motivate Big Accomplishments," in Behance Team, "Top 20 Insights, Talks, and Quotables On Making Ideas Happen," 2013, accessed February 12, 2016, from http://99u.com/articles/7263/top-20-insights-talks -and-quotables-on-making-ideas-happen.

CHAPTER 6

1. Annie Murphy Paul, "Highlighting Is a Waste of Time: The Best and Worst Learning Techniques," *Time*, January 9, 2013, accessed February 28, 2016, from http://ideas.time.com/2013/01/09 /highlighting-is-a-waste-of-the-best-and-worst-learning -techniques/.

2. Paul, "Highlighting Is a Waste of Time."

3. Joe Cuseo, "Academic-Support Strategies for Promoting Student Retention and Achievement during the First Year of College," University of Ulster Office of Student Transition and Retention, accessed September 4, 2003, from www.ulster.ac.uk/star /resources/acdemic_support_strat_first_years.pdf.

4. Cuseo, "Academic-Support Strategies."

5. Jonathan D. Glater, "Colleges Chase as Cheats Shift to Higher Tech," *New York Times*, May 18, 2006, accessed February 28, 2016, from www.nytimes.com/2006/05/18/education/18cheating.html.

6. Gerardo Ramirez and Sian L. Beilock, "Writing About Testing Worries Boosts Exam Performance in the Classroom," *Science* 331 (January 14, 2011): 211–213.

7. Paul D. Nolting, *Math Study Skills Workbook* (Boston: Cengage Learning, 2012), 57.

8. This article incorporates detailed suggestions from reviewer Frank Baker.

CHAPTER 7

1. Robert Manning, "Hemingway in Cuba," *The Atlantic* 216, no. 2, August 1965, 101–8.

2. Leon Festinger, *A Theory of Cognitive Dissonance* (Palo Alto, CA: Stanford University Press, 1957).

3. L. W. Anderson and D. R. Krathwohl, *A Taxonomy For Learning, Teaching, and Assessing: A Revision Of Bloom's Taxonomy of Educational Objectives* (New York: Addison Wesley Longman, 2001).

4. Candy Chang, "Before I die I want to . . ." TED Talks, November 2012, accessed February 24, 2016, from http://www.ted.com /talks/candy_chang_before_i_die_i_want_to.

5. Peter M. Gollwitzer, "Implementation Intentions," National Cancer Institute, accessed February 24, 2016, from http://cancercontrol .cancer.gov/brp/research/constructs/goal_intent_attain.pdf.

6. Arthur Koestler, *The Act of Creation* (New York: Dell, 1964), 35.

7. Martin E. P. Seligman, *Authentic Happiness: Using the New Positive Psychology to Realize Your Potential for Lasting Fulfillment* (New York: Simon and Schuster, 2002).

8. Quoted in Alice Calaprice, ed., *The Expanded Quotable Einstein* (Princeton, NJ: Princeton University Press, 2000).

9. David K. Reynolds, *A Handbook for Constructive Living* (New York: William Morrow, 1995), 36.

10. Byron Katie, *Loving What Is: Four Questions That Can Change Your Life* (New York: Harmony Books, 2002).

11. Mortimer Adler and Charles Van Doren, *How to Read a Book: The Classic Guide to Intelligent Reading* (New York: Simon and Schuster, 1972), 164–5.

12. Center for Human Resources, *National Evaluation of Learn and Serve America*, July 1999, accessed February 24, 2016, from http://cyc .brandeis.edu/pdfs/reports/NatlEvalofLearnandServeAmerica99.pdf.

13. Lauren Mechling, "The Trouble With Writing About Islam," *New York Sun*, November 26, 2004, accessed February 23, 2016, from http://www.nysun.com/on-the-town/trouble-with-writing-about -islam/5417/.

14. Irshad Manji, "Under the Cover of Islam," *New York Times*, November 18, 2004, accessed February 23, 2016, from http:// www.nytimes.com/2004/11/18/opinion/under-the-cover-of-islam .html.

15. Irshad Manji, "The Quranic Solution To The 9/11 Abomination," *Huffington Post*, November 8, 2011, accessed February 23, 2016, from http://www.huffingtonpost.com/irshad-manji/quran-911-10 -years-later_b_935585.html.

CHAPTER 8

1. Lawrence M. Brammer and Everett L. Shostrom, *Therapeutic Psychology: Fundamentals of Actualization Counseling and Psychotherapy* (Englewood Cliffs, NJ: Prentice Hall, 1968), 194–203.

2. Thomas Gordon, *Parent Effectiveness Training: The Tested New Way to Raise Responsible Children* (New York: New American Library, 1975), 114–59.

3. Sidney Jourard, *The Transparent Self* (New York: Van Nostrand, 1971).

4. Marshall Goldsmith, "Try Feedforward Instead of Feedback," 2002, accessed February 28, 2016, from http://www.marshallgoldsmithlibrary .com/cim/articles_display.php?aid=110.

5. Daniel Goleman, *Emotional Intelligence: Why It Can Matter More Than IQ* (New York: Bantam, 1995), xiv–xv.

6. Stephen Covey, *The Seven Habits of Highly Effective People: Power Lessons in Personal Change* (New York: Fireside, 1989), 95–144.

7. "Europe Should See Refugees as a Boon, Not a Burden," *New York Times*, September 15, 2015, accessed March 10, 2016, from http://www.nytimes.com/2015/09/19/opinion/europe-should-see -refugees-as-a-boon-not-a-burden.html.

8. Sophia Kerby and Crosby Burns, "The Top 10 Economic Facts of Diversity in the Workplace," Center for American Progress, July 12, 2012, accessed March 10, 2016, from https://www .americanprogress.org/issues/labor/news/2012/07/12/11900 /the-top-10-economic-facts-of-diversity-in-the-workplace/.

9. Maia Szalavitz, "Race and the Genome," Howard University Human Genome Center, March 2, 2001, accessed March 19, 2013, from www.genomecenter.howard.edu/article.htm.

10. Diane de Anda, *Bicultural Socialization: Factors Affecting the Minority Experience* (Washington, DC: National Association of Social Workers, 1984).

11. Quoted in Richard Saul Wurman, Loring Leifer, and David Sume, *Information Anxiety #2* (Indianapolis, IN: QUE, 2001), 116.

12. Peter Elbow, *Writing with Power: Techniques for Mastering the Writing Process* (New York: Oxford University Press, 1981), 13–19.

13. Jakob Nielsen, "How Users Read on the web," October 1, 1997, accessed February 28, 2016, from https://www.nngroup.com/articles/how-users-read-on-the-web/.

14. M. T. Motley, *Overcoming Your Fear of Public Speaking: A Proven Method* (New York: Houghton Mifflin, 1998).

CHAPTER 9

1. "Education Pays," U.S. Department of Labor, February 12, 2016, accessed February 28, 2016, from www.bls.gov/emp/ep_chart_001.htm.

2. Suze Orman, *Suze Orman's 2009 Action Plan: Keeping Your Money Safe & Sound* (New York: Spiegel & Grau, 2009), 125.

3. Erin El Issa, "2015 American Household Credit Card Debt Survey," Nerdwallet, accessed February 26, 2016, from http://www.nerdwallet.com/blog/credit-card-data/average-credit-card-debt-household/.

4. "Paying Down Credit Card Debt," Federal Trade Commission, August 2012, accessed February 28, 2016, from https://www.consumer.ftc.gov/articles/0333-paying-down-credit-card-debt.

5. "Be debt savvy with credit cards," Sallie Mae, accessed March 19, 2013, from https://www.collegeanswer.com/manage-your-money/managing-credit/credit-cards/choosing-a-credit-card-wisely.aspx.

6. "Education Pays 2013," College Board, accessed February 28, 2016, from http://trends.collegeboard.org/education_pays.

7. Snider Advisors, "Why Buy Term Life Insurance and Invest the Difference," NASDAQ, August 30, 2010, accessed February 25, 2016, from http://www.nasdaq.com/article/why-buy-term-life-insurance-and-invest-the-difference-cm34371.

CHAPTER 10

1. K. Anders Ericsson et al., "The Making of an Expert," *Harvard Business Review*, July–August 2007, accessed February 23, 2016, from https://hbr.org/2007/07/the-making-of-an-expert/ar/1.

2. Adam Grant, *Give and Take: A Revolutionary Approach to Success* (New York: Viking, 2013).

3. Josh Kaufman, *The First 20 Hours: How to Learn Anything . . . Fast!* (New York: Portfolio, 2013).

4. Teresa Amabile and Steven Kramer, *The Progress Principle: Using Small Wins to Ignite Joy, Engagement and Creativity* (Boston: Harvard Business Review Press, 2011).

5. Kate Zernike, "College, My Way," *New York Times*, April 23, 2006, accessed February 28, 2016, from http://www.nytimes.com/2006/04/23/education/edlife/zernike.html.

6. Lydia Ramsey, "Minding Your Global Manners," Business Know-How, 2005, accessed March 11, 2016, from http://www.businessknowhow.com/grow"h/globalman.htm.

7. David Allen, "How Can People Reduce Stress In Their Jobs?" *Productivity Principles Newsletter #94*, May 28, 2009.

8. Richard Bolles, *The Job-Hunters' Survival Guide: How to Find Hope and Rewarding Work, Even When "There Are No Jobs"* (Berkeley, CA: Ten Speed Press, 2009), 8, 92.

9. Ira Progoff, *At a Journal Workshop* (New York: Dialogue House, 1975).

10. Yevgeny Yermakov, "Ben Barry," 5 Questions for 100 Designers, June 25, 2014, accessed February 23, 2016, from http://5questionsfor100designers.com/ben-barry/.

11. Jake Cook, "Facebook's Ben Barry On How To Hack Your Job," 99U, accessed February 23, 2016, from http://99u.com/articles/7118/Facebooks-Ben-Barry-On-How-To-Hack-Your-Job

12. Jake Cook, "Facebook's Ben Barry On How To Hack Your Job."

Additional Reading

BOOKS

Allen, David. *Getting Things Done: The Art of Stress-Free Productivity*. New York: Penguin, 2015.

Belsky, Scott. *Making Ideas Happen: Overcoming the Obstacles Between Vision and Reality*. New York: Portfolio, 2012.

Bissonnette, Zac. *Debt-Free U: How I Paid for an Outstanding College Education Without Loans, Scholarships, or Mooching off My Parents*. New York: Portfolio, 2010.

Bolles, Richard N. *What Color Is Your Parachute? A Practical Manual for Job-Hunters and Career-Changers*. Berkeley, CA: Ten Speed, updated annually.

Bronson, Po. *What Should I Do with My Life? The True Story of People Who Answered the Ultimate Question*. New York: Random House, 2003.

Colvin, George. *Talent Is Overrated: What Really Separates World-Class Performers from Everybody Else*. New York: Portfolio, 2010.

Coplin, Bill. *10 Things Employers Want You to Learn in College: The Know-How You Need to Succeed*. Berkeley, CA: Ten Speed, 2004.

Covey, Stephen R. *The Seven Habits of Highly Effective People: Powerful Lessons in Personal Change*. New York: Simon & Schuster, 2013.

Cushman, Kathleen. *First in the Family: Advice About College From First-Generation Students*. Providence, RI: Next Generation Press, 2006.

Davis, Deborah. *The Adult Learner's Companion*, 2nd ed. Boston: Cengage, 2012.

Downing, Skip. *On Course: Strategies for Creating Success in College and in Life*, 7th ed. Boston: Cengage, 2014.

Duhigg, Charles. *The Power of Habit: Why We Do What We Do in Business and Life*. New York: Random House, 2014.

Friedman, Thomas. *The World Is Flat 3.0: A Brief History of the Twenty-First Century*. New York: Picador, 2007.

Glie, Jocelyn K. *Manage Your Day-to-Day: Build Your Routine, Find Your Focus, and Sharpen Your Creative Mind*. Amazon Publishing, 2013.

Godin, Seth. *Linchpin: Are You Indispensable?* New York: Portfolio, 2011.

Godin, Seth. *Purple Cow: Transform Your Business by Being Remarkable*. New York: Portfolio, 2009.

Greene, Susan D., and Melanie C. L. Martel. *The Ultimate Job Hunter's Guidebook*. Boston: Cengage, 2015.

Hoffman, Reid and Ben Casnocha. *The Start-up of You: Adapt to the Future, Invest in Yourself, and Transform Your Career*. New York: Crown Business, 2012.

Kaufman, Josh. *The First 20 Hours: How to Learn Anything...Fast!* New York: Portfolio, 2013.

Kaufman, Josh. *The Personal MBA: Master the Art of Business*. New York: Portfolio, 2012.

Levy, Frank, and Richard J. Murnane. *The New Division of Labor: How Computers Are Creating the Next Job Market*. Princeton, NJ: Princeton University Press, 2004.

Light, Richard J. *Making the Most of College: Students Speak Their Minds*. Cambridge, MA: Harvard University Press, 2001.

Newport, Cal. *How to Win at College*. New York: Random House, 2005.

Newport, Cal. *So Good They Can't Ignore You: Why Skills Trump Passion in the Quest for Work That You Love*. New York: Business Plus, 2012.

Newport, Cal. *Deep Work: Rules for Focused Success in a Distracted World*. New York: Grand Central, 2016.

Nolting, Paul D. *Math Study Skills Workbook*, 4th ed. Boston: Cengage, 2016.

Orman, Suze. 2009 *Action Plan: Keeping Your Money Safe & Sound*. New York: Spiegel & Grau, 2009.

Peddy, Shirley, Ph.D. *The Art of Mentoring: Lead, Follow and Get Out of the Way*. Houston, TX: Bullion Books, 2001.

Robinson, Adam. *What Smart Students Know: Maximum Grades, Optimum Learning, Minimum Time*. New York: Crown, 1993.

Sethi, Ramit. *I Will Teach You To Be Rich*. New York: Workman, 2009

Toft, Doug, ed. *Master Student Guide to Academic Success*. Boston: Cengage, 2005.

Trapani, Gina. *Lifehacker: 88 Tech Tricks to Turbocharge Your Day*. Indianapolis, IN: Wiley, 2007.

US Department of Education. *Funding Education Beyond High School: The Guide to Federal Student Aid*. Published yearly, http://studentaid.ed.gov/students/publications/student_guide/index.html.

Watkins, Ryan, and Michael Corry. *E-learning Companion: A Student's Guide to Online Success*, 3rd ed. Boston: Cengage, 2011.

Wurman, Richard Saul. *Information Anxiety 2*. Indianapolis: QUE, 2001.

WEBSITES

99U
99u.com
Strategies for taking creative projects from planning to completion

Annie Murphy Paul—Brilliant: The Science of Smart
anniemurphypaul.com/
Insights from the latest research on effective learning and strategies for using them

Art of Non-Conformity Blog
chrisguillebeau.com
Strategies for personal development, life planning, and becoming an entrepreneur

B J Fogg
bjfogg.org
Practical, research-based strategies for habit change from a professor of psychology at Stanford University

Brain Pickings
brainpickings.org
Connecting art, philosophy, science, and technology—an Internet-powered engine for cross-disciplinary learning and creative thinking

College Info Geek
collegeinfogeek.com
Strategies for success and work from Thomas Frank, a 2013 graduate of Iowa State University

GTD Times
gettingthingsdone.com
A community of people interested in Getting Things Done®, centered on the work of David Allen, author of Getting Things Done: The Art of Stress-Free Productivity

I Will Teach You To Be Rich

iwillteachyoutoberich.com

Guidance from author and entrepreneur Ramit Sethi on job hunting, taking charge of your money, and finding your dream job

James Altucher

http://www.jamesaltucher.com

An entrepreneur's guide to "choosing yourself" and thriving in the new economy

JobHuntersBible.com

jobhuntersbible.com

A rich set of online resources from Richard Bolles, author of the best-seller What Color Is Your Parachute? A Practical Manual for Job-Hunters and Career-Changers *and* The Job-Hunters' Survival Guide: How to Find Hope and Rewarding Work, Even When "There Are No Jobs"

Josh Kaufman

joshkaufman.net

Essays, courses, and resources from the author of The First 20 Hours: How to Learn Anything...Fast! *and* The Personal MBA: Master the Art of Business

Lifehacker

lifehacker.com

Tips and tricks for success at school, work, and home, geared to people interested in technology

Open Culture

openculture.com

Links to free ebooks, audiobooks, videos, and courses for lifelong learning

Study Hacks

calnewport.com/blog

Unconventional ideas for succeeding in school and planning your life from Cal Newport, author of How to Win at College *and* So Good They Can't Ignore You: Why Skills Trump Passion in the Quest for Work You Love

Index

A

Abbreviations in note-taking, 186
ABC to-do list prioritization, 74–77
Abstract conceptualization for learning, 34, 38, 42
Academic integrity and plagiarism, 311–313
Accreditation, 367
Achebe, Chinua, 318
Acronyms, 127
Acrostics, 127
  Muscle Reading, 140
Action, 11
Action goals, 267
Active experimentation for learning, 34, 38, 43
Act of Creation, The (Koestler), 248
Adichie, Chimamanda, 318
Adler, Mortimer, 261
Adult learners, 83–84
Advanced Placement (AP), 368
Affirmations, 250, 251
Affordable Care Act, 337, 349
Agendas, 195
"Aha!" experience, 243–244, 249
Allen, David, 91, 380
All-or-nothing thinking, 253
Alphabetical order, 119
Alzheimer's Association, 115
Amabile, Teresa, 198, 365–366
American College Test (ACT), 368
Americans with Disabilities Act (ADA) of 1990, 299
Amygdala, 122
Analogies, faulty, 253
Analyzing
  on essay questions, 212
  and thinking, 237
Annual fees, 340
Annual percentage rate (APR), 340
Antiprocrastination plan, 95
Anxiety
  math, 219–220
  tests, 216–218
Appealing to authority, 253
Appealing to the people, 255
Application errors, 225
Applying learning, 237
Appreciation, expressing, 361–362
Apps
  encyclopedias, 162
  flash cards, 122, 205
  habit change, 19
  memory aids, 130–131
  money, 324
  for money, 349–350
  note-taking, 196–197
  pronunciation aids, 160
  reading webpages, 146, 148–149
  research paper topics, 162, 163
  for time management, 92–93
  visuals for presentations, 315–316
  word processing, 308
Arguments, 239–240
Articles, 188
Articulation agreements, 367
Assertions, 239
Associate of arts (AA), 367
Associate of science (AS), 367
Association for Psychological Science, 155
Assumptions, 240
Attachment, 202
Attacking the person, 252–253
Attitude checks, 283–284
Attitudes, 250
  reprogramming, 251
Attrition, 367
Audience to a public speech, 314
Audio recorder, 171, 178, 185
Auditory learning, 52, 54
Ausubel, David, 190
Authority, appealing to, 253

B

Babauta, Leo, 352
Balance due, 340
Balance transfer, 340
Ball, Lucille, 227
Bankruptcy, 340
Bank statements, 350
Barry, Ben, 396
Beatles, The, 227
Begging the question, 254
Be here now, 60
  and note-taking, 174
Benefits, employer-provided, 331
Beyond the grade, 203
Bias and critical thinking, 234
Big-ticket items, 333
Bills, 350
Blog reading, 148–149
Bloom, Benjamin, 235–236, 237, 363
Bloom's taxonomy, 237
Bodily/kinesthetic intelligence, 48, 50
Boldface, 239
Books, 188
Booth, Lalita, 228
Boyle's law, 120

Brain, care of, 115–116
Brain Pickings, 134
Brainstorming
  goals, 71, 73, 244
  for idea creation, 245, 263
  questions, 262
  solutions, 259, 287
  for to-do list, 74
Breaks and memory, 123–124
Breathing
  and math anxiety, 219–220
  and test anxiety, 217
Brin, Sergey, 296
Budgets, 332
Business, starting a, 331–332
Buzan, Tony, 179

C

Calendars
  apps, 92
  monthly, 85–87
Career, creating, 369–371
Career plans, 371, 377
Careers, learning modes and, 44
Careless errors, 225
Car insurance, 349
Car shopping, 348
Cash advances, 339
Categories and memory, 119
Causes, false, 253
Cell phone bills, 334
Channels of communication, 273
Character, as a skill, 358–362
Cheating on tests, 215–216
Checklists for tests, 204
Chew, Stephen, 81–82
Chronological order, 119
Chunking data for memory, 118
Civil Rights Act of 1964, 299
Classes
  daydreaming in, 174
  learning modes and, 43
  missing, 173
Classroom civility, 294
CLEP (College Level Examination Program), 367, 368
Cognitive biases, 254
Cognitive dissonance, 234
Collaboration, 358
  technology for, 285
Collectivist cultures, 297–298
College Level Examination Program (CLEP), 367, 368
Commitments, 22, 272

Commonplace books, 153
Communicating, 358
    channels of, 273
    complaining effectively, 292
    and conflict management, 287–289
    and cultural differences, 289, 297–300
    and emotional intelligence, 282–283
    as a first-generation student, 302–303
    in groups, 283–286
    with instructors, 293–295, 302
    and listening, 274–277
    open to, 273
    for positive relationships, 271
    Power Process, 272
    practicing critical thinking, 273
    public speaking, 313–317
    saying "no," 290
    skills, 361
    skills snapshot, 320
    on social networks, 303–305
    speaking, 278–280
    writing, 273, 288, 306–310
Communication orientation, 316
Communication styles, 281
Compare, on essay questions, 212
Complaining effectively, 292
Compliments, 300
Comprehending, 237
Computer-graded tests, 213
Concept errors, 225
Concept maps, 190–192
Conclusion of a speech, 315
Concrete experience for learning,
    34, 38, 42
    and memory, 114
    and procrastination, 99
Confirmation bias, 254
Conflict management, 287–289
    and learning styles, 45–46
Consolidation and memory, 124
Constructive criticism, 292
Content and form, 294
Contracts, 348
Contrast, on essay questions, 212
Contrasting pairs, 129
Convergent thinking, 243, 246
Cooperative learning, 209–211
Corequisite, 367
Core values. See Values
Cornell Method, 178–179, 180–181, 182
    on reading material, 187
Corporation for National and
    Community Service, 266
Corson, Dale, 150
Corson technique, 150
Course equivalents, 367
Covey, Stephen R., 62, 284, 312
Cramming for a test, 205
Crazy Busy: Overstretched, Overbooked,
    and About to Snap (Hallowell), 99

Creative thinking, 237, 358
    ideas, 245–249
Creativity, 243–244
Credit cards
    balance pay-offs, 336
    take control of, 338–341
Credit report, 339–340
Credit scores, 338–339, 340
Credit terms, 340
Critical thinking, 233–235, 358. See also
    Practicing critical thinking
    creativity, 243–244
    evidence and, 241
    process for, 238–241
    questions for, 261
    service-learning, 267
    and test anxiety, 217
Criticism
    constructive, 292
    from instructors, 295
Criticize, on essay questions, 212
Cross-curriculum study strategies, 223
Cue columns, 178–179
Cultural differences, 295–300
    and communication, 289
Culture learner, 301
Curriculum, studying across, 222–223
Cuseo, Joe, 209
Cyberbullying, 303

D

Daily practice, 205–206
Data, collecting and playing with,
    247–248
Daydreaming in class, 174
de Anda, Diane, 298
Debate, 281
Debt consolidators, 337
Decision making skills, 257–258
Declaration of Independence, 240
Declare What You Want journal
    entry, 19
Decoding glitches, 115
Decoding memories, 113, 114, 115
Deductive reasoning, 239–240
Deep mind, 309
Deep processing, 82
Default, 340
Defiers as procrastinators, 94
Define, on essay questions, 212
Degree plans, 384–385
Delegation and procrastination, 100
Delivering a presentation, 316–317
Dendrites, 117
Denny, Jimmy, 227
Describe, on essay questions, 212
Designing Web Usability: The Practice
    of Simplicity (Nielsen), 307
Design mind, 179

Desks, standing, 247
Detachment, 202
Diacritics, 157
Diagram, on essay questions, 212
Diagrams and note-taking, 177
Dialects, 159
Dialogues, 281
Dickinson, Emily, 227, 243
Dictionaries, 157
Diet. See Food choices
Digital aids. See Apps
Disabilities, students with, 299
Discounts, student, 333
Discovery, 8–9
Discovery Statements, 8–9, 11, 122, 249
    and emotions, 283
Discovery Wheel, 28–32, 388–392
Discrimination, 296, 300
Discuss
    on essay questions, 212
    and understanding, 236
Disney, Walt, 227
Distractions
    and listening, 275
    from the real issue, 255
    technological, 60, 62, 82, 174
Distributed learning, 123–124, 205
Divergent thinking, 243, 244
Diversity, 295–296
    in the workplace, 378–379
Downtime, 107
Drafts, writing, 308–309
Dreamers as procrastinators, 94
Drug usage, 103
Duhigg, Charles, 21

E

Eat Move Sleep: How Small Choices Lead
    to Big Changes, 103
Edison, Thomas, 246
Education
    and adult learners, 83–84
    goals of, 2
    language of, 81
    paying for, 343, 344, 346–347
    value of, 343
Effective writing, 306–310
80-20 principle, 151
80-20 prioritization method, 75–76
Einstein, Albert, 259
Elaboration for memory, 119
Elbow, Peter, 308
Email
    and time management, 82
    writing, 307
Embrace the new, 232
Emergency funds, 345
Emotional arguments, 253
Emotional health, 102–103

Emotional intelligence
  and communicating, 282–283
  and social networks, 99
Emotions, 249, 283
  and conflict, 288
  in groups, 286
  and listening, 276
Empathy, 282
Employment. *See* Jobs
Encoding errors, 114
Encoding memories, 113, 114–115, 118–124
Encyclopedia apps, 162
English as a Second Language (ESL), 159–160
English language, mastering, 159–161
English Language Learner (ELL), 159–160
Entrepreneurs, 369–370
Enumerate, on essay questions, 212
Environment and note-taking, 174
Errors on tests, 224–225
Essay questions, 212–213, 214
Estimate, and understanding, 236
Ethics, and cheating on tests, 215–216
Etiquette, 305
Evaluate
  on essay questions, 212
  and learning, 237
Evidence and critical thinking, 241
Exercise, 102
  and brain health, 116
  and memory, 123
  and writing, 309
Explain, on essay questions, 212
Extracurricular activities, 81
Extroversion, 281
Eye contact, 274, 317

F

Facebook Analog Research Laboratory, 396
Facts and opinions, 254
Failures, notable, 227
Fallacies, logical, 252–255
False cause, 240
  pointing to, 253
Fast pace of conversation, 281
Fatal flaws, 255
Faulty analogies, 253
Fears
  loving your, 112
  of public speaking, 316
Federal Deposit Insurance Corporation (FDIC), 336, 345
Federal Trade Commission, 339
Feedback, mistakes as, 225–226
Feedforward, 280
Feelings
  describing, 277
  and memory, 122–123

Feynman, Richard, 153
Feynman technique, 153
FICO score, 340
Fill-in-the-blank tests, 214
Finance charge, 340
Financial aid, 329, 343, 350
Financial planners, 345
First-generation students, 302–303
First 20 Hours: How to Learn Anything ... Fast! (Kaufman), 362
First Step technique, 25–26
Flash cards, 121–122
  and test preparation, 205
Fleming, Alexander, 246
Flexible reader, becoming, 155–156
Focus and let go, 245–246
Fogg, B. J., 18
Food choices, 101
  and brain health, 116
Fool, risk of being a, 322
Foreign languages, 223
Form and content, 294
Forster, E. M., 308
Franklin, Benjamin, 248
Free fun, 334
Free writing, 308–309
Fun, 334, 335

G

Gardner, Howard, 48, 49
Germanotta, Stefani, 356
Getting Things Done: The Art of Stress-Free Productivity (Allen), 91, 380
Give and Take: A Revolutionary Approach to Success, 360
Givers, 361
Goals
  action, 267
  brainstorming, 71, 73, 244
  creating effective, 73, 394–395
  and memory, 123
  outcome, 267
  and procrastination, 94
  setting and achieving, 70–72, 246
Goldsmith, Marshall, 280
Goleman, Daniel, 282
Gordon, Thomas, 278
Gowin, D. Bob, 190
Grace period, 340
Grade point average (GPA), 368
Grades
  failing, 225
  meaning of, 203
Graduate Record Examinations (GRE), 368
Graduation, 364–366
Grant, Adam, 360–361
Graphic organizers, 120
Graphic signals, 178

Graphs and learning styles, 38–39
Groups
  communicating in, 283–286
  creative thinking in, 248
  presentations by, 317
GROW acronym, 361

H

Habits, changing, 17–20
  money, 342
  practicing critical thinking, 21
Hallowell, Edward, 99
Happiness, 231
Hasty generalizations, 240, 252
Heading of an outline, 180
Health
  choices, 104–105
  and employment, 380–381
  making time for, 101–103
Health insurance, 337, 349
Hebb, Donald, 113
Hemingway, Ernest, 233
Heraclitus, 232
Hidden jobs, 373–375
Hierarchy of needs, 13
Higher education
  adult learners and, 83–84
  transition to, 80–83
Highlighting text, 143
High performers, 332
Holmes, Sherlock, 172
Home ownership, 348
Hot spots, 238
How to Get Control of Your Time and Your Life (Lakein), 75
How to Read a Book (Adler and Van Doren), 261
Humanities, 223
Humor and public speaking, 315
Hypothesis of Recording Glitches, 178

I

"I create it all," 170
Idea files, 247
Ideas
  creating, 245–249, 263
  and memory, 115
  as tools, 24
Identity theft, 350
Idioms, 159
Illustrate, on essay questions, 213
Images and memory, 114
"I" messages, 277, 278–279
  and conflict, 287
  and group meetings, 286
  practicing critical thinking, 280
Implementation intentions, 246
Inboxes, 91

Income
  increasing, 330–331
  self-employment, 331–332
Index cards
  note-taking, 183, 188–189
  outlining writing, 307–308
Index funds, 348
Individualist cultures, 297–298
Inductive reasoning, 240
Informational interview, 371, 374
Information literacy, 161–165
Inner voices, 60
Inquiry-based learning, 260–262
Instructors
  communicating with, 293–295, 302
  math, 220
  and note-taking, 174, 175, 185–186
  and study groups, 210
  and test questions, 208
Insurance, 348–349, 350
Intelligences, multiple, 48–51
Intensive Journal System, 382
Intentions, 9–10
  communicating, 277
  and listening, 276
  and memory, 122
Intention Statements, 8–9, 11, 122, 249
  and emotions, 283
Interest rates, 340
Internet
  and procrastination, 99
  thinking critically about information
    on, 256–257
  and time usage, 68, 82
Interpersonal intelligence, 48, 51
Interpret, on essay questions, 213
Interruptions and reading, 152
Interviewing skills, 376–378
Interviews, 357
  information to record about, 188
Intrapersonal intelligence, 48, 50
Introduction to a speech, 314–315
Introversion, 281
Intuition, using, 258
Investments, 336, 348
Italics, 239
I Will Teach You To Be Rich (Sethi), 108

J

Jargon, 159
Jenner, Edward, 246
Jobs, 337, 380–381
  hidden, 373–375
  while in school, 329
Jobs, Steve, 296
Johnson, Samuel, 130
Jordan, Michael, 227
Jourard, Sidney, 279

Journal entries
  brain, care of, 115
  career planning, 370
  commitment, 22
  communication styles, 281
  convergent thinking, 246
  Declare What You Want, 19
  Discovery Statements, 8–9, 11
  divergent thinking, 244
  excuses, letting go of, 208
  Intention Statements, 8–9, 11
  learning styles, 34, 55
  lectures, value from, 175
  money, experience with, 325, 330, 342
  Muscle Reading, 146
  not-to-do list, 107
  online reading habits, 148
  purpose statement, drafting, 47
  reflect on learning, 393
  relationships, recreating, 289
  technology and time usage, 68
  tests, 206
Journals, 382
  and idea creation, 247
  and memory, 114
Jumping on the bandwagon, 255
Jumping to conclusions, 252
Jungle of memory, 116–117

K

Katie, Byron, 261
Kaufman, Josh, 362
Key words
  defining, 239
  and note-taking, 176–177, 179–180, 182
Kinesthetic learning, 52, 54
Kite of learning style, 38–39
Knowledge and critical thinking, 235,
    239. *See also* Thinking
Koestler, Arthur, 248
Kolb, David, 33, 35
Kramer, Steven, 365–366

L

Lady Gaga, 356
Lakein, Alan, 75
Language of education, 81
Laye, Camara, 318
Leaders, group, 284
Learn and Serve America, 266
Learning
  from asking questions, 260–261
  and evaluating, 237
  and memory, 113–116
Learning Style Inventory (LSI), 34–39
Learning styles, 33–34
  and decision making, 257–258

journal entry on, 34, 55
and math, 222
modes of learning, 39–43
other people's, 44–46
and procrastination, 99
school and career, 43–44
and study groups, 210
VARK System, 52–54
Lectures, value from, 175
Left brain, 179
Letting go, 246
Levels of thinking, 236
Lewis, Carl, 227
Library resources, 164
Life insurance, 348–349
Lifelines, creating, 71
Lifetime learners, 332, 386–387
Lincoln, Abraham, 356
Liquid money, 345
List, on essay questions, 213
Listening, 274–277
  in groups, 286
List managers, 92–93
Loci system, 128
Logic, mistakes in, 252–255
Logical thinking, 239
Long-term goals, 71, 73, 394
  saving for, 345
Long-term memory
  creating, 114
  as a jungle, 116–117
Long-term planner, 88–90
Love your problems power process, 112
Loving What Is (Katie), 261

M

Macy, R. H., 227
Main body of a speech, 315
Major, choice of
  learning modes and, 43–44
  thinking about, 263–265, 365
Manji, Irshad, 268
*Manners that Sell: Adding the Polish That
    Builds Profits* (Ramsey), 379
Manzano, Matias, 166
Market demand, 369
Maslow, Abraham, 13
Massive open online courses (MOOCs),
    368
Master monthly calendar, 85–87
Master student in you, 7
Master student profiles. *See* Profiles of
    master students
Mastery, qualities for, 4–7
Matching tests, 214
Math, 223
  reading, 220–221
  tests, 218–222

Mathematical/logical intelligence, 48, 49
Math Study Skills Workbook (Nolting), 220
McGwire, Mark, 227
Mediators, 289
    cultural, 298–299
Meetings
    for group projects, 284–285
    note-taking during, 195
Memory
    as jungle, 116–117
    names, remembering, 132–133
    retooling, 130–131
    6 key principles, 113–116
    skills snapshot, 136
    trapping, 126
Memory tricks and techniques
    antiprocrastination plan, 95
    mnemonic devices, 127–128, 131
    25 techniques, 118–124
    VARK System, 52–54
Mentors, 382–383
Metacognition, 55
Midterm goals, 71, 73
Mind mapping, 179–180, 181, 183
    on reading material, 187
    and study groups, 210
    for test preparation, 205
Minimum payment, 340
Missing classes, 173
Mistakes as feedback, 225–226
Mnemonic devices, 127–128, 131
Models, 299
Modern Language Association (MLA), 310
Modes of learning, 39–41
    developing, 42–46
Money
    apps for, 324, 349–350
    and education, 343, 344, 346–347
    experience with, 325, 330, 342
    for the future, 345
    making more, 329–332
    skills, 361
    skills snapshot, 354
    spending less, 333–335
    tools for, 349–350
    and tough times, 336–338
    and values, personal, 351
    worries, end of, 323
Money monitor/money plan, 324–328
Monthly calendars, 85–87
Mood meters, 283
Most Important Task (MIT), 79
Motivation, 15–16, 282
Motley, Michael, 316
Movement. *See* Exercise
Multiple-choice questions, 212–213
Multiple intelligences, 48–51
Multitasking, 62–63

Murphy's Law of Computer Crashes, 193–194
Muscle Reading
    concept map of, 191
    described, 139–145
    leaner approach, 145
    web pages and ebooks, 146–147
    at work, 147–149
Musical/rhythmic intelligence, 48, 50

N

Naikan, 260
Names, remembering, 132–133
National Credit Union Association (NCUA), 336
National Endowment for the Arts (NEA), 139
National Foundation for Credit Counseling, 337
National Service-Learning Clearinghouse, 266
Naturalist intelligence, 48, 51
Natural sciences, 223
NCUA (National Credit Union Association), 336
NEA (National Endowment for the Arts), 139
Negativity bias, 254
Netiquette, 305
Networking, 373–375
Neurons of the brain, 113
Newport, Cal, 155
New Year's resolutions, 72
Nielsen, Jakob, 307
Noise and communication, 273
Nolting, Paul, 220
Nonlinear reading, 148
Nontraditional students, 83–84
Nonverbal communication, 273, 279
Nonverbal listening, 274–275
"No," saying, 290
Note-taking, 161, 165
    apps for, 196–197
    concept maps, 190–192
    for math classes, 220
    during meetings, 195
    and observing, 171, 172–175
    online coursework, 192–195
    and PowerPoint presentations, 175, 177, 184–185
    practicing critical thinking, 182, 186
    process flows, 171–172
    and reading, 187–189
    and review, 181–183
    skills, 360
    skills snapshot, 200
    software for, 196–197
    techniques for, 176–181

Note-taking groups, 209
Notice your pictures and let them go Power Process, 138
Not-to-do list, 107
Novak, Joseph, 190
Numbered lists, 129

O

Obligation in communication, 272
Observing, 277
    and note-taking, 171, 172–175
One-minute mental exercise, 231
Online coursework, 192–195
Online privacy, 304
Online readers, writing for, 307
Online reading habits, 148
Open-book tests, 213–214
Openness in communication, 281
Opinions, facts and, 254
Organizing for memory, 119
Orman, Suze, 336
Outcome goals, 267
Outcomes, focusing on, 106
Outlines, 130–131
    and analyzing, 237
    on essay questions, 213
    and note-taking, 180
    and reading, 141
    on reading material, 187
    for writing, 307–308
Overdoers as procrastinators, 94
Overlearning, 122
Over-preparation for tests, 217–218

P

Paper and note-taking, 177
Paper mills, 311
Paragraphs for note-taking, 177
Paraphrasing, 311–312
Passion
    in career choice, 369
    in communication, 272
Path of mastery, 398
Pauk, Walter, 178, 179, 183
Payment due date, 340
Peak energy and memory, 122
Peer editing, 309
Peg system, 128
Perfectionists as procrastinators, 94
Performance orientation, 316
Performance reviews, 329, 331
Periodic rate, 340
Persistence
    in mastery, 381–383
    Power Process, 356
Phone bills, 334
Physical activity. *See* Exercise

Piano analogy for perfection, 99–100
Pictures
    and memory, 120
    and note-taking, 177
Plagiarism, 189, 311–313
Planning, 106, 357
    applying learning, 237
    in communication, 272
    effectiveness of, 78–80
    long-term planner, 88–90
Planning sessions, 209–210
PLUS loans, 341
Pointing to a false cause, 253
Pollan, Michael, 101
Pomodoro Technique, 94
Popova, Maria, 134
Possibility in communication, 272
Post-purchase rationalization, 254
Power of Habit, The (Duhigg), 21
PowerPoint, 315–316
    presentations with, 175, 177, 184–185
Power Process
    be here now, 60
    communicating, 272
    creating success, 170
    detach, 202
    discover what you want, 2
    embrace the new, 232
    ideas are tools, 24
    introduction to, 14
    love your problems, 112
    notice your pictures and let them go, 138
    persistence, 356
    risk being a fool, 322
Practice sessions
    for math, 221
    for public speaking, 316
    for skill learning, 362
Practice tests, 204–205
    math, 221
    and study groups, 210
Practicing critical thinking
    academic plans, 384–385
    attitude reprogramming, 251
    and Bloom's taxonomy, 237
    career planning, 377
    communication, 273
    culture learner, 301
    education, 344, 346–347
    emotional reactions, 249
    first step, taking the, 27
    goals, creating effective, 73, 394–395
    habits, changing, 21
    health choices, 104–105
    "I" messages, 280
    lifelines, creating, 71
    major, trial choice of, 365
    master monthly calendar, 85–87
    the master student in you, 7

math and learning styles, 222
mnemonic devices, 131
money, saving, 335
money monitor/money plan, 324–328
note-taking, 182, 186
problems to solutions, 133
Q-cards and memory, 125
reading assignments, completing, 154
remembering keys or others, 126
scenarios, 241–242
skills, 359, 363
textbook reconnaissance, 3
the time monitor/time plan, 63–68
to-do lists, 76–77
20 things I like to do, 227
using this book, 387
very important persons (VIPs), 291
Preference in communication, 272
Prefixes, 158
Prejudice, 300, 303
    and critical thinking, 234
Prerequisites, 367
Presentations, 313–317
Presley, Elvis, 227
Preview reading, 141
Primacy-recency effect, 145
Primary sources, 165
Priorities, establishing, 257
Privacy online, 304
Problem solving, 258–259
Process flows and note-taking, 171–172
Process speech, 313–314
Procrastination, 93–95, 99
Productivity porn, 108
Profiles of master students, 55
    Adichie, Chimamanda, 318
    Amabile, Teresa, 198
    Babauta, Leo, 352
    Barry, Ben, 396
    Booth, Lalita, 228
    Manji, Irshad, 268
    Manzano, Matias, 166
    Popova, Maria, 134
    Sethi, Ramit, 108
    Williams, Joshua, 55
Progoff, Ira, 382
Progress Principle, 198
Progress Principle: Using Small Wins to Ignite Joy, Engagement, and Creativity at Work (Amabile and Kramer), 365–366
Promising in communication, 272
Pronunciation aids, apps for, 160
Propositions, 190
Prove, on essay questions, 213
Pseudo-skimming, 155
Psychology of Meaningful Verbal Learning, The (Ausubel), 190
Public speaking, 313–317
Purpose statement journal entry, 47

Q
Question Cards (Q-cards), 125
Question-opinion-support charts, 120–121
Questions
    asking, 235, 383
    15 to try, 261
    generating, 261–262
    learning from asking, 260–261
    and listening, 276
    and reading, 142–143
    on tests, predicting, 207–208
    that are not questions, 279
Quizzes and test preparation, 208
Quotes, attributing, 311

R
Raise, requesting, 329–331
Ramsey, Lydia, 379
Rath, Tom C., 103
Reading
    English language, 159–161
    flexible readers, 155–156
    information literacy, 161–165
    math, 220–221
    muscle, 139–145
    note-taking while, 187–189
    roadblocks to, 151–153
    skills, 360
    skills snapshot, 168
    vocabulary, expanding, 156–158
    web pages and ebooks, 146–147
    when tough, 149–150
    at work, 147–148
Reading groups, 209
Read/write learning, 52, 54
Recall and memory, 123–124
Recency bias, 254
Recite and repeat for memory, 118–119
    while reading, 144–145
Recorders, group, 284
Recording and note-taking, 171, 178, 185
Red herrings, 254
Reflection and listening, 275
Reflective observation for learning, 34, 38, 42
Reflect on learning, 393
Rehabilitation Act of 1973, 299
Relate, on essay questions, 213
Remembering, 126, 236
Repetition
    for memory, 118
    and note-taking, 175
Requests and listening, 276
Research
    for paper topics, 162, 163
    for writing, 307

Research groups, 209
Research notes, 188–189
Reserve in communication, 281
Responsibility, taking, 170
Restating
  and memory, 121
  and understanding, 236
Resting, 102
  and test preparation, 218
Résumé, creating, 372–373
Retirement savings, 345
Reviewing
  for memory, 119
  and note-taking, 171–172, 181–183, 187–188
  and reading, 145
Revising a draft paper, 309–310
Rewrite the book, 3
Rhymes and memory, 128
Rico, Gabrielle, 179
Right brain, 179
Risk being a fool, 322
Rogers, Carl, 275
Roles in a group, 284
Roots, 158
Rowling, J. K., 356
Ruth, Babe, 227

S

Salary negotiations, 331
Sales pitch, 14
Sapadin, Linda, 94
Scheduling study groups, 211
Scholastic Assessment Test (SAT), 368
Screensucking, 99
Secondary sources, 165
Secret of success, 12
Seinfeld, Jerry, 19, 227
Self-actualization, 13
Self-awareness, 282
Self-deception, 234
Self-discovery skills, 360
Self-employment, 331–332
Self-experimenting book, 11
Self-knowledge, 58
Self-management skills, 360
Self-regulation, 282
Senses and memory, 114
Serendipity, creative, 246
Service-learning, 265–267
Sethi, Ramit, 108
Setting and achieving goals, 70–72, 246
Sexually transmitted infections (STIs), 102
Shaking hands, 358
Shallow processing, 82
Shaw, George Bernard, 260
Short answer tests, 214
Shorthand, 186

Short-term goals, 71, 73, 394
Short-term memory
  as a meadow, 116
  and note-taking, 181–182
  trap, escaping, 118–119
Side projects, 387
Sign mind, 179
Silver dollar system, 183
Single tasking, 63
Six kinds of thinking, 235–237
Skills
  communicating, 361
  decision making, 257–258
  developing, 363
  interviewing, 376–378
  practice sessions, 362
  practicing critical thinking, 359
  in relationship, 282
  time management, 360
  transferable, 267, 357–362
Skills snapshot
  communicating, 320
  Discovery Wheel, 32, 392
  memory, 136
  money, 354
  note-taking, 200
  path of mastery, 398
  reading, 168
  self-knowledge, 58
  test taking, 230
  thinking, 270
  time management, 110
Skimming, 155
Slang, 159
Sleeping, 102
  and idea creation, 248
Slippery slope, 255
Slow pace of conversation, 281
Small daily choices, 103
Small talk, 358
Small-ticket items, 333
Smiles, 358
Social change
  and critical thinking, 234
  questions for, 262
Social events, 358–360
Social networks
  and procrastination, 99
  staying safe on, 303–305
  and time management, 82
Social sciences, 223
Software. See Apps
Songs and memory, 128
Sources of information, 165, 188, 189
Spatial order, 119
Speaking, 278–280
  public, 313–317
Specific goals, 71
Speed reading, 155

Sperry, John, 181
Spreadsheet software, 349
SPUNKI acronym, 153
Stafford loans, 341
Standard English, 159
Standing desks, 247
State, on essay questions, 213
Stated assumptions, 240
Stereotypes, 300
Straw man, creating a, 254
Stress
  employment-related, 380–381
  money, 337
Stretch goals, 2
String maps, 191
Student discounts, 333
Student loans, 341
Student services, 364–365
Study areas, 222–223
Study errors, 225
Study groups, 209–211
  and math classes, 220
Study time, effective use of, 96–101
Sub-skills, 362, 363
Substance use disorder, 103
Success
  creating, 170
  journal entry on, 47
  secret of, 12
Suffixes, 158
Summarizing, 312
  on essay questions, 213
  and note-taking, 183
Supporting questions, 162
Support systems, cultural, 299
Synergy, 284

T

Takers, 361
Talking quickly and note-taking, 185–186
Tangram, 243
Target performance level, 362
Tasks, group, 284–285
Taxes, 350
Taxonomy of educational objectives, 235–237, 363
Teachers. See Instructors
Teaching and memory, 124
Technology
  for collaboration, 285
  as distraction, 60, 62, 82, 174
  and note-taking, 171, 179
  and procrastination, 99
  and time usage, 68
Terms, 239
Test mechanics errors, 225
Test review groups, 209

Tests
   anxiety regarding, 216–218
   beyond the grade, 203
   cheating on, 215–216
   follow up after, 224–225
   math, 218–222
   preparation for, 204–206, 208, 218
   questions on, predicting, 207–208
   skills snapshot, 230
   taking, 211–214, 361
Textbook reconnaissance, 3
Thank-you notes, 378
Thesis statements, 306–307
20 things I like to do, 227
Thinking. *See also* Critical thinking
   affirmations, 250, 251
   decision making skills, 257–258
   and happiness, 231
   idea creation, 245–249
   inquiry, learning through, 260–262
   levels of, 236
   logic, mistakes in, 252–255
   problem solving, 258–259
   service-learning, 265–267
   six kinds of, 235–237
   skills, 361
   skills snapshot, 270
   visualizations, 250
Thorough thinking, 234–235
Thought animals of memory, 116–117
Thoughts, communicating, 277
Three Princes of Serendip, The (Walpole),
   246
Three-ring binders and note-taking, 177
3 Tiny Habits, 18
Time boxing, 79
Timelines, 120–121
   group, 284–285
Time management, 61–62, 106–107
   apps for, 92–93
   digital distractions, 82
   multitasking, 62–63
   planning, 78–80, 88–90
   procrastination, stopping, 93–95
   skills, 360
   skills snapshot, 110

techniques for, 96–101
to-do lists, 74–77
values and, 69–70
Time Monitor, 63–68
Timers, group, 284
To-do lists, 74–77
Tolerance, 238
Tools
   ideas as, 24
   for money, 349–350
Topic for writing, 306
Topic-point-details charts, 120–121
Topics for public speeches, 313–314
Trace, on essay questions, 213
Tradition, appealing to, 254–255
Transferable skills, 267, 357–362
   examples of, 360–361
Transferring schools, 367–368
Translators, 298
Transparency, 279–280
Trapping memory, 126
Trouble With Islam, The (Manji), 268
True/false questions, 213
Truth, the key to mastery, 25–26

U

Uncertainty, willingness for, 239
Understanding, 236–237
   and criticizing, 238
Unemployment benefits, 337
Uniform research locators (URLs), 256
Unstated assumptions, 240–241
U.S. Department of Labor, 332
Using the book, 13–14, 387

V

Vague goals, 71
Values
   life consistent with, 69–70, 106
   money and, 351
Van Doren, Charles, 261
VARK (visual, auditory, read/write,
   kinesthetic) System, 52–54
Venn diagrams, 121, 122

Verbal/linguistic intelligence, 48, 49
Verbal listening, 275–276
Very important persons (VIPs), 291
Visualizations, 250
Visual learning, 52, 54
Visuals and public speaking, 315–316
Visual/spacial intelligence, 48, 50
Vocabulary, expanding, 156–158
Voice over Internet Protocol (VoIP), 334

W

Walpole, Horace, 246
Wants, communicating, 277
Weekly practice, 206
Wikipedia, 257
Williams, Joshua, 55
Williams, Robin, 227
Word parts, 158
Word processors, 308
Word stack, 157
Work-content skills, 359
Work flow, 91–92
Working with Emotional Intelligence
   (Goleman), 282
Workplace, diverse, 378–379
Work while in school, 329
Worriers as procrastinators, 94
   studying, 98–99
Writing
   as communication, 273, 288
   effective, 306–310
   and memory, 121
   plagiarism, 311–313
   as transferable skill, 357–358

Y

"You" messages, 277, 278

Z

Zen Habits, 352